HEROIC S

The Automobile and an American Town in the 20th Century

DAVID BALL

ISBN: 978-1-5136-5299-3

Published by The Sinclair Press, Port Huron, MI.
TheSinclairPress@gmx.com

and Movement Publishing

Contents

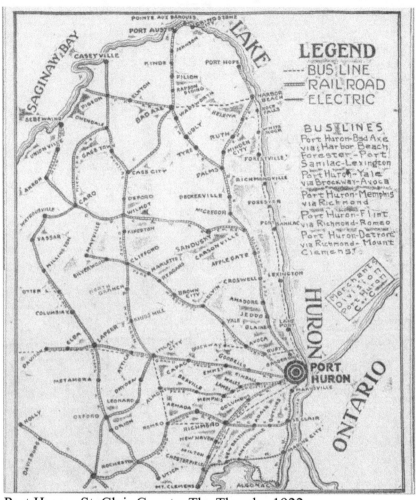

Port Huron, St. Clair County, The Thumb. 1922 map

Chapter 1. 1899: The Story So Far

FORD SAYS HISTORY IS BUNK

- Port Huron Times Herald headline, 1919

Henry Ford was 12 the summer he met the steam tractor on the road to Detroit. He said. According to his memoirs, he and his affluent farmer father William drove a horse team and wagon from their home in Dearborn into the Stove Capital of the World one day in 1876, and along the way ran smack into something known then as a traction engine, basically a steam locomotive that ran on the road. Traction engines were farm vehicles, though not in the sense of later, lighter, gasoline-powered tractors. Farmers didn't use traction engines much for field work like plowing, since these machines weighed several tons (7 tons was typical) and their iron wheels could tear a pasture to pieces, especially given some wet ground. They posed the same threat to roads, very few of which were so much as graveled in the state of Michigan, in America, or in much of the rest of the world. If these steamers got stuck, they remained more or less immovable without monumental effort to free them, usually supplied by animal power. Early traction engines also exhibited problems with "fundamental concepts [like] backing up and steering," in the words of author Patrick Ertel.(1) When owners dared to move them at all, traction engines lumbered slowly from farm to farm as portable power plants for hire, to run threshers, sawmills and what have you.

Henry had never seen one before. At the time of which he wrote, self-propelled traction engines would have been extremely scarce indeed, and expensive, $1,200 - $1,500, more than most farms cost. In a flash, he jumped down off his father's wagon to look it over. He had plenty of time; just passing each other promised to be a tricky business for Dad Ford and the engine operator. Michigan country roads measured about nine feet wide on average, and a good-sized traction engine stood 10 feet high, 8 wide, 20 long. The Ford horses could not have been any too pleased by the encounter with this chugging, smoke-belching threat, and would have needed plenty of coaxing to move around it. They just might decide to depart the scene on their own, with or without the Fords. A single person simultaneously fed the traction engine's burner, monitored the steam pressure, and steered. This multitasking inspired confidence in neither man nor beast, just 12 year-old boys.

The principle fascination for Henry Ford didn't come from the farm applications of the engine. Even at this age he disliked farming and horses and hard physical work in general. His real interest lay in the fact that the machine didn't run where it belonged, on rails. "The engine that ran on the road," he remembered it, though certainly nothing confined it to the road. It meandered any which way you pointed it. He identified it as a Nichols & Shepherd model, built in Battle Creek, Michigan, about 115 miles to the west. Somehow or other William Ford retrieved his son, overcame the reluctance in his animals, circled the clumsy and dangerous mechanism and went on his way.

That was the story, anyway. The event allegedly changed the direction of Henry Ford's life, and he always kept a photo of a traction engine nearby for inspiration. As for William Ford, had someone told him that his son's encounter that July day would help unleash the greatest social evil in American history, he would have been justifiably hurt and skeptical. I'm tempted to say the greatest social evil in the history of the world, but it's early yet, and I don't want to get too rhetorical too soon.

However I'll unlimber enough at this point to say that if most of the households in America each owned a road locomotive or two to drive wherever and whenever they pleased, at speeds up to a dozen times what a horse could manage, with nothing to restrain their vehicles to the road or from the path of other engines except good intentions, filling the highways to the exclusion of all other travelers and all other vehicles and purposes, poisoning the air with a neverending stream of dirt and noise, exhausting natural resources for fuel by the nationful, ravaging city and countryside with their destructive spatial demands and unmanageable clutter, levying an enormous and ever-increasing expense on themselves and a titanic one on the public at large, this would introduce an overwhelming element of chaos, danger, and waste into American life that no pretended advantage of mobility or convenience could possibly justify. It couldn't and shouldn't have happened, but it did.

Turning a traction engine loose on the road in the first place constituted a setback in American transportation progress, the reverse of Henry's appreciation. It increased rather than decreased disorder. It would have been far easier, and far more orderly, to ship cumbersome machinery between farms on a network of light railways and canals, running on a regular schedule, supplementing both the heavy rail system that even by 1876 had made miraculous headway across the United States, and the inland waterways that carried an equally large share of American commerce. Had Henry Ford bent his undeniable talents to the fulfillment of that disciplined ideal he'd have died a happier man, and the 20th Century closed on a far different and better America. Failure to think these things through in the first place bred instead a malign, frenetic, all-consuming selfishness – no, let's ratchet it higher, a narcissism – a sickness – tied directly to the engines that ran on the road. Automobiles.

There, now. How was that for a sweeping statement? Too much? Well, we shall see.

First and foremost among the countless myths about the automobile hatched over the years by its addicts and apologists is that it rescued Americans from a 19th Century dark age of transportational imprisonment. In their vain imaginings, this was a nation practically frozen in place. It was well nigh impossible to go anywhere. Half the land lived in the deep, primitive isolation of the countryside, wracked by soul-searing loneliness, and the other half in the maddened overcrowding of the city, aching to be free. America groaned under the burdens of industrial and agricultural feudalism, cultural arrest, educational retardation, genetic inbreeding, horse-borne contagions, monotony, malnourishment, and the utter futility of human existence. Then the automobile arrived, and boom, everybody got well. This tradition of overripe romantic fabrication includes Ford's steam tractor anecdote, because very likely it never happened at all. It certainly didn't happen the way Ford described it in his autobiography *My Life and Work*, because the Nichols and Shephard Company didn't

6

make self-propelled traction engines until 1891.(2) Virtually nobody did in 1876. Maybe Ford got the year wrong or the make wrong, but he probably made the whole thing up. His Dearborn neighbors didn't call him "Lyin' Hank" for nothing.(3)

In fact the 19th Century was the most successful in the history of transportation in its development of new mechanical mass transit and shipment of goods. But since Michigan became the chief dispensary of the machine built to undo that achievement, this state and a medium-sized city and county in it are going to be the main backdrop of this critical history, to bring some focus to a big subject for the reader, whose indulgence and cooperation I'll have to enlist from here on. Roughly 70 miles northeast of Dearborn lay the boyhood home of Henry Ford's lifelong hero, Thomas Alva Edison: the city of Port Huron, in St. Clair County. These latter communities were just big enough to give us a manageable grasp of what transpired, let us meet some of the average people involved, and understand the spread of carsickness. Unlike Dearborn, Port Huron lay far enough away from the automotive epidemic center, Detroit, to escape its most lethal effects and spare us that distorted viewpoint. The automobile wrecked each American city and county and state in its own special way in the 20th Century, but it shouldn't be difficult to spot the parallels to other locales, and adjust for the differences. Let's take a cursory look at how carless 19th Century people moved around, beginning with the...

WATER

The prior domain for at least 10 thousand years of various Native American tribes, including the Mound Builders, who left dozens of their trademark structures behind to mark their passing, at the opening of the 19th Century the future town of Port Huron in the future state of Michigan consisted of a small collection of cabins at the junction of the St. Clair and Black Rivers, immediately south of Lake Huron on the Great Lakes. French explorers first had examined the site in 1679 from the decks of the *Griffon*, the first sailing ship to be built on the shores of the upper Lakes. Father Louis Hennepin liked what he saw: "The banks of the Streight are vast Meadows, and the Prospect is terminated with some Hills covered with Vineyards, Trees bearing good Fruit, Groves, and Forests so well dispos'd, that one would think Nature alone could not have made, without the help of Art, so charming a Prospect."(4)

It took another 100 years before French Canadian families finally settled there, led informally by a gentleman named Anselm Petit. They traded with the local Chippewa tribe, with the residents of Canada just east across the St. Clair River, and with lumber camps and sawmills beginning to appear up the Black River in that level, fertile, forest-covered section of Michigan's hand-shaped peninsula known as the Thumb. People hauled themselves and their goods in this era by water if possible, preferring this method to pushing their way along the ancient but barely cleared Indian trails that passed for roads. Even in winter months in what became St. Clair County, pilgrims found the frozen surfaces of the four biggest rivers (the St. Clair, Black, Pine and Belle), the numerous smaller streams, and the Great Lakes useful for travel by foot or sleigh. The principle water route ran down the Lakes shoreline southwest to and from the city and fort at Detroit, also originally French installations.

Where water enough existed to float on, marine shipping was abundant and effective everywhere in early 1800's America. The new federal government took a welcome hand in this mode of transportation by establishing national jurisdiction over

7

navigable waterways, declaring them common highways and contributing to their upkeep. As early as 1824, Congress appropriated $75,000 for improvements on the Mississippi and Ohio rivers, and with good reason. A merchant in Pittsburgh, for instance, paid less to send a cargo by water down the Ohio to the Mississippi, down the Mississippi to the Gulf of Mexico, across the Gulf of Mexico to the Atlantic seaboard, and up the Atlantic seaboard to Philadelphia, than to send the same shipment from Pittsburgh to Philadelphia across 300 miles of road.(5)

Flatboats, keelboats and sailing ships had the field to themselves in U.S. waters prior to the arrival of steam. Flatboats were primarily driftboats, slapped together for one trip downstream and converted back into lumber and sold at their their destinations. A keelboat was a more formal, ship-like affair, which when pushpoled or horse-dragged could haul up to 80 tons even upstream. 500 keelboats worked the Ohio River by 1819.(6) Sailing ships plied oceans, lakes, and rivers by the thousands, wherever they had room to maneuver for the wind, and withstood for several decades the challenge from steam in many areas. On the Great Lakes alone more than 1,500 sailing ships, schooners mainly, did business in 1860 and continued to haul most of the cargo on those waters for the remainder of the century.

The powered transportation era in America arrived by water when the first commercial steamboat launched in the US, the *Clermont*, built by Robert Fulton, began service between New York City and Albany in 1807. A thousand steamboats arrived per year in New Orleans by 1836. Eight thousand per year in Cincinnati by 1852. Historian John Stover reckoned the marine industry used "almost every river in the country" for some kind of tranffic by that time.(7)

In 1818 the Fulton-inspired side-wheeler *Walk-in-the-Water* became the first steam vessel to pass through the St. Clair River, followed shortly by the *Superior*, a ship so grand its owners charged a shilling apiece just to tour it. Anselm Petit's boy Edward recalled that the whole community turned out to see the Superior when it stopped by, paid their shillings and "stood in mute admiration of the most beautiful thing we had ever seen. We thought we were in heaven."(8) The considerably less heavenly *Argo* provided the first regular steamer service on the St. Clair in 1829. Built of just two 55 foot logs fastened together side-by-side, with a steam engine sitting on top of them, this unstable vessel, if it even deserved the name, nearly capsized when passengers wandered too far to port or starboard. Many of the early powered Great Lakes ships used both sail and steam.

The benefits of marine transport impressed early Americans so profoundly that where feasible they eagerly set about improving, adjusting, connecting, and manufacturing waterways for travel. Among the Founding Fathers, Washington, Hamilton, Jefferson, and Franklin all declared themselves dedicated canal men. Said Ben: "Rivers are ungovernable things, especially in hilly countries. Canals are quiet and very manageable."(9) Prior to his election as President of the United States, George Washington served much more happily as president of a company organized to canalize the Potomac River, and another organization to build a canal through the Dismal Swamp. The first major American canal opened in South Carolina in 1800, and four thousand miles worth had been built around the country by 1850, of which far and away the most important was the Erie Canal.

The energetic backing of New York City mayor and later New York State

Governor DeWitt Clinton helped push construction of the Erie across 360 miles between the Hudson River and the Great Lakes. The Erie took eight years to build and was finished two years ahead of schedule in 1825, despite some serious setbacks, like the deaths of a thousand construction workers from malaria during a single summer's work in a Syracuse swamp. America had no trained canal engineers available when the Erie project began, but suffered from an oversupply of lawyers, so an attorney, Benjamin Wright, assumed charge of the work. Wright succeeded so well he won for himself the sobriquet Father of American Civil Engineering, whereupon he left the practice of law and thereafter led an honest life.(10) The Erie cost $7 million of public money, but made an immediate and dramatic economic impact. It opened up the entire Midwest to the Atlantic coast. The price of shipping a ton of goods from Buffalo to New York City fell overnight from $100 by wagon to $10-$12 by water. The initial canal rates of about 8 cents per ton-mile fell with time to as low as 1/2 cent.(11) Travel time between the two cities sped up from 20 days to 8.(12)

Mulepower kept things moving on most canals. A team of 2 or 3 mules easily pulled a 90 foot canalboat loaded with 300 tons, the cargo equivalent of 3 railroad freight cars or 15 semi-trailer trucks in the year 2000.(13) Children as young as 6 sometimes did the mule driving, and the smarter mules became so accustomed to the work that they stopped on their own initiative at familiar lock gates, and stopped pulling entirely when their six hour shift ended. Human beings should be so muleheaded. Inexpensive mules kicked the cost daylights out of engine-powered canal craft for decades.

Canals also furnished a valuable source of water power for industry. On the Chesapeake and Ohio Canal, stonecutters, foundries, cement makers and flour mills all tapped into the flow. Like all transportation methods, of course, canals had their drawbacks. Through difficult country building costs escalated, to between $30,000 and $80,000 per mile. While travelers ran little or no chance of a bad collision on a canal, and it was downright difficult to drown in one, the maintenance issues included variable water levels from the feed rivers, the necessity of manning the lock gates, wall and lock repairs, ice, and cleaning out silt.

Inspired not just by the Erie, but by a 320 mile long Ohio canal finished in 1832, and by the Pittsburgh to Philadelphia Main Line Canal which opened in 1834, the brand new state of Michigan decided to take a crack at building its own major canal across itself in 1838. The Clinton-Kalamazoo Canal connected at its eastern end to a river named in honor of Dewitt. Plans called for digging a 200 mile-long, 32 foot-wide, 5 foot-deep channel to the west. Alas, a bum financial climate following the Panic of 1837 left the project somewhat panic stricken, and four years of construction only completed 12 miles before the money ran out. When even this small section opened, a canal boat promptly jammed a lock in the town of Rochester and permanently crippled the whole system.

This embarrassing flub didn't erase for Michiganders the appeal of a well made canal. Even the small, newly organized village of Port Huron thought a canal through town would be a helpful idea, to carry sailing ships around the rapids at the head of the St. Clair River. Community businessmen floated a plan in 1841, but nobody dug it. The lack of money again held up action. Further west, the burgeoning city of Chicago had better luck with a canal to the Mississippi River, completed in 1848, which

9

spurred forward the town's phenomenal growth.

At this point it might be helpful to point out that no systematic, national plan for canal mapping, financing, or construction existed in the United States. Or for water transport as a whole. Or any transport. The whole question of how much the federal and state governments should involve themselves in what were called then "internal improvements" – transportation in other words – provoked one of the great disputes that led to the creation of America's first political parties. The Federalists, led loudly by Hamilton and more discreetly by Washington, favored federally directed works. The Jefferson Republican-Democrats opposed them. The historical verdict can hardly be more plain: the Federalists were right, the Democrats wrong. Unfortunately, in this case the correct men lost. The Congress dispensed transportation aid occasionally, even commissioned some construction, but did not take overall command, seriously defaulting on its responsibilities. The very nature of a federal government required some kind of direction over interstate transportation. No one could expect the states to arrange a balanced network by themselves, taking into account not just their own individual needs, but those of states as much as a thousand miles away. And they didn't.

Canal backers beat every conceivable public and private money bush to get the work accomplished. They built some canals as private stock concerns. Others were entirely state projects, like Michigan's. Local governments built a few. The federal government handed out 4 million acres in land grants and purchased $3 million worth of shares in canal projects to help things along. $125 million of public and private capital had been invested by 1850.(14) As far as obtaining the rights-of-way, some canal builders secured government charters that granted them condemnation powers, others just agreeably paid the asking price of landowners. Taken all together, American canal-making involved a welter of public and private enterprise that some might call creative and diverse and others haphazard and crazy.

When railroads began to compete with canals, and by 1850 even began to drive some out of business, or buy and close them down, government made little effort to protect this immensely valuable tool of transport that favored efficiency, cleanliness, and orderliness over speed. Instead of treating canals as permanent highways, the nation abandoned many, even those which qualified as navigable waterways, supposedly under federal oversight and protection. Canal abandonment in favor of railroads indicated early on how easily American infatuation with new transportation technology could lead the nation to foolishly discard something good in the process. New canal construction became a rarity after 1850, except in cases of smoothing out major natural waterways, like the Sault Ste. Marie canal in Michigan, opened in 1855 to link Lake Superior with the lower Great Lakes. The state paid for this valuable improvement by selling 750,000 acres of federal land grants. Eventually the Soo Canal became the busiest in the world, and perhaps the single most critical transportation facility in the United States.

St. Clair County's first big man in transportation circles knew a good thing like a canal when he saw it. Samuel Ward, a 40 year-old transplant from Ohio, took his newly built schooner St. Clair through the Erie Canal almost as soon as it opened, with a load of gypsum, furs, and fish to trade in New York City. Heading the other way on the Erie came a tide of immigrants who quickly settled the Michigan territory and propelled it to statehood in 1837. To handle the increasing commercial traffic on the Great Lakes, Samuel Ward and his nephew Eber rapidly built up a fleet of dozens of

10

ships, including the first steamer built in the county, the *Huron*, constructed in 1839. Shipping made Eber Ward Michigan's first millionaire, and a force to be reckoned with in lumber, mining and manufacturing.

The shipbuilding industry started by the Wards at the mouth of the Belle River grew big enough that residents of the village of Newport, which Samuel founded, renamed it Marine City. Shipwrights eventually built vessels of one kind or another in about every nook, cranny, and inlet along St. Clair County's 105-mile shoreline. Twenty miles north of Marine City, the federal government erected a Great Lakes lighthouse at Port Huron in 1825, and schooners and steamboats called regularly. Both kinds of craft penetrated the interior of the Thumb via the Black River as early as 1831. They sailed ten miles and more up the Black, occasionally in the process having to dodge gigantic log floatdowns launched by the dominant lumbering industry. Once Port Huron's seven sawmills finished with this timber, most of the resulting lumber products departed by ship. Some of this wood, however, fed Port Huron's own commercial shipbuilding industry, which started work in 1838. During the remainder of the century five different shipbuilders in town assembled some 170 craft, ranging in size up to 2,000 tons.

By the 1850's daily passenger and freight steamboat service connected Port Huron to Detroit – 25 cents, about 4/10 a cent per mile. Captain James Moffet, an early Port Huron go-getter, also replaced his horse-driven ferry with a steamer to cross the river to the Canadian city of Sarnia. The St. Clair River rapidly became one of America's principle route, a fact confirmed when the Congress appropriated $45,000 in 1856 to deepen the channel. Work continued after the Civil War, and during the next 50 postwar years eventually dredged the channel down to 20 feet, at a total cost of $1 million. Nationwide, Congress appropriated "rivers and harbors" cash of this kind regularly right through the 19th and 20th Centuries. The government distributed this money, it should be said, in something of a hit-or-miss fashion. Often, if you had a well-connected Congressman, you got some. If not, forget it.

By the outbreak of the Civil War, the interior waterways of America carried more freight than all the ships in the British Empire combined. The Union's control of the major rivers, and its blockade of ocean coastal waters played a critical part in busting the Confederacy. Business only accelerated further after the peace. Sailors tired of waiting for southerly winds to blow them through the Port Huron rapids, or mules to pull them, up into Lake Huron got relief when tugboats appeared in the 1860's, and the sight of a tug towing a train of schooners upriver became commonplace. Steam-powered iron-hulled freighters came next, and multiplied. In 1872 a railroad company ordered a 210 foot-long English-built railcar ferry for its Port Huron operation, which the manufacturer shipped across the Atlantic and through Canada's Welland Canal in pieces for reassembly. Once put together, this ferry took up duty carrying an ever-increasing number of trains across the St. Clair River.

The relative safety of various forms of transportation is going to be an important part of this history, and occasional wrecks and drownings were part and parcel of life on the water. After all, that first sailing ship on the upper Great Lakes, the *Griffon*, hadn't lasted long. A storm on Lake Huron swallowed it up with its crew and a load of fur pelts less than two months after its launching. The Great Lakes could be profoundly violent in bad weather, or even in good weather, and over time hundreds of ships and thousands of people disappeared into them. The still temperamental steam

11

engine added an explosive element to the mix. In one spectacular early accident, the St. Clair County-built steamer *Goliath*, one of the first screw-propeller freighters on the Lakes, blew up in 1848 while traveling north of Port Huron with a load of 200 barrels of blasting powder destined for the mines of the state's Upper Peninsula. The blast annihilated 22 men with a bang heard 50 miles away. 25% of the 2,500 commercial ships on the Great Lakes suffered some kind of major or minor accident per season as late as the 1870's. From further off, news of the explosion of the steamboat *Sultana* near Memphis, Tennessee marred Port Huron's celebration of the Civil War's end. 1,800 people, many of them Union POW's heading home, died in the worst transportation disaster in American history.

One man's disaster is another's opportunity, and a Port Huron family named Reid made the most of the Great Lakes' contrariness. Captain James Reid and his sons Thomas and William originally wrangled logs to the sawmills on the Great Lakes, like those in Port Huron. Their tugboats on one occasion maneuvered an immense raft that held 6.5 million log feet of wood.(15) But when Canada cut off this timber supply to America, the Reids switched their efforts to ship salvaging, a much more lucrative line of business. They clinched their reputation as salvagers by raising a $125,000 steamer from the St. Clair River, and charging the owners $50,000 in the process. Prices like that led one historian to describe James Reid as an amiable pirate who would blarney you while robbing you blind on a wrecking job.

Slowly but surely safety measures progressed, and enough people and cargoes made it through in one piece that 37,000 vessels of all kinds docked in, departed from, or passed by the 6,000 person city of Port Huron in 1873.(16) The town provided a home base for 50 commercial craft. As many as 150 more laid up there in winter, together spending $100,000 and more for refitting while they awaited the spring ice breakup. Michigan firms operated 979 cargo carriers by 1881, one of the largest totals in the nation, a natural in a state encircled by the Great Lakes, with more coastline than any other state but Florida.(17) More than 110 large package freighters plied the Lakes in the 1880's. "Package" in this case meant ships carrying several different discrete cargoes at once. The Port Huron and Duluth Steamship Company began package freight operations in the late 1890's, backed by a wheeler-dealer named Henry McMorran, who also took over the ferry service to Sarnia. He was perhaps the most enterprising businessman Port Huron ever knew, of whom more later. Just as with canal traffic, though, speed began to outweigh cost concerns and railroad service cut into this business late in the century. Another consideration, ice, put the Lakes out of action for many vessels for three months per year. The number of package carriers fell to about 90 in 1900, many of them owned by railroads.

In addition to stoves, Detroit by the late 1800's built more ships than any city in America, turning out many of the state's commercial vessels to carry lumber, grain, ore, salt, and a wide variety of other manufactures, like the barge load of bricks sent upriver to build Port Huron's first Methodist church. Ship construction in Port Huron reached its zenith at this time through the efforts of the Jenks family. They'd built the Phenix Boiler Works in Port Huron in 1857 to furnish marine engines, then progressed to constructing whole ships. Their yard on the Black River launched the largest vessels ever assembled in Port Huron, including the first locally built steel-hulled models.

Port Huron's three drydocks for ship repair and redesign included what for a time was the biggest such facility on the Great Lakes, the Dunford and Alverson, later taken over by over by the Reids. Many hundreds of other people in Port Huron made a water-connected living as ship chandlers, longshoreman, fishermen, agents, deckhands, mates, engineers and captains. So many top boat hands called Port Huron home that the Shipmasters Association chartered a local branch in 1888. The very names of the city's major dock-lined streets reflected the importance of shipping in Port Huron: Water, Quay, River, Merchant, Commercial.

During the century's last quarter, while it grew to a city of 19,000 people, Port Huron developed a reputation not just as a commercial destination but as a pleasantly-situated, relatively modern, and welcoming excursion spot for passenger ships in the Detroit region. As many as 2,500 people, both daytrippers and long term vacationers, clambered off a single side-wheeler at the docks, to enjoy themselves around town. Those departing Port Huron by water could choose service not just to Detroit but to a dozen Michigan cities on the Lake Huron shoreline by 1879, as well as timely connections to Toledo, Cleveland, Buffalo, Chicago, Milwaukee and a laundry list of other Michigan and Canadian destinations on the other Lakes. Fares usually ran about 1.5 cents per mile.

If you just wanted to skip over to Sarnia you took the 5 cent, half-mile trip on McMorran's ferry boats, as half a million people did in 1899, a sizeable number, considering the two communities mustered only a combined total population of about 25,000. This international crossing was so convenient some people went over and back just to buy Canadian bread which they found especially tasty. Downriver from Port Huron, ferry service crossed the river to Canada at four more towns, and passenger ships serviced large, luxurious summer hotels and clubs on the southern shores of St. Clair County, like the enormous 500 foot-long Oakland Hotel. By the end of the 90's the White Star steamship line commenced building for its customers a huge amusement park, Tashmoo, on Harsens Island at the very southern tip of the county, part of the largest freshwater delta in the world. Residents called this area the "Venice of America," for its many boat docks and residential canals along the waterfront.(18)

As to the quality of passenger travel on the Great Lakes in the 19th century, we can call on the expertise of Mark Twain. In 1853, as a 17 year-old boy, he sailed east across Lake Erie from Monroe, Michigan to Buffalo, New York in a single day, 250 miles, aboard the steamer Southern Michigan, and pronounced the ship a "palace." Forty-two years later, as America's greatest author, he sailed back west from Buffalo to Duluth, Minnesota, right past Port Huron, and said of the Lakes ships, "I have never seen any European steamers inland that approached them for speed and comfort. In fact, the European steamers are cattle boats in comparison with these."(19) And this veteran of the Mississippi River service, and subsequent world traveler, knew whereof he spoke. For journeying amenities – food, sleeping quarters, entertainment, just the sheer ability to move around the conveyance – no stagecoach, railcar, automobile or airplane would ever come close to a well appointed passenger ship.

So as the 19th century drew to a close, Port Huron was familiar with and used to traveling comfortably on the water, and shipping raw materials and finished products across it, and enjoying the low costs and convenience of a genuinely open system, as anybody with a boat was welcome to use it. And still the real possibilities of water transit in a country such as America, with 25,000 miles of inland waterways, plus the

Great Lakes, plus 12,300 miles of continental coastline, had barely been scratched. Not a single river or stream in St. Clair County had been dammed or locked or interconnected with another by canal.

RAIL

Henry Ford's Dream Ride, as we might call his alleged 1876 adventure with the steam tractor, came at a time when the race for supremacy between the two alternatives for motorized land transportation, road or rail, seemed to have been settled. By the time of America's Centennial, railroads looked like the winners. Henry and his dad just as easily could have caught the train into Detroit that year as driven a team and wagon. Dearborn had had regular railroad service for almost 40 years, long before the Ford family even arrived in America. Road engines were another story. As we've mentioned, they hardly existed in the United States.

Two of the earliest models of functional railroad and road engines appeared almost simultaneously at the beginning of the 19th century, in England, both from the hand of a remarkable inventor named Richard Trevithick. This man of genius demonstrated his steam-powered stagecoach for roads in 1803 and his railroad locomotive in 1804. At the steamcoach debut the machine immediately suffered the world's first recorded self-propelled vehicle traffic accident, when Trevithick plowed into a fence while doing 10 mph over a short stretch of cobblestone street in the city of Oxford. Tellingly, Trevithick and partner Andrew Vivian had cleared the street of potential victims before the trial run began, which said a mouthful about their level of confidence in the device.[20] Trevithick took no such precaution for the railroad demonstration since its basic control, a defined path, was built in. That trial took place along a 9.5 mile long Welsh tramway, with the locomotive hauling 10 tons of pig iron and 70 men. It took four hours to cover this distance, slowed by Trevithick's having to remove obstacles and cut back trees along the tracks.[21] But he made his point about the physical advantage of a powered vehicle moving on metal wheels along metal tracks. To flash forward for a moment to the year 2000 for a comparison, a steel railroad wheel on steel rails generated as little as 1% of the rolling friction of a truck tire on pavement.[22]

Another twenty years or so passed before the two land machines got significantly past the experimental stage. The English father and son engineering team of George and Robert Stephenson built and operated a modern steam rail locomotive in 1828, an engine they named the *Rocket*. Locomotives, like ships, received the sentimental honor of names right from the start. In America, Peter Cooper's one-ton engine, the *Tom Thumb*, in 1830 reached the speed of 18 mph pulling a passenger coach on a completed section of the Baltimore and Ohio railroad. In the words of historian John Dilts, "some of the passengers pulled out notebooks and wrote down their thoughts to prove that human beings could function normally at such high velocities."[23] The B&O originally had intended to use horses to pull its railcars, but *Tom* won the day for the iron horse.

After that, events moved full speed ahead. Only 100 miles of American track existed in 1830, but by 1833 just a single company, the Charleston to Hamburg line, stretched 136 miles across the state of South Carolina, making it the longest railroad in the world. Advancing technologically by leaps and bounds, just three years after the *Tom Thumb's* 18 mph record, U.S. locomotives achieved top speeds of nearly 60.(24) Put that in your high speed notebook. America's railroad network covered 3,000 miles by 1840, 7,500 miles by 1850, 30,000 miles by 1860 – more rail line than existed in the rest of the world combined. As of 1860 half the nation's freight moved over its railroad system, in which $1 billion dollars of largely foreign capital had been invested.(25)

Not everything in the train world progressed smoothly during these startup years. The state of Michigan chartered 15 railroads before a company actually built one, the Erie and Kalamazoo. After some warmup trials with horses, the first steampowered E&K train pulled out of Port Lawrence, Ohio one day in 1837 and to the joy of the company actually arrived the same day in Adrian, Michigan. It made 10 mph at top speed along the 33 mile route. These early trains carried both passengers and freight, but eventually the railroads segregated the two services to speed up passenger travel. E&K riders paid a fare of $1.50, about 4.5 cents per mile, while freight shipment cost 30 cents per hundredweight, about 18 cents per ton-mile.(26) Typical railroad passenger fares retreated to 2 or 3 cents per mile on most American lines during the 19th Century, while freight rates declined phenomenally to 3/4 cent per ton-mile.(27)

In the early days of Michigan railroading the limitations of the equipment produced some lively times, dangerously lively. Occasionally passengers had to get out and push a balky locomotive, or they choked on the engine smoke drifting back into the open passenger compartments, which resembled stagecoaches. Sparks from the engine sometimes set the coaches or travelers' clothing on ablaze, and left a trail of brush fire behind in the countryside. Once in a while one of the flimsy early track rails worked its way loose from the ties and smashed suddenly through the floorboards of a passing train compartment – an event known as a "snakehead." After a few of these unnerving incidents the railroads put down solids T-rails, and introduced longer, taller, wider, fully enclosed passenger cars that seated patrons four abreast with an aisle up the middle to stroll through.

Just like steamboat engines, locomotives posed operational challenges at first, the boilers especially. The very first U.S. railroad fatality occurred when a novice fireman monkeyed with a safety valve on an engine and blew himself up. Run in a cavalier fashion, trains also jumped the rails, or rammed each other; harming people and property in pretty dramatic fashion. A good many collisions arose from the inherent difficulty in coordinating traffic running in opposite directions on a single set of tracks. However, the vast majority of railroad casualties occurred not on the trains themselves but when human or animal "trespassers", as the railroads defensively called them, wandered heedlessly onto the tracks (which were eventually standardized at 4 feet 8.5 inches wide) without bothering to check first on what might be coming down the line. The whole novel set-up of a train baffled these early victims.

Locomotives regularly made mincemeat of wild and domestic animals. An entire train derailed near Marshall, Michigan after it rammed an ox, killing not just the animal but the engine fireman as well. Not content to just run over it, one engineer on another early train shot "game," wild or not, from his engine window and halted the train to pick it up. The domestic livestock slaughter became so serious that it sparked a near revolution in Michigan. A gang of irate farmers came to town and burned down the Michigan Central Railroad depot in Detroit in 1850. The state legislature ordered the fencing of rural railroad rights-of-way as a result.

Although they made a majestic appearance at a distance, closer up railroad engines could be pretty dirty contraptions, spewing smoke, soot, and cinders all along their paths, an especially unwelcome side effect in big cities. They weren't very fuel efficient, either, and had to stop frequently for coal or wood and water. About 95% of the energy in the firebox went up the chimney, only 5% actually drove the train. The very lack of rolling resistance that allowed huge weights to be pulled easily on tracks also made trains difficult to stop, as the ox discovered. But even with these drawbacks, one ride convinced most people that a fantastic leap forward in travel had been made, and there was no stopping the railroads' expansion.

In the first year of Michigan railroading, 1837, a fateful year, the brand new state's 25 year-old governor Stevens Mason persuaded the legislature to launch a $5 million plan to build three separate state-owned railroad lines across the lower part of the state. He also wanted to deepen three major rivers for improved navigation, build the Clinton-Kalamazoo canal already mentioned, and tackle other internal improvements, too. These grand ideas struck a popular chord, and the project budget eventually escalated to $8 million. The state christened the three east-west rail lines the Southern, Central, and Northern railroads. For our purposes, the interesting part of the plan involved the designation of the railroads as common highways. From the earliest days, railroad charters in Michigan contained the clause that privately built lines could be purchased by the state from their developers. This principle of treating rail beds just like any other "roads," controlled and maintained and sustained by the government, didn't last long, and its abandonment proved to be a catastrophic error in judgment that bedeviled railroads in Michigan and the U.S. right through the 20th Century.

As previously noted, misfortune fell on the state of Michigan as a result of the Panic of 1837. Perhaps from a lack of sophistication, or too much optimism, Michiganders hadn't counted on the business depression developing in the East when the state laid out its ambitious railroad plan. Only when Governor Mason went to New York City to scare up the money did he get the word to expect worse terms on a $5 million loan than anybody had reckoned. At first the deal seemed like a good gamble. Plenty of customers lined up when the first 28 miles of the Michigan Central Railroad opened in 1838 heading westward out of Detroit. The Central soon carried a thousand passengers and a quarter million pounds of freight per week.(28) It called regularly at Dearbornville, a full ten years before Henry Ford's Irish grandfather John ever set foot in the place.

Despite these good initial results, the bad times that rolled into Michigan by 1839 hampered the ongoing railroad construction, even after the sale of a half million acres of federal land donated to help out the project. $61,000 worth of groundwork began in 1839 on the Northern Michigan RR, designed to run between Port Huron and the community of Grand Haven 200 miles away. At the Port Huron end, Daniel Harrington organized things. A genuine town father, this lumber king was the man who had pulled four separate town plats together and named it Port Huron. Harrington cleared and graded about half the Michigan Northern path, but hadn't put down a single tie or rail before the work halted when the money ran out. Eventually the state turned the Northern into a wagon road.

The Michigan Central made it two thirds of the way across the state as an

16

operating railroad, and the Southern about halfway, before the heavily indebted legislature ordered them both sold in 1846 to private companies for considerably less than cost. The new owners completed the two lines to Chicago and earned substantial profits within a decade. Looking back, historian Willis Dunbar blamed the Michigan government for taking on too much internal improvement work too soon, and it was not the only state at the time to do so. Over in Illinois a similar scheme came to grief in the same way, much to the vexation and embarrassment of one of its main backers, state legislator Abraham Lincoln. To atone for the financial punishment Michigan suffered from all this, the authors of its new constitution written in 1850 forbade the state government from spending virtually anything at all on transportation.

And so Michigan fell into step with the rest of the country in a fateful combination of employing government authority in order to charter railroads, and to empower them in many cases with eminent domain authority, and sometimes to award them land grants and to authorize their bond issues, but leave the resulting train lines entirely in private hands. Though these companies had to operate as "common carriers," granting equal access to customers big and small, they still gave off an unfortunate smell of special privilege right from the start. Americans found the whole idea of private roads of any kind distasteful, and the public aid for private profit arrangement further alienated them, no matter how efficiently the railroads might operate (and railroad freight rates, even during these formative years, declined 50% between 1830 and 1860).(29) Small towns with just a single rail line also objected to the monopoly the train company held over them. Communities across America commonly begged for the establishment of railroad service, then denounced it after it appeared. It's easy to see in hindsight that the government should have built out the track systems, then leased them to competing private train operators.

After four different companies tried and failed, Port Huron and St. Clair County finally obtained their first railroad service in 1859, with help from Canada. The Montreal-based and English-financed Grand Trunk Railroad crossed into America from Sarnia to Port Huron. It eventually pushed two lines through the city and across the state, one south to Detroit, and the other west to Chicago (already the rail center of America), absorbing other lines as it went. The GTRR built its 60-mile Port Huron to Detroit connection at a cost of $27,000 per mile. The first train, packed with 200 jubilant passengers, make its 4-hour run to Detroit on November 21, 1859.(30) All the Port Huroners on board confidently expected rail service to further boost the economy of their newly incorporated city, now 4,000 inhabitants strong, as the forests receded and more farms and industry sprang up.

The track gangs had hardly driven the last spike before 12 year-old Thomas Alva Edison of Port Huron wangled a deal to sell newspapers and refreshments on board the Grand Trunk's Detroit train. When Edison one day pulled a telegrapher's son out of the way of an oncoming boxcar, the boy's grateful father offered personally to instruct Al – as people first called him, not Tom – in telegraphy . With that training Edison launched himself on an electrical life path which eventually won him a worshipful acolyte named Henry Ford.

This happened right in time for the Civil War. It is no idle speculation to suggest that had America been bound together more tightly with a nationally designed transportation network, the fabled "internal improvements," the Civil War might never have occurred. The war crisis, and the firm backing by that dedicated internal improvements man, and former railroad lawyer, Abraham Lincoln, spurred the Congress to authorize in 1862 federal support for the construction of the first transcontinental railroad to securely tie east with west. The overwhelming railroading advantage of the Union, and its corresponding ability to rapidly move men and materials, spelled the doom of the Confederacy before the rebels had fired a shot. With a 2-1 advantage in mileage, and with the industrial might to add more trackage whenever and wherever needed, the North emerged the clear victor in what historian Bruce Catton called the first of the "railroad wars." The South added not a single new mile to its rail network during this conflict. At best it managed to tear up a line here and re-lay it there. Union army railroad builders, on the other hand, added mileage so adeptly that they joked about carrying spare bridges and tunnels in their pockets.

During the war year of 1863 – the gravest year of American peril during the entire century – busy Northern railroads enjoyed their greatest profits ever. That same year, the Michigan Central Railroad's engineers decided in the face of the heavy traffic that it might br wise to organize the nation's first trainmen's union, the Brotherhood of the Footboard. What with hand brakes and manual coupling mechanisms and other dodgy procedures, working on the railroad in war or peace killed and injured so many employees that they couldn't get insurance, so they organized to provide their own. The four operating personnel unions that eventually formed up proved to be a formidable force for railroad owners to contend with.

As phenomenal as the growth of American railroads had been before the Civil War, the postwar boom dwarfed it. Mileage doubled again, to 70,000 miles by 1873, and again, to 156,000 miles by 1888. That included five transcontinental railroads built within a generation. A total of $9 billion had been invested by now.(31) In Michigan, railroad mileage increased 1,000% in 40 years, to 8,000 miles, reaching all but a handful of communities in the state.(32) On our home front, Port Huron's first mayor, William Bancroft, a lawyer and journalist and banker and state legislator and general eager beaver, resurrected the charter for two never-built railroads and built one, all the way west 70 miles to Flint, Michigan by 1871. Part of the money for this came from the city of Port Huron, which put up $42,000 in bonds; part came from investors, and part from land grants – 3,500 acres in St. Clair County.(33) Federal and state governments eventually handed out a total of 180 million acres in land grants to railroad companies. If calculated at the standard federal land price of that era, $1.25 per acre, it came to roughly $225 million worth, though some estimates put the value at twice that.

Many of these land grants predated the Civil War but weren't put into use until the smoke of battle cleared. Railroad developers used some of the property to build on and sold the rest. Grants in Michigan totaled 5.5 million acres, about 9% of the state's land area, an immense slice. Although land deals had been used for canal and road construction, the railroad grants in particular didn't sit too well with some of the public. But others argued that the introduction of railroad service promoted development and increased everybody else's property values for miles around. In exchange for the land, the federal government also received reduced railroad shipping rates that lasted for decades, saving taxpayers hundreds of millions of dollars in the process.

Land grants helped all right, but the really savvy rail entrepreneur got by without them. In 1878 an assortment of nine of Port Huron's leading businessmen

18

organized a new railroad without grants. The backers list included virtually every big name in town, starting with Daniel Harrington again. These men had learned by this time the primary lesson from the Northern Michigan Railroad fiasco, and from the 19 other St. Clair County companies which obtained charters but never built anything: keep expenses down. This ingenious team built a narrow gauge system (about 3/4 the size of standard) to interconnect the Thumb region, one affordable piece of trackage at a time. This narrow gauge idea had been pioneered in Michigan by the lumber industry, to move logs out of the woods where they couldn't be floated out. In four years time the Port Huron & Northwestern Railroad spread out to 254 miles, with stops in almost every village and town of any size in the district. Overjoyed Thumb communities showered the company with spontaneous subscriptions amounting to tens of thousands of dollars; subscriptions not for stock ownership, but simply to help with construction. In the village of Croswell, residents donated $20,000, 12 acres of land on which to build a depot, and 65,000 feet of lumber for a grain elevator. The total cost of the PH&NW came to $3.2 million, about $14,000 per mile, including equipment. In 1882 the bottom line showed a profit of $133,000, thanks to the efforts of the general manager, 38 year-old Henry McMorran, whom we've mentioned already as a prominent ship owner. Hereafter, we'll call this train the McMorran Line in his honor.

Why get so excited, in Croswell or any place, about railroads? In these postwar years rail travel became ever more comfortable for the average passenger, with the addition of steam heat, electric lighting, dining cars, and at the top of the line, the Pullman sleeping car (first built in Detroit by George Pullman). Railroads safety steadily improved, too, with better signaling, air brakes, automatic car coupling, telegraphic controls, double trackage, better bridges and more solidly built cars. Freight rates continued to fall, as engines grew bigger and more powerful and freight cars quadrupled in size, carrying up to 40 tons apiece. The development of livestock cars, refrigerator cars (another Detroit invention), and tank cars all helped facilitate an explosion of American railroad freight service that reached 79 billion ton miles by 1890, eight times the amount carried at the end of the Civil War. And speed, that alternately seductive and destructive siren song for us sometimes shortsighted Americans, continued to increase. Speed on the rails and speed in the factories. Passengers on the McMorran Line might be satisfied with 30 mph, but a test locomotive reached 100 mph in America in 1893, and in 1899 Professor Oberlis Smith told the American Society of Civil Engineers about his plans for a 200 mph train. In Detroit, which had become the largest railcar manufacturing center in America, the Michigan Railcar Company used assembly lines to turn out units faster. An employee named Henry Ford worked there briefly.

In Port Huron the tangible benefits of railroad expansion included a big workforce for both RR lines in town. The McMorran Line built a sizable freight and passenger depot and an 11-engine roundhouse on the riverfront downtown. The Grand Trunk, which swallowed up the Bancroft railroad while opening service to Chicago, erected a huge car repair shop in Port Huron in 1882. The GTRR also built large freight sheds of its own, even a grain elevator, and by century's end employed up to 800 people in a city of 19,000 residents. The true dimension of the economic and landscape-changing muscle of the railroads came home to Port Huronites when the Grand Trunk dug the first ever international rail tunnel beneath a mile of the St. Clair River, linking the U.S. and Canada. Cost: $2.7 million. This facility spared the company the trouble of ferrying 600 railcars per day across the water.

The tunnel project was no picnic for the workmen involved. Pick and shovel men earned 20 cents an hour, digging for 14 hours per day. Workers had to be relieved every half hour due to bad ventilation and the 40 lb. per-square-inch air compression maintained to keep the water out. Three workers died. Ten feet of progress was a good day's work.(34) The project took three years to complete, made the pages of *Scientific American* magazine, and caused such a stir that Port Huron became known for a time as "Tunnel City." A whole new neighborhood called just "the Tunnel" sprang up around this iron-lined hole in the ground. The Grand Trunk built a grand new passenger depot near the tunnel's mouth, next to its extensive marshaling yards. The Biograph Company used one of Edison's latest inventions to make an early movie of this tunnel in 1899.

Just as the GTRR did in Port Huron, railroads consistently built some of the most handsome as well as functional buildings in the country, structures large and small. Stations in major cities rated among the most ravishingly beautiful structures ever erected in America. Railroad historian Willis Dunbar likened them as status symbols to medieval cathedrals. Even in middling cities the size of Port Huron the main depots stood out, and in many towns they served virtually as community centers. Several unincorporated towns grew up in the Thumb around the railroad-built depots. Fargo, for instance, a depot stop, eventually included a sawmill, gristmill, grain elevator, creamery, hotel, pharmacy, dance hall, and general store.

Railroads impacted American life in other ways as well. For all practical purposes the railroads introduced modern postal service and package delivery in America. Mail clerks staffed four Grand Trunk trains leaving Port Huron every day. Railroads brought year-round fresh fruits and vegetables to millions of the nation's tables, and imposed the four time zone concept across America in 1882, an idea that Congress didn't catch up with until 1918. People set their clocks by the trains, and the whole concept of running to time could be said to have been a railroad invention. As early as Henry Thoreau's day, the 1850s, he wrote: "Have not men improved somewhat in punctuality since the railroad was invented? To do things 'railroad fashion' is now the byword..."

The railroads played an indispensable part in opening up for settlement much of the middle and western U.S. They also greatly expanded tourism. The railroad industry heavily backed creation of the national park system to foster vacation destinations like Yellowstone, Yosemite and Grand Canyon National Parks. Railroads promoted summer holiday spots in Michigan, like Port Huron, and in 1887 helped erect the massive Grand Hotel on the former fur trading post, British fortress, Confederate POW prison camp, and now Great Lakes glamour retreat, Mackinac Island.

Railroads also, unfortunately, played a part in the reintroduction of racial segregation into the nation, when the Supreme Court upheld a Louisiana law mandating separate railroad cars for blacks in the disastrous *Plessy vs Ferguson* decision of 1896. And, as we've touched upon, the enthusiasm for railroads and their greater speeds seriously impaired the development and maintenance and useful exploitation of American waterways, especially in cases where railroads acquired canals and shipping companies primarily to eliminate competition.

The single biggest complaint made all across the land against railroads involved discriminatory freight rates. Big shippers got better rates than little shippers; heavy traffic lines charged less than thin traffic lines. This simple practice of volume discounting annoyed a public that wanted the railroads rigidly run as single-rate common carriers, though operating a railroad or any other enterprise that way eventually led to serious financial trouble. The public also wanted lower passenger fares. Neither sentiment was lost on federal or state lawmakers. The first Michigan regulation on fares came as early as 1855. Other states also got active, imposed hundreds of fare and freight and profit regulations, and established state railroad commissions to back them up. In 1887 the federal government joined the party by creating, primarily to watchdog railroads, the Interstate Commerce Commission, an agency which, while begun with good intentions, in time became infamous for its byzantine, contradictory, and often inscrutable rulings. A Michigan judge, Thomas Cooley, served as the ICC's first chairman.

On top of this, though they paid their taxes at the state level, Michigan railroads often had to deal with nitpicking local officials bitching about operations in every city, village, township and county along the right of way. Backbiters wielded a typical weapon, an 1885 law forbidding a train from blocking a road for more than five minutes.(35) In essence, the government wanted the luxury of regulating railroads to a fare-thee-well, without any of the responsibility for their upkeep, as it kept up roads and waterways. A plainly unfair arrangement.

As railroading grew into the second biggest industry in America, next to farming, it frequently got the blame for the entire country's business cycle. By the 1870s 700,000 people worked for US railroads, and 5% of all American families depended on railroad employment for support. Hotheads blamed the depression of 1873, the worst of the century, on railroad overexpansion, though the train lines suffered just as badly as the rest of the nation during the slump, and some bounced in and out of receivership like tennis balls. The next business contraction, in 1893, replayed exactly the same scenario on an even bigger scale.

Attempts by the RR's to cut down wages or employment levels to deal with business reversals could and did lead to strikes and riots. Regulators frowned on mergers meant to increase efficiency because they also decreased competition. When railroads raised money by issuing stocks and bonds based on their estimated future earnings capacity instead of just their physical plant – a financial practice that became commonplace for all corporations in the 20th Century – critics accused them in the 19th of watering their shares, though these securities remained among the most coveted investments in America.

All this downside persuaded Henry McMorran and friends to get out while the getting was good, and they sold the Port Huron and Northwestern RR to some bigger out-of-town boys, the Pere Marquette Railroad, in 1889. The PMRR somewhat recklessly then blew $1.2 million converting this narrow gauge division in the Thumb to standard gauge tracks and equipment, more capacity than it really needed.

So far, we've talked about American heavy railroads but this is as good a place as any to back up and consider the light rail systems that developed right alongside steam railroads during the 19th Century: streetcars. The first horse drawn city street railroad in America opened in New York City in 1832, a 40-passenger rig which did about 12 mph at full gallop, though more often 5-6 mph, about twice walking pace.

21

These streetcars quickly took over the traffic of the unrailed buses which had preceded them. Eighteen million passengers boarded the NYC streetcar system in 1855, 180 million per year by the 1880's. Ever the fashion leader, New York's example inspired New Orleans to install streetcars next, then a flood of other cities followed, and by 1881 400 street railway companies operated in America. They owned 3,000 miles of track, 18,000 streetcars and 100,000 horses to shoe and shovel up after.(36) Detroit's streetcar company started in 1863; Port Huron's City Railway in 1866, co-founded by Thomas Edison's brother.

Pitt Edison originally built the Port Huron system to link the Grand Trunk railroad station with the downtown riverfront business district about two miles away. Fare: 10 cents by day, 25 at night. The streetcar line at first looked like something of an extravagance. After all, customers just as easily could have walked, or taken a ferry downtown. But business on the City Railway boomed so quickly that a competing line sprang up in 1873, sparking a terrific court fight and a bonanza of legal fees. The whole mess went to the Michigan Supreme Court and back again before a merger could be arranged. It is a recurring and important plot point to note that the street railway in Port Huron remained entirely a private enterprise right down to the tracks, but one requiring a city franchise and fare approval. Also, the streetcar company made no effort to set up a complementary line for freight delivery, missing a chance to bring some regularity and order to the commercial life of the city's streets.

The horse, who, after all, hadn't volunteered for the job in the first place, had worn out his welcome in some American streetcar circles by the 1870's, and the search started for replacement power. Cablecars briefly came into vogue. These vehicles mechanically clutched and released a continously circulating cable loop that ran through trenches in the streets, dragging the cars along in San Francisco, Chicago, Washington, DC and two dozen other cities.(37) However, the wave of the streetcar future proved to be an electromagnetic wave, and after Ernst von Siemens launched the first electric railway system in Germany in 1881, American designers got busy. One of Thomas Edison's ex- assistants, Frank Sprague, and a former Detroit furniture maker, Charles Van DePoele, both came up with overhead-wire electric trolley systems for streetcars. They both felt overhead lines would be safer for city use than the ground-level electrified "third rail" system first used by Siemens. Pedestrians and horses who came into contact with a third rail agreed, those that survived the tremendous electrical shock.

A trio of Port Huron brothers – Henry, John and James Talbot – saw a DePoele system operating in Windsor, Ontario across the river from Detroit. The Talbots made a living as paving contractors, also ran a weekly newspaper, and knew nothing about streetcars, but the 19th Century entrepreneur was nothing if not adaptable. The brothers promptly scared up $40,000, and bought and electrified the Port Huron streetcars in 1886, keeping a few horses in reserve at first, just to be on the safe side. The Talbots began operations with four cars and two miles of track, and their inexperience with electricity led to excessive amounts of juice buzzing through the cars at first, magnetizing a few passengers' watches. One man claimed the current did his rheumatism good. The power came from the new Excelsior Electric Company plant, co-owned by the ever adaptable Henry McMorran, a concern built originally to offer electric lights.

The City Electric Railway succeeded as one of the first electric streetcar lines in America, and expanded steadily. The six cars on the route in 1892 covered a combined 1,000 miles per day. By 1899 ridership amounted to as many as 60,000 passengers per week, 1.3 million per year, on a dozen miles of track. The trolley didn't win everybody over, however. Sam Edison – Pitt and Tom's father – took one ride on the electric and found the 20 mph clip too much for him. "That was traveling too fast!" said Sam. "After this give me a horse." He declined to reboard a streetcar thereafter. 99% of American streetcars had unhorsed themselves and switched to lightning by the end of the century.

The marriage of electricity and rail now gave American cities a clean, quiet, smooth, efficient method of moving around large numbers of people (and goods, where the idea occurred to anybody) on a fixed system that served not just as a transportation matrix but as a surefire basis for intelligent urban planning. It worked perfectly not just for ground level but for elevated and subterranean rapid transit trains, too. Unlike Sam Edison, William Ford, Henry's father, embraced electric mass transit and served on a committee advocating it for the Dearborn area. He and others recognized that electric streetcars wouldn't stay confined to cities for long. City-to-city trolley lines called interurbans (IU) very quickly followed. Interurbans promised to fill the the gaps in the American landscape where neither railroads nor boats ran, in what could have been and should have been the master pattern for ground transportation in the United States. In historian William Middleton's words: "The interurbans were bright and clean, stopped almost anywhere, and ran far more frequently than steam trains, for one car made a train. Once in town, the cars usually operated through the streets and went right downtown. They were almost always cheaper than steam trains, too."(38)

The first true interurban, in Middleton's opinion, opened between Portland, Oregon and Oregon City in 1893. But long distance electric rail really came into its own with the introduction of alternating current and improved transmission power in 1896, courtesy of the ideas of former Edison assistant Nikola Tesla and the largesse of railroad airbrake inventor George Westinghouse. By 1898, the interurban service established between Cripple Creek and Victor, Colorado, which negotiated 7% grades and reached elevations over two miles high, demonstrated that if IU service could go there it could go anywhere.(39)

An interurban line began to push northeastward out of Detroit in 1895, heading toward St. Clair County and Port Huron. A frenzy of negotiation and wrangling over franchises and contracts slowed this project down considerably before the last phase of construction began in 1899 on what came to be called the Rapid Railway. Plans also called for another interurban linking Port Huron to the Lake Huron shoreline communities to the north, which had no railroad service. The backers wanted the village of Lexington, with only a few hundred residents, to put up $5,000 in support, and the *Lexington News* proclaimed it would be worth 100 times that.(40)

With no one in America's national or state capitals in charge of trying to work out some complementarity between the nation's transportation systems, neither the steam railroads nor the shipping companies exactly welcomed the interurbans. Rather than work together to each others strengths, they too often spent time at each others throats. Nevertheless, counting city and interurban streetcar systems and the odd heavy railroad that converted to electricity, America by 1899 had built 22,000 miles of electric

23

rail service, an amazing accomplishment in 13 years.(41) And as of that same year, the United States enjoyed the world's premier steam railroad system, worth $11 billion, with the best service, lowest rates and fares, and highest wages on earth, covering a network of more than 250,000 miles. It moved half a billion passengers, and almost a billion tons of freight per year.(42)

ROADS

This subject of roads is a good spot to re-emphasize the four tiers of government at work in Michigan, because they all had a hand in roads eventually: federal, state, county, and the locals – meaning cities, villages and townships. As one of the first things on the agenda at their first meeting ever, the three County Board members of the Michigan Territory's brand new St. Clair County ordered a road built in 1821. Pretty ambitious for a county with fewer than 400 people in it. Member George Cottrell, the son of an Indian massacre survivor, had somewhere acquired previous experience with roads, and persuaded his colleagues to build one between the mouths of the Belle and Pine Rivers, connecting the two ports of Marine City and St. Clair City, a sensible combination of transportation methods. Very likely Cottrell laid out his road along an aboriginal shoreline trail. Many of the primary Michigan territorial roads, which later became important state highways, also were built along Native American paths; the products, after all, of thousands of years of field testing.

When one says "build" a road, this simply meant stripping the proposed route down to bare earth, leveling and grading it. Then, if you wanted to get fancy, you put a layer of stones on it, maybe crowned it to ensure the water ran off, and ditched the sides. The stones made it an "improved" road. You might in addition be called on to fill in depressions, surmount hills, drain swamps, and bridge rivers and ravines to carry your road along. In the 20th Century the stonework and drainage and compacting and paving and curbing and signage got very fancy and expensive indeed, but the stones-on-a-dirt-path schematic pretty much covered roadmaking. Some early American builders substituted logs for the stones, creating what were known as corduroy roads. Others put boards on the ground to make a plank road. Some used gravel mixed up with clay or tar, a mixture called macadam, after the method's inventor. The railroads, of course, laid wooden ties with metal rails spiked to them on top of the stones.

Road construction during much of the 19th Century in Michigan remained primarily a local affair. At first the federal government used its authority to build or assist in building postal and military roads. In 1827 Uncle Sam decided to construct a military road between Fort Detroit and an army installation at Port Huron named Fort Gratiot. This was in case the British and Canadians ever got frisky again and tried to reignite the War of 1812. It's lucky they didn't, since it took all of six years to complete the 60 mile Fort Gratiot Turnpike, later known simply as the Gratiot Pike. Cost: $500 per mile.(43) Other federal turnpikes interconnected the rest of the outposts in the Michigan territory. Federal road building then ceased following statehood in 1837, and these pikes eventually ended up under state control. State roadmaking in Michigan also stopped when, as we'll recall, the 1850 Michigan constitution dried up all spending on new internal improvements. Even county officials in Michigan, like George Cottrell, lost their powers to create roads in 1827, which left most roads and streets in the hands of townships and cities.

24

One of the principle reasons that the responsibility for 19th Century Michigan's roads devolved onto the hands of local authorities was the continuous and exasperating cost of maintenance. Even the meagerest road or street required attention of some sort, often year-round, if for nothing else than just to beat back the jungle. The fancier the road, the more traffic it generated and the more attention it demanded. To introduce a familiar concept into the story here: it wasn't the purchase price that killed you, it was the cost of upkeep. A barren, vegetationless piece of ground like a dirt road easily rutted and easily flooded. Even an improved road if left unattended gave way over time to the most powerful physical force on the planet, moving water. Moreover, roads and streets presented a wide surface for wear and tear, whereas the impact of a train or streetcar focused very narrowly on almost indestructible metal rails which were easier and cheaper to fix. That advantage, plus the fact that the rails largely were in private hands and no drain on the public treasury, made them the ground transportation of choice. The rise of the railways seriously slowed down the construction of improved public roads in Michigan for much of the second half of the 19th Century. In fact, according to the general consensus, the state's roads got worse during this period.

For the overall mapping of roads, the federal government early on ordered the Northwest Territory, including Michigan, to be surveyed in rectangular-grid fashion. Once the surveyors completed their work in a section of Michigan, its occupants built roads mostly along the grid lines, dropping the example of the Native American-style trail system, which everyone had used up until then in the eastern U.S. Cross-hatching the entire state of Michigan this way presented some problems. The grid didn't always directly connect where people were with where they wanted to go, and roads built on this plan resulted in a lot of roundabout travel. But it certainly made construction simpler and helped coordinate the work between adjacent sections.

In executing this plan, Michigan matched each township to a road district in which every able bodied male aged 21-45 worked off his annual road tax at the discretion of the highway supervisor. Henry Ford's father William served as one of these township road bosses, who required up to 10 days work per year per body. Men who brought their horse teams along to help out got extra credit and fewer days on the job. Very few citizens knocked themselves or their horses out on this assignment. In most cases they constructed and maintained roads as good as they needed them to be at a minimum, no better or worse. By 1899 they'd built 1,500 miles of road across St. Clair County's 837 square miles, excluding city streets. The results typified those described by historian George May: "The most familiar sight in Michigan was a quiet country dirt road running past fields of the rich agricultural region of Southern Michigan."(44)

As far as functionality went, minimal roads usually didn't do too well in the spring. In 1841 St. Clair County's governors couldn't meet due to impassable springtime roads. This situation – impassability – became an annual event somewhere or other in the county for the next 159 years, almost a roving spring festival. Winter, somewhat counter-intuitively, offered the best time for horse-drawn travel because the roads froze solid. If you used a sleigh, then snow and ice lubricated the runners. Port Huron's most prominent doctor of the era, Cyrus Stockwell, first president of the Michigan Medical Society, once drove his sleigh to Detroit and back,120 miles round trip, in a single winter's day, with no appreciable damage to the horse, which lived on to the ripe old age of 37.

19th Century Americans in many ways adjusted far more patiently to nature's moods than their 20th Century descendants, especially those engaged in agriculture, timing their travel plans to seasonal variations in road conditions. And more than enough food always got through. America never recorded a significant food shortage anywhere due to transportation issues. Nor did farmers suffer economically from road quality. Here again, the scenarios later concocted about the anguished plight of the pre-automobile farmer don't quite jibe with the reality. The cost of wagoning grain or produce or lumber or fiber, or herding livestock over the roads to town, or to the ship dock, or to the railhead, added less than 2/10 of a cent per pound to the farmer's costs. Some people calculated it at much less, about 25 cents per ton-mile.

When it came to laying out city and village streets in St. Clair County, townspeople used rectangular grid patterns again. We might as well list the rest of these communities here: apart from Port Huron and Marine City they included St. Clair City, Algonac, Yale, Capac. The grid gave them an ancient way of attacking the problem of creating orderly thoroughfares. This method had been used as far back as the days of the Babylonians, the Romans, and the Mayans. In contrast to a grid, winding city streets typical of Classical Athens and medieval Europe looked more picturesque, and could confuse an invading army, but since no one expected a siege of Port Huron anytime soon, the Roman way won out. The right angle layout didn't allow for a city center to which the main streets all naturally led, as in a wheel pattern, and some pretty tight corners resulted here and there, but at the speed of a pedestrian or horse or bicycle or streetcar, sharp turns caused no insurmoutable difficulties. 110 miles of streets reached into most but not all of Port Huron's 11 square miles in 1899. The municipal government put down some board and gravel surfaces on major streets, followed later by cedar blocks and bricks, but on most avenues the good earth sufficed.

You couldn't very well create dirt sidewalks, however. Sidewalks also were a very old idea. Excavators had uncovered some among the ruins of Pompeii and Knossos. Port Huron built its first board sidewalks in the 1870's, and cement versions by the 1890's. In 1899 the city put down 8 miles of new cement walks at a cost of $16 per 50 feet, and banned any more plank ones. Unexpectedly, the length of women's dresses spurred sidewalk installations. These garments in the late 19th Century reached to the ground, and women didn't want to drag their hems through the dirt. Merchants liked sidewalks because they drew shoppers up close to display windows, and Port Huron retailers erected a solid bank of awnings over the walks to further enhance them. The sidewalk system didn't cover the whole town, though, and gaps in the walks forced pedestrians back into the streets. And just as with streets, maintenance caused problems. Fallen pedestrians tripped up by bad sidewalks sued the city with regularity.

First and foremost the sidewalks, streets and roads belonged to walkers. Those travelers who employed foot locomotion, the product of six million years in evolutionary development, which exercised 60% of the body mass, benefited from the most natural and healthful transportation in the world. The more you walked, the better you felt and looked and it was almost impossible to do too much. In fact, walking played an absolutely indispensable role in good health, though just how much a person needed hadn't been quantified. Thomas Jefferson thought two hours per day, and he safeguarded the health of his slaves by insuring that they did five to six times that much. In his honor, we'll call this two hours the Jefferson Minimum.

26

Port Huron, St. Clair County, the state of Michigan and the American nation did the vast majority of its traveling during the 19th Century on foot. One of the first great American pedestrians, Estwick Evans, left behind some thoughts about the early days in the Michigan territory. In 1818 he published the story of his "Pedestrious Tour," a four thousand mile walk from New Hampshire to New Orleans and back. "...I met no tract of country which on the whole impressed my mind so favorably as the Michigan territory. The soil of this territory is generally fertile and a considerable portion of it is very rich. Its climate is delightful and its situation novel and interesting."(45) Behind Evan's observations lay a simple truth that came to be forgotten later in America: only someone who walks a place really knows it, whether it's a neighborhood or a nation. One of the wonderful things about America was that nobody would ever walk it completely, so no one would ever really know it completely. Henry Thoreau often put in 30 miles per day. Mark Twain thought nothing of walking nine miles up the side of Mt. Davidson to get home to Virginia City in one night. Young Henry Ford often walked the eight miles into Detroit after school, and caught the train home.

Pedestrians occasionally excited popular adulation during the 1800's. Another of the leading lights of American footsters, former newspaperman Edward Payson Weston, took up extreme walking after the Civil War. Weston put in 30 to 40 miles per day along an announced route, then at his destination delivered a temperance lecture, and passed the hat to cover expenses. Weston wasn't above competitive race walking for money. Sometimes these races covered fixed distances; he did 550 miles in 142 hours at one event. Another time, walking against a field for 24 hours to see who could pile up the most miles, Weston picked 'em up and laid 'em down for 109 miles. Even Port Huron staged walking races from time to time. Sam Edison regularly took part, and so did a speed hoofer named Patrick Newell. Newell once wagered $100 – a huge sum then – that he'd walk the 25 miles round trip to St. Clair City and back in three hours, almost jogging pace. He won, despite having to deal with staged distractions along the way put on by the other bettors, like a girl fighting off a make-believe masher.

According to historian Dorothy Mitts most Port Huron pedestrians made no big deal of walking. "Those were the days when the pioneer thought nothing of walking from Port Huron to St. Clair City or out to Clyde Mills [10 miles] when there was no other means of transportation, when he had to carry...25 to 100 pounds." An elderly lady once refused a wagon ride into Port Huron from two miles outside of town, saying, "No thank you, I'm in a hurry and better walk."(46) Clyde Township farmer Alex Jacobs regularly walked the nine miles into Port Huron until he turned 102 years old. Unfortunately, he suspended this healthful habit at that age, and, sure enough, he died two years later. After him we'll name this phenomenon the Jacobs Effect: when you stop walking, you start dying.

Because walkers built it,19th Century Port Huron remained a relatively compact community. Its full corporation limits measured 7 miles north to south, 2 miles east to west at its widest, but a pedestrian could march between its furthest two points in about two hours, and most errands took just a few minutes. The multitude of elementary schools made a striking example of this accommodation to walking. Thirteen of these schools, scattered about a community of fewer than 20,000 people, guaranteed that young children could easily walk to school.

Most of Port Huron's homes and businesses and public buildings sat close

27

together, which gave the streets an intimate but still, in an automobile-free city, an uncrowded feeling. The streets were 20-30 feet wide in most cases. The widest, at 66 feet, was the main downtown thoroughfare, the old Military Road built between the forts in Detroit and Port Huron. For convenience we'll call it Main Street. The ease of walking around Port Huron raised the question in the minds of people like Sam Edison of just how necessary the streetcars were. Did they make life too easy, if such a thing were possible, and undercut the necessity for healthful exercise? As well as spread the city out too much? Was there such a thing as overtransportation? There certainly was, as we will see.

Even with rudimentary roads, the typical horseback pace in St. Clair County in the 1820's achieved 7-8 mph, compared to the average walking pace of 3 mph. In the eastern states American stagecoaches reached a measure of considerable velocity by 1820. A traveler could ride from New York to Philadelphia by stage, get to a business appointment, and return home the same day the same way, 200 miles all told.(47) The first public stagecoach in Michigan went a lot slower than that. In 1822 it took a whole day to cover 20 miles, for a fare of $1, a day's wage for a working man, who could have walked faster. Gradually, though, the Michigan stages ramped up speed to about an average 7 mph range, which made the standard 5 cents per mile passenger fare defensible. Four horses pulled the 2,500 pound coaches, which carried up to nine passengers. The first stage clattered into Port Huron from Detroit in 1837. These large vehicles posed a couple of problems which will loom large later in this history. They took up a lot of space on Michigan's narrow highways, endangering foot traffic. And even before the first Port Huron stage arrived the state legislature had taken the precaution of passing a law against drunk stagecoach driving, and drunk carriage driving to go with it.(48)

With extended stagecoach travel came the introduction of privately-owned plank toll roads, an innovation only possible in a state awash in cheap lumber, like Michigan. A state franchise holder built the first plank road in 1837. Workmen nailed eight foot long, three inch thick boards side by side to sunken beams along the route. It gave a great ride, at first, and plank roads were very popular, "...virtually hummed with traffic," according to historian David McCormick. Entrepreneurs eventually built 200 of them around Michigan, including three leading in and out of Port Huron, to the west, northwest, and south. Franchises lasted for 60 years. Toll-keepers exacted 3.5 cents per mile for a stagecoach, 1 cent for horse and rider or carriage, 2 cents for a score of cattle. Most didn't bother charging pedestrians, who sneaked onto the plank highways easily enough.

As one can imagine about a wooden road, maintenance proved to be a serious handicap. When in 1868 Mark Twain took a Michigan trip from Grand Rapids to Kalamazoo on a plank road, he remarked "It would have been good if some unconscionable scoundrel had not now and then dropped a plank across it." Railroad competition stole much of the plank road traffic over time, especially from stagecoaches. Port Huron's stage service traveled five different routes as late as 1871, but faded away as most of its customers climbed aboard trains instead. Only 23 of Michigan's 200 plankways remained by 1899 and gravel had replaced the board surfaces.(49)

The graveled toll roads won no travelers' awards, either. In describing one of

28

the three leading into Port Huron, farmer Henry Van Luven said he and his wagon team negotiated stones as big as coconuts or pumpkins, "...the most conscientious saint in the township fills the air with profanity as he dodges Scylla and runs into Charybdis."(50) In 1898 St. Clair County District Attorney Joseph Walsh hauled the owners of a Port Huron toll road into court to cancel their franchise due to poor service. Impetuously, Walsh then tried to revoke another toll road license held by Henry McMorran, who didn't aim to be deprived of his investment by Walsh or anybody else, and beat off the attack.

Michigan played a major role in the evolution of the horsecarts and wagons that plied the country roads and city streets of America. It is here that a major contemporary and competitor of Henry Ford makes his entrance into this history. Born in 1861 in Boston, the grandson of an early Michigan lumberman / railroad builder / and governor, William Crapo Durant moved with his mother to the city of Flint as a boy. Just to fix its relative location on a map for the reader, Flint anchored the western point of a equilateral triangle joining it with Port Huron to the east and Detroit to the south. Always known familiarly as Billy, Durant's own ascent as a businessman began in 1886 when he spotted a horse cart of a new design which took his fancy. Flint already manufactured wheeled vehicles in abundance – some 30 different carriage and wagon brands eventually – and Durant wanted his share of that action. He got it. Borrowing $1,500 to buy the cart plans, and enlisting as a partner a hardware merchant and former schoolmate of Henry Ford's named Josiah Dort, Durant in a dozen years built one of the largest carriage companies in the world, demonstrating powers of salesmanship and financial legerdemain that fell nothing short of wizardry. Durant-Dort helped turn Flint into America's self-proclaimed "Vehicle City."

Michigan manufacturers mass-produced 379,000 horse-drawn vehicles in 1899. The leader, Durant, shipped tens of thousands of his "Blue Ribbon" buggies by railroad to a network of dealers all over America. A four-passenger Durant-Dort surrey set its owner back $64. Blue Ribbons would have been a common sight in Port Huron and on St. Clair County roads. Of course, typically of that era, a town the size of Port Huron had half a dozen of its own carriage and wagon builders, but none worked on Durant's scale. Flint's huge success in this trade made some Port Huron businessmen thoroughly envious. They couldn't understand why the local wainwrights built only to custom for individual clients like Henry McMorran. Some people wanted very fancy rigs. Folks like the Daniel Harrington clan took a good deal of competitive pride in a handsome buggy and animal turnout. "The Harringtons used to drive their two horses down the street and had their dogs trained to walk right along behind the carriage," remembered one Port Huroner. "Made quite an impression."

Virtually every American farm family owned a wagon and carriage, and a horse or mule or two to pull them. Far fewer of these animals lived in towns. Keeping a horse on a typical home lot in the city didn't provide it with enough grass. If you couldn't find in-town grazing for the animal, and had to buy feed, a horse could get very expensive – $3 a week board at Lawlers livery stable in Port Huron. City horses belonged mainly to businesses, government, the wealthy (Henry McMorran owned 18), and liveries, which rented them. Port Huron still encompassed several farms within its city limits at that point, but still only counted about one horse for every 20 people in 1899, say 1,000 animals. Approximately 11,000 horses and mules resided in St. Clair County. Nobody knew for sure how many millions of horses there were in all of

America. The horse census was not especially meticulous and estimates ranged between 13 and 30 million. The government valued the average horse at only $37, but good ones cost far more.

The alleged tempermentalism of the horse plays a large role early in this story. As man evolved to walk, so the horse spent 50 million years or so perfecting its running technique, and it got precious little chance to exercise this facility pulling a plow, milk wagon, or carriage. The whole domesticated arrangement got on a horse's nerves now and then, and it sometimes galloped off for a good leg stretch if so much as a piece of paper blew by. In 1872 a jumpy horse he had taken out for a ride dragged home 9 year-old Henry Ford with his foot caught in a stirrup, permanently alienating Henry from the species. An 1899 runaway in Port Huron ended with Henry McMorran tossed from his carriage onto his head. Then there were the occasional problems of the horse kicking or biting you, or pitching you from its back and rolling on you. The horse's carefree habit of relieving itself whenever and wherever it chose, and the attendant result, flies, also brought it into disfavor. Fed, watered, harnessed and saddled, currycombed, shoed, blanketed, barned, the horse sometimes seemed to be a little too much trouble.

But on the plus side, for your $37 you got an immensely strong riding and pulling creation (a team of four Michigan draft horses once pulled a sleigh loaded with 100,000 lbs of logs out of a forest), adaptable to a phalanx of farm machines or a myriad of other vehicles. James Watt paid tribute to this beast by measuring the steam engine against it, coming up with the unit of horsepower, or the ability to move 550 foot-pounds per second. The animal rendered up to 25 years of service in exchange for good treatment, operated on grass and water which it converted into excellent fertilizer, repaired and replicated itself, and could be converted into a dozen useful items when dead, and even eaten. The fact that the horse, although a tool, remained a living being with a personality, was for some people its charm, for others its curse. Professional team drivers put up the stoutest defense of the horse. These workmen organized themselves into the Team Drivers International Union in Detroit in 1899, and they needed it badly. Typically, to that point, the Teamsters worked 12-18 hours days, up to seven days per week, at $2 per day, and saw the price of lost or damaged goods taken out of their pay. (51) As labor leader Samuel Gompers observed, even the horse had it better.

The sporting side of the horse captivated many 19th Century Americans, who made horse racing the most popular spectator sport in the country. Two different race tracks, called driving parks in those days, operated in the Port Huron area. Several prominent businessmen founded the premier track, a half-mile long oval within the northwest city limits, and named as its director the city's biggest horse fan, John Petit, a direct descendant of Anselm. Petit also ran a driving park in Detroit, and he owned a livery stable in Port Huron besides. Local horsemen didn't limit themselves to just track racing. They often matched their nags on vacant streets, or even in winter on the frozen Black River – a slow moving, commodious river 150 feet wide that froze as level as a floor for much of its length. This racing took place between the dozens of frozen-in ships that wintered in the Black. Off the track, given a good length of river or road, the very best cart horses kept up a 15 mph pace for as much as an hour.

So maybe you didn't admire horses as much as John Petit or the Teamsters, or couldn't afford one. A personal-sized road alternative for the horseless or the horse averse, one that when perfected proved to be the most energy efficient form of

30

transportation ever created, first saw the light of day in America in 1866. French mechanic Pierre Lallement brought his pedal bicycle design to the New World that year and patented it. This rickety 70 lb. wooden machine, nicknamed the boneshaker for its rough ride, cost $75-$150. It used no gearing; riders pedaled the front wheel directly. The bicycle didn't make much impression right away, but technological progress improved the product very quickly, adding within three years tubular metal construction, rubber tires, wire spoke wheels, and ball bearings.

The resulting, better bike enjoyed a relatively big sale in 1869, and the man who got the patent away from Lallement pulled in $80,000 in royalties on the 16,000 or so bikes built that year. Several bicycle riding schools opened in America during this fad, including one in Detroit. On city streets early bikes, if pedaled with a frenzy, reached 12 mph. Via country roads, determined bicycle tourists traveled 5-8 mph and sometimes covered 50-90 miles per day.(52) But these speeds and distances came very hard to the average cyclist. Continued uncomfortable riding, low speeds, and control problems all dissipated American interest for a few years after the 1869 bicycle boom.

With the direct pedaling design, to reach higher speeds you needed a bigger drive wheel. This led to the development in Europe of the strikingly unstable and dangerous "penny-farthing" bicycle with its gigantic front wheel (48-54 inches, typically) and smaller trailing one. This device was an accident waiting to happen, but it was undeniably fast. In 1878, a high-wheeler bicyclist outran horseback rider Albert Pope one day in Bostom, and Pope decided to import big wheel bikes as a sideline to his shoemaking business. Then he turned to building two-wheelers himself, and within four years Pope had become the world's largest bicycle manufacturer.

Despite the dangers in big-wheel bikes, enough people loved their wheels to found the League of American Wheelmen (the LAW) in 1880, and they set as one of their first goals the construction of better roads to bike on. The American Road Builders Association organized in the same year, 1880, to pursue and profit from the same idea. Albert Pope naturally backed good roads. He paid to pave a stretch of a Boston street with asphalt as a demonstration project, and gave the Massachusetts Institute of Technology $6,000 to found a road engineering department.(53) In Port Huron some early bicycle enthusiasts got together to form their own club, led by Albert Dixon, an English immigrant wholesale grocer, and his sons Harvey and Fred.

The real bike breakthrough came in 1885 with the appearance of English designer James Starley's so-called safety bicycle. The combination of identically sized wheels and chain-driven gearing on this model added speed and stability both, and kept the rider low enough to the ground to spare him any serious falling distance. Add to that the invention in 1888 of easy-riding pneumatic tires by John Dunlop in Belfast, Ireland, and the combination put riders in bike heaven. The explosion in popularity which followed eclipsed completely all previous interest in bicycles. Within a decade 10 million people in America were riding bicycles and 300 factories were building them, making it one of the country's leading industries.(54) Albert Pope's company finished assembling another 800-part bicycle every minute at his 17 acre, all-in-one factory, where each of the 2,000 workers had his own bicycle parking stall.(55) Across the river from Detroit in Windsor, Ontario, two former Port Huron machinists, John and Horace Dodge, designed and built their own brand of bicycles. Bike makers who didn't have the Dodge brothers' mechanical skills could easily buy the components from various

31

suppliers and assemble their own bicycle brands, with maybe one or two novel features of their own thrown in to set them apart from competitors. American dealers sold 2 million of all kinds in 1897.

Bikes got progressively lighter (down to 27 lbs. or so), cheaper ($25 models could be had, and used ones a lot cheaper), faster (track riders sometimes exceeded 50 mph), more reliable, more stoppable with better brakes, and easier to pedal. Shops sprang up all over the country, including a Dayton, Ohio establishment run by brothers Wilbur and Orville Wright, and two in Detroit run, respectively, by a man named William Metzger and a farm implement dealer named Horatio Earle. Earle became a major force in the LAW in Michigan, a consul no less. As part of the war for better roads he helped persuade the state of Michigan to backtrack a bit in 1893, and give counties the option to take back road control from townships. That same year, at the LAW's suggestion, the U.S. Agriculture Department opened a road information office, as part of the effort to tie the good roads movement to farming.

In 1893 George Yokom, stepson to a member of the Jenks shipbuilding family, decided to devote part of his Port Huron electrical shop to bicycles. He had plenty of competitors, mainly hardware dealers like Boyce's, Sturmer's, Beard & Goodwillie's, and Sperry's. Even Patterson's Music Store sold them. If you didn't have the cash, Yokom would sell you a bicycle on credit, with easy terms. One unidentified Port Huron dealer, probably Yokom, told a local newspaper in 1898 that he'd sold 1,400 bikes in a single summer. Even allowing for George's habit of wild promotional exaggeration, and discounting his statements by half, he'd still moved a lot of wheels. So intent did wheelmen and high speed "scorchers" become about getting the latest bicycles that Port Huron dealers held a collective new model show in the spring.

The Dixons and the rest of the Port Huron Bicycle Club raised the money to build a graveled bicycle path covering 12 miles downriver to St. Clair City. Hundreds of riders used it, and got thoroughly annoyed when farmers let their cows and horses wander across it, impeding the oncoming riders. Even without their own bike paths or the asphalt roads of the future envisioned by Albert Pope and the road contractors, many bikers found long distance riding now a pleasure with safety bikes. Two Chicago boys, Elliot and Chris Stevenson, aged 14 and 12, rode all the way over to Port Huron in 8 days, doing better than 40 miles per day. Four riders from Buffalo came charging through town heading in the other direction toward Chicago, covering 85 miles per day.

Of the bicycle, *Scientific American* magazine rhapsodized in 1896, "As a social revolutionizer it has never had an equal. It has put the human race on wheels, and has thus changed many of the most ordinary processes and methods of social life."(56) Progressives heralded the two-wheeler variously as the liberator of women, the working class, children, and anybody else who needed liberating. Bicycles went into common use everywhere in the world and in every conceivable weather and terrain condition from the Australian outback to the Klondike gold fields. Everyone from John D. Rockefeller to the Russian Czar to Henry Ford to Henry McMorran rode them. The bicycle gave them a convenient, cheap, reliable, adaptable and healthful form of personal transportation, and in terms of travel per energy unit bicycling even beat walking. Port Huron's 4th of July in 1899 starred the bicycle both in races at the Driving Park and in a nighttime parade. The bike was too attractive, to some extent. Thieves stole them for "joy rides" in Port Huron 83 times in 1899, though police usually recovered the machines. Impudent bicycle rustlers even took McMorran's a couple of times.

The bicycle had its drawbacks and risks, naturally. Balance played a far more critical role than for any other travel method. This made steering imperfect, and the chance of a bad spill or collision something more than negligible. Some critics claimed that irresponsible cyclists invented the hit-and-run accident. Bicycles seemed to make horses especially tense and prone to bolt. Flats frequently crippled the butt-friendly pneumatic tires. A dispute arose over whether Port Huron bicyclists had any right to ride on the sidewalks, slaloming around walkers, or should be confined to the streets. Some people objected that bicycles went too fast for city use at all, and posed a danger at all times to pedestrians. Port Huron's City Council split the difference and set speed limits for bikes at 8 mph on sidewalks, 10 mph on streets, and ordered night riders to carry lights. These regulations didn't stop a few people from getting injured each year, though virtually never killed.

Because so many of the methods and practices of the bicycle world interfaced with the coming automobile, it brings us back to the subject of engine-powered road transportation. We left it in the early years of the 19th Century, in England, where Richard Trevithick's road steamer made its abbreviated debut. That incident did not mean the end of it, though. Trevithick and other tinkerers persisted until a passenger-carrying road steam stagecoach, or steamcoach if you like, got rolling commercialy in Britain in 1831. A machine built by Sir Goldsworthy Gurney ran between Cheltenham and Gloucester for a period of four months. Four times a day it covered the nine miles in 40-45 minutes, and during those months it hauled a total of 3,000 passengers.[57] The British Parliament, at the urging of the horse lobby, promptly put the operation out of business by special taxation. The tax amounted to as much as 10 times what a regular stagecoach paid, outraging the steamsters, but in fact the wear and tear inflicted on even an improved macadam road by a multi-ton self-propelled vehicle like a steamcoach easily equaled 10 times what a stage pulled by four horses would do, as future generations discovered. Not to mention the proportionate risks this vehicle posed to the passing public.

And there had been incidents. Alarmed residents and travelers along the highway who didn't cotton to sharing it with Gurney's menacing contraption tried to wreck it by occasionally dumping boulders in the way. Or, demonstrating more initiative, they picked up the boulders and stoned the steamcoach as it went past. Dodging these missile and tax issues, other steamcoach operators started service from London to destinations in the cities of Bath, Brighton and Birmingham later in the 1830's, at speeds of up to 20 mph. Then came the inevitable. History's first big motor vehicle road wreck occurred in 1840 when an enormous coach designed by steamship builder John Scott Russell lost a wheel while running between Glasgow and Paisley. Packed with 40 people, it flipped over and exploded, killing five, and shredding and scalding with red hot metal and steam another 20 victims.[58] This did a serious though not mortal injury to the road locomotive industry. Enough of them remained on the highways for travel and farm purposes in 1865 to inspire Britain's Red Flag Act, which set a speed limit of 2-4 mph. It ordered each machine to be preceded on the highways, like a leper, by a man waving a red flag.[59]

In America, the very minor efforts made at developing steam powered passenger vehicles for the road during the first 80 years of the 19th Century are scarcely worth mentioning. A couple of St. Clair County mechanics, father and son John and Thomas Clegg, in 1884 fooled around with one such vehicle they built in their shop. Local lore much later claimed it carried four passengers at up to 12 mph, and that the Cleggs drove it a total of 500 miles. But the Cleggmobile had to be fueled and watered every couple of miles, and the Cleggs gave up on it after a year's work.(60) Similar stories could be told all across America. Successful self-propelled steam vehicles – for farm work, not for passengers – like those that caught Henry Ford's attention, didn't appear in any great numbers until the late 1880's.

One of these traction engines happened to be produced by the Port Huron Engine and Thresher Company, which moved to its namesake city in 1884 at the enticement of many of the same businessmen who'd backed the McMorran Line. PHET became a respected brand name in farm machinery, with sales offices across the Midwest. It's 200 employees, who included for a couple of years those future bicycle builders John and Horace Dodge, built corn huskers and shellers, hay presses, plows, portable sawmills, wagons, water tanks, and threshers. An 1899 jingle about the Port Huron thresher came aggressively right to the point:

When you want a threshing rig that does the biz
You'd better get the very best there is;
It's strictly up to date
Every Thresherman will state
And he don't want any yellow streak in his.

The PHET also built traction engines, which chugged around the company's property on the west side of town, and provided most Port Huronites their first glimpse ever of self-propelled road vehicles. The firm branched out into making its own brand of road construction equipment as well, to better facilitate the movement of its elephantine products across the countryside.

It wasn't steam but a different fuel that cleared the way for the introduction of the automobile: gasoline. Oil distillers once regarded this explosive, flammable, and deadly poisonous leftover from kerosene production as a waste item. Late in life, John D. Rockefeller reminisced wistfully about how his early Standard Oil Company refineries dumped hundreds of thousands of barrels of gasoline into rivers just to get rid of it in the 19th Century. The people of Port Huron knew all about this gas disposal subject, because right across the St. Clair River stood the Imperial Oil Company's Sarnia refinery, controlled by Standard Oil, constructed in 1871 to handle some of the petroleum pumped from wells in the nearby Ontario cities of Oil Springs and Petrolia. These wells produced 2 million barrels in 1899.

The search to find a constructive use for gasoline and ease Rockefeller's conscience about waste resulted in its harebrained promotion for use as a cleaning solvent. Another madman invented the gasoline stove, the single most dangerous appliance ever introduced into the American home. It found its way into several incautious Port Huron households:

A gasoline stove at the residence of Steven Sheehy...sprung a leak on Friday afternoon
and an explosion occurred. Mrs. Sheehy was badly burned about the hands and face,
and her clothes caught fire. After burning up a couple of suits of clothes owned by her

husband she managed to extinguish the flames.(61)

For German inventor Nikolaus Otto, gasoline furnished just the fuel he needed to develop his internal combustion engine in 1876. The ratio of explosive power to volume of gasoline couldn't be beat, as Mrs. Sheehy could tell you. Early gasoline engines only managed about 13% running efficiency, but that was enough. Nursed along by other European experimenters such as Gottlieb Daimler, Karl Benz, and Emile Levassor, the Otto engine was powering a light horseless carriage, a recognizable automobile, on the streets of the Continent by 1891. Early automakers in Europe muscled their way onto public highways to test and promote their machines by staging races. They especially looked to France, which boasted the best network of graveled roads in the world, with a history of good maintenance stretching back to the passage in 1836 of national legislation on the subject. In the 1890's, sadly, impetuous France lacked the good sense to protect its roads by banning autos immediately.

Emile Levassor starred in the 1895 Paris to Bordeaux race, averaging 15 mph for 732 miles in his Panhard Levassor automobile. He received worldwide acclaim as the first of only 9 finishers in the 22 car field. A technicality disqualified Levassor from victory in that competition, and a dog disqualified him from life the next year when it ran in front of Emile's car during a race to Marseilles. Levassor swerved to avoid the animal and piled up his vehicle, suffering the lingering injuries which claimed his life. Symbolically, Levassor became the first of millions of automobile drivers to die from the unfounded expectation of a clear road ahead for their personal progress. In point of fact, neither Levassor nor anyone else, then or ever, could react quickly enough at the controls of an automobile to cope with unexpected obstructions at even modest speeds. Especially a living obstruction, say a dog or a person. And turning the issue around, no dog or person in the road could anticipate what the oncoming automobile driver planned to do. Truly double jeopardy. In memory of pioneer Levassor we'll name after him long, drawn-out auto fatalities as Levassor deaths.

Gasoline autos started menacing the streets of the U.S. in 1893, when buyers acquired the first imported Benz models from Europe. Also that year, two bicycle mechanics, the Duryea brothers, turned out the first of their own cars in Springfield, Massachusetts. Frank and Charles Duryea were the first Americans to get this type of vehicle on the road, but plenty more followed close behind. Tinkerers had filed for 500 different automobile patents in America by 1895. These included an application from a Michigander named Ransom Olds, who had extensive engine experience, and one from a future Port Huron industrialist, Oscar Mueller.

In imitation of the Paris-Bordeaux automobile romp of 1895, the *Chicago Times-Herald* newspaper later that year organized a race of its own in its hometown, the first such race in the USA. After the city of Chicago unwisely lifted its ban on automobiles for this competition, 83 vehicles entered. Exactly two showed up at the starting line: a Duryea driven by Frank, and a Benz driven by Oscar Mueller. The Mueller car had been modified by Oscar and his father Hieronymus as a hobby. Normally they made a living manufacturing highly-regarded plumbing equipment in Decatur, Illinois. Due to the poor turnout of automobiles on the scheduled race day officials postponed the formal event and held a preliminary two-car contest to whet public interest. Mueller copped a $500 prize by beating Duryea. Two reporters covering this "race" on a tandem bicycle had to slow down to let the cars catch up.(62)

Race Day #2 arrived in Chicago in the aftermath of a three-day November blizzard. Duryea and Mueller were again the top men in the field, which wasn't saying much since only 4 other cars joined them. Trouble at the starting line on the Mueller vehicle gave Duryea an hour's head start. The race took 11 hours of driving in uncovered cars and freezing cold to cover 53 miles. Unimpressed spectators frequently pelted the drivers with snowballs. Benumbed from these missiles and exposure after several hours at the wheel, Oscar Mueller collapsed and had to be replaced by the race umpire assigned to his car, Detroit engineer Charles King. King sportingly drove the Mueller vehicle the rest of the way to a second place finish. Duryea won the $2,000 first prize. Mueller won $1,500 and a trip to the hospital.

On the strength of this experience, come the following spring of 1896, the Duryeas asked Charles King to drive the Chicago race-winning Duryea automobile around the Detroit Riding Club's indoor arena during a horse show. They meant this to be a sort of a special treat for any club members who wondered what a horseless carriage actually looked like, and might want to part with some cash to acquire one of their own. The demonstration left the riding club cold, in George May's words: "...its presence created mixed if not outright hostile emotions among the assembled horse-lovers, especially because the fumes from the car's exhaust provided a good deal of coughing among the occupants of ringside seats."(63) Had the horse crowd wanted one, a two-seat Duryea cost $1,000, a four-seater $2,000. Charles King also built, and drove, the first local automobile ever to make it onto Detroit's city streets. He found little difficulty in attaching a gasoline engine to a wagon he owned and taking it for a little turn around the neighborhood at about 5 mph. In support, one of King's friends followed behind the creeping Kingmobile on a bicycle: Henry Ford.

Here we should recap what Henry had been up to during the intervening 20 years since his imaginary big day with the steam tractor. Like most boys of that era, Ford left school at 15 and restlessly tried a number of occupations. He worked a couple days in a shipyard, a few more in the railcar factory, in a machine shop, and in a watch store. He worked as a demonstrator and repairman for Westinghouse steam engines, and also took some business courses in Detroit against the day when he might want to run his own company. Ford cut and sold lumber from some land his father William had given him in an effort to keep his son down on the farm. After several years of these varied activities Ford and his wife of three years, Clara, finally took a decisive step and left the Ford farm for good in 1891, abandoning a beautiful home Henry had designed and built for them. They subsequently bounced through ten rented homes in Detroit during the next ten years.

Ford accepted a position as a mechanic with the Edison electric power company in Detroit, undaunted by the interviewer's first words, "A man was killed down at our substation last week and we need someone in his place right away."(64) Ford made an immediate success at Edison, not simply for his own considerable engineering ability and innate ingenuity, but for his heretofore unsuspected and enormously powerful leadership skills. This job unleashed in Henry a new self-confidence, and an uncanny knack for wielding authority and couching orders in an agreeable way, simultaneously befriending his subordinates while directing them. He often recruited the same men to assist him with his personal projects at home, and persuaded them to perform much of the actual work for free. Although he was excellent with his hands and enjoyed experimenting, when an interesting job crossed the line into

36

tedious labor, Henry Ford preferred to supervise. Within two years he became the Edison company's chief engineer, with plenty of free time on his hands and a very ample salary.

After reading a magazine article on how to build an Otto engine at home, and riding herd on Charles King's autowagon experiment, Henry constructed his own "quadricycle" in the shed behind his rented home on Bagley Street. Ford aptly named the quadricycle because much of the know-how for the early automobiles came from the bicycle/tricycle industry, including, in Ford's case, the wheels and the differential gearing that allowed one wheel on an axle to turn slower than the other, making for smoother cornering. Ford assembled basically a motorized buggy, from bits and pieces he purchased or fabricated. At 2 a.m. on the morning of June 4, 1896, he hacked a bigger opening in the shed doorway with an ax to let the vehicle out (he had forgotten to allow for its size), and drove it a short ways around the streets, accompanied by Edison co-worker Jim Bishop on a bicycle. The quadricycle broke down quickly, and the two men pushed it to the Edison works for repairs.

The next day Henry took Clara and two year-old son Edsel out for a ride. The first Ford car weighed 700 lbs, could travel 20 mph, and had no brakes. Loaded with three people, moving at top speed, it would have hit with the force of a player piano dropped from a third story window. Only this "piano" could follow the victim around the street, or up onto the sidewalks; no outdoor place offered a refuge. By contrast, a streetcar or train followed a narrow, defined path, appearing at regularly scheduled intervals. It took an act of carelessness to get hit by one. A horse-drawn vehicle typically didn't make half the quadricycle's speed, nor did a bicyclist. Ford demonstrated complete indifference to the dangers to which he exposed himself, his family, and his neighbors with his device. In the grip of automobile euphoria, he never worried over the onboard risks, and as for the occupants of the street, they'd better stay out of his way. This absolute self-absorption became a hallmark of the American automobile industry, and its customers.

Mr. and Mrs. Ford indeed did run down a pedestrian not long thereafter. Ford biographer Sidney Olson jocularly described the victim as "slow-moving," absolving the Fords. This reverse blame game, which dated from the earliest days of the automobile, served as a very effective tactic in the auto's campaign of terror to take over the streets. Apparently the Fords weren't going top speed, since the man manage to slide down beneath the machine to escape death. Pinned there, the unnamed accident victim discussed with Henry how best to extricate himself, before Ford finally enlisted some helpful bystanders to lift the vehicle off. No legal action followed. Perhaps Ford talked him out of it. But if less amiably this first person in a line of millions to be run over by a Ford automobile had sued, Henry might have disappeared from our history.

Next, Henry persuaded Charles King to ride with him in the quadricycle out to Dad Ford's farm that summer of '96. The trip didn't go well, according to King. The car broke down several times, panicked a few horses along the way, and when the duo arrived the apparatus failed completely to impress the Ford patriarch. "The door opened and there was the tall form of his father, William Ford, Justice of the Peace, Church Warden and Farmer. He stood there, saying nothing. He was certainly lacking in enthusiasm."(65) Sensibly, Justice Ford refused to ride in the quadricycle. But following this fatherly rejection, Henry got much more encouragement from Thomas Edison, whom he met later that year at an Edison utilities convention in Atlantic City. Though he hadn't brought it with him, Henry eagerly described the quadricycle to the great man. Ford's idol hammered the table and said loudly, "Young man, you have it!" Of course, this was something of a snap judgment on Edison's part. He hadn't yet seen it, ridden in it, smelled it, been run off the street or struck by it. Ford applied for a patent.

Ford also made a believer out of the mayor of Detroit, William Maybury, who stopped by Bagley street, took a ride with Henry, and promptly issued him the first driver's license in Detroit history. The Maybury and Ford families had known each other for 50 years in America and Ireland. Mayor Maybury, an attorney by trade, wielded a lot of clout with a lot of flush people in Detroit, entrepreneurs with serious money. Under the spell of Henry's persuasiveness Maybury and three other backers put up $2,000 in development money with which Ford built more prototypes. In 1899 an assortment of two dozen stockholders, including some of the biggest names in the state, several with railroad connections, incorporated the Detroit Automobile Company (DAC). Mark Hopkins of St. Clair County, whose uncle helped build the first transcontinental railroad, joined them. Ford quit his Edison job and went to work for the DAC full time, as chief engineer, at a higher salary. Henry also proved to be very adept at handling the press. *Horseless Age* magazine did a fawning feature on his work in 1898, and in 1899 the *Detroit Journal* followed suit.

Others gasoline automobiles started disturbing the peace around Michigan. A model showed up in Port Huron in 1898, the first ever seen there, and although nobody fell down in wonderment, it did arouse curiosity. Built by an inventor whose name has been lost, it came to town at the behest of prominent businessman Wilbur Davidson. Davidson had made his fortune not so much in the dry goods business in which he started, but in the electric industry. He'd brought electric light to Port Huron in 1883, as a sideline at first, then he emerged as the leading light, so to speak, of the Excelsior utility company, which also powered the streetcars. Davidson went on to design and build more than 50 electric lighting systems in other communities in Michigan, taking an equity stake in many as part of his compensation. A prime example of the honorable profession of "capitalist," as the city directory called them, Davidson served as an officer in 30 different corporations. This was despite the fact that he'd once been squeezed accidentally between two railroad cars, and understandably he didn't feel as spry as he might, but he still had a nose for an opportunity.

Davidson brought the auto to Port Huron as a potential product for the Standard Novelty Company, which he served as secretary-treasurer, under its president Henry McMorran. Primarily, Standard Novelty made men's pantaloons, but they were game for anything. The *Port Huron Daily Times* described the vehicle only as a "horseless wagon." Standard Novelty passed on it, but the next summer Davidson brought in yet another automobile to assess, a 900-pounder with three fixed forward speeds of 5, 10, and 20 mph, and one reverse. There is an outside chance it belonged to Michigan engine manufacturer and inventor Ransom Olds, who shopped an auto around at about this time, looking for a good deal on a factory site. Publicly Olds talked nothing but the auto's big future. Privately, when asked by his partners about the prospects for delivering a safe, reliable, stink-free car he replied, "You shouldn't even expect it."(66) That was probably the last entirely honest statement ever made by an American automaker about his product. Olds recruited another St. Clair County native for a backer, a mining and railroad tycoon named Samuel Smith, who eventually poured

$1 million into what became known as the Oldsmobile. But Olds didn't build it in Port Huron.

Wilbur Davidson's automobile project in Port Huron came to nothing, but the *Daily Times*, a vigorously pro-auto and anti-horse paper, hailed the new invention anyway. The editors predicted that in the coming auto age Port Huron's "streets will be clean, there will be less noise in them, and pavements will last twice as long as they do now." If not with gold, perhaps the streets would be paved with boiler iron, suggested the *Times*, to accommodate the new chariots. As for risk, "The danger that some profess to feel of more frequent accidents from the use of automobiles is imaginary."(67) On the contrary, added *Automobile* magazine, the motor vehicle "will lead to a distinct lessening of human suffering."(68) The *Daily Times* then went completely over the top by claiming that the greater speed of automobiles would make the streets less crowded. That statement must have given readers some pause. Crowded with what? By no stretch of the imagination could Port Huron's streets have been described as crowded in 1899.

Only the very largest cities, the New Yorks and Chicagos, suffered from a failure to restrain the number of horse-drawn vehicles that operated in town, and then only in certain districts. For Port Huron, and most of America, even with horses, carriages, wagons, streetcars, and bicycles using them, the streets remained open, hospitable public places, where, day or night, people walked largely with ease and safety, stopped and chatted, shopped and sightsaw; crowds gathered, children played, teenagers dallied, vendors hawked. A city could be a city. In Detroit, the fastest growing big city in America, whose proud residents embraced the "City Beautiful" movement, and called themselves without embarrassment the "Paris of the Midwest," a photographer climbed to the top of a downtown eminence and captured just such a panoramic scene one fine day late in the 19th Century. Barely noticeable in the frame, a small but singular nuisance, tooling along on one of his homemade automobiles rode Henry Ford, taking the measure of the community he and his mount would help to destroy.

Chapter 2. 1900: Baseline Port Huron.

The effort was prodigious, and many mistakes would be made in building a transport system that was both fast and efficient and that would link the entire nation. But it was accomplished by 1900; just as a new transport technology, the internal combustion engine, was being developed, which would call for a completely new system.

– Willard Cochrane (1)

As the last year of the 19th Century opened, Horatio Earle had some good news for the city of Port Huron. Real good news. Because the Port Huron chapter of the League of American Wheelmen had signed up in record time a total of 200 new dues-paying member bicyclists, the fastest haul in the state, the entire LAW division of Michigan was coming to town to hold its annual state convention for 1900. But even more unspeakably exciting, this convention would be held in conjunction with the world's first International Good Roads Congress, also organized by Earle. He expected 5,000 – no – 10,000 delegates from all 45 states and Canada to flood Port Huron during the 4th of July week. They'd celebrate bicycling, raise high the good roads banners, listen to speeches from experts, look at a mile of demonstration good (meaning stone) road built at a cost of $2,800 at the city limits, and incidentally watch some automobile races. The first auto races ever held in Michigan.

All this came as a very pleasant surprise to the people of the state's 8th largest city, even those who had to ask, who is Horatio Earle? He was a 44 year-old transplanted Vermonter now living in Detroit, who'd made his fortune in an earlier incarnation selling and designing farm equipment. During this period some hooligan unwisely had copied Earle's patented grass-cutting sickle, and Horatio had wrung a $110,000 infringement judgment out of the culprit.(2) Earle had not been hardened nor made cynical by his experience with the patent-jumper. Though he was nobody's fool, Earle remained an open-countenanced man, resolutely cheerful, determined, and optimistic in a way that would have put that other Horatio, Alger, to shame. In fact, Earle's enthusiasm occasionally overflowed, and led him to make outlandish promises and predictions. Thanks to the sickle suit this indefatigable promoter enjoyed the freedom to lavish time on his bicycle business, called the Earle Cycle Company, and the LAW, which he presided over as Michigan Consul, state chief.

Both the business and the LAW needed attention in 1900. After a dozen years of red-hot expansion, faddish excitement, overproduction, and saturation marketing of bicycles in America, demand took a breather. The USA had bought about all the bicycles it could readily absorb. Public interest in bicycle issues waned. Hence the need for the LAW membership drive that won Port Huron the Congress. Even Earle's affections started to stray. His addition of the auto races to the Good Roads Congress was an ominous sign. The Consul didn't understand yet the absolute incompatibility of bicycles and automobiles, nor the destructive impact of automobiles on his precious good roads. Earle could be forgiven for having a shaky grasp of these matters because in 1900 few automobiles encroached on the roads, perhaps 3,000 in all America. They really didn't play a big part in bicycle affairs. Growing competition from electrified wheels seemed more of a threat to members of the LAW. They blamed the rapid expansion of streetcar and interurban systems for seducing bicyclists away from the highways.

Another issue depressing the sales curve at the Earle Cycle Company was the durability of the bicycle product. A well-made bicycle could last a lifetime, maybe absorbing new tires and parts along the way, but not needing full replacement, unless the buyer wanted some new technical feature. At the same time, if manufacturers built junky bikes that wore out quickly, in order to keep demand up, disgusted buyers wouldn't shell out for another new one when the first collapsed. Too many mass-produced American cycles fell into the flimsy category. Moreover, the big trust formed by several bicycle makers in 1899 put a lot of people off. This unpopular trend of setting up monopolies in America illustrated to many people Adam Smith's theory about combinations – a "conspiracy against the public and a contrivance to raise prices." Admittedly, if higher prices had been the aim, the trusts didn't get the job done. Consumer prices had been falling in America since the Civil War, and bicycle prices went with them.

Things might be shaky elsewhere, but Horatio Earle happily discovered that bicycle sales in Port Huron still thrived in 1900. Dealers would put you on a wheel, as people called them, "from $20 up", or rent you one. Competition was tough. "Underhanded methods" of one dealer shut off the Patterson Music Store's supply of bikes completely, and ran Patterson right out of the business, he claimed. That tactic sounded like George Yokom in action, but Patterson wouldn't name names in making his accusation. Dealer S. L. Boyce took the dramatic and expensive step of actually placing a photograph of one of his bicycle models in the *Port Huron Daily Times* newspaper, one of the first consumer products so honored. Used bicycles also found a ready market, according to thief George Ford, who rode 40 miles into Port Huron that summer on a stolen bike, which he sold for $5 before the cops nabbed him.

New bicycle inventions and accessories cropped up all the time in the Port Huron stores and in the news, like the rig that let you ride your bike illegally on railroad tracks. Best to be careful with that one; if a train came up behind you the chances of outrunning a locomotive looked heavily problematic. With a recently invented front wheel ski attachment a rider could pedal his bicycle across the ice of his favorite river or pond, provided he could get any traction on the rear wheel. The ingenious Talbot family of Port Huron, who'd electrified the streetcars, planned now to let bikers ride across the sky on their bicycle-powered aerial tramway across several miles of southern St. Clair County. Much as they admired the Talbots, the public did not hold its collective breath in expectation of seeing that project completed.

From a more practical point of view, cushion frames and coaster brakes and chainless transmissions scored big bicycle selling points in 1900. Port Huron rag merchants outfitted the well dressed rider with bicycle suits, pants and hose, for men or women. A few trouser-wearing female bicyclists around town impatiently tried to break out of some of the Victorian strictures of that time. Alarmed, responsible authorities repeatedly cautioned women to avoid overexciting themselves while bicycling. Who knew what depth of moral depravity a bicycally overexcited woman couldn't sink to?

41

Port Huron's City Councilmen worked to hammer out bicycle rules for the road in 1900, with limited success. They insisted that bicycles be licensed, and promised their constituents to put the license money into a trust fund, for building bike paths around town. 700 wheel owners paid $1 apiece for licenses, and this allowed them to ride on streets and sidewalks. Many hundreds more bought no licenses, and these people also rode on the streets and sidewalks, and dodged the police. No bike paths appeared. The sidewalks seemed like ready-made bike paths anyway, smoother than virtually any street in town. Port Huron put down 11 miles of cement sidewalks in 1900, more than in all previous years combined. Some villains even drove horse carriages along the sidewalks to avoid rough-riding streets.

It proved to be just about impossible to enforce the license or speed laws on Port Huron's numerous, speedy cyclers, a foretaste of what came along later with automobiles. Scorching concerned the most people, as immortalized in a verse reprinted in the Port Huron press from the *Daily Oregonian*:

I ride in front of trolley cars,
And they reverse their power;
I never use my handle bars
At thirty miles per hour.
The children all with terror shriek
When I go past them humming;
Their mothers are too scared to speak
Whene'er they see me coming.
I ring my bell to terrify
The walking population,
For when I'm in condition
I can frighten all creation. (3)

Cops based an arrest for bicycle speeding entirely on a judgment call: how fast Joe Scorcher peddled between points A & B, indicating his velocity. In addition to the necessity of proving this point in court, authorities faced the problem of first catching Joe. Speeding bikes caused such a nuisance in America that the LAW abolished its racing department so as not to be associated with these bad actors. Yet bike racing, official or unofficial, remained a popular sport.

Another bone of contention in Port Huron over "the steel steed" involved the law requiring a bike rider to carry a lantern at night. After a few jouncing bike lanterns exploded in the faces of riders, most stopped carrying them. The cops cracked down on unlit bikers and issued tickets, including some to rather prominent and irritated men, like piano dealer John Bell. The night riders complained that buggies didn't need lanterns, so why should bicycles? The lantern law for bikes was promptly dropped, except for sidewalk cyclists. The City Council tried a new tack to keep the streets orderly at night. They ordered bikers to ride on the right hand side on the streets, night or day.

Just as John Bell did, many another of the city's important names regularly bicycled back and forth across town in pursuit of their affairs. Henry McMorran, insurance man Edgar Spalding, and shipping agent, landlord, coal dealer, garbage collector, sometime newspaper publisher, and customs inspector Heil Buckeridge all used bikes. At the busy customs house Buckie often found that people departing in a hurry grabbed the first bikes they could lay their hands on and rode off, whether they owned them or not, which resulted in a lot of false stolen bicycle reports to the police from dismounted owners. It seemed ungentlemanly to use a bicycle lock.

A bicycle occupied about a tenth of the street space a horse carriage did, and there weren't all that many of those in Port Huron. Even if Consul Earle's full 10,000 visitors turned up for the Convention & Congress on bikes they'd have plenty of room on the streets. The more the merrier. If the conventioneers didn't *all* pedal into town there'd still be no problem transporting them in and out and around the place. Travelers had their choice of five round-trip passenger trains daily to and from Detroit, which took as little as 90 minutes en route. Plus five trains to Chicago (the world's largest railroad hub) running on a seven hour schedule. And seven trains to the eastern US and Canada. Half a dozen more went to various towns throughout the Thumb. Through any one of these destinations, a delegate could make rail connections to almost every part of the continent.

The White Star line expected to have its new vessel, the *Tashmoo*, running between Detroit and Port Huron in time for the Congress. This 300 foot-long, lavishly appointed passenger ship, constructed by the Detroit Shipbuilding Company, if jammed full could carry 4,000 people at 22 mph for a fare of 75 cents, or $1 round trip. The Detroit and Cleveland Navigation company offered its usual exemplary service from other Great Lakes towns to Port Huron, as did four other shipping lines that serviced the city, not to mention Mr. McMorran's four cross-river ferry boats that went back and forth to the Canadian side of the St. Clair River.

Backers of the new Rapid Railway scheduled its completion for Congress time, so those interurban electric trolleys between Port Huron and Detroit could wend their way north and south through the shoreline towns of lower St. Clair County (which previously had had no rail service), picking up and unloading LAWmen and Good Roads fanatics at any one of 94 potential stops. Once visitors arrived in Port Huron, the 30 City Electric Railway streetcars stood at the ready. They'd proven themselves capable of picking up and moving a whole Congress in a single day, with ease. Most of the time the single truck, 2-man streetcars ran on the half hour, but the company could put on extra cars at a moment's notice and even lay temporary rails and switches in the streets to accommodate big events. It had done so for the Ringling Brothers' Circus, an event roughly comparable to the Earle circus. The CER also mulled over plans to build its own 20-acre amusement park up along Lake Huron as an added draw, with swimming, a theater, and a dance pavilion, to entice the whole tourist race and stir up hometown biz, too.

And apart from these methods of mechanical movement, the old reliables, foot and hoof, still were good enough for many people. As had been demonstrated times without number, if anything really worth seeing or doing popped up in Port Huron, like the Buffalo Bill show or the annual farmers' picnic, the Chicago Symphony or a good stage production of Uncle Tom's Cabin, carriages and wagons (sleighs in winter) and pedestrians poured into town from neighboring communities and townships by the hundreds, or thousands, from scores of miles away, over the allegedly unacceptable roads that according to Horatio Earle were denying America the good life.

Port Huron's excited city fathers worried only about where to house Earle's 10,000 delegates when they showed up. A turnout that size would swamp the town's dozen or so hotels – the biggest and fanciest of which, the five-story Harrington Hotel, had only 125 rooms – as well as all the rooming houses and resorts in town. This meant a lot of delegates might have to commute from surrounding communities. However, Port Huron's leaders relished just this kind of logistics problem. They'd already landed the Michigan Democratic Party's state convention for 1900; now, this! could you believe it? In short order a roster of local influentials like *Daily Times* publisher and editor Loren Sherman signed up to help sponsor the LAW Convention and Good Roads Congress. Sherman had been running good roads articles for years in the pages of the *Times*, rebuking Michigan for its backwardness on the subject. Only a handful of eastern states employed state road aid programs of any kind in 1900 but Sherman badly wanted Michigan to join them.

Bicycle Club stalwarts Albert, Fred, and Harvey Dixon and attorney William Jenks also played a leading part in sponsoring the Congress. The four of them now owned both the streetcar line (replacing the Talbots) and a big chunk of the Rapid Railway. Dozens of other business people in the Port Huron Excursion and Convention League, and the 300-member Merchants and Manufacturers Association climbed aboard the Earle bandwagon. Tourism booster and resort owner Marcus Young talked of building a new 200-room, $200,000 hotel on the beachfront if the Congress proved to be the publicity bonanza everybody hoped for. Charles Lauth did more than talk, he ordered construction of the handsome new Lauth hotel and livery stable downtown, located on the streetcar line for the convenience of guests. Cornelius Gillespie pressed ahead with his 42-room Gillespie Hotel across the street from the Grand Trunk railroad station.

Horatio Earle, ace promoter, pulled a number of tricks from up his sleeve to get people excited about the coming saturnalia. He called on showmanship, in the person of trick bicycle artist Captain Paul Quincy, who brought his 120 foot-long stair chute to Port Huron's Lakeside Park. Before fascinated audiences the Captain repeatedly plunged into Lake Huron aboard his Yale bicycle after a bouncing descent of the enormous stairway, a pretty dramatic metaphor for bad roads. Quincy's sponsors – the Yale company and the Beard-Goodwillie hardware store – couldn't have been happier. The "Beard" in Beard-Goodwillie stood for Frank Beard, a member of one of the wealthiest Port Huron lumber families, and now the city's biggest buggy and sleigh dealer. In anticipation of a new wave of sales, Frank stocked up on bikes, including his own custom-made models, the Beard and the Beard Special.

Earle sent out a blizzard of press releases and invitations to his Good Roads get-together. One typical blast announced a scheme of his to impose a $1 poll tax throughout Michigan just for roads, and to build a thousand miles of good roads a year using stone crushed by convicts. Though this plan got people to talking, just as Horatio hoped, it didn't quite add up. The Earle Plan intended none of this money or manpower for city streets, just country roads, so that aspect of it turned off town folks in places like Port Huron. And considering that the entire state budget came to just $3 million per year, the idea of blowing $600,000 annually on roads seemed pretty extravagant. Even at the rate of re-building 1,000 miles of roads per year, it would take more than 60 years to finish the mileage already in place. Plus the costs looked painfully underestimated, and the constitutional problem remained, forbidding any kind of state government support for transportation.

Just one local enthusiast came forward to the support of Earle's poll tax and chain gang scheme. Port Huron Police Court Judge Carl Wagner liked the idea of putting jailbirds to work, and suggested that St. Clair County buy a stoneyard to sell road gravel pounded out by the "drunks, wife beaters and criminals" who otherwise just sat around the cells. Earle's plan had scope, all right, but it wasn't the only Paul Bunyan-sized road proposal floating around America in 1900. The miniscule American Auto Club wanted the federal government to build a 3,500 mile coast to coast highway at a cost they estimated at $10 million. The feds had given up on a national road project like that back in 1838 – one only half as long – after first dumping $14 million into it. "A little chimerical," commented the normally road-positive *Daily Times* about the Auto Club's transcontinental idea.

The subject of road and street construction and surfaces and pavements interested the public considerably in 1900. The Mayor and 20 Port Huron City Councilmen hashed over the various options endlessly every time they faced paving or repaving another stretch of street. That happened whenever enough streetfront property owners petitioned for paving, or the council declared it to be a public necessity. The city and landowners split the costs through bonding and special tax assessments. At one time or another the community had tried nine different paving methods, including planks, cedar blocks, gravel, macadam, asphalt blocks, concrete, bricks, and various combinations.

Cost, of course, both to lay and replace the paving, was a vital consideration. A macadam experiment executed on a lakeside avenue priced out at $6,500 per mile. That didn't cover the whole width of the street, either, just an 8-foot strip of it. It came to quite a bill. Port Huron spent only $11,000 per year on street maintenance for the whole town. Wilbur Davidson, the man who'd brought the first test autos to town, raged over the assessment he got for the macadam poured in front of his beachfront cottage, and said he'd refuse to pay it. Most city residents favored brick pavements in 1900. Brick didn't make the most even surface and could get slippery when wet, but brick looked good, lasted for decades, and you could get at the subsurface and underground utilities beneath it without making too much of a mess.

Brick cost too much for country roads, and so did cedar and asphalt and macadam. Only 200 miles of country roads in all of America had been paved with anything.(4) Even gravel strained the rural budget. Out past the Port Huron city limits dirt was still king of the road. Here Horatio Earle's Good Roads agenda bumped up again against reality, at the very seat of his Congress. The $2,800 mile of stone road he built for demonstration purposes (and virtually everything about it had been donated) cost plenty by rural standards. A public subscription had raised $800 to gravel a few miles of the Lake Huron shoreline road north of Port Huron in 1900. But $2,800 per mile? And what about good road maintenance? By one estimate, every mile of graveled good road required 32 cubic yards of new stone added to it *annually* just to keep it in shape. Forget it, Mr. Earle, said the skeptics. The shoreline road, we should add, served the same stretch of country where people had been crying for rail service. Talk good roads all you wanted, railroads beat them hands down, and everyone knew it.

Earle remained undaunted. To further his case, he started up a scintillating new magazine, *The Road Maker*, under the editorship of former Port Huron City Engineer Frank Rogers, with the backing of the Port Huron Engine and Thresher

Company. In addition to the wherewithal for the magazine, the PHET put up most of the money, and almost all of the machinery, to build the good road demo Earle had promised for the Congress. Not coincidentally the road ran right past the PHET factory. The firm practically salivated at the profit potential of the Good Roads movement. While the company sold its fair share of the 5,000 steam tractors built for farms in America in 1900, and did good business on the rest of its implement catalog too, it didn't take a wizard to calculate the potential bonanza in road-building machinery the nation would need to upgrade and maintain 1.3 million miles of roads if Horatio Earle's ideas caught on.(5) The PHET meant to get out in front of this development but quick.

After some persuasion by the Convention and Excursion League, some farmers out at Goodells, a railroad depot community about a dozen miles west of Port Huron, donated the good road gravel. The railroad shipped the rock, gratis, into town. From there the ever-versatile streetcar company delivered it to the road site. Under the direction of Frank Rogers, and with the sage advice of an aging luminary from the U.S. Agriculture Department road office, E. J. Harrison, a heavy PHET steam roller ran back and forth, over and over the mile-long, 10 foot-wide, 7 inch-thick pile of wet stones and dust which had been dumped on Port Huron's 24th Street. PHET superintendent and engineer George Conner, who'd acquired more than 50 patents on company gear, had designed this machinery. Harrison assured the press during the rolling that despite some qualms he had about the drainage situation and questionable gravel quality (thanks a lot, Goodells), the resulting mashed stone road would only get more solid with regular use and the passage of time.

Despite all the ballyhoo associated with it, or maybe because of it, the Michigan LAW Convention & International Good Roads Congress bombed completely. Only a handful of delegates turned up, too few for the embarrassed *Daily Times* to put a number to. The uninundated hospitality industry of Port Huron felt especially put out, and said some disparaging things about Horatio Earle. Trying to retrieve the situation, on the 4th of July the PHET put two of its traction engines to work, and towed a few hundred delighted locals around in wagons, first in the annual Independence Day parade, then out to the good road worksite for a looksee at this modern day marvel. Then they came back again, at a considerably slower pace and with a bumpier ride than the streetcars would have given them, but with a good deal more engine smoke and chugging, the kind of noisy demonstration everybody loves on the 4th.

The state championship bicycle races staged on the 4th at the crowded Driving Park also furnished some good entertainment value. By contrast, when only two automobiles appeared for their races the next day, the 37-acre Park was nearly deserted. These steampowered vehicles, which carried the redundant brand name of Mobile automobiles, had been furnished by an investor friend of Henry Ford's named William Murphy, and by William Metzger, otherwise known as "Smiling Billy," the Detroit bicycle dealer who now operated what he called the first auto "repository" in Michigan. Distributorship, he probably meant.

"Locomobile" is what people called steam autos like the Mobiles. The name had started out as the trademark for a single manufacturer but turned into a generic term. The "loco" in locomobile was meant to suggest the power of the locomotive, not insanity, but it was a pretty loco contraption nonetheless, which used a gasoline fired, high pressure boiler to quickly raise steam for the engine, sometimes too quickly, combining the worst explosive threats of both propulsion methods. A modified version might have made sense in streetcar service, providing power where there were no electric lines, but it had no future in automobiles. Metzger avoided driving this product himself. The New York-based Mobile company paid a bicycle racer, Eddie McDuffie, to travel the country and do the driving honors for hesitant dealers.

Horatio Earle had intended the time-trial auto racing to take place on the good road sample just built on 24th Street. One look told McDuffie that, good or not, the road clearly wasn't up to it. Instead he skidded his locomobile around the horse track twice, a total of one mile, in just under two minutes. "This is considered a record for automobiles for that distance," reported the *Daily Times*, without much conviction. On the strength of this one mile demonstration and what must have been a whale of a sales pitch, Metzger signed up Frank Beard as Port Huron's first ever car dealer. A typical locomobile, one of the cheapest cars on the market, cost about $600, cash, more than a year's pay for the average workman. First year's sales in Port Huron: 0. The attempt to excite the local public in the automobile fell as flat as the rest of the Congress. Without further ado, the resilient Earle returned to Detroit and that fall got himself elected to the Michigan State Senate, where he could work his magic on the legislature through his Good Roads Association.

The whole Earle episode had been a major letdown for those proud Port Huroners anxious to show off their community to the world. But in place of those missing 10,000 visitors we can take a walking tour around Port Huron's quiet and orderly streets ourselves, and see how well this typical American city got along in the year 1900 without the automobile. "It was a carbon copy of most other small communities in the Nation," a reporter remembered 70 years later. St. Clair County's seat of government was no longer the lumber town it once had been, before, sadly, rampant overcutting and fire claimed most of the Thumb's forests. Only a single sawmill, the Howard company, struggled on. But in many ways the city worked better now with a wider-ranging economy.

Railroading was the biggest enterprise in town, followed by shipbuilding, the world's largest chicory processing plant (backed by Henry McMorran), a vegetable fiber works, the Engine and Thresher company, the Kern brewery (makers of Cream of Michigan beer – "Good for nursing mothers"), several grain elevators and mills (Henry McMorran owned the biggest until it burned down in a $250,000 fire shortly after the Congress), commercial fishing, printing, paper pulp processing, cigar rolling, clothing manufacture, harness making, and much more. The city came as close to full employment as it ever would in peacetime, with more than 5,000 people at work, and that didn't include the 800 or so on the Great Lakes boats. No fewer than 205 manufacturers in Port Huron and vicinity employed 3,500 people to turn out $5 million worth of goods per year. American industry paid the highest wages in the world, and the average Michigan factory man made $1.39 per day, working a, granted, much too long 10 hour day, six day week, about 46 weeks per year. Railroad men averaged 50% higher earnings than that.

As far as new industry went, the business community did a lot of crowing in 1900 about the startup of the Port Huron Salt Company, a huge salt plant built south of town on the St. Clair River near the village of Marysville, assembled with 2 million board feet of locally cut lumber. The salt company built an entirely new shortline

47

railroad, the Port Huron Southern, to service the plant. Most large manufacturers had their own railroad sidings, or waterfront dock access, or both, and the salt company soon was moving 4,000 barrels of product a week by rail and ship. On top of this favorable news, the PHET announced plans to construct an all-electric industrial park on some farmland at the south end of Port Huron, complete with a new neighborhood of homes within easy walking distance of the planned factories. Here again, rail service played a key role. The Port Huron Southern, the new Rapid Railway interurban service, and the other train lines and streetcar system, all furnished critical transportation for the industrial park. So did a new dock built on the river.

Port Huron's white collar economy continued to grow in 1900, its financial sector considerably enhanced by the ready means of transportation. The missing 10,000 conventioneers had not seen the massive, multi-domed, copper-roofed Maccabees Temple on Main Street, newly renovated that spring. This palatial establishment, designed by the city's leading architect, George Harvey, served as headquarters for a 400,000 member national fraternal insurance society overseen from Port Huron by the city's former four-time mayor, school board president, state legislator, realtor, and Civil War cavalry veteran Major Nathan Boynton. The Major's resume also included experience as a carpenter, whipmaker, farm laborer, postmaster, newspaper publisher and traveling medical salesman of an "electrical apparatus with curative powers". He also claimed to have invented the hook-and-ladder fire truck, and founded the city of Boynton Beach, Florida.

His anachronistic billygoat beard well suited the Major, a man somewhat hot-tempered like a billygoat, who occasionally was inclined to headbutt opponents, figuratively speaking. Esteem for Boynton ran so high that a brass band and two streetcars of dignitaries met him at the train station and threw a banquet in his honor in 1900 simply to welcome him back to Port Huron from his winter vacation in Florida. A Detroit newspaper said Boynton had the widest circle of friends and admirers of any man in the state. He'd been a prominent name on the Good Roads Congress executive committee.

Among the 85 officers and clerks working alongside him in the Temple, Boynton employed a young size-large protege, former high school teacher Bina West. An equally dynamic figure, maybe even more so than the Major, West organized the Ladies version of the Maccabees. The daughter of an early St. Clair County road contractor, West traveled the country on business to towns large and small, moving relentlessly and easily by train. She earned a reputation as a platform speaker second to none. However far she roamed, though, Bina always came home to Port Huron claiming it offered the best climate in the country.

The Maccabees amounted to the biggest financial enterprise in town, outstripping the six local banks by several millions of dollars. Like the railroad unions, members of the 'Bees relied not on insurance companies but on each other in times of sickness and death, as well as for good time socializing and moral support. At a gigantic Mac's Labor Day picnic in 1900, in front of both Michigan gubernatorial candidates, Mrs. Parleigh. M. Holmes sang to the assembled hosts the "Battle Hymn of the Maccabees":

My friends, there lives no Order
Like the modern Maccabees,

Its truth and noble virtues
Have outlived all rivalries;
It protects the orphan children,
It maintains the home bereaved,
And it leads the van today.

The Maccabees led the van of well over 60 social clubs and chapters of one kind or another whose members met regularly in Port Huron. So did more than 30 labor union locals. Virtually every trade in town had a union, from shipbuilders to clerks to teamsters to cigarmakers to plumbers to bootblacks. If shoeshine boys could have a union, the city's streetcar workers figured they too deserved one and organized in 1900. The Labor Day parade in 1900 mustered hundreds of marchers and took 25 minutes to pass by the reviewing stand.

The Good Roads Congress absentees missed the chance to examine Port Huron's growing utility structure, which included the Excelsior power plant, where workmen busily installed the new Tesla alternating current system to more efficiently drive the streetcars. A new 1,000-customer Michigan Telephone Company exchange, a big artificial gas plant, and a steam-driven water works also kept things up to date. The stay-at-homes missed out on the entertainment offered at the City Opera House, where new thespians and vaudevillians arrived by train or passenger ship weekly. That week the Opera House featured the Marks Brothers Dramatic Company, in repertory with "The Major's Bride," "The Prince of Liars," and three other plays. The few people who showed up at Horatio Earle's confab enjoyed the hospitality of the three year-old City Auditorium, where all the conventions that hit town headquartered, and where Port Huronites roller-skated or played indoor baseball, danced or attended events like the annual poultry show in between congresses.

No summertime visitor to Port Huron could fail to have been delighted by the regular performances of the musicians at the 20-acre Pine Grove Park on the St. Clair River, a major stop on the streetcar line. At one memorable musicale 27 bands performed during a competition at the park's enormous pavilion, before 2,000 concertgoers. In a prior era the park had been the scene of an 18th Century cannibal banquet, at which some of Chief Pontiac's men ate British Commander Charles Robertson during the French and Indian War. But in 1900 Pine Grove Park welcomed more civilized picnickers, who preferred chicken and deviled eggs along with their music. "These people are happier than Carnegie or Rockefeller, and having a better time," said grocer Henry Nern on one such occasion. Music played a big part of the city's life. Virtually every home in town had at least one musician in it, and the city band received an annual stipend from the government. A carriage track, gardens, ball field and tennis court also lured people into Pine Grove, where pleasure craft and passenger boats docked along its river frontage.

Continuing a circuit of town, the visitor would have been impressed by the large, dignified stone Federal and City/County government buildings in Port Huron, the 30 other brick office structures, the 20 churches, plus the half dozen large fountains placed decoratively here and there. Who wouldn't have enjoyed spending some time spending in the 10 block long downtown shopping district centered along Main? Or grabbing a streetcar out to the golf links on Griswold Street? Or lolling along the beaches in the expansive uptown Lakeside Park on Lake Huron, whose enchantingly

49

blue waters were already a Port Huron trademark?

Among the thousands of regular beach visitors and cottagers in 1900 who effortlessly found their way to this delicious Lakeside spot without auto transport, 13 students from the University of Michigan worked out to prepare for the coming season of what the *Daily Times* denounced as "Foot ball...a barbarous game which numbers its victims, killed or crippled for life, by the score every year...". This dark opinion didn't stop Port Huron city teams from playing football themselves, hosting and visiting rival teams by railroad. The trains facilitated other sporting contests between cities and schools the same way. A six-city baseball minor league in which Port Huron fielded a team started up in 1900, stretching 600 miles across Michigan and Ontario, a well nigh impossible arrangement without the railroads.

You wouldn't have taken the full measure of Port Huron's prosperity without walking the street of dreams along lower and upper Main Street, residential areas bordering the business district, where the town swells had built dozens of large Victorian mansions (Henry McMorran owned by far the grandest spread), fronted with broad sidewalks and serviced now by both streetcar and interurban service. Mass transit access at that point in time actually enhanced real estate values. "I would like to see a streetcar on every street in the city," said Eugene Schoolcraft, the city's top realtor. Less than 10% of the city's streets were tracked for the streetcar system. Not everyone shared Schoolcraft's level of enthusiasm. Residents on 20-30 foot wide residential streets thought the full-sized streetcars a little too large for their confines, and they preferred living "steps from the car line," as real estate ads phrased it. Port Huron needed some smaller trolley version, something that didn't require overhead wiring everywhere, and this was a spot where the gasoline-steam engine of the Locomobile might actually have found a useful life, powering smaller cars on side street tracks for utility work, deliveries, trash collection and the like.

Wooden frame single family homes intermixed with some apartment and business buildings lined most of those other 90% of Port Huron streets which Schoolcraft wanted added to the streetcar routes. Most homes measured less than 1,000 square feet in size. The earlier settlers had built their wood homes of solid timbers and wood pegs, and built them to last. But as historian James Kunstler has pointed out, the board and nail "balloon" frame homes going up in America by the year 1900, while respectable, didn't seem quite so carefully built or so sturdy.(6) Brick homes were very rare, a prejudice from the lumber era commonplace in much of the United States. Row houses, and what anyone could reasonably call a tenement, were virtually unknown. At the worst, a few small shacks stood here and there in the poorer areas. A typical home cost $600-1000. You could rent one for $10 per month, and about 40% of the populace rented.

Under no circumstances did the city's banks write a mortgage for more than 50% of a home's value – at a stretch 60% – but sometimes private financing offered more flexibility. Port Huroners desired of all homes, huge or humble, a front porch. American homes, at least Midwestern ones, differed from those of the old world in this way. Families kept tabs on the passing parade from the front porch in good weather, and sometimes even in bad, and were assumed to be at home to casual visitors when seated there. Coal, wood, or oil heated these homes, kerosene or gas lit them, with electricity running a distant third, but gaining gradually. Contractors George Yokom and D. J.

Stephenson vied to see who could wire the most homes for electricity, but it was slow going. Barely 5% of American homes used electricity in 1900.(7)

Port Huron for the most part liked things quiet. Train and tugboat whistles and occasional banging at the shipyard prompted the only serious noise complaints. The city kept a reasonably tidy appearance, but enough vacant lots grew wild that enterprising boys sometimes cut the grass on them and sold it for hay. Too much trash for anybody's liking accumulated on the working commercial frontage of the waterfront. Port Huron was an international city. Canadian visitors from across the river moved comfortably around town and traveled back and forth by the ferry with such facility and in such numbers that Port Huron merchants put out Canadian flags on the Queen's birthday.

Despite the availability of bicycles and streetcars and horsemobiles, most people walked where they went in Port Huron. Thousands of pedestrians daily crossed the downtown Main Street Bridge over the Black River, one of four bridges spanning this waterway which essentially divided the city in half. This bridge marked the central spot in town. Port Huron residents knew their neighbors and neighborhoods and the layout of their city so well that many buildings lacked visible address numbers and the streets formal name signs. Local newspaper stories often dispensed with addresses and sometimes even business advertisements did, too. If you didn't know where a business was, just ask somebody, otherwise your trade probably wasn't worth bothering about. Folks navigated by landmark – homing in on such points as the Baer block, the Grace Episcopal church, the Jackson school, Major Boynton's house, and most iconic of all, the City Hall clock tower.

On our tour, we can be gratified to find that Port Huron and St. Clair County ate perfectly well, and affordably, largely through local agricultural efforts. The rich plains of the Thumb, just recently emerged, in geological time, from the bottom of the receding Lake Huron, proved to be outstanding farmland once the trees had been cut down. 3,800 county farms provided plenty of just about every food staple year round, including some hothouse produce. Though they would have welcomed better roads and more trains and boats at no additional expense, farmers encountered no real problems in moving their wares to city markets or the neighborhood elevator or railroad depot or ship dock. A typical farm family, the McKennas from the city of Yale 25 miles distant, thought nothing of driving a wagonload of grain and dressed hogs all night into Port Huron, selling them, then returning home. Many farmers delivered directly to the grocery stores, circumventing any middlemen. Others dealt with an agriculture exchange in Port Huron which quoted daily wholesale prices, or with the grain and bean elevators in town. At a single cold storage warehouse 36,000 eggs arrived by wagon, ship and rail daily during peak periods, and one hay company shipped out 200,000 tons to eastern markets per year. Agriculture readily absorbed casual labor not employed in other endeavors, and part-time farming balanced the budget in a lot of households. Small scale farms on Port Huron's outskirts earned a good income from just a few acres. Neighboring Fort Gratiot Township numbered so many of these producers hat it came to be known simply as Gardendale.

Serious financial trouble visited only those farmers who – as Thoreau had found 50 years earlier in Concord, Massachusetts – took on too much land, livestock, machinery or debt in an effort to get ahead. Overproduction, in a word, which drove farm prices down for 30 years after the Civil War before they turned around in 1897.

The farm sector accomplished all this in 1900 without the artificial fertilizers or chemical pesticides or gasoline tractors so beloved of future industrialized American farmers. Historians delight so much in describing 19th Century agriculture as "backbreaking" that it seems a shame to point out that few if any St. Clair County farmers suffered from broken backs, unless they fell out of a hay loft. Nor did famine threaten the population due to the amount of land grazed by horses, as some automobile fantasists later claimed. Instead, as farm historian Willard Cochrane put it, "...the typical family-owned-and operated farm [of 1900] was an efficient and productive unit. What more can be said?"(8) Nevertheless, if one tired of farming, a farm usually could be swapped even-up for a middle class home in Port Huron.

Many Port Huron residents helped feed themselves by keeping gardens, a fruit tree or two, and even chickens, cows and goats in the backyard. People at times drove livestock through the streets to pasture on the vacant land in the city. Tiring of their home diet, tame backyard critters from time to time wandered away to raid a neighbor's garden. The neurotic dread of the latter 20th Century that these animals might visit some pestilence or unendurable odors on the human population would have seemed laughable in 1900. The one exception: police regularly shot dogs running at large. Rounding out the balanced diet of the community, commercial fishermen caught so many fish in Lake Huron that they not only satisfied the local market but shipped thousands of pounds weekly to New York.

Port Huronites shopped at one of 90 general grocery stores or dozens of produce, butcher, fishmonger, bakery or dairy stores in the city, and if they wanted exotic items or delicacies like California oranges, or Cape Cod cranberries, or Central American bananas or Russian sardines – there they were, railroad-delivered year round. Port Huron manufactured its own bread, ice cream, candy, soda pop and beer. Almost every grocer in town offered home delivery, and like most other merchants ran a weekly or monthly tab for customers. Or you could shop from one of the horse-drawn door-to-door produce wagons, or go over to the farmers' market grounds.

The scarcity of the gold-backed American dollar meant that without a surfeit of currency in circulation the rest of Port Huron's retail economy, like the food sector, ran on credit. Now and then a merchant like hardware dealer John Sperry declared a policy of "cash only." Most then reluctantly backed down when customers disappeared. This money policy was another reason a lot of cash-carrying Good Roads delegates would have been a welcome sight in city stores. One enormously influential political figure who appeared in Port Huron that year, Democratic Presidential candidate William Jennings Bryan, hero of the Populists, wanted to put more money into circulation, a lot more, based on silver, but businessmen dreaded inflation even more than specie starvation. Even without silver, in 1900 America prospered, and ran a large trade surplus behind a barrier of heavy tariffs, like the 45% levy against imported automobiles. Virtually all the retailers in town owned their single-store concerns. Shopkeepers might carry national brands, but nobody told them how to run their stores. A Detroit store owner, Sebastian S. Kresge, picked out Port Huron in 1900 as the spot to open the first branch of his nickel-and-dime chain store idea, which eventually grew over the years to 670 locations. The *Times* stood by its local advertisers and discouraged readers from catalog shopping by mail via the railroads. Those persons and businesses that traded out-of-town often used the three railroad express companies that served the city – American, National, and Canadian Express – whose agent Ira Clark arranged pickup

52

and delivery out of his Main Street office.

A police force of 15, nine of them patrolmen, looked after law and order and without much difficulty kept things quiet, under the direction of Chief of Police Marshall Petit, another descendant of the city's earliest settler Anselm Petit. The town usually stayed so calm that the board of estimates wanted to cut back the police force. The chief expressed no qualms at all about handling a 10,000 person congress, if one ever showed up. Cops had made 1,000 arrests in the latest fiscal year, almost half of those drunk-and-disorderlies. Boozehounds who reeled home along the sidewalks from one of Port Huron's 59 saloons were somewhat figures of fun, like Happy Jack Welch, Old Joe Powley, and Maggie Kinney, who each landed in the city/county jail again and again. And Fred Kamul, the man who fought the bulldog:

[Kamul] *divested himself of his coat, got down on his knees like a dog, and the bull dog was then let loose at him. With nothing but his elbows and teeth the man knocked down and shook the animal around the yard in a manner that is disgusting to describe. A woman, seeing the crowd, looked over the fence and with one cry fainted away.*(9)

Rowdy sailors off visiting ships sometimes had to be restrained from busting up a watering spot or one of the bordellos near the docks. Not everybody laughed at that or the antics of people like Powley, who gave away his children so he could concentrate on alcoholism full time. A growing number of prohibitionists made their views heard in the county. Larceny ran second to carousing as the most frequent criminal complaints.

City patrolmen, led by 70 year-old Billy Reynolds, the town's oldest, walked or rode bicycles around their beats as visible, familiar, and trusted figures known to everyone in town, young and old. When a cop asked bystanders for help in corralling a troublemaker he got it in a hurry. Police walked their arrested parties to jail or sometimes took them by streetcar, and that seemed sufficient, though they talked of getting a paddy wagon if the budget allowed. The three fire stations kept the fastest working horses in town on standby to pull the fire trucks. Residents hurried to get out of way once the alarm went off, since fire, whether accidental or intentional, threatened a disaster that made it a force to be reckoned with. The racing trucks were showy, but most fire losses really stemmed from low water pressure in the hydrants, and too many dry wooden buildings.

Everyday street traffic posed little problem and police spent next to zero time on it, in fact spent more time patrolling the sidewalks. There were no such things as traffic signs. There was no category of arrest for traffic violations in the annual police report. Fifty independent hacks and drays - carriages and wagons for hire - needed permits to work the town, but this was the only limit Port Huron placed on the number of horse-drawn vehicles allowed in the city. Police kept no hard statistics on the subject, but about one impatient civilian horse per week ran away with its burdensome rig. Townsfolk did not overly resent this, in fact they rather relished the dramatic spectacle, so long as it wasn't their horse:

There was a runaway on Main street on Thursday afternoon in which Miss Helen Black displayed considerable nerve. Miss Black was driving down the street near Griswold when the cutter overturned. The horse ran a distance of thirty rods [about 500 feet]. The young woman, notwithstanding she was dragged through the snow, hung onto the reins until the horse stopped. At times she was almost submerged with snow. When the animal was brought to a standstill Miss Black righted the cutter, got in and proceeded home.(10)

After an episode like that Miss Black might have been forgiven for an outburst of temper against her steed, but anybody caught going too far and abusing a horse in Port Huron, like farmer Jay Shaw, who left his animal standing outside all one February night, was hauled in promptly by the cops and jailed. Many people felt downright sentimental about the family horse. Druggist George Coppernoll went into mourning when his 17 year-old mare died after pulling him 30 miles to Port Sanilac one day, and saw to it that she was buried her next to her mother. "That best of friends, the horse," the *Woman's Home Companion* magazine called the species.

Good treatment or bad, a horse never quite knew what to expect next from its unpredictable masters. Let an *equus caballus* run wild on the Port Huron Driving Park track, like the popular local pacer Jimmie Dude, and the sporting crowd hailed it as the very spirit of the wind. Let another run wild on the city streets, slam its owner into a tree and kill him, as Capac resident Richard Lee's did, and an angry citizenry denounced the beast as practically a murderer, fit for the rendering plant up on Black River. It could be an exasperating life. One day a frustrated horse belonging to the International Tea Company almost executed a spectacular somersault on Main Street, and untangling the charger from its broken harness occupied 50 men. The Tea Company had its choice of numerous harness shops and 13 different Port Huron blacksmiths to make good the damage.

Here we should reiterate that while auto-loving historians have frequently cited horse hysteria, horse abuse, and horse hygiene as three of the evils removed by the automobile from America's largest cities, those concerns were thoroughly atypical of the nation at large. In cities the size of Port Huron, somersaulting horses simply didn't present a major problem, nor should they have in the larger metropolises. Clearly, the horse and the big city didn't make an entirely comfortable fit, but it was a question of degree. By 1900, 38 cities in America numbered more than 100,000 residents, and these metropolises did not take enough steps to limit horse access, such as the number of animals and under what conditions they were welcome. Julius Caesar had had sense enough to ban horse-drawn wheeled vehicles during the daytime in Rome 1900 years earlier, though admittedly he found it easier as a dictator to decide that. America didn't operate on the Caesar plan in 1900 AD, and suffered accordingly from bad urban horse management. By exchanging the horse for the automobile without fully exploiting the better alternative of rail, the United States gave up one brand of disorder for another much worse. And there would be plenty of auto hysteria and auto hygiene problems to dwarf those of the horse in the years to come.

At the St. Clair County level, law enforcement took the same relaxed approach found in Port Huron. Sheriff Harrison Maines employed a grand total of four people in his department, mainly to assist township constables, serve court papers, retrieve and deliver prisoners (accomplished by train, boat or buggy), and to run the jail, which did double duty as a free crash pad for hoboes. After giving them a night's lodging and breakfast, Maines allowed bums 20 minutes to get out of Port Huron, and he wasn't the sort of man you wanted to dispute the point with. The sheriff enlisted more manpower when he needed it by deputizing, but St. Clair County pretty much abided by the laws, in part because there weren't as many laws as came later. Traffic control in the

54

countryside amounted to even less than that in town, none at all. The total county population of 55,000 lived half in the city, half on the rural scene, spread among 24 townships and six incorporated cities and villages. The 1900 census showed two thirds of the townships lost population during the 1890's, while all the cities and villages gained some. All six of the incorporated units and 22 of the townships enjoyed regular railroad and/or interurban service by the end of 1900.

City and country life overlapped in places like Goodells, donor of the good road gravel whose quality that ingrate E.J. Harrison had badmouthed. It boasted, of course, the train depot, plus several stores, a post office, a hotel, fraternal hall, bank, two schools, a farm elevator, a couple of factories, two churches and the county poor farm, where 60 or so guests worked 200 acres to help support themselves. Goodells is a good spot to stop briefly to deplore again the idea that winter imprisoned Americans during the 19th Century, without the automobile around. If you put any stock in Henry Ford biographer Sidney Olson's version you might think so:

When winter came, you stayed put until spring opened the roads...in those days winter put a profound stop to everything. Winter mean isolation, loneliness, hibernation ...When the first huge battleship-gray snowclouds of November stood along the horizon and the first fat fluffy snowflakes began to drift down...everyone nodded goodbye to the outside world and went inside for the winter's indoor sports.(11)

When he wrote this passage in the 1950's, Olson had before him the written evidence that long before Henry Ford ever assembled the quadricycle, he'd met his future wife Clara at a countryside New Year's Day dance that neither of them found the slightest difficulty in getting to, nor did a couple of hundred other people in the Greenfield Dancing Club. As Henry himself might have put it, Olson's winter history was bunk. In Goodells, or Port Huron, or anywhere in St. Clair County the sledders, skaters, ice-fishermen, hockey players, hunters and trappers, farmers, syrup gatherers, horsemen, pedestrians and, look out, even wintertime bicyclists testified to the nonsense of it. Schools, stores, businesses, churches, clubs all operated as usual, the trains and streetcars ran, so did some boats if the ice wasn't too bad, the announcement columns of the newspapers filled up with notices of social goings-on, hundreds of cutters filled the countryside and the county seat on a snowy Sunday.

Returning to Port Huron, we discover underway in 1900 the biggest public works project in the city's history: a mile-long canal to connect Lake Huron with the Black River at the city's north end. The city did not, sadly enough, undertake this $100,000 effort for transportation purposes like the Erie or Canada's Welland canal, nor for hydroelectric power, like the huge new power canal up at Sault Ste. Marie, Michigan. Instead the community intended it as a public health measure, a sanitary canal, to flush out the sewage and industrial waste draining into the Black Rver from the city's ill-designed drains. The animal rendering plant and paper pulp factory in particular dirtied the river up plenty.

A torrent of pure Lake Huron water, officials hoped, would sweep the muck out of the Black and into the St. Clair River, then downstream for somebody else to drink. A Pere Marquette Railroad engineer, W. B. Sears, warned Henry McMorran and others that the mismatched elevations at either end of the canal didn't support this idea, but they ignored him. The Black River Sanitary Canal took as long to dig as the Panama Canal, and it accomplished nothing in the end, as its meager, shallow waters obstinately refused to flow uphill. It didn't carry enough water to float anything larger than a dinghy. This fiasco marked a sad comedown from the ambitious Port Huron plans of the 1840's, to interconnect two major waterways for shipping. The project also poisoned relations, in a manner of speaking, between Port Huron and the downriver towns, who complained about this pass-the-pollution scheme long and loudly to the state government.

Port Huron enjoyed tolerably good health for the day in 1900. The St. Clair Count Academy of Medicine promoted construction of a new $30,000 hospital in the city, and promised that doctors who normally charged $1.50 for house calls, would donate their services at the hospital absolutely free. No one counted how many laughs that promise got. Even the desperately sick went to American hospitals, which were virtually infection centers, with reluctance in 1900. Doctors of that era might charitably be described as underachievers. Enthusiasm for replacing the old barracks style hospital (which charged patients about $1 per day) with a brand new building didn't catch fire. Instead of hospitals, many Port Huron locals favored mineral springs for preventive medicine. A proposal for a new bath house in which customers could soak themselves in heated salty waters pumped up from beneath Port Huron prompted Loren Sherman, Henry McMorran, and more than 40 other stockholders to put up $30,000 in a flash. The Deepspring Mineral Bath House opened, while the similarly priced hospital idea languished.

Once stricken with the miseries, most patients stayed away from doctors and hospitals and relied on remedies like Port Huron's own "Knills Pills. Cure all Ills. Save you money and doctors' bills." Local pharmacist and prominent Good Roads man H. C. Knill manufactured his red, white, and blue pill varieties from secret ingredients. People actually worried more over weight loss than fat in 1900: "Thin people will find a 50-cent bottle of Sylvester's Beef, Iron and Wine a great flesh builder." Wilber Sylvester, another Port Huron druggist, mixed up this revolting brew. The patient who felt run down all over could try Beecham's Pills: "Those unable to exercise suffer from Sick Headache, Dyspepsia, Liver Ills, Constipation, Drowsiness and the Blues. Beecham's Pills rid the system of impurities and thus are a substitute for exercise." And there were many, many more such nostrums. Port Huronites who needed stronger stuff used morphine and cocaine as a painkiller and stimulant, respectively, available at any of the city's 18 drug stores. Cocaine also made a useful dandruff treatment.

Dirty water, tainted milk, infection, and contagious diseases posed the biggest health threats. America's median age stood at 23 years. High infant and childhood mortality depressed the life expectancy to 47 years. Something as simple as a fever or diarrhea could be fatal to a youngster. Parents braced themselves for the sad likelihood of the death of one or two of their children. Mayor Fred Moore's little girl Joan, 6, died of typhoid at about this time. A thousand children in Port Huron were insured for burial expenses.

Farm folks, like Alex Jacobs of the Jacobs Effect, generally outlasted city slickers, despite living further away from the ministrations of doctors and hospitals. The rural set got bigger daily doses of grandma's sure cure for what ailed you, fresh air and exercise. The claims for Beecham's Pills notwithstanding, nothing substituted for exercise, especially the essential exercise, walking. This had been perfectly well known for centuries. As far back as the 18th Century a medical writer popular in America, Dr.

William Buchan, "counseled repeatedly that exercise, fresh air, a simple regimen, and cleanliness were of more value in maintaining health than anything medicine could do," according to historian Paul Starr.(12) Starr also observed that the good health of their supposedly primitive Native American neighbors surprised the envious early American settlers from Europe. The natives hadn't even invented the wheel yet, and may well have been the healthier for it.

St. Clair County's earliest settlers paid little heed to doctors because there weren't any around. According to William Jenks, a historian as well as an interurban builder: "If nature was not too much interfered with, the patient generally recovered, and for the most part the pioneers were a sturdy, active, strong, out-of-doors folk, entirely ignorant of many of our modern diseases."(13) The county's first doctor, Harmon Chamberlin, who set up practice in 1820, found so little demand for his medical services that he also worked as a clerk, lumberjack, home repairman and as the county sheriff. Yet slowly but surely, this good sense about health slipped away during the Victorian era, and urban Americans in 1900 increasingly gave way to a growing appetite for patent medicines, a tendency to hypochondria, and a positive delight in any labor-saving device however trivial or idiotic.

Especially when it saved walking, a considerable paradox. Lest anyone think that they were first invented for 20th Century airports, we'll note that Port Huronites read in the *Daily Times* of 1900 about the moving sidewalks at the Paris Exposition, which carried fairgoers around the grounds at 2-4 miles per hour, rather than have them resort to walking. E.J. Schoolcraft's streetcars-on-every-street suggestion seemed to show the balance tipping in favor of riding instead of walking. In a couple of telling incidents that year, when electrical problems knocked out the streetcars in Port Huron for an hour or two, some patrons acted as though they had been paralyzed by the disaster, and summoned hacks and private carriages from every direction to carry them home rather than simply walk. Even physically robust working men fumed over one such forced march. Happily-named attorney Eugene Law's daily exercise of walking a couple miles before breakfast also made the newspaper, for its novelty value.

Photographs of the day show most people in Port Huron were fit enough, and even the slackards rarely got beyond the stout phase. Yet even without stomach-busting obesity, even before the appearance of the automobile, people occasionally talked in 1900 of whether they saved ourselves too much labor. Granted, the farmer didn't have this problem, nor the hundreds of railroad men in Port Huron, nor those Jenks shipyard workers pulling 60-hour work weeks, nor the thousands of housewives who manually cleaned, cooked and washed for their families without electric power. But as the urban white collar ranks grew, even in a city the size of Port Huron, their routine of jockeying a desk all day, combined with riding everywhere they went instead of walking, or at least pedaling a bike, looked like no way to stay healthy. Were modern people becoming physically degenerate? Could you have a society so completely mechanized you didn't have just the idle rich, but the idle everybody, making themselves sick in the process? Stay tuned.

Politically, both Port Huron and St. Clair County straddled the fence. Republicans held only a small plurality. Partisanship sometimes got noisy, especially at election time, but hardly ever personal. Those two bosom business pals, Henry McMorran and Wilbur Davidson, vehement Republican and Democrat respectively, still got along. Nevertheless, the rabidly Republican *Daily Times'* derisive treatment of Bryan when he visited town that spring for the Michigan convention so incensed Port Huron Democrats that they promptly organized their own newspaper, the *Daily Herald.*

This didn't alter the fact that everybody knew, liked and respected the *Times'* Loren Sherman. He had plenty of Democratic friends he loved like brothers, but he knew which side his bread was buttered on. In Sherman's spare time he served as Port Huron's postmaster at a salary of $5,000 per year, a lucrative and virtually work-free federal patronage plum he plucked by vigorously backing the McKinley presidential ticket in 1896, and which he meant to keep in 1900. Sherman wore several other hats as well. He ran the biggest printing company in town, and sold books and stationary and 10-cent color photos of President McKinley through the Sherman Store, located in the Sherman office block.

Nobody in 1900 seriously believed journalists to be politically impartial, making it easier to understand why 55 year-old Loren Sherman satisfied even the Democrats' *beau ideal* of a dedicated newspaperman; first, last and always foursquare for Port Huron. Virtually nothing happened in the city that he didn't hear about, and care about, and he made sure to pack each edition of the *Times* with the kind of local news and gossip and commentary that made it must reading. The paper often mounted loud campaigns on municipal issues, such as for the LAW convention and Good Roads Congress, and for the Black River canal. This drum beating could be annoying but could not be ignored. Sherman liked gadgets, too, and promoted them. He'd installed Port Huron's first telephones in his office and home, and he and his son Fred ran frequent laudatory stories in the paper about bicycles and the coming of the automobile. The paper included regular comprehensive columns of railroad and marine news, detailing new improvements and services. The final newspaper product that came off the Sherman presses every day suited Port Huron so well that to a considerable extent the new *Daily Herald* just copied the *Daily Times* format, but with a Democratic twist.

The *Herald's* backers recruited a 23 year-old Port Huroner working at the *Detroit Free Press*, Louis Weil, to return home and help run the new journal. Born in Brooklyn, New York, Weil as a young boy had moved with his Jewish family to Port Huron where his father Abram opened a haberdashery on Main Street. The Weils lived in the ethnic-rich 1st Ward along the waterfront, whose residents spoke 15 different languages and made it the most interesting section in town. In high school Louis edited the school paper, the *Tatler,* and played football. Then after graduation he worked briefly in a law office before taking up journalism professionally.

Nobody in Port Huron gave Weil's religious background a second thought. Though overwhelmingly Christian, the city lived under an easygoing ecumenism. Port Huron had elected a Jewish mayor, clothier Joseph Jacobi, as far back as 1880, and local Christians often dropped in on Jewish services just for a change of pace. Of course, this brotherhood of man attitude stopped short of the hereafter; Protestants, Catholics and Jews each ended up in separate cemeteries. Eventually Louis Weil decided to switch graveyards; he married a Catholic girl and converted to her faith, which resulted in some tension among the Weil clan.

In running the *Herald* Weil really found his feet when the paper dumped the Democratic affiliation, and declared itself "independent," so anyone could read it with a clear conscience. Weil wasn't really an in-your-face sort of guy anyway, and he approved the decision to soft-pedal the politics rather than alienate half the potential customers. Louis and his colleagues also hatched the bright idea of regularly putting local news on the front page, which the *Times* would not do. Sherman reserved it instead for world and national events, even when his readers became profoundly bored with the Boer War. The two Port Huron newspapers soon ran neck and neck in circulation, and via train and interurban delivery reached a readership across much of the Thumb.

A handful of St. Clair County men managed to make the front page in both papers in 1900, fighting with the 60,000 American pacification troops in the Philippines. Since a considerable number of Filipinos declined the blessings of American rule, the U.S. Army sometimes encountered tough going in that distant tropical locale. 24 Americans died in a single battle in September. The bloody, expensive, and inexcusable Philippines campaign, which led to the deaths of an estimated 200,000 Filipinos, stemmed from the recent Spanish-American War, when the United States took several properties away from Spain, including Cuba and Puerto Rico. Port Huroners turned out by the thousands twice in 1898, to send off and welcome back their national guard troops from the main show, a short fight in Cuba. The home folks little dreamed of the consequences this American adventure in international meddling would have during the years to come, consequences with a direct bearing on this history. Anti-imperialist sentiment remained a minority opinion at home, though a respected one.

Politically and religiously Port Huron always gave you a break, but racially the city hadn't always been so hospitable. Few blacks lived in town in 1900, only 90 in the whole county. Little wonder after the 1889 lynching in Port Huron of an innocent mulatto, called an "octaroon" in those days, an event unanimously regarded eleven years later as the most shameful day in the county's history. Drifter Albert Martin had been charged with attacking a white woman in an adjacent township, a crime to which another man later confessed. A mob of the victim's neighbors dragged Martin from the Port Huron jail, beat him senseless, hanged him from a Black River bridge and shot him 32 times just for good measure. Authorities indifferently donated his unclaimed corpse to the University of Michigan medical school for dissection, after which one med student extracted the gold from Martin's teeth to have a ring made and another used the skull for a tobacco box. Readers of the two Port Huron newspapers occasionally were reminded of this atrocity by ghastly stories of black men being burned at the stake without trial in 1900 America, in addition to garden variety lynchings.

Out of Port Huron's 6,000 school age children 3,800 attended classes. "There is still plenty of work for the truant officer," commented the *Times* archly. Those Port Huron children who stuck out grammar school's eight grades often received a better grounding in the basics than their high school graduate descendants obtained 100 years later. Most American children, like Henry Ford and Al Edison and Henry McMorran, left the classroom before they ever reached a high school. Port Huron High, a prominent downtown landmark, graduated a class of a mere 28 students in 1900, only five of them boys. The City Council, which ran the schools, spent about $13 per child annually. Port Huron employed 73 public school teachers, almost entirely single females, paid about $300 a year to tame classrooms of up to 40 children. These ladies left teaching immediately after they married. Those rare birds, college graduates, roosted mainly in the legal and medical professions.

In the St. Clair County countryside children used 150 one-room schoolhouses. Student Hazel Ketelhut attended a typical one near Capac. Hazel walked 1.5 miles to and from school, spending about an hour on the road per day. Sometimes her dad took her to school by sleigh in winter. 40 children of all ages attended class from 9-4 daily, after entering the school by sexually segregated doors. During the lunchtime break kids played outdoors in virtually all weather. Hazel loved school, comparing it to the proverbial "one big happy family," in which older children looked out for the juniors, helping them with their winter clothing, gear, and class work. Hazel's father had attended the same school, as later did her daughter, grandchildren and great grandchildren. Only cities maintained high schools, and Ketelhut later went to Capac High by carriage. Others went by train. A few rural kids roomed-and-boarded in St. Clair County cities while attending high school, and for some it was an important step on their road to independence.

When not in the classroom Port Huron children had the run of the streets. The coming 20th Century's idea of fencing urban youngsters into backyards or playgrounds or even restricting them to the sidewalks to protect them from traffic would have been unfathomable in 1900. Port Huron kids spent much of their idle time doing what children most want to do, imitate adults, and they had the freedom to do so. Most took full advantage of it, sometimes to their parents' alarm. One day that summer of 1900, 10 year-old Harry Moss got onto his brother's new bike to go out for a test ride. Several hours later his startled parents learned by telephone that Harry had arrived in Croswell, 25 miles away, where his voyage had been halted by the police. In another incident, Deputy Sheriff Robert Woolley's 6 year-old son's disappearance had his father out combing the city for him, until the boy nonchalantly reappeared after a roundabout trip to the candy store. Mr. and Mrs. Robert Dove raised a full-fledged panic over their missing 2 year-old daughter, only to find that she simply had wandered down the street and fallen asleep on a neighbor's porch.

Some children, as one would expect, pushed their luck too far even in a largely safe town like Port Huron. Half a dozen boys drowned in the rivers and Lake Huron in 1900. One of them, 7 year-old Fred Cheney, toppled into the Black River behind his father's blacksmith shop while sailing a toy boat. Others kids came to grief from passing conveyances. Eight year-old Erick Nuski tried to climb onto a passing hay wagon and instead fell under the wheels to his death. Non-fatal injuries occurred in wide varieties. A passing streetcar whacked Wilbur Inslee's 7 year-old daughter pretty badly while she played too close to the tracks on Main Street one evening. A trolley motorman had to keep his eyes peeled for children every inch of the route in Port Huron. Police shooed adolescent boys out of pool halls and taverns, or hauled them in for breaking street lights or pelting pedestrians with snowballs. Chronic troublemakers landed in reform school. But for the most part the city indulged its children. Their type of risk-taking and exploration, of push-and-pull interaction with each other and the world around them was absolutely essential for their normal development, a fact that parents of 1900 fully appreciated.

Having mentioned Henry McMorran again in this context as a Port Huron boy who made good with basic schooling and healhy upbringing, and having pointed him out so often, it's time to pause and expand a little on such a signal figure. Born in 1844 practically at the very center of town, this tailor's son left school by age 13 and worked in several local stores. He eventually caught the eye of Nelson Mills, a wealthy gentleman from the neighboring village of Marysville. A self-made shipping and lumber baron, Mills among his numerous sidelines also owned the streetcar system in the state capital of Lansing. Mills took the ambitious young McMorran under his wing, and after having taught him the business ropes, backed him in setting up as a Port Huron ship chandler, to sell supplies to visiting vessels. This springboard eventually catapulted Henry McMorran into indisputable first place in Port Huron's commercial community.

In 1900 McMorran had so many irons in the fire that people wondered how he kept track of them all. Aside from those investments already mentioned, he toiled as president of one bank and director of another, ran a ship salvage company, sold insurance and real estate, owned property in virtually every ward in town, and held minority stock interests in numberless other firms. He hadn't done much in the way of public service, but he would redress that balance in 1902 when he reluctantly accepted a Republican nomination for Congress as "a protectionist first, last and always." McMorran served five straight terms, a considerable obligation for a man as busy as he was. Happily married, he had two daughters to marry off, Clara and Emma, and a son, David, to succeed him in business.

But to return to our main theme. Leaving behind the disappointment over good roads and the automobile, Port Huron that summer of 1900 celebrated the arrival of the interurban connection to Detroit, the Rapid Railway, when service began in early July. Construction of the souped-up trolley line over the last 40 miles to Port Huron cost $2.5 million, including a quarter million for a new Westinghouse electric power plant. The Dixon family and William Jenks didn't fool around in pushing the last leg of construction through, and built about a mile of line per week. On one leg of the Rapid, workmen cut a recalcitrant farmer's barn in half to make way for the tracks. People who donated land got free passes, and they were a lot more numerous than the barn owner. The track crews also cut in half some Indian graves, to the fascination of Jenks, the amateur historian. Regret over this desecration of Native American resting places would have to wait for a later generation.

Once they were up and running, the IU cars left Port Huron hourly from 6:30am to 9pm. The Rapid charged a fare prorated according to how far you were going; $1 all the way to Detroit, $1.50 round trip, a sum competitive with railroads and ships, adjusting for their different speeds and amenities. In addition to passenger service, the Rapid made two package freight runs daily. Two routes to Detroit offered riders a choice, one which ran along the shoreline, and a second, the shortcut, which made a quicker trip. A local IU – that is, one which halted at each stop, as opposed to a limited, which did not – took 2.5 to 3 hours to cover the 72 miles to Detroit. Rapid cars usually averaged about 20 mph, including stops. Sometimes the motorman cranked it up to 60 mph on the straightaways on the Rapid Railway. Other IU systems in Michigan reached speeds as high as 90. Like the Port Huron streetcars, two employees handled the Rapid Railway vehicles, a motorman at the controls and a conductor to take fares and keep order.

The Rapid service made such a hit right from the start (generating $40,000 per month in revenues) that occasionally a jam packed 66-passenger car which couldn't fit any more on board had to bypass people waiting at a stop, which led to some fist-shaking and heated letters to the *Daily Times*. One group of infuriated passengers stranded in this fashion built a fire in the middle of the tracks to halt the next car. A number of derailments on the line also plagued the new service at first, and the unanticipated strain of capacity passenger loads led to the hurryup installation of bigger electric motors, which gave the cars 300 horsepower. Some collisions occurred along the line with people and livestock not yet Rapid ready. Nevertheless in August the community threw a grand banquet at the Harrington Hotel in honor of the Rapid's completion, chaired by Loren Sherman himself. After they'd eaten their fill and taken their bows, the Dixons and Jenks sold out their interest in the Rapid Railway and the City Electric Railway to a group of out-of-town financiers, netting the quartet about $75,000 apiece.

After some financial juggling among big money interests, both the Rapid and Port Huron's streetcars became part of the massive Detroit United Railways company, the DUR, which blanketed southeast Michigan, and included Detroit's streetcar system as well. This sale had both bad and good results in Port Huron. On the down side, the fact that local owners no longer controlled the streetcars in Port Huron cut quite a few ties of loyalty among city patrons. Positively, though, the new ownership gave the interurban service a further boost, because it interconnected the Rapid with networks spreading fast all over Michigan and the Midwest.

20 IUs already operated in Michigan in 1900, a dozen lines in and out of Detroit alone. City after city – Lansing, Ann Arbor, Jackson, Battle Creek, St. Joseph, Bay City, Flint – reported new interurbans either under construction or in design. Promoters promised service connecting all these points to Chicago to the west and dozens of other major cities north, south and east. The sky was the limit. In Port Huron, patrons realized another benefit when a fare war broke out between the Rapid Railway and the Grand Trunk for travel to Detroit, one of many such confrontations between electric and steam trains.

A trip south along the St. Clair River on the Rapid Railway moved *The Daily Herald's* John Murray to something approximating poetry, though his muse didn't find its way into many anthologies:

Let's go forth and join the moving throng
Cheerful as larks and pipe a jovial song;
And down the swirling river you and I will go
And see the waters as they ebb and flow..

...Through farms and rich alluvial lands we pass;
Through rye and oats and corn and wheat and grass;
Through orchards with luscious fruits laden,
Pink and white as the first blush of maiden;

...Over rivers, railways, gullies, brooks and bridges;
Along green plains and close cropped ridges;
And, anon, on some clean swept village street
We see a mother's smile and hear the childrens' feet.
Southward, ever southward...

A great ride, if not a great poem, no question. Electric light rail service of all kinds expanded across much of the USA in 1900. Apart from the interurbans, 850 streetcar systems operated in American cities. 300 miles of streetcar lines spread across the island of Manhattan alone. The Louisville, Kentucky system gave such a comfortable ride that a doctor prescribed a 2-hour streetcar trip just before bedtime as a cure for insomnia.(14) Internationally, electrics increased their mileage in Canada, where Port Huron's neighbors in Sarnia began electrifying their streetcars in 1900. It was the same story in Mexico, Europe, Asia, Africa and Australia. Foreign streetcar companies often emulated the world-leading mass transit development of the United States by building according to American specifications and using American equipment.

Now, in view of these trends, the people of the upper Thumb wanted to know: if they can build these lines in Africa, why not out to us? The frustrated Lake Huron shoreline towns north of Port Huron felt left out of the party, and it rankled. The Rapid Railway stopped short in Port Huron and never proceeded another inch further, despite the pleas of people like Thumb resident Jane Kinney, who promised a "passenger at every farm gate" and plenty of freight traffic, too, if somebody, anybody, would build a line into their neck of the woods. The *Port Austin News* foresaw the day when an interurban system would make "one grand summer resort" of the whole Thumb shoreline – when and if the blamed electrics ever appeared. According to another press report, citizens in the town of Lexington offered up daily prayers to a merciful Providence for some kind of rail service.

A new company did indeed propose to build an interurban into the upper Thumb, and it meant to add additional streetcar service to Port Huron as well, just as Mr. Schoolcraft the real estate man had urged. The backers of the proposed Detroit, Lexington & Port Huron included William Canham (past president of the City Electric Railway), and attorney John McIlwain (a former Port Huron mayor). They claimed to have the necessary franchises, rights-of-way and financing from English investors all sewn up. But the DL&PH ran into some powerful opposition from the holders of the existing city streetcar franchise. These opponents logrolled mayor Fred Moore into vetoing the laying of any more streetcar tracks in Port Huron, or at least laying them too close to the existing tracks, on the grounds this would carve up existing city passenger business too many ways. If built, the new interurban would have to pay tribute to the DUR and lease the latter's lines in Port Huron. This kind of imbroglio, in effect a replay of the 1870's Port Huron streetcar war, could have been avoided had the government owned the tracks, as it did roads and streets.

Cooperation between the two companies and City Hall could have extended Port Huron's light rail trackage to more streets, developed more package and freight service around town through a neighborhood depot system, and given the signal for the northward march of trolley service into the Thumb. Just the sort of coordinated, balanced rail picture America could have achieved, and spared itself the automotive nightmare that lay ahead. But the nation came to a fork in the future and took the wrong path. In retrospect it seems scarcely conceivable, but not another inch of streetcar or interurban line would ever be built in Port Huron or St. Clair County during the 20th Century, a tragedy that loomed ever larger as the years passed.

If only Horatio Earle in 1900 had drummed it up for public rail tracks by convening a Good Tracks Congress in Port Huron, he'd have had something. His poll tax and convict labor scheme made far better sense if applied to publicly-owned railroad, streetcar and interurban tracks (and, for that matter, canals). The vaster efficiency and durability of the rail network compared to road transportation admitted of no debate. In load-bearing capability alone rails made a farce of even the best paved road or street. The heaviest wagons on Port Huron's streets weighed from 5-10 tons, and they broke up the pavements as fast as the community laid them. The Rapid Railway cars weighed 40 tons, and didn't so much as dent the street rails carrying them.

A change in the tax weather for rail enterprises which took place in Michigan in 1900 placed further obstacles in the way of new construction. When voters went to the polls in November, they approved taxing rail companies by property values once again instead of by revenues, reversing a policy of almost 30 years. Just by themselves, the 59 steam railroads in Michigan owned one-third of all the taxable property in the state, including not only the rights-of-way but almost 1,400 stations and a great deal more besides. During the next few years this switch effectively hiked Michigan railroad taxes 200%, to $3.5 million per year, not a penny of which went to the upkeep of the tracks or to much of anything else connected with rail transportation.(15) In fact, railroads got so little service out of the government that they often had to maintain their own police and fire departments.

For all the superb service they offered, Michigan took its railroads for granted by this time, and many of them struggled financially in 1900. This concerned the more perceptive observers like Loren Sherman. Stalwart Republican he might be, The *Daily Times* boss favored government ownership of the tracks. The Great Commoner, Bryan, called for outright nationalization of the entire American railroad system when he came to Port Huron to address the Democratic state convention in May. 3,000 people turned out at the Auditorium to listen to the most influential American politician of his day. The city of Detroit had made an unsuccessful effort in 1899 to municipalize that city's streetcar system, along the lines of the Bryan plan. It failed, because the courts ruled that Michigan's constitution still outlawed government-owned rail systems, even rails put down for private companies to use. Why it should be legal for cities to own the streets and pave them, but not to put rails on them, was one of those mysteries accessible only to the seers of the law profession.

Port Huron's #1 employer, the Michigan division of the Canada-based Grand Trunk Railroad, actually went into receivership in 1900, after lenders foreclosed on a $6 million loan. The company called it a "friendly foreclosure." Nobody feared for the GTRR's future, it was just too vital a resource, and it managed to get its finances straightened out before the end of the year. But the situation reflected growing industry problems. The other major steam railroad operating in Port Huron, the Pere Marquette, completed in 1900 the last of what had been close to 100 mergers over the years, including the 1889 buyout of the McMorran Line. Now the Detroit-based PMRR took its final form as the biggest railroad in Michigan, with 2,000 miles of track, 215 locomotives, and 7,600 cars. It had carried 3.8 million passengers an average of 37 miles each, and 6.2 million tons of freight during the latest fiscal year. Its 1900 profit totaled $2 million. But financially the Pere, too, looked a little unsteady on its feet at times, like Happy Jack Welch.

Underappreciated American railroads shouldered a larger and larger burden as the economy grew, under a growing load of taxes and regulation. The average freight train at this time moved 2,000 tons in 40 cars, manned by a crew of five. The Grand Trunk dispatched up to 1,600 trains per month in Port Huron, putting up to 2,500 cars a day and 21,000 passenger cars per month through the tunnel to Canada. Railroads carried 5 million bushels of grain out of Port Huron in 1900 and another 1 million could have been handled had enough cars been available. At one point a million board feet of sawn lumber sat in the Port Huron freight yards awaiting rail shipment. 46 million tons of freight rode Michigan railroads in 1900, as did 12 million passengers.(16) Nationwide, steam railroads handled 141 billion ton-miles of freight business in 1900, and transported 576 million passengers, or about the whole American population eight times over.(17) Plus they carried the bulk of the nation's intercity mail, and millions of express packages as well. The railroads had another 60,000 miles of new trackage on the drawing boards, and needed it all.(18)

The many hundreds of trainmen in Port Huron loaded, unloaded, repaired, built, rebuilt, connected, disconnected, fueled, watered and serviced hundreds of thousands of railcars and locomotives annually, everything from freight to passenger to dining to sleeping to mail cars. Just marshaling a train required considerable effort and skill to coordinate. It took 30 minutes simply to fire up a steam locomotive, and you were going nowhere without one. Shepherding the hundreds or thousands of passengers who daily came and went aboard the trains also needed careful attention to detail. On a single day in 1900, in addition to its regular traffic, and without paralyzing the system in the process, the Pere Marquette trains from Saginaw delivered 2,000 excursionists to Port Huron, led by Republican gubernatorial candidate Aaron Bliss. Bliss that year defeated Henry Ford's friend and benefactor William Maybury, who also campaigned by train through Port Huron.

Railroading extracted a human toll from its professionals. The year 1900 scarcely had opened before an accident in the Port Huron marshaling yards crushed and scalded to death veteran engineer William Riggs and yardmaster John Burke. A little later in the year 21 year-old yard worker Mark Windover met his fate when caught between two engines ("Windover's Head Was Squeezed" explained a headline). During this especially bad year in the yards half a dozen men died, and several more local railroad men were killed on the job elsewhere. Port Huron conductor Michael Fleming slipped while trying to re-board his train after a water stop at Goodells and was cut in half. Risks like these motivated railroads to open the first company medical departments in America. A convention of the International Association of Railroad Surgeons paid a visit to the Tunnel in 1900. Dr. Charles Stockwell of Port Huron worked as a railroad surgeon. The son of Dr. Cyrus Stockwell – the pioneer St. Clair County medicine man who did house calls by sleigh – Charles graduated from the Harvard Medical School, and came to be called the Singing Surgeon because he was a singer of some note, though not, one hopes, while operating on railroad men.

In 1900, a bad train accident somewhere or other in America was almost a weekly staple of the news. Two reasons accounted for much of the damage: tracking and signals. Most railroads, interurbans and streetcar systems traveled on single tracks, with sidings to let opposite-bound traffic pass. Double tracks existed only in busy areas, like the streetcar lines down Port Huron's Main Street. The Grand Trunk planned to double-track its line between Port Huron and Chicago, to keep up with the rising demand and make things safer. Another crucial safety element, train signaling, had improved enormously following the advent of first the telegraph then the telephone; but nevertheless a blown signal could set the stage for collision on a terrific scale. Thomas Edison had nearly caused a crash on a Canadian railroad when he bungled a traffic message as a young telegrapher thirty years earlier, and the same sort of thing still happened in 1900. A carbon copy of the Edison incident led to a seven-fatality wreck in Michigan.

It was still too easy to become confused. Patrolman Billy Reynolds' nephew, a Port Huron engineer also named Billy, died in a head-on freight train crash that summer due to a bad signal. Young Billy stood at the controls, like Casey Jones, trying to avoid disaster right to the end. The Rapid Railway relied on telephone orders to keep things straight, but not long after operations began two cars came within two feet of slamming into each other before halting just outside Port Huron. Another safety problem involved the quality of the steel rails, which didn't always keep pace with the greater speed and weight of the trains running across them. They spread apart, multiplying derailments.

It's hard to imagine that a steam locomotive, streetcar, or interurban could sneak up on you, but it did happen. Occasionally a civilian carelessly walked or drove or bicycled in front of one inside the city of Port Huron, despite the obviousness of the tracks and the frantic sounds of bells, gongs and whistles announcing the approach of these vehicles. Their warnings didn't always register soon enough with people too used to hearing them as just background noise. Teamster Joseph Biggers failed to take heed one day, and a Pere Marquette train moving a mere 4 mph nailed his wagon. Biggers lived through it with the help of generous doses of morphine. Train engines ran slowly enough in Port Huron that they usually just knocked the unwary out of the way. On the other hand, more numerous railed vehicles coming and going at higher speeds in a city the size of Detroit, 12 times as large as Port Huron, made accidental civilian deaths there a regular fact of life.

In rural St. Clair County, too, faster moving trains did not forgive as they did in Port Huron. A Grand Trunker running full speed crashed into Lewis Evans and his horse team as he was on his way into town to vote as a precinct delegate in the Republican caucuses. Evans instead was "ground under the car wheels," and even morphine wouldn't help that. Country pedestrians often preferred to walk the more direct routes of the tracks instead of the roads, and a daydreaming track walker got picked off now and then. A train killed the somewhat deaf 70 year-old Reverend W. B. Rowe while he walked on the rail line at Goodells in 1900. John McKinney failed to beat a Rapid Railway car across a trestle while out for a stroll one day, and the 40-tonner launched John into the troposphere for some distance before he returned to earth in "a dazed condition."

Other less dramatic, day-to-day rail-related mishaps occurred in Port Huron, primarily with the streetcars. Edison's sister Mary sued the streetcar company for $5,000 after she was flipped to the ground while trying to exit a moving car. Damage suits like Mary's rarely went to trial; plaintiffs usually settled for a fraction of the claim. Since the streetcars ran down the middle of the avenue, bicyclists and carriages illegally passing a stopped trolley sometimes collided with persons stepping off, provoking more court action. And the live electric streetcar wires strung in the sky posed another risk. If a wire fell, or something metal fell across one, the danger could be considerable. Contact with a fallen telephone line draped across the streetcar wires briefly paralyzed two Port Huron boys and badly burned florist Matt Ullenbruch when he came to their rescue just outside his shop in 1900.

Michigan steam train accidents in 1900 killed or injured slightly fewer than 800 people. The national toll was 7,865, consisting of 249 passengers, 5,000 trespassers, the rest employees. Injuries totaled 50,000. This in a nation of 76 million people, 5 million of whom, incidentally, lived on railroad wages. That came to about 1 passenger killed for every 2 million carried, 1 hurt per 139,000. Despite the industry's growth, the dangers it presented steadily decreased, while the efficiency of American railroads of all kinds increased. Six tons of coal sufficed to send a 2,000 ton train from Port Huron to Durand, Michigan, a distance of 85 miles. By doing some forward comparison we see that the weight of, say, a 4,000 lb. automobile of the year 2000 could be transported by that train in 1900, on a comparative fuel weight basis, at a rate of 56 miles per gasoline gallon. The fuel for moving that two tons in 1900 cost about 3/100 of a cent per mile. This illustration also gives some idea of what a train fireman's workday involved – a little matter of shifting six tons of coal with a shovel in an open moving conveyance, in every conceivable weather.

So what did America's steam railroads get paid for providing the world's best land transportation service in 1900? $1.487 billion. Operating expenses ran to $961 million. Subtracting out an additional $47 million in taxes (Michigan steam railroads paid $1.2 million in taxes in 1900) and $252 million in debt service, and additional monies for various other charges, $227 million remained for dividends and retained surplus, on an investment reckoned to be worth about $11 billion. A return of just over 2%. Even including on the profit side of the ledger the monies spent on debt service – a sore point for railroad haters convinced the companies deliberately overloaded themselves with bonds – the return came to less than 5%.(19) In the electric rail industry, the City Electric Railway in Port Huron grossed about $70,000 for transporting well over a new record of 1.5 million people in 1900 (about 80 trips per capita) at 5 cents per head, plus carrying packages and mail and some freight. Neither the steam nor the electric rails exactly qualified as get-rich-quick schemes unless the stocks appreciated dramatically.

Along the Port Huron waterfront the Jenks Shipbuilding Company did record business of its own in 1900. To the delight of thousands of onlookers, most of whom arrived on foot, by bicycle, and in small boats, Jenks sent two large steel freighters sliding down its shipyard ways into the Black River that year. One of thesse ships, the 440 foot *Thomas Wilson*, was the company's biggest project ever. The *Wilson's* capacity of 250,000 bushels of grain or 6,200 tons of iron ore per trip equaled more than three trainloads, carried at a top speed of 12 mph. Using the fuel weight figures cited above for railroads, the *Wilson* could move that imaginary car the equivalent of 65 miles per gallon. 160 million bushels of grain and 18.5 million tons of iron ore crossed the Great Lakes by ship in 1900. It would have taken a train 750 miles long to carry the grain alone. The lake freighter charged $1.25 for moving a ton 500 miles, about 1/2 to 1/3 the railroad rate.

It all looked pretty good, but the Jenks firm had to turn down an order for a 500-foot vessel, the biggest on the Great Lakes. The property they leased from the Grand Trunk Railroad for the shipyard couldn't hold a vessel that large. Jenks wanted to relocate to the St. Clair River, but needed a lot of money and a lot of land, perhaps overreaching available local capital in the race to stay even with big shipbuilders in Detroit and Bay City. In the meantime the 250 Jenks workers took advantage of William Jennings Bryan's rouse-'em-up convention visit to Port Huron in 1900 to call a strike. They won a pay boost, to $1.50 per day, and half days off on Saturday. On a smaller scale, at the other end of St. Clair County, a company opened in Algonac in 1900 by

67

duck boat expert Chris Smith concentrated on building personal-sized watercraft, brand named Chris Craft.

The new passenger ship *Tashmoo* closed out its first operating year in 1900 after having carried, in less than a full sailing season, 100,000 passengers between Port Huron and Detroit. Spanish-American war hero Admiral George Dewey of "You may fire when ready, Gridley" fame made the trip on the *Tashmoo's* maiden voyage as a promotion. A total of 480,000 passengers departed Port Huron by various steamships that year. Elsewhere on the city's miles of docks 1,400 ships from foreign ports and 1,900 from domestic came and went. Every time one of Henry McMorran's Port Huron and Duluth package carriers hit town a couple hundred laborers went to work unloading and loading it. Union longshoremen made 40-60 cents per hour, some of the best wages in town. A single McMorran steamer's cargo amounted to four railroad cars worth of bran, two of lumber and shingles, and 50,000 bushels of wheat. The same ship took back 8,000 barrels of salt on its return trip.

In an average day on the riverfront half a dozen sailing schooners might unload. Sadly, the race to build bigger and bigger steel steamships signaled to men like customs man Buckie Buckeridge the coming demise of the smaller, white-sailed schooner. That seemed a shame, considering the sailing ship had served so well and so faithfully, on what a later generation would call clean energy, and cut a wonderfully picturesque figure in the bargain. Promotional material about Port Huron frequently and proudly featured schooners sailing the St. Clair River and Lake Huron. By schooner or steamer or ferry (or rail), so much foreign cargo and so many travelers entered the U.S. through Port Huron that a major station for the U.S. Customs Service operated there. Agents like Buckeridge together collected $240,000 in duties during the 1900-01 fiscal year.

Buckie also worked on the side as the agent for six different shipping companies. He kept his finger firmly on the waterfront pulse, and knew that, just as in the railyards, on the water haste often made waste. Boat collisions in the St. Clair River in August and September of 1900 killed half a dozen sailors and temporarily obstructed the channel. The wreckage of the principle vessel victim, the schooner *Fontana*, had to be dynamited out of the way when no salvage company, neither McMorran's nor the Reids', would touch it. A lot of lake men chewed their nails with anxiety when skirting the wreck, but the river ferries took loads of curious Port Huron civilians, who thought of themselves as strong swimmers, out to look at the *Fontana* with the demolition still in progress. Another marine disaster touched St. Clair County that season. The weather forecasting on the Great Lakes still left something to be desired, as Marine City's Captain Albert Senghas discovered when his steamer *John B. Lyon* went down in a September storm on Lake Erie. He and three of his Marine City crewmen perished along with four others. 110 people died in Great Lakes shipping accidents in 1900, out of the 5-6 million travelers that year.

Despite the large business operating on Port Huron's major waterways, the federal government in 1900 did little to improve the navigable lesser streams that ran for many miles back into the Thumb. The Congress had spent $42,000 during the 90's to dredge occasionally a two mile stretch of the Black River above its mouth, within the Port Huron city limits, mainly to facilitate wood shipments to a paper pulp company. Nothing happened further upstream, and by now no regular commercial boats serviced

68

the upper Black. Similar situations prevailed on the county's two other rivers, the Pine and the Belle. The idea of interconnecting the Thumb's rivers with canals, dams, locks, and deeper channels lay stranded, high and dry. Some idle talk of harnessing these rivers for hydroelectric power failed to get anything done about that either.

Readers of the *Daily Times* learned that New York Governor Theodore Roosevelt took a much more aggressive approach about inland waterways in his state, when he urged the legislature in Albany to spend $60 million improving and enlarging the state-controlled Erie Canal, to let bigger craft through. Roosevelt: "...in the most highly developed portions of Europe there has been an immense positive and relative increase in the canal systems, and in the traffic upon them...[It] is desirable and profitable to keep up the development of the canals as fast as railways are developed."(20) If only Michiganders, who lived in America's most watery state, had shared the governor's insight.

This kind of big thinking got Roosevelt noticed. His ideas weren't always as judicious as the Erie project, but big. He'd scarcely presented this plan when the Republican party, to Roosevelt's intense annoyance, drafted him to run for Vice President behind President William McKinley. But the Erie canal improvement plan finally did go through. Other prominent men besides Roosevelt felt America neglected its waterways. University of Michigan engineering professor Lyman Cooley, who'd worked on a big canal project in Chicago, counted up 7,000 miles worth of new canals and channel improvements needed in the eastern United States. But he couldn't engineer the cool $1 billion they would cost.

Now as to the automobile. As we've seen, it made little retail or sporting impression on Port Huron in 1900. Apart from the follies at the Driving Park in July, just a handful of other autos appeared around town that year. An electric delivery truck made a promotional appearance on behalf of the Swift Meat Company. According to the meat wholesaler this red and gold wagon weighed 3,000 pounds, traveled at up to 14 mph for 30 miles between charges, and cost $2,250. The Swiftmobile warmed some hearts when it carried a live carcass, stevedore Guy Sink, over to the hospital one day after he broke his leg on the docks. Ambulance cases in those days often went to the hospital in a hearse, not exactly a confidence builder for the patient, so Sink appreciated the truck ride. More electric and steam automobiles occupied the streets of America in 1900 than gasoline-powered. Electrics like the Swift Meat truck ran more simply, quietly, and cleanly but their limited range curtailed the long-term prospects. Henry Ford paid no serious attention to either electric or steam cars.

Another auto seen around Port Huron belonged to the Cornell Concert Company, which appeared at the Opera House. Stage shows like Cornell's, as well as circuses, sometimes featured automobiles, working them into their acts or driving them around town for publicity purposes. Across the St. Clair River in Sarnia, stovemaker Thomas Doherty built a gasoline car of his own for fun. He defrayed costs by giving rides around town in it for 50 cents apiece, before putting the project on the back burner. (21) Considering the many occupations and backgrounds that automobile builders hailed from, one can pretty much set aside the notion that assembling one required some kind of extraordinary ingenuity or magical mechanical skill.

Apart from these fleeting appearances, news about the automobile mainly trickled into Port Huron through stories in the press. Down in Detroit, Henry Ford messed around with construction of a commercial delivery truck at the Detroit Automobile Company in 1900. Only three autobuilding concerns existed in the state of Michigan at that point, 60 in the entire nation. With his usual flair for priming the public, Ford managed to get another favorable press write up, this time in the *Detroit News-Tribune* in February. "Swifter Than a Race-Horse It Flew Over the Icy Streets" ran the headline. The unnamed reporter claimed he'd taken a spin with Ford in a DAC truck, in conditions bad enough that the journalist threatened to jump out when the vehicle reached 25 mph.

Bang, bang, went the warning bell under the seat. A milk wagon was coming ahead. The horse shivered as though about to run away. "Ever frighten horses?" I asked Ford. "Depends on the horse," he replied...With a simple twist of the wrist the big machine turned gracefully just sufficiently to allow a loaded brewery wagon to lumber on its way. I began to have a creepy feeling and told Ford I wanted to get out. "Nonsense," he replied. "No danger. All you have to do is keep a sharp look-out ahead. It's like a bicycle, you see..."(22)

As we've seen previously, this wasn't the first time, nor would it be the last time, that Henry Ford demonstrated his indifference to the dangers he posed to the community while behind the wheel of an automobile, or behind the tiller we should say at this stage. No such person as a good automobile driver existed in 1900, and never would, but beyond his operational incompetence, driving transformed Henry into an arrogant bully and a menace, the kind of person he deplored at any other time. The automobile often brought out the worst in the personality of the operator, one of its most singular and ugliest powers. Too often a driver lost all consideration for everybody and everything else on the road. They ceased to be fellow human beings, harmless animals, valuable public or private property, and became instead impediments to the driver's progress, obstructions in an obstacle course to be run as fast as possible.

In this case the *News-Tribune* writer recovered his composure and went on disingenuously to assure his readers that despite Ford's reckless driving among the civilians and other vehicles on the slick streets, and with the exception of one cursing teamster, "...everywhere people had a welcoming smile and an expression of delight."(23) Fewer expressions of delight turned up at the sales office. Ford historians differ as to how many trucks the DAC actually sold – Ford himself claimed 20 – before the annoyed shareholders shut the company down – $86,000 poorer.

In his first entrepreneurial venture, which lasted just over a year, Henry Ford swifter than a race-horse had earned a reputation from his investors for maddening, self-defeating procrastination. Ford simply didn't have a clear idea of what he wanted to build, or how to build it, or if a market even existed for the product. What he did build was junk. In fact, if the memories of the DAC workmen are any guide, the *News-Tribune* story may have been another Ford fabrication, contrived with the assistance of the press. According to Sidney Olson, these workers couldn't remember the truck ever covering more than a block before it broke down. As to Henry's later claim that he'd built 20 such vehicles, we will treat it with a dignified but skeptical silence.

It's a shame that at this point Ford didn't hie himself from the DAC over to the DUR and go to work on streetcars. But the automobile delusion wouldn't let go of him. From Henry's perspective one positive development did come out of the wasted year at the DAC. He'd put his mesmeric powers to work and picked up for very little salary a part-time assistant, C. Harold Wills, a 22 year-old jack of all trades with some experience as a toolmaker, draftsman and commercial artist, who also studied engineering and metallurgy on the side. Wills served Ford as a critical right-hand man during the next two decades, and later made a huge impact on Port Huron and St. Clair County all by himself.

Elsewhere on the Detroit scene in 1900, 36 year-old Ransom Olds proved to be more decisive than Ford and settled on a design for a simple lightweight gasoline automobile with a curved dashboard; a one-cylinder 700-pounder which he planned to build for $300 and sell for $650.(24) The average American passenger car at the time cost $1,000, or about the price of a good middle-class Port Huron house. Ransom decided to go low on price to undercut the competition.(25) In view of the fact that he leap-frogged everybody else in America in the automobile game, Olds deserves a little more background in this history.

Like Henry Ford a former farm boy, Ransom Olds' career started at his father's machine shop in Lansing, Michigan in the 1880's. Dad Olds had traded in his farm for this business so he could drop out of agriculture and divorce the horse. Ransom shared this prejudice. The Oldses developed and sold their own brand of small steam engines for industrial use, and Ransom soon started tinkering with powered road vehicles. In 1892 he put a barely functioning gasoline-fired locomobile on the road. He then pioneered the auto industry's practice of buying favorable and dishonest publicity when he purchased advertising in *Scientific American* for the engine company, and in exchange the magazine printed a hoked up story about the car. To be fair to Olds, he did not invent this well established gambit in journalism, employed on behalf of a wide range of consumer products. The Port Huron papers were rich with this kind of planted, paid-for story.

The resulting fairy tale about the first Olds automobile contained the egregious lie that the vehicle cost 1 cent per mile to operate. This precedent-setting deceit about the price of ownership laid a foundation of crookedness that stood the automobile industry in good stead for the next 100 years and beyond. Carmakers *never* realistically appraised the operating cost of their products. The *Scientific American* tale also concealed a considerable shortcoming of the loco. Whenever Olds couldn't avoid a hill while driving his underpowered vehicle, and tried to ascend it, his wife had to follow on foot, carrying a block of wood to jam under the wheels in case of a stall, to prevent the car from rolling back down the hill out of control. Just which of the couple this maneuver placed in greater jeopardy looked like a tossup. On the strength of this story, Olds promptly sold the car to some English suckers and shipped it to India, as far away as possible. The first American auto export.(26)

Olds then took up gasoline-only engines, and built more automobiles as a sideline during the 90's. Finally he decided to get into the car business whole hog. He started a separate auto manufacturing concern in Detroit in 1900, where his assistants whipped out plans for the curved dash Oldsmobile. In ordering parts for the new car, Olds drew into his orbit several men who later became very prominent indeed in the automobile industry. For some reason Olds decided not build the engines himself, but contracted instead with a prominent Detroit machinist named Henry Leland to supply some of them. A man known for his painstaking exactitude, Leland had been one of the few speakers to actually show up and address the Good Roads Congress in Port Huron.

71

Olds also ordered engines and transmissions from those former Port Huron mechanics, John and Horace Dodge. The Dodges by this time had returned from Canada, founded a machine shop in Detroit, and now gave up bicycle-making for automobiles.

The wheel bearings for the Oldsmobile came from the Hyatt Bearing Company in Newark, New Jersey, where the sale left partner Alfred Sloan "beside himself" with excitement. The 25 year-old Massachusetts Institute of Technology graduate had gotten off to a slow start in the business world, until his father more or less bought him a job by investing in Hyatt. In Utica, New York, Charles Mott's company won a sizable Olds contract for wire wheels, of the kind used on bicycles, similarly delighting Mott, who was a Spanish-American War vet and bicycle enthusiast.(27) Parts makers happily welcomed the fact that the automobile needed a lot more pieces than a bicycle, and were bound to wear out a lot more quickly. Olds ordered his parts on credit, but he intended to sell the cars for cash, in effect financing much of the venture through his suppliers. That, too, became standard operating procedure for automakers of the future. With a potential profit margin like the one Olds figured on, the auto gold rush in the States picked up speed. In December 1900, the National Association of Auto Manufacturers organized a lobby on behalf of the industry, to furnish a steady stream of misinformation to the press, public and government.

Additional wide-ranging press accounts about the automobile captured the interest of Port Huron readers in 1900. They learned with a certain gruesome fascination about the first fatal automobile crash in Michigan. It took the life of 33 year-old C. Kirk Eddy of Saginaw, whose two brothers lived in Port Huron, sons of a lumber and salt tycoon. While racing in a car against a horse one day Eddy slammed into a curb and was catapulted out of the vehicle onto his noggin. The papers issued remarkably detailed reports about Eddy's subsequent brain operation, in case any surgeons happened to be interested:

Saturday convulsions set in, denoting trouble at the base of the brain, and a second operation showed a stellate fracture of the skull on the left side, the cracks running off in various directions from the center. A circular piece of skull was removed, disclosing that the membrane covering the brain was badly torn and that an artery had also been severed. The operation relieved the convulsive condition, but the patient gradually grew weaker, until the end.(28)

Coincidentally, the National Automobile Racing Association in 1900 held its first ever competition. This event at Newport, Rhode Island went off somewhat more successfully than Eddy vs. Horse or the Horatio Earle Good Roads 1-Miler in Port Huron. William Vanderbilt, Jr., who owed his immense fortune to the fabled Vanderbilt shipping and railroading interests, drove his automobile named the White Ghost a distance of five miles on the Newport course in about nine minutes. The spectators on hand declared him national champion, for what that was worth. Vanderbilt's everyday street racing won him no awards. Driving an automobile transformed Vanderbilt, like Henry Ford, into a fairly vile character. He bragged about his hit-and-run driving almost as if it were his right, and later barely escaped lynching at the hands of an Italian mob when he nearly turned a six year-old boy into a white ghost by recklessly running him down with a car near Florence during a European motor tour.(29)

Speaking of ghosts, the plumbing profession bowed its head in 1900 at the news that a distinguished pioneer of piping had gone up in smoke. Oscar Mueller's dad

72

Hieronymus had continued to experiment with automobiles during the five years following Oscar's ludicrous 1895 races in Chicago. Hieronymus got a little sloppy in the auto workshop in Decatur one day and apparently lit up a pipe while working on a gasoline carburetor. Firemen surmised as much anyway from looking at his charred remains. This would not be the last devastating impact the automobile made on Oscar Mueller's family life.

Headlines from the nation's capital reported more automobiles on the streets of Washington in 1900. Word was that U.S. Senator Edward Wolcott of Colorado spent a whopping $125 per month maintaining his private motor vehicle, which should have been ample warning in itself about the impracticality of these machines for the average American. The enormous auto "victoria" favored by the elites like Wolcott stood almost as big as a stagecoach, with both a chauffeur and a footman to operate it. These land yachts often carried no more than one or two passengers at a time. The niece of the Russian ambassador, Marguerite Cassini, dispensed with the chauffeurs and drove herself, according to newspaper gossip: "She is said to hold the record among Washington women for high speed and skillful driving." Stripped of the press gloss, this probably meant that she drove as badly as Ford and Vanderbilt.

Automobile taxis in Washington gave the horse cabs some serious competition, though the city really needed neither thanks to its excellent streetcar system. America's military leaders in D.C. took note of the fact that both the French and German armies used automobiles in their war game maneuvers of 1900, driving officers and messages back and forth at up to 40 mph. It looked as though the automobile might play an important part in war before long, ventured the *Port Huron Daily Herald*. It certainly did. But the coming automobile war on the streets would kill far more Americans than the auto-assisted wars in the trenches during the next 100 years.

Washingtonians discovered that gasoline engine automobiles "make a noise like a cotton mill and leave a trail like a polecat," in the words of one observer. In Detroit, Henry Ford's buddy and auto enthusiast Barton Peck came to the same conclusion: "...there is one great obstacle that must be overcome and that is the offensive odor from the gasoline that has been burned and that is discharged into the air. It is a sickening odor and I can readily see that should there be any number of them running on the streets, there would be an ordinance passed by the council forbidding them."(30) America did not overcome the great obstacle, or forbid gasoline automobiles. Instead it just got used to the sickening odor, as much as people can get used to poison gas. Individual coal burning steam engines were even dirtier, of course. Three men had choked to death on the smoke in minutes when a locomotive stalled in the St. Clair River Tunnel in 1897. But the growing numbers of automobile engines, and their ability to penetrate into every street and road, made them a much worse health threat.

Stink, racket, and all, the automobile muscled its way into the 1900 New York Bicycle Show, much as it had the Port Huron LAW convention and Good Roads Congress. One attendee reported about the auto crowd:

The vehicles ranged from the heavy truck to the light, handsome and sporty runabout built for the lady whose husband or papa has a large bank account. Manufacturers representatives in full dress explained and exploited their goods to men wearing high hats and women in tailor-made suits and rich furs. The bicycle was by no means neglected, but its votaries presented a more democratic appearance.(31)

Later in the year class conscious automobilists staged their own New York show, entirely without the presence of the democratic bicycle. 48,000 people paid 50 cents each to see the 50 auto exhibitors. Among those on hand, Henry Ford, laying his plans. With that, I think the stage is crowded with as much background as it can hold, and it's time to forge ahead into the next century.

Chapter 3. 1901-1910: Conceit.

...the investment of an exceedingly modest sum in the purchase of a perfected, efficient, high- grade automobile would cut out anxiety and unpunctuality and provide a luxurious means of travel ever at your beck and call.

– Ford Motor Company, 1903

The automobile business [in 1903] *was not on what I would call an honest basis...but it was no worse than business in general.*

– Henry Ford, 1922 (1)

Angus Carpenter came down with the first case of automobile sickness in Port Huron, and bought one. The secretary-treasurer of the Jenks Shipbuilding Company, and by no coincidence a son-in-law to the Jenks family, lived a 10 minute walk from the company's main office downtown. It took 25 minutes to walk from his home or office to the shipyard. As a deskbound executive, the 40 year-old Carpenter needed this exercise walking to and from these places. In a pinch, by bicycle, he could cover those distances three times as fast. On top of that, the streetcar stopped a block from his home or office. Virtually all Carpenter's business and social contacts lay within ready reach by foot, bicycle, hired carriage, streetcar, interurban, train, or boat. Not to mention mail, telegram, or telephone. Or any combination. So why buy an automobile? Conceit. In the fall of 1901 Carpenter ordered his machine.

It wasn't unprompted. The first local advertisements for motorized vehicles hit the Port Huron newspapers in the spring of 1901, though not for automobiles. Hardware and bicycle dealer John Sperry offered for sale the Pattee motorcycle, which promised to carry a rider anywhere he wished to go at a speed between 4 and 30 mph, sans peddling. A hustler like competing bikeseller George Yokom couldn't let the Sperry challenge pass by, and he began hawking the Auto-Bi, short for auto-bicycle. The Auto-Bi, *the 20th Century wonder,* built by the renowned Cleveland-brand bicycle firm, consisted of a Cleveland bike with a small gasoline engine slapped on. Yokom mentioned no price. Buyers did not rush the doors.

The considerable risk to the user of a motorcycle could not have escaped the notice of Port Huron people who could afford one, like Angus Carpenter. Not only did the possibility of falling off an Auto-Bi at 30 mph sound ominous, but suffering this with one of the gasoline engines of the day clattering away between your legs seemed a doubly dangerous prospect. As in the Port Huron automobile market of the previous year, motorcycle sales in 1901 amounted to nothing. George Yokom once had done a stretch as a theatrical promoter, and he wanted eagerly to use the same methods in this case by announcing any Auto-Bi sales in the press, but he made none to announce. As a stepson to one of the Jenkses, Yokom knew Angus Carpenter well, but couldn't get his in-law mounted onto an Auto-Bi.

So Angus didn't want a motorcycle, but perhaps the hoopla which took place

75

down in Detroit that autumn convinced Carpenter finally that he needed an automobile. On October 10th Smiling Billy Metzger, now almost wholly occupied with automobiles instead of bicycles, put on an "Automobile Day" in Detroit. He mustered, so the excited press reported, 100 car owners to parade their vehicles through the city on the way out to the Detroit Driving Club's horse park to watch, what else, auto races. Some of the new Oldsmobile runabouts emerging at the rate of one per day from Ransom Olds' Detroit factory helped flesh out the parade ranks. Olds closed down the most active auto plant in America for the occasion to allow his workers time to attend the "Day" festivities.

The biggest name in American auto racing, Alexander Winton of Cleveland, Ohio, came to Detroit to compete in Metzger's 10 mile Grand Challenge Race. Winton expected to face a list of 25 announced opponents, including the relatively unknown Henry Ford. After the formal dissolution of the Detroit Automobile Company early in 1901, Ford had whiled away months at his remaining investors' expense by supervising the construction of a $5,000 racing vehicle. Persuading these people to put up for such a project after the ignominy of the DAC collapse showed how Henry could still shake the money tree. Ford worked on the new car mainly out of frustration, hoping to capture the racing crowd's fickle fancy. "I never thought anything of racing," said Henry with some exasperation," but the public refused to consider the automobile in any light other than as a fast toy."(2)

History repeated the experience of the 1895 Chicago race at the 1901 Detroit event, when out of the 25 entrants – including that automobile terror of two continents, William Vanderbilt – only two men, Ford and Winton, showed up at the starting line for the Ten-Miler in the Detroit suburb of Grosse Pointe. Henry had not driven his two-cylinder racer, powered by pistons as big as beer steins, in the automobile parade that day because a) it was so loud it couldn't be driven in the city's streets and b) like the quadricycle, it had no brakes. The Ford machine had to be horse-towed to the track. With absolutely no experience in racing, Henry nevertheless climbed behind the tiller himself and drove ten laps around the mile-long track at an average speed of 40 mph, with his mechanic Ed "Spider" Huff hanging onto the outside of the car as human ballast to keep it from rolling over in the turns. When Winton blew his engine trying to keep pace with his competitor, Ford roared home the winner, to the near delirium of the spectators. Himself nearly delirious from fear, shock, and deafness after the experience, HF vowed never to drive a race car again, and one can imagine how Huff felt.

Instead of the $1,000 Smiling Billy typically had over-promised, Ford took home a more modest first prize. "Well of all the things to win, a cut glass punch bowl!" said a disappointed Clara Ford, who very much more wanted the thou.(3) Dry goods dealer Edgar Boice of Port Huron witnessed the whole thing from the grandstand, then returned home to report that, all-in-all, he preferred horse racing. But the general enthusiasm and the growing involvement of many of Detroit's biggest business names with the automobile no doubt made its impression on both Boice and Angus Carpenter. Angus made his decision.

A Detroit salesman named V. F. W. Neuman personally delivered Carpenter's car to him. Neuman drove the gasoline powered yellow vehicle, whose model name has been lost to posterity, in a roundabout course through several St. Clair County towns on his way up to Port Huron. Might as well get a little free publicity out of the sale as long as he was going up that way, though it couldn't have done the car any good. The machine readily attracted the attention Neuman wanted. Marine City residents, for instance, positively swarmed over it. Customers expected driver education to be included with the product in those days, though many salespeople knew little enough themselves about it. When Neuman reached his final destination he put in enough time instructing Carpenter that within a week Angus was creating alarm by the speed with which he drove his fast toy through Port Huron's streets.

He had introduced an immediate and obvious menace, just as Henry Ford did when he first rolled the quadricycle through Detroit. This was no bicycle of limited impact potential, no streetcar or train held in place by tracks, no horse to be overawed by human intervention. Not to mention the accompanying noise and smell. Port Huron's indulgent citizenry had tolerated the handful of cars that flitted briefly through town to this point. But Carpenter's automobile looked like a permanent, and ugly, addition to the city, made all the more obnoxious because a familiar face had sprung it on them. Just who did Angus think he was, anyway? At first, only the *Daily Times* rooted for him, "A. M. Carpenter is fast becoming an expert automobilist. He is using it in his business and it is proving a great convenience."(4) Convenient for him; for everybody else on the streets, a potential death threat.

Conceit disguised as convenience, the very essence of the automobile. If Angus Carpenter was entitled to this convenience, excused of any responsibility to coordinate with the rest of the community his use of this barely-controlled street machine, wasn't everybody entitled to it? Multiply one man's convenience by millions and what would you get? When America rejected the rationality of powered mass transit on land via rail, and chose instead the anarchy of individualized motor vehicles pouring across the landscape, it became an over-transported society. Angus Carpenter acquired his auto as a thoughtless expression of Yankee independence, but in doing so he and others like him blundered through the practical limits to individual freedom. Millions of others followed through that breach.

The spectacle of Carpenter's conceit in full flight along the streets that autumn, before he stored the machine for the winter, apparently intrigued enough people to change some minds among Port Huron's wealthy, once they got over their first fear and annoyance. With his ear to the ground, Frank Beard, who'd struck out trying to sell cars two years earlier at his hardware store, tried again in the spring of 1902 and posted the first automobile ad in Port Huron. *Do not fail to visit the Automobile Show in Detroit...Examine the Olds Mobile, Mobile Steam Carriage, Baker Electric, Winton Gasoline Automobile.* Beard didn't mention any prices, suggesting some flexibility there. At last, success. Mrs. J. H. Broad, the spoiled trophy wife of a Chicago can magnate who summered in Port Huron, scooped up the second car in town. The Broad's stable space behind their Main Street mansion housed 7 horses, and the streetcar ran right outside their front door, but nevertheless the Mrs. had to have an automobile. After that, John Sperry and George Yokom immediately secured auto dealerships to compete with Beard, and the battle was joined.

Four more sales followed quickly. The buyers included lumberyard owner John Howard, head of one of Port Huron's oldest families, and Dr. George Treadgold, the latter seduced by Frank Beard's suggestion that, *Automobiles! are just the thing for a doctor to use...* Automobiles! as it turned out were just the thing to supply doctors

77

with more patients as well. George Yokom fanned this brief rush of spring excitement by offering to rent automobiles for parties, and he opened what he called an "automobile livery" for car owners. He'd feed, water, oil, and bed down your vehicle and deliver it at any hour day or night for $10 per month.

Somewhat surprisingly, the idea of substituting automobile buses for trains and streetcars cropped up even at this early stage, 1902. Some Lake Huron shoreline residents, who still couldn't get rail service, talked about regularly running a bus down to Port Huron. The Engine & Thresher company promised to put its own bus on the streets if the DUR didn't extend the streetcar lines to the factory. Then, just as suddenly as this flurry of auto enthusiasm had broken out, it cooled off. Sales stopped, the market had been saturated. Yokom despaired. "It seems almost impossible to sell automobiles in Port Huron. In every town of similar size they are as thick as flies." No buses appeared either. It marked the first boom and bust automobile sales cycle to hit the city.

The dangers posed by six cars in town aroused the concern of Port Huron Mayor Fred Moore, who took his mayoral duties seriously. Sometimes too seriously. People liked the 39 year-old banker well enough, but thought him something of a prude, especially about breaking the Sabbath. He'd once stopped a Sunday baseball game as illegal fun, then hassled some Sunday golfers, and he was pure poison to any saloons that served on the Lord's Day. On the 4th of July, a Friday fortunately, Moore asked George Yokom to give him a ride in an automobile to judge for himself what to do about them. The two didn't have to go far at 30 mph for the mayor to come to a negative conclusion. Even allowing for Independence Day exuberance, the car traveled two to three times faster than any other vehicle in the city. Yokom's driving compounded Moore's alarm. Like everybody else, George was a novice automobile operator, and a bad one at that.

Mayor Moore immediately asked the City Council for an auto speed ordinance, to complement the oldest law on Port Huron's books, the train speed limit. But baseball-, golf-, and liquor-loving voters retired Moore from office that November before his request had been answered. The new council didn't respond with an automobile law for another two years. Port Huron probably passed the point of no return in 1902 as far as banning automobiles went. It wouldn't have been the first Michigan community to take that step. Up at Mackinac Island, automobiles had been ordered off the premises in 1898, an act which eventually secured for that island a rich prosperity as a auto-free refuge and vacation paradise.

Others in Port Huron also urged a crackdown on cars. The *Port Huron Daily Herald* seconded Moore's views about the need for regulation, and sarcastically advised some drivers to "take out a license as an undertaker" and "get an ambulance attachment for your auto and save time, trouble and expense." The local press noted the numbers of auto dead already piling up in bigger cities like New York. In one memorable Gotham incident, society figure Edward Thomas ran over and killed 7 year-old Henry Thiels, while driving along NYC streets in that notorious vehicle the White Ghost, which Thomas had bought from William Vanderbilt. An avenging, screaming mob of boys later attacked Thomas and his wife in their car, pelting the couple with a hail of hardware, boiler pans, pails, stones, sticks, finally knocking Mrs.Thomas out cold with a thrown kettle lid. The $3,100 Thomas paid to Thiels' father as a settlement for flattening the child appeased almost nobody. Mr. Thiels had wanted $25,000 compensation.

As the Thomas/Thiels matter demonstrated, the arrival of the automobile quickly clouded up the whole issue of road rights in America. The courts at this time gave the pedestrian first possession to a road or street. While standing or walking in it he had no obligation to get out of the way of an oncoming wagon, or stagecoach, or bicycle, or the White Ghost. Vehicle drivers had to avoid *him*.(5) But did he want to bet his life on it? As a practical matter, the escalating numbers of automobiles, their size and speed, and the impossible task the police faced in exercising effective control over them, eroded in short order not only the pedestrian's rights but those of everybody else on the road. Trains and streetcars presented a different matter altogether, a clear cut and far safer matter. Their franchises gave them the right of way along the predictable path of their tracks at all times, but they shared streets and roads, while autos virtually expropriated them from curb to curb for their exclusive use.

Port Huron hesitated when the temptation of a getting a share in the auto manufacturing business first flashed past in 1902. Henry Spaulding of Buffalo, N.Y. approached some community leaders about moving his auto factory to Port Huron's new industrial area called South Park. Spaulding promised to employ 200 workers. But he'd only been operating in Buffalo a year, and his proposal (probably just a fishing expedition for more money) sputtered out within a month. Spaulding went out of business in 1903, and later accidentally drove one of his cars into the Erie Canal and drowned, which didn't say much for the car's maneuverability or Spaulding's presence of mind. 4,000 automobile makes like the Spaulding came and went in America during the 20th Century.

Ransom Olds fared far better than Spaulding in 1902. Shortly after the Automobile Day in Detroit he dispatched assistant Roy Chapin on a publicity-seeking endurance test drive from Detroit to New York City, a little over 600 miles, in one of the small new 2-seater Oldsmobile models. Chapin took seven days to cover a distance a train traveled in 20 hours. The Oldsmobile broke down repeatedly along the way and overheated like a tea kettle. Unlike Henry Spaulding, Chapin found the best driving conditions along 150 miles of the Erie Canal towpath, which he negotiated without drowning himself. Chapin admitted to using 30 gallons of gas and 80 gallons of water in the Oldsmobile en route.

As was his wont, Olds played up this completed journey in unabashedly dishonest car advertisements: *A child can operate it safely. Speeds up to 25 mph without fear of breakdown..* This creative merchandising (in layman's terms – lying) helped Olds sell 2,500 cars in 1902, and 4,000 in 1903. Company profits in 1903 totaled a phenomenal $900,000 out of $2.3 million in sales, almost a 40% margin, and the firm paid dividends of $327,000 on an original capital of $350,000, or about a 93% return.(6) Compared with the single-digit profits the railroads labored mightily to achieve, Olds' seemed little short of miraculous. George Yokom, his spirits revived and faith in the future restored, enthusiastically joined the Olds sales ranks as the company's Port Huron dealer.

Three other American automobile brands that eventually survived the other 4,000 first appeared in 1903. A former plumbing equipment inventor, rather like Hieronymus Mueller but more cautious around gasoline, David Dunbar Buick organized a $100,000 company in Detroit to build his eponymous vehicle. The Cadillac also hit the market, originated by none other than Henry Ford. Immediately following the Punch Bowl race in 1901, Ford made a second stumbling effort to build passenger cars, this time with a new organization called the Henry Ford Company. It ended in an even worse disaster than the Detroit Automobile Company. Ford didn't finish a single car, he quit the HFC after four months, and he permanently alienated the last of his original backers. These money men called in Detroit's top machinist (and Oldsmobile supplier) Henry Leland to run things. They renamed the company Cadillac (after Detroit's founder), and went ahead with Ford's design and Leland's engines. Cadillac's sales director Smiling Billy Metzger wrote 1,000 orders for the promised model at the 1903 New York Auto Show.

Again Ford turned to building race cars as a way to mark time and keep his name before the public. Under commission by international bicycle racing star Tom Cooper, Ford constructed two vehicles, the *Arrow* and the *999* (named for famous locomotives). These appalling machines, each basically a couple of girders mounted together on wheels with an engine on top, alarmed even Henry Ford, after he broke his no-racing pledge and test drove the two: "The roar of those cylinders alone was enough to half kill a man. There was only one seat. One life to a car was enough. We let them out at full speed. I cannot quite describe the sensation. Going over Niagara Falls would have been but a pastime after a ride in one of them."(7) Cooper desired none of that kind of pastime, so he enlisted his less prudent bike racing colleague, Barney Oldfield, to drive the *999*. "This chariot may kill me," Oldfield said with some trepidation but went ahead nonetheless. Once more the Ford team cheated death and won a big competition at the Grosse Pointe track in the fall of 1902.

This bought Ford great publicity, but wouldn't pay for yet another passenger car company. Desperate for new capital, Ford switched on his personal magnetism again and bore down on his coal dealer, of all people, Alexander Malcolmson, who had connections around town. Ford did the same with the Dodge brothers, John and Horace. It worked. Malcolmson put up $3,000 and began twisting the arms of potential investors. The Dodges not only forsook Oldsmobile but agreed to swallow $40,000 in retooling costs at their machine shop in order to build chassis, engines and axles for Ford. The Dodges also subscribed for 10% of the shares of the Ford Motor Company (FMC). Working together, Henry, his assistant Harold Wills (now chief engineer), Spider Huff and the Dodges designed and built a prototype.

When incorporation day arrived – June 16, 1903 – the FMC had raised only $28,000 in cash out of a nominal capitalization of $100,000. Just a handful of Malcolmson's friends, relatives and colleagues invested, and they put up more promises than money. The biggest chunk of actual coin - $10,000 - came from banker John Gray, Malcolmson's uncle, who in return was made company president. Malcolmson's office clerk James Couzens managed to scrounge up $1,000 cash to invest. Ford and Malcolmson took a combined 51% of the stock as the main organizers, although Henry didn't contribute so much as a penny of his own money, nor did any Ford friend or relation. This pathetically small kitty looked especially puny against the $350,000 the company already owed in parts contracts.

The FMC bank account fell as low as $223 that summer before the first cars were sold. With two flop companies behind him, this time around Ford saw to the recruitment of some dealers, he advertised nationally in *Harper's* and *Leslie's Weekly*

80

magazines, and most importantly he made sure to actually assemble and ship the vehicles. In this he had the enthusiastic help of the 30 year-old Couzens, whom Ford quickly and completely converted into his own man and into an automobile firebrand to boot. Couzens, a one-time carchecker with the Michigan Central Railroad, is often credited with having curbed Ford's dawdling perfectionism. It's more likely Henry realized that with two strikes against him, one more whiff at running an auto company and he'd be out of the game.

There certainly was nothing perfect about the Ford Model A. This two passenger wooden-bodied cracker box, mounted on a steel chassis with wooden wheels and a four cylinder engine, weighed 1,250 pounds and had a wheelbase six feet long, although Ford told the artist drawing up the first illustrations to fake them and make the car seem longer. Uneconomical, unreliable, unsafe, in the odd moments when it actually ran the A could reach 30 mph. Ford tried toning the speed issue down in the first ads, promising *...an automobile which will attain to a sufficient speed to satisfy the average person without acquiring any of those breakneck velocities which are so universally condemned.* But that pitch didn't really jibe with his racing rep, so Henry also hastened to assure the propsective buyer, *You can - if you choose - loiter lingeringly through shady avenues or you can press down on the foot-lever until all the scenery looks alike to you and you have to keep your eyes skinned to count the milestones as they pass.* (8)

Henry Ford's disinterest in public safety vis-a-vis the automobile hadn't changed a bit. He found it amusing, for example, to teach his 10 year-old son Edsel to drive a model A, oblivious to the risks this posed to anyone else on the street. The FMC aggressively proclaimed the car, *The Boss of the Road...It is positively the most perfect machine on the market, having overcome all drawbacks such as smell, noise, jolt, etc., common to all other makes of Auto Carriages.* Later, much later, Henry came clean about the early days of the auto industry:

..there was not much concern as to what happened to the car once it had been sold. How much gasoline it used per mile was of no great moment; how much service it actually gave did not matter; and if it broke down and had to have parts replaced, then that was just hard luck for the owner... if the repair man were a shiftless person, with an adequate knowledge of automobiles and an inordinate desire to make a good thing out of every car that came into his place for repairs, then even a slight breakdown meant weeks of laying up and a whopping big repair bill that had to be paid before the car could be taken away. The repair men were for a time the largest menace to the automobile industry.(9)

The first Ford units were laughably bad. Horace Dodge, in fact, punched out a laughing street bystander as the fellow watched the stranded Dodge struggle to crank a "Boss of the Road" to life. Rather than try to troubleshoot the A's at the factory, Couzens decided it would be cheaper to send a mechanic to the buyer's home, or wherever the Ford happened to break down, a practice pioneered by Ransom Olds. Other companies in other industries picked up on and mocked the general unreliability of automobiles, like the makers of Force breakfast cereal:

Jim Dumps an automobile bought
Which didn't auto as it ought.
No skill could keep it in repair
And bills increased poor Jim's despair.

Such trials now glance off from him
For "Force" has made him Sunny Jim.(10)

The new Fords had one additional problem, they were illegal. The FMC refused from day one to pay royalties to the holders of the Selden Patent on all automobiles, one of the most preposterous patents ever granted in America, on an unworkable design that dated all the way back to 1879. In a paroxysm of rage, the excitable Couzens, definitely no Sunny Jim, told the Association of Licensed Automobile Manufacturers, headed by Ransom Olds, to go to hell when it demanded patent payments. The ALAM launched a campaign to inform customers that "If You Buy a Ford, You Buy a Lawsuit." HF countered by promising to indemnify any sued customers, and thereafter a long and profitable (for the attornies) legal action commenced.

Priced at $750 without a top and $850 with one, the Ford Model A, or Fordmobile as the company briefly called it, produced a $150-$200 profit per vehicle. Only $20 of the $600 production cost went to FMC assembly workers. In that first year, the company hoped to sell as many cars as possible as quickly as possible, and if demand carried over into a second year, well and good, if not, too bad. According to historian David Brinkley, company president John Gray, "sincerely believed the automobile craze was a passing fad and that the average citizen would tire of the work and bother required to operate and maintain a car."(11)

Ford sold A's not just in Detroit, but shipped them by reliable rail and water means to Philadelphia, New York, Chicago, San Francisco, even as far away as Hawaii. Port Huron soldier Robert Krenkel recently had written home from Honolulu, calling it the most beautiful city he'd ever seen, neat and clean, with beautiful paved streets and buildings, and a railroad that encircled the island. The automobile soon would fix all that. None of the first batch of A's made it to Port Huron; the FMC at its inception didn't have a dealer there or in any city of that size, though you could order an A from the factory direct.

In the meantime, Loren Sherman became the next notable name in Port Huron to join the auto owners' ranks. In the spring of 1903 he purchased a $2,500 six seater touring car, which his own paper called the "finest in the city." While he'd been promoting automobiles for years in the pages of the *Daily Times*, it took some horse trouble to finally convince Sherman to part with his $2,500. A horse took a friend of his, Mrs. Richard Bloodgood, for a runaway ride in the Sherman carriage, after a passing automobile panicked the animal. Although the horse had been perfectly correct in running away, this experience didn't go down too well with either Mrs. Bloodgood, who'd been slammed into a phone pole during the adventure, or with the publisher, who decided he'd rather dish out auto intimidation than take it. Car ownership changed Sherman's perspective on the rights of pedestrians in a hurry. Less than two months after his purchase, the *Times* complained editorially that people in the street made it "exceedingly difficult" for vehicle drivers. The reverse idea that vehicle drivers made things exceedingly difficult for pedestrians receded from Sherman's point of view.

The large amount of advertising the auto dealers placed in his paper during the spring selling season also worked on Sherman's sympathies. These car ads easily covered several times as much space as the modest daily schedule notices placed by the trains, ships and streetcars; and promised much more to come. During the first decade of the 20th Century, publications all over America faced the choice of hobbling their editorial consciences and reaping the bounty of auto ads, or rejecting the auto income by forthrightly calling a spade a spade. The vast majority failed the test. *Collier's* magazine turned over its whole January 1903 issue to adoration of the automobile, and won the reward of 13 big auto ads, among them Oldsmobile's. The farm journal *Breeder's Gazette*, on the other hand, didn't warm up that quickly, and called automobile drivers "a reckless, blood-thirsty, villainous lot of purse-proud, crazy trespassers upon the legitimate avenues of trade."(12) The BG editor couldn't reasonably expect his ad salesman to overcome that.

The attitude of another prominent Port Huron man toward automobiles changed dramatically in 1903. Ex-mayor Fred Moore, who'd been so alarmed at the velocity of automobiles in the streets less than a year earlier, by now had been separated completely from his reason by car sickness. Moore bought John Howard's auto from him and promised, perhaps facetiously, to make the street in front of the Moore home, Court Street, one of the oldest and most prominent thoroughfares in the city, his "favorite speedway." This did nothing to reassure the public, who read at the same time about the Paris-Madrid automobile road race in Europe, called off after 10 drivers and spectators had been killed. When Moore took his car and family out for a spin one Sunday, his favorite day, and tried making a speedway out of some of St. Clair County's country roads, he got stuck in a mudhole. The Moores had to walk home, and in the minds of many Port Huroners it served them right.

George Yokom now blazed fresh automotive trails in Port Huron, by setting up the first auto repair shop in town, one of those menacing but all too necessary extortion parlors Henry Ford had warned about. Yokom also ran the first used car ad, for a National electric runabout, "as good as new." That wasn't saying much at this stage. It's a telling point that after barely a year's use some Port Huron owners, either fed up or bored with their flimsy cars, wanted to get rid of them. And gamble that next year's model night have more things right with it. The practice of buying a new car every year, and trading in the old one, appeared at the very dawn of the auto industry. Compared to the one-year-and-out automobile, a railroad locomotive commonly lasted 20 years and ran 2 million miles, a passenger railcar about half that. As to reliability, Vermont doctor Horatio Jackson needed 64 days to make the first ever transcontinental auto trip in 1903, while U.S. Steel executive Henry Lowe crossed the same continent by train in a record 73 hours.

Yokom also made an unenviable but inevitable record in Port Huron in 1903, when he ran over a boy on Main Street, the city's first reported collision of an automobile with a human being, though no doubt there'd been others. The *Daily Times* leaped to the defense of its generous advertiser, and told readers that the victim (whom it didn't bother to name or ask what had happened) had escaped unhurt, even though the car ran entirely over him. The *Times* absolved Yokom of any suggestion of malice or carelessness. Had George landed in court over this, the responsibility for traffic accidents in these early years often could be shifted from the driver to the misbehavior of the automobile itself, since none of the motorists of the day exercised much real control over their machines. The public regarded autos somewhat like horses in that respect; you never knew what the thing might do next.

William Wilson for instance, a prominent Port Huron capitalist, colleague of

Major Boynton, and a secret embezzler, was dragged around his yard by his new car on the second day he owned it, after the engine re-started while Wilson was climbing out. The steering gear on merchant tailor Herman Appel's week-old automobile failed at a rather critical moment, while Appel's friend, jeweler Henry Fair, in his first attempt at driving, barreled down Main Street. The unsteerable Appel vehicle subsequently hit the curb and flipped over. Mr. Fair also, per the press, escaped unhurt, though these lucky escapes from "hurt" couldn't last forever. Port Huron's auto community kept the faith and defiantly stuck together in the face of these discouraging incidents. Five autos at one time hobnobbed together in Pine Grove Park that summer of 1903, birds of a feather who the next year formed their own Auto Club.

Discouragement found no home at the Ford Motor Company as 1904 arrived. After surmounting the most crippling quality control problems, which led to furious shouting matches between Couzens and the equally volatile Dodge brothers, the company sold 1,700 cars during the first fiscal year and declared an amazing 100% in dividends on the company's $100,000 in stock. The payout covered the unpaid personal notes that made up most of the company's first investment capital; rather like pulling an auto company out of a hat. Ford drafted plans for the 1904 models, put together a Canadian division, and moved the FMC to a factory 10 times as big. This turn in his fortunes delighted the company namesake so much that he reneged again on his "no more racing" pledge, got back into one of his speeders, and drove it to a record 91 mph on a straightaway mile laid out across the surface of frozen Lake St. Clair, located at the southern end of St. Clair County. After this dubious achievement, HF treated himself and Spider Huff to a muskrat dinner at a nearby hotel.(13) Suffice to say, the automobile's relationship to ice would not always be so fortunate.

The growing FMC dealer network extended its reach into Port Huron in June, 1904 when Rex Cole, an electrical contractor competitor of George Yokom's, took command of local Ford sales. He sold his first Ford to Joseph Walsh, a stalwart officer in the National Guard, a Spanish-American War veteran, a dedicated bad roads foe, a prominent barrister, and Port Huron's part time city attorney. The very same week that Walsh bought the Ford, he drew up the first Port Huron automobile ordinance, duly passed by the City Council. This would not be the last time that a government official favorably disposed toward the auto industry played a key role in drafting the public regulations of the automobile.

The new law decreed a speed limit of 12 mph inside the city limits, and 8 mph in the business district, about the same as bicycles. It set the minimum driving age at 16, disqualifying Edsel Ford. A mandatory, tiny 4 inch by 3 inch license plate costing $1 had to be affixed to every car. Good luck reading it as it went by. Autos had to keep to the right side of the street as they traveled, and carry two lights at night. Though headlights made the car visible to others they were largely useless for lighting the road ahead of the car. 100 years later, headlights were still inadequate for night driving, as University of Michigan researcher Paul Olson concluded, "You can't see worth a damn at night!"(14) The 1904 auto ordnance prescribed penalties of up to $100 in fines and 90 days in jail, the same as for all misdemeanors. Walsh himself took out the first license, followed by Fred Moore and Loren Sherman. Eighteen drivers signed up during the first few days.

The *Port Huron Daily Herald* applauded these measures: "The life of any little child on our streets, or the safety of pedestrians of any kind, that they may not be run down or maimed or killed, is of far more importance than the comfort, convenience or pleasure of any of the automobile owners of our city..."(15) However, the most important restriction, the speed limit, proved the most difficult to obey or enforce, just as with bicycles. Since not all early cars carried speedometers, some motorists had no way of knowing how fast they traveled. Some wouldn't have paid any attention if they had known. As they did with bikes, police officers used a stopwatch to time a car driver as he passed two fixed points, then calculated the speed, then lit out after the lawbreaker on foot or bicycle, or tried to catch him at home later, or if that failed wrote him a letter.

The naive faith that an ordinance would bring lasting auto civility to the streets was dashed in a week's time, when George Yokom ran down Edgar Spalding, by clumsily backing a car into the 60 year-old bicyclist. That was the only way cars could be backed up, then or ever, clumsily. The incident shocked the city, and Yokom's car career might have come to a halt had he not been so well connected. One of Port Huron's most admired men, Spalding had enlisted at age 18 as a private during the Civil War, and then energetically worked his way up to the post of company commander just a year later. Wounded and captured at the battle of Chickamauga, he'd spent 18 months in various Confederate prison camps. As at Chickamauga, the attack by this new automobile enemy left Spalding badly bruised and shaken up but unbroken. The same *Herald* editorialist who had welcomed the auto ordnance now cried out: "All the automobiles in the city could not compensate for an injury to such a citizen."

In addition to the Spalding affront, complaints came pouring into Port Huron police headquarters from all over town about wild drivers. Police Chief Henry Marx at first issued one empty threat after another to crack down. This became an annual rite of spring for years, the police chief's declaration of war against speeding. But Marx proceeded cautiously with actual enforcement at first because automobile owners included some of the wealthiest and most influential people in town, and the chief held an appointive office. When the cops finally did catch their first auto varmint they made sure to grab somebody of no importance, a vacationer named E. K. Stewart, who paid a mere $5 fine. The estimated average speed of Port Huron motorists escalated to 15-20 mph, then 20-25, and even 35 mph.

The general ineptitude of Port Huron's earliest drivers, who sometimes shouted "Whoa!" while trying to stop their cars, frayed nerves still further. The auto ordinance made absolutely no provision for testing driver skill or even physical capacity to handle an automobile. Neither did the first Michigan state automobile license law passed the next year, 1905. The 60 year-old Loren Sherman fainted at the wheel of his 3,000 lb. touring car one day and it roamed free for a while around Main Street before finally ramming a tree. "It was fortunate that the street was clear..," Loren admitted editorially.

Port Huron's police filed no criminal charges against George Yokom for the Spalding rundown, but George decided to make himself scarce for a while, and he took one of the new Oldsmobiles out on a demonstration tour of St. Clair County. At one stop the *Yale Record* reported that while some residents "...never tired of examining the wonderful thing. Every part from the headlight to tires was examined with the most minute scrutiny." Other citizens exhibited more caution, "Many a timid creature was seen to go around by the M.E. church rather than face the panting Red Devil."(16) The

Red Devil meant the car, not Yokom, but George bragged to the Yale populace that an Oldsmobile could travel 45 mph. The implication was pretty clear: if you didn't want to end up like Edgar Spalding you'd better get out of the way.

Dr. George Treadgold also took advantage of his summer vacation in 1904 for a little spin around the Thumb. He reported covering 250 miles on this trip, 110 in a single day, without a hint of trouble. A month after he returned home to Port Huron from this marathon, the doctor's car collapsed under him in a cloud of dust with a broken axle, depositing Treadgold onto the street in a very undignified manner. Refusing to take the hint, the doctor arose, brushed himself off, and immediately ordered another automobile.

Joseph Walsh's Ford quickly ran into trouble, literally. Just two months after he bought it, the Ford met its match when Yokom mechanic Charles Ballmer crashed it into a moving streetcar while ironically driving it in for repairs. The trolley dragged the Ford for 150 feet and beat it up to the tune of $200. Walsh took the tragedy hard because he jus had erected the first "automobile house", or garage, in Port Huron behind his home, with a cozy concrete floor to hold his Ford at night. Wiping away his tears, Walsh sued Yokom for $1,000, Port Huron's first reported automobile lawsuit. The bulk of the damage request came because Walsh had been "deprived" of the use of his automobile companion for the precious days it took to be rebuilt. This is how quickly a screwball emotional attachment formed between automobiles and some of their owners.

The emotional attachment ended in 1904 between Ransom Olds and the company he built. Olds disagreed with his majority stockholders over whether to discard the little curved dash Oldsmobile and make bigger, more expensive, and more profitable cars instead, following the trend at several other companies, including the FMC. Olds said no, and the company said, "Go." Although Olds never regained the center stage in the auto industry, he successfully founded another vehicle firm named after him, REO. Another significant name, David Buick, disagreed in 1904 with the wagon and carriage makers in Flint who had obtained financial control of the Buick automobile company. Things were in such a mess at Buick that the Flint boys appealed to their competitor, Billy Durant, to step in and take over. The multi-millionaire Durant preferred spending his time in New York at this point, playing the stock market and enjoying life, and he hated automobiles on top of this, so he took some convincing.

After making a couple of test drives in the Buick around Flint, Billy changed his mind and swung into action. Entirely devoid of any mechanical expertise, he put to work his awe-inspiring ability at selling and financing. Durant took orders for 1,100 Buicks at the next New York Auto Show, even outdoing the peddling record of that other Billy, Cadillac's Metzger. Next Durant ballooned Buick's capitalization to $1.5 million, far exceeding its assets, the sort of finagling railroads regularly were accused of. Durant built the world's biggest auto factory in Flint, one with 14 acres of floor space. He even started his own Buick racing team, a la Henry Ford, and found a man as foolhardy as Barney Oldfield to drive for him, Louis Chevrolet.(17) From a standing start Billy built Buick into America's biggest car company in four years. He did not always select his sales agents with care, though. In 1905 he awarded Port Huron's Buick franchise to William Wilson, the con man, who'd been dragged around his yard by his first car. Offered an opportunity tailor made for a swindler, Wilson set up the first stand-alone business in Port Huron dedicated entirely to automobiles.

The Port Huron auto count in 1905 reached 25. Five of them belonged to local doctors like Treadgold and Dr. Theodore Heavenrich. Though automobiles had been hailed by their manufacturers at first as a blessing to the profession, in San Francisco that year a doctor reported to the American Medical Association that his new $980 car had cost him $566 in repairs in its first four months and the tires had lasted a mere 1,000 miles.(18) The average doctor in America made $1,000-$1,500 per year at this point, and couldn't absorb costs like those. So, many a doctor's auto bills went straight onto the patient's bills.

Automobile-injured patients started to generate more business for Port Huron's medical profession at about this same time. Patients like store clerk Myron Brown, carstruck while bicycling across the Main Street bridge. The guilty motorist, saloonkeeper Martin Newell, first blew his horn at Brown from behind, then ran over him when the startled cyclist fell over. This pretty clearly demonstrated the uselessness and downright danger of the automobile horn right there. Brown couldn't tell exactly where the horn noise came from, what it meant, who it was meant for, or what to do about it. Neither could 150 students at the Washington School, who bolted from their classrooms one day after mistaking a passing automobile horn for a fire alarm. Nevertheless, the horn quickly established itself in the motoring public's mind as a fair warning for everybody else on the streets, the first line of defense in case of accident: "After all, I blew my horn at him!"

Loren Sherman made his the first two-car family in Port Huron when he bought a an "electric surrey" for his wife Stella in 1905, probably a Waverly model sold by George Yokom. To their great credit, most American women detested the internal combustion engine from the moment they laid eyes on it and overwhelmingly favored electric autos. The gals found particularly distasteful the broken arms and shoulders some gasoline-powered cars inflicted on their owners when the machines backfired while being crank started. Clara Ford said no thanks to the crank and drove an electric, although even electrics still often left their distaff owners hopping mad over a breakdown or a flat tire or an exhausted battery.

When motoring, a woman of 1905 expected to dress the part, just as in bicycling. "Automobile Costumes: They Are No Longer Hideous, Hats and Veils Being Dainty," reported the *Times*. Since most cars operated entirely open to the elements, especially dust, which they raised in choking clouds, most car inhabitants needed protective clothing, dainty or not, for a trip of any length. Properly outfitted, Stella Sherman managed pretty well driving the Waverly around town until she struck a policeman's son bicycling on Lapeer Avenue. Predictably, the *Times'* headline reversed the blame: "Fred Mills Ran into Mrs. Sherman's Automobile."

Loren Sherman also bought the first truck in Port Huron for his Riverside Printing Company, after one the Riverside delivery horses bit a chunk out of his hand. Some people called the truck an auto buckboard, though it ran far less reliably than the horse kind. Almost any other delivery method would have been quicker than a 1905 truck, which might travel 5-10 mph when loaded, if it could be started. The lumbering, solid-tire trucks of that year hadn't improved much since the Swift Meat vehicle days, and sometimes they had to zigzag back and forth or even back up a hill to get over it. But the smarting Sherman made the purchase on principle.

Even in its earliest form, the usefulness of the truck came into dispute in the debate about the automobile. The influential French automaker Henry Fournier claimed streetcars had failed to handle the problem of local package and freight delivery, which made the truck the only recourse to the horse. In view of the facts that America's hundreds of electric streetcar and interurban systems were not yet even 20 years old, and that they'd been built primarily by private interests for passenger traffic, built without government support or direction, and that in some locales these systems were forbidden to carry cargo, in view of all this Fournier jumped to a premature and insupportable conclusion. The truck solution for freight delivery proved to be a disastrous error. The disorder and danger delivered on American streets and roads by large, noisy, dirty, and destructive trucks, some of them already in this first decade weighing 10 tons and more, driven erratically by personnel of dubious competence, went a long way toward making America a worse not a better place in which to live.

The growing menace from cars and trucks on the streets played into the show business hands of the Ringling Brothers Circus when it stopped in Port Huron in 1905. One special act, the "Dip of Death," milked the "Look out!" aspect of motor vehicles for all it was worth. First, circus personnel chauffeured one of their lions around town in the back seat of an open touring car to get people's attention. Having gotten it, featured Ringling performer Mademoiselle De Tiers performed the "Dip" in an automobile (without the lion) in front of 10,000 spectators under the big top. Dressed in an evening gown, Miss De Tiers strapped herself into a car with a body harness, then drove through a 30-foot high vertical loop-the-loop, for which feat Ringling paid her $500 per night. Despite De Tiers' good results with automobile seat belts the general public waited another 60 years for them, and hundreds of thousands of people didn't survive the wait.

An additional, unlooked-for brand of automobile excitement roared into Port Huron that summer of 1905, its first ever high speed police chase. A deputy sheriff from a neighboring county had pursued a car thief all the way from Detroit, over 60 miles, breaking the new state speed limit of 25 mph most of the distance, only to find that the stolen vehicle had been wrecked at the end of the chase. Michigan policemen now had to deal with the question of whether it posed a greater public danger to pursue a lawbreaking driver in another car or to let him go. This incident also gave Port Huron its first real experience with car theft, a troubling crime to say the least. No other material possession stood so ready to help a thief steal itself as an automobile.

And the opportunities to grab one grew apace. By 1905, 34 companies employing 3,900 workers built automobiles in the state of Michigan, a 1,000% increase in five years. This made the state the auto center of America, producing more than half the 22,800 cars constructed that year. The young industry already thought enough of itself to organize a Society of Automotive Engineers. It also mustered enough political muscle to help get a constitutional amendment on the ballot to overturn the 55 year-old ban on Michigan state aid for transportation, the old internal improvements issue. Automakers looked at it as a straightforward sales proposition: they'd sell more cars if there were better roads, and by and large somebody else would pay for the roads. The measure passed easily on election day, in Port Huron by a 10-1 margin. It seemed appropriate to local auto men to celebrate. On the fifth anniversary of the embarrassing 1900 Good Roads Congress, which had taken on a nostalgic glow for auto lobbyists, car racing made its return to the Port Huron Driving Park, this time under the auspices of George Yokom. He rented the park for the 4th of July for another try at exciting the public pulse with speed, in case people weren't getting enough of that on the streets.

After a parade of 18 vehicles motored out to the track, and several thousand people filled the grandstands, who should appear but Henry Ford. Introduced as the "world champion" because of his ice record on Lake St. Clair, Henry did a couple of demo laps in one of his racers, sort of a sentimental journey. Ford didn't try anything fancy or record-breaking this time out. He didn't want to get laid up in a hospital at that particular moment because he had more important matters on his mind, a corporate showdown. In 1905 Henry proved to be infinitely more adroit at boardroom infighting than Ransom Olds or David Buick or even Billy Durant ever were. He slickly maneuvered his equal share partner Alexander Malcolmson right out of the Ford Motor Company. When company president John Gray obligingly died in 1906, HF took over the presidency himself, holding 58% of the FMC stock, in near-total command, beholden, he felt, to no one.

Ford undoubtedly had planned something of the sort at the FMC right from the start. Once accomplished, it cleared the way for him to tackle, virtually without interference, his plans to forsake building the higher-priced models in the FMC lineup, and instead produce a utilitarian "Universal Car." As a first step, the company debuted the rough riding but relatively cheap $600 Model N, a sales hit. The FMC plant spit out as many as 25 N's per day, and Henry bought up a 60 acre horse track in the nearby community of Highland Park on which to build an even bigger factory. Exuberantly, Ford declared the company's third 100% dividend and gave each of his 300 workers a $1,000 bonus at the end of 1905, which amounted to a good deal more than 100% of their annual wages.(19) Henry must have regretted the bonus immediately, since he could have bought each worker a cut glass punch bowl for a lot less. The FMC never again awarded its factory workers so proportionately large a sum.

Meanwhile, reports of the gigantic profits being made in the lightly taxed and entirely unregulated auto manufacturing business by the FMC, Oldsmobile, Buick and other firms awakened some envy in the normally conservative business circles in Port Huron. Envy too of sister cities in Michigan like Detroit, Flint (where 18 different motor vehicle models were built at one time or another), and Lansing (home now to both Oldsmobile and REO). Temptation passed through Port Huron in the person of several more auto entrepreneurs, each of these pitch men looking for money.

Local mechanics also got busy with their own car designs. George Conner, the equipment mastermind at Port Huron Engine and Thresher, claimed he had a plan in mind for an automobile with an automatic transmission, and shock absorbers. Conner further told the Chamber of Commerce that he already held a patent on the transmission, he just needed startup money, so let's get going. Despite his impeccable credentials Conner's idea went nowhere. George Yokom also worked on a prototype of his own car, and so did some men at the Lee Manufacturing Company, which usually just supplied carburetors to the car business. The Lee team somewhat fancifully called their car the Trout. Neither the Yokom nor the Trout ever made it into the ranks of the American automobile 4,000.

Finally a realistic proposal appeared in 1906. The Northern Automobile company of Detroit, an actual going concern, offered to install a factory in Port Huron if local people subscribed for $100,000 in stock and put up the building. Northern didn't make clear why it needed a second assembly plant so close to its main operation, but the company did have some weight in back of it. Both Henry Ford's pal Charles King and everybody's pal Billy Metzger had helped organize Northern, with the support of the well-heeled owners of the Detroit Stove Works. Inaccurately advertised as *The Silent Northern...Absolutely Noiseless,* the touring car version – the one to be built in Port Huron – cost $1,700. Fred Moore bought an even bigger Northern model, and gleefully described it as the most powerful car in Port Huron, capable of doing 65 mph, which no doubt sent shivers down a few spines.

The deal at hand offered work for 250 men in the Port Huron factory, generating at least $200,000 in total wages annually. Eventually 400 might be employed. This would make it as large as the Jenks shipyard once had been, and Jenks unfortunately had closed recently. The new Northern Auto plant would fill this gap as one of the biggest employers in town. Dazzled, the Chamber of Commerce raised the $100,000 in two days from a full roster of bigwigs like Moore, Yokom, and Loren Sherman (though some of the contributors later welshed and had to be sued for the money). Workmen completed the 50,000 square foot factory, with full railroad service, in just two months, right next door to the Driving Park.

Many Port Huroners were of two minds about this arrangement. On the one hand, building, selling and servicing automobiles seemed to promise solid financial returns. Several companies in Port Huron, like Lee Manufacturing, already furnished parts, castings and auto bodies to other carmakers. Property values around the Northern factory site jumped immediately after the deal was announced, according to E. J. Schoolcraft, on the prospect of future expansion. At retail, a hundred cars, new and used, changed hands in Port Huron in 1906. Revenues from new vehicle sales alone came to $35,000. George Yokom sold as many as one per day during the 1906 spring rush. As to service, automobiles required an enormous support system to keep running. Given the large amount of repair work, fuel, lubricants, tires and replacement parts needed for just a few dozen vehicles around town, the aggregate spending total mounted very rapidly.

On the other hand, the Northern product, like all cars, was undeniably an obnoxious and dangerous extravagance. The number of cars operating on the streets of Port Huron had doubled in a year's time, to anywhere from 60 to 75, the public had lost count. That number doubled again during the tourist season when visitors brought their own vehicles to town. "They keep the pedestrian dodging..." said the annoyed *Herald*. The paper ran back-to-back editorials in the same edition, one welcoming Northern, the other saying, "While talking about automobile factories it may not come amiss to notice that the automobile ordnance is violated daily and in such a way as to threaten a serious accident at any moment."[20] Many Port Huron mothers increasingly feared for the safety of their children, especially after a hit-and-run driver administered a broken shoulder to 13 year-old Fred Smith, while the boy, minding his own business, walked along the formerly calm Griswold Street.

A prominent English psychiatrist of the day, Sir James Crichton-Browne, accused some drivers in 1906 of "homicidal mania...A confirmed motorist must become sluggish in intellect and excitable in temper." Just how excitable even Crichton-Browne never imagined. Certainly nothing prevented a maniac from climbing into and driving away a car, now or ever during the 20th Century. And broader social objections came into play. The advent of autos amounted to a kind of class warfare, in which working people built them while the rich drove them, and the rich used them to drive working

90

people off the streets. This moved Princeton University president Woodrow Wilson to write, "Nothing has spread socialistic feeling more than the use of the automobile. Automobilists are a picture of arrogance and wealth, with all its independence and carelessness."(21) An avid bicyclist, Wilson helped draw up a law banning automobiles from the island of Bermuda, his favorite vacation spot.

Dr. Royal Dunn of Port Huron didn't cut so much a figure of wealth and arrogance as of notorious clumsiness. He had a fondness for alcohol, and showed a kind of goofball detachment that didn't inspire much confidence in him as a physician. He made horses uneasy, too, and they did everything in their power to rid themselves of his company, employing the usual assortment of kicking, biting, bucking, rollover, and runaway tactics on him. This campaign finally persuaded the doctor to buy an automobile from George Yokom in 1906. Police subsequently stopped Dr. Dunn three times that summer for speeding. He spent nary a single day, a single hour in jail for this chronic lawbreaking. Virtually nobody went to jail for speeding in Port Huron during this decade. When his car's wooden body caught fire and burned up while he made a house call one day, Dr. Dunn walked home, caught the train to the 1907 Detroit Auto Show, and drove a new automobile back. Within days he'd been arrested for speeding again. It was to this man that the responsibility fell for first killing a Port Huronite with a car.

Dunn ran over 60 year-old Joseph Turner while the Grand Trunk shop mason biked home from work. "Dr. Dunn is caring for the injured man," reported the *Herald,* "and stated this morning no serious results would ensue." Serious for Dunn, that is. Turner must have wondered about this, and he hung on for nine months, long enough to file a $15,000 lawsuit against Dunn, before dying, the first Levassor death in Port Huron. Nobody else witnessed this collision, but it's entirely likely that Dunn's speeding and inattention to his driving killed Turner, habits fostered by the sheer boredom and monotony Dunn experienced in regularly driving a car over the same route again and again. The American car industry preferred to describe driving as exciting, healthy, fulfilling, endlessly fascinating. The opposite was the case.

It's also possible that Dr. Dunn had been drinking, seeing as how drunk driving had not been banned yet in Port Huron. As early as 1904 a study in the *Quarterly Journal of Inebriety* found that 19 of 25 drivers in fatal wrecks in their "automobile wagons" drove under the influence. Looking forward a bit, automobiles killed 20 people per month in the United States by 1910. And that figure probably missed a lot of Levassor victims who suffered lingering deaths. Police didn't always update their files when the Turners of the world relocated to the cemetery. Nobody in 1910, or thereafter, had a clear picture of how many non-fatal car injuries occurred. Too many to conveniently count.

Despite the well-founded reservations in the community about the ultimate product, the Northern car factory in Port Huron opened in April 1907. To begin with, about 170 workers built 12 units per week, and to their surprise the unexpectedly dangerous work inflicted three injuries per week on the labor force. Northern tested the first completed cars on the streets of Port Huron, mainly Main Street, which ran right by the plant. Immediately the company insisted that the city raise the speed limit to accommodate this testing. It was not a timely request. Justice of the Peace Chester Benedict had just dished out the biggest auto speeding fine yet, $25, and threatened the son of William Canham, ex-president of the streetcar company and a Northern shareholder, with 65 days in the Detroit House of Corrections, a notorious institution. "No more light fines, I'll stop this mad racing," said JP Benedict. "Speeditis" he called it.

The scope of speeditis in Port Huron needed addressing. By now, Police Chief Marx's men didn't arrest anybody doing less than 20 mph, well over the limit, and even under that lax arrangement they issued up to 20 warrants a week. One of the guilty parties, Dr. Albert Irwin, chief medical officer of the Maccabees, petulantly refused to apologize for his speeditis. "There is no pleasure in driving an automobile through the streets of Port Huron at the present time, on account of the interference by the police," said the doctor. He further pronounced driving an automobile so slow as 8 mph to be almost impossible. A *Daily Herald* editorial promptly roasted Dr. Irwin in print as a "speed fiend." Wary of the charge of speeditis, the Northern company tried the alternative of testing cars on its own property, until one of the drivers mistook an accelerator for the brake and slammed into the factory wall, wrecking the car. So, the company went back onto the streets, seeing as how the cops unofficially had raised the speed limit anyhow.

Now that the Northern factory was actually up and running, some of Port Huron's local money men felt encouraged enough to get behind another new startup automotive venture, the Cass Truck Company, which they owned 100%. But Cass and Northern both ran almost immediately into an economic roadblock, the 1907-1908 depression in America, the first national financial setback in a decade. This slump began in the railroad industry, and we'll explore that aspect more fully later, but by September 1907 half the Northern employees in Port Huron had been laid off while the Cass project had been adjourned. Eight sizeable automakers failed nationwide, and Cadillac, one of George Yokom's suppliers, suspended production. The five companies in Port Huron making auto parts felt the breeze. "Wall Street 'Panic' is Hard on Auto Business," admitted the *Daily Times*. A reported 2,000 New Yorkers sold their cars and another 2,000 canceled orders valued at $15 million. In Port Huron, the Wilson Buick dealership went temporarily into receivership, and George Yokom found he had way too many trade-ins on hand, "So call early if you want a cheap car." Anyone who cared to look saw that even at this early stage in the auto industry's history, many car owners, even ostensibly wealthy ones, had purchased and maintained their vehicles with savings they should have held in reserve. They couldn't really afford them.

With the onset of bad economic times in Michigan, popular opinion turned a little more decidedly against automobile owners for making a bad situation worse by their shenanigans on the roads. Port Huron editorial cartoons lampooned car drivers by comparing them to Mr. Football Season and the Grim Reaper as notorious killers. In one front-page drawing, motorists lined up to buy that joke of the day, Auto Insurance: "Get insured in case of a blow up, smash up, collision, break down, in case of arrest, assault by irate natives, etc. No auto trip should be made without our auto insurance tickets."(22) Yes, in 1907 this concept qualified as a gag. "Is the automobile to disappear as a fad?" asked a Port Huron editorial in the midst of the national slump. Unfortunately, no.

At the FMC, Henry Ford met the depression by the expedient of shipping unordered cars to his dealers and demanding payment for them. Desperate times called for desperate measures, so he also hired a convicted embezzler, Norval Hawkins, as the company's sales director.(23) In Flint, Billy Durant also kept on building Buicks, and putting the vehicles aside to sell when the panic subsided, or perhaps we should say when the sheep again were ready to be shorn. "He was one hell of a gambler," said Durant's admiring colleague, Charles Mott, who had relocated his wheel and axle company from Utica, NY to Flint to build only for Billy. As calm as they may have seemed on the outside, both Ford and Gambling Billy Durant felt enough anxiety that in early 1908 they met with Ransom Olds in Detroit to discuss a $35 million merger of their three companies, a discussion organized by financier and trust builder J. P. Morgan. The deal sounded okay at first, until Henry and Ransom demanded $3 million each up front. They didn't get it, and went home.

Many other carmakers weren't so obdurate under the circumstances. The depression forced Northern Automobile into the arms of the Wayne Automobile Company, also of Detroit. Or perhaps it was vice versa. In any case the Port Huron branch factory of Northern now became just a parts supplier for the combined company, called EMF, the "M" of which stood for that man about town, Smiling Billy Metzger. EMF liked to call its product, like the Auto-Bi, "a twentieth century miracle," but some wags claimed EMF really stood for "Every Mechanical Fault", or "Every Morning Fix it."(24) EMF workman Harold Vance of Port Huron said the car "could go as far as 30 miles without developing trouble." He meant this remark facetiously but plenty of models couldn't even manage that much. And their shortcomings were by no means always trivial, but often vital to life and limb. The first auto advice column to appear in the Port Huron press, under the pseudonym of "A. Crank", advised motorists, "It is a good plan to have always a little powdered resin in the toolbox of the car. It is mighty useful on the brakes when they do not hold sufficiently in a hilly region...". That presumed, of course, that the driver survived the initial discovery that his brakes weren't holding and had time to apply the resin.

The brakes on one car in Port Huron needed some resin the day it knocked Circuit Judge Eugene Law flying on Main Street, interrupting the jurist's daily walk. The 50 year-old Law landed 30 feet from the point of impact and the car then ran him over as well. "Notwithstanding the fact that a man has a much right to the road as vehicles," said the battered, chastened judge, "I think it is better judgment for the man afoot to take to the nearest tree when he hears an automobile coming."(25) Police filed no charges against the driver. A car fought the Law and the car won. To make matters worse, the driver who mowed down the jurist worked for Buick dealer William Wilson. Before Judge Law could get a lawsuit filed, auditors discovered Wilson's $125,000 swindle of Major Boynton's savings and loan society. Wilson went bust. So Port Huron's scandal-tainted Buick franchise landed in the hands of George Yokom.

Neither the setback of the depression nor the bad news of the situation in Port Huron could hold Billy Durant in check for long. When the clouds parted for the automobile industry later in 1908, and it looked as though Buick sales were picking up, Durant shifted back into high gear. He flew "high, wide and handsome," in the words of one friend. Durant incorporated the General Motors Company (GM) on September 16, 1908, mainly, so an associate said, to create a new stock issue to "dicker and trade." Wheeling and dealing like mad, over the next two years Gambling Billy bought up Oldsmobile and Cadillac and more than two dozen other car, truck, and parts companies that looked to be promising, although he himself still had no clear idea of how GM actually designed and built automobiles. He jacked up the company's capitalization to

$60 million.

For his part, once he squeezed through the slump, Henry Ford turned his attention to the design of the ninth model to be produced by the Ford Motor Company, the T. He made it two feet longer than the A, and bolted it together from no fewer than 5,000 parts. The first ads for the T hit Port Huron in December '08, describing it as a *big handsome powerful speedy reliable family car,* but not exactly a steal, for the customer anyway. The FMC quoted prices of $850 for the touring car version, $900 for the coupe, and $1000 for the town car. Buyers had to put at least a 50% deposit down and pay the balance on delivery.

The T carried up to five people, but the occasions when that many rode in one together were few and far between. This meant the owner dragged around excess capacity for 3-4 people almost every time he cranked up. In fact, right from the auto era's beginning, Americans typically drove their cars, no matter how big, with just one full person aboard, plus an occasional half a passenger, statistically. Henry Ford reckoned that farmers when not transporting their families could use the backseat for milk cans, and to rural customers he marketed the T as half car, half farm truck.

Owners found starting the T to be difficult and sometimes dangerous. Its high ground clearance made it top heavy and prone to roll over. The standard wheels couldn't be detached from the axle, so the numerous flats had to be fixed by prying the old tire off the rim, a monumental task even in good weather. Once the tires wore down beyond repair a new set cost $74, a major expense. The transmission and brake bands required weekly adjustment. The T had no front doors (Henry himself always vaulted into cars), and no shock absorbers. No more reliable or better built than any other car on the road, the T could claim one saving grace: its simple design made it, aside from flats, the most easily and cheaply repairable of automobiles, often do-it-yourself, a considerable advantage.

Alfred Sloan, the New Jersey bearing maker who sold his products to both the FMC and General Motors, couldn't quite understand why anyone bought Model T's, or Buicks, or EMF's, or any of the other hundreds of makes on the road, they were all so bad. Neither could Ford's buddy Thomas Edison – too flimsy, he said of the cars of these days. Sloan claimed hat he'd learned to swear after he bought his first automobile in 1903. After cussing it out in his native Brooklynese for all he was worth, Sloan sold this lemon to a friend who subsequently in a fury blew it up with dynamite. Years later Sloan enjoyed a mellow chuckle at the expense of the car buyers of the 1901-1910 decade.

Many bright automotive ideas ended with a horse, a towline, and laughter. Although progress was expensive, American motorists cheerfully paid the bills for it. In their enthusiasm for individual transportation, they bought the cars, reliable or unreliable, and thus provided the source of a substantial portion of the risk capital for experiment and production. Not many industries have been so well favored by their customers. (26)

Just how Americans raised this "risk capital" increasingly concerned bankers in the still shaky post-depression financial world of 1909. Sloan marked this period down as the dawn of the mass vs. class automobile market. Most of the "mass" didn't have the ready cash to buy automobiles. The average working man in America earned $500-600 per year; the typical savings account held $237. Ignoring the experience of the previous two years, carsick buyers turned to decidedly reckless means to pay for them, by withdrawing savings, selling bonds, mortgaging homes, taking out loans, offering personal notes, trading in horses, pianos, maple syrup, anything for an automobile.(27) In exchange they received a depreciating, typically non-productive asset, which cost an average of $1,500 to purchase, plus 17 cents per mile to operate, about eight times the passenger railroad rate. A very fortunate buyer might get 20,000 miles from a vehicle, if he drove it till it dropped.

In Port Huron the Elks Club became the first organization to use the fundraising gimmick of raffling off an automobile, a $950 REO, but the far more valuable prize would have been the REO's operating bills. Port Huron City Assessor William Denler called determining the value of the 125 autos in town a "ticklish" business. "Today they're worth so much and tomorrow they are not worth anything. They deteriorate rapidly, you know."(28) Alternatively, for about the price of a Model T, you could have bought two small houses in Port Huron, or a 40 acre farm with a home and two barns just south of town.

One of every 44 American households owned an automobile by the end of the decade, including the White Household. President William Taft, not quite so stretched financially as many another car buyer, plunked down $7,000 for the first auto ever stabled at the Executive Mansion. He needed a heavy duty set of wheels to handle his 320 pounds, and really should have walked instead. Trouble arose one day when Taft's son Robert took the family vehicle out for a spin, blew the horn to clear a street repair crew from his path, then ran over one of the scrambling laborers, fracturing the man's skull. The headline read: "Young Taft is Anxious – Forgoes Yacht Race to Attend Workman He Injured," which seemed pretty sporting of Robert. President Dad eventually paid off the victim with the equivalent of the man's yearly wages, all medical bills, and a free trip to Italy.

By 1910 the registered automobile population in America reached nearly half a million, 15,000 of them in the state of Michigan. The figures included an increasing volume of trucks, whose numbers in Port Huron multiplied with the addition of these vehicles at the Troy Steam Laundry, Howard Furniture, and the Port Huron Creamery. Some companies still needed more convincing. The White Star boat line tried out a truck in Port Huron, then dumped it, saying the firm could keep six horse-and-wagon teams going for the price of running one truck.

The FMC sold more than 10,000 vehicles in the 1908-09 fiscal year, then 18,000 the next year, then 34,000 the next. The company dropped all other model lines except the T, and demanded that its dealers sell no other brands but Ford. Henry celebrated by building Clara a Detroit mansion, after having dragged her from one rented home to another for 17 years. He also began buying land, 1,000 acres and more, around the old Ford farmstead near Dearborn. The FMC opened its huge new Highland Park assembly plant, big enough for 4,000 workers. Detroit architect Albert Kahn designed the structure, one of his relatively new glass wall and reinforced concrete factories. During the next 40 years Kahn created 1,000 buildings for the FMC. At one point his company designed 20% of all the architect-drawn commercial buildings in the United States, plus hundreds in foreign countries. Much to Kahn's surprise and even shock, other architects adopted his auto factory look for every use under the sun, from office buildings to schools to hospitals to churches to homes and apartments. Frank

Lloyd Wright (who designed a home with a three-car garage as early as 1906) wound up the sentimental favorite as America's most influential 20th Century architect, but in practice Kahn took the title, hands down.

Kahn also finished a big new Dodge Brothers plant in 1910 in another Detroit suburb, Hamtramck. The brothers still supplied parts to the FMC, but they intended eventually to say *sayonara* to Henry Ford and build their own automobiles in this factory. Two Port Huron contractors reaped substantial rewards from the auto industry's expansion program. Scottish immigrant Andrew Smith and his son Maynard pocketed a $75,000 fee, and employed 50 Port Huron workers, on their first Ford project. A good many more auto plant commissions in Detroit came the way of the Smiths, and their billings grew to $300,000. Andrew counted himself lucky still to be in one piece to benefit from this. He'd lost control of the first car he ever tried to drive in Port Huron and crashed it into a tree, nearly running down in the process ex-police chief Marshall Petit's daughter Frances. Andrew occasionally let his 11 year-old son Earl illegally drive around town, a bit of father-and-son fun in the tradition of Henry and Edsel Ford.

Just one more hiccup disturbed the equanimity of Henry Ford during what remained of the decade. The FMC lost the Selden Patent suit in 1909, despite Lyin' Hank's having gone to the trouble of perjuring himself by misdating an evidentiary photo of his original quadricycle.(29) In a moment of despair over this legal setback, the company founder nearly sold out again, this time to an offer from Billy Durant and General Motors. GM by now included 10 brand names selling 21 different models, but Billy always had eyes for more. This time, though, with his credit badly stretched, Durant couldn't come up with the $8 million cash price demanded by Henry. So Ford soldiered on, vowing to appeal the Selden business to the end.

This providential decision may have spared the life of the Ford car name. The very next year General Motors teetered on the brink of bankruptcy, thanks to Durant's crazy spending habits, and a Ford acquisition might well have destroyed it. Some East Coast bankers bounced Gambling Billy out of the GM driver's seat in 1910. They brought in fresh executive help to shore up the GM management ranks. One of the newcomers, the former superintendent of the American Locomotive Works in Pittsburgh, Walter Chrysler, found automobiles so fascinating that he took a 50% pay cut to move to GM.

It took some time for Ford Motor's fortunes to get settled in Port Huron. Dissatisfied with the first Ford dealer, James Couzens and Norval Hawkins tried out a couple more sales agents, including one named Eugene O'Neill, and they even gave George Yokom a go briefly. But Yokom insisted, like Billy Durant, on having as many car brands to sell as possible, not just Fords. Moreover, dealers changed auto franchises as often as their BVD's in the early days, and Yokom didn't want to be tied down to any one company in particular. Finally, the FMC found its man. John Petit of the Port Huron Petits, the oldest family in town, agreed to run the Ford agency. The FMC scored a coup in getting such a recognizable name pitching its wares, although Petit wasn't entirely an automobile man. Contrary to the Ford philosophy, Petit loved horses, and opened his dealership in a former livery stable on 6th Street. This didn't jibe with the FMC ideal about its showrooms: "Absolute cleanliness throughout every department. There must be no unwashed windows, dusty furniture, dirty floors." But since that mandate hadn't been met at any automobile sales premises anywhere in the world, the

Petit family remained the Ford dealers in Port Huron for the next decade.

Like Ford, the EMF company also rode the post-depression wave of auto sales to new heights, and racked up a $1 million profit in its first 11 months of operation, a 100% return on the company's $1 million capitalization. 300 men now worked at the Port Huron plant, including youngsters like Harold Vance and Charles Rettie, most of them making about $2 per day. The black ink at EMF attracted the attention of the Indiana wagon building company Studebaker, which was plunging into auto manufacturing in a big way. Studebaker orchestrated a takeover of EMF in 1910 and paid off the original Port Huron Northern investors with a 440% profit after three years. Word around town about that kind of gravy quickly reignited plans for the Cass Truck idea. 150 shareholders raised $40,000 in a week for Cass and one of them donated a factory site.

At the same time, local venture capital launched still another auto enterprise in Port Huron, the Havers Automobile Company. The Standard Oil Company's Port Huron agent, Frank Havers, convinced his designer brother Ernest to come over from Flint where he'd been working in the auto industry, and bring his car idea with him. The usual roster of big names, topped by Henry McMorran, bankrolled Ernest in preparing his six-cylinder, $1,250 Havers automobile. The company incorporated on Halloween, 1910, using the by-now familiar FMC-style of financing to get auto companies started – credit. Shareholders had paid in only $6,200 out of the promised $60,000 capitalization by the first day of business.

The Havers company arrived a little late to the party. 270 companies already manufactured automobiles in America at that point, and as the *Daily Herald* admitted, pretty plainly the country didn't have room for all of them. Half of the U.S. car companies started up before 1910 already had gone out of business. Nevertheless to McMorran & Co. it seemed worth the risk to try elbowing their way into Michigan's second largest industry, which had turned out 67,000 motor vehicles in 1909. The Havers board of directors bought a building from Port Huron Engine and Thresher to start work in. They named Frank Beard as Havers' first president. Beard apparently merited this post in recognition of his honorific title as Port Huron's original auto dealer. Nobody else on the board besides Ernest Havers knew a thing about the car business, and for some reason the board wouldn't give Havers control.

Like John Petit, Beard still had a foot in the horse camp, doing nicely for himself selling buggies, wagons and sleighs – about 700 cutters in a good winter. Horse vehicle builders dwarfed the American auto output numerically in 1909, producing 2 million units, compared to 120,000 motorcars. Billy Durant's partner in the carriage trade, J. Dallas Dort, said stoutly, "We still rally around the standard of the horse drawn vehicle, for you cannot beat the horse. You can put anything you want parallel with the horse, but you can never put it ahead of him."(30) This noble but purely allegorical sentiment didn't do one unfortunate Port Huron animal much good. At about this time George Yokom beat a horse by driving a car into it and killing it.

Yokom continued to lead the automobile retail sales field in Port Huron, operating from his new headquarters in the former National Guard Armory on Main Street opposite the Harrington Hotel, a hot spot. He also operated a light trucking delivery business from there, and dropped bicycles sales altogether by the end of the decade. George staged Port Huron's first auto show in 1909, hiring an orchestra to serenade shoppers, and he built his first branch showroom 70 miles further up the Thumb, in Bad Axe. Yokom also lapped the field in speeding tickets in Port Huron, racking them up year after year after year, but authorities never stripped him of his license or punished him with even a minute in jail.

John Sperry gave up selling automobiles from his establishment, preferring instead to run a straightforward department store, which he gradually expanded into the biggest in the Thumb, a magnet for shoppers from several counties. Paul Grenier, one of Loren Sherman's right hand men, tried filling the Sperry vacancy in the auto dealer ranks for a while, selling Oakland-brand cars from a downtown store, probably with Sherman's backing. This enterprise didn't last long. Greiner drunkenly rolled one of his $2,000 Oakland models over a 20-foot embankment outside town one night, breaking some ribs and barely escaping with his life when the car, which landed on top of him, caught fire. The four friends who'd been riding with Greiner took a bad beating, too. Shortly thereafter Greiner sold the business.

Enough automobiles roamed the streets of Port Huron by 1910 for the first car-to-car crash to occur, when John Petit's brother Earl rammed into laundry owner Herb Smith at the corner of 7th and Court, right in back of the new Carnegie Library, a collision heard a block away. Automobiles had a near-magnetic attraction for each other in this way. The only two motor vehicles in the length and breadth of Kansas City ran into each other in 1910. These bright omens convinced realtor E. J. Schoolcraft to start his own independent car repair shop in Port Huron as a sideline, the Quick Reliable Garage. Schoolcraft erected the first electric sign in town to advertise it, but his mechanics apparently worked neither quickly nor reliably enough for customers, and the Q & R went out of business within a year. Other more knowledgeable establishments took its place, and just as Henry Ford had feared, repair work became one of the juiciest profit centers in autos.

The used car confidence game paid off nicely, too. A used vehicle seemed to the gullible to be a less expensive way to satisfy one's auto conceit, and by now the three retailers in new automobiles in Port Huron offered an ever-growing assortment of trade-ins for resale. Up to 20 at a time sat at one establishment on Water Street, one of the principle Port Huron thoroughfares. These heaps sprawled all over the place, and it took no time at all for the cluttered used car lineup to become one of the most singular and repulsive nuisances in the city. Buyers ignorant about how an automobile functioned knew nothing about a used vehicle's real condition and accordingly paid a very great deal more for it than the dealer did.

As of 1910, automobiles outnumbered horses by about 2-1 on Port Huron's Main Street on an average day. Police assigned patrolman John Mills, whose boy Fred had been flattened by Stella Sherman, to be the first full time traffic officer. Standing at his post in the middle of Port Huron's major intersection, Main and Water, Mills had his hands full. To begin with, nobody – neither automobile driver nor horse nor biker nor pedestrian – wanted to obey the keep-to-the-right law. Next, speeds hadn't slackened a bit. Some motorists hit 40-50 mph in town. Police chief Marx announced for the umpteenth time: "The auto owners of Port Huron are getting so careless about how fast they drive that I have decided to enforce the speed ordinance..." The street racing bug spread too, after Thumb native Bob Burman won the first race at the new Indianapolis Speedway in Indiana, where five people died during the first three days of competition.

A few Port Huron boys who'd once helped themselves to somebody else's bicycle or buggy for fun, now enjoyed the new fad of "joy-riding" in cars they'd stolen; cars which might or might not be found in one piece by their owners the next day.

None of the preceding events happened in a vacuum, of course, and we need more context to give us the full picture. Gasoline, for example. America needed a huge increase in gasoline production during the decade to meet the automobile demand. Fortunately for men like Ford, they did business in a country swimming in oil. A total of a billion barrels already had been pumped out of the ground in the United States by 1900, and there was plenty more where that came from. Ten days into the new century drillers struck a gigantic field at Spindletop, Texas. It gushed 100,000 barrels per day to start with, more than all the other oil wells in the country combined. Besides Texas, other petroleum hot spots kept producing in Pennsylvania, California, and Ohio. Next door, in Mexico, oilmen made a colossal strike of their own during this decade. Even the state of Michigan had a drop or two. A wildcatter drilled a dozen wells in the Port Huron area, tapping into part of the field that stretched over into Ontario, where the Canadians had been pumping for more than 30 years. The Port Huron wells produced only a barrel a day each, pretty lame by Texan standards.

Port Huron paid a surcharge in pollution for the automobile age when the demand for gasoline supercharged the growth of the Imperial Oil refinery right across the river. With Ontario's petroleum output already in decline, Imperial Oil looked for other sources of supply for its Sarnia refinery. The Canadian government came to the rescue in 1904 by abolishing the duty on imported American oil. This policy triggered a new flow from fields in Ohio, and a $200,000 building boom in what eventually came to be called Sarnia's Chemical Valley, right on the St. Clair River. The 16-acre Imperial works made a malodorous and poisonous presence on the riverfront, so far as Port Huron was concerned. As early as 1907 people on the Michigan side complained about the stink from the Canadian refinery every time an east wind came up. Imperial went right on, producing 32 million gallons of gasoline per year, blithely unaware yet of the 225 toxic or carcinogenic elements in the product, though obviously it wasn't mothers' milk.(31) Standard Oil, Imperial's parent, also built a 6,000 square foot warehouse along Port Huron's waterfront to adequately supply the local market.

The tidal wave of oil products that washed across America entirely distorted the national outlook on automobiles, by reducing the price of fuel practically to a non-issue. Cheap gasoline came to be seen as the norm, even a right, by motorists and auto manufacturers alike. The slightest interruption in gasoline supplies aroused the deepest anxiety among some auto owners, like the overstated "gasoline famine" reported by the *Daily Times* during just a few days in the fall of 1906. Port Huron bought 2,000 gallons of gas per day by 1909. Demand for gasoline everywhere increased so dramatically that Standard Oil, which once had thrown the stuff away, in 1909 set its top chemist William Burton the crash project of getting more gasoline out of each barrel of oil. When Burton eventually doubled the output the company hailed him as virtually the Pasteur of petroleum. In 1910 US gasoline prices averaged about 12 cents per gallon; in oil-poor Europe, between 50 cents and $1.(32)

The gasoline stove, however, fell from favor. One spring evening in 1907 Mr. and Mrs. Fred Hicks returned home in Port Huron to find their three children – Ethel, Paul and Reynold, ages 11, 9, and 1 – all had died in a flash fire when Ethel tried to light the gasoline stove. Port Huron was still so closely knit a community that the accident staggered the entire city. Complete strangers to the Hickses wept in the streets. 3,000 people visited the funeral home. That kind of bond eventually became another casualty of the automobile age. Like many another workman who'd been drawn to the south end industrial park, Hicks worked in an automobile parts plant.

The growing number of influential car owners proved to be a stronger and stronger voice for more paved city streets and graveled county roads as the decade moved along. Even so, government had a hard time keeping up with the improvements already laid. Port Huron spent $22,000 on new paving in 1901, but four times that amount for repaving. This fortune, compared to the city tax revenues of $168,000, had to be paid for with more debt. The pushing and shoving among councilmen about materials and methods also continued. Should they use blocks, bricks, macadam, asphalt, concrete, gravel, etc., etc.? When the annual paving tab hit $200,000 in 1903 the *Herald* pointed an accusing finger: "Of course the few automobiles in the city may delight in a long stretch of nice pavement on 10th Street, but some 22,100 people in Port Huron cannot afford automobiles. Most of the taxpayers have to walk..."(33)

Contractor Andrew Murphy led the charge of the pavers. Originally from Ohio, Murphy arrived in Port Huron in 1901 to fulfill a contract for his family's paving company, and never left. He vigorously lobbied the City Council, and in his spare time courted and married Emma McMorran, Henry's 31 year-old daughter. This connection didn't harm Murphy's business prospects any. The price of paving took another leap upward in 1904 with the adoption of the method of putting sheet asphalt over concrete. Just over a mile of it on Main Street cost $57,000. That price tag led the *Times* to say enough, no more paving, ever, would be needed in Port Huron. But more kept coming. The equally vexed *Herald* fumed: "The city is in the hands of a paving combine whose only object is to make all they can out of it and make it as speedily as possible." In some cases the paving assessments against vacant lots amounted to more than the lots were worth. 25 miles of city streets, about 1/5 of the total, had been surfaced with something or other by the end of the decade.

Great Lakes Captain Frank Danger assessed the situation from his home:

They took a little gravel and they took a little tar
With various ingredients imported from afar.
They hammered it and rolled it and when they went away
They said they had a pavement that would last many a day.
But they came with picks and smote it, to lay a water main
And then they set themselves the task to put it back again.
To run a railway track along they took it up some more
And then they put it back again just where it was before.
They took it up for conduits to run the telephone
And then they put it back again as hard as any stone.
They took it up for wiring to feed the 'lectric light
And then they put it back again, which was no more than right.
Oh, the pavement's full of furrows, there are patches everywhere.
You'd like to ride upon it but it's seldom that you dare.
It's a very handsome pavement, a credit to the town.
They're always diggin' of it up and puttin' of it down.(34)

100

All this activity warmed the heart of that Good Roads champion Horatio Earle, and he made a triumphant return to Port Huron in 1905 as Michigan's first official State Highway Commissioner. In the five years since his appearance of 1900 Horatio had not been idle. He'd served as national head of the bicycling League of American Wheelmen, which organization unfortunately had collapsed under him and disbanded. He'd founded the American Road Makers Association (ARMA). He'd been appointed head of a Michigan State Senate roads committee. He'd toured Michigan with a trainload of Port Huron Engine and Thresher road building equipment, creating more demo roads, including one near the William Ford farm. And finally he'd taken considerable deserved credit for the election victory that erased the Michigan constitution ban on internal improvements, and cleared the way for state road aid. Horatio claimed that state aid now could relieve local governments of some of the costs for improving "public wagon roads," a false hope for the man who eventually paid for everything: Mr. Taxpayer.

Earle came back to Port Huron for a meeting of the ARMA. In some ways the same old Horatio, he predicted the descent of 10,000 delegates and 500 automobiles on the city for this convention. "Whizz Wagons Will Gather in Groups," marveled reporters, who should have known Earle better by this time. The automobile cause had won Earle over completely by 1905 and he shilled relentlessly for the industry. He offered a prize for the car doing the fastest time between Detroit and Port Huron to get to the ARMA conference, only to be blasted by the farmers of the Michigan Grange for making a race track out of a public road.(35) 300 delegates and 20 out-of-town autos appeared in Port Huron for the meeting, which on the Earle discount scale made a pretty good turnout. Horatio outlined for the eager road makers how he would distribute Michigan's state aid on a basis matching it with local money, between $250-$1,000 per mile, depending on how fancy the road.

Michigan helped pay for 200 miles of mainly 9-foot wide macadam and gravel roads during the first two and a half years of Earle's administration, with state assistance amounting to $322,000, plus some federal money, too. At that rate the state could look for the job to be finished in another 500-600 years. Immediately outside the Port Huron city limits, Port Huron Township snapped up the offer of state dollars and put down seven miles of macadam in a single year at a cost of $21,000, the first township in the county to get so serious about road paving. Neighboring Kimball Township followed suit and bonded for $25,000 to build roads, all on the promise of state aid. Elsewhere, Wayne County's road commissioners, who included Henry Ford in their number, approved a mile of concrete road for one of Michigan's oldest roads, Woodward Avenue just outside Detroit. Nobody seemed to notice the double set of interurban tracks along Woodward, which if left in place would outlive a concrete road many times over.

It is worth noting again the huge discrepancies in efficiency which existed between rail and marine travel vs. roads. One of Horatio Earle's closest associates, Martin Dodge, who headed the federal road office in Washington, acknowledged as much. Dodge had appeared as one of the few speakers at the 1900 Port Huron Good Roads Congress, after which he named Earle his special agent. According to Dodge, freight traveled by rail 50 times more efficiently than over bad, unimproved roads. By water, 200 times.(36) So, even if Michigan improved its road quality tenfold, trains and water would still surpass road transport by a vast margin. For the best return on its money, Michigan needed more rails and canals, better rivers and harbors, before it needed better roads.

Significantly, the Michigan state road aid Earle handed out went entirely for construction, nothing for maintenance. Keeping the good road in one piece remained entirely a local headache. On the upkeep subject Highway Man Earle had his eyes opened in a hurry to the destructive effect of motor vehicles on roads, especially trucks. "It is simply burning up money," said Earle, " to build a first-class road and then allow the hauling of three, four, and in some cases, six tons over them on tires two or two and a half inches wide."(37) He admitted that engine-driven wheels inflicted far more destruction on a road's surface than those of a horse drawn vehicle, just as English lawmakers had said 70 years earlier. And the better the road, the more traffic it attracted, and the faster it wore out. The old problem of traffic generation.

Earle wanted strict truck weight limits set for Michigan roads, enforced by experts who actually weighed the vehicles. Here again, his unquenchable optimism ran afoul of reality. Keeping track of the weight of loaded trucks as they moved back and forth over 80,000 miles of Michigan roads would prove to be next to impossible. Vehicle weight control remained one of the insoluble problems that road officials in Michigan quietly gave up on over the years, and made only token efforts to enforce. Then they moaned and groaned when roads rutted, pavements buckled and bridges collapsed. Then they called for higher road taxes.

Under Earle's guidance the state of Michigan in 1907 abolished the in-kind road tax system. From now on, farmers had to put up cash for road taxes, not just a few day's work per year. This switch didn't go down too well with St. Clair County's George Ferguson, who called it "the biggest curse on the farming community that ever was known...before the automobile was invented nothing was mentioned about good roads as nobody cared whether the farmer got to town or not."(38) Cash road taxes provided another windfall for the professional road-builders in ARMA who made out just fine with their founder Horatio running the state highway office in Lansing.

Horatio Earle was a real dynamo all right, but as we've seen his reach occasionally exceeded his grasp. His ego got the better of him in 1908, and he ran for governor against the incumbent who had appointed him State Highway Commissioner in the first place, fellow Republican Fred Warner. When Warner won renomination, after campaigning extensively by automobile, he dropkicked Earle right out of the highway job. Although always good for entertainment value, Horatio Earle never again occupied any kind of government office. His protege succeeded him. Frank Rogers, the former Port Huron city engineer and PHET executive, a man of considerably more tact than Earle, adroitly expanded the highway office into the single most powerful branch of Michigan's state government during the next 21 years.

The good times in road building prompted Rogers' ex-employers at the PHET to set up an affiliated company, Good Roads Construction, which landed 30 miles of road contracts in Port Huron and St. Clair County in a single year. What with building roads, road machinery (sales increased 50% in 1909 alone), farm gear and auto bodies, the PHET became the biggest non-railroad company in Port Huron, capitalized at $2 million. The road building bonanza also employed any number of smaller contractors around town, like teamster Herb Campbell, who did very well indeed at the public's expense.

102

For the railroads, the worst thing to happen to them during the decade occurred on September 6, 1901, when an assassin shot President William McKinley in the stomach in Buffalo, NY. McKinley died eight days later, and his doctor blamed the president's flabby physical condition for helping to kill him. "You know he rarely took exercise, except in his carriage." That epitaph came to apply to a lot more auto-sickened Americans during the next 99 years, even those who weren't gut-shot. In place of the even-tempered, diplomatic, and popular McKinley, Theodore Roosevelt took charge, a much more energetic but often impulsive leader, whose anti-railroad bias played havoc with America's system. It's possible that Roosevelt's outlook on trains was negatively influenced a year after he assumed the presidency, when his carriage collided with an interurban, the latter traveling at 40 mph, killing the carriage driver and putting TR in the hospital. It didn't help, anyway.

Roosevelt adapted much of his "Square Deal" domestic policy from William Jennings Bryan's Populist agenda, but as far as the railroads went, Roosevelt's watered down Progressive program of slow strangulation was definitely worse. Instead of outright government ownership of the railroads, Teddy opted for tighter and tighter regulation, with no government support at all for operations. A new series of federal laws, culminating with the Hepburn Act in 1906, effectively gave the Interstate Commerce Commission control of rates on interstate rail traffic, rates it had no competence to set. In one especially ludicrous example not long after Hepburn took effect, the feds charged a Michigan railroad agent with 23 counts of allowing illegal discounted rates on the shipment of ice, with a potential fine of $423,000.(39) Fortunately for the agent, the case just melted away.

In the same city where Roosevelt relentlessly tightened the regulatory screws on the railroad industry, Washington, D.C., Australian delegate Hugh Maclachlan told the 1905 International Railway Congress that "America has far and away the cheapest rates in the world."(40) Neither Roosevelt nor U.S. lawmakers chose to listen, baffling Maclachlan and his fellow delegates. 1.3 million American railroad employees furnished the world's best service and received the highest wages, on a system three times as long as those in the UK, France and Germany combined. The already low freight rates declined further, and passengers paid just 2 cents per mile, with frequent discounts and excursion fares for as little as half that (like a $1 round trip fare offered from Port Huron to the 1907 World Series in Detroit). Demand for more and more railroad service galloped ahead in America during much of the decade, faster than investment could keep pace.

While blithely ignoring the auto industry's devil-may-care money-changing, the government increasingly hampered railroad financing. James Hill of the Northern Pacific, perhaps the world's greatest railroad expert, warned that the industry needed $5.5 billion in new capital (to bolster the $17.5 billion already invested), and wouldn't get it unless President Roosevelt wised up. Far from being the exclusive currency of "malefactors of great wealth" as Roosevelt claimed, half a million people across the country owned railroad securities. "It is not by accident," said Hill, "that railroad building has declined to its lowest within a generation at the very time when all other forms of activity have been growing most rapidly."(41) America required another 75,000 miles of track, a one-third increase. Railroad business had soared 110% during the past ten years, but trackage had expanded by only 25%. Even under the Roosevelt regime, the railroads did invest, substantially, in existing infrastructure, with heavier

103

rails, bigger locomotives and railcars, bigger stations, and experiments in new motive power, like electric and gasoline engines.

Failing to take Hill's advice, Roosevelt doubled down on his railroad bashing in 1907, and that, plus his lawsuit to break up Standard Oil, put the economy on the canvas. Ironically, Roosevelt had no other way to see the country except by train, and he took a railroad tour of the Midwest in 1907. The President pulled into Lansing, Michigan during this tour, and in a pointed contrast to his animosity toward the railroads, he alternately motored around the state capital in both REO and Oldsmobile cars, one after the other, so as to give no offense to either of the local autobuilders. Back on the train and spitting fire again, Roosevelt returned to Washington, where private capital was building Union Station, the world's largest railroad passenger facility. The president had covered 1,774 miles by rail in four days, often requesting special whistle stops, but encountering no delays or trouble, having made the entire run on regular trains, running regular schedules. Roosevelt later mustered the temerity to accuse railroads of an "inability" to meet the country's transportation needs.

This railroad industry owned one-eighth of all the wealth in the country, more than all the other industrial corporations combined. It spent more on wages and materials than the American nation paid in taxes. Even the railroad unions, who collected a lot of those wages, thought Roosevelt had gone too far. TR then pulled another blooper by first denouncing railroad securities as overvalued, then throwing his mouth into reverse and saying they were fairly valued after all, or even undervalued. After months of wobbling, in October the stock market went into a freefall, arrested only after weeks of frantic effort by men like banker J.P. Morgan. America's latest depression followed, the 1907-1908 railroad model. For a time during the following spring hobo camps lined the tracks for miles outside Port Huron, and tramps crowded the county jail. Within 4 months 300,000 railroad cars and locomotives, more than 10% of the country's total, had been idled. New railroad construction in America had been permanently slowed, according to historian John Stover.(42) Michigan added only 45 miles of new train and electric line track in 1909.

One of the three steam railroads servicing Port Huron had an especially wild time of it during this decade. At first the Pere Marquette RR expanded like mad to keep up with demand, buying a Canadian subsidiary, commissioning a 350-foot railcar ferry to cross the St. Clair River, and drawing up plans to build a bridge across the same waterway (it couldn't use the Grand Trunk's tunnel). The PMRR built new lines into the Thumb and rebuilt others, and laid seven miles of new tracks along the Port Huron waterfront. The crush of business forced the railroad to open and close its bridge over the Black River downtown up to 60 times per day, a real headache for ship traffic. Then in a wave of railway consolidation in 1905, the PMRR merged with an Ohio line which promptly fell into receivership.

Denunciations flew thick and fast, mainly of the financiers who so badly miscalculated the merger. The Pere Marquette had been "hawked and peddled about for speculative purposes," proclaimed one state official. The new Michigan Railroad Commission acquired additional regulatory power, though it assumed no responsibility to assist train companies in trouble. We'll point out here that mergers and buyouts and bankruptcies happened with equal abandon amomg automakers, but no such thing as a Michigan Automobile Commission pestered them about it. The *Times* editorial writer warned, "The extremes to which states are going in their efforts to regulate the operations of railroads will bring on disaster," and eventually they did.(43)

The other major railroad through Port Huron, the Grand Trunk, after weathering its own brief bout of insolvency, operated free and clear again by 1901. It, too, handled increasing amounts of traffic during much of the decade. A good share of the new business came from the Michigan auto industry, the railroads' mortal but as yet unrecognized enemy. By 1910 the Grand Trunk obligingly had ordered 500 units of a new type of rail car, the automobile carrier. Although it shifted its locomotive works to another city, 1,200 or so GT workers in Port Huron still operated trains and rebuilt freight and passengers cars at the St. Clair River shops. The GT paid $60,000 in wages per month in Port Huron (and launched its first pension plan for retirees, at $200 per month minimum). The monthly PMRR wage bill of $7,000 paid for its 200 workers in the city. Together these companies shepherded 115 trains per day through town, and both ranked among the four largest of Michigan's 57 railroads.

The idea of building a new steam railroad across 114 miles of the Thumb, between Port Huron and the town of Bay City, got some attention in 1904. Some entrepreneurs in Bay City promised to put $1 million into it. The dickering over the route into Port Huron and the site for the new depot lasted a year. Proponents like wagon builder Marshall Buckeridge said you couldn't have too much train service. Why, he'd been in Wichita, Kansas recently, a town crisscrossed by four railroads, and he'd seen more life there in a week than Port Huron had in a month. The opponents were mainly homeowners not very keen about the idea of a train chugging directly down their streets every now and then. Couldn't the new line share tracks with the Pere Marquette? And better yet, go electric? Port Huron finally granted the company a franchise, the promoters promised construction would start before the snow flew, the snow flew, no railroad was built.

Many in the public and press urged once more the extension of the Rapid Railway interurban to the north, rather than have the route covered by a new steam railroad line. "No steam railway could ever do for Port Huron what the Rapid has," said the *Herald*. John Sperry claimed that more intercity electric rail service would be of far greater benefit to Port Huron than the Northern automobile factory, and he was one of the chief backers of the factory. "The time is not far distant when people will be able to travel from Port Huron to all points via the electric railway," promised Lincoln Avery, one of the top lawyers in town.

By 1907, almost 1,500 electric interurban and streetcar companies in America carried 10 billion passengers per year, or about the entire US population 115 times over, plus an increasing amount of freight, across 34,000 miles of lines. Between Port Huron and Detroit the Rapid Railway hauled 3.2 million people back and forth in just its second year of full route operation. The Detroit United Railways ordered six new 120-passenger cars, twice as big as the originals, and traffic on the Rapid soared to 4.8 million fares in 1908. Connecting service from Port Huron via Detroit put all of lower Michigan and cities as far away as Cleveland within IU reach, the latter only 8 hours away. IU equipment designers talked of future 120-140 mph trolleys spanning the entire country. The DUR built a new freight house in Port Huron to facilitate express service that often beat that of the steam roads.

But nothing in the way of new electric rail mileage appeared in St. Clair

County. Perhaps the lure of the easier money to be made by investing in the virtually *laissez faire* automobile industry had something to do with it. The Rapid netted $51,000 in 1901, its first full year, and $144,000 two years later, a good result, but not spectacular compared to returns being reported in the auto game. When William Canham, who'd talked and talked about constructing a Thumb IU north of Port Huron, instead bought an eight-seat automobile, the biggest in town, people took it as a sign of his waning interest in the trains. Canham's automotive folly broke down on a county road one day, and the farmer who towed it home for him upbraided Canham, and advised him to trade the car in on a wagon and two oxen.

New York City won the decade's national championship for new civic transportation by opening its $32 million electric subway in 1904 after four years of work on one of America's premier engineering feats. It triggered "one of the great civic blowouts in New York history," per William Middleton. 400,000 people a day rode the subway by the end of year one. New York continued to operate ground level streetcars, but mistakenly allowed further invasion by automobiles, which increasingly got in the streetcars' way. In retrospect, New York should have banned automobiles at this point, and left motorized transport to the rails and boats. 80 years after the fact, historian and architecture critic Jane Holtz Kay observed that railroads, interurbans, and streetcars had "formed a splendid tripartite system of mobility" by 1910. "The efficiency...of railed movement set the outlines that produced the finest streetscapes and architecture in America."(44) Late in his life, prominent magazine publisher David Lawrence found he preferred the transportation world of 1907 to that of 1967: "On the weekend one could get on a streetcar and for a ten cent fare go to a suburban park several miles away. The areas en route were full of trees. Beautification came naturally then."(45)

America's railroad performance trailed that of the rest of the world in just one way, safety. For example, railroad mishaps killed and injured 10,000 and 84,000 people respectively during the 1904 federal fiscal year, mostly railroad workers and trespassers. American rail workers suffered accidents four times as often as English trainmen. The federal government made one welcome intervention in railroad affairs during the decade by setting shorter working hours in an effort to get safer.

A single year's railroad casualties included a variety of people in and around Port Huron. One of them, engineer Leonard Neil ,had told his wife that he planned to retire from the Grand Trunk right after that very day's run to Detroit. The distraction of this prospect may have contributed to Neil's locomotive colliding with another one halfway there. "He was literally cooked by escaping steam," reported the *Times* with some relish. In another case, Port Huron Township's Buck Sloan, so plastered after a winter night's bar crawl that he started driving his sleigh down the railroad tracks toward home, met an oncoming express train that decisively removed him, his two sleigh horses, and his dog from the right-of-way. Michigan's worst crash of the decade involved The Wallace Brothers Circus trains, bound in a week for Port Huron, but which crashed instead at Durand, Michigan, killing 26 people and a lot of exotic animals.

The steam railroads still posed a pollution problem, what with all the smoke and soot they shot into the air. A Grand Trunk freight train broke apart in the St. Clair River tunnel one day in October 1904, and within minutes five trainmen choked to death on the smoke, along with tunnel supervisor Alexander Begg, who ran into the

106

passageway to almost certain death in a futile rescue attempt. Heartsick, the railroad immediately switched tunnel train operations to electric power, something which had been on the drawing board for months.

Though incapable of choking anybody, the electric interurbans met with their own share of accidents, enough that the Michigan legislature ordered them to fence their right-of-ways, like steam railroads. Four people died on the Rapid in '02, including motorman George Morrish of Port Huron, killed when somebody forgot to close a switch, which led to a collision. Open switches did a lot of damage on all kinds of rail lines. The local casualty toll inspired this pithy though exaggerated comment from the usually pro-interurban *Herald*:

I've jes' been readin' up about them Rapid Railway wrecks
A-sendin' people right an' lef' from this world to the nex'.
I really ain't a-feelin' quite as envious as before.
An' Mandy ain't complainin' 'bout the bay hoss any more.(46)

Mandy's qualms notwithstanding, 219 million people per year rode Michigan's steam and IU railroads by 1910.

Even Mandy would have felt safe on the Port Huron streetcars. Operations claimed only a single life during the entire decade. They achieved this marvelous performance while regularly moving 1.5 million people per year, and as many as 22,000 in a single day, along the 12 mile circuit at 10-20 mph, while motormen increasingly put up with the dangerous antics of automobile drivers going a lot faster on the same streets. The current franchise locked fares in at 5 cents through 1929, and package delivery cost a dime. Many and often came the calls by the community for more streetcar lines but they fell on deaf ears at the headquarters of the DUR in Detroit. This unwillingness to expand counted as one of the principle drawbacks to the loss of local control of the Port Huron streetcars after the DUR took over. An additional point: Horatio Earle's 1905 constitutional amendment cleared the way legally for the Port Huron city government to build its own extension of the streetcar lines and invite the DUR to use them. But Port Huron failed to do so in lieu of putting down more pavements.

Having dropped the ball so disastrously on the subject of railroads, President Roosevelt tried to pick it up again by enthusiastically backing greater development of marine shipping in the United States. In 1907 he appointed an Inland Waterways Commission (IWC) to study and recommend ways for expanding the use of this, the cheapest and most efficient traffic method. The IWC findings: more than $400 million federal dollars had been spent on waterways by the opening of the 20th Century. One half of the American canals built in the 19th Century had been abandoned. The federal government needed to spend $50 million annually on water transport.

Enthused, some Michigan promoters took the President's cue, and outlined a plan for a 150 mile-long, 120 foot-wide, 21 foot-deep hybrid waterway to run from the Thumb clear across the Lower Peninsula, deepening existing rivers and connecting them together with canals, locks, and dams. It looked eminently feasible. Riverboats already made extensive use of the west end of the proposed Trans-Michigan route, the Grand River. On this waterway a 400-passenger river steamer ran from Lake Michigan 50 miles up to Grand Rapids, the state's second largest city. Other vessels on the Grand carried freight in as little as 34 inches of water. So with this example before them, what couldn't be done with a first class water route clear across the state? Now how about some of that $50 million a year in federal cash for a big dig? It never materialized. This made a sharp contrast to the distant Panama Canal construction, for which Washington during this decade wrote virtually a blank check.

Shipping continued to play a big role in St. Clair County affairs during the decade; tonnage on the St. Clair River doubled during this decade. But ship construction fell off considerably. Fire ravaged the Jenks shipyard on the Black River in Port Huron in 1901, and no satisfactory arrangement could be reached for moving the yard to the roomier banks of the St. Clair River. The Jenks team hadn't lost its touch at construction. It turned out many excellent watercraft, including the *Eastland*, the first four-decker steel passenger ship on the Great Lakes. Schools and businesses closed for the launch of this vessel, whistles blew and bells rang, and 6,000 people looked on.

But Port Huron didn't have the location necessary for construction or repair of the larger and larger steel ships taking over on the lakes. Great Lakes shipping companies built 40 new 500 foot-long freighters in 1905-06, none of them in Port Huron. Jenks went out of business in 1906. Fred Moore bought the Jenks machinery for a song, and started an automobile engine company with it. Business at another big shipyard in the county, Great Lakes Engineering at St. Clair City, also tailed off, although it diversified by crafting the 10 gigantic immersible tubes, each 260 feet long, which made up the Detroit River Railroad Tunnel, assembled in 1910.

Hundreds of Port Huroners still earned their livings as sailors, and during the decade the newly inaugurated Shipmasters' Ball quickly became the social event of the winter. The lakemen, who had a long history of knowing how to enjoy themselves, on one occasion jammed the Harrington Hotel to the rafters with two orchestras and 250 couples. "There was such a crush at the doorway of the dining room that several ladies fainted. It was nearly 5 o'clock this morning before the last of the weary dancers started for home," reported the *Times*. Many mariners made their homes in the city's 1st Ward, and children ran down to the shoreline to talk by megaphone with Dad as he sailed past town.

Ship passenger numbers in and out of Port Huron climbed to more than 700,000 per year, not including the ferry. Those heading to Detroit still paid $1-$1.25 per round trip. Though unaffected as yet by the automobiles, the boats lost some business to the interurban, which, though more expensive and not nearly as comfortable, did the Detroit run in half the time. To defend its cargo traffic, the White Star shipping line offered free land delivery for freight from its Port Huron dock to the package destination, and built a second landing. On the safety side, Great Lakes drownings from commercials vessels averaged about 100-110 per year; almost all of the victims sailors. The worst local calamity involved the Reid salvage company's tug *Annie Moiles*, which capsized in the St. Clair River in 1904. Port Huron's Tom Reid had to take a rest cure after fishing the bodies of seven of his employees out of the wreck. (47)

Although local businesses still used bikes heavily, bicycle numbers in general declined during the decade in Port Huron. As early as 1902 the *Times* could see "no rational explanation" for the eclipse of recreational cycling among adults around town, especially women. The LAW went out of business that year and the big bicycle trust, the American Bicycle Company, also failed. No doubt the street menace of the automobile

108

accelerated bicycle abandonment in subsequent years as local victims like Edgar Spalding spread the word about their peril. Bicyclists now were hunted by motorists who themselves formerly had ridden bikes, like George Yokom.

But plenty of two-wheel progress occurred elsewhere in the world during these years. The international standard in bicycles, England's three-speed Raleigh, appeared in 1903, and nothing ever surpassed it for beautiful, lightweight, rugged design. In other countries, bikes moved massive cargoes and enormous numbers of people. But increasingly auto-conceited America came to regard bicycle-riding as an activity beneath an adult's dignity. Two Dayton, Ohio bike dealers gave up their trade not for dignity, but to execute the most thrilling and daring invention in American history, the airplane. After eight years of work, the Wright Brothers gave public demonstrations in 1908, but practical passenger travel seemed a long way off, and planes played no part yet in civilian transportation.

A number of other changes in daily life in Port Huron during the decade will come to have greater pertinance later in this story. Port Huron shed its ward system of government in 1910, and a panel of five allegedly non-partisan representatives elected at large replaced the 22 ward heelers, effectively disenfranchising in city matters many of the poorer sections of town, and giving special interests like automobile owners and dealers a more manageable number of politicians to lobby. This new arrangement, so Loren Sherman and others claimed, put government on a "business" basis.

The first inkling of automobile-assisted urban sprawl occurred, when a realtor subdivided a section of Lake Huron shoreline north of town, beyond the streetcar line and off the railroad route. The developer advised the public that the property was easily accessible by auto. Louis Weil and partner Elmer Ottaway triumphantly completed a 10-year conquest of the *Daily Times*, bought it from Loren Sherman and son, and merged it with their own sheet to form the *Port Huron Times Herald*. This left city a one-newspaper town, just as the real explosion in all kinds of newspaper advertising, especially automobile advertising, really began.

Major Nathan Boynton pushed through construction of a massive new Greco-Roman style Maccabees building in Port Huron, and 18,000 people, including the governors of Michigan and Florida, flooded the town in 1906 for the dedication. However, no sooner had the cheers died than the fraternal order moved much of its business away to the bigger city of Detroit. Adding the loss of this venture to the Jenks shipyard shutdown, the transfer of the Grand Trunk locomotive works, and the '07-'08 depression, Port Huron and St. Clair County ended the decade with fewer residents and going businesses than in 1900. 350 homes and 40 stores stood vacant in the city in 1910. Which made it all the more susceptible to automotive overtures.

The townscape didn't stand still during this decade. Many new buildings went up in addition to the auto factory: a flour mill and commercial bakery, a knitting mill to take advantage of the county's wool production, a new high school and a new elementary school – Lincoln – in a neighborhood so friendly teachers competed to be assigned there. Plus the new $40,000 Carnegie library, the Salvation Army Citadel, and the Masonic Temple. Thomas Edison helped out his old hometown by recommending Port Huron to his former assistant Edward Acheson as a spot to build an abrasives and lubricants plant.

Tourism, though disorganized, held up well, and an informal study found it to be one of the biggest industries in the city. The Woodmen of the World, the National Cash Register Company, the Colored Baptists, the Methodists, and too many more groups to list paid a holiday call in Port Huron, some setting up vacation camps in the parks. Virtually none of them drove to town. Of the 92,000 counted tourists in 1909, 36,000 came by boat, 55,000 by the rails.

The business of entertainment prospered in good times and bad. A big new amusement park, the Keewahdin, opened in 1905 on Lake Huron directly at the northern end of the streetcar line. The number of theaters in Port Huron quadrupled to four during the decade. The new 1,500 seat Majestic Theater was the biggest private building in the downtown area for a while. The four theaters started mixing their live entertainment with moving pictures. Movie mogul Thomas Edison titled one of his earliest films simply *Automobile Parade*, and the auto quickly became an important motif in both comedies and dramas. Movies also made a surefire selling tool. The B. F. Goodrich tire company sponsored free movies at a Port Huron picture house, featuring the deadly opening of the Indy Speedway. Just the thing to get more folks on four wheels.

Automobiles quickly took their places in the arts of all kinds. The occasional fiction printed on the *Times* women's page included the dramatic story of *Her Canine Chauffeur.* In this tale a young lady departed innocently on a date in her suitor's automobile. Her pet bulldog Puffs loyally chased them down the road. The fellow announced that the date was really a surprise elopement, he improbably pulled a pistol, and said he'd use force if necessary. Puffs arrived on the scene and bit Mr. Boyfriend on his gun hand, after which the abductor contritely drove the girl and dog home. A little too fantastical. Most Port Huron girls in 1903 would have asked "Who needs a gun?" and gone off happily with a man rich enough to own a car. In fact one of the first popular songs dedicated to automobiles, *In My Merry Oldsmobile*, celebrated just such an elopement in 1905. This is also the time to mention that the American custom of the guy *always* driving while the gal rode already had been settled.

The eventual destination of thousands of merry automobile patrons of the future, the new Port Huron Hospital, opened in 1905, stimulated by a gift of cash and land from furniture dealer Charles Baer. The first Port Huron child ever born in a local hospital arrived soon thereafter. Hospital income skyrocketed 600% the first year. St. Clair County's doctors did *not* make good on their pledge to work in the hospital for free, and in fact doubled their uniform schedule of fees. Doctors of the day accepted price-fixing, regarded as a mortal sin for railroads, as a matter of course. The medical community stayed notably silent on the question of alcohol prohibition during this decade, an issue which came to have considerable automobile significance later. St. Clair County voted prohibition down in 1910, by a 2-1 margin in Port Huron.

Also on the health front, as they abandoned bicycles and took up autos, an increasing number of well-to-do Port Huronites worried about their weight. It didn't make them feel any better to read the first regular cartoon panel published in the *Times*, "Nobody Loves a Fat Man", about a capitalist so obese he blew out the tires on an automobile when he climbed in. In the column next to "Nobody" the paper's classified ads offered a "Remarkable Fat Reducer. No dieting, exercise or exertion." Just swallowing. The Reducer consisted of a few doses of poke root and toasted bread and

110

came by mail order from Battle Creek. It had plenty of competitors. Clothier Phil Higer, a Packard automobile owner, reassured Port Huron's flabby business ranks that "Stout Men are among our Best Friends," but Professor J. B. Roche found a ready audience for Physical Culture classes when he brought them to Port Huron. He addressed Louis Weil, Judge Law, ex-bicycle champion Albert Dixon, and many others:

Why is it that few people die of old age? Ask your doctor. The great law of nature says that in order to be healthy we must exercise. But this we often fail to do, and the cry is, 'Can't spare the time, too busy!' Poor physical wrecks...although your credit is A No.1, your physical bank has collapsed and your bodily credit is ruined.(48)

The tried and true physic, walking, still had plenty of advocates. The *Herald* quoted *Women's Life* magazine on the subject:

Girls do not appreciate the advantages of walking as they should. It has been said by an eminent physician that walking is the exercise most conducive to physical beauty in women.

Less reliably the same article claimed that tennis made a girl's arms too long and bicycling left her clumsy on her feet. On another occasion the syndicated author "Jane Story" urged her audience to "Walk, Ladies, Walk!" Jane estimated that half the women in America led sedentary lives:

You have not time? Take it. What is time for if not for us to use a proper amount in getting good health and good looks? With some practice you will presently be able to walk 15 and twenty miles a day.

As we've mentioned before, thousands of Port Huroners needed no encouragement or practice to walk, it was built into their lives. Walking to work, to school, to shop, to visit, to play, or just to promenade. Nor did they allow themselves to be bullied by automobiles without resistance. Some people scattered nails and broken glass on streets that became too busy with autos. Anti-auto gagsters at Halloween put a horse hitching block in the middle of the street and Dr. Treadgold's vehicle crashed into it in the dark. A car knocked down habitual drunk "Hickory" Bennett and lost a headlight in the crash. Hickory defiantly hurled the light back at the driver, and yelled, "You'll have to hit me harder than that to hurt me!" A neighborhood correspondent for the *Times* got ornery on the walker's rights subject: "With bicycles on the sidewalks and autos on the streets, pedestrians are wondering if they have any right to any parts of the public thoroughfares, especially on Sundays." Indeed they did have that right, the state Supreme Court reiterated in 1909: "There is no imperative rule to require pedestrians, when lawfully using the public ways, to be continuously looking or listening to ascertain if auto cars are approaching..."(49) No imperative rule except survival, of course.

Bank clerk Fred George made a name for himself as one of Port Huron's top pedestrians. Fred walked 34 miles down to New Baltimore one winter's day, and often went for the 12 mile stroll up to Lakeport and back just to relax. He sometimes put in 40 mile training days, and on his 1909 vacation walked 280 miles up to that automobile-free retreat Mackinac Island. Some elderly walkers kept up the pace. 73 year-old Mrs. George Buzzard walked the 12 miles into Port Huron to visit her husband's grave at Lakeside Cemetery. Ephraim Potter often covered 30 miles round trip to see his sister

Phoebe at the poor farm at Goodells. For this the *Herald* deemed him "eccentric." "Tall, patriarchal Henry Hope, with the aid of a cane, still walked to town from his home on Rural Street to look in at the grocery...of which he was proprietor from near Civil War days," historian Dorothy Mitts recalled.(50) Nor should we forget the U.S. Mail carriers, who often walked 25 mile routes daily in Port Huron. The city gave them an assist by steadily lengthening the sidewalks, adding 7 miles in 1902 alone.

All of the marching millions in America could look to one amazing man for inspiration at the end of the decade. Edward Payson Weston still walked strong at the age of 70. To prove it, he embarked on a hike from New York City to San Francisco in the spring of 1909, leaving New York at such a furious foot pace that two policemen assigned to escort him to the city limits couldn't keep up. Weston budgeted 100 days for the 3,900 mile walk, taking Sundays off, averaging an incredible pace of more than 40 miles per day. He entered San Francisco to the peal of bells and the roar of cannon. But the trip had taken him 104 days, not good enough. Six months later Weston turned around and walked back again, Los Angeles to New York, in 78 days. Now *there* was something to be conceited about.

Chapter 4. 1911-1920: A Code Word for Happiness

...Georgie's undoing was not a big and swift and momentous car...it was a specimen of the hustling little type that was flooding the country, the cheapest, commonest, hardiest little car ever made. It was not moving very fast but it went all the way over George. He was conscious of gigantic violence, of roaring and jolting and concussion; of choking clouds of dust, shot with lightning, about his head; he heard snapping sounds as loud as shots from a loud pistol, and was stabbed by excruciating pains in his legs...the policeman said, looking down on George..."It's wunnerful the damage them little machines can do - you'd never think it..."

Booth Tarkington – *The Magnificent Ambersons,* 1918

Let's park this history here briefly and take a look around some of the vistas of the automobile landscape of 1911.

Every Fifth Car Sold in This Country is a Ford Model T – the Car Sold without 'Extras'. That's what the Ford Motor Company proclaimed to Port Huron in 1911 through some whopping big ads placed in the local press by John Petit's dealership. Credit for the FMC's achievement, these bulletins declared further, properly belonged to the "inventive and mechanical genius of Henry Ford." Now, neither this genius Henry Ford nor John Petit guaranteed anything, but a Model T, they thought, "should go" 20-25 miles on a gallon of gas. It "may well run" 3-10 thousand miles on a set of tires. The Model T price of $680 for a runabout, $780 for the touring car, included an "automatic brass windshield," as well as a car top, speedometer, and acetylene or oil burning headlamps. The chief of the New York City fire department drove a Model T; could you beat that for an endorsement? If the unthinkable happened, and your T broke down, no fewer than 3,000 Ford dealers stood ready across the United States to revive it, each stocked with a full supply of parts. End of message.

Apart from the brass in a Model T windshield, the FMC put plenty of brass in its advertising that year of 1911. As far as being the automobile sold without "extras", the copywriter did some hair-splitting there. A barebones T lacked so many practical necessities and creature comforts that an accessories industry grew up around it offering 5,000 extras.(1) Given the amount of regular, often weekly maintenance required but usually skipped, and the amount of time an owner left his Model T idling rather than go through the rigamarole of restarting it, it's very unlikely that typical drivers obtained the gas mileage predicted for the Universal Car. The 60 pound psi tires might run 3-10 thousand miles, provided the operator properly patched them after they ran over anything sharp in the road. America's 900,000 vehicles used up 4 million tires per year at an average cost of $30 apiece. Inner tubes without number usually blew out every few hundred miles.

These ads raised the troubling question of why John Petit needed to keep so many replacement parts on hand for the supposedly reliable Model T. Did he really jam every one of the thousands of pieces onto the shelves of his Port Huron shop? John could have started building the car himself in that case. In a marked contrast to the optimism of its advertising, the FMC privately advised dealers to keep the repair shop well separated from the sales floor, and Petit obeyed that advice to the letter. He discreetly hoisted sick T's up to the second floor of his facility with a freight elevator.

As to pricing, it seems fair to ask just how affordable did customers find a Model T at this time? Or any car? Former bicycle maker John Willys, now the builder of Willys-Overland cars, addressed that topic in 1911 in a tub-thumping New York speech. By my figures, said Willys, there are 5.5 million households in the U.S. that make at least $1,200 per year, that's about one quarter of the country, and every blessed one of them should own a car. Automakers rapidly got into the habit of calculating car affordability by the amount of annual wages it took to buy one. On the Willys scale, a Model T runabout cost at most seven months wages for top tier people, if they didn't bother to feed, clothe, or house themselves or spend a red cent on anything else during those seven months. In reality, it took years for all but high income American families to raise the capital to buy an automobile.

If you couldn't shell out the entire purchase price, maybe John Petit would sell you a T on time, say, over one year. He suggested as much. Then again, maybe he wouldn't. As previously explained, much of the retail economy in Port Huron ran on credit. Depending on whether he trusted the customer, and whether he could carry the loan or sell it, the auto dealer alone set the size of the down payment, the installments payments, and the interest rate. Banks in Port Huron did not yet make auto loans to consumers; perish the thought. One way or another, Petit sold 275 Model T's during the first two years he handled them, earning a 15% commission, plus a small bonus for volume.

After taking delivery of a new T, or holding one's nose and buying a used one, the owner received a real shock about the cost of operating it. Writer Herbert Ladd Towle, an out and out automobile idolator, admitted in a 1913 *Scribner's* magazine issue dedicated to the greater glory of motor vehicles that running even the smallest car cost at least $1 per day, and a Ford wasn't the smallest. By Towle's conservative measurement, the annual expenses would amount to 50% of the T's purchase price. For the overwhelming majority of American families, above and below the Willys income line, buying and maintaining Henry Ford's Universal Car threatened to put them on the quick road to the poor farm.

Allowing his own company's advertisements, like the full-pager for Petit's, to refer to him as a genius reflected the ego inflation in Henry Ford. Auto conceit grew in him to breathtaking proportions. Perhaps the FMC founder got carried away with himself in early 1911 because he'd finally won the Selden patent lawsuit. A federal court in New York overturned the decision which had cast down Henry's spirits so deeply just two years earlier. Automakers didn't have to license their machines any longer with the Association of Licensed Automobile Manufacturers. Somewhat surprisingly, the plaintiffs and the defendants held a joint celebration banquet following the court ruling. (2) Turned out they all were fed up with Selden anyway, and Ford must have seemed like a genius for thumbing his nose at the whole patent scheme for eight long years.

Now, with Selden sidelined, Ford and his company exuberantly promised that you could rest easy legally, financially, and mechanically while driving one of its products. But in practice it didn't pay the prudent Model T owner to relax much behind the wheel. A hundred years later America's premier auto magazine called driving a surviving Model T "an archaic and dangerous experience," and it took a lot to frighten *Car and Driver.*(3) Looking back from the 1970's, P*ort Huron Times Herald* writer Floyd Bernard, who'd experienced the process of running a T first hand in its heyday, reminisced about starting and operating one.

It was a real trick to set the spark and gas levers on the steering column, go around to the front of the car, grasp the crank in the right hand with thumb tucked out of the way in case the engine kicked, hook a finger of the left hand into the choke wire which came out through the radiator, and nurse the thing to life.

The steering wheel bucked with each passing rut in the road...There was little obstruction to the winter wind...Disgusted owners [were] *known to push them off cliffs and over river banks, just to be rid of them.* (4)

The Model T tested its driver's adroitness and patience in any number of ways. For example, operating the transmission involved manipulating three different mechanisms. Then, instead of a foot-activated accelerator, the T employed a hand throttle perched on the steering column, so some of the most critical steering took place with one hand fumbling with the speed control. Drivers in general had been cautioned to keep both hands on the steering wheel ever since it had replaced the tiller on American automobiles in 1903. Next, the brakes, which acted on the transmission instead of the wheels, didn't work too well. Braking had never been Henry's strong suit. Another item: if the gravity-fed fuel system ran too low (there was no gas gauge) the T would stall going up a hill, which brought the brake issue into play again. Or the Universal Car could just plain ran out of gas without warning if you lost track of the last time you'd filled it. Finally, the handcranked windshield wipers added to the harried operator's responsibilities.

Ford fatuously claimed that he had given the Model T owner *Control – to hold its speed always in hand, calmly and safely meeting every emergency and contingency either in the crowded streets of the city or on dangerous roads.*(5) But the T had even less control to it than many other models. All automobiles were inherently unstable because the turnable front wheels, covered with deformable air-filled tires, naturally followed the uneven contours of the surfaces they traveled, unless continually corrected by the driver, at speeds which did not allow sufficient time to react to every "emergency or contingency." Especially while simultaneously coping with the transmission, throttle, brakes, gas attitude and windshield wipers. The first automobile ever rescued by the inventor of the tow truck was a Model T that had flipped into a creek.

The bold but dishonest claim of Henry Ford and many other manufacturers about the perfect control in their machines didn't fool their victims forever. An auto accident in 1911 in New York State led to a successful lawsuit against Buick for its dangerous design.(6) Later in the decade the mayor of Munising, Michigan, Dr. George Trueman, tagged the FMC with a $100,000 suit over the busted skull he suffered when his Ford failed to calmly and safely deliver him from a contingency. The battle had commenced over who to blame for the destruction taking place on America's roads: car or driver.

It may have been the imperfect control of Model T drivers on increasingly auto-filled streets that inspired Henry Ford's former colleague on the Wayne County Road Commission, Edward Hines, who also had worked once with Horatio Earle in the League of American Wheelmen, to come up with the idea in 1911 of painting a stripe down the middle of paved highways. This at least gave motorists an imaginary target zone of possession on the road. Without visual help, the mandate of "Keep to the Right" didn't get the job done. Hines faced an entirely novel problem: large numbers of mechanically powered, unrestrained land vehicles moving simultaneously at relatively high speeds in opposite directions on the same narrow, entirely undifferentiated route. Unlike, say, two train tracks, the stripe couldn't stop an oncoming T driver from veering into your lane and crashing headlong into you if he had some difficulty with "Control". But he might be deterred from downright recklessness by the so-so chance of himself being mangled in the bargain. Dread is what really invented the striped highway, dread of what a later generation called, in a different context, mutual assured destruction, or MAD.

Striping also formalized the issue of passing. When an automobile driver overtook another vehicle while traveling on the same half of the striped road, he either had to decelerate and plod along behind it, or veer across the center stripe into the oncoming lane to pass the obstruction, trespassing as it were into the adjacent right of way, endangering motorists coming the other way and perhaps exceeding the speed limit to boot. Observers saw early on that even the most civilized motorist could be provoked into an almost demonic rage by the frustration of traveling mile after mile behind somebody going more slowly. Which made passing an absolute must. Hines no doubt wondered about the legal ramifications of all this. More work for the automotive lawyers, who already had their hands full. In 1911 a District of Columbia attorney, Berkeley Davids, had enough legal material on hand to publish a 700-page volume on the *Law of Motor Vehicles*.

Passing power became the ready-made excuse for automakers in refusing to curb the speed of their vehicles. Why, one might ask, did Port Huron allow George Yokom to sell a Willys-Overland that "can easily take you fifty miles an hour if you so desire," when Michigan law limited motor vehicles to 25 mph? Why not fit automobiles with speed governors to prevent them from exceeding the limit? The pat answer: passing power. A driver needed the potential to go twice the legal speed limit in order to pass other vehicles obstructing him, or, more nebulously, to get himself out of any other undefined trouble that might loom up on the highway. The fact that excessive speed got far more drivers *into* trouble than *out* never made the slightest impression on the industry. Not a single state government, nor the federal one, ever mustered the guts to limit the speed capability of American automobiles during the balance of the 20th Century.

The authorities in Port Huron took a few years to catch on to the striped street idea, and of course they couldn't stripe a dirt street. In the meantime, they purchased six iron dummy policemen to set up in the middle of busy intersections with "Keep to the Right" signs stuck to their helmets. Drivers kept knocking the iron cops down, and metal officers like "John Doe" and "Silent Harry" spent as much time in the repair shop as on the beat. A 66 year-old deaf city employee, Patrick Bennett, couldn't be repaired so readily when a Howard Furniture delivery truck ran into him while he did some street work in 1911. The Howard driver civilly took Patrick back to the Bennett home after clobbering him, where the victim died four days later. Port Huron had suffered its second auto fatality, one of more than 1,500 which occurred in Michigan during these ten years.

Bennett's death received little notice around town because he wasn't prominent enough. The demise of the Harrington Hotel's manager Arthur Stuart caused much more excitement. He died a few days after Bennett, while riding as a passenger in a car over in Canada. Reports said that Stuart had beseeched the driver to slow down, but not convincingly enough apparently, before the vehicle plunged into a ditch. "A majority of the automobile accidents may be traced directly to two causes – reckless driving or liquor," intoned the *Times Herald* wisely on this occasion. Incidentally, in this history we will *not* record systematically every auto death in Port Huron and St. Clair County going forward, just the most interesting, instructive, amusing and bloodcurdling ones.

While fatalities made headlines, the number of survivable automobile injuries less noticeably built up to fantastic numbers. From the day Henry Ford wheeled the quadricycle out of his garage, virtually everyone who owned an automobile eventually suffered an accident with one. Port Huron contractor Alexander Treacy's own mishap came when he plowed into a crowd of pedestrians while driving drunk in Toronto in 1911, knocking down six people in one fell swoop. Here were reckless driving *and* liquor working hand in hand, just as the *Times Herald* had warned. When offered a $1,000 fine or six months in jail Treacy complained of the severity of the sentence. After all, it wasn't like he had killed anybody.

Speaking of automobile injuries and ditches, when he'd recovered from the broken ribs, burns, and other extensive bruising suffered after his car landed on top of him in a ditch in the last chapter, former Port Huron car dealer Paul Greiner decided the accident hadn't been his fault at all. Nor the car's. The blame belonged to the people of Clyde Township, for maintaining the ominously named Wildcat Road with a 20-foot steep embankment running alongside it for Greiner to drive over. In 1911 he sued the township for $6,000. Just a few hundred people lived in Clyde Township, with probably a combined annual income of about $25,000. Their 50-60 miles of road hadn't been designed for automobiles, or speeds of 25 mph, or for drunk drivers like Greiner. Yet by his new breakthrough reasoning Greiner now expected every inch of these roads to be maintained in a condition to handle motorcars in every mechanical state, as well as drivers of all levels of intelligence, competence, and sobriety, like himself. Neither Clyde Township nor anyplace else in America achieved this impossible dream during the 20th Century. Luckily for the Clyde side, it came out at the trial that Greiner's accident had been the first on this stretch of Wildcat in 50 years, and the plaintiff lost. Nevertheless, the lawsuit inaugurated a new front in St. Clair County, this time against the government, in the automobile culture's perpetual campaign to shift both the blame and the costs for its failings to somebody else. The folks in Clyde Township still had the power in 1911 to ban autos, but they didn't do so, and they would soon lose that power.

A week after the filing of the Greiner lawsuit shocked Clyde Township, New York City received its own unsettling news about the civic costs of the automobile: a $15 million street repair bill, chiefly due to auto traffic, which occasionally reached levels of 240 vehicles per minute in congested spots. Some people suggested paving the NYC streets with metal to try to stem the destruction, and indeed they should have been, with metal rails. "Officials blame enormous trucks for much of the damage," came the word from New York, "and have already found that widening the streets only accentuates the problem."

When it came time to talk of improving streets and highways in order to adjust for the automobile in 1911, the talkers avoided the topic of maintenance like the plague. Good Roads types confidently quoted a figure of $3 billion as the ultimate price tag for improving the 1.9 million miles of American dirt road that hadn't been touched yet. But how about upkeep? From all resources, the U.S. spent $140 million on roads and streets in 1911. No one calculated how much of that went for maintenance. Though only a quarter of Port Huron's streets had been paved or graveled, and needed an ever increasing amount of repair or repaving, attorney Lincoln Avery now promoted construction of an 18-mile "automobile boulevard" from Port Huron up the Lake Huron shoreline, in order to boost tourism. Typically, he didn't get specific about the upkeep costs.

If we look at the role that Port Huron played in automobile manufacturing in 1911, we find that if Ford sold every fifth car in America, the Havers company was selling every 1,500th. The latest Port Huron car company began actual production during this year and managed to turn out about 100 six-cylinder Havers vehicles of dubious merit during the first season, and 200 the second. Prices started at $1,500 for the roadster, $1,650 for the touring car, and inched up to $1,850 and $2,250 in two years. Henry McMorran's son-in-law Andrew Murphy, a total novice, actually ran the company. To try to whip up interest in the Havers, Murphy copied a couple of familiar stunts out of the auto marketing playbook. Somebody drove a Havers from Grand Haven, Michigan across the state to Port Huron. It took 2 1/2 days to cover just over 200 miles, which a train could do in 5-6 hours. Not exactly world-beating performance. Murphy dispatched his assistant Alexander Theisen to attend the New York Auto Show with a Havers display model, and Theisen dutifully reported back for public consumption about all the "excitement" the car had created. Somehow Murphy managed to sell a Havers to a customer in St. Petersburg, Russia, and made of big deal out of crating up the vehicle in front of the Harrington Hotel and having a horse and wagon team haul it to the train station. When Studebaker shut down the one-time Northern-then-EMF-then-Studebaker auto parts factory in Port Huron in 1912, bringing that five year enterprise to an end, Havers moved in, supposedly a sign of its rising fortunes.

Both Ransom Olds and Henry Ford could have told Andrew Murphy about the importance of striking the right tone in automobile advertising. That is, lie it up. But Havers ads practically put people to sleep at first: *...the physical comfort and mental security which are founded in the reliability and smoothness of its mechanism and its ease of control are valuable adjuncts.* Adding some pepper to the pot, Murphy next portrayed Havers as the persnickety car company, in a manifesto published in the *Saturday Evening Post* magazine: *Naturally – The HAVERS factory has never been able to meet the demand. It has never tried to. Nor did it wish a national market until the car was fortified by the test of time and the year of the 'SIX' should come.* But the year of the SIX came and went and no national market for the time-tested Havers ever developed, nor much local market either. Frank Beard, the company president, quickly gave up on selling the Havers at his store, and dropped out of the presidency too, not exactly a vote of confidence. Even George Yokom couldn't get rid of them. Thereafter

118

Murphy sold the cars factory direct.

No real automobile mastermind remained at Havers by this stage. The designer himself, Ernest Havers, had departed the scene after spending less than two years in Port Huron. No real reason existed to buy a Havers, a car with no life support system. Price and cylinder numbers aside, those 3,000 Ford dealers made the real difference between the Havers Six-44 and the Model T. Finally, in 1914, the salvation of fire visited the Havers factory, wiping out 20 cars and mercifully bringing production to an end. Murphy gave out a ringing declaration that the firm would rebuild, but McMorran instead put up just a new foundry, which successfully made car parts. The Havers automobile left barely a trace behind. 60 years later local historian Helen Endlich, who'd grown up in Port Huron during this period, couldn't remember the Havers had even existed. Hundreds of similar stories about similar auto brainstorms could be told in cities big and small all across America. Stories about the Washington, Roosevelt, Dolly Madison, Napoleon, Blackhawk, Iroquois, Mohawk, Custer, Success, Cyclone, Meteor, Tiger, Fox, Gopher, Bug, Duck, Coyote, Bull Dog, Yale, Harvard, Knickerbocker, Rickenbacker, and Pneumobile cars.

Running right alongside the Havers on the highway to oblivion came the Cass truck of Port Huron design and manufacture. Four years after it first had been announced to the world, a one-ton yellow Cass stake truck finally lumbered out of the assembly plant in March, 1911. Again, promoters staged an endurance run to bedazzle potential buyers. The Cass drove south down to St. Clair City, 13 miles away from Port Huron, in 90 minutes, burning eight gallons of gas on the way. A Cass skeptic remembered that 20 years earlier shoe clerk Norman Gray had bicycled the same route in 34 minutes.

This underwhelming performance by the Cass led to an immediate company reorganization (George Yokom became one of the directors). A retooled Cass undertook two more promotional runs, one an emergency delivery of 600 lbs. of ice cream to a big dance in Memphis, Michigan, 25 miles away. According to its specifications the Cass could have carried 2,700 lbs of ice cream to those demon dancers in a pinch, but somehow this fact failed to entice more than a few local firms into buying one. Gruel & Ott, local bottlers of their own brand of soda and that new "bracer," Coca Cola, tried out a Cass. So did Howard Furniture; it was their Cass truck that killed Patrick Bennett. But the City Council of Port Huron spurned Cass' offer to build the community's first automobile fire engine in 1912, and they ordered one instead from a company in Columbus, Ohio. Cass lingered like a ghost for a few more years, through another reorganization, and under another name, Independent Truck, but come mid-decade it, too, had joined the ranks of the vanishing 4,000.

Though not impossible, it usually took big money and often a big name to start a successful new car or truck firm in 1911. Billy Durant began his comeback in this year, when he launched a new motor vehicle company, the name of which resounded unpleasantly in Henry Ford's ears for the rest of his life, Chevrolet. Durant's startup methods had a familiar ring to them. His former race chief at Buick, Louis Chevrolet, helped design the new car, giving it the same racing allure that had worked so well for Buick and Ford. But Durant bid the Swiss-born Louis *au revoir* when the two men differed about what future course the business should take, the same way David Buick and Ransom Olds had exited their namesake companies. Durant intended to give Ford some real competition in the low-priced field with the Chevrolet, while Louis wanted his name on something grander. Gambling Billy sold 3,000 Chevies the first year, and in short order the company turned such handsome profits that by 1916 Durant could use Chevrolet stock to take back General Motors from the bankers who had ousted him in 1910. GM had lost almost two-thirds of its market share during the intervening five years. In the process of this maneuver Durant picked up the General Motors Truck division, also founded in 1911.

But now, it's time to take the 1911 handbrake off this chapter, and see how fast this baby can go.

After building more than 30,000 T's in 1911, Henry Ford saw plainly that increasing production had outstripped the supply of skilled and semi-skilled labor manning his Highland Park, Michigan factory. Somehow, to meet the demand, he had to get entirely unskilled workers into the act of car manufacturing, people as dumb as a fence post. That meant making the jobs so easy anybody could do them, breaking the process down into the simplest steps. And it meant hurrying things up. Over the course of about two years, these two notions led to the adoption of the moving assembly line at the FMC, first in the sub-assembly parts lines, then in the general assembly process. Ford claimed later he'd gotten the idea from watching meat cutters in a Chicago slaughterhouse.

The net result of the application of these principles is the reduction of the necessity for thought on the part of the worker and the reduction of his movements to a minimum. He does as nearly as possible only one thing with only one movement.(7)

To pull this off, HF used the help of two aides known as the Great Danes – William Knudsen and Charles Sorensen – as well as that of handy Harold Wills. Ultimately, Ford rooted his workers to the spot on the factory floor, so that they barely budged, moving not a step in doing their jobs nor even bending over, repeating the same task hour after hour after hour. Henry permitted no chairs on the floor for their repose, and limited lunch breaks to 15 minutes. This cut assembly time by 85% as of 1914, and the cost of the Model T fell with it, down to $525/$600 for the roadster/touring car duo, to $500/$550, to $440/$490, to $345/$360 by 1916 at John Petit Ford in Port Huron. The cost to the workers rose as the price fell. It was unspeakably boring, but so what? Ford never made any secret of his contempt for anyone so brainless and unambitious as to take a job in an auto plant.

Repetitive labour – the doing of one thing over and over again and always in the same way – is a terrifying prospect to a certain kind of mind. It is terrifying to me. I could not possibly do the same thing day in and day out, but to other minds, perhaps I might say to the majority of minds, repetitive operations hold no terrors. In fact, to some types of mind thought is absolutely appalling. To them the ideal job is one where the creative instinct need not be expressed. The average worker, I am sorry to say, wants a job in which he does not have to put forth much physical exertion – above all, he wants a job in which he does not have to think.(8)

Ford could have said the same thing about his car customers: they wanted to avoid exertion and not think about the consequences. In that respect, the description fit himself. Auto critic Kenneth Schneider later observed that Ford's factory methods limited people movement in order to maximize efficiency, the opposite of the automobile's social impact, maximizing uncoordinated movement and inefficiency.(9)

The Highland Park labor force didn't remain so docile as Henry claimed. After the moving assembly line came in, the worker absentee and turnover rates, already high, went through the roof. The FMC hired 53,000 workers in a single year to keep 14,000 bodies on the line, and they weren't all able bodies either. Ford put the blind, the deaf, epileptics, amputees, convicts and consumptives to work. Immigrants from 22 different countries, speaking 14 different languages, assembled the T in that plant.(10) Desperate to stabilize the manpower situation, James Couzens announced in January, 1914 that the FMC would double its minimum daily wage and shorten the work day – to $5 per eight-hour day – provided the candidate met some qualifications, like learning English. This magnanimous offer triggered a tsunami at the Highland Park employment office the very next day, as 10,000 men tried to apply for jobs. The fire department had to hose them down when things turned rowdy. Overanxious job applicants even turned up at Henry's home in Detroit, and accordingly he sped up plans to evacuate his family to his new residence, a $3 million, 31,000 square foot castle he was building out in Dearborn.

In looking back in his memoirs, Ford glossed over somewhat the reason for the 5 buck-a-day offer:

It was to our way of thinking an act of social justice, and in the last analysis we did it for our own satisfaction of mind. There is a pleasure in feeling that you have made others happy – that you have lessened in some degree the burdens of your fellow-men... (11)

But it didn't make typical new probationary hire Charles Madison any too happy to be told that he wouldn't get the $5 a day of social justice until he'd toed the company line for six months. In the meantime, stopwatch-wielding efficiency experts goaded him with demands to go faster and faster. Madison quit, saying, "For some time thereafter the painful Ford interlude was a rancorous memory – a form of hell on earth that turned human beings into driven robots."(12) Enough people remained dissatisfied that Ford had to start up a "Service Department", really a security force, to ensure order among his fellow men at the factory.

The falling prices and rising wages at the FMC (if not the working conditions) succeeded in placing Henry Ford, and the automobile, squarely in the middle of the Progressive movement in the United States, when just six years earlier Woodrow Wilson had reviled the motorcar as a rich man's plaything, an incentive to socialism. Now, at the same time they endorsed the persecution of the railroads, Progressives knighted Henry Ford because allegedly he had liberated the Universal Man from the toils of the train and streetcar companies, and furnished him with personal motorized transportation. Actually, Henry had ensnared the U-Man in the Ford toils, undermining the best transit system on Earth, and unleashing the worst.

Undeniably, the Ford Motor Company worked a considerable logistical achievement in pulling together the thousands of necessary parts into 1,000 Model T's per day, an achievement which, incidentally, would have been flatly impossible without efficient railroad service. But the FMC necessarily sacrificed quality in its ever accelerating manufacture of a complicated product like a car by an alienated workforce. And automobile quality had been bad enough to begin with. More and more enterprises adopted the Ford method of mass production, a term he himself coined, which others clumsily called Fordism.

On simply-assembled products Fordism worked adequately, making a wider variety of material goods of varying quality and usefulness available to the public. At its best, it brought solid improvements like refrigerators and washing machines into virtually every home. At its worst, it flooded the nation with a river of junk, especially automobiles, which eventually inundated every corner of America. The tenets of Fordism also spread into other, less appropriate areas of American life, like agriculture and education, with deplorable results.

Ford converted President Woodrow Wilson to the cause. Immediately after winning election in 1912 Wilson laughingly told reporters, "It goes without saying I can't afford an automobile and never could." Within months of his inauguration the next year, Wilson was motoring around Washington, and promptly ran over bike messenger Robert Crawford, crushing the fellow's bicycle in the process.(13) The conscience-stricken Wilson, no doubt remembering his own carefree days bicycling around Bermuda, visited Crawford in the hospital and bought him a new bike. Shaking off the incident, as most motorists usually did faster than their victims, Wilson later entertained Henry Ford at the White House. But not everybody in the Progressive camp fell for the false promises. Ford's own governor, Michigan's Chase Osborn, gave away his seven passenger touring car and stable of horses at this time, vowing to walk everywhere. "From now on I am going to travel and see more of the world than I have ever seen in the past," said Osborn. "But I am going to enjoy the beauties of nature in my travels by walking instead of being shut up in an automobile going so fast it is all one can do to catch his breath."(14)

Henry Ford paused in his own labors in 1914 to catch his breath and to pay a visit to Port Huron alongside his hero Thomas Edison, the last time the Wizard of Menlo Park ever returned to his boyhood home. The press hailed Ford upon his arrival as "the genius of travel," though both men came by train. Edison interested himself in the electric locomotive now smoothly, cleanly and efficiently moving as many as 1,000 railcars daily through the St. Clair River Tunnel. For his part Henry found a booming Ford automobile business going in town, but with plenty of competition.

During the first five years of the decade half a dozen men abandoned their trades and started Port Huron car dealerships, in competition with Petit and Yokom and Frank Beard. No experience at all was necessary. Grain and feed dealer Bert Hyde, traveling salesman Avery Hill, newstand owner Bert Mooney, marine engineer George Roin, former shipping executive William Barkell, and mechanical engineer Frank Church, all rank amateurs, joined the auto game. More kept coming. A one-time newspaper publisher and school superintendent from the Thumb by the name of John Cawood arrived a bit later. By 1920, 13 auto dealers offered 22 different brands for sale in Port Huron.

Most annoying to Ford in 1914 must have been the Port Huron Dodge dealership, which Frank Church fittingly set up in an old church. John and Horace Dodge still owned 10% of the FMC, but they no longer supplied Henry with parts. They instead pocketed FMC dividends while building their own Dodge cars directly in competition with Ford, a situation the genius of travel didn't intend to tolerate for long.

The number of motor vehicles in Port Huron by the time of Ford's visit had grown to 500, a 2,000% increase in 10 years. The assessor reckoned them worth about $500 apiece. Other St. Clair County residents owned about 1,500 additional cars; more of them, proportionately, owned by rural than city people. Circus day in Port Huron now attracted dozens of farm families traveling in cars alongside their neighbors in horse rigs. Conservatively, about $2 million had been invested in the purchase of all these motor vehicles; enough money, had better sense prevailed, to have added scores of miles of railroad, interurban, and streetcar lines.

They became future allies in the cause much later, but for now banks and auto dealers battled each other for Port Huron's hearts and minds on the subject of auto spending. Take heed, said the banks, we'll give no credit for cars. "It Is Our Duty In This Community To Preach Thrift," proclaimed a Community Bank newspaper ad. On the next page Bert Mooney suggested, "Why Not Buy Your Car Now And Pay For It Next Year!" While his dealers, like John Petit, wheeled and dealed, Henry Ford put on a little puritanical act over the idea of buying cars on the installment plan. Said Henry: "The Ford Motor Company is not interested in promulgating any plan which extends credit for motorcars or anything else." Here Hank set aside for the moment the fact that the company itself had been founded largely on credit.(15)

Many, various, and clever were the overtures made to entice Port Huronites into the auto sales offices:

– *Why Don't You Own a Motor Car?*
– *The Ford: this car has made the horse and carriage a lavish extravagance.*
– *Oakland, the Car with a Conscience.*
– *65 mph in 30 seconds from a standing start.*
– *The Answer is Here to that oft asked question: "What will Howard E. Coffin do when he builds a 'Six'?*
– *Slaughter Prices on Automobiles.*
– *Your Neighbor's Car: Suppose he buys a Hudson Super-Six. One thing we can't forget in buying cars. That is the pride of ownership. The car is a pleasure vehicle. And it spoils the fun to be hopelessly outrivaled in about the same-class car.*
– *Today, 8 out of 10 merchants need motor trucks and don't realize it.*
– *Studebaker: The Safe Car for Women.*

Dealers even used children for bait. *Picture your own little ones riding in the great outdoors, cheeks aglow, eyes sparkling, blood pulsating with the tonic of sunshine and fresh air.* Yes, the industry actually promoted the idea of driving children around as inert baggage in an open automobile for their health. Eventually, after enough of this treatment, sparkling-eyed kids supposedly could take the wheel themselves: *For the growing boy or girl, from 14 years old up, there is no gift that can equal a Saxon roadster. It brings health and happiness, self-confidence and resourcefulness. It is the gift ideal. Young people – if father doesn't want to give you a Saxon outright perhaps you have saved enough money to partly pay for one. Why not get him to loan you the difference and pay it back by doing certain tasks about the home?* If all else failed: *There is nothing better than an automobile for a Christmas present.*

Motor vehicle ads of all kinds drenched local newspapers and national magazines alike during the decade, and began to enter a more impressionistic phase. Some featured drawings of the latest machine posed stock still, perhaps at a yacht club or beside the steps of a mansion, with dapper men and women basking in its glory.

When portrayed in motion, the product moved in an imaginary plane of what we might call Empty Roads motoring. Spotless cars and motorcycles sped easily along smooth, level, unobstructed roads and city streets, without another vehicle in sight to trouble the driver or passengers (or the reader) with even the hint of potential conflict ahead.

Samuel Lane, Port Huron's Harley Davidson dealer, placed one such fantasy before the Port Huron public: a natty young man piloted his motorcycle, with his girl in the sidecar, out among the quiet pastures in Goodells, or someplace like it, and smiled with genial condescension as he passed a cowherd:

Co' Boss! Co' Boss! Shut your eyes a moment! Carry yourself out into the cool, green countryside, any place you will. Can you hear that call echoing and re-echoing in the still afternoon? Can you hear the tinkle of the bell as the herd ploddingly responds? Say, for instance, you're on a Harley Davidson, for 14 years the Master Mount. A farmer lad calling the cows waves with an envious grin as you sweep by. Farther along the winding road you, too, turn off into a lane to spend the week end with friends. Let us help you make every leisure hour your fondest dream come true.

Nobody with livestock to tend in the real world, who heard how much noise the Master Mount made a-coming, likely welcomed it so cheerfully. But that's advertising. The Harley ad played up one-half of the auto industry's city/country switcheroo approach. In one version, city car owners barreled out into the fresh air, open fields and contentment of the country. Henry Ford himself had said it: "We will leave the city!" In the reverse version, country car owners raced into the pulsating excitement, variety, and adventure of the modern city. Carried to extremes, these two autofied populations would pass each other on the road, heading in opposite directions, only to find the city and country deserted when they got there. In the real America, although people drove both ways, they usually ended up in suburbia, the worst of both worlds.

Specialized businesses devoted to the care and feeding of automobiles sprang up left and right in Port Huron, like the first Standard Oil service station, followed by another and another, then no fewer than 10 stations belonging to the locally owned Star Oil Company. Their owners built these pit stops in spite of loud objections from the neighbors about the traffic, stink, and danger of having a gasoline store next door. Stations could be built virtually anywhere at first since no zoning law existed to prevent them.

Auto equipment shops hawked everything from spark plugs to antifreeze to new upholstery to new auto horns ("They'll Get Out of Your Way When You Cut Loose with a SEISS") to garage heaters ("Saves the Engine, Saves the Bearings, Saves the Batteries, Saves the Varnish, Saves the Tires"). The Cut Rate Tire Store offered a hot item, "non-skid" tires. To skid or not to skid, that was the question. Should a driver choose speed or grip? This kind of philosophical question absorbed the automotive mind. The Huron Radiator Repair shop, John Petit's "Auto Laundry," Angus Carpenter's "Invincible" self-starter agency ("frees you forever from the labor and danger of cranking"), and general emporiums like former mayor Cyrus Hovey's Garage all waited to take your money .

Hovey aimed a typical proposal at that ultimate sucker, the used car buyer: *Let us figure on making your old car new by putting on a brand new body, top and*

124

fenders and painting the running gear. All for $275. Hovey charged 60 cents per hour for repair work by his mechanics, and also kept bonded chauffeurs and taxis standing by. The taxis cost 50 cents per mile, compared to the 5 cents you paid a streetcar for going all over town. Hiring a whole car and driver on an extended basis cost $3 an hour. An attorney by training, what Hovey himself actually knew about cars the public never discovered. They discovered plenty about the reliability of Hovey mechanics, and all auto mechanics of this time, courtesy of another Michigan governor of this decade, Woodbridge Ferris:

Average garage men are not sufficiently familiar with the different makes of motor vehicles to properly analyze a defect to a motor vehicle by accident or misuses or carelessness in operation, consequently the door is open to make unreasonable charge. (16)

For do-it-yourselfers who wanted to close the door on unreasonable charges, the Port Huron Library now carried the volume *Diseases of a Gasoline Automobile and How to Cure Them.* But entirely curing the owner of his automobile disease required a complete amputation, as former Governor Osborn had decided.

Incurable car owners now often found automobile insurance, once a joke, to be a practical necessity. Coverage cost about 1 3/4% of a new car's value the first year, not including injury or liability protection. The percentage went up as the car got older. Louis Weil collected a claim on a run-in he had with a Rapid Railway train while out motoring one day with his son Louis, Jr. The porch of Moore's Drug Store caved in from the impact when the interurban slammed Weil's auto into it. Fortunately, both Louies survived without serious physical damage. Theft insurance came in handy too, as about one car per week in Port Huron either disappeared for good, or, in Weil's case again, turned up stripped after joyriders had finished with it.

Eventually, as it must to all mankind's conceits, death came to Port Huron's automobiles. The Goldman Brothers junkyard held funeral rites for about two corpses per week. About 20% of all the 2 million American motor vehicles in operation at mid-decade met a similar end every year. Probably a lot more should have been scrapped annually, but instead drivers pushed them on, dispensing increasing amounts of smoke, noise, and danger until these cars dropped in their tracks. Many ended their days rusting away in a field, a backyard, or a vacant lot, as the Great American Eyesore. "The waste due to the comparatively short life of the average automobile has, in the past, been of staggering proportions, and continues to be enormous," admitted the *Times Herald.* (17)

Though Port Huron no longer built whole automobiles, car parts manufacturing still occupied several firms besides McMorran's. Fred Moore built hundreds of engines for Detroit customers with machinery left over from the Jenks shipyard. William Lee, he of the stillborn Troutmobile, took orders for as many as 150,000 pistons in a year. Even Port Huron Creamery owner John Ruff built auto engines on the side. The premier parts maker in town, the Holmes Foundry in the industrial park, poured castings for the FMC and other automakers. Founded by former Henry Ford associate Lyman Holmes, in two years the foundry became one of the biggest of the 92 manufacturing factories in Port Huron, eventually taking over the empty Northern-EMF-Studebaker-Havers plant.

125

Foundry work taxed workers far worse than auto assembly, and Lyman Holmes couldn't get enough white men to do it, so he hired a large complement of Negroes. He backhandedly helped to integrate Port Huron racially to a modest extent. Things got so chummy for a while that the cops had to break up some mixed race dances, performed to the strains of the William McKanlass Orchestra, a unique nearly all-white ensemble led by a black Port Huron musician and composer. High dudgeon reigned at the *Times Herald* about this dancing:

There will be no more 'black and white' tangos, bunny hugs, or turkey trots at Society Hall on State Street. White women and negroes danced together and white men and wenches went through the graceful movements of the 'bunny hug'. The decency of many north end residents was shocked...(18)

Louis Weil's paper carried an ever expanding amount of automobile display advertising as the decade went by, often an entire page or two of it on automobile Saturdays. The classifieds booked lots of lucrative used car buy and sell notices as well ("Ford. Looks so good stolen by joyriders twice. $300"). Weil gave away Model T's as first prizes in *Times-Herald* subscription contests, though he left the T's operating bills to the "winner." Weil and his editorialist now firmly planted their flag: automobiles and streetcars had priority in the streets, wagons and bicycles came second, and pedestrians should only set foot on streets to cross them, and only at street corners. "Pedestrians rightly have the first right of way in crossing streets but it should be under such regulations as may be necessary for the guidance of drivers of vehicles for which the roadways are made and maintained."

And that went double for kids: "...in a city the size of Port Huron where we have so many beautiful yards, parks and other playgrounds it should not be necessary for the little one to use the pavements as places for play." But even if these preventive steps were taken, the fourth estate warned readers not to expect miracles: "No matter how careful the driver of a motor car might be, he finds it difficult to avoid accidents even under favorable conditions."(19) So in a complete reversal of its view of just a few years earlier, the *Times Herald* now held that Port Huronites should accept meekly the seizure of the heretofore public property of the streets for the principle use of automobile drivers, who might or might not be able to avoid killing or maiming people should they even venture to cross the street.

Given this new order in he civic heirarchy it came as no surprise when the automobile put its first Port Huron child in her grave. Clothier John Wolfstyn drove some of his family out to Lake Huron one July evening in 1912. He parked his Ford alongside the avenue beside the growing numbers of car owners who crowded the thoroughfare, parading their conceit and forsaking the streetcar which would have carried them safely out to that neighborhood. The youngest of Wolfstyn's eight children, 6 year-old Margaret, excitedly hopped out of her father's vehicle directly into the path of another oncoming car, driven by Norman Gray, the former bicycle champion. "She passed away in the arms of her grief-stricken mother...," according to the *Times Herald*. The paper rated Margaret's death as "unavoidable," a pretty strange epitaph, considering how easily it could have been avoided. A few weeks later the paper reached a verdict of "absolutely blameless" for driver Beth Mills, when 12 year-old Earl Ludington went down for good under her wheels, child fatality #2. That assessment more or less left the blame up to Earl, whose side of the story we'll never know.

126

The punishment an auto meted out could be gauged by the speed at which Gray and Mills nailed these kids, 6 miles per hour, which still crushed the victims' skulls. For a brief time Port Huron drivers felt a little anxious about kids in the streets. After the Ludington killing, prank-loving Port Huron boys preyed on this anxiety by dropping stuffed dummies under the wheels of passing cars to terrify their drivers, and it worked like a charm. Occasionally the boys substituted nail studded boards for the dummies. Some underage boys climbed illegally behind the controls of cars themselves, like 13 year-old Jack Kelley, who then ran over his 14 year-old neighbor Hugh Bonner, inflicting a crushed skull, two broken legs, and a lingering death on Hugh, another Levassor victim.

Even when they stood still, the sheer size and numbers of skullcrushers caused trouble in Port Huron. In summer they jammed up Lakeside Park so badly that the first dedicated parking area in town had to be set up. This happened after Mayor John Black, a streetcar conductor, on a single day witnessed first a fender-bender between motorists at the park, and shortly thereafter "..two other automobile drivers engaged in a word battle, in which foul language was used, as to who should back out first." As a result the city roped off some of the most beautiful landscape in town, to use for automobile parking, an abuse which eventually consumed a third of Lakeside.

Automobiles crowded pedestrians on the cross-river ferries to Canada. The vessel owners quickly posted "No Smoking" signs, for fear the weed would ignite gasoline fumes stewing from the tanks on these cars. "Pretty soon we won't be able to ride on a boat unless we own an auto," said a disgusted patron. "It seems as if we must knuckle to those machines wherever we go. On the street it is duck them continuously and on the boat it is don't smoke in the presence of them." Automobile-based businesses took up enormous amounts of room downtown and began to push the once orderly district outward in a haphazard fashion. The Yokom dealership alone, which could hold 300 vehicles, occupied almost half a city block. Autos parked every which way downtown, the favorite destination, clogging the curbs, obstructing other travelers, and hampering the streetcars.

Port Huron's street parking regulations, just two years old, needed a rewrite in 1914, part of an auto ordinance overhaul almost entirely authored by the local Auto Club. It limited parking on Main in the busienss district to an hour (some businessmen wanted just 10 minute parking). The one hour limit posed any number of enforcement problems, a commonplace failing of auto laws. Were the police supposed to march up and down Main and Water streets memorizing where and when each vehicle had been parked an hour earlier? If you pulled your car out of one space and pulled into an adjacent one, did you get a restart on your one hour? Another heated debate dealt with angled parking versus parallel parking relative to the curb. Angled was a lot easier. Parallel saved street room but sometimes required a backward-and-forward automobile tango to get close to the curb between other vehicles. The nonsense about parking pandered again to auto owner's conceit, the idea that driving a car entitled one to convenient room to stash it when arriving at any destination.

Port Huron's new auto law, which grew by the end of the decade into 40 different sections and subsections, got around to banning drunk driving, 13 years after the first auto appeared in town. The inebriate might be a figure of fun on foot but get one behind the wheel of a car and the party was over. Trouble was, preventing a drunk

127

from driving before the fact didn't seem possible, unless you prevented the drink. Prohibitionists made drunk drivers a favorite argument of the movement. A crazy man with a revolver posed far less danger than a drunken man with an automobile, according to the *Times-Herald*.

Such a man, with a car not a gun, the former foreman of the Havers automobile plant, Henry Drago, caused a wild seven-injury crash on Main Street one summer night, when driving his Havers while plastered. Police already held several outstanding traffic complaints against Drago at the time. The last bartender he'd dealt with at the Metropole Hotel before the crash had advised Drago not to drive and had summoned the cops to stop him, too late. After the wreck Drago skipped town, then snuck back a year later and humbly worked as an auto mechanic before the cops re-collared him. Total fine: $50 and a couple days in jail. At about the same time of the Drago incident, the Safety First Federation of the U.S. and Canada met in Detroit, and called for a lifetime driving ban for anyone caught drunk behind the wheel twice. To no avail. The two countries fell short of this level of sanity for the balance of the 20th Century.

Port Huron also now forbade the mischievous and frankly infantile practice of some auto enthusiasts in altering their mufflers with what were called "cut-outs," to make the car noisier. The nuisance of auto noise on busy streets was already bad enough to persuade some wealhy Main Street mansion owners to sell their homes to landlords who cut them up into apartment buildings. Many of the rich evacuees ended up at the north end of town, and rebuilt former cottages along Lake Huron into full time homes, well back from the street. Others went further north into the township auto suburbs which were multiplying north of Port Huron, like Cedarcroft, Lakeview Beach, and Shady Shore. Or they went south, and displaced farms along the St. Clair River. These people tried to use automobiles to escape automobiles, but in the words of American city designer Frederick Olmsted Law, it couldn't be done: "Their very numbers begin to distill the poison that blights the paradise they seek."[20] These new homes also started to wall off the lake and river from public access or even from view.

Another section of the revised auto law reaffirmed Port Huron's ban on passing stopped streetcars embarking or debarking passengers. Since the trolley lines ran down the middle of the street, an exiting customer faced increasing risk from auto traffic impatiently zipping past, and the possibility of ending up like Margaret Wolfstyn. Eventually, one did. Driver Henry Hentzman struck and killed 18 year-old Mattie Balmer as she got off a streetcar. Prosecutor Shirley Stewart charged Hentzman with manslaughter, the first such charge ever made against an automobile driver in Port Huron. Lawyer Joseph Walsh, the first Ford buyer, got Hentzman off the hook. Just one sympathetic car owner on a jury greatly improved the odds of acquittal in criminal driving cases. If nothing else, a motorist could plead brake failure, and no one wanted to send a man to jail because his brakes "failed."

The 1914 auto ordinance also bumped up Port Huron's automobile speed limit to 12 mph downtown, 15 elsewhere. The limit went up again to 15/20 mph by the end of the decade. It might just as well have doubled or tripled for all the good it did. Each time it went up Port Huron got another dose of the phenomenon of speed limit creep: the higher the speed limit, the faster people went in breaking it. The *Times-Herald* waffled mightily on this issue. One week it cried "Stop the Speed Fiends," the next it said sadly of speed limits that "strict enforcement is a practical impossibility." The Port Huron police department still made its annual declaration of war against neuromobilitics, as one psychiatrist called speeders, and bought a motorcycle with which to chase them, then two more, and even rented a patrol car from George Yokom for $25 per month. No doubt they occasionally chased speed fiend Yokom with his own car. But the city employed only 10 patrolmen, and put a maximum of 5 on duty at any one time, and they couldn't be everywhere.

On one occasion a motorcycle cop stopped a car doing 68 mph on Griswold, faster than Barney Oldfield clocked at the Driving Park when he dropped by for a race. Another time policeman James Alloway had to shoot out a tire on an auto doing 50 mph on Main Street at midafternoon, to halt malefactor George Keeley. Salvage man Tom Reid broke the speed law plenty. After scoring a 3,000% profit on a big ship rebuild at his Port Huron drydock, Reid rewarded himself with a brand new Packard, and promptly ran over his daughter Virginia while racing the vehicle up his own driveway. Virginia recovered, with a few permanent physical reminders of the incident, and Reid's wife Anna really let her husband have it on this subject, often.(21) Reid's car later ignited itself with a backfire and burned up on Lapeer Avenue, to general public satisfaction.

Some people thought the Port Huron streets resembled the "Monkey Speedway" brought to town by the Parker Circus, where trained monkeys drove miniature cars furiously around a 1/8 mile track. A good many Port Huron drivers had less training than the monkeys. The state of Michigan took over the licensing of all drivers in 1919 (truckers in 1918), but required no instruction in automobile operation or a test of any kind to get a license, just a written application accompanied by your police chief or sheriff's endorsement. Half the state's 800,000 drivers didn't even bother to get licensed at all. The state also for a time lowered the driving age to 14, which cleared the way for a lot more monkey shines.

With auto accidents and traffic tickets now a daily occurrence, not just in Port Huron but all over St. Clair County, the court system set aside regular traffic case days. About a dozen drivers appeared weekly (compared to as many as 500 per day in New York City). The recurring cast of characters at the bar included Reid, Yokom, John Petit and the Dixons. Judge Clair Black hollowly vowed over and over to get tough with speedsters, but only dished out meager fines, suspended jail terms, and virtually no license repeals. Black and fellow judge Harvey Tappan themselves belonged to the Auto Club and agitated on the side for even higher speed limits in Port Huron.

The public found the George Caton case a particularly galling example of outrageous leniency. For knocking over at 40 mph on the wrong side of the street two boys bicycling on Griswold, Caton paid a $28 fine, that was all. But even if dispensers of justice had slapped every speeder with the maximum, the jail couldn't hold them all. The same situation prevailed in the big cities. During the first 11 months of 1913, 227 people died in New York City auto accidents, for which there were 39 arrests, no indictments, and no driver's licenses revoked. Civil lawsuits about automobile mayhem multiplied, sometimes two a day were filed in Port Huron, but most plaintiffs still settled for pennies on the dollar. Alvern Bollo's parents pitched their hopes high when they sued the city of Port Huron for $5,000 after the city's lone police car, while pursuing a speeding Model T, rammed the 14 year-old bicyclist instead.

129

It took citizen pressure in Port Huron to get the first speed limit signs put up, and the first centerline painted, and a hand-operated stop light installed for the traffic cop at the Main and Water intersection. Enforcing the law in the middle of Main and Water gave a cop some serious jitters. Apart from the hair-raising physical peril, he endured a wave of heckling: "The officers have had to stand considerable abuse from auto drivers and truck and express men." Down in Detroit, fed-up policeman William Potts built an electric, automatic, four-direction stoplight device out of red, green, and amber railroad lamps, to try bringing order out of chaos on the streets at less risk to cops. With imperfect success. "The Murder Goes On," said the *Times Herald* after Detroit's auto death toll hit 85 in 1915.

Except for the Main and Water stoplight, no other traffic signals or stop signs troubled drivers anywhere else in Port Huron yet. The auto ordinance simply directed a motorist approaching an intersection to yield to a vehicle approaching from the right, assuming one saw it in time. Then proceed, and hope for the best. Pedestrians had the dubious right to halt motor traffic at intersections by walking in front of oncoming vehicles and signaling them with an upraised palm. Not many walkers chose to bet their lives on this procedure, and it's unlikely 5 year-old Glenn Thomas knew about the correct procedure when he unsuccessfully tried to cross the street near his home. Glenn dodged one car, but another coming the other way clipped him: "He was thrown to the pavement and most of his teeth were knocked out, his body bruised and he received two gashes on the head. He was not seriously hurt." So went the report on Lucky Glenn.

Had he been a little older, Glenn might have known that only two things reliably slowed drivers down in Port Huron: a street crowded with other cars (the only benefit of auto congestion), and a really bad surface (the benefit of ruts). And not only children, women, and men, risked life and limb in front of Port Huron's autos, but how about dogs? Harry Goseline wanted to say a word on that subject: *"With eyes upturned, his master's look to scan / The joy, the solace, the aid of man / The poor man's guardian, the rich man's friend / The only creature faithful to the end.* Did you ever stand among a bunch of men, in the barber shop or garage, and hear a fellow brag 'I got one today'?"(22)

More and more public officials figured they now needed cars to execute their jobs, first and foremost the police. Sheriff Harrison Maines bought the first full-time police vehicle in St. Clair County, out of the belief that automobiles gave lawbreakers a disturbing measure of mobility. A trio of autoborne thieves who raced around the streets of Port Huron at 50 mph while exchanging gunshots with sheriff's deputies cemented Maines' opinion. A 1920 report to Michigan's governor made autos sound like the greatest aid to crime since the invention of lawyers:

Raiding small town banks, stores and homes has become a fairly common practice among criminals, who, with their high powered cars, can strike into the interior of the state miles from their haunts and hiding places in the cities...[creating] *practically a reign of terror.*(23)

To cut short terror's reign, 300 officers of the newly formed Michigan State Police (MSP) started roaming the roads from border to border. A few of them operated out of a post on the St. Clair River 15 miles south of Port Huron. State MSP Commander Robert Marsh didn't take long to issue the first in the department's never-ending series of anxious demands for more men and more equipment to handle the booming growth in auto crime.

The automobile immediately and effectively exploited those two Progressive pratfalls of the decade, the Prohibition of narcotics and alcohol. Smuggling is practically as old as civilization, and a tailor-made tool for it like the automobile turned Prohibition into the greatest criminal money making opportunity in American history. At first the federal narcotics law of 1914 produced only a yawn in Port Huron, since there weren't enough users around to notice. Within four years, however, the *Times Herald* reported that narcotics use in America had actually increased since passage of the Harrison Act. Thanks in large part to U.S. automobility.

As to booze, Michigan beat the national prohibition law by two years, voting in 1916 to go dry, effective in 1918. Judge Eugene Law reckoned he'd seen the last of any drunks in his Port Huron courtroom, and indeed liquor cases and the jail population in general dwindled dramatically at first. But once the large minority who wanted to drink got organized, liquor flowed again faster than the St. Clair River. It flowed across the river, actually, from Canada. Port Huron police regularly stopped autos stuffed with hundreds of quarts of joy juice tail-dragging their way up the river banks from the clandestine boat landings where they'd met their Sarnia connections. Cops got a further jolt when they found that the first big home distillery they uncovered belonged to their own traffic officer Charles Yearn, who sold alky out of his 10th Street address. Yearn no doubt felt the need of a tightener now and then to face up to his duties tangling with the auto population.

The list of official and semi-official motor vehicles lengthened steadily. Port Huron Fire Chief Frank Schaller obtained a city car, but the motorized fire truck from Ohio proved to be something of a disappointment. Because other auto traffic obstructed the fire engine, it saved only a negligible amount of time in getting to a fire, compared to a horse rig. The city bought three more general purposes trucks, and provided school truant officer Andrew Spring ("not as agile as he used to be") with a $30/month car allowance for chasing the hundreds of artful class dodgers. Ben Karrer started transporting Port Huron's sick in the first motorized ambulance. Undertaker Albert Falk acquired the first auto hearse. Falk still offered to do horse-drawn funerals on request, but under protest. He had taken against horses after a Boy Scout band on Main Street panicked an animal one day, and the beast rammed Falk's personal automobile head-on, doing it major damage.

What hath Ford wrought? Port Huron might have asked that question of its famous visitor in 1914. But the genius of travel couldn't stay long enough to consider it. After all, he had a business to run. Once he got back to Highland Park from Port Huron, Henry Ford decided to deal with two nuisances plaguing him. First, the Dodge brothers' stake in the FMC. The solution dovetailed with another idea Henry had, of eliminating all outside contractors, and manufacturing all the parts of the Model T himself. Fordism run wild. The Dodges rightly mocked this impossible scheme, then sued Henry when he cut off all dividends to FMC shareholders to divert $58 million into building a gigantic new factory complex on the Rouge River. The site lay about four miles from the new Ford family estate, Fair Lane, outside Dearborn.

While this legal fight raged, John and Horace Dodge, who after just two years on their own operated the fourth biggest auto company in America, paid their own sentimental call on Port Huron in 1916. They arrived in Horace's 200-foot yacht, and

131

visited the Port Huron Engine and Thresher plant where they'd worked as young men. They also looked in on the former Dodge family home which they'd built by hand, and finally stopped by Frank Church's Church of Dodge dealership. The trip went off smoothly, something not always guaranteed if the Dodges got to bending an elbow. John in particular. He'd once forced a Detroit saloon owner to dance on a tabletop at gunpoint while Dodge smashed the establishment's mirrors with shot glasses. With his limitless supply of auto cash, John settled legal claims against himself left and right, including one for a hit-and-run collision he'd committed while driving around town with his drinking buddy Detroit Mayor Oscar Marx.(24) In their high spiritedness, the Dodge brothers sometimes played automobile polo on John's hobby farm, using Model T's instead of horses.

The other potentially bad-for-business annoyance on Henry Ford's mind at mid-decade arose from the dustup in Europe commonly known as World War One. HF came out decisively and loudly against it, and he flatly refused to make any war vehicles for the belligerents. He was having none of the anti-German propaganda circulating in America. After all, Kaiser Wilhelm personally owned 30 different cars and trucks, so he couldn't be all bad. This attitude made a considerable break from that other apostle of Progressivism, Theodore Roosevelt, who much as he had before the Spanish-American War, now ranted like a demented person in his eagerness to see the United States join the fight for the Allies against the Central Powers. For his intransigence, Ford was denounced in pro-Roosevelt newspapers like the *New York Times* and *Chicago* Tribune, and, mildly, in the *Port Huron Times-Herald*.

Unfazed, Henry pledged $10 million to get a peace conference going, and for this purpose sailed in 1915 with fellow pacifists to Scandinavia where they meant to hold armistice talks. It availed them little. The war roared on. For this honorable failure his antagonists subjected Ford to even more mockery and abuse. James Couzens resigned from the FMC at about this time, in large part due to his disagreement with the boss over the war. Couzens' automobile enthusiasm also had been tempered a bit after he gave his son Homer a brand new Model T for his 14th birthday, the gift ideal, and the boy promptly rolled it over and killed himself. Couzens gave up automobile work forever and went into government. Though Stormy Jim had no qualifications for the job, Mayor Marx appointed him as Detroit's police chief on the strength of his FMC record. With his usual flair, Chief Couzens described the city as "lousy with criminals," though naturally he didn't cast any blame for this on automobility. Then in 1918 Couzens succeeded Marx as Detroit's mayor. Mayor Couzens, too, paid his own visit to Port Huron, a city which he'd frequented as a boy working on the Canadian railroads. For once in a reasonably benign mood, Jim reminisced happily about summers he'd spent swimming in the deep blue waters of Lake Huron.

President Woodrow Wilson lacked Henry Ford's determination in standing up to the interventionist lobby, and he obtained a Congressional declaration of war in April 1917. At this point Wilson coined the unfortunate phrase "We must make the world safe for democracy," though no directive about this existed in the Constitution. The war faction in America then and later tried to portray the country as unanimously behind the WW1 fight, a wild exaggeration. Though a tumultuous crowd hurrahed Port Huron's National Guard volunteer troops to the train station when they left for Europe, 36 of the first 37 army draftees who appeared for examination by the local induction board asked for exemptions.

132

Enough people in Michigan agreed with Henry Ford's skeptical view of the world war that without asking for it or lifting a finger to get it he won the Republican Presidential primary in Michigan in 1916, which he gratefully acknowledged but did not pursue. Then *both* political parties put Ford on the U.S. Senate primary ballot in 1918. He faced the distinct possibility of running against himself in the fall. Ford won the Democratic nomination, but narrowly lost the Republican primary, then the general election, to Truman Newberry, a former U.S. Navy Secretary under Roosevelt, and a co-founder of Packard Motors. St. Clair County went Newberry in this election, and the *Times Herald* noted that many a war supporter, especially the farmer, drove his Model T to the polls to vote agin' Ford.

President Wilson placed no war restraint of any kind at first on the auto industry, which clanked along merrily making 1.7 million passenger cars in 1917. Finally, well into 1918, the administration ordered a 50% reduction of automaking, cutting the year's output to *only* 925,000 cars.(25) But the production of trucks increased astronomically during the war. First, of course, these went to the truck-happy military. Commanding U.S. General John Pershing barely had set foot in France with an initial supply of 2,400 trucks before he demanded 50,000 more, at a cost of $1,200 apiece, plus an unlimited supply of spare parts. To clear the way for this land navy the army assigned 10,000 soldiers to road-building duties in Europe. More constructively, American engineers also built 1,000 miles of new railroad line in France to help the war effort. When the army returned home in 1919, his superiors ordered Major Dwight Eisenhower to lead a 42-truck convoy on a coast-to-coast run across America to find out just how useful these machines would be in a war on the home front. The answer: not very. The trip took 62 days, the vehicles broke down everywhere, and the deeply irritated Eisenhower described most of the roads as "average to non-existent."(26) This trip would have considerable consequences 40 years later.

America's wartime truck boom made its greatest and longest-lasting impact on civilian life. During the first seven years of the decade up until the war, most trucks in the United States carried local loads. Though the bay hoss still held an important position at the old dray stand next to the Port Huron City Hall, several trucks had moved in alongside the horses and wagons, waiting for a job to move something around town. Trucks owners charged three times the rate of horse-pulled service, but owners claimed their machines handled twice the load in half the time. Oscar Richards, a former railroad freight agent, became one of these trucking freelancers. Several more businesses also purchased their own delivery trucks, like Sperry's department store.

And apart from local service, World War One marked the start of long-distance trucking in America, intended at first as a supplement to railroads. For the first time cargo in large amounts traveled by truck hundreds of miles between cities and states. Compared to rail or ships, long-haul trucking wasted everything – fuel, manpower, load, material, time – but there seemed little alternative at that moment. The federal government helped bring this about through its complete mismanagement of the railroads during the war, which we'll get to presently, coupled with the traditional lack of any overall transportation plan for the country. As they do so often about these years, statistics vary, but one American Trucking Association history estimated that the number of commercial trucks increased from 300,000 at the beginning of WW1, to 1,000,000 twenty months later, at the Armistice in November, 1918.(27)

As war biz boomed, trucks smashed up more roads, even concrete ones put down by the federal government as a war measure. A 20-tonner punched a large hole in the brand new bridge over Port Huron's Black River Canal, infuriating the City Council. Michigan set a loaded truck weight limit of 30,000 lbs in 1917 (eleven years after Horatio Earle had called for one) but nobody actually started weighing trucks to enforce this until 1923. After the war, the state of Michigan began licensing intercity trucking companies to try to get a handle on this traffic, but didn't set very strict requirements, and offered for an extra $50 to throw in a bus permit, too. Several Port Huron entrepreneurs, including Richards and a former auto industry employee named Myron Ogden, started regular trucking service between Port Huron and Detroit, dispatching trucks in two-vehicle convoys to back each other up in case of trouble. Operating alone, a truck might get stuck for an entire day or even two on the beaten up gravel-covered Gratiot Pike.

Even on decent roads, a good many men found driving one of the open cab trucks of this era to be an ordeal, according to a Teamsters Union history:

A driver now had to have clear knowledge of the best route where roads would be safe, places to get fuel, possible weather hazards that might affect the motor or handling of the vehicle, and how to complete any number of repairs. Rainy days did more than make a driver damp and miserable. Water in the engine could cause it to stall out, and rubber tires were much less 'sure-footed' on the road than a horse. Trucks were equipped with simple heaters for cold weather, which was a step up from the lap robe, but offered little true comfort, a situation that was not remedied until many years later. Countless drivers recall driving with one hand on the wheel and the other warming up in a coat pocket. Most drivers could also show off smooth, hairless knees and calves, because a very hot engine with no protective barrier singed their legs on a daily basis.
(28)

Truckers in St. Clair County, who earned about $20 per week, didn't easily recognize the best routes because they had no road signs to go by. A 21 mile drive between Port Huron and the city of Richmond required 21 navigational checks against church steeples, school houses, bridges, phone poles and crossroads. Even those with driving experience often had their hands full with the clumsy rigs, as truck salesman Frank Tacie found out when he inadvertently steered a new demonstration model in front of the train in Port Huron, which killed him. A truck design with interchangeable front and back ends, the semi-trailer, appeared by 1920, and although even longer, taller, and more dangerously unstable than earlier models on the road, the industry embraced its versatility, which, of course, the railroad already had enjoyed for 80 years with far greater safety and efficiency.

The FMC added the Model TT, a 1-ton truck, to its product line in 1917, some of the 700,000 vehicles it produced that year. Henry Ford relented on his pacifist view for the war's duration once America joined the fracas, and eventually furnished 127,000 Ford vehicles to the Allies. Ford also built airplane engines and submarine chasing ships, and he had a plan in mind to build 90,000 tanks, but the fighting ended before this could be cranked up. None of this made Henry very happy. Even after the Allied victory, Ford's spirits remained somewhat depressed, particularly by the deaths of 116,000 American troops, 48 of them from Port Huron, who in his view had sacrificed their lives for nothing. Smarting from some of the nasty remarks made about him by the

134

pro-war press, Ford sued the *Chicago Tribune* for $1 million for calling him an anarchist. Former Port Huron Mayor Elliot Stevenson defended the *Tribune*, at a trial conducted in Mount Clemens, Michigan by visiting Port Huron judge Harvey Tappan. After Ford famously testified that "history is bunk," he won 6 cents in damages.

There'd been plenty of problems in the nation's factories during the war, Ford's included. Anti-war feeling, draft opposition, the Communist takeover in Russia, and soaring prices at home triggered hundreds of strikes across the country during the 18 months of the American war effort. As Ford had foreseen, wartime inflation pushed up the prices of the Model T line by as much as 100%, and top wages at the FMC climbed to $7 per day. Things got more unsettled after the war ended. Even with higher wages at Ford Motor's main factories, one-third of the workforce – 16,000 men – quit or were fired in 1919. The situation looked even worse at the Willys-Overland auto plant down the road at Toledo, Ohio, where a massive riot killed two people, injured 19, and brought out the National Guard.

It left Ford feeling a little mixed up. After all, the war hadn't been *his* fault, and everybody knew the score by now with Fordism.

We expect the men to do what they are told. The organization is so highly specialized and one part is so dependent upon another that we could not for a moment consider allowing men to have their own way. Without the most rigid discipline we would have the utmost confusion.

In labor's view, that didn't quite jibe with Henry's earlier pronouncement about the happy factory floor he allegedly wanted.

Because there are no titles and no limits of authority, there is no question of red tape or going over a man's head. Any workman can go to anybody, and so established has become this custom, that a foreman does not get sore if a workman goes over him and directly to the head of the factory.(29)

Ford got more bad legal news when the FMC lost the Dodge brothers lawsuit (Elliot Stevenson also represented the Dodges), forcing Henry to cough up some of the millions in dividends he'd hoarded away for the Rouge project. That did it, in the Founder's mind. Time for a thorough house cleaning. HF informed the other Ford Motor shareholders that unless they agreed to his offer of a buyout he'd start another car company on his own and let them sink or swim. He furthered this charade by resigning the company presidency in favor of his son, Edsel. Henry had used a similar squeeze play against Alexander Malcolmson in 1905 to run him out of the company, and this time Stevenson called Ford's actions a pure bluff. But after some hemming and hawing, the Dodges, Couzens, and the rest of the gang of '03 all tendered their shares to Ford in 1919.

Even chief engineer Harold Wills departed. Although he owned no shares, Wills redeemed his contractual arrangement with Ford for a $19 million jackpot. The buyout, dividend payout, and the startup of the Rouge plant construction amounted roughly to a $120 million spending spree by Ford, $75 million of which had to be borrowed. But aside from that debt, Henry, Clara and Edsel now owned the entire Ford Motor Company lock, stock and barrel. It's a significant testimony to Ford's personal magnetism that he remained on friendly terms with all these ex-partners after they parted ways. And why not? He'd made them some of the richest people in America. Henry attended as an honored guest the funerals of the Dodge brothers, after John and Horace both died the next year, 1920, from pneumonia and liver trouble and maybe too much auto polo.

With plenty of time on his hands now, Harold Wills and another FMC alumnus, former personnel director John Lee, took a little sail on Wills' yacht up the beautiful St. Clair River to Port Huron. At some point the two men hatched a plan for a new automobile venture of their own, the Wills Sainte Claire company. It looked simple enough. They had the model of Ford Motor to work from. The two men bought up 4,000 acres of land immediately south of the city of Port Huron, including much of the unincorporated 200-person village of Marysville. In May 1919 they announced plans to build a 40,000-worker auto manufacturing complex, which would balloon the new, incorporated village of Marysville into a metropolis of 100,000 people. "It won't be long before the St. Clair River is lined with smokestacks," proclaimed Harold proudly, in a time when people still welcomed smokestacks.

The power of the Ford name by now, even by past association, lent enough credibility to this crazy scheme that the news left Port Huron gasping with excitement. Real estate prices doubled overnight and half a dozen developers raced each other to City Hall to get their plats approved. Realtor Stanley McFarland won big. He sold out 300 home lots within 10 days of the Wills announcement. In the biggest housing boom the town ever saw, 500 new residences went up in Port Huron during the next 10 months, and hundreds more changed hands. Property taxes soared. Louis Weil made sure to get in on the land rush, reaping a rich harvest of advertising from his brand new weekly builders' page, which inaugurated a regular house-plan feature to entice prospective home owners.

In part, Wills and Lee had chosen the Marysville site because its ready railroad, interurban, and waterfront access made it a simple matter to start promptly building streets, sewers, utilities, and what they planned as a 1.5 million square foot assortment of Wills Sainte Claire factories. 60 railcars full of material soon arrived daily at the site. Wills set prejudice aside to also press a large complement of horses into service. The partners built workers homes and apartments (with no garages) close enough to walk or bicycle to work, on streets as much as 150 feet wide. They laid out plans for future streetcar service, and built a new 500-foot dock on the river. They erected a community house in a big one-day building bee using dozens of Wills-Lee employees shipped up from Detroit via the Rapid Railway. Wills himself did some of the roof shingling that day.

Wills and Lee started a bank, and a real estate company, and re-sold some of their land holdings back to 150 different companies who wanted a piece of the Marysville action. At the front of the line stood a Canadian auto parts maker named Pressed Metals, which employed 500 people. It's not likely Pressed Metals got a rock-bottom price for the property it bought from Harold. Like Lyin' Hank and most other people in the auto industry, Wills did not always hew strictly to honest dealing. According to some ex-colleagues at Ford, Harold had enriched himself beyond his deserts by buying up commodities ahead of FMC orders he knew would inflate prices.

Wills clearly intended the Marysville project to put him on the same plane with Ford and Billy Durant, who shaped not only their car companies but whole car making cities as well, in Dearborn and Flint. And indeed, just as in those communities, the first shovel had barely turned the sod in Marysville before auto troubles arose. Speeding cars on the hitherto quiet streets became such a serious problem that the police-less city bought a motorcycle for traffic control and deputized a dozen Wills-Lee men to use it. Auto-equipped crooks staged robberies and break-ins. In one instance looters emptied a new house of everything but a piano and a cook stove and carried the swag away in a truck. Heavy trucks used in the construction phase destroyed Marysville streets as fast as Wills built them. One of the guilty parties, Myron Ogden, bought the first dump truck ever seen in Port Huron, one far too heavy for the streets of the day, to fulfill a Wills contract.

Having learned steadfastness, some might say obstinacy, at Henry Ford's feet, Wills did not allow these difficulties to deflect his purpose. He quickly took personal charge of most of the project, sweeping his partner Lee into the background. Looking to ensure proper promotion for the firm, Wills started up a Wills Sainte Claire film company, starring himself, just as Ford had done at the FMC. Rhapsodically, the *Times-Herald* predicted that the names of Marysville and C. Harold Wills would outlive those of movie stars Douglas Fairbanks, Mary Pickford, and Charlie Chaplin. After he'd spent 17 months getting everything ready, in October 1920 Wills unveiled his prototype automobile to an assembly of eager government officials, reporters, and business people.

Wills personally had designed his namesake car, and carried around a stethoscope to listen to its engine. The state of this power plant occupied much of his attention. When one of his visitors asked Wills to start the vehicle up, Harold proudly replied that it *was* running. Nothing else much distinguished the automobile which came to be called the Gray Goose. Except the price. Wills announced that the various models would cost between $3,000 and $5,000. He expected to build 7,000 units the first year. Disquiet spread through the crowd like auto exhaust. This looked nothing like the Ford Motor Company stepchild Port Huron had hoped for. These would be some of the most expensive autos in America. How could a 40,000-worker factory arise on that kind of foundation? "If you want to make money, make quantity," Henry Ford once said. Some Port Huronites thought they smelled another Havers episode in the making, and on a much grander scale.

As Ford and Wills had stayed active during the last half of the decade, so had Billy Durant. Somewhat too active, in the opinion of Alfred Sloan, the New Jersey bearing maker. Sloan sourly observed later that once Durant got back behind the wheel at General Motors in 1916, "The big show was on again." The big show concerned Sloan because he'd sold his own company to Durant in 1916 for stock worth millions, and went to work for Billy as well. This left Sloan with a lot of GM shares and a top executive post, but also with a lot of qualms. Why Alfred didn't sell up and depart at this point can only be credited, first, to Durant's own considerable powers of persuasion, almost the equal of Henry Ford's, and second, to GM's still robust profits as the Number 2 auto company in America. Even running a distant second to Ford enriched everybody in the GM executive suite, because the number of motor vehicles in America increased 300%-400% between 1914 and 1920, reaching a total somewhere between 8 and 10 million, depending on who counted.

During his second GM reign, Durant added a refrigerator company, Frigidaire, a tractor company, Samson, an auto body maker, Fisher Brothers, and an electrical parts company, Delco, to his motley GM family, along with many other acquisitions. He boosted the company capitalization to $1 billion. Delco originally belonged to Charles Kettering, perfector of the automobile self-starter, who soon became a buddy within the GM upper echelon to the trio of Alfred Sloan, Buick boss Walter Chrysler, and axle man Charles Mott. Durant's wobbly management methods often left these four men almost beside themselves with concern, until Billy confounded them with another of his unpredictable strokes of brilliance. Durant's greatest coup came when he took the opposite course from credit-hating Henry Ford, and okayed formation of the General Motors Acceptance Corporation (GMAC) in 1919 to finance the sale of motor vehicles to dealers and customers. The word "acceptance" struck a reassuring note, as though customers were being admitted to an exclusive club when they took out auto loans. Actively sponsoring the purchase of cars on time proved to be the American auto industry's single most important non-mechanical breakthrough ever.

Installment financing became the indispensable backbone of America's auto culture. It could hardly be otherwise, because the average family simply could not afford one of these machines by any strict set of criteria. The typical household earned just $800-$900 p.a., and only about 10% of Americans maintained a savings account, which held less than $500. Just as John Petit and thousands of other individual dealers had done heretofore on an irregular basis, by breaking the cost into monthly payments, GMAC, the pioneer taskmaster, convinced people to indenture themselves for their automobiles. The company wrote $2 million worth of loans the first year, on terms of one-quarter down and a year to pay.

And just how good were the cars GMAC wrote loans for in 1920? You wouldn't hear this at George Yokom Chevrolet in Port Huron, but 40 years later Alfred Sloan allowed himself a little honesty on the subject:

It had a four-cylinder engine whose crankshaft and associated connecting rods and pistons were inherently unbalanced. Ordinarily this car had two-wheel brakes with braking confined to the rear wheels; it had no independent springing of the front wheels; it had a sliding-gear transmission, and an engine of low power. It vibrated and often shimmied; it veered and sometimes skidded when the brakes were applied; it rode hard and rough; the clutch grabbed; the gears often clashed in the shifting, and, owing to the low power available, they always had to be shifted on hills of substantial gradient. But the car usually got somewhere and back; fortunately it was unable to go far enough for many of its deficiencies to become serious drawbacks. (30)

In this same vein, the Auto Club's Port Huron representative, A. L. Westgard, furnished some advice to motorists preparing for an out-of-town trip in 1920. Be sure to take along wrenches, pliers, a hammer, screwdriver, files, wire, nuts and bolts, tire valves, a tire pressure gauge, spark plugs, rim lugs, talcum powder, tape, grease gun, an extra valve and spring, and spring clip and bolts. Also one or two spare tires, extra tubes, blow out patches, tire pump, a small plank, weed chains, a towing rope, collapsible canvas bucket, five gallon water bag, rubber hose, lubricating oil and grease. Make sure to lubricate all parts and fully charge the battery. Once in motion, keep the car's load down, distribute weight equally on the springs, use soft water for the radiator, watch the brakes and adjust them as needed, don't strain the motor, watch the wheel alignment, repair small tire cuts, don't drive in ruts, don't adjust the chain too tightly,

138

keep the tires inflated, and test those tires daily.

While installment selling worked wonders in attaching automobiles to people who didn't really want to know their true costs, at the corporate level easy financing proved again to be Gambling Billy's downfall. When America encountered a post-WW1 depression at the end of 1920, and car sales fell down a well, Durant found himself in the same sort of financial bind that had tripped him up in 1910. This time he had to answer to General Motors' biggest shareholder, the enormously wealthy, chemical-making DuPont family. Even as Durant's $20 million monument to himself, the Albert Kahn-designed Durant Building, the biggest office building in the world, rose up at GM's expense in Detroit, the DuPonts ousted Billy from control of his brainchild, this time completely and permanently. GM Chairman Pierre DuPont, who knew even less than Durant about automobiles, eventually settled on Alfred Sloan as the man to run things. Had Walter Chrysler still been around he probably would have gotten the job, but Chrysler had bailed out on Durant and GM months earlier. Charles Mott made an even better candidate, easily the most broadminded executive at the company, already a three-time mayor of Flint, and a sometime skeptic about the benefits of the automobile. In that way Mott may have been *too* broadminded to suit the DuPonts. In any case, Sloan it was to be.

The depression proved to be no easier for that one-man band, Henry Ford, to handle. Sales dropped off just as $70 million in various loans came due, with the FMC $38 million short. After an unpleasant discussion with Wall Street about refinancing, which threatened to strip him of control, Henry instead resurrected a tactic from the 1907 slump and dumped 100,000 unwanted cars on his (by now) 7,000 dealers and demanded payment for them. He shut down production and instituted the sort of draconian cost cutting program only a corporate dictator could mount, shedding personnel, buildings, furniture, telephones, order blanks, anything he could toss overboard. It surprised Ford to find out that the biggest savings came from improved use of the FMC's rail and ship connections.

After a close call, Ford Motor survived. It had been a nervous time as well for Henry's new Port Huron dealer Albert Parfet, who just before the crisis arrived had commissioned a big new $135,000 Ford showroom and repair shop on Main Street. Rather uniquely, the architect put a test track on the two-story dealership's roof. The new Ford palace occupied the former site of one of the Jenks' family mansions, and though Parfet built a decidedly handsome and solid structure, on balance it represented another sacrifice of the city's graciousness to the spatial demands of the auto.

What had become of the former Ford dealer, John Petit? He'd died in a 1917 crash on the Rapid Railway traveling between Port Huron and Detroit. On this occasion, the swifter, surer, cheaper method of going between the two cities, even for an auto dealer, failed to prove safer. Due to a blown signal, two Rapid cars met on the tracks near St. Clair City one June day, and Petit tried but failed to jump clear of the collision, leaving an arm behind. The doctors couldn't save him. Four other people died as well. Petit had been ticketed for speeding in his automobiles so many times it seemed especially pathetic to go out this way. Given his druthers, he'd probably have preferred a good street wreck. The Petit family held on to the Ford agency for two years before selling out to young Parfet, a University of Michigan graduate who'd worked for the FMC prior to taking over in Port Huron.

By 1920 the number of motor vehicles in Port Huron had multiplied to 3,000. Nobody took a make and model census, but it's a good guess that half of them were Fords, as were half the rest of the cars in America, and half the cars in the world. The FMC constructed one million vehicles in 1920. Opinions of Henry and his products varied considerably across the country. Port Huron minister J.T. Charlton thought "The farsightedness, the humanitarian spirit, and the moral courage of Henry Ford are worthy of emulation." Thirty different song composers agreed, and turned out hits like *Hurrah for Henry Who Built the Model T.* But life would be insufferably dull if everybody agreed on everything, and U.S. Senator John Sherman of Illinois had this song to sing: "I regard the Ford automobile as an international pest. It destroys more useful material than any other sink hole in the world. It is a waste of time and substance."(31)

Ford had one more trick up his sleeve which he played during this decade - his own version of the gasoline tractor. The gas tractor wasn't new, the first one in St. Clair County fired up at the Daniel Foley farm in 1911. Neither Foley nor any other farmer really needed one. Tractorless American farmers prospered so handsomely during the years of 1910-1914 that this period became the benchmark used by the U.S. Department of Agriculture for most of the rest of the century as a period of perfectly balanced production and prices. Anxious to solve this non-problem and further avenge himself against the horse, Henry put the Model T of tractors, the Fordson, on the drawing board by 1915.

He built several thousand of the 2,500 pound, steel wheeled Fordsons for British use during the war. U.S. distribution began in 1918. $750 Fordsons soon drove General Motors' Samson tractors right off the market, at a loss to GM of $30 million. The Fordson also marked the beginning of the end for the Port Huron Engine and Thresher Company's steam-powered gear. They didn't notice it at first, since the world war had eaten up everything American farmers could grow, but the gasoline tractor permanently fastened the problem of overproduction around their necks. In 1920 American sodbusters, with 240,000 tractors in the field, and 2 million automobiles in the barnyard, started sliding into their own special depression, the likes of which no one could readily imagine.(32)

Car, truck or tractor, you couldn't use 'em if you couldn't fuel 'em. The Imperial Oil refinery across the river from Port Huron labored day and night to prevent that calamity from happening. Anywhere from 200,000 to 1,000,000 gallons of oil arrived every two days at Imperial in an assortment of nine different ships sailing from Ohio. Eventually the oil flow swelled to such proportions it required a pipeline laid directly from the Ohio oil fields. The refinery expanded over and over again, until the $15 million installation covered 110 acres of former Indian reservation on the south side of Sarnia. The largest refinery in Canada, with 500 storage tanks, miles of its own railroad tracks, its own water plant, and 1,200 workers on hand, Imperial cranked out gasoline, kerosene and any other petroleum products it could think of, including 3 million wax candles per year.(33) Gratefully, the Sarnians dubbed their town "Imperial City." Just how much product leaked dangerously away at Imperial nobody knew or cared much about yet, but in California a refinery built in 1911 dripped 250 million gallons of gasoline into an aquifer during the next eight decades.(34)

American oil production quadrupled from 60 million barrels per year in 1900 to 250 million by 1914, and kept on rising.(35) As of 1911, gasoline in Port Huron sold

140

for 13 cents for gallon, and during the decade the price fell to as little as 11 cents, until WW1 intervened and briefly tripled it. Alongside regular gas, retailers started marketing higher octane fuel, like Hi-Test, with Hi prices, holding out the hope that it made an engine run better and faster. Neither Hi-Test nor any other gasoline gimmick fooled Henry Ford: "All the world is waiting for a substitute for gasoline. When oil is gone, there will be no more gasoline, and long before that time, the prices of gasoline will have risen to a point where it will be too expensive to burn as a motor fuel."(36) Teetotaler Henry thought booze would be better to run automobiles with than to drink, and after Michigan voted in consumable alcohol prohibition in 1916 Ford suggested that distilleries convert to fuel production. This fantasy about the nation's automobiles running on hooch outlived prohibition and Ford both.

If nothing else, WW1 fully illuminated the extent of the American car culture's oil habit. Three months after the USA's entry into the world war, before its armed forces had scarcely lifted a finger in anger, Standard Oil of New Jersey president Alfred Bedford announced that the country already was running an oil deficit, producing 300 million barrels per year while consuming 335 million, dipping into its 165 million barrel reserve. Bedford blamed the joy-riding that motorists did in their 4 million automobiles even in the face of the war emergency, during which time America also furnished 80% of the oil used by the Allies.(37) St. Clair County's 2,600 vehicles each gulped an average of a gallon of gas daily in 1917 to push their 3,000 lbs. around for 13 miles. Despite Bedford's warning, more than a year went by before the Wilson administration, which seemed more frightened of the driving public than of Germany, ordered gas stations to close at 6pm six days a week and completely on Sundays. Not really emergency type measures.

In August, 1918 authorities timidly suggested a ban on Sunday driving east of the Mississippi, but the public ignored the request so completely that, in St. Clair City for instance, residents nicknamed the busy main street "Slacker Avenue." In the face of the same attitude everywhere the government called off the Sunday ban after just three weeks. The Central Powers surrendered to the Allies two months later, so America's reluctance to face the music over civilian automobile driving in war produced no major repercussions, this time.

The automobile's insatiable thirst spurred more crazy oil policy from the United States in the postwar world. While America pumped out yet more petroleum, a million barrels per day, it simultaneously imported it from Mexico and exported it to Canada (refineries like Sarnia's). Even in these relatively early days, oilmen worried about exhausting domestic supplies, and in order to keep filling those filling stations they proposed to extract oil from shale rock if the liquid wells ran dry. Some companies wanted to look for oil in the nations of the notoriously unstable Middle East. U.S. gasoline production increased an overall 560% during this decade, to 4 billion gallons in 1920, two thirds of which disappeared first into the tanks of automobiles, then into the spacious skies.

Moving such gigantic amounts of an explosive product from the refinery to the gas tank posed some problems. Much of it traveled by rail. In getting his new Port Huron service stations supplied, Star Oil boss James Wilson discovered that railroads regarded gasoline as such a hazardous cargo they charged a stiff premium to carry it. It took a brief 1920 wildcat strike on the railroads to do what the war couldn't do, bring

141

gasoline rationing to Port Huron. Authorities limited gasoline to doctors, taxis, trucks and public utility vehicles during the strike. Some drivers not on the list tried adding "Speedoline" to their tanks, an additive positively guaranteed to increase gas mileage 25-40%, the first time that type of scam had appeared.

Automobile owners really needed a Speedoline for their bank accounts to magically increase the balances. According to a rough, and envious, estimate by *Railway Age* magazine, Americans spent $500 million for gasoline per year by the end of the decade, the third largest annual expense in owning a car, behind depreciation ($1.8 billion), and tires ($1 billion). Throw in a $73 per car insurance bill, 8 gallons of motor oil per year per car, repairs and loan costs and whatnot, and the total national tab came to $6 billion.

And that didn't include roads and streets. "...it is quite possible to spend too much money on pavements and their maintenance," said the *Times-Herald* at the beginning of the decade, a prediction that came true in spades. The most disastrous example occurred when the City Council chose to lay three miles of new pavement on 10th Street, a major north-south artery, at a cost of almost $120,000, one of the biggest outlays in the city's history, rather than use the money to quadruple the size of Lakeside Park. The lost opportunity never recurred. The council made this boneheaded decision in order to relieve traffic "congestion" on Main Street, by funneling some of it onto 10th. The move failed completely, it just congested both Main and 10th, gave police a new trouble spot in the bargain, and put 10th on the regular pavement maintenance list. Had 10th simply been railed for streetcar traffic it could have maintained its orderly ways and very likely the city could have afforded to expand the park as well.

In the minds of public officials, most of whom owned automobiles, nothing now equaled traffic congestion as the certified, unquestioned, #1 civic taboo which overrode all other municipal concerns. Decongestion efforts progressively tore up more and more of Port Huron, and led to the neglect of other more worthwhile improvements. The City Council repeatedly postponed building a sewage treatment plant in favor of ordering more street work. As early as 1912 the local Auto Club demanded that Port Huron's "dangerous" streets – dangerous for drivers – be widened, the sidewalks narrowed, the trees and shrubs felled, just to accommodate the sight lines and turning abilities of motorists. This made these streets more dangerous and unpleasant for everyone else but what did that matter to the auto lobby? In essence, the rights of drivers now superseded the rights of fixed property owners. No one's home, business, safety, or peace and quiet could be allowed to stand in the way of automobile emancipation.

Here the reader is entitled to a warning that during this decade the road issues of the day first engaged the full attention of American government at every level. By 1920, road programs of one kind or another operated at the city, township, county, state and federal levels. As a result a baffling multiplicity may creep into the narrative. It would take a forensic CPA to sort out where all the money came from and where it went to, but no such expert is available for this history. The main point to keep in mind is that the automobile prompted this melee. We'll try to keep to the major events and make things as simple as possible.

St. Clair County voters, after a long and contentious process, finally agreed in 1913 to set up a three-man Road Commission. It might as well have been called the

142

Automobile and Truck Commission, because it paid no attention whatsoever to the needs of pedestrians, bicyclists, or horse owners in administering county roads. The Road Commission picked up a bad reputation right from the start. The first chairman, Charles Bailey, owned shares in the Good Roads Construction Company, run by his son. This blatant conflict of interest embarrassed even the most fervent auto people. They replaced Bailey with Frank Beard, the Port Huron car dealer and former Havers president, by way of another backroom deal only slightly less seamy than the first.

After some debate over ways and means, the Road Commission secured a county road tax, added state aid money into the pot, and issued bonds as fast as the presses could print them. They bought St. Clair County's roads on the installment plan in this way, just as most buyers did their cars. The Road Commission hired an engineer, D. D. Worcester, and bought him a Model T to supervise from. Worcester had no systematic plan to go by in choosing where to start work. Petitions from landowners willing to pay an extra helping of the costs under special assessments, called the Covert Plan, received first attention. One of the first truly big projects involved rebuilding the road leading northward from Port Huron up the Lake Huron shoreline. Designers intended it to be the first phase of a driver's delight, an 18-foot wide concrete road showpiece encircling the entire Thumb, a scenic highway. Of course, once you built a highway through a landscape it wasn't scenic anymore, but what's in a name?.

Sadly, from the perspective of this history, the Scenic Highway followed roughly the course of the unrealized railroad proposed as far back as 1870s, and several times thereafter; the train service people had begged for. The first installment of the Scenic encompassed 10 miles or so up to the St. Clair County border. The Road Commission opened it with great fanfare, marred only by a first-day accident when Frank Dixon slammed his car into a bridge abutment. The Scenic project stalled out at this point, and it took another 60 years to complete the circuit of the Thumb, but the local section played a very large role in auto affairs of the future.

Another notable early Road Commission effort took place in 1915, the big Gratiot Pike Road Bee. 700 volunteers, mainly from Port Huron, with 200 horse teams patiently assisting, managed to gravel four miles of this old military road to Detroit in a single day. Movie cameras captured the Herculean effort, which made it to the screen at the Maxine Theater: "Popular Port Huron Business Men shoveling gravel. They are all there and plainly seen." Okay, it wasn't *Birth of a Nation*, but it tickled local movie fans. Off camera, contractor Andrew Murphy put his employees to work improving county roads while he pocketed $11,000 per mile in fees from the government. So did builder Herb Campbell, who with his son Marshall employed up to 50 horse teams of their own, and got rich on the roads.

Unmoved by the shoveling movie stars, and annoyed by the absence of action on their own particular township roads, St. Clair County farmers began howling, claiming discrimination against them. The county road tax that farmers paid benefitted them nought, they said, it just diverted cash away from their neighborhood roads to a few select ones favored by motorists. "The trunk line highways are for the rich people with automobiles..." said one township supervisor, John Shepherd, meaning the Gratiot Pike and Scenic Highway. In the opinion of some of Shepherd's constituents, the plain farm roads had never been so bad.

In referring to "trunk line highways" Supervisor Shepherd meant the 3,000-

mile highway system set up by the state of Michigan in 1913. By and large, officials in Lansing created this network by simply anointing select existing roads as state highways. From this point forward, we'll use the term "highway" to refer only to state and federal roads. Main Street and the Scenic became state highways. So did the Gratiot Pike, and the former east-west plank road out of Port Huron, known within the city as Lapeer Avenue, and outside town as Highway 21. The original plan interconnected all the 83 county seats in Michigan, but over time the trunk lines expanded to 9,000 miles, and connected whatever the automobile and Good Roads lobbies wanted connected.

It is pertinent to point out that by 1915 every single member of the Michigan legislature owned an automobile. They made sure to spend on roads and nothing else the millions of dollars collected in auto license fees. They also appropriated general tax money for highways. By 1917 Michigan's State Highway Commissioner, Frank Rogers of Port Huron, was promising road building ahead of "such magnitude as to dwarf the fondest dreams of the most enthusiastic highway boosters." Plus the bills to go with it. Rogers helped put a special $50 million bond issue for new roads before Michigan voters in 1919, and Governor Albert Sleeper, the first Thumb man ever elected governor, asked ministers across the state to beseech the faithful on Good Roads Sunday to vote yes come election day. The electorate answered those prayers by a 4-1 margin in St. Clair County, 3-1 across the state.

Last but never least, the federal government joined the road renaissance by enacting in 1916 a Federal Highway Act that matched the state sums expended in building or improving post roads. This contribution turned these roads into Federal Aid Highways. The *New York Commercial* outlined the ultimate aim: "The whole country should be covered with a network of concrete automobile roads which would not wear out in a century if reserved exclusively for motor traffic."[38] Initially, Congress expected this federal aid to cost $15 million per year, but the program exploded in size to more than $100 million annually by 1920. Compared to an estimated $43 million in 1914, the states and federal government together spent $1.3 billion on roads in 1920.[39] A direct subsidy for the automobile.

Boiling this down to St. Clair County's portion, it meant the Road Commission ordered $2.5 million of work of one kind or another in 1920. For years travelers crossing the county's 1,200 miles of road encountered a crazy, spreading patchwork of different road surfaces, which Frank Rogers honestly admitted cost the following annual amounts *per mile* to maintain: dirt ($138), gravel ($252), macadam ($490), and concrete ($659). And those figures didn't include snow plowing, which Rogers wanted to inaugurate, to help out the new long-distance trucking industry.

At no level did the government launch a comparable effort to build the superior and saner alternative of public rail lines to intertie with the existing systems. No 10th Street rail extension in Port Huron, no St. Clair County Rail Commission, no Scenic Railway, no Rail Bee, no Good Rails Sunday, no $50 million Michigan rail bond, no Federal Railbed Act. Instead a steady drumbeat of government interference with and downright hostility towards American train and trolley companies continued throughout the decade.

This gloomy era for railroads began symbolically with two serious fires in Port Huron. First the Pere Marquette Railroad station on the riverfront burned in 1912. Then, even more disastrously, the Grand Trunk repair shops went up in smoke in 1913,

144

a $1 million catastrophe. The GTRR conflagration idled a workforce of 600 men, and the community wasted no time in raising a $100,000 bonus to convince the company to rebuild on donated land west of town. The PMRR, on the other hand, received no bonus, and lacking the cash didn't rebuild its downtown station until ordered to do so by the Michigan Railroad Commission two years later.

A number of people, including Henry McMorran, who'd sold the Thumb division to the Pere Marquette 20 years earlier, crabbed about the inadequate service they felt the McMorran Line now gave them. Michigan's largest railroad staggered toward another bankruptcy, its second in seven years, and seventh overall. PMRR president Newman Erb had no doubt about where the blame really lay, with the government: "Michigan burdens the railroads with greater taxes and lower rates than any other state in the country. 75%-80% of Michigan mileage is unprofitable."(40) The Grand Trunk and Michigan Central railroads both seconded Erb in this opinion, and they also pointed out that railroad taxes paid more than a quarter of the state budget.

Although critics still claimed the railroads' owners manipulated finances to put on a poorboy appearance, a Michigan legislative report confirmed that the PMRR's passenger rates, 2 cents per mile, were indeed inadequate, since it cost the line 2.1 cents to carry people. The resulting loss totaled $600,000 per year. The Pere Marquette went into receivership again in 1912, this time for five years. It had plenty of company. One-sixth of American railroads worked under court control or in receivership by mid-decade.(41) Although in somewhat better financial shape than the PMRR, the Grand Trunk said every railroad in Michigan faced potential bankruptcy.

The Pere Marquette closed three rural St. Clair County stations to save money. Passengers drifted away. Helen Endlich and her Port Huron schoolmates began the decade by taking Pere Marquette trains to their favorite picnic grounds, and ended it by driving cars to them. Governor Woodbridge Ferris suggested the state take over the company, but the *Times Herald* doubted that government-run railroads would do any better. Dr. Fred Lohrstorfer of Port Huron, though an automobile owner (and bad driver), nevertheless spoke up against "railroad whacking": "The state of Michigan through its lawmakers has fixed the rates for passengers and freight so low in order to curry favor with the voters that the result is starvation. Hundreds of laws are on the statute books, and other hundreds are introduced every year which are designed to hamper or harass the railroads."(42) When Michigan's railroads asked for a 5% rate increase in order to assure a 6% return on capital, the attorney general filed a 26 page brief against it. Meanwhile, the auto and gasoline industries raised and lowered their prices with abandon, the FMC earned 60% on its capital in one year, and 45,000 Michigan railroad workers for performing an invaluable service made less than half of what Ford's $5 per day men did for turning out junk.

92% of Michigan's population lived within five miles of a railroad station.(43) Most of the nation, by the more colorful measurement of historian John Stover, within the sound of a train whistle. Across 260,000 miles of track, freight moved at the rate of 366 billion ton-miles annually at mid-decade, like the 3 million oranges which landed one year in Port Huron. A 10 lb. package could be expressed from Port Huron to New York for 40 cents. U.S. rail passengers racked up 35 billion yearly miles, including those on the 40 passenger trains in and out of Port Huron daily. Railroads built showplace new train stations across the country. In 1913 the Michigan Central opened

145

its 17-story cathedral in Detroit, with a lobby supported by 68-foot pillars almost on an Egyptian scale of grandeur. The giant Pennsylvania and Grand Central stations in New York City made their debuts, and so did the humble but sturdy Pere Marquette brick rebuild in Port Huron.

At the railroad cash register, the 1916 gross of $3.8 billion resulted in a net of $1 billion, for a 5% return on the $21 billion invested in America's system. According to historian Stover, the trains "were clearly taking care of the nation's transportation needs, even though those needs were growing with explosive speed." They helped especially take care of Henry Ford's explosive needs at his new Rouge River auto factory. Universal Henry bought his own railroad, the 454-mile Detroit, Trenton, and Ironton, to bring raw materials in and carry automobiles out. "The railroads will always continue to be the great democratic highway for the mass of the people," said the *Times Herald*, but the Michigan Central RR hedged its bets, and ordered hundreds more automobile carriers in 1916.

Valiantly, a trio of Bay City, Michigan brothers, the Handys, actually built a new steam railroad across the Thumb in the face of all the railbaiting during this decade. Their Detroit, Bay City and Western railroad, usually called just the Handy, methodically worked its way from city to city, opening a new section every year or so, heading for Port Huron and eventually, they hoped, Detroit. The pace of American railroad building had slowed to such an extent that the 100 miles of track the Handy laid down between 1912 and 1917 amounted to 10% of all the new railroad track in America during those five years. The Handy built its line to last, with sidings every mile and masonry train stations along the route. The Commercial Bank in Port Huron welcomed this by proclaiming "We Cannot Have Too Many Railroads Entering This City."

Oh yes we can, said enough auto-warped people, and Port Huron refused to allow the Handy to build any new tracks into the city or erect a new train station. When the Handy Line arrived in Port Huron in February 1917, it had to use facilities owned by the Pere Marquette and Grand Trunk, not an ideal situation. On top of that, the Chamber of Commerce reneged on a $40,000 bonus it had promised the DBCW. Nevertheless these trainmen pushed on for another 20 miles, as far as Marine City to the south, before the world war intervened. This halted construction for good on one of the last new railroads ever built in Michigan. When another group of financiers tried to launch a $3 million, 235-mile railroad connecting 40 different communities through mid-Michigan in 1919, regulators practically laughed them out of the state capitol, by then controlled lock, stock and barrel by the automobile industry.

In spite of all the brave talk about cars, trucks, and tanks changing the face of war in WW1, the railroads actually decided the outcome. A superior railroad system brought the Central Powers to the brink of what would have been history's most incredible military victory. A wave of material and manpower reinforcement assembled by America's rail network for shipment to Europe eventually carried the Allies to their ultimate triumph. Freight loads on some American railroads surged 25% almost overnight after the war declaration. To stop some of it, German agents plotted but failed to blow up the St. Clair River Tunnel in Port Huron to destroy a vital pinch point on the rail network. American railroads functioned so quickly in the war crisis that they delivered supplies to Eastern seaboard ports faster than ships could take them away. Loaded freight cars sat idle, a situation for which, incredibly, the government blamed the train companies. 25 years later the Michigan Railroad Association still seethed about this, and a spokesman let loose at a Port Huron luncheon:

The trouble then arose from a misuse, not a proper use, of the railroads by the government that finally caused the standing on sidings of 224,000 loaded cars that could neither be unloaded nor moved for months. War hysteria, not war traffic, caused the problem.(44)

In December 1917 Woodrow Wilson authorized the government takeover of the railroads for the war's duration (compared to the hands-off policy on auto companies). He appointed his son-in-law, Treasury Secretary William McAdoo, to run them. McAdoo had acquired some practical railroad industry experience before entering the government, and probably knew the administration was completely unprepared to handle this task, but under the circumstances he couldn't give Wilson a flat-out no. An utter fiasco ensued, as McAdoo aides ordered both higher wages and new equipment without adequate rate hikes to pay for them. They neglected maintenance, muddled scheduling, and even with dictatorial powers only managed a 2% increase in railroad delivery performance.

America's 2 million railroad workers got into the habit of telling customers infuriated by the McAdoo mess, "Don't blame us, the government is running things now," until McAdoo ordered this finger-pointing stopped. The federal train overseers incurred a $1.8 billion loss in a little over two years of operation, then after grabbing additional permanent regulatory control, handed back to private ownership in 1920 a railroad system so utterly fouled up it took years to recover, and in some respects never did.(45) The war experience clearly demonstrated the need for federal financial support in maintaining the track system so vital to the nation's defense, to put it on the same open pocketbook basis the nation's highways now enjoyed. Instead, Washington looked the other way.

On the light rail/trolley scene during this decade supporters made a final effort in 1911-1912 to realize the lingering dream of interurban service running north from Port Huron. Big-timers Henry McMorran, ex-streetcar boss William Canham, and Louis Weil all put their shoulders to the wheel in a futile effort to get the IU extended, and this seemed especially big of McMorran, who'd been banged up in a recent Rapid Railway crash. The Thumb District Improvement Association, 200 businessmen strong, agreed new service would be a boon to the entire region. Virtually every burg in the Thumb endorsed the interurban plan, more than 17 in all, offering subsidy money and even free rights-of-way.

His mass transit interest revived, William Canham ingeniously proposed using gasoline-powered interurban cars as a cost-saving measure, rather than string electric cables along the route. Port Huron voters approved by an awesome 18-1 margin a franchise for Canham's new interurban company, the Port Huron & Northern. But the enthusiasm waned when Canham revealed that he still needed a $100,000 stock subscription to get going. That money never appeared. A regional government alliance in the Thumb might have forged an arrangement with Canham to lay down publicly-owned tracks and lease them to him, but the public initiative needed for such an effort couldn't be mounted, as automobile conceit ate up more and more resources.

The top interurban man in the state, native Port Huroner George Moore,

147

admitted in 1911 that IU construction in Michigan had come virtually to a standstill, despite the fact that more than 20 existing systems carried a combined 200 million passengers per year, demonstrating the demand. As many as seven passenger cars at a time linked together on the Rapid Railway to handle the mob during busy periods. The Rapid carried more and more freight as well, everything from coal to newspapers to iron castings to broom corn to package express.(46) So what held up expansion? Said Moore: "Unfavorable legislation and the attitude of municipal authorities have combined to retard the construction of interurban railroads in Michigan to such an extent that the state is today farther behind in interurban railways than any of the populous states in the central west. The state today needs several hundred miles of interurban railways constructed to serve its needs and to keep it abreast with the trolley development of its sister states."(47)

Moore ran one of the best engineered IU's in the country through mid-Michigan, but he envied those in Indiana and Ohio. Ten different trolley lines, for instance, used Toledo for a hub. That meant Port Huron passengers could take the Rapid to Detroit, then on to Toledo, and eventually as far as Indianapolis, 350 miles away, on electric rail sleeper service overnight. The excellent Indianapolis IUs promised same-day express package delivery anywhere within 75 miles of that city. Surpassing even the service in the Midwest, or any in the world for that matter, out in exotic Los Angeles the Pacific Electric Railway, with 1,600 trains daily, gave that region the finest ground transportation system America ever had, or ever would have during the 20th Century.(48) Later historians pegged 1917 as the high water mark for service on America's streetcars and interurbans.

The service high water started to recede in Port Huron. The meager profits of the government-hobbled Detroit United Railways (7% in a good year) didn't allow the DUR to meet requests from its customers for wider Port Huron area service. 200 west side families petitioned for a streetcar extension. So did people living farther out along the banks of the Black River west of town, where Captain William Bonnan offered to donate half a mile of frontage on the Black and 40 acres for a park if the streetcars ever ran out that way. Another 1,700 riders asked for more streetcars on existing routes inside the city. The DUR had no capital to do any of these things. Though Port Huron's streetcars carried 5 million passengers in 1920, the company lost almost five cents per head due to the five cent fare frozen into the 1899 franchise. The inflation brought on by WW1 made that an unsustainably low price. Especially in view of the competition on the streets. When President Wilson appointed a federal commission to look into the electric rail industry's future at the end of the decade, its report named the automobile as one of the main threats.(49)

Port Huron's marine fortunes had a mixed decade. Still indisputably the cheapest way to go (Port Huron to Detroit round trip $1.25 on the *Tashmoo*) passenger lines on the Great Lakes managed to withstand the onslaught of the automobile. Some lines experienced their best years ever. A popular amusement spot on the boat routes like St. Clair County's Tashmoo Park was "plastered with people" on busy days. Whether for pleasure or business or convenience 360 million passengers traveled by steam vessel on the Great Lakes in 1920, 99.9999% of them in complete safety.

Freight business continued in a healthy state. And efficient. Sending a bushel of grain 1,000 miles on the Lakes cost 2 cents. The Port Huron and Duluth shipping line's massive warehouse in Port Huron sometimes held more than 300 railroad cars worth of flour. One of the grain elevators in town bulged with a million bushels. Hundreds of men still made their living working on the docks and ships, drawing a total payroll from local shipping companies of more than $600,000 a year. Dozens of vessels in winter and summer made Port Huron their home port. An important government marine inspection station licensed 160 officers and inspected 65 vessels in 1920.

It's true that a once-in-a-century anomaly, the monstrous Great Lakes storm of 1913, destroyed 19 vessels across the region, including three 500-footers, stranded many more, and drowned over 250 sailors, large numbers of them in wrecks near Port Huron. But nothing stopped 48 million tons of iron ore from transiting the Soo Locks in that same year of 1913, much of it destined for the auto industry. Or stopped the 1913 construction near Detroit of the big new *North American* and *South American* passenger ships, familiar sights in Port Huron for the next 50 years.

In the matter of local ship construction things didn't go so well in Port Huron. The last attempt to rejoin the big leagues occurred when the New York-based Foundation Company took over the city's largest drydock from the Reid family. Foundation planned a huge expansion at this St. Clair River facility during the frantic shipbuilding boom of WW1, when other yards on the Lakes built 400 new merchant ships.(50) Foundation landed a big contract of its own, and obliging Port Huron officials actually re-routed Main Street around the shipyard to give the place more room. Then came the unexpected: peace. The fighting stop before a single ship could be launched. After a few feeble efforts to get some civilian business, Foundation threw in the towel, and shut down. The Reids meanwhile decided to reallocate their capital into entertainment, and bought the Family movie theater and City Auditorium.

Did America make enough use of its inland waterways during this decade? It didn't seem to, according to a 1912 federal report. Investigators said railroads exerted too much influence over domestic shipping and canals (they controlled 90% of private canals) and stifled both to eliminate competition. This report originated from an order given by Theodore Roosevelt during his presidency, so its anti-railroad theme can't be relied on entirely. In any case the passage of Panama Canal Act during this decade subsequently banned railroad ownership of ships and canals unless okayed by the Interstate Commerce Commission. This did not do much to reinvigorate canal-building. The trans-Michigan canal idea which had been proposed a decade earlier didn't budge an inch.

To get illustrative here, the federal government threw $22 billion away on WW1. That kind of dough could have built the equivalent of four Panama Canals worth of waterway improvements in America, and spurred a concomitant increase in marine activity. Or it might have doubled all the railroad, streetcar, and interurban track mileage in the country. Compared to the $7.5 billion tab Americans paid for automobiles and roads per year by 1920 the idea doesn't seem so outlandish.

One other important transportation method of the future landed from time to time in Port Huron during the decade. For 25 cents per head aviator Jimmy Ward amazed the populace with some demo flying in his Curtiss biplane at the Driving Park in 1911. In 1914 noted pilot Lincoln Beachy barnstormed through St. Clair County, and announced that, "Within ten years there will be few automobiles except for trucking purposes. They will all be flying, and it will far safer than any earth or water transportation..."(51) Nine months later Beachey died in a plane crash in San Francisco. A Detroit native, William Boeing, started his own airplane company in Seattle in 1916, with money his family made in lumber. The federal government tried to get commercial use of airplanes off the ground in 1918 by awarding some air mail contracts, with pathetic results. The tiny deliveries arrived no faster than on railroads, and pilots often had to use train tracks to find their way across the countryside. Nevertheless 15 federal air fields had been established coast to coast by 1920, yet another sad contrast to the railroad non-support in Washington.(52)

St. Clair County's bicyclists came under increasing automobile attack on the streets and roads during this decade. When a woman motorist ran down Joseph Brown while he pedaled along in Port Huron, she paused only long enough to tell him, "I am glad I hit you," before driving away; a fairly convincing example of the callousness that automobiles unleashed in even the fair sex. Pavements made drivers ever more reckless and impatient, but about three-quarters of Port Huron's streets remained unpaved, and bicyclists found them somewhat safer, except for the dust. Cars using the dirt streets in summer kicked up so much dust, choking bikers, walkers, and homeowners alike, that Port Huron in 1912 resorted to applications of calcium chloride to try to keep the dust down.

Business still made extensive use of the bicycle in delivering groceries and whatnot around Port Huron. Western Union bought 5,000 per year for its messengers all over America, and these cyclers sometimes covered as much as 120 miles per day.(53) Commuter biking enjoyed a brief revival during WW1, when the streetcars filled up with war workers while auto production tailed off slightly. Sturmer Hardware, one of 10 bike dealers and repair shops in Port Huron, made the point.

A Good Bicycle for the Man who Works – In the office, shop, or factory, one that will get you to work on time and bring you home early. No trouble on the way, no cars to wait for, just the smooth, easy peddling, economical way of transportation. A good bicycle offers greater returns to you, both through the big saving in car fare and the health giving rides which it renders to you.

Health giving, unless some nincompoop in an automobile got you in her sights, as Joseph Brown found out. No such thing as bicycle rider insurance appeared in Port Huron, though motorcyclists could get some. After the Armistice America largely relegated bicycle use to the young, and the government at every level wholly ignored two-wheelers as a practical method of transportation.

The obnoxious presence of the automobile intruded more and more into the lives of pedestrians, as we've seen. This alarmed even the Census Bureau, which warned in 1920: "Each year it becomes more and more dangerous for a person to walk the streets." Port Huron school children walking to class, even along the city's 110 miles of sidewalks, took some real chances, since they had to cross one of the increasingly dangerous streets someplace, and might end up like Grant Thomas. Teenage girls read conflicting advice in the *Times Herald* about the advisability of country walking among the growing numbers of motor vehicles. One week it said: *... for the average enthusiastic, wholesome American girl, nothing could be more of a lark, afford greater pleasure, nor be of more real benefit than a hike of a week or ten days through the country.* But on second thought, a couple weeks later it suggested: *For the athletic college girl, looking for an opportunity to spend her vacation in some healthful,*

150

profitable and enjoyable manner, what would be more delightful than for her to secure a position as chauffeur for some woman who owns a car, and does not care to drive it herself.(54)

Many a fool credited the automobile with improving the nation's health during this decade and later, with which it had nothing to do. Just the opposite, in fact. It inflicted thousands of deaths (9,100 in 1920), hundreds of thousands of injuries, and the Jacobs Effect on the riders who made 5 billion automobile journeys in 1920. Some eugenics promoters expected the automobile to improve American mating habits and thus intelligence, by bringing a wider variety of gals within driving range of guys. But no super race appeared. Michigan Governor and eugenicist Woodbridge Ferris wanted lovers to pass an IQ test before getting a marriage license. He should have demanded an intelligence test for a driver's license. But then, if you wanted to drive an automobile in the first place, you'd already failed.

The automobile became more prominent in the arts. Movies gradually began displacing much of the live theater in Port Huron, and many patrons watched director D. W. Griffith make a hero out of a car in his 1916 film *Intolerance*. In this tale, the relatives of an innocent man facing the gallows recklessly chased down by automobile a train carrying the state governor, in order to halt the execution. Griffith wasn't intolerant of madcap driving, obviously, and suffered from the same moral tunnel vision most motorists did, never questioning whether the fate of one person justified the endangerment of scores or hundreds of other lives along the roads.

Much of the time, though, movie cars tickled the funny bone, driven crazily around by the Keystone Kops and others, colliding, running over cliffs, or occasionally knocking people down for comic effect. Comic, since the "victim" never bled to death in her mother's lap like Margaret Wolfstyn. Charlie Chaplin's film *A Day's Pleasure* milked the mechanical failings of the auto for all they were worth: "Talk about self-starter! There's laugh ignition in every spin of Charlie's sick-cylindered engine."

In literature, the tragedy of the automobile furnished America with one of its greatest novels of the 20th Century, *The Magnificanet Ambersons*, published by Booth Tarkington in 1918. The veteran author made his fictional automobile entrepreneur Eugene Morgan, someone not unlike Henry Ford, the finest man in town. A spoiled, shiftless brat by the name of George Minifer played the automobile hater. Despite this ironic twist, Tarkington made no secret of where his own loathing lay, when he described an automobile disturbing the quiet of a summer's evening in a Midwestern city which could have doubled for Port Huron:

Then, like a cowboy shooting up a peaceful camp, a frantic devil would hurtle out of the distance, bellowing, exhaust racketing like a machine gun gone amuck - and at these horrid sounds the surreys and buggies would hug the curbstone, and the bicycles would scatter to cover, cursing; while children rushed from the sidewalks to drag pet dogs from the street. The thing would roar by, leaving a long wake of turbulence; then the indignant street would quiet down for a few minutes – till another came.(55)

As well as noisier, Port Huron by 1920 had grown bigger, to about 25,000 people, a 37% increase from the 1910 census. This didn't compare to the mad expansion down in Detroit, which almost quadrupled in population to nearly a million people between 1900 and 1920. Oldtimers in Detroit didn't entirely welcome this. When the auto men congratulated themselves for backing a new city symphony, one veteran Detroiter said he'd rather do without the symphony and without the auto industry, and just get his quiet town back.

As to whether Port Huron became more prosperous, it depended on how you defined prosperity. Auto-related businesses employed an increasing number of persons, but the local economy expanded in other ways, too. New businesses big and small sprang up during the decade, notably the Port Huron Paper Company (founded by the Haynes lumber family), the new bean warehouse downtown, and especially the Mueller Brass Company. None other than Oscar Mueller, the racing flash from Decatur, Illinois, the hero of the country's first auto race in Chicago in 1895, opened his family's branch factory in Port Huron to make brass shell casings for the war, and he stayed on afterward to manufacture a wide variety of plumbing devices, and auto parts.

The men's Maccabees fraternity may haved moved away, but the ladies version remained, and their leader Bina West ordered a huge new classical-style headquarters built at the south end of the business district. Bina indulged her passion for pageantry at both the groundbreaking and the dedication, overflowing the city hotels with thousands of Lady Macs, moving them across town to the building site in a snakeline of automobiles on the big day. Bands, choirs, speeches, and prayers rent the air before the ladies enjoyed a final soiree at Bina's riverfront mansion, Westhaven. She'd never leave Port Huron, said Bina.

Plenty of other people still found their share of contentment in the city. Visitor William Nicoll's family spent 8-10 weeks every summer at the Windemere Hotel on the lake. "Port Huron was such a delightful place," said William, who remembered "many, many pleasant trips to Detroit on the *Tashmoo*, even now and then on the interurban line." In its hotels and 400 waterfront cottages Port Huron continued to entertain several conventions a year plus tens of thousands of vacationers. Foolishly, one such couple chose to drive their automobile all the way from Independence, Missouri on their honeymoon, ignoring a dozen better transportation alternatives. But, according to their daughter, after checking into the Harrington Hotel, they found it had been worth the journey:

From Chicago the honeymooners motored to Detroit and Port Huron, Michigan. North of that city there were (and still are) miles of golden beaches on vast Lake Huron. The air was marvelously free of summertime Missouri's awful humidity and scorching heat. For the rest of his life, whenever Harry Truman wanted to regain the radiance of those first days with Bess, he simply wrote: 'Port Huron.' For him it was a code word for happiness. (56)

152

Chapter 5. 1921-1930: The Hour of Bedlam

It is the hour of bedlam on the boulevard – 5 o'clock in the afternoon. As far as the eye can see, one seething stream of motor cars – humanity at the end of the day fighting its way home – fender to fender, Running The Rapids of a modern Rush Hour. All the traffic confusion is just one meaningless blur. There is no focus. You see no one person in particular – no one car in particular attracts your attention. You are conscious of automobiles milling In The Mass. And subconsciously you feel rather than see in the set jaws and sharp eyes the Strain of it all – for driving today, by and large, is less of a joy and much more of an ordeal than it once was. Will the brakes hold? Is there space wide enough for two fenders? Instinctively you know that everyone is thinking these same thoughts – experiencing this same dread. And the miracle of it all is that anything could come out of it intact – that shining fenders and burnished glass can endure – that any man-built, man-handled machine can battle its way through for one single block And Live. (1)

So said the Wills Sainte Claire company in one of its sales brochures as it commenced building its Gray Goose models in Marysville. Yes, Harold Wills meant this all-too-accurate description of American city driving, a sobering dose of the real world behind the usual Empty Roads advertising fantasy, to promote automobile sales, by convincing the mark that the Wills' Goose could wing its way through the bedlam of the boulevard in some magical way unknown to its competitors. Wills rolled the first production versions of his 10-foot long, V8-powered, 3,000 lb. car out the door of the Marysville factory on February 19, 1921. Port Huron's civic leaders put aside their qualms about the project for the moment and surrendered themselves to dionysian riot.

"Rejoice, rejoice, the day of days is at hand!" is how the auto dealers association put it. The real estate board said: "The new day is dawning. The metamorphosis is here. Port Huron today stands on the threshold of unlimited possibilities as the result of the faith, the will power, the ability and the stamina of C. Harold Wills, John R. Lee and their associates." The Ford Motor Company ponied up for a full-page congratulatory ad in a *Times Herald* supplement packed full of them. A staff writer lovingly profiled Wills himself as the meticulous craftsman, ever watchful over the busy bees of the assembly line:

As the engine purred away on the testing block, Mr. Wills pointed to a few drops of oil, a slight leak. "We can easily stop that up," suggested a mechanic. Instantly Mr. Wills turned to him. "That isn't the way the Wills car will be built," he replied. "Take it down and do it right."(2)

Later, suspecting another unacceptable flaw had crept in, the obsessive Wills rammed one of his cars backwards into a sandpit 50 times until an axle broke. "I knew something wasn't right," he said.

153

300 people crowded their way into the Harrington Hotel five days later for one of the biggest banquets in memory, a regular bacchanal in honor of the Wills Sainte Claire. In the custom of these occasions, the Chamber of Commerce singers serenaded the guest of honor:

Howdy-do, Mr. Wills, howdy-do.
Is there anything that we can do for you?
We are with you to a man.
We'll do anything we can.
Howdy-do, Mr. Wills, howdy do-do-do.

$12 million had been invested in the Wills company thus far, and 1,000 men put to work at the factory, the vanguard of the expected 39,000 to follow. John Black, who had succeeded Frank Church as the local Dodge dealer, signed up as the Wills Sainte Claire man in Port Huron, one of 150 representatives nationwide. Smiling Billy Metzger handled the Wills brand in Detroit.

Yet, once order and sobriety had been re-established in Port Huron after the inauguration festivities, the uneasiness over the Wills project resurfaced. With a shyness befitting a June bride, Wills withheld the exact car prices from his advertising. Instead his first messages of allurement somewhat bafflingly described the Goose as the "Mol-lyb-den-um Car," a nod to Wills' interest in metallurgy, and a replay of the big noise made over the vanadium steel used in the Model T. When the Elks lodge gave away a Wills during a St. Clair County Centennial contest that summer, the winner said he would sell his molybdenum car and get a cheaper brand. Sales started slowly. Wills had launched into the teeth of the 1920-21 depression, and found the market overloaded with high-priced cars like Cadillac, Packard and Pierce Arrow.

Even before the day of days arrived Port Huron's increasing economic dependence on the erratic performance of the auto industry, especially during this latest business slump, had prompted concern. "Resumption of work in automobile factories will do much toward returning Port Huron's manufactory to normal," reported the *Times Herald* hopefully, "as many of the local plants are engaged in manufacturing parts for various automobile concerns."(3) Insiders claimed that Port Huron produced parts for virtually every car in America, which even allowing for hometown exaggeration equaled a lot of parts. 300,000 Americans now made their livings in auto assembly plants, millions more worked to turn out and sell auto parts and accessories. 35,000 car dealers employed 100,000 salesmen and phalanxes of repairmen. The true total included several slippery figures, things like steel and glass and gasoline, but some calculators reckoned that one tenth of the country's wage-earners toiled directly or indirectly on behalf of its 3rd largest industry. The percentage naturally was massively higher in Marysville, a company town through and through. Disconcertingly, just six months after his howdy do-do-do, Wills cut his workforce back to 600 men, and sliced Goose prices by $400, meaning the roadster, coupe and sedan now retailed for $2,875; $3,750; and $4,100; or six times a Model T's tab.

Wills then reached 20 years back into the past for some kind of attention-getting stunt, and revived the Detroit-to-New York City endurance run used by Ransom Olds for his Oldsmobile in 1901. In Wills' case, he did the driving himself, leaving Detroit in a Goose at a speed-limit-shattering pace that left a trail of frightened motorists and furious traffic cops all the way to New York. Wills blew out a tire at

Mount Clemens, Michigan, barely 20 miles into this odyssey, and in making up time afterward spectators saw just a "whizz of dust" as he passed his Marysville factory at more than 60 miles per hour. After pausing in Port Huron to get chewed out by the police for speeding, Wills unmindfully forged ahead into Canada at a similar velocity, where the unkempt roads administered a savage beating to him and his passengers. Battered reporter E. A. Batchelor testified, "Probably no car ever has taken such bumps at such a rate of speed for so long a time before; none probably could have stood it." Somehow Wills covered the whole 689 miles in 20 hours and 36 minutes of bedlam, And Lived. He averaged just over 33 miles per hour. This impressed nobody, since Wills still could have taken a train and gotten there faster, a lot more safely, and a lot more comfortably.

Sales and production of the Wills Ste. Claire rose and fell in the following months. Sometimes 1,000 workers went back on the job and completed 80 cars a week, sometimes nobody and nothing, a complete shutdown. Wills cut prices another $400, and issued one optimistic statement after another, hoping the 1922 rebound in the car industry would float his boat, too. But only 6,000 Geese had been delivered when bankruptcy dropped by Wills headquarters in November 1922. A "distinct feeling of depression" hung in the air of Marysville at this point. Wills' partner John Lee took to the lifeboats and departed. Rumors flew that Henry Ford planned to come to the rescue, and buy up the Wills as an expensive addition to the FMC line. Maybe Henry thought about it, but he decided instead to purchase the bankrupt Lincoln car company, and make it the Universal Car for the rich.

Wills rebuilt his leaky enterprise with fresh funds. He took it down and did it right, he hoped, and pressed on for four more dispiriting years, refusing to admit defeat. "We have turned the corner and nothing can stop us now." Another endurance drive, this one in 1925, crossed the entire U.S., New York to San Francisco. A 50 year-old ex-bicycle racer named Louis Miller, "...riding and driving without sleep or rest of any kind," pulled into Frisco after 102 frazzled hours at the wheel of a Wills. In the Himalayas of American stupidity about cars, Miller's drive certainly ascended one of the notable peaks, but no law anywhere in the country limited how long a driver could remain continuously at the wheel of a private automobile, unlike, for instance, a locomotive engineer. Commerce had imitated Hollywood with this Miller-Wills stunt. Not long before it took place, *The Drivin' Fool*, starring Wally Van, a motion picture of this era in tune with automobile follies, appeared at the new Desmond Theater in Port Huron, promising movie fans "You will follow him from coast to coast in a wild dash to save his father's fortune."

That fool Miller's drivin' marathon saved nothing. The last Goose gasp came in November 1926 when the company closed. In six years Wills had built 14,000 cars, fewer than the FMC turned out in a week. Many other firms suffered a similar fate. While the number of motor vehicles in America tripled during the 1920s, to more than 26 million, the number of automakers shrank from 108 to 44.(4) Compounding his woes, Wills' Marysville Land Company also went bankrupt. Some of its building lot customers sued. Wills had promised them a city of 100,000 people – ok, where was it? After peaking at a population of 2,000, Marysville deflated to a town of 700 lost souls. (5)

It's doubtful if Wills' travails wrung more than a *tsk-tsk* or an occasional chuckle out of Henry Ford. Apart from building one million passenger cars in America and Canada combined in 1921, then 1.8 million in 1922, plus trucks plus tractors, Ford busied himself completing work on his autobiography, *My Life and Work*, one of the most fascinating memoirs ever published by a great man.(6) It's futile to expect complete consistency from anyone telling his life's story, great or small, and readers of *MLW* certainly didn't get it from Ford. Nevertheless, this concoction of some genuinely brilliant insights and business maxims, some self-serving contradictions and untruths, some musings and meanderings and just raw independence of outlook, made compelling reading. Ford's was a mind unlike any other.

My *Life and Work* found its way onto the book tables of everyone from church ministers to Adolph Hitler. Ford won special admiration in the USSR, and during the 1920's he signed a $30 million contract to build a car factory there. The automobile furnished *My Life and Work* with both its major theme and its major flaw, as Ford awkwardly tried to rationalize this device. The inefficiency and waste inherent in the auto, and the disorder it spread far and wide, just weren't congenial with his character, and a kind of defensiveness about this ran through the entire book. In one tail-chasing passage, Ford simultaneously hailed the automobile as both an economy and an indulgence. One should save to spend, spend to save. Spending was the "sap of living." And so on.

I've probably been a little too pejorative of Henry Ford to this point and it's only being fair to this remarkable if misguided man to look more closely at some of his good points, and he had very many. So many that he stood at the pinnacle of his popularity in America in the early 20's, and there was considerable enthusiasm to see him elected President. Both political parties urged him in 1924 to run for the top job, which he graciously declined, prompting a rare outburst of genuine emotion, gratitude, from the eventual winner Calvin Coolidge. People couldn't help but admire a man who'd made a billion dollars from scratch in 20 years, whose empire spread into 21 nations by the end of the decade.(7) "Activities of Henry Ford Embrace Nearly Every Conceivable Sort of Undertaking," said one newspaper profile seen by Port Huroners, and it didn't overstate the case. And Ford's fearless opposition to the world war by now had converted the country almost completely. Public revulsion for that debacle turned the U.S. against the one good thing that might have come from it, the League of Nations. Without American support the League withered away as surely as the Wills Sainte Claire.

Almost everything in life interested Henry Ford. Unlike General Motors' Alfred Sloan, who regretfully admitted to being a very narrow man, scarcely a topic of his time failed to excite Ford's curiosity. Good health, for instance. What could be more important than that? It all began at home. No coffee, tea, tobacco, liquor or white bread. Drink plenty of water and don't neglect enough "mastication" at chow time. His son Edsel's later indulgence in the smoking and alcohol vices disgusted Ford, who promised to fire any employee except Edsel caught drinking in a speakeasy or even at home. Henry ate abstemiously, he liked his vegetables, and he kept himself in superb shape. He remembered to use his feet often. While building his Dearborn estate Fair Lane he occasionally walked the 11 miles from his Detroit home out to the building site, stopping to chat with friends along the way.(8) Well into his seventies Ford regularly challenged both young and old visitors at Fair Lane to foot races, and entertained them with handstands. He ice skated, he chopped wood. If not a tireless worker, he tirelessly

156

supervised workers, and regularly wore out subordinates at the office, the factory, and the laboratory.

Given this, it hardly could have escaped Henry's notice that the automobile sometimes negated a healthy lifestyle in a flash. All his life Ford drove dangerously, ran up a pile of speeding tickets, raised his own whizz of dust that could be seen a mile away along country roads, and occasionally launched his car airborne over raised railroad crossings.(9) Ford euphoria gripped him when he got behind the wheel, certain in his mind that nothing could harm him. Nothing that is until he finally suffered a bad accident. In March 1927, while out for a Sunday evening drive, Henry ran off the road, down an embankment, and slammed into a tree. Dazed and confused from some sort of unspecified head injury, like many another victim of his products, Ford stumbled home to Fair Lane on foot, and had to be carted to the Henry Ford Hospital in Detroit for an operation. It's entirely possible that some of the strokes he reportedly suffered during the last 20 years of his life stemmed from the after effects of this wreck, sustained at the age of 63.

Happily for Henry, the hospital named for him stood ready to administer this aid. Part of Ford's thinking on healthy living concerned medical care. Hospitals served a useful purpose in cleaning up after car accidents alright, but as Henry saw it they needed to clean up their act as well. "It is not at all certain whether hospitals as they are now managed exist for patients or for doctors," said Ford.(10) When the movement to build a general hospital in Detroit ground to a halt for lack of money in 1914, Ford shouldered the burden himself, and spent $9 million during the next seven years to complete it. At Ford's, all the doctors worked on staff at fixed salaries, all the patients occupied private and identical rooms and paid a flat $4.50 per day for them. A major operation, if that's what Henry needed for his headbone after his crash, cost him a standard $125. Ford also built a hospital at the Rouge River plant, where busted up employees sometimes did light work in bed in order to stay on full wages.

Ford's were two of the 9,000 hospitals across America at the opening of the 20's. By then the 1905 version of the Port Huron Hospital had doubled in size to 60 beds. The annual number of patients and revenues had multiplied another 400% at this nominally "non-profit" facility. It hadn't grown as fast as the Ford Motor Company, but considerable. Americans now spent $1.5 million per day on doctors and $3 million per day on hospitals. How much of that they wasted (as Henry suspected) no one could say. A traffic accident victim limped or was carried through the doors at Port Huron Hospital every few days. The staff did its best, for instance, with 75 year-old minister John Lomas, run over by an auto on Main Street, but he gave up the ghost following a short stay, after having had both legs amputated.

Henry Ford did not neglect public health measures, which added most of the 10 years to increased American life expectancy between 1900 and 1930. He'd been miles out in front on the subject of purifying drinking water and milk, two of the most important medical improvements of the century. Port Huron chlorinated its water and pasteurized its milk by the 1920's, but Ford had begun corresponding with his old boss George Westinghouse as early as 1911 about treating these beverages with ultraviolet rays.(11) Ford built a water filtration plant on the Rouge River at Fair Lane, which furnished clean water not just to himself but to the city of Dearborn, the fastest growing city in America during the 20s. Yet here again, Ford's products cut across his

Progressive beliefs. Just a couple of miles down the Rouge, the 2,000 acre FMC plant, which operated the world's largest steel foundry and a dozen other divisions, converted the river at that point into a filthy orange mess. Building an automobile required one of the dirtiest manufacturing processes in existence, right up there with gasoline refining.

Henry Ford the nature lover served as a board member of the Audubon Society, built 500 birdhouses all over Fair Lane, and lobbied for federal protection of migratory species. He practiced selective timber harvesting on the half a million acres of Michigan's Upper Peninsula forest land he'd bought to obtain wood for his car bodies. To husband the resources he extracted from the land, Ford became one of the great original American recyclers. Sickened by any kind of waste, he converted leftover automaking remains that didn't end up in the river into everything from fertilizer to 100 tons of charcoal briquettes a day.(12)

To commune with the natural world, Henry regularly sallied forth on camping trips into the semi-wilderness in the company of Edison and tire king Harvey Firestone. He cooled his feet in a Maryland stream for one photograph captioned "Henry Ford, the Barefoot Boy." But Henry naturally made his celebrated camping trips by automobile, the very ruination of America the Beautiful. Ford simply couldn't see the disconnection Frederick Olmsted had warned about, between the arcadia he sought and the desolation he left behind. Ford owners despoiled America's national and state and municipal parks with exactly the kind of mechanical, visual, and environmental clutter the parks had been established to keep out. Port Huron changed what once had been a pleasant lane through Pine Grove Park into parking spaces, and similarly the new Lakeport State Park half a dozen miles north of Port Huron leveled several acres of woods to make room for 1,500 parked cars. America sometimes wrought monumental destruction on itself in the name of the automobile. "Face of Mountain Blasted Off to Make Way for Scenic Motor Road Along Coast Near Los Angeles," ran one headline.

By the end of the 1920's Ford had to plant lines of trees across Fair Lane to shield his 56-room home from the automobile racket on the state highway that ran past his property. Millions of Model T owners routed and pulverized the wildlife in the suburbs and countryside, while trashing the roadsides with junk. The St. Clair County Road Commission raged not only at the auto-deposited garbage but also at the illegal gas station and restaurant signs that appeared overnight along its improved highways almost before the gravel settled or the concrete cured. Autos similarly fouled every street and alleyway in the cities. Abandoned Model T's posed such a nuisance in New York City that Queens Borough president George Harvey wrote to Ford that he should try recycling his cars for a change: "We have yet to find an effective method to combat this Frankenstein monster...I think your company should bear a large part of the responsibility of the abandoned car problem."(13) The truth was plain as day by this time: nobody who owned or drove an automobile could be a nature lover or a conservationist.

He hadn't dazzled anybody in school himself, but Ford kept the subject of education close at heart. He built a trade school that flourished for decades, and on one memorable occasion during the 20's he pledged $100 million dollars and re-dedicated the rest of his life to building schools all across America. This latter outburst of pedagogical enthusiasm came during another visit with Edison, whose company often inspired Henry to flights of fancy. Ford didn't go through with re-dedicating his life or spending the $100 mill, but he did keep up a strong interest, and he constructed another unique and lavish town school at his huge living museum named Greenfield Village, near Fair Lane.

Yet, at the same time, two of the most destructive products of the automobile age – the school bus and the misapplication of Fordism – began their mischievous invasion of American education. In 1922 St. Clair County's rural school supervisor Elmer T. Blackney targeted some one-room primary schools for the first in what came to be a countywide wave of consolidation. He'd round up the children, then subject them to the daily risks, discomfort and boredom of riding a school bus into the city of Yale to attend schools there. This relieved them of the exercise they'd gotten walking to school, the familiar personal instruction at the neighborhood schoolhouse, and the unique atmosphere of working among different aged pupils in a single classroom. Great work, Elmer.

18,000 rural school districts across America had adopted similar plans by the early 20's. The payoff from mass production and economies of scale in education supposedly came from better facilities and specialized teaching, but according to historian Willard Cochrane, the country really didn't need it:

The graduates of rural primary schools could read advertisements and catalogs with some judgement, understand the content and conditions of contracts they entered into, make rough calculations of enterprise costs and returns, compute simple interest, and in general behave like rational businessmen in the operation of their farms. They could also read their state and local newspapers with pleasure and interest, follow national and community affairs, and participate in an informed way in the political and social affairs of their nation and their community.(14)

Graduates of rural primary schools like Henry Ford.

Ford played a major role in introducing aviation in America. He admired to no end the feats of daring and ingenuity of the Wright brothers, and completed one of his most prized additions to Greenfield Village during the 20's, the original Dayton bicycle shop where the Wrights had invented the airplane. Fascinated by flying, which he said would end war, Ford built one of the first commercial airports in the country in Dearborn and installed a novel radio beacon navigation system. He obtained one of the federal government's first privatized air mail contracts.(15) He helped launch passenger service in the United States with the production of his reliable all-metal Tri-Motor airplane. The Tri fortified the nerves of the air-skittish public primarily because it had two more engines aboard than a Model T did.(16) As reliable as the Tri might be, the federal government took the precaution of testing commercial pilots regularly for vision, coordination and balance, something never done for Ford land pilots.

Charles Lindbergh honored Ford by taking him up as the first ever passenger in the *Spirit of St. Louis* following its transatlantic flight. Lindbergh ordered a dozen Tri-Motors for the nation's first transcontinental air service, and together with Ford helped multiply the number of commercial air travelers in America by 7,000% in four years, to 417,000 by 1930.(17) Ford toyed with the idea of building a single engine Model T-type airplane for mass production, an air flivver, until his test pilot let him down and cracked it up, killing himself. Perhaps even Henry could see what the chaos the automobile had introduced in America at ground level would translate to if put into

159

the air. Ford abandoned the small airplane to small fry builders, like the Buhl aircraft company, which manufactured 1,000 of its Buhl Bulldog single seaters, priced at $12,000 apiece, in the Wills Sainte Claire Marysville factory after Harold Wills gave up on his car.

Of all his various enterprises, nothing quite so confused the farm-raised Henry Ford as his feelings on the subject of agriculture, and this too became part of his legend. Over-production, falling prices, soaring taxes, and new expenses like tractors and artificial fertilizers beat American farmers lower and lower during the 1920's. In 1920-21 alone, crop and livestock prices fell 40%, farmers lost $7 billion, and they abandoned 450,000 farms.(18) The decline of the small farm drove people by the thousands into the factories of industrialists like Ford, and Henry couldn't decide if he liked that or not. It deepened his quandary about how large businesses should be. Sometimes he favored small scale, sometimes huge scale. In *MLW* Ford he said he distrusted large businesses, they robbed owners and workers alike of the personal touch, and at times he felt uneasy over the gigantic size of the FMC. He felt the same way about farms. He ransacked the country for memorabilia to reconstruct at Greenfield Village the family farm life he had known as a boy. Yet he worked diligently overseeing his no-horses experimental farm in Dearborn, trying to bludgeon yet more yield out of thousands of acres with his fleet of Fordson tractors.

For what little respect Ford gave it, you'd have thought the horse had vanished from the face of America by the 1920s. Far from it. 20 million were still in harness, 17 million of them on farms, 13,000 in St. Clair County. The Horse Association of America claimed these animals still did 97% of all field work, which if true pointed to the relative pointlessness of introducing tractors on small farms, which already turned out too much product. "No tractors yet devised have been able to approach the horse in adaptability, reliability and economy in farm work," said the HAA, defiantly. You could buy an average horse for about $70. "I could plow more with five horses than I could with a Ford tractor," said Ray Mudge, who ran the St. Clair County poor farm's 240 acres. It might disgust Henry Ford, but the horse had enough rural friends left to make an annual plowing match inaugurated in St. Clair County in 1924 a fan favorite for decades to come.

In the cities, though, Ford's equine enemies definitely were in retreat. Port Huron horses still pulled vegetable carts and milk wagons, vans for the Michigan Cartage Company, newspaper boys Jack and Wilbur Hamm around their route, grocery and other delivery rigs, even sleighs. But carriages had almost disappeared, according to cartwright Asa Wright, who shifted to auto repair after having built buggies in Port Huron for 57 years. Interest waned in local trotting horse racing, so its owners sold the Port Huron Driving Park for redevelopment. The last horse trough in town was removed.

In search of a farm compromise, Henry Ford tried setting up some small-scale combined factory and farm communities next to the hydroelectric dams - another interest of his - that he'd constructed around Michigan. This way he intended to give auto workers the chance to spend at least half the year farming small plots in the sunshine. Working full time in someplace like a car factory, thought Henry, clearly could be as bad for your health as liquor or white bread.

Men who do the same thing continuously the year around and are shut away from the

160

health of the sun and the spaciousness of the great out of doors are hardly to be blamed if they see matters in a distorted light.(19)

But then, at the end of the decade, as the U.S. farm situation got steadily worse, and even President Herbert Hoover blamed this on the automobile and tractor, Henry did another about-face and reverted to his mass production ethic. He called for the abolishment entirely of the family farm and the total industrialization of agriculture. This kind of spin-o-rama was pure Henry Ford.

Ford also packed this decade with work on a dizzying array of other projects. He managed by remote dictate a 2.5 million acre tire rubber plantation in Brazil, in a spot he named Fordlandia. He experimented with mass produced housing construction. He expanded his film company into the world's largest, and he briefly owned and operated his own radio station. And speaking of seeing matters in a distorted light, Ford published his own newspaper, the *Dearborn Independent*, which regularly lashed imaginary Jewish conspirators for trying to take over the country. And he undertook much more still, but we'd better veer off here, or this thing will turn into a Henry Ford biography.

Back to the T and back to the Thumb. The Willsmobile may have dominated the local headlines in this region for a while, but the Model T still ruled the sales roost in Port Huron for the first half of the decade, competing against two dozen other makes. Albert Parfet sold more than two Fords a day in his dealership during the worst of the 1921 slump, and as many as four per day in the 1922 recovery. Parfet did not wait for the Ford Motor Company to follow General Motors and get into installment lending, he did it himself, selling new Fords for half down and 12 months to pay. Parfet and several other Port Huron dealers banded together to set up their own auto finance company, the Huron Acceptance, one of 110 motorcar moneylenders across the country, some of them charging as high as 22% interest. By 1922, 73% of all cars in the country were sold on time payments.(20) Huron Acceptance accepted 478 car buyers for financing in 1922, for an average loan of $670.

Americans by 1924 owed $2 billion on cars, while they junked $2 billion worth of them annually. Enough Fords and other brands collapsed forever in Port Huron during the 1920's to keep four auto wrecking yards busy. Credit expert J. Harry Tregoe laid it on the line when he said that the dramatic expansion in the car market came not from some sort of unfathomable miracle, but from borrowing: "The installment plan of buying automobiles is neither an entirely safe nor economic plan because it means the mortgaging of a future income for immediate satisfaction."(21) Port Huron's own credit bureau manager Arthur Miller issued a similar warning: "Over-estimation of their ability to pay for merchandise purchased on credit is the reason why many people find themselves deep in debt."

Rowing against the tide, Sperry's department store adamantly refused all credit, proudly advertising "No one is in debt to Sperry's." Americans still bravely talked of thrift. "Thrift – no word more familiar in the American home unless it is 'Mother'," said one bank president. But even "Mother" wasn't heard as much these days when almost 10% of married women worked outside jobs to help make ends meet in debt ridden homes. Overall, the total credit tab in America reached $15 billion by the end of the 20's. Household Finance found takers for $100-$300 loans at 2.5% interest *per month* through its Port Huron office.

161

As we've seen, the widespread use of credit in America predated the auto era, and besides cars Port Huron households stocked up during the 20's with new electrical appliances as well. They purchased refrigerators, washing machines, and radios on time, happily urged on by the Detroit Edison power company, which took over Port Huron Power and Light. Closets filled up after the National Clothes Store introduced Port Huron customers to the immortal words: "simply say CHARGE IT." But nothing else bought on credit came close to the running cost or the rapid depreciation of a car, the second most expensive item most families ever bought. Even a house looked like a bargain compared to an auto. Port Huron realtor John Rawlings tried pointing this out to those innocents waylaid by the Parfets of this world: "A home of your own, a permanent roof over your head in times of prosperity or depression is much more reassuring than an automobile." South Side Lumber agreed: "Own Your Home – Even If Obliged to Mortgage Your Automobile."

Still loath to offer credit itself, Ford Motor encouraged debt-wary potential customers in Port Huron to enroll in an official Ford savings plan at their local banks, and save not for a rainy day but for a Model T. "One day, one dollar, one year, one Ford," is how the slogan put it.(22) You didn't need even that much stash if you settled for one of the growing number of "Certified, Renewed" T's around. A/k/a used. Parfet offered a five day guarantee on his used cars, a pretty clear statement of how much he'd renewed 'em. The story of one such recycled T involved some of Henry Ford's distant cousins living in the Thumb. An especially observant young boy named Ford Bryan grew up in the town of Columbiaville in the 1920's, about 60 miles from Port Huron. Despite the excellent rail service in Columbiaville, Bryan's father caught the automobile sickness and invested in a Certified, Renewed Model T in 1922, incautiously spending $300 for a 1920 sedan that had lost two-thirds of its original $900 value in just two years.

Even at that reduced price point, it disappointed the Bryan family to discover that the Model T, their first car, along with its many other shortcomings which we've already examined, had no heater ("We all had feet and fingers numb with cold on long winter trips," remembered young Bryan); the magneto-powered headlights dimmed when the vehicle slowed, sometimes blacking out the road ahead at critical moments; the passenger compartment often stank of gasoline from the fuel tank under the front seat; and the flimsy tires occasionally blew out just standing in the sun on a hot day.

On one 10-mile T trip to the county seat of Lapeer, a route covered by a couple of trains per day, the Bryans suffered 3 blowouts. At even moderate speeds theseincidents could make your hair stand on end, Ford Bryan recalled, "A blowout could very well mean the ditch on one side of the road or other for a Model T driver because maintaining steering control was very difficult with a flat." And in this era the 20-foot embankment still yawned wide along the roads in some parts of rural Michigan. After successfully bringing the vehicle to a halt, and rummaging around in a trunk containing one mounted spare, a jack, a socket wrench, tire irons, inner tubes, tire boots, spare valves, tube patching kit, hand pump, tire pressure gauge, screwdriver, pliers, monkey wrench, rags, spare timers, fan belt, spark plugs, and a radiator hose, Mr. Bryan senior set to work in something of a bad temper: "Pumping up a tire was strenuous work, and if there were two men in the party, they would alternate at the job. Women and children would sit at some distance from the roadside to avoid dust from passing cars (and profanity emanating from the worksite)."

162

Mr. Bryan found that owning a Ford furnished him with a continuing education in auto mechanics because, his boy recalled, "...the car could sputter and stall anywhere on the road. There were few garages, no tow trucks, and miles of almost deserted roads in the rural districts where the Model T was especially popular." Once he felt well-versed enough in the Ford's little quirks, Mr. Bryan ventured to drive his family 700 miles to Richmond, Virginia on a vacation trip. They slept in the Model T at night, despite the objections of his wife and daughter to these accommodations, especially the daughter, who had to sleep crowded among the pedals under the dashboard. Bryan discovered how incomplete his Tin Lizzie expertise really was when he burned out the car's feeble brakes going down a serious hill in Ohio. This required a garage visit.

Further on, the Bryans took several hours to ascend a 2,600 foot mountain in Appalachia, often backing their way up because the T couldn't handle the grade running forward. During this climb, speeding hillbillies regularly passed the Bryans going the other way, driving their T's at breakneck speeds downhill so the momentum would carry them up the next rise ahead. Cars wrecked in this practice sat perched in the treetops in mountain ravines below the roadside. Finally the Bryans arrived in Virginia to find their host, an uncle, flat on his back from injuries suffered in an auto accident.(23) If taken by train, the Bryans' trip would have cost the four of them a total of 8 cents per mile, with, again, much more speed and comfort, versus the 12 cents per mile that auto travel cost, not including the Ohio brake repairs.

To celebrate the Universal Car, Albert Parfet organized a "Ford Day" in Port Huron, modeled on similar jubilees in other cities. Not unexpectedly, the rest of the auto dealers association showed a marked lack of enthusiasm for this project. Parfet estimated that 9,000 Ford owners lived in his two-county sales district, and he expected 2,000 Model T's to appear for "the biggest day Port Huron has ever had." He offered prizes for the muddiest, noisiest, most dilapidated Fords, as well as the oldest, tallest, heaviest drivers, the most beautiful girl, and the flappiest flapper to appear in a Ford. As it happened only 400 Fords showed up, but that many formed a parade that took an hour and a half to pass the reviewing stand. Harold Wills joined 15,000 spectators at this event, looking on, no doubt, with decidedly mixed feelings.

Not content with this coup, Parfet bought up the first radio station in Port Huron, which had been established in John Bell's music store by his son Irving. Parfet moved the station to his Ford building and renamed it WAFD, for "We Are Ford Dealers." He made the first local connection between the auto industry and the new electronic media, which promised to be a lucrative future partnership. Two 14 year-old Port Huron boys, Ralph Powers and Henry Brown, already had installed their own radio receiver in a car as a further distraction from the boredom of driving.

With all these developments running in his favor, to Parfet's Port Huron competition it seemed for the moment to be a Ford Universe. Against this onslaught Chevrolet dealer John Cawood could only fight back feebly, hiring from a passing vaudeville show a psychic known mysteriously just as Kodah: "The Girl Who Sees Without Eyes. Watch for Her Monday Noon. She will drive through the traffic of Port Huron streets blindfolded. To do this feat she has chosen the new Chevrolet 4-Passenger Coupe."(24) Watch for her and watch out for her Monday noon.

Fordism drove the price of the Model T back down from its war-inflated price, then lower and lower during the opening years of the 20's. Six price cuts pushed the cheapest model as low as $260 in 1924. By comparison, the average new car among all other brands cost about $1,800. Henry Ford at this point still made "the Model T forever" his motto: "We want to construct some kind of a machine that will last forever. It does not please us to have a buyer's car wear out or become obsolete."(25) But it's a long road that has no turning, or blowouts, as the Bryan family might have put it. The barely spartan comforts of the Model T began losing their appeal for many people as early as 1922, when some FMC's dealers first grumbled that the thing needed a makeover.(26) The novelty of an automobile in and of itself pretty much had ended by then. An entire generation which had grown up around The Perpetual Car now found it too familiar, too plain. It was boring.

At General Motors the profit-minded Alfred Sloan, who did not spread his energies nearly as thin as Henry Ford did, noted disapprovingly that GM accounted for just 12% of American motor vehicle sales in 1921, while Ford took 60%. But Sloan marked the coming of several automobile changes which he hoped eventually would pull the rug out from under the Boss of the Road. The closed automobile body gave Sloan his first reason for hope:

For twenty years we protected ourselves with a variety of rubber coats, hats, lap robes, and other makeshift things. For some reason or other, it took us a long time to realize that the way to keep dry in a motorcar was to keep the weather out of the car.(27)

Sloan conveniently forgot here the marketing claim he and other auto mavens had made previously that nature's tonic of fresh air, sunshine, dust, rain, wind, and snow pouring into an open car did passengers a world of good. "Motoring is one of the most effective forms of health insurance that modern life has produced," said New York City's health commissioner Royal Copeland in 1922. Copeland obviously had not gotten the word yet from Detroit about the U-turn on health. Now the open car became an invitation to heat stroke, to hay fever, to pneumonia. *Don't Drive That Open Car - This winter weather demands closed car comfort,* proclaimed John Cawood. It may have protected them, but the closed body cocoon also further detached people inside it from the automobile reality, the destructive path they carved through the rest of the world. Sloan noted with satisfaction that Ford hadn't designed the Model T to accept a closed body, and by 1927 87% of the new cars sold in America were closed.

Sloan also favored a low car, unlike Ford. The closer one rode to the pavement the better Sloan liked it. He in fact replaced the wheels on his own Cadillac with smaller ones just to get low, and this low profile came into vogue during the 1920's. It ignited another one of those auto debates which persisted for the rest of the century: high versus low. Should a buyer choose a low-slung car, faster, more stable, more nimble, which occasionally lost its muffler going over a curb or bottomed out on bumps in the road, choked in the exhaust of other cars, and might get caught beneath a higher-pitched vehicle in a crash, threatening the occupants with decapitation? Or should one ride somewhat slower and higher, like in the bouncing, swaying, upright Model T, with better visibility, more clearance over rocks and ruts and such, better able to punch it out with another car in a collision, but with the tendency to roll over at moderate speeds on modest curves or inconvenient slopes?

Sloan saw balloon tires coming along, which really didn't suit the Model T either. Wider, softer, with about half the air pressure of the old style, balloons gave a more comfortable although somewhat more unpredictable ride:

The engineers had to deal with front-end instability, scuffing of the treads, squeals on turns, diving under fast braking conditions, and a peculiar condition known as wheel tramp, caused by a slight imbalance of the rotating mass of tire and wheel. These phenomena did not show up as major problems until car owners began to take long road trips at high speeds.(28)

Balloons also whined at those high speeds, they increased drag and decreased gas mileage, which hovered in the 12-13 miles per gallon range.

Perhaps most importantly, Sloan also foresaw how social climbing and regular superficial styling changes could supercharge American automobile sales. With more brands on hand to work with, thanks to the departed Billy Durant, Sloan wanted to prompt the typical new-car family into exchanging one barely-paid-for vehicle for another every year or two, in the process gradually working its way up the GM price ladder: Chevrolet, Pontiac, Oldsmobile, Buick, Cadillac. Once carrying a car loan became a regular household expense in America, auto owners needn't suffer the humiliation of being seen around town in last year's passé Chevrolet. They could revel in the splendor of a new Chevrolet, or better yet, a Pontiac. Buying upward marked the family's social ascent in the world, though it might be accompanied by a steeper descent into debt.

It further benefited GM for owners to dump new motor vehicles after just two years use, so the company wouldn't need to build them to last forever, as Hank Ford rashly claimed he did. Sloan made a virtue of the automobile's innate flimsiness, and he often got the credit, or blame, for the throw-away car, a concept somewhat grandiloquently called "planned obsolescence," or Sloanism. Annual car model changes weren't new, nor were rapid fire trade-ins, nor better-buggy envy, but Sloan succeeded in enrolling the middle class in this ridiculous game. *Times Herald* house poet Ed Snover condensed it into rough verse:

As far as chaps who fabricate
The automobile are concerned
They'd be in a most wretched state
If none of us for new cars yearned...
It's mighty seldom any scout
Who owns a modern motor car
Drives it until he wears it out.
But fewer still of us there are
Who do not crave to own a brand
New bus built on the later styles
Although the one we have on hand
Is good for many thousand miles.(29)

Fewer and fewer people cared about the inner workings of automobiles, or wanted the do-it-yourself hassle of a car like the T. As GM's master engineer Charles "Ket" Kettering put it: "At first, when cars were novelties, people were interested in what made them go. Now they want to be unconscious of the mechanism."(30) Looks and comfort became all-important to most customers, so Sloan set up a styling department at GM in 1927, very much like a dress design house. He first called it the

Art and Color Department, recognizing that color alone challenged the all-black, all-the-time Model T. Despite its innocuous name, eventually this department became the most important in the company, overruling the production and engineering people at will, sometimes with fatal results for GM customers.

GM's five brands of cars differed little from each other, usually just in size, sometimes with a bigger engine, different curves on a wood body or a few wrinkles of sheet metal as steel bodies came in, plus additional seat padding, and assorted knicknacks. They were so basically similar that even exec Charles Mott couldn't always tell GM vehicles apart at first glance.(31) One thing, however, all the Sloan boys knew by heart about their products: the more expensive the car, the less value the buyer got for it, and the more profit GM pocketed.

Sloan's strengths and weaknesses as an executive stemmed from his strict adherence to profits first. The first stirrings of public demand for safer cars (like safety glass windshields) left him cold. As his biographer David Farber recounted: "Sloan did not buy the idea that safer automobiles were more desirable automobiles, (saying) '...irrespective of accidents or no accidents, my concern in the problem is a matter of profit and loss.'"(32) This must have been a tough sell to finance director John Raskob, the father of GM's loan wing, whose 19 year-old son died in a car crash. Less egotistical than Ford, the methodical Sloan relied heavily on a team of men like Raskob, Kettering, and Mott to do business. The other helping hands included Charles "Engine Charlie" Wilson, Harley Earl the styling boss, and ex-FMC production manager William Knudsen. Henry Ford rather ungratefully had kicked Knudsen out the door in 1921 for allegedly getting too big for his britches. The Great Dane landed as head man at Chevrolet, with blood in his eye, determined to sell Chevies "vun for vun," as he put it, with Fords.(33)

One of Sloan's former GM colleagues, Walter Chrysler, after walking out on Billy Durant in 1920, lost not a moment in getting back into the auto game which had made him, too, enormously wealthy. But Chrysler avoided making the mistakes Harold Wills had made in starting from scratch and, even worse, in risking his own money. Instead Chrysler used the backing of other investors to revive the fading Maxwell brand in 1921. He combined it with the similarly downcast Chalmers car company, and used the resulting organization to build his own vehicles: Chryslers, DeSotos and Plymouths. In Port Huron, Bert Hyde took on the Chrysler dealership, and got straight to the point: *Walter P. Chrysler Announces 25 Miles to the Gallon, 58 Miles per Hour, 5 to 25 miles per hour in 8 Seconds. $895-$1345.* Bert had a word for the ladies, too: *Women Who Have Found Driving a Tiring, Joyless Task now are turning to the car which makes driving a delightful, thrilling, healthful pastime.*

Chrysler quickly turned a delightful, thrilling, healthful profit, but his big coup came in 1928 when he bought up the Dodge Brothers auto empire left behind by the lamented John and Horace of Port Huron memory.(34) The resulting Chrysler Corporation, the last of the Big Three American automakers to take shape, joined Ford and GM as the only three to outlive the 20th Century. Together, they held 80% of the market by the end of the 20's. To celebrate himself, Chrysler ordered an enormous skyscraper built in New York City, just like Billy Durant had done in Detroit. His former colleagues, Alfred Sloan, Charles Mott, and Charles Kettering, each bought 1,000 shares of Chrysler Corporation out of affection for the big lug.

None of these men – Ford, Sloan, or Chrysler – suffered from excessive modesty when it came to hawking their wares during the 1920's, but in Port Huron at least, even the wildest excesses of auto advertising couldn't outstrip the *Times Herald* editorialist:

The true ideal of American life will not be reached until every family in the United States not only theoretically but actually owns its own automobile. It is American opportunity; it is the American idea of justice and equality. Why shouldn't the chore boy and the scrub woman ride to and from their work in a motor car? ...Is it any great stretch of the imagination to the time when every boy and girl in the family shall have an automobile for personal use, just the same as they now have their own bicycles and roller skates? (35)

Admittedly, this new ideal compared awkwardly with news leaders like, "The headless body of Mrs. Elizabeth J. Beem, 77, lies on a slab at Falk's morgue today..." after Mrs. Beem's car happened in front of a train at the Port Huron city limits. Or details of how the corpses of Mrs. Earl Minnie and Mrs. A. E. Gerrie had been fished from the Black River after their car plowed through the stop gates at the 10th Street bridge. Or the alarming news that St. Clair County Sheriff Harrison Maines had killed his 68 year-old wife Dora by slamming their car into a phone pole while driving home from a church supper. Or the grim irony that Oscar Mueller, 1895 race car driver and now head of the big, booming Mueller Brass plant in Port Huron, had lost his only daughter in a car crash. Or the remark of Babcock Dairy driver Fred Rebeske after he ran over and killed 9 year-old Harry Jackel (who apparently hadn't gotten his own car yet), then drove away to finish his Babcock route: Rebeske "thought somebody else would report it," as though he'd flattened a dog.

Aside from an abundance of advertising about motor vehicles and their upkeep (sponsored by the 48 gas stations and 50 other auto-related businesses in Port Huron by mid-decade), every *Times Herald* edition now carried details of fatal local, regional, state, and national auto accidents, a toll which interfered with the true ideal of American life. Even when accidents failed to kill, or took on a kind of slapstick hilarity ("Bee Scares Driver, Car Plunges Over Bank, Three Hurt"), it seemed to Louis Weil that this kind of carelessness at the wheel seriously delayed the dawn of auto nirvana. His mighty journal impatiently peppered the public with safe driving tips, threats, demands, pleas, and advice. One adage warned that "Every year many children are killed or maimed for life because they neglect to look both ways on a street before crossing." From Harry Jackel's squashed viewpoint it looked as though drivers neglected to look both ways for children. Weil sometimes resorted to sarcasm. "The undertakers and physicians are planning for a busy season, and it is probable that we will have to station a reporter on the turnpike Sundays to keep tab on the casualties." This remark came after a $2 million paving job on the main highway to Detroit, the Gratiot Pike, promptly boosted its auto accident rate to 1,000 crackups of varying degree per year.

Weil should have taken his own warnings a little more to heart, since not long afterward he drove his own car off that very Gratiot highway into a phone pole, breaking his arm and slicing up his head. In the process he bounced around his passengers pretty badly, Mr. and Mrs. William MacArthur, who happened to be his sister Lorene and her husband, the president of the Port Huron Auto Club. Very embarrassing. Weil insisted his car inexplicably had swerved off the road, like a runaway horse. The same edition of the *Times Herald* in which Weil absolved himself of any blame for this wreck reported that between 1919 and 1926 auto accidents had killed 137,000 Americans and injured 3.5 million.(36) And these were very conservative estimates, especially the injuries, since no central bureau collected this data, as one did for railroads.

Acting as U.S. Commerce Secretary, Herbert Hoover convened the first National Conference on Street and Highway Safety in Washington in 1924. One of the most intelligent and dedicated men who ever served in American government, Hoover called the automobile a "malefactor against public safety." He didn't identify executives like Ford or Sloan or Chrysler personally as the malefactors, just the car, but the machine didn't manufacture itself, so you could draw your own conclusion. The conference didn't even make a dent in the problem, which grew continuously worse. In 1927 the estimated economic loss from serious auto accidents in America, leaving out fender-benders entirely, reached $627 million. The country shoveled under another 28,000 auto dead in 1928 and 31,000 in 1929, and treated one million people for auto injuries in '29 alone.

The automobile in 1929 killed three times as many people, and injured 10 times as many, as the railroads had during their most heavily-traveled years. Or nautically speaking, automobile fatalities in 1929 amounted to a Titanic sinking every three weeks. William Eno, one of the first Americans to systematically study automobile sickness, suggested that delayed deaths from traffic injuries, Levassor deaths, effectively tripled the automobile toll, which would have made 97,500 dead in 1930. Delayed deaths like that of 47 year-old John Wolfe of Port Huron, who went over a bad bump in a car, smacked his skull against the roof, and two years later packed it in. How many auto accidents of all kinds took place annually? No one had the faintest idea, but the Auto Club of Southern California estimated 2.4 million in that state alone in 1927.

Not idly did Aetna insurance man Edward Moore warn Port Huron motorists:

Do You Dread to Drive? Every time you take out your car do you worry – What if it is stolen? Suppose it burns? Might I injure somebody? The car may be ruined in a crash. What if I damage property of others? Maybe I'll get hurt.

Moore's solution: "Aetna-ize." Only about 28% of U.S. drivers insured themselves for liability, which offered Moore a wide field of opportunity. Howard Furniture also had a warning for drivers of the 20's: you need a better mattress.

Remember! every car you pass – or passes you – holds in the passing a potential possibility of an automobile accident, all because either one driver or the other did not get a proper rest the night before, and therefore the mind would not function fast enough to meet the emergency.

Everywhere you looked the evidence mounted up, that even under the most benign circumstances imaginable, in the hands of experienced people who drove them every day, people who had the best mattress money could buy, the automobile was unpredictably dangerous. John Cawood learned his lesson the hard way when a car ran him over as he stood innocently on his own sales lot. The offending vehicle, driven by a salesman for a neighboring dealer, Cawood's ex-partner Earl Paige, invaded Cawood's turf at an estimated 15 mph and clobbered John. He suffered a broken leg, dislocated

168

knee, several muscle, nerve and ligament rips, and a "fractured head." Unwilling to forgive his friend this insult, Cawood sued Paige for $50,000, and won $22,000 in the biggest local automobile damage judgment up until then.

Cawood found plenty of company in the Port Huron courts, as other auto casualties, or their survivors, lined up to file lawsuits. However, some members of the public still took the more stoical "unavoidable" viewpoint about car accidents, as though the victims had been hit by lightning. When a truck crushed Louis Austin's 12 year-old son Charles to death as he bicycled to school on 10th Street, his father hastened to reassure the public: "Understand me, I am not complaining or protesting. What has happened to our boy was to be. Nobody is to blame, and I do not hold anyone responsible." "You must be brave," was Coroner Albert Falk's manly advice when he reported one day to Goodells resident Emil Klandowsky that Mrs. Klandowsky and their two daughters had been killed when their car collided with a train. At which point Emil disagreeably fainted. If only they'd been Aetna-ized.

Automobile sickness often blinded its victims to the obvious, like Kodah, or prompted otherwise normal persons to take diametrically opposed positions without the slightest difficulty. The *Times Herald* admitted that its reportage of the death toll on the roads had become "trite": "...we are amazed and bewildered by the apparent failure of all our safety propaganda...to make more than a casual and feeble impression upon the number and the seriousness of automobile accidents." At the same time, Louis Weil campaigned for raising the "absurd" 35 mph state rural speed limit, and he applauded when, almost unimaginably, the Michigan legislature abolished the limit completely in 1927. This in a state with more automobiles than in all of Europe, a state in which 1,088 people died and $10 million in property damage resulted from car accidents in 1925. Go ahead, drive as fast as you could push your buzz wagon on any road in the state outside city limits. And most of these roads were still 9 -16 foot-wide dirt jobs traveled as well by pedestrians, bicyclists and horse drawn vehicles. But feel free to floor it.

Carmakers like the Essex company happily seized on this new unlimited speed liberty as a sales tool: *Real Car Joy must include...50 Miles an hour all day long and far greater speed when wanted.* So did REO: *A tidal wave in power...a hurricane in speed...a summer cloud to ride...The Reo Flying Cloud.* The no-limit law contained a lot of subjective phrases directing drivers to proceed at "prudent", "careful", "reasonable" and "proper" speeds, but this flying cloud of balderdash flew directly in the face of the experience of judges like Detroit's Charles Bartlett, the terror of Motor City leadfoots, who jailed them by the hundreds. Bartlett had just called for mandatory speed governors on cars, not limitless accelerators.

Port Huron Police Court Judge Fred George, the champion pedestrian of years gone by, expressed similar doubts about no speed limits: "It will be practically impossible to convict motorists of reckless driving, excepting in cases of gross recklessness," whatever gross recklessness now meant. St. Clair County Assistant Prosecutor Arthur Mann gave what amounted to a shoulder shrug and said, "Let your conscience be your guide." Pioneer auto victim Judge Eugene Law, still jumpy after being belted by that car back in 1908, also saw more legal trouble ahead. He nervously pointed out that cars already had inspired a welter of law textbooks and "thousands" of opinions to baffle the most astute attorney.

Even before the inauguration of this crazy speed policy Michigan's legal system had had its hands full, because another true ideal of American life, alcohol prohibition, the Progressives' apotheosis, just wasn't progressing very well. "There is no place for alcohol in the age of efficiency, mass production and excellence," said Rev. R. N. Holsaple, superintendent of the Michigan Anti-Saloon League, in a speech to Port Huron Kiwanis members. Henry Ford endorsed this view but a substantial and growing minority did not. In 1926 Port Huron cops arrested more drunks than ever, 520 that year, including 38 drivers for breaking Michigan's new state drunk driving law. Half the criminal arrests in America involved dry law violations. Up to 100 prisoners a day crowded the St. Clair County jail, where 20 had been thought a lot in 1900.

In a little over one year the state police post on the St. Clair River grabbed 52 booze-hauling cars, trucks, and boats and 30,000 quarts of alcohol. The pitifully few federal liquor cops assigned to St. Clair County attached 7,000 gallons of beer, 320 quarts of whiskey, 30 boats, and 30 cars. The Port Huron customs house pulled about 3,000 quarts off cross-border travelers, including 10 quarts of whiskey tucked into a baby carriage by Grand Trunk worker John Hammond. A single car, a Buick, stopped by police in Port Huron, carried 14 cases of whiskey worth $1,000. Occasionally entire boxcars full of white lightning rolled through the train yards, and machine gun-wielding gangsters escorted away trucks full of Canadian booze loaded from barges at the Port Huron docks.(37) Home brewers dumped so much spent mash down their drains it clogged the sewers. Drivers who wanted one for the road found plenty of refreshment at any one of Port Huron's 100 blind pigs.

Illegal imbibers in Michigan now drove in increasing numbers on highways without speed limits, a sobering thought. He may have been slightly nuts on the subject of unlimited car speed, but Louis Weil had no patience with drunk drivers, and he resolutely printed every convicted offender's name in his newspaper, even when begged by family members of these "potential murderers" to lay off. The *Grand Rapids* (MI) *Press* agreed: "Driving while intoxicated is always intending manslaughter, unless the culprit is so great a moron or idiot as not to be able to foresee the most obvious possible consequences."(38) Less intolerantly, Michigan's legislature in 1921 created a new kind of reduced criminal charge for intoxicated killer motorists, "negligent homicide," or manslaughter lite, because juries were so reluctant to convict drivers of full manslaughter. Michigan prison commissioner Arthur Wood condemned this as chickening out:

Automobile manslaughter, commonly termed negligent homicide, slays its thousands, costing the nation more lives annually than the Mexican or Spanish wars, yet only 16 automobile drivers have been sent to Michigan prisons to pay the penalty for this crime during the past year. The usual sentence is from six months to five years, with the average around 18 months.(39)

Bruce Fairman's slaughterer didn't even get the average. The 71 year-old teacher and former rural schools superintendent of St. Clair County died in front of hit-and-run drunk driver Roy Smith while walking home from visiting two pupils in the hospital, where *they* had landed after being hit by a car. Having convicted Fairman's killer of involuntary manslaughter, the jury took a backward step and recommended leniency. The defendant walked away with a $750 fine, 1 year suspended prison sentence, and a 5 year driving ban. Smith paid less for killing Fairman than a popular Port Huron businessman, Jesse Lamphere of the Mecca Cafe, paid for breaking the

170

prohibition act at about the same time, $1,000. Many felt that Smith should have gone to *The Big House*, the prison in a popular movie of the day, in which actor Robert Montgomery's character landed, like one of the unlucky Michigan 16, dazed at the prospect of actually going to jail for killing somebody with a car. A real life crash later so badly mangled the film's director, George Hill, that he committed suicide.

In the Port Huron courts judges still used plenty of leeway in assessing fines or jail time for the morons or idiots brought before them. Judge Fred George couldn't quite make up his mind about drunk drivers. First he opposed mandatory jail for this crime because, he said, it would negatively affect innocent spouses, children and parents. Then George reversed gears and said drunk motoring should be made a felony. He called violators who pleaded with him in court a bunch of "sobbers." Defendants unlucky enough to appear before Judge Eugene Cote for drunk driving got the slammer, no exceptions. No exceptions, that is, until the jail filled up. In that case, sentence suspended.

Apart from drunk driving and rum running in the 20's, cars furnished indispensable tools for a wide variety of other crimes. Police now distinguished between *auto thieves*, criminals who stole cars, and *auto bandits*, criminals who used cars to get to and from stickups, burglaries, murders, bank robberies, or any other job that needed doing in a hurry. Some auto thieves satisfied their needs just by taking and re-selling the car, like former policeman Charles Thornton, who ran Port Huron's first chop shop. Auto bandits on the other hand relieved Albert Parfet's dealership safe of $3,400, blew up a bank vault on Port Huron's south side, and hit Harold Wills' Marysville Bank for $4,000. Some thugs combined both practices. On one occasion auto thieves first stole a Ford, then turned auto bandits and held up the Sperry's department store in downtown Port Huron in broad daylight and shot up the place. Bandits picked on Parfet again by stealing his Lincoln from in front of his home and using it in an $8,000 Detroit bank heist.

Michigan's mobile underworld favored bank jobs in particular. To meet this threat, the sheriff, state police, and the bankers association organized the St. Clair County Vigilantes. 50 deputized men, armed with .45's and automatic rifles, were assigned three each to the county's rural banks. At least one vigilante had to hang around his bank's vicinity during business hours, on the lookout. The vigilantes furnished their own cars, in order to help out the sheriff, who only commanded two radio-equipped patrol units. "Banks will be further protected by death traps and gas throwers located at strategic positions," promised the county bankers association, who offered a $1,000 dead or alive reward for bank busters. The possemen frankly looked forward to a merry chase across the countryside if and when called into action, though the very day the vigilante scheme was announced 52 year-old special Marine City policeman Walter Peterson drove into an unexpected death trap, a ditch, crashed headlong through his windshield, and expired.

Robberies of that cash-cow fixture of the automobile age, the gas station, also flourished. Bandits could rob three or four filling stations around the Thumb in a single evening thanks to the mobility of their stolen getaway cars. During one wave of gas station holdups Port Huron police staked out some likely targets on a night in October 1930. Sure enough, they nabbed two crooks in the act: 18 year-olds Russell McComis and William Brown. These two already had killed a man in an Akron, Ohio robbery, shot and blinded a man in Ann Arbor, Michigan, and robbed two Oakland County, Michigan sheriff's deputies. While being driven to the jail in downtown Port Huron, McComis pulled out an undiscovered pistol and killed 41 year-old police sergeant and former railroad engineer Roy Shambleau, the only city policeman to be murdered during the century. The infuriated police wasted no time in extracting a confession, and a judge sentenced McComis the next day to life in prison at hard labor, a sentence that, much to Port Huron's anger, an appeals court reduced years later for having been a little too swift.

Aside from their criminal misuses, the rabbitlike multiplication of motor vehicles on Port Huron's city streets made the town more difficult and expensive to manage. The Port Huron police department now employed 25 hands. Some officials wanted an additional 15 men, along with more Ford patrol cars (at $45 each per month) and motorcycles. Even with extra bodies on duty and wheels to carry them, Mayor John Bell frankly acknowledged that the department could not enforce all the traffic laws. The abridged combination of state and local auto codes took up an entire page of small print in the *Times Herald* when the latest complete version appeared. No policeman or driver could keep up with it all.

Despite the limited scope of their resources, police officers hauled in so many impounded and abandoned cars that the city had to rent warehouse space to keep them in. Taxpayers also forked over $14,000 for a city garage. The municipal government owned 40 motor vehicles, not including the public works department's collection, nor the eight fire trucks. To pay for auto culture expenses like these, property taxes in Michigan had soared 700% in the 20 years ending in 1922, and kept on climbing. Port Huron's taxes were stiff enough that in 1928 $260,000 of them went unpaid. A Presidential commission named the automobile and inflation as the two biggest reasons for runaway taxes in America.

Auto congestion, suggested the national Auto Club, cost the USA $2 billion annually. On Saturday nights in Port Huron traffic on Main Street sometimes lined up for blocks, barely moving, and the City Council wondered if that new panacea, one-way streets, would help. The first automatic traffic signal went in on Main Street in 1924, followed quickly by three more. Installers set these signals with 2-minute stop and go intervals at first, but that quickly drove the waiting motorists crazy, and the lights rolled back to one and a half minutes. Pedestrians won an important "victory" of sorts during this era when a federal court ruled that pedestrians had the right to finish crossing the street if a traffic light changed against them while they were halfway across. What else were they supposed to do, fly out of the way?

City Councilmen also decided to install street name signs, 400 of them. The more people drove, and the faster, the less familiar they became with their surroundings, and needed more guidance. 5,000 vehicles entered and left Port Huron daily, and nobody wanted them driving around and around lost. The Auto Club lent a hand by paying to put up 200 metal stop signs at intersections. Previously, the few stop signs in town had been painted on the pavement, a little hard to read under leaves, or after a snowfall, or at night. Not too many drivers yet expected to see important messages for them written on the ground. The Auto Club also sponsored a free safety check for motor vehicles in Port Huron, and rather alarmingly found that half of the 3,300 inspected cars needed repairs. A specific brake test flunked one-quarter of the cars tested. That

172

dovetailed with the Hoover Highway Safety Committee's finding that 15% of traffic deaths resulted from mechanical defects in vehicles, primarily brakes, lights, and steering gears. The committee suggested that these auto elements needed regular state inspection. It was enough to make a mechanic's mouth water.

Had 60% of the households of Port Huron owned a horse and carriage in 1900, and 7% of them two or more, they would have made a shocking mess of the city. By the end of the 20's, this percentage of households owned automobiles, with a far worse result. Parking space downtown came at an ever greater premium during business hours. City officials put up additional "No Parking" and "One Hour Parking" signs, and even tore out some of the street landscaping near City Hall to try to clear space at the curbs in front of public buildings. In the tightening grip of their automobile sickness, far more debilitating than any liquor or narcotic, some drivers refused to walk so much as a block from their vehicles to their destinations, let alone from a streetcar stop, or from their homes. They demanded parking directly in front of wherever they went. Syndicated poet Breton Braley addressed this fanaticism in "The Motorist's Dilemma", which seemed to suit Port Huron, about a Model T owner driven mad after four days of circling town in search of a parking spot: *Then off ye dock the Motorist / Propelled his dusty flivver / And then the cop arrested him / For parking in the river!*(40)

First National Bank grappled with Port Huron's auto placement problem by renting a vacant piece of property and converting it into that blight of blights, a parking lot, one of the first in the business district. Customers could rest their weary vehicles for 30 minutes in the bank lot while attending to affairs. Nobody held a stopwatch on them, or checked if they were indeed bank customers, or punished transgressors. It ran on the honor system. Several more businesses quickly followed suit in setting up their own lots, and the Chamber of Commerce laid its hands on enough space to establish a 100 car parking corral. It began to dawn on some observers that parking lots carried a lot of disruption potential. At this rate, quite a few buildings would need to be erased from the Port Huron landscape to make room for them. They'd spread everybody much further apart.

"It is not going to be long, apparently, before the business of providing parking space...will demand convenient and valuable property in the very center of the city's business district," said the *Times Herald.* Or else, added the paper – and this hardly bore thinking about – "the people who ride in automobiles must learn to walk again."(41) Faced with the threat of walking, Louis Weil promptly bought and tore down a neighboring building for his paper's own parking lot. A vertical solution for parking opened in Detroit during the 20's, an 11-story 800-car parking garage. Another answer to the problem, Country Club Plaza, a "shopping center" with plenty of auto pasture attached, started business in the Kansas City area in 1922, the first in the nation.

Be they driving or parking, the squirrely habits of Port Huron's motorists in this decade wore especially hard on kids. Children walked a gauntlet of moving and stationary vehicles in arriving at and departing from just about anyplace, but especially school. Parents demanded the city assign traffic cops to schoolhouses, and not without reason. During the 1920's children made up one-third of the victims killed by autos in America, and 90% had been pedestrians. Some parents of Washington Junior High pupils proposed building a pedestrian tunnel beneath 10th Street, so children could get to their playground across the street alive. Authorities in Highland Park outside Detroit

173

actually constructed these escape tunnels for their children near the Ford assembly plant.

Chevrolet neatly turned parents' concern about their kids' safety on its head, suggesting that driving children to school now made better sense. Only a bad parent allowed his child to walk: *Why worry about the safety of your little ones on the highways or crossing city streets on the way to school? The low price and small upkeep of a Chevrolet is cheap insurance against such risks.* Did an American child run a greater risk of dying inside a car or in front of one? Chevrolet didn't get that specific, but many Port Huron parents took the advice anyway. Driven or walking, Port Huron's children slowly became prisoners of the automobile age, robbed of their liberty inside a claustrophobic car or surrounded by a maze of auto-menaced streets.

Often Port Huron car owners treated their vehicles better than their children, insisting on a large domicile of its own for the automobile at home, or "A Residence for Your Buzz Wagon," as Haynes Lumber called the garage. If you had no barn or chicken coop to convert, Haynes advised that you build over the backyard lawn or garden with one of their garage kits. About one new garage went up per week around town, at a cost of $250 apiece. For something the size of David McMorran's 6-car garage at his Main Street mansion, price slightly higher. For Edsel Ford's 27-car garage, much higher. Without an alleyway available from the rear, so the auto could get into its kennel that way, a driveway from the street to the garage had to be fitted between houses, a very tight squeeze on some of the older, narrower lots. In order to cope, lot sizes for new homes expanded to allow both garages and driveways, pushing these houses further apart, as in the new Covent Gardens subdivision on Port Huron's north side.

Some homebuilders put the garage inside the house, like a very large baby's nursery. The "attached" garage appeared in the weekly Times Herald house plans, and in some instances replaced the old-time front porch. Architect Hedley Stevenson didn't think much of that design breakthrough: "...this onslaught - the garage in the house and to the front...has swept the country like the other pestilence, jazz-music, and is now enthroned in the high seat and termed 'modern.'"(42) With an attached garage the automobile owner need not expose herself to raw nature, red in tooth and claw, even for a second in transiting from the house to the closed car before departure. A Port Huron inventor, Norman Gray, Jr., son of the man who killed Margaret Wolfstyn, came up with a spring-loaded automatic garage door opener, triggered by a pressure plate on the driveway, so the driver needn't get out of the car on the way home either, until safely within his castle walls.

Garageless autos left on Port Huron's streets had to be marked from dusk to dawn with a light, a real nuisance for the owner. Even with a light on it, if left out too often all night long another car likely would smack into your Gray Goose eventually, or hooligans joyride it away. In addition, overnight street parking fostered a regrettable lessening of public decorum, if you took Police Chief Byron Buckeridge's meaning:

I refer to the large number of automobiles which are parked at all hours of the night on dark streets. Their mission is usually anything but of a moral nature, and it is common knowledge that many of our younger folk are implicated in activities which lead to disgrace in many instances.(43)

The same week Buckeridge made his declaration, the Reid Family Theater presented the

174

motion picture "*Camille* – Fresh Perversion, Fresh Credulity, Fresh Passion, Fresh Pain!" so the chief didn't have to get too specific here. It was *Camille* on wheels, or as one judge called it, cathouses in cars.

A big meeting of worried parents talked over the whole issue of automobile carousing. "Tales of alleged midnight escapades among the high school pupils of Port Huron were told in indignant voices of shocked parents Tuesday evening at a meeting of the Parent Teachers Association..." Some Moms and Dads expressed more resentment than shock and said it would be nice if their kids would let them use the car once in a while. General Motors stepped in here as a mediator, urging an "end to breakfast table arguments about 'Who is to have the car today?'" The answer: *Today the American family is discovering that a second or third car is not only a convenience but an economy.*

For those intent on spending the night in their cars, sleeping or whatever, the Port Huron Chamber of Commerce felt it would be far better for them to stay in an auto tourist camp than on the streets. The C of C persuaded the city to convert 8-acre Palmer Park into one such camp, similar to thousands of others set up by municipalities across America during the 20's. The city installed hydrants and lavatories and charcoal grills, and eventually 100 campers per week settled in, from a dozen different states. For free. Naturally, it didn't do the park much good, but it gave automobile travelers like the Bryan family someplace to stay when they snoozed in their Model T's.

"Free" turned out to be entirely too cheap, however, and the tourist camp soon attracted an undesirable class of car bums who didn't just travel in their vehicles but lived in them. This arrangement thrilled not the park's neighbors nor hotel or resort owners, and Port Huron closed the camp down for a rethink, then relocated it near the century-old Fort Gratiot lighthouse property. With fees and a caretaker this time the camp became a fixture for 25 years, but the automobile presence made an ugly blot on one of the most beautiful lakefronts in America.

Automakers, dealers, flacks, and other industry shills claimed their product bound the nation closer together by travel during the 1920's. Automobiles had "taken the curse off urban living," and "knit together farming communities," and drawn city and country happily together, declared the *Times Herald.* The city/country switcheroo again. In fact, the car bound the nation together in jackassery. 300 miles from Port Huron, in another infected Midwestern town – Muncie, Indiana – social researchers turned up some nice quotes from auto nuts that could have come from anywhere in America. "We'd rather do without clothes than give up the car," said one. "I'll go without food before I'll see us give up the car," offered another. One family told a farm agent they'd bought a car before a bathtub because "you can't ride to town in a bathtub."(44) A puzzled Muncian asked the research team, Robert and Helen Lynd, "Why on earth do you need to study what's changing this country? I can tell you what's happening in just four letters: A-U-T-O!"(45)

Instead of being knit together with anybody, once an American family bought a car they often became a lot less neighborly, and zipped past people they'd lived near for years but now avoided. People they'd formerly met on the sidewalk every day:

We have nothing whatsoever to do with my neighbors [said one Los Angeles resident]. *I don't even know their names or know them to speak to. My best friends live in the city but by no means in this neighborhood. We belong to no clubs and we do not attend any local church. We go auto riding, visiting and uptown to the theaters.*(46)

Farm families not only drove past their neighbors but past their small town stores for the bigger selection in the cities. When their neighborhood stores failed as a result, the longer shopping trips become a necessity rather than an adventure.(47) The automobile loosened club and church and union ties when people skipped meetings in favor of road cruising. And internally, families of all stripes didn't knit any tighter together because of the automobile. The American divorce rate doubled between 1910 and 1928. One couple divorced for every four married in St. Clair County in 1930, almost twice as many as in 1900.

One of the curses of urban living the automobile failed to take off, its own stink, grew worse the more cars moved into Port Huron. In his "How's She Hittin'?" newspaper column, Israel Klein advised auto owners to take advantage of this drawback: "Many difficulties in the running of the automobile can be detected by odor." Keep your nose to the wind for evidence of burning rubber, burning insulation, gasoline raw or burned, or the smell of frying grease, the latter of which meant a leaking universal joint. Even when working perfectly the automobile emitted a blast of carbon monoxide which the *Times Herald* seemed surprised to learn at this late date did some harm. "Our very atmosphere is already badly befouled by the deadly gas from our automobiles. It is suspected of being the cause of some of our mysterious human ailments – to say nothing about certain death in a closed garage."(48)

The rising crescendo of automobile noise befouled the very atmosphere too. Port Huron's Hotel Metropole promised that "...a minimum of traffic noise is assured patrons because the hotel is located just outside the congested traffic district. " But many formerly peaceful neighborhoods could get no such assurance, and by the end of the decade eight more of the grand old mansions along Main Street's once-fanciest way, now a state highway, had been carved up into apartment buildings for people too poor to afford quiet. John Sperry, the department store boss, up and moved to the lakefront north end, next to assorted other big names. No street in Port Huron now lived entirely safe for more than a few minutes at a time from the noise and fumes of a motor vehicle passing by. And the older the car, the more it discharged. At 6-8 years old, the average auto on the streets dished out plenty.

This noise situation lent sales pizzazz to some of the suburban home developments a-building out in the townships. McDonald's Garden Acres featured one-acre homesites off a paved road, a "10 minute drive from down town," in the once-bucolic (but not for long) Gardendale. John Cawood built his own suburban housing project called Forrest ("For Rest") well outside the city limits, offering buyers a car and a lot in a package deal. "People thought we were losing it when we moved here," one Forrest buyer said later. "It was so far away from town." Port Huron's water department started running lines outside the city limits to feed these projects, a practice which had major consequences in the future.

Next, possibly, to motorcycles, trucks made the biggest road racket. They tripled in number during this decade, to 3 million.(49) Apart from local delivery vehicles like the American Railroad Express and *Times Herald* route drivers and Fred Rebeske's killer Babcock Dairy truck, more tradesman such as Watson Brothers plumbers now carried half their shops around with them in trucks, rather than scope out a job in

176

advance for the really necessary materials, then fetch them. At the intercity level 1,500 dedicated trucking companies operated in America. Half a dozen intercity firms ran fleet operations from Port Huron to Detroit and to several other big Midwestern cities. Many of their semi-trailers couldn't safely fit onto the city's streets. The state of Michigan loosely restricted truck length to 60 feet, about twice as long as most Port Huron city streets were wide, too long even to negotiate a simple turn at corners. The new auto carrier trucks also cleared a substantial path when they pulled up at Parfet Ford with four cars stacked on them. Pedestrians stepped back if they knew what was good for them when one of these monster trucks swung its hind end up and over a curb. Grocery delivery boy Norman Stephen didn't back off quickly enough one day and died under a gravel truck on 10th Street.

Big trucks tore up the city streets in Port Huron and elsewhere with next to complete impunity. In the same newspaper edition in which George Yokom's dealership offered customers the 5-ton General Motors' *Big Brute – a truck like men have never seen before,* there appeared a story about a 5-ton truck which had caved in a street in Los Angeles. Users of the open highways of St. Clair County also dreaded big trucks as notorious road hogs, operated by not always well-rested hog drivers. Michigan's Public Utilities Commission didn't get around to regulating truck driver hours until 1930, when supposedly it limited drivers to 10 hours of driving in every 18, one of the most systematically flouted laws in the state.

The Pressed Metals company decided to accept the risk of sleepy drivers, and hired trucker Oscar Richards to haul auto parts to Detroit (one of his first big contracts) rather than send them by train any more. Usurping the proper role of the railroads, lightly taxed trucks used the public roads for peanuts, comparatively speaking. The Ogden and Moffett firm, Myron and Dale to you, ran alongside Richards at the front of the growing Port Huron truck pack, with a fleet that swelled to more than two dozen assorted vehicles. They hauled 100 tons of castings per day from Port Huron foundries to Detroit auto plants, and returned with 120 tons of groceries for chain stores across eastern Michigan. Grocers like Kroger's and A & P and Port Huron's own H. A. Smith chain.

These retailers did little direct dealing with local food producers anymore, buying instead from wholesalers food heavily processed to withstand lengthy transportation and long shelf life. Fordism in a can. In fact, a Kroger ad carried a Henry Ford endorsement:

Mass production is the answer to questions such as the price of food. We have it in the chain stores which have developed tremendously in the last five years. Their principle is sound and they should be encouraged.(50)

Chain grocery store sales quadruped during the 20's, and even independents banded together to form their own cooperatives, like the Independent Grocers Alliance (IGA). Other Port Huron businesses, like Sperry's department store, and the First National Bank, tried affiliating with retailing and banking chains to get in on the supposed magic of Fordism.

Henry Ford may have been proud of grocery store chain growth, but in carmaking things suddenly turned sour for the FMC in the middle of the 1920's. General Motors' chief weapon against Ford, the sale of Chevrolets, boomed in 1925 and 1926, while Model T sales stalled. All due to the new design changes and sales strategy Alfred Sloan had greenlighted years earlier. 70% of Ford dealers lost money in '26. Edsel Ford, a phlegmatic man of almost limitless patience where his father was concerned, finally put his foot down and insisted on their producing more closed cars, balloon tires, and some new car colors besides black. Despite the changes, sales suffered a fatal crash, so to speak, in early 1927, declining by two-thirds from the previous year. As coroner Falk had put it, "You must be brave," and the Fords decided to bury the Model T in May of '27.

During an elaborate, drawn-out, and tear-drenched wake for this lousy product, Ford Motor published an obituary emphasizing the T's bigness. During 19 years of production $4.8 billion worth of materials and $1.9 billion of wages had gone into building 15 million T's, which burned up 60 billion gallons of gasoline during their lifespans, etc., etc.. Mournful Henry shut down his factories completely, stopping a $1 million per week payroll in Detroit alone, while he and his staff scrambled to come up with a replacement. General Motors' sales zoomed past the Ford Motor Company's, and stayed there for the rest of the 20th Century.

Ford gave the new car the recycled name of Model A, the same as the FMC's first product in 1903. For clarity's sake, we'll call the second version the A2. Henry set the design just three months after ditching the T. Improvements, such as they were, came hard. Ford himself, still recovering from his own recent car wreck, took the A2 out for an off-road test drive. This adventure shook up both the car's chassis and Ford's own so badly he immediately ordered a better suspension. Another test driver, Harold Hicks, had his head rammed into the windshield in a crackup, cutting him badly enough to warrant the installation of safety glass. Welding replaced the bucket of bolts formerly used to hold the T together. Ford toyed with the idea of using an automatic transmission, but decided against it, to his later regret.

The finished A2 came in nine different body styles in three colors (Raven Black, Washington Blue, Stone Brown), unrealistically priced at first at $385 for the cheapest version.(51) With one thing or another the price crept up until the "new Ford" cost about the same as any other average "low-priced" new car in America, $600. Ford okayed a huge publicity campaign in November 1927, placing full page ads over his signature in 2,000 newspapers. The FMC even reluctantly created its own car loan arm, Universal Credit, to get the A2 off the launch pad. On Opening Day 6,000 people went through Parfet Ford in Port Huron to take a look. They saw pretty much the Standard Car that every automaker in America already built and continued to build with increasing complications for the next 70 years. It just had the Ford name on it.

Henry Ford gave away free A2's to Edison, to comedian Will Rogers, and to old FMC sidekick James Couzens.(52) 400,000 orders rolled in, even before the unveiling. Spirited debate about the new design broke out across America. In the Thumb, a Saginaw, Michigan household quickly chose up sides:

Argument over the respective merits of the Chevrolet motor and that of the new Ford car Friday night sent Mrs. Emeline Acceti to the hospital with a bullet wound in her hip and landed James Candella in jail. Candella, calling at the Acceti home, lauded the merits of the new Ford motor while Thomas Conrad, Mrs. Acceti's brother, defended the Chevrolet motor as superior. Candella drew a gun to support his argument. Mrs. Acceti and her mother...rushed between the two men and Candella's bullet hit Mrs. Acceti. (53)

178

The temporary shutdown of the gigantic FMC triggered a small recession in America in 1927, but when Ford got back in the game, building 5,500 A2's per day in 1928, auto sales roared back to new heights. Herbert Hoover, who'd once called them the malefactors of public safety, now made "two cars in every garage" a theme of his successful Presidential campaign. In 1929, America built a new record of 5.3 million cars and trucks (three-quarters of them in Michigan), and accounted for 85% of all those built in the world. Americans borrowed to buy cars with increasing abandon, $1.9 billion in 1929 alone, against a backdrop of nearly full employment, gimme-gimme consumption, a rocketing stock market, and a $1,500-$1,700 median household income. 80% of those households didn't have a penny in savings.

Subtracting the 22 persons killed in and by motor vehicles in 1929, St. Clair County's 67,500 residents now owned 19,200 automobiles and trucks. Auto-related stores in Port Huron did $5 million in business, about 25% of all retail trade. Americans drove their motor vehicles about 198 billion miles that year, according to historian James Flink. Said the Ford Motor Company, *...we do not have automobiles because we are prosperous, we are prosperous because we have them.* This theory was about to be put to the test, in very short order.

America did not have gasoline because it had automobiles, it had automobiles because it had gasoline. A lot of it. To get some at the opening of the 20's cost Port Huron drivers about 23 cents a gallon, and they spent an average of $125-150 per year to keep fueled. Unlike railroad prices for instance, the government placed no controls on gasoline prices. Plentiful supply and ferocious competition kept them low, about one-quarter of what European nations paid. American touchiness about even a modest rise in gasoline prices could set off a nationwide outcry, as it did in 1922, when a six cent per gallon increase over the course of six weeks led to an investigation by U.S. Attorney General Harry Daugherty. Many more similar witch hunts followed during the rest of the century. Usually by the time the investigators got up off their chairs, prices had retreated again. Allowing for some regional variation, gas pretty much cost the same at the 120,000 filling stations in business across America at the end of the decade.

That being the case, gasoline retailers took some pains to set themselves apart from one another. Their most ridiculous gimmick involved cutting one-tenth of a cent off the price, down to, say, 17.9 cents, to make it look a penny cheaper, and this became a standard practice. Companies also exaggeratedly promised better performance from their brands. Standard Oil combined forces with General Motors to add one of the world's most dangerous chemicals, tetra-ethyl lead, to gasoline, to try to cure engine knock, at the expense of flooding the atmosphere with an even more poisonous exhaust. When Standard persuaded motorists to "fill 'er with Ethyl," both the car and the bloodstream got a dose. White Star gasoline countered with its own "Knockoline" additive to keep pace.

New stations popped up regularly all over Port Huron, obliterating in the process familiar structures from the past. The Edison Hotel and the Mineral Springs Bath House on Main Street, both in the heart of town, fell to make room for two more filling stations. Star Oil Company, the star of Port Huron gas station operators, owned 14 of the 60 in the city. Star sold 3 million gallons per year, and kept 120,000 gallons in storage along Port Huron's waterfront. Leaky storage. About 6 million gallons of gasoline evaporated from holding tanks every month in the U.S. Other interesting

179

methods of waste: (1) inefficient burning sacrificed 30% of all gasoline pumped into a car, just blasted it unmolested into the air; (2) idling cars burned 400 million gallons per year, going nowhere in America.

400 refineries across the country distilled gasoline from the 440 million barrels or so of native oil pumped annually in the early 20's. That barrelage grew to 1 billion by 1929. Across the river from Port Huron, Standard's Imperial Oil refinery couldn't expand fast enough. It built in a single year eight new 80,000 gallon storage tanks, and commissioned a $1 million research lab. A 62-cent barrel of oil bound for these tanks took about three days to make the 155 mile trip to Sarnia through the pipeline from Ohio. Not even a colossal explosion at the Sarnia plant in 1930, which killed two workers and injured five more, and threw flames hundreds of feet into the air, slowed production appreciably. It just gave Port Huronites a bad case of the jitters. Many residents awakened by the 3 a.m. blast assumed at first their own city had caught fire, and fire trucks confusedly drove around town looking for the scene of the disaster.

Oil might be dirty and dangerous, but President Warren Harding admitted that America now found itself "utterly dependent on a future abundance of petroleum." Guesses about the amount of petroleum left in the ground varied so wildly nobody could put any faith in them. The Federal Trade Commission in 1923 warned of rapidly depleting oil reserves. The American Petroleum Institute begged to differ, guaranteeing a practically inexhaustible supply for centuries. Drillers made several big discoveries in the U.S. during the 20's, culminating in another spectacular oil find in Texas. They also started work in remote Alaska in 1922.

Like Moses to his wandering flock, Chevrolet handed down the 13 Commandments for Better Gas Mileage. 1) Don't race your idling motor. 2) Turn off motor for stops of more than one minute. 3) Don't speed. 4) Drive slower. 5) Don't overuse the choke. 6) Get brakes adjusted frequently. 7) Avoid excessive braking. 8) Have your valves ground regularly. 9) Adjust carburetor regularly. 10) Don't overfill the gas tank. 11) Don't ride the clutch. 12) Check gas line for leaks regularly. 13) Check the spark. Obey all these steps and you might save 2-5 miles per gallon, though any monetary savings obviously would be wiped out by the cost of all the regular garage work. In good times or bad throughout the decade gasoline sales in America kept rising. By 1930 Americans bought 26 million gallons of gas per day, at a daily cost of $5 million. Ed Snover observed:

...he who retails gasoline
Displays no sad, unhappy mein.
His trade is booming all the time
For folks who cannot spare a dime
To purchase twenty pounds of coke
Are ne'er, it seems, so flatly broke
That they can't find two bits, or so,
To make the family flivver go.(54)

With all that money flowing over the counters of gas stations, it seemed to some people a natural idea to tap into it to help pay for the roads underlying the motoring public. In 1919 Oregon passed the first state gas tax, and 35 other states soon did likewise. Michigan's legislature passed a 2 cent per gallon levy in 1923. It didn't at first win universal acclaim. "Unconstitutional, unjust, vicious and unnecessary," said

180

Governor Alex Groesbeck in vetoing it. Groesbeck, who'd read law in Port Huron as a young man, all but accused Highway Director Frank Rogers of hatching the gas tax to cover up his own department's waste. A "deplorable mess," is how Groesbeck described the highway office. The governor hadn't reckoned with the political clout behind the mess, however. His outlook matured, shall we say, during the next two years, courtesy of the road lobby, and in 1925 Groesbeck signed the same 2 cents per gallon law. Combined with weight taxes, this raised $21 million per year. Two years later the gas tax went up to 3 cents per gallon.

Government needed every tax penny it could lay its hands on to keep up with street and highway construction, improvement, and maintenance, the 2nd biggest public expense in 1920's America.(55) Even with gas taxes in place, motorists directly paid only about a third of the costs of roads, which reached $2.5 billion per year by 1929.(56) A lot of lettuce. None of it, of course, went for rails. Business statistician and columnist Roger Babson warned the nation against going "tax crazy" over roads, which took up 40% of St. Clair County's overall budget in 1929. Port Huron's bonded indebtedness crossed the $2.5 million level, mainly for streets and sewers. Its individual property owners carried another $1 million in special street assessments. Though stupefied by these figures, the *Times Herald* refused to turn back: "Whether we can afford it or not, and whether we are getting the worth of our money, there is nothing else we can do except to keep right on with our road building program."(57)

Some weary St. Clair County taxpayers took offense when Port Huron's Chamber of Commerce presented Road Commission Chairman Frank Beard with a $3,000 gift in cash in 1921, and threw a huge banquet in his honor at the Harrington Hotel. What was that all about? they wondered. In explanation the *Times Herald* cheerfully claimed that Beard had transformed the county into a "...compact community unit bound together by miles of concrete ribbon, 18 feet wide..(as) concrete mixers spew white stripes across the country and wipe away the great reason for the desertion of the farm by young people.."(58) At that point perhaps 150 miles of road had been graveled or paved, out of a total of 1,500 miles in the county.

This business about roads saving the farm gave one correspondent from Capac a good laugh. And a good cry, too. In fact, taxes absorbed about 17% of total farm income, and road taxes drove some farmers right off the land:

There is no denying the fact that perhaps more than two-thirds of the farmers bought cars during the prosperous war time but the majority of them are scarcely able to keep them in tires now with crop failures and deflated prices. The farmer can get his crops to market over poor roads easier than he can take a chance on losing all he's got. (59)

Transportation of the product still played a negligible part in farm costs, but nothing could get this simple fact into the heads of Good Roads groupies. Another dissenter yearned for the good old days of purely local road making: "The farmer-built gravel road will always stand up under the use the farmer gives it. It is only the city man's truck that needs anything better." Farmer B. N. Clark wrote that his property taxes had gone up from $60 to $300 in ten years, two-thirds of it for roads. He'd been sucker-punched when he signed a Covert petition for a better road past his place, which ended up costing nine times its planned price. Clark also correctly blamed the undertaxed trucking companies for not paying their fair share: "We require the steam roads to furnish their own right of way at great expense while the trucks by paying a small tax

181

have a paved road quite as good for their purpose, provided for them."

Though people like Clark suspected that they worked hand in glove together, road directors frequently found themselves at war with the trucking interests over the subject of weight. Load limits on trucks (15,000 pounds normally) sparked very heated battles. Many of the heaviest vehicles in the Thumb hauled auto parts between Port Huron and Detroit or Flint. Although himself an auto man through and through, nothing steamed Frank Beard quite like the idea of overweight trucks crushing the life out of his improved roads, particularly the newly paved Gratiot Pike and Highway 21. Beard estimated the spring damage done by trucks at $2,500 per day in St. Clair County. It was true that the weight limits, which varied by season, were so complicated that the Michigan Attorney General could hardly figure them out, let alone a truck driver. Nevertheless, when inspectors found a truck stopped at Marine City to be three tons overweight, and a judge fined the driver a measly $3.50, Beard saw red.

On other occasions, cops just turned obese trucks loose without so much as a penny in fines. The Road Commission started operating its own patrol car, but its weight cop sometimes had a fistfight on his hands when he stopped one of these scofflaw trucks. The Michigan Highway Department set up permanent weigh stations on busy roads, and tried sending out roving scale crews to check truck weights on state highways at random, but for the most part the trucking fraternity easily evaded them. The industry fought back with lobbyists of its own as well as its fists. In 1928 Port Huron's Myron Ogden helped found the Michigan Trucking Association, which became a force in the state capitol. The whole weight problem remained just as insoluble as it had been for Horatio Earle 20 years earlier.

Bravely, Frank Beard toiled on. As many as 1,000 contractors' men labored during roadbuilding season on the Road Commission's behalf, and by decade's end they had graveled or paved one-third of St. Clair County's 1,500 miles of roads. Nationally, progress came slower; only 10% or so of roads and streets had been "improved" by 1930. Beard often daydreamed of the coming of "super highways" for more and more traffic. The supers would be 4 lanes, or 6 lanes, or who knew how many lanes wide, with cars and trucks divided into their own dedicated slots. There'd be no stop lights, no speed limits, only infrequent entrances and exits, and for real car joy a motorist could drive between Port Huron and Detroit like a bat out of hell.

Beard also wanted to see a "bypass" road built around Port Huron, so that a driver wouldn't have to wade through downtown traffic before continuing the next leg of his mad dash. Beard could afford to dream large. He'd turned the Road Commission into the biggest single government enterprise in St. Clair County, aside from schools, with a growing fleet of every imaginable type of road pampering equipment, including 10 snowplow-fitted trucks. The state demanded round-the-clock plowing from Beard if so much as 1.5 inches of snow fell on its highways, until those trunks were as clean as a whistle.

I wish that I might live within a town / Whose pavements were securely fastened down / So that no man or any group of men / Could tear them up again and yet again.(60) Ed Snover expressed a widely-shared distaste over the endless cycle of street work in Port Huron during the 1920's. No one yet dreamed that this continuous hacking away at road beds had become a permanent, expensive fact of automobile life in the 20th Century. If street crews weren't putting down new surfaces they were repairing the

182

old. The cost of paving a Port Huron street averaged $60,000 per mile, and the city spent about $300,000 per year on it. 43 miles of streets had been paved by the end of the decade, not yet one-third of the city, at a total cost of $3.5 million, about $100 per person.

The watchword these days about important Port Huron streets was "wider." Workmen chopped three to six feet off each side of the Main Street and Water Street sidewalks downtown, to make more room for cars (called a "desperate necessity" per Louis Weil). They also cut down a dozen large trees which shaded those walks. The city rounded off street corners so motorists needn't slow down so much in making a turn. This further endangered pedestrians, but what did they matter anymore? On school days cars backed up so deep in front of the High School that the street there required 14 feet of widening. A heavily traveled avenue along the lakefront doubled in width to 36 feet, despite a property owners' petition against it.

Another taxpayers rebellion broke out over individual tax assessments for street rebuilding and repaving. Henry McMorran himself led the charge against it, one of his last public stands. He argued that once the city paved a street, then subsequent maintenance or repaving of it became a general municipal obligation. This opinion eventually carried the day. Despite having to navigate those rounded off street corners, McMorran still regularly walked the 3 miles round trip from his expansive Main Street mansion "Deerfield" to his downtown business headquarters, until his death at age 84 in 1929. Death from old age, not a car rundown, lucky for Henry Mac.

Port Huron's automobile and street obsession continued to delay the cure for its massive water pollution problem during the 20's. Sewage fouled the Black River so badly by now that its waters killed a state scientist's boxful of test fish in eleven minutes. In a ruinous merry-go-round, the state of Michigan's Streams Commission demanded repeatedly that the city erect a $1.5 million sewage treatment plant, only to be put off just as often by city officials pleading poverty due to the high debt levels incurred largely by street paving and sewer construction, both of which just added to the pollution levels.

Notably, one major Port Huron street project failed to get off the ground – the street in the sky – a toll bridge over the St. Clair River connecting Port Huron with Sarnia. This brainstorm originated from onetime auto factory and road builder, now president of the New Egyptian Cement Company of Port Huron, Maynard Smith. The ferry system still easily handled car and pedestrian traffic across the river, so Port Huron didn't really need a bridge. But America built a lot of things it didn't need during the flush 1920's. Had a new connection really been needed, Smith had before him the ready example of the Grand Trunk railroad tunnel under the river, a durable crossing vastly superior to any bridge. But Maynard wanted something a little more visible, with plenty of cement in it.

Smith planned the 1,100 foot-long bridge to carry autos, streetcars, pedestrians, and bicyclists across an arch 150 feet high over the ship traffic passing below. That meant tearing up several blocks of downtown Port Huron on which to build the bridge approaches, and that idea didn't sit too well with some people living and doing business in the kill zone. Once it had been paid off in 30 years or so, Smith said he would hand the whole works over to the government as a toll free bridge. Estimated construction cost: $4-$6 million. With some heavy duty lobbying help, and the

183

distribution of $250,000, Smith fought off three competing plans and managed to get okays from the Canadian and American governments. He signed up Frank Beard and Louis Weil for his bridge commission, and got set to start pouring the foundations. At that point his bankers ran into an untimely financial difficulty at the end of the decade which we're still coming to.

Port Huron's system of clean, efficient, comfortable, convenient and affordable light rail mass transit expired at the end of this decade, a victim of automobile-induced American brain failure on the subject of transportation. The Detroit United Railways company, owner of Port Huron's streetcars and the Rapid Railway interurban, experienced serious financial trouble as early as 1921. First and foremost this stemmed from the massive government subsidization of automobile traffic, and second from the failure of the authorities to underwrite the rail networks in the same way they did roads. Irresponsible government control of rates and business practices also played its part, like the untouchable 5-cent fare on Port Huron's streetcars.

In addition the war for passengers became a 3-way battle, rails vs. autos vs. buses. Private bus companies incorporated left and right to run routes parallel to the trolleys and trains, but run cheaper on the publicly maintained streets and highways. A Port Huron to Flint bus service started up with as little as $16,000 in equipment, followed quickly by buses to Detroit, and to virtually all the cities in the Thumb. In very short order, DUR president Elliott Stevenson, the ex-Port Huron mayor and Henry Ford court nemesis, had to complain about buses "bleeding us white." 108 bus lines around Michigan carried 16 million passengers annually by 1925.(61)

Though Roger Babson called streetcars and interurbans the "ideal form of mass transportation," more than 130 electric rail systems in America failed in the four years following the end of WW1.(62) 16 billion passengers rode electric rail service in 1923, but expansion had come to a standstill, and service quality in many places slipped backwards. For instance on major city streets clogged with automobiles, streetcar travel time slowed down by as much as 50%. Electric rail operators abandoned 6,000 miles of line between 1923 and 1933.(63) Mayor James Couzens forced the DUR to sell its Detroit streetcar system to the city, for a price less than half its $40 million value. This swindle immediately created the largest municipally-owned streetcar operation in America, in a city in love with automobiles, dedicated to their propagation.

The financial setback that Couzens handed the DUR didn't bode well for the company's future in Port Huron. The Rapid Railway faced its own rate troubles, and jousted continually with state regulators about whether the company should be permitted to hike fares half a cent per mile, or pay shareholders even a tiny 2.5% dividend. Highway officials also kicked the Rapid off its rights-of-way in some areas to allow for wider roads. To draw a familiar comparison again, General Motors, Ford and Chrysler faced no such regulatory animosity, and they raised and lowered their prices, wages, and dividends with complete freedom. The DUR began substituting buses for its trolleys in Port Huron and St. Clair County in 1924. It didn't take long for these vehicles to negatively impress the public. DUR bus driver Dennis Daley almost immediately crashed into a gravel truck on the way to Detroit, killing himself. Shortly afterward, the first "Breaking News Photo" ever published by the *Times Herald* showed a fatal bus wreck at the north end of town, in which 85 year-old passenger Wilson Pace died when his driver hit a phone pole.

They weren't as safe as streetcars, and for comfort, rider John Currie compared the Port Huron city buses to riding in a concrete mixer. Many years later author Jan Crawford didn't see much improvement: "Everybody hates buses. The're slow, they stink, they're noisy, they take forever to board, they lurch, and the small, hard seats pinch your butt."(64) Jane Holtz Kay insightfully observed late in the 20th Century that streetcar lines provided a solid framework around which a city might design and structure itself, while buses were nothing more than junky multiple-passenger automobiles, with all their crazy failings and impermanence. The route "flexibility" of buses only encouraged directionless sprawl, overtransportation on too many routes, and the casual starting and stopping of service on a civic whim.

The *Times Herald* jumped the fence on the rail-vs-bus issue several times, hailing the advent of buses as "inevitable" at one point, then on another occasion calling streetcars the method of "first importance" in city transportation: "...it is hardly to be conceived that the steam railroads and the electric railroads are to be put out of business ..." Hard to conceive or not, the DUR came to the end of its rope. In the space of two days in 1925 company president Stevenson died and the DUR went into bankruptcy, neither to emerge again. The company struggled on for five more years in the hands of receivers, its streetcars still carrying 2 million people per year around Port Huron in 1928, but even the introduction of higher fares failed to turn the tide. Both the City Electric Railway and the Rapid Railway ceased operations in January 1930. Streetcar service in many Michigan cities – Lansing, Kalamazoo, Battle Creek, Jackson, Muskegon – went the same way.

The question then in Port Huron became: what next? Should the city run its own streetcars, or buses, or look to private enterprise, or do nothing? Tempers flared. So bitter became the debate that Mayor John Bell, who'd served six terms in office, died of an apoplectic fit. His successor, Fred Kemp, opposed a city takeover of the streetcars, and instead Port Huron enfranchised entrepreneur and former Great Lakes sailor Frank Carpenter to operate a bus-only system. As for the Rapid Railway, neither the state of Michigan nor the three counties it had served so brilliantly for 30 years offered to continue it as a public conveyance. Buses replaced it, too. "It is a tragedy to see a property which only 20 years ago was the marvel of the country junked in this way," said one DUR official about the rail system. It was a far cry from the day when passengers packed into the streetcars so "there was hardly room to breathe." Much of the trackage in rural St. Clair County the receivers sold for scrap, while Port Huron just paved it over.

Just five years after its first train pulled into Port Huron in 1917 amid welcoming cheers, the Handy Brothers Bay City to Port Huron steam railroad failed. Almost immediately after its inauguration the Handy Line fell into the hands of McAdoo's maladministration during WW1. Afterward, diminishing passenger numbers and the loss of freight business to trucks halted Handy service entirely by the mid 20's. Some bits and pieces of the system survived as short-line freight operations, including the resurrected Port Huron & Detroit, the salt plant railroad built in 1900, which ran 20 miles south to Marine City.

The other two railroads operating through Port Huron, the Grand Trunk and Pere Marquette, also lost passengers steadily. "Mr. and Mrs. August Flebelkorn, of Stanton Street, will leave Saturday for a two week motor trip over the Northern

185

Michigan pike," ran a typical social item in the newspaper, right next to the story, "Travel Light On Railroads – Automobile Believed To Have Taken Much Business." Ten, or even five years earlier the Flebelkorns would have made that trip by train.

In 1921, Pere Marquette president Frank Alfred predicted the replacement of much of Michigan's intercity passenger rail service by buses due to the open road cost advantage. Then, having prepared the ground, Alfred cut service in the Thumb, which he said lost $800 per day. This left just one passenger train per day servicing the old McMorran Line. A correspondent reported: "Where once the arrival and departure of a train from the village station was an event that natives gathered around the depot to see, it is now attended by no more interest than a passing automobile – and sometimes less." Alfred had performed a near miracle in pulling the PMRR out of receivership and putting it back in the black, and he wanted to keep it there. He did such a good job of this that a wave of consolidation in America's railroads swallowed up the 10,000-employee PMRR. It became a branch of the Chesapeake and Ohio Railroad system.

The Grand Trunk reduced passenger service from Port Huron to Detroit from four trips daily to two by 1930. Several trains still headed east every day to New York or Toronto or west to Chicago, and the GT occasionally ran excursion fares of $6 round trip to Chicago, less than one cent per mile. However, the hotels and other businesses clustered along Port Huron's Railroad Street near the Grand Trunk passenger station faded with the passenger count. The fewest American passengers in 20 years, 788 million, took the train in 1928, traveling an average of 264 miles each. By the end of the decade 75% of intercity travelers went by auto, 18% by bus, which didn't leave much for the trains.(65) Those who did entrain enjoyed 60,000 meals served in dining cars daily, while 40,000 people bedded down in Pullman car comfort every night, something Ford Bryan's family could only dream of.(66) Even while they lost passengers, the railroads worked closely with Charles Lindbergh to set up combined domestic transcontinental air-and-train travel, precursor to the airline-only system.

Things shaped up a bit better for American railroads on the freight side. In 1929 trains carried 75% of all U.S. freight volume, while 16% went by inland waterways, 4.9% in pipelines, 2.5% on trucks. The steam trains moved almost triple the amount they had in 1900, and the GTRR built a new $250,000 warehouse in Port Huron for freight operations. Train speed rose 40% during the 20's, and fuel efficiency increased 20%. It took only two ounces of coal to move a ton a mile, 26 times the fuel cost effectiveness of an automobile.(67) Trains ran so punctually that Alfred Parfet had the effrontery to compare his Ford repair garage to a train timetable ("Parfet Service is Like Train Service"). Former railroad worker James Couzens, who'd been promoted again by the public from Detroit Mayor to U.S. Senator, lauded the train systems for being "very efficiently and economically managed." Not everyone agreed, and under continuing anti-railroad pressure from federal and state regulators, Michigan train companies abandoned 10% of their track during the 20's. Expansion plans stood no chance at all, as the ICC demonstrated when it shot down a proposal for a new beltline railroad to encircle the Detroit suburbs.

The 24 members of the Michigan Railroad Association minced no words in blaming many of their problems on a pro-automobile assortment of government paper-shufflers:

These bodies fix our rates for carrying freight and passengers – pass judgment on all or our security issues and other financing – specify the working hours of our employees and the wages we must pay them – limit our profits, when there ARE profits, to a small and definite maximum – have full jurisdiction over our tax assessments – restrict rigidly our methods of competition – hedge about, with a multitude of restrictions, every department of our operations.

Give us a square deal – an honest chance.(68)

At one point during the decade 92 bills waited in Congress to further regulate railroads. A single train company in Michigan spent $125,000 per year just making out government reports. But the public seemed unmoved, or uninterested in these affairs, and the regular railroad news column disappeared from the *Times Herald.*

While still just a naive rookie railroad owner, Henry Ford gave some friendly advice to the industry early in the 20's: get rid of your stockholders, lay off workers, and impose one-man rule, like mine. Soon, however, the genius of travel found himself and his railroad "hogtied in a mass of rules and regulations," of the kind he never tangled with in the automobile biz. When the ICC blocked the incredulous Ford from *lowering* freight rates on his line, he'd had enough. After eight years at the throttle, Ford sold the Detroit, Toledo, and Ironton Railroad for an enormous profit in 1929, and went right on doing business with the DTI. The railroads rendered indispensable service to Ford and everybody else in the auto industry, carrying as much as 3 million carloads of materials and finished cars for automakers per year. Why should railroads provide service to an industry that undermined them? Because as "common carriers" they couldn't refuse. And needed the money.

Railroads did strike back at individual automobiles violently on occasion, colliding with 584 of them in Michigan in 1923, killing 164 people. A train emptied the St. Clair County Drain office in a trice when Commissioner Ira Chase drove his official car in front of an oncoming express while conversing with his assistant Howard Large. Some locomotive engineers retired from service with their nerves shattered from watching car drivers impatiently or even playfully race them to crossings, and lose. Just as bad were balky motor vehicles stalling on the tracks, as used car dealer George Porter's did one day in Port Huron, with fatal results for him and his wife Martha. Safetywise, the Porters should have taken the train. Riding a train in America was safer than crossing the street on foot in a major city, thanks to pedestrian-stalking automobiles.

The railroads continued to make heavy investment in their existing plant, as much as $1 billion per year, virtually all private money. 1,750,000 people worked in the $25 billion industry. Port Huron remained an important post for Grand Trunk. Its railcar shops, tunnel, and marshaling yards employed up to 1,700 men at a time, with an annual payroll well in excess of $2 million. On the civic side the company also built an athletic field and amphitheater, ran recreation leagues and social clubs, and even sponsored a band for its Port Huron employees. Louis Weil played toastmaster at a general thank-you banquet at the Harrington Hotel for GTRR president Sir Henry Thornton. But when its 1 million bushel grain elevator burned on the riverfront, Grand Trunk didn't replace it, a setback for the city. The Pere Marquette also put up big money to improve its Port Huron operation, bought the world's largest railcar ferry for crossing the St. Clair River, and earmarked $500,000 for a new lift bridge across the Black River in downtown Port Huron.

187

In Port Huron's marine circles during the 20's the situation looked like a watery reflection of what happened to the rail industry. 52 U.S. and Canadian passenger vessels still plied the Great Lakes, but passenger traffic declined throughout much of inland America except in special cases like ferries. Speed naturally tilted the playing field in favor of automobiles against ships. Some long-time shipowners saw more heavy weather ahead. After spending a fortune to adapt his St. Clair River ferries to automobiles and build a new terminal, and to replace the ferryboat *Conger* after it blew up and killed four people at the Port Huron dock in 1922, Henry McMorran prudently sold out when talk started about building Maynard Smith's automobile bridge across the river.

The White Star Line continued to offer passenger service between Port Huron and Detroit, but dropped its package freight business by mid-decade due to the inroads of truckers. The company also sold off one of its passengers ships, whose new owners converted it into an automobile carrier. White Star travel still gave the ultimate in value ($2 round trip to Detroit), comfort, and safety. During a long career Captain Burton Baker made 65,000 dockings along the Port Huron-Detroit route without a single mishap. No longer could you catch a passenger boat calling on the small Lake Huron towns north of Port Huron around the arc of the Thumb shoreline. They had bus service instead. But weekly boats still ran to many of the larger cities on the upper Lakes. Enough of a luxury market remained that the Detroit and Cleveland line launched a huge new 650-room steamer, the *Greater Detroit*, at a cost of $3.5 million, for overnight runs between those two cities. But the D&C no longer called at Port Huron.

As far as cargo carrying went, Commerce Secretary Herbert Hoover called for a total upgrade of 9,000 miles of American lakes, rivers and canals during the 1920's. As President he celebrated the completion of the massive canalization of the Ohio River, and signed a $140 million dollar waterways appropriation which included $29 million for the Great Lakes and a federal takeover of the Erie Canal. Mr. Hoover could be satisfied that bulk shipments of materials like coal, ore, grain, and oil continued to grow on the Great Lakes, 87 million tons of it in 1928. The Port Huron Paper Company, run by executive Edgar Kiefer, who held a shipmasters certificate, operated its own freighter, which regularly trundled up the Black River bringing pulpwood to the plant. The proud Kiefer called the Black River Port Huron's "ace of diamonds" for future industry. A second paper company organized by businessman Theodore Dunn built a large new plant in Port Huron during this decade to take advantage of the same shipping efficiency. The Mueller Brass Company owned a quarter mile of water frontage for the same reasons.

Much of Port Huron's vital coal supply to heat and power the city arrived by ship. The New Egyptian Cement dock on the St. Clair River busied itself with raw materials coming in and finished product sailing out. St. Clair County's salt industry favored the water for getting to market. Harold Wills sent his cars that way, as long as they lasted. Further downstream, just off the Detroit River, so did the Ford Motor Company, whose Commodore Henry Ford bought up a fleet of freighters and canal vessels in the 20's to service the Rouge River plant. A single 260-footer carried enough parts to assemble 3,000 Model Ts. Henry enjoyed one of his boats so much – the *Henry Ford II*, named for his grandson – that he sometimes commandeered it as his personal 600 foot-long yacht.

188

An attempt by the Jenks family to boost Port Huron's slipping package freight fortunes started well. Their Port Huron Terminal company handled 175,000 tons of cargo in its first year of 1924, including a lot of foodstuffs. But the firm had all but shuttered by 1930. The *Times Herald* lamented, "It is probably a fact that we are not making use of the traffic opportunities of our inland waterways as we should and might with advantage and profit." A couple of dry docks continued to operate on a modest scale in Port Huron, but the Reid family merged its salvage interests with a Canadian firm and moved away. The last builder of big commercial ships in St. Clair County, McLouth, shut down its Marine City yard. Two sport boat makers, Chris Craft and Gar Wood, managed to thrive. Recreational sailors kept their faith in traditional canvas alive. While wearing his Captain's hat, Edgar Kiefer helped organize the Port Huron Yacht Club's participation in an annual 300-mile sailboat race to Mackinac Island.

Few people in Port Huron still had the stamina to walk to Mackinac Island by the 1920's, as Fred George had done 20 years earlier. Shame on us, the press occasionally chided the community. "There is one door to good health to which every man and woman, rich or poor, holds a key," proclaimed an article in the *Times Herald*. "That is walking...a healthful exercise which brings every muscle in the body into active use. It has, moreover, a tonic effect on the entire system, overcoming constipation more effectively than any other method."(69) What's wrong with a little constipation? countered the Ford Motor Company: *Again We Say - Why Walk? Why Walk When You Can Drive This New Car for Only $100 Down.*

One expert of this decade suggested that good health required five miles a day of walking. That was about a mile short of the Jefferson Minimum, but a diminishing number of Americans even got five in. Parodying the growing national laziness, in his 1924 film *The Navigator* Buster Keaton played a spoiled young millionaire who took his chauffeured limousine literally across the street to propose to his neighbor's daughter. When she rejected him, Keaton told his driver "I think a long walk would do me good," and re-crossed the street on foot. Keaton lived long enough to see this splendid gag become a depressing reality in America.

Partly as a result of this trend, by the opening of the 1920's heart disease had supplanted tuberculosis and pneumonia as the number one killer of Michiganders. Port Huron city physician Gertrude O'Sullivan reported that "constantly increasing" heart trouble had dropped 52 people in their tracks in 1926. Hardening of the arteries also increased apace. President Warren Harding's doctor fruitlessly advised him to get in more exercise a full year before the Prez died of a stroke in 1923. Bina West, who'd spent a lifetime selling life and health insurance, opened 38 health centers across America for her lady Maccabees, now called the Women's Benefit Association. She brought in a Swedish exercise expert to work out the office gals in the WBA's Port Huron headquarters. But Bina didn't always practice what she preached, she drove too much, and put on weight, and she'd been no sylph to begin with.

Jumbo mamas fell hard for chimerical fat solutions. Phil Higer's Port Huron store offered camouflage: "For the Larger Woman – Special Purchase of Slenderizing Fall Frocks." The larger woman also might try opening her mouth wide for: "Rite-Wate: Vegetable Compound Fat Reducer. It is now an easy matter to lose your extra weight. No exercising, dieting or massaging required. Guaranteed absolutely harmless. No Thyroid!" Or she could try scrubbing it off: "Wash off Those Rolls of Fat. Reduce

Your Ankles, Legs, Arms, Hips, Double Chin with Dr. Folt's Soap." Fat men showed little more sense about their situation. In Detroit, doctors removed 36 pounds of fat surgically from 20 year old Edward Morine. His mother told Ed that blubber ran in the family. So did stupidity, evidently.

No, *forward march* provided the only sure path to health. 160 miles of sidewalks invited Port Huron pedestrians to take a hike by 1930, built for only 4% the cost of the paved streets. Maintaining these walks cost a pittance compared to streets. Twelve horses pulling cheap board snowplows could clear all the sidewalks in Port Huron of snow in four hours, while clearing just Main Street for cars required an army of laborers, horses, and trucks, sometimes struggling for days. Professionals like mail carrier Arthur Carlisle welcomed clean walks. He covered 300,000 miles in 37 years before retiring at age 69 in 1929. If you kept your wits about you, ready to dodge those no speed limit motorists, and traveled only during the day, you could walk St. Clair County's country roads with something approximating safety. Judge Fred George kept on walkin,' and sometimes ordered drunk drivers to do the same: "In court this morning Ledsworth started to argue with Judge Fred George over the suspension of his drivers license. 'You can't suspend my license because I will have to walk three miles to work.' The Court reply was 'Walk'."(70)

Eleanora Sears took her place among the noteworthy national walkers. A Boston athlete and society figure, Sears walked the 44 miles home from Providence, Rhode Island in 10 hours on a challenge, then made an annual event of it. First Lady Grace Coolidge put in a minimum of four miles per day, rain or shine, summer or winter, around the Washington neighborhoods. 78 year-old Fanny Straiter of Virginia dropped in on her daughter in Oregon after a 3,000 mile walk. The amazing Edward Weston continued walking almost to the end. He leisurely covered the 500 miles between Buffalo and New York City in a month in 1923, at age 83. "I did it for the sake of Young America – to spread the doctrine of keeping well by walking, instead of trusting to doctors." It was his last great outing. A taxi ran down Weston in New York in 1925, and he never fully recovered his health or his senses. Instead of trusting to doctors he aimlessly walked the streets and slept in doorways. Playwright Anne Nichols rescued the grand old pedestrian with a pension, and Weston died in 1929, his life's work, for a time, less and less heeded.

People heeded the bicycle less and less as well. Makers built only about a quarter million U.S. bikes annually, and Xmas priced them in 1927 at $30-$40. Most bicycle ads aimed at children, but some adult riders remained steadfast. 71 year-old Emil Lenly rode 1,250 miles from New Jersey to St. Louis in 18 days. In Port Huron, worthies like Judge Carl Wagner, bakery owner John Endlich, and the chief Episcopal rector, John Munday, all regularly cycled around town. The spectacle of Munday pedaling about Port Huron in his flowing ministerial robes did not meet with the approval of some of his car-addled parishioners. When Munday rode his bike four miles out to Thomas Reid's beach home one day, the appalled marine captain started a fundraising campaign to buy the minister an automobile. The auto had become the very hallmark of respectability. Munday wouldn't own a car because he was a minister, he would be a minister because he owned a car. Somewhat surprisingly, Frank Beard's hardware store still sold bikes, and he rejected Reid's reasoning: "Bicycles are not out of date. Bicycling is not now a craze. It is a good business proposition." And a good business proposition in America at the end of the decade suddenly became very

190

welcome indeed.

"The United States is reaching a point in its financial and business structure where panics are becoming impossible."(71) This revealed wisdom of 1927 came from Norval Hawkins, the former crook and ex-Ford Motor Company sales manager. Hawkins' views accurately reflected the feeling in Detroit as the decade drew to an end. The city was awash in automobile money. Skyscrapers grew there like dandelions. Up went the Penobscot, the Book Cadillac, the Guardian, and the ultimate, a General Motors project designed by Albert Kahn, the Fisher Building. These structures competed with each other in marbled and gilded ornateness. So did the Institute of Arts, Orchestra Hall, and the world's largest Masonic Temple. Detroit's extravagance reached its zenith in the construction of what may have been America's most wildly elaborate theater, the $10 million Fox, described by its future owner, who first saw it as a boy, as "another world, a fantasy, another planet."(72)

Detroit completed a dozen annexations during the 20's to swell its land area to six times that of 1900. Investors built both a new bridge and a new tunnel across the Detroit River to Canada to make way for the marvelous future ahead of limitless auto traffic. On the drawing board aviators crafted a plan to build the world's largest airport in Detroit, to service a civic population of 1.5 million. About the only transportation item Detroit officials rejected, a $54 million subway idea, lost out even though Henry Ford endorsed it. Perhaps Henry down deep really wanted to answer a higher calling, rapid urban mass transit. We'll never know.

Port Huron's 31,000 residents, too, seemed on balance to be having a successful decade. Even given the Wills Sainte Claire collapse, the city population went up 20%, the home count up 25%, new businesses started, new schools opened. And after all, look at all the cars in town, and all the car commerce, didn't that prove something? So it seemed. Hindsight is always 20-20, but in retrospect there were some signs of tottering as the 20's came near their end. The Port Huron Community Welfare League busily searched out jobs, food, clothing and coal for growing numbers of needy families. Not all the auto firms in Port Huron made money. Dealer Earl Paige left the car trade and became the new city bus company manager. Garageman Clair Green hanged himself. Some other long-time enterprises failed, like the Port Huron Engine and Thresher Company, undone by the gasoline engine.

Port Huron readers of Roger Babson's financial column got two specific warnings in 1929 to get out of the stock market, which had reached crazy heights on borrowed money. When the crash occurred in October it made Babson's reputation for life; but Port Huron paid more attention to the golden jubilee of Edison's electric light than to the latest shenanigans on Wall Street. "The stock market is just wind anyhow," said Henry Ford. In this case, an ill wind. Within a month of the collapse in equities, automobile sales and production in America tanked completely, and the FMC built up the biggest unsold inventory in its history. Layoffs followed, by the gross.

Both Ford and Alfred Sloan expressed bafflement. Things had been going so well. 1929 had been a record year. Why didn't everybody just keep on borrowing and buying? Only a small percentage of potential customers owned cars, said Ford. Let's get the rest of them into the ring. However, another auto exec, REO sales manager Clarence Eldridge, made an open confession decrying the industry's "insatiable ambition," and "blind worship at the goddess of 'quantity production.'"(73) Very quickly it became

191

apparent that America had entered a business depression. This was nothing new, nor especially alarming, at first. The country had survived sharp, brief depressions in 1907-08 and 1920-21 fairly well. This "temporary lull" looked like a replay, according to the Port Huron Chamber of Commerce: "Port Huron is not dead industrially. It is very much alive!"

Roger Babson advised the unemployed to catch up on their rest and do odd jobs around the house until the temporary lull passed. But in March 1930 100,000 rested-up people in an ugly frame of mind turned out for an "Unemployment Day" march in Detroit that escalated into a riot. 2,000 cops tangled with the "Day" trippers, and the melee produced 12 injuries and 23 arrests. Citizen outrage over the whole affair led to the recall of Mayor Charles Bowles. An energetic Detroit judge who'd been born in the Thumb, Frank Murphy, succeeded Bowles as the new mayor of America's fourth largest city. It was not a job to be envied at that moment. Murphy promised "drastic measures" to stop job seekers from flooding Detroit, because the city had no work for them. The world headquarters for the automobile industry was ground zero for this business contraction, and not just in the factories. Between one-quarter and one-third of all American car dealers closed in 1930.(74)

Port Huron's faith in the auto industry revived a bit that summer when the Auto-Lite company decided to relocate a factory and 300 jobs to our town, to make electrical wire for Ford. This was tough luck for the factory's former home city of Muskegon, Michigan, but under the circumstances dog must eat dog. Louis Weil played a prominent part among the movers and shakers who'd engineered this coup. Auto-Lite took over the old PHET factory. A little more speculative good news arrived: the Pittsburgh Plate Glass company had bought 300 acres of Marysville property from Harold Wills, on which someday it wanted to build an auto glass plant. At a golf banquet in Port Huron, Michigan Bankers Association president John Harrer tried firing up a crowd of businessmen: "This so-called depression is mainly mental. We must kiss the bag of pessimism goodbye. We're through the worst of it now. From now on we're going up."(75) He predicted a big comeback in 1931, especially in automobiles.

But the old bag wouldn't be kissed off that easily. Car sales continued to tail off, even though prices were cut. Unpaid property taxes in Port Huron and St. Clair County hit record highs. A bank failed in Capac. Financing for Maynard Smith's bridge to Canada evaporated. The Grand Trunk cut hours drastically at the repair shops. More old-time stores like Boyce Hardware closed. There were no reliable unemployment statistics available in those days, leaving many people to wonder, just how bad *are* things?

The answer in Port Huron came the week after Labor Day, 1930. The Commissioner of Public Works, 50 year-old Charles Rettie, mosied down to the *Times Herald* to plant a little item in the Saturday edition, that he'd be hiring 25 temporary ditch diggers on Monday to lay a new water line at the north end of town. Just a few days work, no wage rate was mentioned. You had to look hard just to spot this tidbit in the summary of goings-on around town. A veteran of the auto industry, Rettie had worked first in the Havers plant, then went partners with his brother in the successful Rettie Garage. He eventually took on the duties of public office as well. In business or public affairs, folks recognized in Rettie the outgoing, opinionated, and voluble nature of a born politician. But his gregariousness failed him Monday morning when he

192

arrived at the water job site to find 500 desperate, destitute men milling around, waiting to take one of the 25 pick-swinging jobs for a few cents an hour. They'd come from all over St. Clair County and the Thumb. Nervously surveying this mob scene, it doubly shocked Rettie to see that 300 of these applicants had arrived in their own automobiles. They didn't own these cars because they were broke, they were broke because they owned them.

Chapter Six. 1931-1940: This So-Called Depression

Because of the widespread use of [automobiles] *there has been a noticeable increase in mental alertness, physical ability, health, judgment, courtesy and good habits. It has brought* [the driver] *realization of the rights and privileges of others, taught him courtesy, quick thinking, immediate determination of pressing problems, and to a certain extent it has even disposed of any deliberation or conscious thought about the solution of any particular proposition...The age of deliberation and of easy-going, well-thought-out, logical determinations, where as much time as might be needed could be taking for decision, passed with the horse and wagon...and it probably is not too much to assert that notwithstanding all the damage and injury which the motor vehicle has brought in its train, its use has been a tremendous boon to individual and national character.* (1)

Well, everyone to his own opinion, as the old man said when he kissed the cow. The above opinion came from the former commissioner of highways in the state of Connecticut, Robbins Stoeckel, lately a research associate at Yale University, as expressed in an article reprinted in the pages of the *Port Huron Times Herald* in early 1934. The same edition carried the news that Michigan's state school superintendent Paul Voelker had run over and killed a 64 year-old musician in Detroit after mistaking some neon store signs for traffic lights. U.S. Attorney General Homer Cummings' son Dickinson lay in a Connecticut hospital with a fractured skull after a one-car wreck that killed one of young Cummings' fellow passengers and left the driver charged with manslaughter. In Port Huron a trio of weekend traffic accidents had involved several residents, including City Engineer Earle "Wide Streets" Whitemore, and also 25 year-old Angus McKay, who paid a $50 fine after colliding with another vehicle while driving drunk on the wrong side of the street. And finally, from Watertown, New York: "Four Nuns And Man In Car Plunge To Death In Canal." All part of the daily roll call of 100 Americans killed and 3,000 or so injured by automobiles as part of the boon to the individual and national character.

Stoeckel's meditation on America's automotive blessings appeared in a special section mounted by the newspaper to celebrate the 1934 Port Huron Auto and Food Show and Recovery Exhibit. The nine new car dealers still standing in the city held this event in Alfred Parfet's Ford dealership. Along with "Bigger" and "Longer," the industry embraced "Streamlining" as the important buzz words for carmakers that year. Streamlining meant simply that designers had rounded off a few exterior corners on their cars, like airplanes. Chrysler, which led the way in exaggerated advertising among the Big 3, practically hyperventilated over its streamlined Chrysler "Airflow":

Nothing that has previously existed in transportation gives any adequate idea of the sensation of riding in this car...The periodicity – or rate of movement – of the springs has been slowed down to the point that is most agreeable to human nerves...The doors are as wide as house doors. Both front and rear seats have the spaciousness of divans.

So as the automobile driver's thoughts were speeding up, the seat springs in his house on wheels were slowing down to ease his nerves via his butt. Another Chrysler claim struck what became a familiar chord during the 30's, that this product wasn't a thing at all, but a being. Like, well, a horse:

A Chrysler is more awake, more alive, quicker in response, more facile in suiting its pace to match your mood. Two high gears instead of one – a high gear for flashing sprints in city driving and another high gear for the open road.

Ford Motor said the same: *There is always less strain and less likelihood of tight situations when you drive an alert, obedient car.*

As if streamlining and animalizing weren't enough, the auto industry bombarded the buyer with adjective-loaded trade names for the various and nearly identical mechanical parts in all models of cars. "Knee-Action Wheels," "Floating Power," "Gliding Ride," "Quadripoise Suspension," "Starterator," "Syncro-Mesh Gear-Shift," "Shockproof Steering," "X-Bridge Type Frame," "Blue Streak Engine." They offered new gizmos like turn signals, theft alarms, and automatic transmission (*It's As Catching As Measles*). Engine horsepower crossed the wholly unnecessary 100 threshold. Tradesmen continued to sell this excess both ways: power to drive like a happy hellion, or, as a safety feature, power to pull you out of the way of trouble, like that oncoming happy hellion.

Dr. H. C. Dickinson, the president of the Society of Automotive Engineers, predicted everyday blue streak car speeds ahead of 120 mph. However, the doctor didn't sound quite as sanguine about expanding mental alertness as Robbins Stoeckel, or about spring-pacified human nerves as Chrysler, or about evading tight situations as Ford. "One shudders to think of two cars passing each other on an 18-foot strip of highway at any such speed," said Dickinson about 120 per. "Progress in highway travel has so outstripped the imagination that none of us can think clearly on the subject."

Some discrepancy existed there between "none of us can think clearly on the subject" and "immediate determination of pressing problems." Meeting the challenge halfway, Penn State University physicist H. L. Yeagley claimed that a properly designed car could hit a wall head on at 115 mph without injuring the occupants. Among Yeagley's ideas: move the dashboard to within three inches of the driver's nose. How would that help? Details to follow, said Yeagley. The professor hadn't tested this theory personally, it seemed, but by the 1930's the flapdoodle of the automotive experts, meeting themselves coming and going, a technocratic car wreck so to speak, didn't seem much out of the ordinary.

Forget about it, advised the Nash car company, which probably captured as well as anybody the automobile ethos of the 1930's: "At 5, or 85 miles an hour, you have never driven a car that performed so sweetly."

If you're looking for a fourth for bridge, or company for the movies, don't call up that friend who bought a Nash. His house is dark. The door is locked. Something has happened to him! He's been shanghaied – by a car that refuses to stay in a garage. And that's the way it happens. There's your new Nash – long and rakish, gay and glittering, so restless it can hardly stay at the curb. Next thing you know, you're out of town with your heart singing with excitement.

195

And if wanderlust gets the better of you – if you can't get that proud hood headed home – well, just park beneath a star and go to bed. For it's that simple with a Nash. With its convertible bed, you can live in it – anywhere – for weeks on end. Too bad you're missing all the fun that Nash owners have. If it's money that's holding you back – forget it!

At his Nash showroom in Port Huron, dealer Harvey Kimball wanted $700 for this auto kidnapper. If truth be told, Harvey really didn't have any trouble from Nashes that refused to stay on the lot, and he wasn't going to forget about the purchase price, either.

Plenty of people slept in their cars in 1934 in the United States, but not from wanderlust. The auto show shebang at Parfet's bore the supplementary, hopeful title of "Recovery Exhibit" because the pressing problem requiring quick thinking and immediate determination in Port Huron as we concluded the last chapter, the Great Depression, had entered its fifth year and still dragged along in 1934. Now that the age of deliberation had ended, few in the nation drew the damning conclusion that the drainage of America's private and public financial resources through the unparalleled profligacy of the automobile had caused and prolonged the depression. An admission of that sort would have triggered an earthquake in the carsick American psyche which nobody wanted to face. There were already enough troubles.

A delegation of Soviet Union officials on a tour of the States in '34 took a flabbergasted look at the American auto industry and the circus of waste involved in the annual model changes which continued right on through a bad economic slump. What's going on here? one baffled Russian, Stephen Dybetz, wanted to know: "Either you don't know what to do with your great national resources or you don't know how to make them go around. We are not so rich as to spend $10-$15 million to start a new model, just for style."[2] Instead of facing up to it, the automakers bragged about being the black hole of the country's wherewithal. "As a consumer of raw materials the automobile has no equal in the history of the world," said General Motors' Charles Kettering, proudly.[3]

But here we need to go back a few years in the history of the world.

Shortly after the end of the last chapter in 1930 Charles Rettie managed to pacify the unhired 475 ditch-digging applicants in Port Huron with some vague promises of help. Mayor Fred Kemp and Louis Weil called together a committee of top Port Huron business leaders to organize special relief efforts. Although there'd been official city and county administrators of the poor in Port Huron and St. Clair County for years, they weren't prepared to handle times like these. Eventually the 1930's supercharged, to put it in automotive terms, the growth in the government welfare bureaucracy until it became as big as the road bureaucracy, but that came later. By the opening weeks of 1931, the Kemp-Weil relief committee had registered 1,200 unemployed Port Huroners, well over 15% of the local labor force. The American Federation of Labor estimated 20% of its St. Clair County members were on the sidelines. More guesswork put Michigan's total unemployment rate at 29%. These unfortunates floundered around in a sea of 5-7 million jobless workers nationwide.

Family man and unemployed Port Huron landscaper Elvin Arnold found himself in a tight spot typical of many. The Port Huron poor commission paid rent on homes for 350 families, and although he qualified for this assistance, Arnold sounded a little fidgety. "I hope I don't have to go into the Negro section," he said, "where they tell me the poor commission sends everyone when they have to pay rent for them. I don't like to have my wife and children live in that section, because we have always lived in a clean, respectable neighborhood."(4) Having ingratiated himself in this fashion with his prospective new neighbors, Arnold went on to add that the poor commission had given him four loaves of bread, a head of cabbage, two pounds of beans, two cans of condensed milk, two pounds of oleomargarine, three pounds of salt pork and two bars of laundry soap with which to feed his family of four for a week. And no matter how hungry they were, laundry soap made pretty poor fixings. When Arnold protested about this allotment to the relief director in Port Huron the man asked Arnold to step outside a minute, then locked the door behind him.

The equally downcast 24 year-old Elmer Muter hadn't held a steady job in three years, and as a result now had three children on his hands, aged 2 weeks to 2 years. Muter told a reporter he'd work 48 hours per week for $5, what Ford men in boom times had been making per day. Enough Arnold and Muter families lived in similar circumstances to triple in one year St. Clair County's spending on the indigent to $250,000, and it kept on rising. 12% of the county went on relief, and this later increased to 18%. There were limits to this largesse, however. When administrators discovered that some people on the poor list still owned automobiles, they delisted the car owners PDQ. Joseph Klenefeter had the gall to park his car outside the city limits, then hike down to the jail and ask for lodging as a bum. As attitudes hardened further, the city and county put welfare recipients to work for their stipends, mainly on roads. A hundred at a time could be seen scraping the streets in Port Huron.

American car production skidded 75% in three years, to 1.4 million vehicles in 1932. Which meant Detroit had the highest unemployment rate in America, as near as could be figured. Automakers laid off half of the almost 500,000 auto workers in the Detroit metro area, while most of the rest worked part time. The average annual pay for these workers sank from $1,639 in 1929 to $757 in 1931.(5) 120,000 Detroiters went on the dole, costing the city $1.8 million per month. The handsome handout for food relief in the Motor City allotted $2 per adult, $1 per child per week, compared to the $15 worth that the average self-sustaining family ate. U.S. Senator James Couzens donated $200,000 of his ill-gotten Ford gains for Detroit aid, while less sentimentally the Ford Motor Company lent the city $3 million at 3.5% interest. A breathtaking $500 million worth of Detroit property sat on the delinquent tax list.

Plenty of country brethren also lived in fear of the tax man. Michigan Governor Wilbur Brucker painted a disheartening picture in 1932 of the burden that cash road taxes placed on the farmer. Especially onerous were the special assessment road taxes, known as the Covert plan, once hailed as the emancipation of Old MacDonald. St. Clair County alone had built 100 of the Covert road swindles, which Brucker now denounced.

The Covert road situation in some of our counties has become acute in the last few months. It has been established beyond question that special assessments...have frequently far exceeded the total present value of the property assessed; that thousands of our citizens will be turned out of their farms and homes; that whole districts will be laid waste by tax sales. Words can hardly express the ruination that faces these people.
(6)

The lowest farm commodity prices in 20 years, thanks to overproduction, further compounded the farmer's miseries. So did the expenses of the automobiles and trucks owned by 92% of American farm families. Many of them also owned tractors and attachments they couldn't afford. Farmers needed to work tractors 75-100 days per year just to break even on them, and figured on an overhead for these vehicles amounting to 20% of the purchase price, plus gas and oil. A tractor at the Port Huron Sears store cost $1,100, once again more than many depressed farms were worth. American tractors didn't do just financial damage, but in the Plains states tore up the soil and contributed to the Dust Bowl conditions there. From one astringency or another, Henry Ford's brother William, a tractor dealer who incidentally refused to own an automobile, declared bankruptcy under the weight of $400,000 in business debts.

America's agriculture dilemma reached such a pitch that one official warned of the potential for "civil strife." 5,000 dairy farmers from around the Thumb trooped into the city of Yale to raise some strife about getting a meager 4 cents per quart for milk, and paying exorbitant 15%-25% rates to truckers to haul it away. This especially annoyed producers who had lost their train service. Amazingly, with these odds stacked against them, the number of farm families in America actually grew by 2 million during the first five years of the decade, by 10% in St. Clair County, because conditions in some cities were even worse than those in the sticks.

The grim reaper of insolvency stalked the Port Huron business ranks. In the transportation sector, the bus line from Port Huron to Detroit left over from the old DUR, now known as the Eastern Michigan Lines, declared bankruptcy. The shipping line on the same route, the White Star Line, reorganized, and sold off its big Tashmoo Park resort on the lower St. Clair River. The Port Huron Terminal for cargo handling on the riverfront went bankrupt. The Buhl Aircraft Company, formerly building its skywares in the old Wills Sainte Claire car plant in Marysville, vanished as completely as did Amelia Earhart. The McMorran Foundry closed forever, while the Holmes and the Auto Lite factories, while not dead, went into deep hibernation along with several more auto parts makers. So did manufacturers Mueller Brass, the paper makers, and Peerless (formerly New Egyptian) Cement.

Retailers in Port Huron collapsed like ten-pins. Even the biggest guys shuddered. The stress and strain may have hastened the death in 1931 of John Sperry, the department store king of Port Huron, and in his place his son Clare took over the helm. One of the late J.B. Sperry's aphorisms, perhaps in sympathy with the dairymen, had been "Do not develop into a milker unless you're willing to go out and take care of the community cow."(7) Such had been his dedication to the cow that Port Huron's biggest downtown store survived on its customers' loyalty.

Smaller fry did not. Clothing stores turned into ghost stores: Pearce Knitware, Henson Clothing, Field's Clothing, Checker Shoes, all said goodbye. Bowman and Johnson Shoes kept the wolf from the door by appealing to women to please wear out more footwear: "Don a pair of TREADEASY shoes and you too will take a new-found pleasure in that most healthful of all exercise – walking." B&J illustrated this with a drawing of an attractive gal passing up a ride in a dude's sports car with, "Thanks, Bob – but I'm out for a walk." More commercial casualties piled up: Brown Credit Jewelers, Economy Furniture, and one of the city's grand old emporiums, home furnishings veteran J. A. Davidson and Company. A desperate Howard Furniture offered to sell

198

furniture for wheat. Food stores had to deal with a 16% decline in shelf prices in a single year and many fell from the ranks.

Rieman's Radio & Tire store closed, but Fred Dole's Goodyear Tire shop hung on, defiantly parading the world's largest tire, all 12 x 4 feet of it, through downtown Port Huron. Dole dolefully warned the motoring public about being too stingy with rubber in this penny-pinching hour: "Do you knock on wood every time you set out for an airing in the car? Is your heart in your mouth when you swing into a curve at a little more speed than the law allows? There's nothing like a set of junky old tires to take the joy out of driving."(8) Another company that bucked the tide, Kerr and Calhoun Collision, actually started business in the teeth of the depression and soon kept 12 mechanics busy ironing the wrinkles out of 25 motor vehicles at a time.

Cutbacks in municipal expenses became the the order of the day. Under the watchdog glare of the newly organized Port Huron Taxpayer Association, the city rolled its budget back to 1920 levels, turned off 300 street lights, slashed wages, laid off one-third of its 50 firemen, and gave the remaining firefighters and cops unwanted, rotating, no-pay 20-day vacations. Police had to raise money for patrol car radios by holding a 4th of July field day fundraiser, while St. Clair County officials talked of abolishing the sheriff's department altogether. Port Huron's school board axed 58 teachers in a single year, firing all married women on the theory that their husbands should support them. The remaining teachers all took pay cuts.

Civic improvements of almost all kinds halted. The latest Port Huron Hospital expansion stopped. Voters twice in two months turned down a $600,000 bond issue to build a sewage plant and clean up the rivers, while Mayor Kemp begged the infuriated state streams commission for more time. Inspectors called the Black River "an elongated septic tank," but Kemp reasoned that with the water already so dirty a little more of Port Huron's tons of annual sewage discharge wouldn't hurt. No clean river lobby existed during the depression in Port Huron, but a loud automobile one did. The slightest slowdown in spending on streets portended the fall of the Republic to these people. They brooked no delay in replacing the 7th Street bridge, one of the principle river crossings linking north and south Port Huron. Auto and truck traffic had beaten the bridge to pieces, but instead of just closing it to motor vehicles, the city pressed ahead with a $200,000 rebuild.

Despite this unhappy panorama before him, publisher Louis Weil remained nothing if not an optimist. Nay-sayers and gloom-spreaders were foreigners in his publishing house. The bag of pessimism sang no siren song for him. Where would he and Elmer Ottaway have been if they had listened to these sourpusses when launching the *Daily Herald* in 1900? Nowhere, that's where. Certainly Weil wouldn't have become one of the wealthiest and most influential men in town, a city father, a stalwart of corporate and charitable and public boards and commissions, across the whole spectrum of the community. A bringer of smokestacks: "It is because the smokestack is the symbol of human progress and human accomplishment...that we will work and work untiringly to bring about the building of more of them in Port Huron." 400 people turned out at a banquet in early 1931 at the Harrington Hotel to honor Louis for his can-do attitude.

For this reason, and naturally to reverse the dramatic shriveling up of automobile ad lineage, Weil's newspaper fed readers mainly a diet of hopeful economic

199

news, especially about the auto industry, during almost nine solid years of depression that stretched across the decade. If you believed the *Times Herald*, good times always waited just around the corner, and American carmakers turned more corners than a barnful of square dancers. Judging from artfully selected statistics and press releases, it seemed as though auto companies called workers back to the job more or less constantly, factories expanded, sales soared. Some typical early pick-me-ups: a record 36,000 people turned out for the first two days of the 1931 Detroit Auto Show; 4,000 people visited Union Chevrolet in Port Huron to see the newest models; Roger Babson predicted a comeback year in 1931 for the automobile, which he somewhat oversold as "an instrument of international enlightenment." Rah, rah, rah.

Only did the sharp-eyed and the skeptical notice the lower-case news that auto ownership in America actually declined at the beginning of this decade, for the first time ever, down by about 2 million vehicles from 1929 to 1931. Enough of them still smashed into each other on the nation's roads to ring up $2.5 billion dollars in accident costs in 1931, and keep Kerr and Calhoun Collision prosperous, but targets of opportunity dwindled in number. 3,000 cars actually disappeared from St. Clair County during this period, and thousands more from around the Thumb. An observer in the community of Brown City reported: "Five years ago a horse and buggy was almost a curiosity here. Now they may be seen frequently. Economic conditions which make it difficult for farmers to support a car and provide for its upkeep, combined with township roads that are almost impassable, are responsible for the revival of the horse and carriage here."(9)

Hard times temporarily left Harold Wills, the erstwhile Gray Goose mastermind, without a car to his name. He'd once owned a dozen. While he didn't resort to a horse and buggy, financial embarrassment forced Wills (if you have tears prepare to shed them now) to ride the *bus* back and forth between Marysville and Detroit while he re-built his fortunes. Harold's long experience in the auto industry continued to stand him in good stead when it came to goosing the public. Relying on the fact that one of his land company employees served as Marysville's mayor, Wills managed to persuade the populace of his invented city, which now numbered about 1,000 people, to borrow $100,000 and buy 35 acres of riverfront land from him for a park. About ten times what it was worth on the market.

In 1931 Wills' former employer Henry Ford offered up to the public from his stable:

The Greatest Value Ever Built Into A Ford Car – $490. (Bumpers and spare tire extra at low cost.) The Beautiful Ford Tudor Sedan...torque-tube drive...three-quarter floating rear axle...four Houdaille double-acting hydraulic shock absorbers...A joy to drive because it is so alert and easy to handle.

A joy to drive but not to sell. Ford Motor Company sales collapsed by two-thirds in 1931, to half a million vehicles, and the firm lost $53 million. At first Henry tried bluffing out the depression with public promises of wage increases, new hiring, re-hiring, and a dealer commission cut, only to have to backpedal with undeclared layoffs, production cutbacks, wage reductions and a dealer commission increase. Ford's doubletalk sparked some impatience with the great man, as in a Muncie, Indiana newspaper editorial, "Henry Ford says that wages ought to be higher and goods cheaper. We agree with this, and let us add that we think it ought to be cooler in summer and warmer in winter."(10)

And Henry received a thorough roasting in 1931 from a member of Detroit's city unemployment committee, economist S. M. Levin, "Hosts of Ford workers are denizens of public soup kitchens and lodging houses, and thousands of others have been reduced to dependence on the skimpy allowances of public and private charity."(11) Dictator Benito Mussolini took some of the sting off this by giving Henry Italy's highest civilian award, the Crown of Italy: "You are the world's fairest and most humane employer of labor." At least one desperate job applicant agreed with Mussolini. Frank Mustrig tried to hire in at the FMC Rouge plant at gunpoint, apparently unaware that the fading numbers of people inside worked a three-day week and not every week. FMC wages fell from a minimum of $7 per day, to $6, to $4, leaving workers worse off than they'd been in 1914. Fordism in reverse. The FMC lost a further $74 million in 1932.

The Fascists may have been in Ford's corner but American Communists switched sides, as they often made a habit of doing. A gang of Reds from an early version of the Auto Workers Union led a march of 3,000 people out to the Rouge factory one winter's day in March 1932 to present a list of demands. With the Detroit riot of 1930 still fresh in their minds, Dearborn police and Ford security men met the paraders with fire hoses, tear gas, and gunfire. The occasion did not end well for the four marchers shot to death, scores of others injured, and the 31 arrested, making it the ugliest single incident in FMC history. Just who started what was lost in a storm of accusations and denials, but this battle cemented the connection in Henry Ford's mind between unions and troublemakers.

Not long after the march Ford supervisors laid off a skilled tradesman named Walter Reuther from his job at the Rouge plant, where he'd been making some pro-union noises. Walter and his brother Victor headed for Europe and the Soviet Union on an exploratory trip, to see how labor and capital got along overseas. But the Reuthers would be back. Further down Henry Ford's annoyance list in 1932, British author Aldous Huxley published his popular sci-fi extravaganza *Brave New World*, with a raft of Ford jokes in it, making Henry out to be some sort of crazy demigod. Typically, Ford bore no personal grudge and later commissioned some travel articles from Huxley.(12)

Ford next found himself mixed up with the near collapse of the banking system in early 1933. The FMC was the biggest depositor in both of the largest banks in Detroit. When cratering real estate values closed the doors of these banks, Henry's atypically gloomy comment came as something of a shocker, "Let the crash come. Everything will go down the chute. But I feel young. I can build again."(13) Governor William Comstock didn't share that youthful outlook, and declared a bank "holiday" which temporarily shut down every bank in Michigan until the mess could be sorted out. In short order a national bank holiday followed to halt the spreading panic. 6,000 banks had already failed across America during the previous five years. Thousands more never saw the light of day again after the holiday, including several in St. Clair County. An average depositor in one of the departed banks, 20 year-old Ruthe Bragg of Port Huron, lost all her money. This reduced her to taking a 77-hour per week waitressing job, which paid $4 for the entire week plus tips and a daily meal. Port Huron's biggest bank, First National, an affiliate of one of the Ford-dominated banks in Detroit, only saved itself with some difficulty. To make matters more painful for him, the president of First National, Stephen Graham, had barely recovered from the death of his son, Junior, in a car crash.

The automobile's unpleasant association with crime also caused Henry Ford some embarrassment during these years, when allegedly he heard from two satisfied but distasteful customers. Bank robber and murderer Clyde Barrow, of "Bonnie and Clyde" fame, supposedly wrote Henry this testimonial: "While I still have got breath in my lungs I will tell you what a dandy car you make. I have drove Fords exclusively when I could get away with one. For sustained speed and freedom from trouble the Ford has got every other car skinned..." From Barrow's perspective his Ford needed just one improvement, bulletproofing. He and his girl died when police shot it full of 106 holes in 1934. Another Ford fan, gangster John Dillinger, dropped Henry a little note: "Hello Old Pal. You have a wonderful car. It's a treat to drive one. I can make any other car take Ford's dust. Bye-bye."(14) Perhaps acting on Dillinger's recommendation, two bandits hit the Marysville State Bank for $5,000 and escaped in a blue Ford. Both of these missives were probably fakes, and certainly no one found it amusing when one of Dillinger's accomplices, Herbert Youngblood, died in a police shootout in Port Huron in 1934, killing Undersheriff Charles Kavanaugh in the process.

Though less dramatically than for the boss, things didn't go much better for Henry Ford's dealers during these years. Port Huron's Albert Parfet and his wife made out alright at first, photographed in 1931 while winter-vacationing on a golf course in the "Sunny South." Parfet determinedly kept the publicity machine humming. On one occasion he dazzled the masses with a demonstration of *The Human Ford – with the Radio Brain. The only automobile in the world that sees, hears, reads, talks, and operates driverless.*(15) The Ford Traveling Show, with the "Ford Mountaineers, a cowboy musical organization" pulled into town and performed for free on Erie Square next to City Hall. Parfet offered free movies at his shop, like the scintillating *A Tour Through The Ford Factory.* He booked a history of the Ford Motor Company, *These Thirty Years*, into the Ritz movie house: "It's real, gripping – an inspiration to young and old. A picture filled with excitement, delightful romance, thrills and fun."

The FMC film division also turned out a singalong music video, in which the new Ford V- 8 swept through the Empty Roads of the countryside, while an upbeat vocalist danced merrily in front of an orchestra:

Speeding along the rolling highway
Singing a song to the rhythm of the road.
The sun in the sky, a heaven of blue,
The world flashes by.
You feel so happy
When you're sweeping along the leafy byway.
You'll never be late if it's a V-8
When you're speeding along to the rhythm of the road.

Soon, however, bad business reduced Parfet to offering not just terms on new cars, but $0 down and 20-month installment plans on used cars, then installment plans on car repairs. He sold his Main Street Ford showroom, moved to more modest quarters, and the new owners of the former Ford building converted it into a combined self-serve grocery and children's clothing factory. Twice Port Huron's Ford man relocated downward during the 1930's, and the second time he admitted, "We have allowed an overdose of optimism to bring about a condition that could be faced in no other manner." At the bottom of the slump, Parfet promised to bring a new Ford to the customer's home for a test drive with just the slightest encouragement. The commission-paid employee ranks at the dealership thinned, and Parfet put out a call for help, "Salesman Wanted – Good opportunity for a hustler."

In Canton, Michigan, practically next door to the Ford Motor Company's Dearborn headquarters, former Ford franchisee and hustler George Monnot also had overdosed on optimism. He didn't sing much to the rhythm of the road these days, though he'd once featured an 11-man tuxedoed dance band at his dealership. Nor did he get in much golf either since he'd given up his country club membership, along with his lakefront summer home, and his yacht. He'd wiped out in the '29 crash, and now begged for handouts. In 1931 he wrote from his alleyway apartment in application to a charity: "For 26 years was in the Automobile business prosperous at one time and have done more than my share in giving at Christmas and at all times. Have a family of six and struggle is the word for me now for a living. Xmas will not mean much to our family this year as my business, bank, real estate, insurance policies are all swept away. Our resources are nil at present..."(16)

C.A. Vane, general manager of National Automobile Dealers Association, admitted the depression had "utterly discredited" the merchandising policies of his members. He blamed "super salesmanship" and "greed" for the "deplorable plight" of America's 40,000 auto dealers.(17) FMC sales manager William Cowling agreed, "We must quit saying you can buy a car for $900 when if you want the whole car you will have to pay $1200. In some selling methods we have tried to outclown the clowns." These confessions fell flat, however, with Chevrolet vice-president H. J. Klingler. Why, that kind of talk stabbed them all in the back, to General Motors' way of thinking. Klingler placed the blame for the auto slump, and the depression, not on the industry, but squarely where GM felt it belonged, on that good-for-nothing, the consumer.

"It has been estimated that half of the 44 million people now employed are in a position to buy a new automobile right now," said Klingler. "Why they have been putting it off isn't important. The fact remains that they can afford to buy but haven't."(18) They could have afforded to jump off the GM building, too, but put that off as well. The "buy or die" pitch amused Robert and Helen Lynd, the sociologists who went back to Muncie, Indiana again, to get an update on that city. Said the Lynds, "This 'underconsumption' note – alternately wheedling and belaboring the individual citizen, overboard in mid-ocean, for not throwing away his life belt – went on year after year through the depression..."(19)

Sometimes the automobile wheedling came through the channels of that booming new medium which prospered even during this troubled decade, radio. A new hometown station, WHLS, started broadcasting to Port Huron. After a slow start in assessing this electrical home companion, the car industry jumped into radio advertising with both feet in the 1930's. Using a disembodied voice to extol the virtues of an invisible product didn't really make much selling sense, but at least it kept the product name in the ears of the public. As to the commercials themselves, Shakespeare they weren't. The memory of that notable 18th Century native Michigander, Chief Pontiac, who'd been resurrected as an automobile nameplate by General Motors, now was subjected to further indignities on radio.

Pontiac, Chief of Value: *Forefathers went to trading post, three long days journey, to*

get powder and shot.
Paleface*: Today I drive my Pontiac to town in a few minutes to see the latest Paris gowns.*
Pontiac: *Before paleface came to prairie, Indian slowly fought through the great blizzard from the North.*
Paleface #2: *In 1932 we don't mind the weather, we go places in a Pontiac.*

The real Pontiac might have been tempted to barbecue these two smart alecks, just as he had Commander Robertson in Pine Grove Park. His radio reincarnation contented himself with working as a front man for dealers like John Cawood, who'd switched from Chevrolet to Pontiac. John temporarily went bust in 1931, closed his branch dealerships in Flint, Saginaw, and Detroit, and then hung on for dear life in Port Huron.

At least the Dodge Brothers managed to escape Pontiac's fate of working as a beyond-the-grave huckster. Chrysler did *not* bring John and Horace back to promote Dodge cars. In this case the job fell to a couple of lesser jokers:

Frank: *When I'm in love I'm just breezing along with the breeze. I never mind the bumps or the ruts along the highway of life. I float through life on a cloud.*
Harry: *And that, folks, is exactly the way you feel in the famous Dodge Air-Glide Ride.*

Listeners heard a considerably more honest slice of automobile life on radio from the enormously popular comedian Jack Benny, who supposedly drove a rattletrap Maxwell car on his show year after year. The tortured sound effects of the Maxwell as it audibly came back to life during a typical episode never failed to convulse Benny's audience, who were only too familiar with real-life automotive asthma of that kind. Although this gag sprang from Benny's pretended miserliness, increasing numbers of auto-poor Americans discovered in the 30's that driving an old car saved them nothing. Instead it cost a comparative fortune in padded repair bills, overpriced replacement parts, and bad gas mileage, not to mention the plain bother of nursemaiding an iron invalid along. But if on his show Benny had walked or taken the streetcar to save money, the joke would have fallen flat due to its inherent good sense. A bicycle might have gotten a laugh.

It didn't come standard yet, and it took up about as much space as a picnic basket, but Potter's Radio Shop in Port Huron could install a Motorola Auto Radio aboard your car for $40. So could Albert Parfet, who unwisely had disposed of his own radio station WAFD, which its new owner promptly had moved to Detroit. Did a car radio dangerously distract a driver from his main duties as onboard pilot, or did its blather help keep Mr. Motorist from snoozing at the wheel? Captain L.A. Lyon of the Michigan State Police thought the former: "Every time you improve a car it seems that something is added which takes the driver's attention away from the highway."

Even worse off than Jack Benny in America's imaginary car life, an erstwhile Oklahoman family named the Joads figured first in the popular novel, then the film of *The Grapes of Wrath*. When the movie opened in Port Huron, viewers saw the story of a clan of displaced sharecroppers unwillingly caught up in the rhythm of the road. After an army of tractors ran the Joads off their land, Pa Joad sank most of their last $200 into buying the story's main character, a dilapidated stake truck. The Joads piled a mountain of belongings and a dozen people onto this machine, and lit out for California. Along the way they endured hunger, humiliation, beatings, sunstroke, endless breakdowns, and farm labor camp squalor that made Alcatraz look inviting. When Grandpa and Grandma Joad kicked the bucket during this odyssey, their kin dumped the bodies into holes by the side of the road; anything to lighten the load and coax more life from their precious truck. The picture might just as well have been called *The Jalopy of Wrath*.

Hollywood spun no farfetched fantasy in the Joadmobile. By one estimate 11 million Joad-style heaps rambled over the nation's roads during the worst of the depression. They littered used car lots from coast to coast. The average value of all vehicles in the country, new and used, came to only $240. The Model Joads clearly weren't roadworthy, and constituted a menace to everyone on the highway, but as yet no vehicle safety inspection programs existed anywhere in America except in New Jersey, which state the Joads took care to avoid.

By common consensus, the United States hit bottom in the Great Depression during the spring of 1933. The Remington Rand company computed that the U.S. had gone, unofficially, broke. As bad off as George Monnot or Harold Wills or the Joads. The nation's assets totaled $138 billion, the debts $141 billion. The national income had declined by half since 1929. Half the home mortgagors in the country had defaulted, though amazingly most auto loans stayed current.(20) The depression's epicenter, the state of Michigan, faced insolvency after collecting only one-third of the property taxes due during the latest impost. Aghast, the legislature offered a 10-year installment plan on paying those overdue taxes, and permanently replaced the state property tax with a sales tax.

Among many cost-cutting moves, Michigan closed 23 of its state parks, including the Lakeport unit near Port Huron, where 400,000 people had stopped by in their 94,000 cars the year before. Seemed a shame to shut it, since so many jobless people now had more time on their hands to visit. A third of the manufacturing firms in St. Clair County had gone out of business, and 40% of all manufacturing jobs had vanished. In an echo of yesteryear, a Port Huron native made the news when the bankruptcy of the Studebaker company rocked the auto industry. Its president shot himself, and stockholders turned the reorganization over to Harold Vance, a veteran of the old Port Huron Studebaker factory of 1912, whose latest owner now used it, get this, as a horse stable.

After one term in office President Herbert Hoover exited the White House under a storm of vilification that never lifted for the rest of his long life. To fight the slump, he'd spent billions of dollars and run up huge deficits for federal relief schemes, including some whopping sums for roads. But he failed to mollify the voters, who discharged him despite a strong endorsement for re-election from Henry Ford. Hoover once had promised every American family two cars, but his valedictory *adios* to the automobile took a more dubious view. His appointed Committee on Social Trends said: "...the automobile has become a dominant influence in the life of the individual and he, in a real sense, has become dependent upon it." That dependence threatened to turn the whole country upside down, "redistributing its citizens, disorganizing its cities, causing random suburban building and blight."(21)

A distant cousin of Theodore Roosevelt's succeeded Hoover, after campaigning against the incumbent's reckless overspending. Lucky enough to have been born before the automobile era, Franklin Delano Roosevelt had bicycled his way all over Europe as a robust young man: "From the time I was nine until I was seventeen

205

I spent most of my holidays bicycling on the continent. This was the best education I ever had; far better than schools."(22) In his case this meant far better than the Groton private school, Harvard, and Columbia Law School. Railroad money formed a large part of the family fortune on which FDR relied to support a privileged life spent in public service. It could not protect him, however, from the bout of infantile paralysis which immobilized his legs for good at the age of 39 in 1921, just a year after he'd run unsuccessfully on the Democratic ticket for U.S. Vice-President. Automobile sickness now was crippling many Americans almost as surely as a case of polio, but for the latter there was no cure, and Roosevelt faced a gradual decline and premature death from the Jacobs Effect unless a medical breakthrough occurred. A lesser man might have been destroyed by the experience, but Roosevelt's supreme self-confidence (some said vanity) swept it aside, and he won first the governorship of New York State, then the Presidency, assuming the latter post amid a crisis Hoover had compared to Valley Forge.

"An immediate and drastic reduction of governmental expenditures to accomplish a saving of not less than 25 percent in the cost of federal government. Maintenance of the annual credit by a federal budget annually balanced. A sound currency to be preserved at all hazards."(23) Roosevelt and a huge Congressional majority won election on that 1932 Democratic Party platform, but it didn't take them long to toss this road map out the window as far as they could wing it. The administration instead abandoned the gold dollar, devalued the currency 40%, and embarked on a deficit spending bash that made Hoover look like Ebenezer Scrooge. Roosevelt launched almost the equivalent of a wartime program in peacetime for relief purposes. And, in essence, America began the systematic debasement of its money in order to prop up the automobile culture.

Roosevelt's New Deal spent $3.5 billion on relief and public works the first year, and similar amounts, give or take a billion, annually for seven more years. Almost half the 2 million people hired for public works projects built roads and streets, at a cumulative cost of $4 billion through 1940.(24) $316,000 in works dough trickled down to Port Huron in 1934, and the city spent 97% of it on streets. Every mile of this kind of construction saddled America with growing future maintenance costs, but officials hoped the sight of a lot of laborers at work would reassure the public that at least *something* productive was happening. Public works didn't keep those laborers at work very long. A $47,000 paving job in Port Huron employed 55 men for six weeks, then cut them loose again. The federal government gave away this road money at a ratio of 20 to 1 over the pittance it only loaned to railroads and streetcar lines. "The American people could not have done worse in 1932 had they deliberately set out to elect a President who was ignorant of the implications of the automobile revolution," according to historian James Flink.(25)

Though he had voted for Hoover, Henry Ford started off on the right foot with Franklin Roosevelt. The President's splendid inaugural address – "We have nothing to fear but fear itself" – repeated what Henry had been telling the nation since 1929. Ford lavished praise on the speech: "A great thing has occurred amongst us. We have made a complete turn-around and at last America's face is toward the future. Thanks for that belongs to President Roosevelt. Inauguration Day he turned the Ship of State around."(26) But mutiny broke out aboard the Ship of State when the National Recovery Administration came aboard. The New Dealers wanted to get more Americans working, and dreamed up a byzantine system of cooperative employment codes to achieve this. It amounted mainly to shorter work weeks, higher pay, and collective bargaining. Ford didn't like the NRA, especially the union part of it. Henry didn't want unions or anybody in Washington telling him what to do. Ford called NRA boss Hugh Johnson a dictator – the pot calling the kettle black – and he refused to play ball. Just as with the Selden patent, Ford and other opponents won the day in court finally. The Supreme Court declared the NRA unconstitutional in 1935. But unlike the Selden decision, this ruling did not end the matter.

The speedy end of alcohol prohibition, abolished by the Roosevelt administration in just a few months, also must have disappointed a dry stalwart like Ford. St. Clair County pretty much decided it had had enough of the 18th Amendment after the James Shamalay incident. This Port Huron bootlegger stopped into a repair shop in the summer of 1932 to find out what was making his automobile engine miss. The mechanic told him it was probably the six sticks of dynamite that Shamalay's competitors had wired imperfectly to the battery, enough to level a city block. Once a defender of the dry cause, the *Times Herald* now admitted that hundreds of blind pigs operated around town, along with gambling and slot machine parlors. The city was wide open. The county voted 4-1 in favor of booze legalization in April 1933 when Michigan became the first state to ratify prohibition's repeal.

The landmark Kern Brewery, which dated to 1879, fired up its kettles on the Port Huron riverfront again, and 85 year-old owner Christian Kern died a happy man not long after this vindication. Trucker Earl Smith, a pioneer rumrunner now poised to make a legal fortune distributing brew, threw a huge beer party at his refrigerated warehouse. Blind pigs morphed into open beer gardens all over Port Huron, which, said the *Times Herald*, "make the old time saloon look like a well-conducted ice cream parlor. There are joints in which colored and white persons mix nightly in the most disgusting and revolting manner." Pastor John Martin of the First Methodist Episcopal Church inveighed against the general "orgy of drunkeness." Even gas stations began selling beer, over the editorial protests of the Weil press: "The roadside dealer who fills an automobile tank with gasoline and then helps fill the driver with alcohol may almost be an accessory before the fact in murder."

Naturally, legal liquor meant more drunk driving. There'd been no shortage of it during prohibition, as we have seen, but Port Huron police now braced themselves for drunker and more aggressive violators. They got one in 22 year-old Clark Bradley, who led the cops on an 80 mph chase through town, stopped only when police fired shots at him, then tried to run over one of the arresting officers. The police subsequently ordered a couple of 120 mph motorcycles to deal with the Bradleys on the road, and inadvertently themselves became as big a potential danger to the public. Fortunately for the constabulary and other motorists alike, 39 year-old Earl Boman didn't need to be chased down because he expired after he drunkenly plowed his car into a house on 16th street.

The most spectacular incident involved 34 year-old Bernhardt Mueller, son of Oscar and heir to the Mueller Brass fortune, who rocketed off the Gratiot Pike at 100 mph following an early morning sloshfest at the golf club. He knocked down a fence and flipped end over end for another 85 feet. This killed outright one of Mueller's sales managers and badly hurt two other employees unlucky enough to be partying with the boss that night. Bernhardt himself died five days later, blaming a dog in the road for the crash, just like Levassor 40 years earlier. Mueller's broken hearted father Oscar, who'd once bragged of being a pathbreaking car racer, now had lost his father, daughter and son to the automobile. Left childless, Oscar turned the Mueller company over to his long-time subordinate Fred Riggin and moved away to Florida. He couldn't live with his memories in Port Huron any longer.

Drunk driving arrests tripled in Port Huron, and in Detroit rose 160% during the first year after prohibition's repeal. With legal booze on board America's traffic score hit a new high in 1934 of 36,000 dead, 1 to 2 million injured. That was enough corpse-making to have wiped the city of Port Huron off the map, and as for the number hurt it just didn't bear thinking about. So nobody thought about it, though sometimes insurance agents thought about it for them. Like the concerned folks at the Wright-Hoyt agency in Port Huron: "Every hour...in fact, every minute...an American tragedy occurs involving some family in these United States. The many cars on crowded highways make inevitable a terrific toll of collisions and accidents with loss and damage. The only certain protection against financial tragedy is Complete Automobile Insurance."(27) Wright-Hoyt was run nowadays by Fred Moore, the ex-mayor and chronic speeder of the city's earliest auto days.

Though they sometimes raged against the drunk driving practice while sober, Americans didn't hesitate for a second to get behind the wheel after a couple of belts, and often laughed about it when they saw this habit portrayed in cartoons or in the movies. The successful film comedy *Topper* opened with Cary Grant's character drunkenly steering a car with his feet. After he and his equally brainless wife, the Kirbys, died in an auto wreck then reappeared as a pair of fun-loving ghosts, their dull friend Cosmo Topper imitated their *joie de vivre* by trying reckless driving himself. The Michigan legislature even gave drunk drivers a helping hand by allowing them, or their survivors, to sue the taverns where they got drunk before their car accidents. Bar owners fired back with the logical challenge: how did bartenders know which of their patrons were too drunk to drive, or even intended to drive, and how could barmen restrain them? A drunk driving conviction now technically brought an automatic driving license suspension of three months for the first offense in Michigan. The courts suspended 9,000 licenses in 1939, but in most cases the guilty parties just kept right on driving. "Show Them No Mercy," said the *Times Herald*, in endorsing a lifetime driving ban for drunk drivers. A ban that never materialized.

After the failure of alcohol prohibition, Americans fell with a frenzy of denunciation on the practice of narcotics use, as though to reassure themselves that abolishment still worked for some vices. And it would have, too – for automobiles. But the subject of automobile addiction never came up. In retrospect, it's instructive to substitute the word "automobile" for "dope" in some of these jeremiads unleashed in Port Huron during the 30's:

If at the time they burned Joan of Arc at the stake, they had known the effect of dope (automobiles), *they would have made her death more horrible by making a dope* (automobile) *fiend of her.*

If I had a child and a choice between placing him in a room of rattlesnakes or a room of dope (automobile) *fiends I would place him with the rattlesnakes.*

Nothing could be more loathsome to a decent human being than a man or a woman who peddles marihuana (automobiles) *to boys and girls. Marihuana* (the automobile) *produces effects that make most other narcotics seem tame and innocent. It destroys the inhibitions that are the foundations of civilized society. And it can transform the most peaceful youngster into a fiendish murderer almost instantly.*

Narcotic prohibition had not lessened appreciably the number of users – 1,000,000 by one estimate. The most frequent imbibers were housewives, followed by laborers, doctors, salesmen, druggists, actors, merchants, farmers, clerks, cops, lawyers, mechanics, gamblers, journalists, and bartenders.(28) Not to mention the butcher, the baker and the candlestick maker. Authorities did no drug screening of driving license applicants and never would in the 20th Century.

In an effort to get the nation, be it drunk, stoned, or sober, to face up to the massacre occurring on the roads, one of the nation's most popular magazines, *Reader's Digest*, commissioned a shockingly frank article from writer Joseph Furnas, "And Sudden Death", in 1935. It didn't take much research. Furnas just described realistically the injuries suffered in an assortment of fatal traffic accidents: "...the pair of youths who were thrown out of an open roadster this spring – thrown clear – but each broke a windshield post with his head in passing and the whole top of each skull, down to the eyebrows, was missing."(29) General Motors' styling boss Harley Earl used to say, "You can design a car so that every time you get in it, it's a relief – you have a little vacation for a while," but Furnas pointed out that the vacation was over if you got into an accident.(30) Then, he wrote, your trip resembled going over Niagara Falls in a steel barrel full of railroad spikes.

Furnas produced one of the most widely read and quoted magazine articles ever. Requests for reprints flooded the *Digest*. But in the end, millions of readers just read it and forgot it. Furnas didn't have the slightest effect on the number of road accidents. Certainly not in St. Clair County, where 30 people died in traffic in 1935, then 39 in 1936, then 47 in 1937. Another story along the same lines also failed to straighten people out. Groundbreaking physician Claire Straith of Detroit told the American Medical Association convention in Cleveland: "For the first time in 2,000 years the male sex can have a handsome new nose by plastic surgery, and the American automobile is mostly responsible for the change...accidents in cars have thrown occupants against windshields, smashing faces, often disfiguring or removing noses."(31) Including those left with no noses, a half million people suffered bone fractures in 1936 car accidents, which crippled one third of them for life.

The Bard of Port Huron, Ed Snover, nosed around the fact that the concept of the automobile itself carried the blame for this bloodletting:

Death rides beside the driver of
Each motor car you see,
Awaiting a good chance to shove
Into eternity
His host and other folks who ply
The pavements of this land –
The prospect's one to terrify
The public and to brand
The automobile as a tool
That's far too deadly, as a rule!(32)

This engine of conceit magnified a hundred times, a thousand times, the everyday failings of even the average driver. Not just liquor, but ill temper, sickness, drowsiness, overexcitement, inattention, poor reflexes, bad eyesight (10% of Americans had bad night vision even without the inadequate headlights on cars), confusion, ignorance, the list ever ended. Lapses which would have counted for nothing in a carless world, now in America resulted in instant dismemberment:

Port Arthur, Texas. Miss Marie Stahl, whose arm was severed Sunday night when she held it out of an automobile window to flick off cigaret ashes, died Monday night. The arm was caught in the uprights of a parked truck.(33)

Simple misplaced pride played a serious role in dangerous driving, according to Harvard University traffic expert Miller McClintock: "If the average person who rides with you is constantly nervous and is moved by apparent hazards to make suggestions frequently, you are probably not as good a driver as you think you are." Detroit insurance executive Otway Conrad maintained that the majority of traffic accidents "happened in daylight, when the weather was clear, streets dry, occupants sober, speed reasonable, brakes and steering gear in good shape," which left poor fallible humanity behind the wheel as the unpredictable variable.

At the beginning of the decade 36 states including Michigan required no driving license examination at all. The Auto Club estimated that 60,000 physically and mentally incompetent people obtained licenses annually in America as a result. 500,000 applicants who flunked licensing exams were allowed to drive anyway until they passed. "On a recent day in Detroit, nineteen men who had been convicted of drunken or reckless driving were examined in the pyschopathic clinic," reported the *Times Herald*. "Eight of these men had defective vision, two were mentally diseased, one was hysterical, two were on the verge of insanity and four were chronic alcoholics."(34) When Michigan finally ordered driving license exams, Port Huron police gave the applicant a rudimentary check, then if he appeared screwy, a driving test. Not one in 100 failed. But even the passably sane person couldn't always be relied on to act that way in an automobile. It stunned the city when St. Clair County's ex-Sheriff Harrison Maines, 75 years-old, died in a road rage fistfight on Main Street over a minor fender-bender accident with another driver.

The inevitability of auto mayhem touched the high and the mighty during the 1930's. Three of President Roosevelt's sons suffered serious wrecks. Movie star and Port Huron native Colleen Moore's chauffeured limo ran over a woman in Hollywood, who successfully sued Moore for $12,000 in damages. Silent film cowboy star Tom Mix died in a crash, and Mix's sound-era successor John Wayne had to jump from a moving automobile to avoid becoming another victim at a notorious "dead man's curve" in California. Entertainer Arthur Godfrey suffered 27 fractures when his car hit a truck. Oil drilling mogul and airplane speed demon Howard Hughes struck and killed a pedestrian with a car. Composer Maurice Ravel died after a bizarre brain operation to try to restore his music-writing ability, which he claimed he'd lost in a car crash. Across the river from Port Huron, Sarnia's mayor Gordon Hodges poisoned himself after undergoing his second car wreck. He'd suffered a permanent leg injury in the first accident. This second time he'd been pinned beneath his vehicle for three hours before being rescued. "It is believed his mind was affected...," suggested the press.

Frank Covert, author of the Covert road taxes which impoverished so many farmers in Michigan, died of a fractured skull when he collided with a truck. Like all Michigan residents by now, Covert had a 70% chance of being involved in an auto accident during his lifetime, a 1 in 60 chance of being killed, and he hit the lottery. Mr. and Mrs. Frederick Sanborn, descendants of an early Port Huron lumber barony, died in a Los Angeles car wreck. They'd left enough money in their wills to build a home for the aged in Port Huron, so it wasn't a total loss. Congressman Jesse Wolcott of Port Huron escaped a crash with just cuts and bruises. Future British Prime Minister Winston Churchill nearly landed in the morgue when struck by a taxicab while walking in New York City. The next President of the United States and former Port Huron honeymooner Harry Truman ran a stop sign in Washington and slammed into another car, nearly killing himself, his wife and his daughter Margaret. Miss Truman admitted that Dad always had been a lousy driver, a speeder, with bad eyesight to boot.

The "slaughter of the innocents," as he called it, on life's highway these days further undermined Louis Weil's confidence in the safety of America's auto habits, and he didn't want to be next on the butcher block. "For one I'm getting to the point where I dread a motor car trip in the country of any length." Getting killed would be bad enough, but Louis also deplored the real chance that his destroyer would get off unpunished. To the astonishment of his readers, the *Times Herald* owner confessed in print that he and other people of influence regularly intervened in traffic cases in the St. Clair County courts to get pals and relatives off the hook. "I know it because I've done my share of it....some 'good fellow' who is, in fact, nothing more than a drunken criminal literally and actually gets away with murder."(35) Louis didn't name names, but he advised folks to look at how many ugly accident cases simply faded away following the first big headlines and arrests.

Coincidentally, the *Times Herald* not long afterward found itself running a syndicated romance serial with a similar theme, "Hit and Run Love":

(Yesterday: Larry admits to Pat that he ran down the woman and child; intends to lie his way out of it.)

She sat frozen within the circle of his arms. "What do you mean, Larry?"
"You can help. People with pull get a break in any court. Get him to go easy. He could even change the charge from involuntary manslaughter to negligent homicide..."
Slowly she drew away, pushing his arms from about her, staring into his blue eyes, now cold and calculating.(36)

Even when these cases made it to court, the leniency by now bordered on the ridiculous. Or crossed the border. Judge Fred George offered drivers convicted of negligent homicide the choice of a fine or a prison term. If the prison term looked to be inconvenient, just pay the fine on an installment plan, about the same way you'd buy a used Oldsmobile. John Seipe of Detroit got this deal after colliding with and killing pedestrian and father of eight John Godzisewski in St. Clair County, at a speed of about 45. Seipe accepted a $300 fine with easy payments of $50 per month, in lieu of 1-5 years in prison. Judge George's attitude on the proper punishment to be meted out to road killers apparently had been modified somewhat when his son Fred George, Junior struck and killed a dentist, who'd been standing along the Gratiot Pike while young Fred was driving by at 40 mph on icy pavement.

211

Port Huron's jurors didn't help matters by turning in inexplicable verdicts in traffic cases, such as the acquittal 17 year-old Velma Knight of negligent homicide for running over a road worker. Velma, who had no driver's license, happened upon the victim while speeding and tailgating in a borrowed car with defective brakes. "We'll just have to let the town run wide open if we can't get convictions," said one disgusted official. Some motorists dodged a trial altogether and bought their way out of a criminal auto charge. 19 year-old Donovan Twiss did so after he slammed into and killed 5 year-old June Cowper, at 50 mph on 10th Street, knocking the child completely out of her shoes. Prosecutors dropped the matter when "Twiss made a settlement satisfactory to the girl's parents..." How to turn a child into quick cash. What did a "satisfactory settlement" amount to? At the time champion Port Huron bowler Chester Statler crashed into a tree and died he faced a $30,000 lawsuit from the family of a man he'd killed in a previous accident. Statler's estate eventually coughed up $2,000, about average. Deliah Schofield didn't get nearly as much. When a car fatally struck the 85 year-old widow on 10th Street, the declaration "May God help me," was all the unidentified driver offered in recompense over Deliah's corpse before fleeing.

The police department got around to formally setting up a full-time traffic bureau, headed by Sergeant Ralph Irwin. Nicknamed "Ham" Irwin, he toured the Port Huron schools with a bandaged dummy he called Careless Tom, and warned little kids that Tom had been run over by a car and they might be next. The press and police cautioned Port Huron drivers to watch out for kids in the street every summer and fall because school had stopped or school had started. Come to think of it, watch out for them any time. Children now had a 1 in 3 chance of being injured or killed by an automobile before finishing school. "Drive Safely. Don't Kill A Child" recommended one police-backed newspaper ad, co-sponsored by 15 businesses, including the Hi-Speed gas stations and Smith Funeral Home, but no car dealers. The warning didn't do 10 year-old Donna Jex much good. Port Huron motorcycle cop Alfred Thomas ran over and killed Donna while she watched a school parade. But sometimes it's the thought that counts.

Authorities claimed that Port Huron children seemed to be "unconscious of danger." As though adults were any better. City and school leaders started a special playground program to entertain kids away from the streets: "Little children who used to scream when they heard the screech of automobile brakes are having a 'grand' time. There's nothing to worry about now... " As children grew older they eventually entered automobile puberty, and like Velma Knight sought to embrace cars, not run from them. The high school began offering driving instruction classes: "Boys and girls grow up automobiles curious. They just naturally expect to drive an automobile as soon as they are big enough to manage a steering wheel, the same as boys and girls a generation ago expected to drive a horse as soon as dad would allow." While getting their bearings behind the wheel, automobile curious drivers under 20 suffered a 39% worse accident rate than the rest of the population. Nobody, but nobody, ever lectured Port Huron children on the advantages of not buying or driving or riding in an automobile.

When not in school or at headquarters Ham Irwin sometimes drove around town haranguing the populace from a loudspeaker on his police car, calling himself the Voice of Safety. Occasionally his department launched a traffic law crackdown, just to show they meant business. One week they blitzed 98 drivers for breaking the now faster 25-35 mph city speed limits, or committing some of the hundreds of other potential auto

212

infractions. Port Huron's Public Safety Director Otto Schmekel thought about enlisting 25 or 50 citizens as traffic spies to rat out bad drivers. But a discouraged Detroit traffic judge named John Maher told a Port Huron audience not to bother, they'd need an army of policeman just to enforce the speed laws. Detroit Police Commissioner Heinrich Pickert added bitterly, "People just seem to be stupid on the streets. They act like animals...lame-brained morons. Just look at the faces of the people in traffic court and you can see why no appeal to them to drive carefully does any good."(37) Despite the best efforts to keep the animals in line, Port Huron reported 495 traffic accidents during the 1937 municipal year, which killed 11 and injured 166. These wrecks involved 882 cars, 66 pedestrians, and 12 bicyclists. Cops arrested 58 people for drunk driving, and issued 1,561 traffic tickets.

Statistics like those made some people want to get away from it all:

Quail's Little Farms. 2 miles southwest of Port Huron. 2.5, 5 and 10 acre lots. Nothing down. Drive Out Sunday. Easy Terms – Low Prices. Restricted – White Americans Only. Happy contented neighbors. Tell the greedy landlord to keep his high priced shack in the smoke, dust and heat of the city. Build your own home where taxes are almost nothing. Where pure spring water has no chemicals added. Where your children play with safety among the trees and flowers instead of in the streets among the automobiles.

The suburban development of Sparlingville, brainchild of ex-Great Lakes captain turned realtor Walter Sparling, also enticed buyers into the land of contentment. And Mueller Farms, the remnants of the Oscar Mueller estate: "Large Choice Lots, Well Restricted, Quiet, Away from Traffic." In his competing though thinly settled city next door to Port Huron, Harold Wills tried to sell off his Marysville land with the same dubious offer of safety: "Give The Kids A Chance...own a home in Marysville where they can really GROW UP!"

But the by now familiar pitch – use an automobile to escape the automobile – offered no real refuge. Suburban living didn't give 7 year-old Bobby Bright much of a chance. A car ran him down on Thanksgiving Day not far from Quail's Little Farms, and he barely survived a fractured skull. The medical report: "The brain tissue was exuding from the wound and small pieces of bone which extended into the brain substance had to be removed." With no speed limits on Michigan's rural roads, 60% of fatal accidents happened beyond the city limits. No one now walked a rural road in St. Clair County with any guarantee of safety. Sheriff Ferris Lucas, a former auto worker, imposed a 40 mph "protection" speed limit around rural schools, as though being hit by a car at that speed gave a kid protection.

When it came to rural traffic enforcement, police went through the motions with no real hope of much effect. St. Clair County's highways and roads stretched for 1,650 miles, about the distance from Port Huron to Santa Fe, New Mexico; or, on an international map, from Paris to Moscow. At the most a total of five sheriff and state police cars patrolled them at any one time. Essentially the cops drove around in circles for hundreds of hours and tens of thousands of miles per month, and usually caught up with the lame-brained morons a little too late. Like Port Huron's Smith sisters, Muriel and Elizabeth, who burned to death when their car slammed into a tree west of town. Or the late Alfeus Townsend and his father-in-law, who met up with another stubborn country tree a week later. Or father of ten Claude Stevens of Port Huron, stopped dead by yet another killer tree, when the driver of the car he was riding in fell asleep.

213

If the road risks didn't scare off the buyer, many of the homes in automobile suburbs qualified for mortgages from the brand new Federal Housing Administration, another in the army of New Deal programs inaugurated by Roosevelt and his Brains Trust. These loans offered low down payments and an unheard-of 20 years to pay. With FHA help, homebuilding doubled in 1936 in the area around Port Huron. Most of it took place in neighboring townships, which grew as much as 15 times faster than the city during this decade. An additional incentive: Port Huron now supplied water to 500 suburban customers, and even offered fire protection, despite Public Works Director Malcolm Patrick's warning that these practices would come back to haunt the city by encouraging taxpayers to move out of town.

Whether because of the New Deal, or because of the stringent economies Americans made in their lives early in the decade, like getting rid of the car, the financial circumstances of several million people improved during President Roosevelt's first term. Alas, Billy Durant wasn't one of them. He declared bankruptcy. Out of his one-time $100 million fortune he retained only $250 in clothing and $1 million in debts. But on the sunny side of the street, Harold Wills persuaded his new employer Walter Chrysler to buy the old Wills Sainte Claire car plant. Chrysler announced plans in 1936 to depot parts in Marysville.

Several hundred local men with short memories showed up the next day at Chrysler to apply for work. In one of those passing ironies of automobile life, the plant foreman, 45 year-old Arthur Ellis, died in a head-on car wreck when he fell asleep at the wheel from all the work he'd been doing in getting the facility ready. This minor setback, the fortunes of war, didn't stop Chrysler from putting 900 men to work in Marysville by the year's end. The Auto Lite plant in Port Huron went back into action as well, spinning 14 miles of automobile wire daily to install into Chryslers. Pressed Metals and several other local parts makers ramped up also.

American automobile production gradually increased from the 1932 barrel bottom to 2 million units in 1933, 2.5 in 1934, 3.2 in 1935, to 4.6 million in 1936. Following the brief decline in the car census during the early 30's, the count climbed to almost 31 million motor vehicles by the end of the decade, at which time St. Clair County owned a record 26,000, for about 76,000 people. Bad habits can be troublesome to break, and as the worst of the depression dissipated auto conceit led people into hock again to buy cars and trucks and tractors, as though the hard times and hard lessons of the past few years had never happened. Families with less than $30 per week income owned half the cars in the U.S. Port Huroners spent about $2 millions on cars and car services in 1936.

This development gave Roger Babson the blues. "I cannot say debt is any less dangerous today than it ever was. Families with scarcely enough income to feed the children are buying big new cars 'on time'. I often see run down ramshackle homes with a spanking new car beside them. Families that could afford neither to own savings accounts nor to build a home are 'investing' their savings in an automobile instead."(38) Some people combined the ramshackle home and the spanking new car into one unit, travel trailers. The first local trailer dealership, Covered Wagon, opened in Port Huron, and within short order 30 trailer parks operated in St. Clair County. Their manufacturers meant travel trailers to be used for vacations, but the city of Detroit experienced enough trouble with permanent trailerites, called "gasoline bedouins," that it tried kicking them out of town.

After that fleeting moment of critical self-examination early in the 30's, America's auto industry went right back to its shady dealing. The Federal Trade Commission accused 21 different car companies of making dirty loans of one kind or another. Their own dealers impugned The Big 3 for backhanded practices, and even the national Auto Club denounced car loans as a "scandal." Revived in the wake of the "holiday" crisis by the introduction of federal deposit insurance, the banking industry hungered to get in on the auto action. "Let Us Finance Your Car!" begged Port Huron's 1st National Bank, which made 20 such loans per week. "I Saved Big Money Buying My New Car with a Loan from the Peoples Savings Bank," said another firm, though Peoples didn't identify the "I" in its story. The consumer could have saved Really Big Money by not buying a car at all, but the hogwash and empty promises reeled in the gullible auto-fixated public again and again.

For those prospects who absolutely couldn't raise the funds to buy new, Port Huron auto dealers staged a used car "Mardi Gras" to help out, with a bevy of shined up clunkers on display at a street circus. This event appropriately featured the entertainment of staged automobile crashes by stuntman Wild Bill Welch, who lost control of his car during his last appearance and suffered an honest-to-goodness crash into some onlookers' vehicles. Port Huron's 21 auto repair garages backed the Mardi Gras to the hilt, holding out to vehicle owners the tantalizing hope that if only they'd allow mechanics to tune this, or fix that, or replace the whatzit, any old car could be made good as new again. A typical appeal: "Sick Motor Cars Require professional attention as humans do. If your car lacks the vim and pep it ought to have, come in and let us test it with our Moto Vita and Mercury Vac." Vita and Vac, that fun couple.

However, just when things seemed to be getting back to normal in the car trade, a major interruption occurred. In the light of the false dawn of 1936, and the apparent fulfillment of his earlier campaign pledge of "Happy Days Are Here Again," Franklin Roosevelt and the Democrats all but annihilated the Republicans at the polls that year. This time, the votes barely had been counted before sitdown strikes broke out at automobile factories all across the country. A wave of unionization washed over the whole economy, both private and public sectors, as the labor movement sought to reverse three decades of backsliding, and called in its IOU's from the President. The unions were through fooling around, and following this second Democratic landslide in four years, the federal government put its full weight behind them in the form of the new National Labor Relations Board.

Given the fact that railroad employees had been organized for decades, and considering the size of the auto industry and the crooked course it steered, the union upsurge didn't come as a complete surprise in Detroit. Superficially, the work done in American auto plants wasn't heavy labor. Heavily tedious, yes. Carmakers paid high if not always reliable wages that averaged 76 cents per hour, compared to the 57 cents of other manufacturers. Some car companies offered rudimentary savings, health, and life insurance plans for employees. But most factory floor men still labored entirely at the mercy of the bosses when it came to issues of how often they worked, how long, how fast, layoffs, callbacks, sick time, break time, discipline, what employees could talk about on company property, or whether they could talk at all. Auto workers could be fired pretty much at will, and sometimes companies let them go for the sin of getting

215

old, when they couldn't keep pace with speed-ups on the assembly line any more.

Charlie Chaplin captured all this in 1936 in the opening of his film *Modern Times*, playing a frantically harassed factory worker gradually going mad. Ostensibly, Chaplin based this scene on life at the FMC. Opponents of unions argued that auto linesmen had no one to blame but themselves for accepting and staying with these jobs if conditions actually were so bad. But the sun was about set on that kind of reasoning.

The small, Communist-riddled United Auto Workers union, affiliated with the Congress of Industrial Organizations (UAW-CIO), took charge of the automotive sitdown strikes. The Roosevelt administration favored this union because, among other reasons, the CIO had put up $300,000 toward FDR's re-election. The UAW's leadership included Walter Reuther, the ex-Ford man, and his brother Victor, back from their expedition to Europe and Russia. The classic sitdown action came at a General Motors factory in Flint just after Christmas, 1936. A small group of UAW men seized control of the plant, and wouldn't come out. After two months of demonstration, riot, gunfire, bullet wounds, vandalism, threats, counter-threats, lawsuits, injunctions, arrests, parades, arson, a National Guard callout, and some serious arm-twisting by Michigan Governor Frank Murphy – the former Detroit mayor and now Roosevelt protege – General Motors gave in and recognized the UAW as the collective bargaining agent for the union's members.

This gave the UAW a foot in the door which the union forcefully exploited to eventually sign up the vast majority of employees at GM, Chrysler and several other automakers during the next four years. But not Ford, yet. The UAW threatened to put the FMC out of business for resisting. Not surrpisingly, when Walter Reuther appeared at his former stomping grounds at the Ford Rouge River plant to do some recruiting and maybe get another sitdown strike going, he and fellow organizer Richard Frankensteen were stomped flat by the security guards.

To say the experiences of 1937 embittered General Motors head Alfred Sloan for life may be an exaggeration, but it certainly took the gloss off the decade. Sloan had been a busy beaver during the 1930's, but a largely successful one. He'd lost his fight against installing safety glass in cars, sure, but despite this additional and, as he saw it, unnecessary expense in auto building, he kept GM profitable and paying dividends right through the worst depression years. To head off the "safer car" nonsense before it went any further Sloan helped found the Automobile Safety Foundation, an auto industry front which successfully ran blame-the-driver and blame-the-streets campaigns for the next two decades, distracting the public from the inherent dangers of autos themselves, while bleeding government treasuries of yet more money for roads.

Further along these lines, Sloan founded the National Highway Users Conference, a lobbying group dedicated to reserving gas and auto taxes for roads only, and to sticking the general public with the rest of the huge costs of the automobile culture. The voters of Michigan compliantly passed a state constitutional amendment tying up gas and auto taxes exactly as NHUC wanted. "We have two common enemies," Sloan told NHUC, "1. The railroads. 2. The legislatures, to which might be added the Congress of the United States."(39)

During the 30's Sloan also hatched a scheme for GM and its corporate partners to buy up and tear out streetcar lines across the country and replace them with dirtier, noisier, less comfortable, more wasteful, more destructive, more dangerous, and shorter lived GM buses. Streetcars still carried twice as many passengers as buses in America at the time. Sloan launched this campaign behind another bland corporate name, the National City Lines, and made one of his first targets the exemplary Los Angeles streetcar system, in 1938.(40) Sloan also did well personally during the decade. As GM's largest individual shareholder, he pocketed as much as $2.5 million in dividends annually, and he often collected the highest business salary in America, $561,000 in 1936.(41) Just as thrifty in his fashion as competitor Henry Ford, Sloan even managed to dodge $128,000 in income taxes by incorporating his yacht. Regrettably, most of his customers couldn't do the same with their cars.

But Sloan's winning streak came to an end when he personally donated several thousand dollars to the Liberty League, a vehemently anti-Roosevelt political group. Sloan also helped pour a torrent of abuse onto the President and the New Deal via the public relations office of the National Association of Manufacturers (NAM). NAM sponsored a radio serial entitled *American Family Robinson*, about fictional small town folks valiantly beating back sinister big-government officials coyly nicknamed the Arcadians.(42) Unlike Henry Ford, FDR had a long memory for that sort of mockery, and when the UAW sitdowners arrived at GM's door, Roosevelt, who personally didn't approve the occupation tactic, didn't lift a finger to stop it.

After a fruitless telephone shouting match with U.S. Labor Secretary Frances Perkins during the Flint strike, Sloan finally realized that the fix was in and GM would have to deal with a unionized workforce and much larger responsibilities as an employer.(43) Not to mention new reforms like federal wage and overtime laws, unemployment compensation, and a new national old-age savings plan called Social Security. The Arcadians had had the last laugh after all. A fuming Sloan gave up the GM presidency, and handed that job to William Knudsen, but he kept the chairman's seat. He also shelled out $10 million to dispense anti-New Deal propaganda through the Sloan Foundation, promising to "diffuse economic facts from the cradle to the grave."

Port Huroners watched with alarm the unionization violence spreading throughout Michigan, in the cities of Flint, Pontiac, Monroe, and the state capital in Lansing. At one point rumors flew that the UAW intended to take control of the entire state government. Unionists targeted not just auto-related companies but electric utilities too, and during one job action UAW men turned off the electrical power to 400,000 people. Frank Murphy, who happened to be a friend, fraternity brother, and occasional Port Huron house guest of Ford dealer Albert Parfet, scurried from one crisis to the next, berated by his critics, who claimed he needed "more backbone and less wishbone." They further mocked the governor when he took time out to accept an honorary degree from Duquesne University, and announced that "nothing new or essentially unusual" was happening in his state.

Murphy's assurances didn't square with what Louis Weil was hearing. When Weil traveled out of state at this time, shocked strangers repeatedly accosted him for information about the "revolution" and "outlawry" underway in Michigan. Teamsters Union truck drivers, including 150 in Port Huron, joined the outlaws and blockaded highways to enforce their own actually pretty modest strike demands for a 9-hour day, 54-hour week, higher wages and a closed shop. Drivers turned back everything except food, mail and newspapers. Nationally, Teamsters membership grew by almost 500% in

217

seven years, to 420,000 by 1939, led by "a small group of devout socialists and communists," according to historian Steven Brill.(44)

UAW sitdown strikers at one Port Huron plant managed to settle without any trouble. The 75 members at United Brass and Aluminum wanted seniority rights, a 40 cent an hour minimum (38 cents for gals), an 8-hour day, a 48-hour week, plus time-and-a-half for overtime, Sundays and holidays. They got everything they wanted except a closed shop, but eventually that linchpin of UAW strategy became standard as well. Things didn't go quite so smoothly later in the year at the Mueller Brass factory across town, when 600 men from rival unions fought hand to hand over a UAW attempt to close down the plant. 25 people had to be treated for injuries and the state police came in to break up the festivities. Right across the Canadian border in Sarnia a UAW sitdown action at an auto foundry erupted into another pitched battle that left 8 combatants hospitalized and 69 under arrest.

Similar scenes wherever they looked unnerved Wall Streeters still jittery from the stock market cliff dive of 1929. This seemed like a serious assault against private enterprise going on here. Stocks crashed once again in 1937. Four million jobs disappeared in four months, and America returned to depression country by the end of the year. Roosevelt admitted that despite the federal government's having spent $14 billion on relief during the past five years, and doubled the national debt, one-half the nation remained "ill-fed, ill-clothed, ill-housed." Not to mention ill-driven, loaded up again with unaffordable cars. One-third of U.S. households lived on $780 per year or less.

Governor Murphy called the situation a "modern famine," and the Michigan government revisited the insolvency brink after running up a $30 million deficit. Owners surrendered half a million parcels of Michigan property for non-payment of taxes, and the city of Port Huron picked up some lots for $1 apiece. Harold Wills lost for unpaid taxes some of his Marysville land, which eventually became the municipal golf course. Half the wage-earners in Detroit's by now emphatically undiversified economy lost their jobs again, including 200,000 of the UAW's new members. Maybe it made the union ranks feel better to know that thanks to their efforts Michigan companies paid the highest average wage in America, $1,100 per year, to those still working.

1,600 out-of-work citizens in Port Huron registered with the new Michigan Unemployment Commission. They lined up to get some of the 88 tons of free food handed out to the poor from the nation's gigantic surplus stockpiles during a single month in St. Clair County: potatoes, citrus fruits, apples, prunes, cabbage, milk, flour, pears, cereal, fish. Enough to make local grocery stores wonder: Why try to sell it (and at prices 30% cheaper than in 1929) when the government gave it away?

All this economic backsliding transpired although taxes gobbled up almost twice the amount of American income they had during the 20's. Higher federal taxes did most of the gobbling. Port Huroners filed almost 2,500 returns in 1939 for the national income tax, a measure introduced 25 years earlier as a modest levy on the rich. People making less than $1,000 per year in the 30's paid one-quarter of all taxes. The only semi-bright spot in the latest economic swoon developed because, again, so many people couldn't afford to run their cars that traffic fatalities fell by more than 20% in 1938, to a mere 32,000.

218

Henry and Edsel Ford took out heartfelt ads in the press commiserating with the nation: "If we knew anything better we could do for the country than make good motor cars, we would do it." Purely to further the nation's welfare, therefore, the Fords introduced a new model line in 1938, Mercury, (*a thrillingly big car inside and out*), to fill up the price range between Fords and Lincolns. Nobody at the FMC dared say it out loud, but this seemed like exactly what General Motors would have done. Privately, one FMC designer disparaged the Merc as a "blown-up Ford," and even the standard 1938 Ford car, introduced in *Good Housekeeping* magazine, looked a little bloated. But, increasingly these days, size mattered:

Open your eyes to the biggest surprise in all your woman's experience. The new DeLuxe Ford V- 8 is definitely the largest Ford ever designed. It stands before you...more than fifteen feet of low, flowing length [compared to the 12 feet of the Model T].(45)

A *Fortune* magazine poll named Henry Ford America's most popular industrial figure; also the second most unpopular. Numerous communities across Michigan celebrated his 75th birthday in 1938. 10,000 children sang "Happy Birthday to You" for Henry at the state fairgrounds in Detroit, reducing to tears the man pronounced by the *Times Herald* as the "world's greatest citizen." Frank Murphy finished out of the money in greatest citizen sentiment, and voters booted him out of Michigan's governorship in the 1938 election after his disastrous two-year go-around with the United Auto Workers. Both sides blasted him. A Republican congressman called Murphy a Communist stooge, and a former Communist UAW member pronounced him a "fence sitter deluxe." But President Roosevelt appreciated a guy who could take punishment in the ring, and named Murphy U.S. Attorney General immediately after the '38 election, then a Supreme Court judge a year later. Before Murph could get on board the Court, its members outlawed sitdown strikes, cold comfort by that time to the ex-governor.

As bad as the depression-bothered present might be, America could look forward to an inexpressibly wonderful future when the auto companies ruled the world, according to their displays at the 1939 New York World's Fair. The fair's overall theme was "The World of Tomorrow," and the Big 3 played a Big Part at the fair, especially General Motors. GM put on a "Futurama" exhibit that would have done Aldous Huxley proud, featuring a massive animated toytown version of the year 1960. Five million fairgoers got a look at GM's brave new world of elevated, four-decker, seven-lane "skyways" full of automobiles careening along at 100-200 miles per hour, crisscrossing the American landscape, snaking their way between 2,000 foot tall skyscrapers.(46) Don't worry about those speeds, said traffic whiz and Futurama advisor Miller McClintock, driverless cars of tomorrow would be steered by a combined "invisible eye" and short wave radio. Given the value of most auto company promises, America really needed not driverless cars but carless drivers in the future.

The estimated construction bill required to translate Futurama into real life came to $57 billion for the highways alone, with no cost figures for maintaining or policing them. Just don't expect GM to pay for it. They left that up to the taxpayer, as always. The main designer, Norman Bel Geddes, previewed Futurama at a National Planning Conference in Detroit. Bel Geddes loved the way the automobile "has given us a chance to tear down buildings, widen streets, and turned our 'blighted' areas into more pleasant-looking places by letting in the light."(47) Letting in the cars, he meant. World's Fair bigwig and New York City's urban planning boss Robert Moses enthusiastically seconded GM's manifesto, and soon thereafter made his name synonymous with bulldozing neighborhoods to clear the way for the automobile paradise of *mañana*.

Daydreamers like Bel Geddes, McClintock, and Moses divorced themselves completely from the reality of the automobile's unrivaled powers of blightmaking. They expected residents of their monstrous Futurama City to dedicate three-quarters of its land surface to cars. In the World of Today, 1939, Detroit endured traffic congestion so bad that "At 5:15 you can almost hop across a street on the tops of cars frozen in the traffic tie-up," according to *Life* magazine.(48) Another wave of street widening and structure demolition to create parking lots availed Detroit nothing in handling this mess on wheels.

Civic leaders in Port Huron crabbed constantly about the jam-ups in their own downtown, where 70% of workers, shoppers, and visitors now arrived by car. The Carpenter bus company tried playing up the squeeze: "Ride The Busses. Downtown Parking Is A Problem! Save Time! Save Money! Save Your Disposition!" Owners graded more vacant lots, then covered them with a repulsive layer of cinders, or raw asphalt blacktop, to create more parking lots, public and private. Sperry's department store put in a 50-car lot, free for customers to use, for everybody else 10 cents. When the first self-serve supermarket opened downtown, owner H.A. Smith assured the public of parking for 300 cars. The installation of another 150 paved parking spaces further defaced Pine Grove Park. A parking lot for dining, Port Huron's first drive-in restaurant, opened in 1939.

The first parking meters appeared briefly on Port Huron curbs, charging five cents for an hour's repose. The City Council reluctantly approved them after an epic, angry debate. Then, after another ruckus, the Council pulled the meters out again. The old dispute about parallel versus angled parking on the downtown streets flared up again for no less than the fifth time. "Parallel Parking – A Menace," insisted local insurance agents, because, they said, jockeying your buzz wagon along the curb to get it parked parallel practically invited a sideswiping. After 80 different businesses, labor unions and property owners joined in the battle, parking switched back again to angled. Then back again to parallel. And so on.

In a way, a slice of the World of Tomorrow did come true for Port Huron during the 30's. Though not stacked four decks deep like the GM Futurama version, the American and Canadian governments revived as a public works measure the automobile and pedestrian bridge across the St. Clair River proposed by businessman Maynard Smith during the previous decade. They called it the Blue Water Bridge this time, along the same theme lines used in the immensely popular Blue Water Festival, which Port Huron inaugurated in 1934 to cheer itself up during the depression. A bridge still made no real sense. The ferry carried a million passengers and 175,000 vehicles per year efficiently. The railroad-proven tunnel option still sat there. But a bridge would make a visible symbol of government in action, it would cost less to build than a tunnel (though not to maintain), and take less time to finish.

Both the old and new generations of Port Huron power brokers supported the skyway. In the lead came Marshall Campbell, that horse-wrangling son of the road contractor Herbert, and now head of the auto-loaning People's Bank, which he'd practically resuscitated singlehandedly after the bank holiday. Campbell also owned Frank Beard's hardware store, which he'd taken over after the Road Commission Chairman for Life went to his reward at age 80 in 1934. Truckman Dale Moffett of the Ogden & Moffett firm buttressed the bridge project. A publicly built bridge, thought Dale, looked like just the ticket for the trucking industry to make more inroads against the railroads, once the Canadians lightened up and allowed American trucks onto their highways. Maynard Smith naturally lent his support, ready to supply the project with cement by re-opening his factory following a four year shutdown. Louis Weil took a place on the bridge builders totem pole and he assigned *Times Herald* reporter Ralph Swan to work full time promoting it.

Scores of Port Huron homes and familiar businesses like Florence's Lunch and North End Billiards had to be condemned and torn down to clear the dozens of acres of ground needed for the Blue Water Bridge and its half-mile of approaches. After two years of rush work, an ungainly, derrick-like assemblage of girders arose that looked as though it had been designed with a child's Erector Set. The finished bridge rattled and boomed like a roller coaster when vehicles crossed it. A shower of noise and automobile exhaust cascaded down on surrounding neighborhoods around the clock. Property values plunged. The State Bridge Commission obtained legal immunity from damages caused by objects thrown or falling off the structure, so anybody beaned while walking under it couldn't sue. The bridge permanently despoiled the view of the St. Clair River which generations of Port Huronites had enjoyed, all to give a thrill to passing motorists who spent a few seconds enjoying the panorama from the bridge's summit.

The Bridge of Tomorrow opened in October 1938 with ceremonies chaired by Weil. 100 marching units, 32 floats, and 48 cars representing every state in the Union paraded through Port Huron. Frank Murphy made one of his last appearances as governor to cut the ribbon. 100,000 people on foot and in cars crossed the bridge for free during the first two days. A newly commissioned song of surpassing insipidity celebrated the "bridge of peace," which had destroyed the peace and quiet.

Across the Blue Waters to you
May we extend a friendly hand
To build a friendship that's been true
And everlasting bind our lands.
So too the nations near and far
May they take heed to this refrain
For may there be an end to war
And may they all join hands again.(49)

The nations near and far didn't pay much attention to this cease-fire invitation in 1938. The total project cost came to $4 million for about a mile and a quarter of single-deck, three-lane elevated highway. $700,000 bought out the St. Clair River ferry for gradual retirement, lest its efficiency provide any embarrassing comparisons with the bridge operations. The tolls to cross the Blue Water Bridge – 60 cents per car and 10 cents per passenger – cost more than twice the ferry's, but the backers promised that once they paid off the skyway bonds in 1953, crossing would be free. The BWB hadn't been open a year before the perpetual job of scraping and repainting its rusting steel

221

began.

Not all the road and street work done in Port Huron and St. Clair County during the 1930's required World of Tomorrow, $4 million per mile treatment. But even on the mundane level of tens of thousands of dollars, it was one great business to be in, because the first generation of automobile-inspired pavements were crumbling left and right. "Harder Pavement Needed," opined the *Times Herald*. "The financial strain of replacing these pavements every ten or fifteen years, which is about the limit of their effectiveness, is terrific...Practically every highway in every direction from Port Huron needs patching, and some of them need actual rebuilding, although very few miles are as much as twenty years old."(50) The Auto Club blamed not traffic for destroying streets but "the ravages of the elements and the horsemen of road destruction that follow in their wake – abrasion, suction and shear." Whatever did it, the U.S. Bureau of Public Roads admitted that two miles of improved roads were wearing out for every new mile put down.(51)

Undissuaded by the horsemen, Port Huron by now had paved half its streets. The city widened virtually every major thoroughfare during the 30's, some by as much as 50%. The Public Works Department sacrificed to the traffic gods more sidewalks, lawns, landscaping and 100-foot tall elm trees. Once the worst of the city budget crisis had passed the street lights came back on, and more traffic signals went up. A single stoplight on Main Street now cost $4,500, as much as a good size house. 150 more stop signs appeared, although a state police study found that two-thirds of Michigan's drivers didn't stop for stop signs and many didn't even slow down.

90% of traffic accidents in Port Huron occurred on just 12% of the streets, mostly the state highways, which supposedly had been engineered for safety. The affluent now shunned homes built along these busy trunk lines, once Port Huron's elite streets. Nash dealer Harvey Kimball fled the raucous effects of his own automotive products on the urban scene, and abandoned downtown living to move full-time in his beach house, as so many high rollers had done before. A large new apartment building constructed on Main Street sat 100 feet back from the curb to escape traffic noise. Any further back and it would have fallen into the river. Across the street, owners of another of the grand old Main mansions being offered up for sale for apartment conversion assured landlords that despite the car flood rushing by the property, the area remained "a good neighborhood."

Some sort of covering, stones or pavement, reinforced three-quarters of St. Clair County's rural roads by 1940. But hold on! the job wasn't done yet. 100 county road bridges needed repair, at an average cost of $10,000 apiece. After a minor staff reduction early in the depression, the Road Commission ranks grew to 150 employees. They manned four king-size depots across the county. A big scheme, once just the wistful fancy of the late Frank Beard, the "bypass" road, got underway during the depression. It was meant to carry north-south traffic entirely around Port Huron's business district, for those drivers bound for someplace else who didn't want to get slowed down in downtown. In the 1900 era as many as 5,000 visitors per day had been absorbed easily by the streetcars, trains, and steamboats, and transited smoothly through the city. Now most of these people fought their way through with cars.

The depression brought two major changes to local road and street administration which had significant consequences. In 1931 the state of Michigan as a cost savings abolished all township control of rural roads. From now on county Road Commissions ruled the boondocks byways, and residents outside the cities had virtually no say in what happened to them. The second change came about in 1937 almost as a second thought by Port Huron Police Chief Herman Nelson. He decreed that all motor vehicles must be removed from city streets each and every night during the four wintertime months to make way for snow plowing. By the 30's the demands of automobile driving had replaced the once cheerful welcome given to the benison of snowfall with full blown snow paranoia. Nothing now could be permitted to interfere with the removal of this white pestilence, this life-threatening car enemy, which one moment immobilized your vehicle while the tires spun helplessly, and the next instant sent you skidding into perdition along an icy avenue of terror.

Just sanding and cindering weren't enough, Port Huron's streets now had to be scraped clean of snow, by up to 14 city trucks and 40 laborers at a time, another endless battle in the automobile's world war against nature. Police ordered 28 cars towed away during the first night of Chief Nelson's Empty Streets plan, and, pronto, cars and trucks of every description, which had no fixed garage abodes, and lived on the streets, pulled up onto sidewalks, boulevards (between curb and sidewalk), lawns, alleys and backyards, making an even uglier spectacle of themselves than usual. Many of these vehicles stayed put right where they were in their new spots year round.

Snow control on St. Clair County's endless miles of country roads was highly problematic. Even the lightest dusting triggered 20 accidents in a single day. During a storm, the Road Commission plowed and sanded top-priority state highways first and left everybody else to wait. Traveling salesman D.J. Fovell of Port Huron got mighty sore about the unsanded road on which his car smashed into a tree, killing his passenger – his mother – who like mothers in cars everywhere no doubt had urged D.J. to slow down, or perhaps take the train. Michigan's newest Highway Director, Murray Van Wagoner, promised all-weather roads someday, in the World of Tomorrow. This Thumb native won election to two successive four-year terms in the highway directorship.

Van Wagoner adopted a simple motto as highway director: keep on building. His wish list included 3,600 miles of trunk lines rebuilt, 1,500 miles of highway divided, 800 miles widened, 275 bridges repaired, and 3,000 miles of gravel highways paved. Total cost $853 million. Plus a $38 million elevated highway through Detroit. Plus a national superhighway system. Even the New Deal team couldn't furnish cash on that scale. Murray, it will not surprise you to learn, served as president of the American Road Builders Association. He won his chief notoriety in Port Huron when he ordered construction of a divided highway on lower Main Street in 1936, despite fears it would create greater speeding problems. Two weeks after its completion police hauled over drivers doing 70 mph. In 1940 Van Wagoner won election as Michigan's governor, the first road engineer ever to take the top spot in the state government.

The Smell of Tomorrow emanating from tailpipes across this modest sized city of Port Huron could be something terrible by the 1930's. "Just how much of this poison we may be taking in more or less continually from the polluted atmosphere of our streets is not at all certain..." worried the *Times Herald*. Port Huron school teacher Kathleen Moore took in enough to choke to death when she fainted while closing her garage doors one day with her car's engine running. Dr. William McNally told the Michigan State Medical Society that if asphyxiation and heart disease weren't enough, motor exhaust could also inflict "headaches, vertigo, shortness of breath, drowsiness, nervousness, muscular weakness, nausea, vomiting, blood alteration..."

A resident could hardly avoid catching the whiff of raw gasoline these days from 117 filling stations in Port Huron, whose numbers seemed overplentiful for a city of 32,700 people. At least, Bina West-Miller thought so. The now-married head of the Women's Benefit Association got a jolt from a real estate agent in 1932 when he told her that a gas station would be built on a lot across the street from the West-Miller riverfront home unless she bought the property herself. Bina immediately marched downtown to confront the City Council over this outrage. She was still a force to be reckoned with at age 65, though she sometimes showed signs of loosening screws – megalomania. At the 1931 WBA convention in Chicago, 75,000 conventioneers had filled Soldier Field for a celebration of the "Dear Leader Bina," complete with marchers, horses, an orchestra, and operatic singing. It concluded with Bina's portrait outlined in fireworks.(52) She set off some fireworks at Port Huron's City Hall right enough, over this gas station business. Officials promptly drew up the community's first zoning ordinance, plus an additional law pointedly regulating where these fuel parlors could be built. The Port Huron school board joined Bina's numerous allies in this campaign, to get gas stations well removed from schools.

Despite these strictures, service station builders replaced several other prominent Port Huron buildings with gas pumps. Like the home of the late Edgar Spalding, on Main Street, once a showplace, the pride of the city's pioneer auto accident victim. Away went the 80 year-old mansion of John Howard, the lumberman and early car customer. And the Globe Hotel, a landmark whose livery barn once had cared for up to 100 horses. The suggestively named Hi-Speed company built a station next to the entrance to Pine Grove Park, despite a public outcry and petitions to run it off. Less visibly than fillings stations, other businesses stored gasoline on their property, as the neighbors of Ogden and Moffett trucking learned when the O&M tanks sprang a leak into the sewers, forcing homeowners to extinguish their furnaces in the middle of winter so as not to ignite the fumes.

Even this seemed a modest risk when compared to the scale of the latest Imperial Oil refinery explosion in Sarnia which killed one worker and injured 11. Imperial's works now stretched a mile and a quarter along the St. Clair River across from Port Huron. The biggest refinery in the British Empire functioned virtually as a city in itself. Its 1,800 workers used as much electricity as a city of 10,000 civilians while processing 24,000 barrels of oil per day. The Imperial blast brought home vividly the interesting fact advertised by the 42 Sinclair Oil dealers in St. Clair County - that a single gallon of gasoline contained enough energy to elevate the Statue of Liberty by 3 feet. A similar reminder came when a gasoline delivery truck crashed just south of Port Huron. The subsequent explosion and fire burned up driver William Basing, who'd just delivered 5,000 gallons of gas to the Hi-Speed station, enough to blow Miss Liberty three miles high. The unfortunate Basing might not have been as alert as optimal with that kind of cargo. Gas truckers commonly traveled 500 miles per day making deliveries.

With so many stations in town, and the prices and product more or less the same, dealers scrapped harder than ever for the loyalty of customers. Given the natural connection between gasoline and fire, Texaco took to the radio to sponsor the Ed Wynn

Show with the 35 piece Texaco Fire Chief Band. In the print wars, Shell promised its gas would chase away "Old Lady Engine Waste." Mobil would give a car "Climatic Control" for all weather driving. Sunoco: "Makes telegraph poles look like a picket fence...the streamlined acting motor fuel." Standard: "Live Power - for quicker get-away, higher speed, richer climbing power..." An artist's conception portrayed both a freight train and a gazelle galloping alongside a symbolic Standard customer's car.

Fresh out of high school, brand-new gas station attendant Bernie Lyons had to *run* to a customer's car, per the boss' orders, and in addition to dosing the vehicle with gas, service without fail the windows, oil, radiator, and tires. All these gas stations and suppliers battled for a total of 6% of America's entire retail trade, a hefty pie. One inspector found that 20% of the Port Huron stations took an extra slice of the pie by using defective gas pumps that charged for more gas than they dispensed. Port Huron consumed 35 million gallons of gasoline per year. A Standard Oil tanker ship delivered a million gallons to its local terminal each month, enough to launch Lady Liberty into orbit. A similar ship went aground in Michigan's straits of Mackinac during this decade, and six men died trying to pump off the gasoline before it fouled the Great Lakes any further.

Like everything else, the price of oil fell drastically with the onset of the depression. A simultaneous glut of overproduction helped push the cost of petroleum down to 18 cents a barrel at one point, and the government stepped in to set production quotas to try to drive it up again. At its lowest level, gasoline cost just 8.6 cents a gallon in Detroit, including the 3 cents state gas tax. To this obviously undertaxed product the federal government added its own 1.5 cent gasoline tax during the 30's. The outraged Michigan Auto Club took this to be a penny-and-a-half holdup by Uncle Sam, and actually started a "ride a bike" campaign in protest. Even in the worst of the depression years, 1932, Americans burned through 18 billion gallons of gas at a cost of $2.8 billion, about $100 per vehicle. Half a billion gallons went into tractors alone. As the nation's prospects brightened a bit, gasoline prices firmed, and reached an average of 21 cents per gallon in 1936, half what it cost in Europe. American demand reached 23 billion gallons by 1939; to power 250 billion miles of driving.

As always, the gasoline production and distribution system in America wasted prodigious amounts of it. The automobile itself positively threw gasoline away. Port Huron learned from "This Curious World," a syndicated newspaper feature by William Ferguson, that only 8% of auto fuel energy actually moved the car. Cooling the engine used 40%, transmission and engine friction 12%, incomplete burning 20%, miscellaneous inefficiencies another 20%. An even dirtier burning type of petroleum fuel, diesel, started gaining popularity among truckers during the decade due to its lower cost, though not to your lungs.

America's oil consumption doubled in the 20 years that ended in 1940. The nation used 62% of all the petroleum pumped in the world, twice as much per capita as Canada, the next biggest consumer. Even the modest Michigan oil fields pumped 23 million barrels in 1939. How much oil was left? Some people idly wondered. One 1935 report pegged U.S. reserves at 12 billion barrels. Citing other sources, the *Times Herald* estimated those reserves as "inexhaustible." The American Chemical Society said at the present rate of depletion oil fields wouldn't last another decade, after that oil shale might work instead, plus imports. "We are fortunate to have vast supplies of crude oil," wrote

225

Roger Babson, "but is that any reason why this generation should exploit them, waste them, use then uneconomically? Just as one generation exterminated the buffalo, so we are exterminating our crude oil reserves."(53) American oil companies burrowed like gophers for more supplies, both at home and abroad. The first big strike in Saudi Arabia came in 1938, from an American wildcat operation. Closer to home, American oil companies and their British counterparts made themselves so obnoxious to the Mexican government that it kicked them out and expropriated their holdings, a foretaste of political ramifications to come involving oil power plays.

America's railroads endured another terrible decade during the 1930's. Between 1929 and 1932 the depression knocked down train revenues 50%, to $3.1 billion. Freight tonnage declined by more than 50%, to 1.1 billion tons. Passenger numbers retreated almost 40%, to 480 million.(54) Fares fell; it cost just $4.95 for an overnight Pullman room, but automobiles now grabbed 87% of all intercity travel.(55) Layoffs among railroad workers topped 700,000 by '32. The major railroads ordered a grand total of 2 new locomotives in 1932, and 1,700 freight cars (the norm was 65,000). Business at the Port Huron freight depots fell 60% in five years, down to $1.8 million worth in 1932. The laws of the time didn't limit the financial losses of railroads, just their profits. America's interstate RRs, for instance, couldn't make more than 5.75% profit on revenues even in good times. As the depression deepened, train companies had to go hat in hand to the Interstate Commerce Commission, and in Michigan to the Public Utilities Commission to ask for permission to raise prices or lower wages. The anti-railroad malice of these agencies made trouble throughout the decade. In 1937 the ICC granted rate increases of only $47 million dollars to America's biggest train systems, whose wage bills had risen $135 million. Only one-half of U.S. rail carriers made money in '37, and by 1938 one-third of the rail mileage in the country operated in receivership.

Railroads lost 15% of their freight traffic to trucks during the 30's, and managers blamed the lack of truck regulation. To illustrate the situation, we'll cite the case of Port Huron's trucker Oscar Richards, who won a General Motors contract away from the railroads to haul auto parts to Detroit. Richards recruited more trucks for the job simply by flagging them down in the street and signing them on the spot. In fact, about the only competitive victory won by the rails during the depression, and a modest one at that, came when they persuaded the federal and state governments to impose some oversight on truck and bus firms comparable to what railroads faced. In Michigan regulators cut maximum truck lengths to 50 feet, banned doubletrailer semis, tightened weight limits, imposed safety rules, and required approval of truck and bus routes and rates. Port Huron beer and meat trucker Earl Smith almost lost his head over this setback. He soon found himself under indictment for lying about a bribe he allegedly offered for a state license. Earl sweated bullets for a while, even in his refrigerated warehouse. He hired Port Huron's city attorney Patrick Kane to defend him, and persuaded the city police commissioner, school board president, and Judge Fred George to testify as character witnesses, before winning an acquittal.

The railroads also proposed banning long-haul trucking as too dangerous, and again asked the government to help pay for railbed upkeep, as it did for highways. Neither idea went anywhere. President Roosevelt refused any suggestion of subsidies for the trains, although American railroads paid more taxes than any other industry. They paid twice as much of their income for taxes as did truck and bus companies, and eight times as much to maintain their rights of way. The 37 railroads in Michigan forked over $9 million in state taxes in 1932 for virtually no government service at all, nothing for maintaining their 7,800 miles of track. Buses and trucks paid $12.6 million in Michigan taxes in 1932 while the government lavished $50 million on streets and highways alone, and millions more on other auto-related support services.

As mentioned above, hundreds of railroads in America had a brush with bankruptcy during the worst of the slump. In St. Clair County one small 19-mile train line failed completely, while the three other remaining lines chopped away at costs and services in order to stay solvent. The Pere Marquette railroad halted its railcar ferry across the St. Clair River in Port Huron and paid Grand Trunk to use the latter's tunnel instead. The PMRR cut passenger schedules in the Thumb back and back until by 1940 no more passenger service existed at all north of Port Huron, the end of an era which began back in 1879 with the McMorran Line. The railroad freight service out that way, once known as the "buttermilk run," which picked up dairy and produce shipments, shrank as well, cutting off once busy farmland stations, to the dismay of those farmers still using them. For many, that left trucking as the only option.

The Grand Trunk system made out somewhat better, though its meager profits didn't average as much as $1 million per year, less than one-fifth its average during the 20's. After four years of skeleton staffing the GTRR railcar repair shops in Port Huron rounded the bend in 1934, so to speak, and put on a near normal staff. Among the jobs awaiting them: refitting 550 freight cars as automobile carriers. By 1936 things had improved enough that GTRR freight trains again rolled once an hour through Port Huron. Its freight sheds expanded and offered 1-day freight service out of Port Huron to Detroit and Chicago, 3-days to New York. It handled 22 million pounds of freight for Port Huron merchants in a single year. The company's local payroll slowly climbed back to 1,200. Grand Trunk still maintained Port Huron to Detroit passenger trains (despite the unfair competition of seven buses on the same route daily), as well as eight east and westbound connections daily to Chicago, Canada and New York. Fares still cost 2-3 cents per mile, and as low as a penny on special excursions.

A veteran Grand Trunk locomotive starred unexpectedly in a special excursion to Port Huron in 1940, hauling movie actor Mickey Rooney, several Metro Goldwyn Mayer studio executives, and Edsel Ford to town for the premiere of the film *Young Tom Edison*. It touched off the biggest civic celebration Port Huron had ever experienced. Collector Henry Ford lent the Edison-era locomotive from his museum for the occasion, in memory of his great friend, who'd died in 1931. Starstruck Rooney fans mobbed the train at every station en route from Detroit, and 75,000 people packed Port Huron and the five theaters showing the film, straining automobile parking space to the limit. A locomotive also co-starred in the move. In the climax, Young Tom somewhat improbably sent a Morse code message by a train's whistle, averting a disaster on the rails.

Even during the national depression-recovery-depression mess of the Thirties, American railroads continued to improve their overall technical performance. Freight train speeds increased 55%, passenger trains by 10%-40%. The newest freight cars carried 110,000 pounds and improved locomotives could pull up to 260 of them, moving a ton of freight at a penny per mile. As far as motive power went, some railroads installed direct electric drive locomotives to replace steam, but the big news

227

came from the development of diesel-fueled locomotives at General Motors, of all places. Alfred Sloan's animosity toward the rails mellowed considerably when his GM colleague Charles Kettering came up with a diesel engine design that promised to replace most of the coal-burners in the country. Just six years after identifying railroads as his #1 enemy, Sloan had this to say:

Improved types of roadbed, the increased use of air conditioning in passenger trains, high speed, light-weight equipment, traffic control systems permitting faster freight schedules, studies in fuel economy, and many other developments, indicate a bright future for the railroad – the backbone of our transportation system.(56)

Just as in the auto industry, streamlining came into vogue in passenger train design. A Union Pacific streamliner with a diesel engine cut 14 hours off the coast to coast record in 1934, running from Los Angeles to New York in 57 hours, at speeds which touched 120 mph, practically World of Tomorrow pace. Passenger service out of Port Huron got faster, making New York in 15 hours. The Grand Trunk tried out a new 100 mph streamliner on the Port Huron to Chicago run. But these improvements didn't compare with the 18 hours it now took to fly coast to coast.(57) Though trains traveled 53 times more safely than airliners, as well as more cheaply and comfortably, 1.8 million people took commercial airline flights in 1933, 3 million in 1940. Here again, the federal government spent millions subsidizing airport construction, and began setting up the national air traffic control system during the 1930's, compared to the policy of only extending an occasional low-interest loan to the train companies. With the government taking control of air travel facilities, Henry Ford decided to convert his airport into an automobile test track.

No commercial air service took off yet in St. Clair County, but aeronauts put together a simple airport from scrounged resources just outside Port Huron, with Louis Weil pushing the project. Two years before she disappeared into the Pacific, aviatrix Amelia Earhart stopped in Port Huron on a 1935 speaking tour to talk up flying. Somewhat surprisingly, she revealed that she'd been driving, not flying, her way around the Midwest this trip. Not the most cautious of drivers, Miss Earhart told her audience that she intended to make the 450 mile ground hop to Marquette, Michigan in a single day, the kind of recklessness that later cost her life.

But back to trains. Safetywise, riding an American train reached a pinnacle in 1935 when not a single passenger died. The Pere Marquette hadn't had a passenger fatality since 1908. A train passenger rode in 8 times greater safety than an automobile one. Railroad employee deaths and injuries, 535 and 15,000 respectively in '35, also diminished. U.S. trains averaged 14 accidents of one kind or another per million miles traveled. Plenty of car-train collisions still took place, "almost invariably" caused by the car driver, according to Travelers Insurance. Five people died in Capac when their Model TT truck pulled in front of a train. The impact knocked the family matron, 200 pound Mrs. Mabel Hendrickson, flying 200 feet. Her son identified the body when he happened by the accident site moments afterward. In Detroit 64 year-old conductor Frank Bray died of the shock two days after his train killed a family of 12 people jammed Joad-like into a single motor vehicle at an Indiana crossing.

Buses and train crossings didn't mix well, either. A freight train hit a school bus during a snowstorm in Utah, killing 26. "People walked up and down, putting parts of bodies into bushel baskets," according to reporter Gordon Kirby. Spectacular crashes of buses – running off roads, diving through open draw bridges, careening into bridge abutments – threatened to replace the news stories of yesteryear about great train wrecks. Nationwide 5,000 bus companies, enjoying the same public subsidies as trucks and cars, carried 1.7 billion passengers per average year in the 30's. One-half of all the buses in the country – the 45,000 school buses – transported 1.5 million children at a cost of $35 million per year. For some strange reason, school officials adamantly opposed the merger of school and public bus systems almost everywhere.

Among the other species of rail transport, the last interubans in Michigan stopped running during the depression, as did many others across America, and awaited their day of recall when the nation regained its senses, if it ever did. When one of the builders of the late Rapid Railway, Albert Dixon, died in Port Huron his meager obituary made no mention at all of his role in founding that excellent system. Port Huron's streetcars were gone, and some people regretted it. "A speedy, well-equipped and efficiently operated electric streetcar system certainly offers the most ideal transportation service for any city," admitted the *Times Herald*.(58)

Detroit's streetcars still operated, as did systems in dozens of other cities, until Alfred Sloan could get around to wrecking them. In the backwards logic of some auto addicts in Detroit it was the streetcars that caused traffic congestion, not cars. Voters on second thought okayed a Detroit subway system to put the streetcars underground, but the federal government wouldn't cough up $87 million to pay for it. For the dwindling numbers of communities lucky enough to have them, the best designed and best built IU's and streetcars ever seen in America went into service during this decade, the Electroline interurban, and the Presidents' Conference Committee streetcar. Some of the PCC's were still running in Newark, New Jersey 70 years later.(59)

Commercial shipping of most kinds slowed to a crawl on the Great Lakes early in the decade. Iron ore shipments fell by 94% between 1929 and 1932. One of Henry Ford's two big freighters tied up at the dock for two years, while the other sailed only part time, and they were not unusual in this. On the Port Huron waterfront, the last drydock, Fitzgerald's, closed during the depression after 70 years in business. The last locally-based tugboat sailed away for good. The last commercial sailing schooner, the J.T. Wing, retired. The U.S. Bureau of Marine Inspection closed its office after 69 years. The ferry to Canada stopped after the Blue Water Bridge went up. The last regular passenger steamer service out of Port Huron halted forever, when the reliable 36-year old vessel *Tashmoo* was wrecked in 1936 in the Detroit River, never to be replaced. The Port Huron Terminal went bankrupt a second time. Visiting Captain Matthew Crawford described the waterfront as a "disgrace."

Things didn't come to a full stop on the water. Freighters still called occasionally at various businesses, like the two paper companies and the Edison power plant in Marysville. The feds relocated a Coast Guard station and 75-foot patrol boat to Port Huron, to assist traffic safety on the Lakes. Pleasure boats aplenty still enjoyed sailing the waters of St. Clair County, and the Chris Craft company in Algonac built enough of them to call itself the world's largest boat factory. The federal government ordered minimum safety and signal equipment for motorboats like Chris Craft products during the 30's, but didn't order any put on automobiles.

Some special passenger cruises occasionally drew customers back to the Lakes. A luxury 4-day cruise to the Thousand Islands in the St. Lawrence River attracted many Port Huron bigwigs like Louis Weil. 2,800 black Detroiters paid a raucous visit to Port Huron in two big chartered lake ships, and left behind three bushel baskets of empty whiskey bottles in Pine Grove Park alone. Ferries still connected St. Clair County to Canada at four other spots on the St. Clair River. Elsewhere regular passenger service still continued between bigger cities, like Detroit, Cleveland, and Buffalo, and travelers could sail for the upper Lakes from Sarnia three times weekly. On the Lake Michigan side, though, the Goodrich passenger line out of Chicago shut down.

One of the loudest voices in Port Huron bewailing the decline in water transit belonged to paper company executive, shipmaster, and Fascist sympathizer Edgar Kiefer. Again and again he told anyone who would listen that the city neglected its shipping possibilities, especially on the Black River, where his factory was located. One of Kiefer's talks unsarcastically outlined "The Possibilities of Port Huron as a Port." Kiefer said that once America and Canada built the St. Lawrence Seaway, Port Huron would become in effect an ocean port. A bushel of grain could be sent from Port Huron to England for a dime.

In Congress the Seaway project, an idea already 20 years old, started and stopped about as often as Jack Benny's Maxwell. It proposed to widen canals and deepen channels to allow the largest ocean going vessels into the Great Lakes. Kiefer enthused so about these prospects that he took passage on a freighter to Europe for three months in the fall of 1939 to scout around, and came back denouncing England for stirring up trouble on the Continent. Elsewhere, the federal government proceeded with improving the Tennessee and Missouri Rivers, the canalization of the upper Mississippi, and work on other river systems around the country, though the investment came nowhere near road outlays.

Inland shipping for hire across state lines came under Interstate Commerce Commission rate control in 1940, about 50 years after the railroads. Congress then directed the ICC to play off railroads, trucks and ships against each other, so than none of the three got too far ahead of the others, a major milestone in American myopia about transportation. This three-way split didn't alter the fact that most marine shippers used navigable waterways for free, a distinct contrast to the railroad system. Unlike the railroads, Great Lakes shippers managed to recover almost completely from the depression by 1939, when 300 freighters moved a record 140 million tons, including hundreds of thousands of automobiles, without the loss of a ship or man. Commercial vessels passed Port Huron at the rate of one every 10 minutes, and there were still enough local professional sailors in town to fill up the annual Shipmasters' Ball.

A transportation *benefit* worked on the country by the depression was the revival of the bicycle. At the beginning of the decade, the idea of adults on bikes hardly rated a contemptuous laugh in Port Huron, as one typical Detroit Edison ad for electric ranges suggested: "You don't do business on a bicycle! You don't make business calls on a bicycle – why should you expect your wife to do her work with equipment just as antiquated?" Special *Times Herald* columnist William Phelps, who was a Yale University professor and Louis Weil pal, noted: "To most Americans today the bicycle means nothing...the omnipresent automobile has made wheeling so dangerous that both for business and for pleasure the bicycle is scarce used at all." But in Nazi Germany, where Phelps was vacationing, he counted 30 bikes to each car in Munich.(60) Since you could snag a new bike for as low as $20 in Port Huron, and for a used one practically name your own price, an increasing number of cash-strapped people decided to accept the risks.

The bike count in Port Huron reached 3,000. Adults rode about one third of them. 1,500 kids biked regularly to school. Extrapolate that ratio and we find that America owned 10-12 million bicycles. Manufacturers built 1 million bikes in 1936. Although Port Huron had none, the big city of Chicago got into the swing of things and blazed miles of bicycle trails.(61) Even the normally auto-centered Murray Van Wagoner wanted bike paths placed alongside Michigan highways, though he failed to produce any. 23 year-old journalist Roland Higgins certainly could have used one. An automobile ran him down and killed him as he bicycled along Lapeer Avenue in Port Huron. Higgins had been in the process of riding 600 miles to New York to take a job, and police found his typewriter amid the crash debris. His 17 year-old killer, Charles Reifergerst, had no driving license and had been motoring along in the rain without windshield wipers. When he pled guilty to reckless driving, the court rewarded his manly confession with 18 months probation. 700 American bicyclists like Higgins died this way in a typical year.

The Higgins case more or less confirmed part of William Phelps' thesis. The rights of cyclists to ride on public roads unofficially had been repealed, they could not be sure of their safety at any time on any thoroughfare in America, and if struck by a motor vehicle they'd get no justice. Port Huron police actually considered ordering all bicyclists under 14 years old off the streets, as though *they* were the problem, instead of the Reifergersts of the road. To survive in a world gone mad, bikers needed to be crafty, clandestine, cautious, like 88 year-old John Bessay of St. Clair City. Bessay credited decades of daily bicycling for his long life. Nobody ever credited riding in a car that way.

The 18 million horses and mules in America suddenly found themselves on the favorite animal list during the depression, hailed for helping to eat up the country's massive grain surpluses. They'd been stigmatized 20 years earlier for allegedly wasting good farm acreage with their appetites, but now the annual upkeep of a farm horse cost only $46 in depression prices. Things weren't all clover, though. A city horse had trouble getting a new set of shoes in Port Huron when the last blacksmith in town, George Cheney, closed up after 50 years in business. Cheney still maintained, like Ray Mudge, that no tractor could do farm work as well as the horse.

Port Huron coal dealer Francis Spencer sold his last horse delivery team and hated to see them go: "It was much more economical to use horses than trucks on short hauls. A team and wagon can be bought for $400 and last about 15 years. A truck which will last three years costs about $850. It is much cheaper to keep and feed horses than it is to buy gas and oil for trucks."(62) Spencer only got rid of his horses because customers objected to their trampling on lawns. Some rural mail carriers still ordered postal buggies in 1935. Even that old horse enemy Henry Ford spent one morning guiding a horse sleigh around Dearborn, picking up kids for the Greenfield Village school after a snowstorm immobilized his automobile offspring. Marshall Campbell started a horse riding stable at his 1,200 acre country estate outside Port Huron for amusement. So did truck honcho Myron Ogden on his 160 acre spread.

The automobile's mass murder of pedestrians continue apace during the 1930s. Cars hit 337,000 walkers in America during 1934 alone, and these victims made

231

up a huge percentage of the auto dead every year. 64 year-old Elias Jones died on Christmas Day of 1937 in Port Huron after a car struck him, the same way his wife Emma had been killed on the 4th of July the previous year. The *Times Herald* verdict on people like the Joneses: "Pedestrians are notoriously reckless on city streets," although reckless pedestrians didn't kill too many motorists in Port Huron. The many threats to walkers now included a new state law ordering rural pedestrians to walk against the traffic, though the law didn't set aside any safe portion of the road for them to do so. The "right turn on red" procedure introduced at some city stop lights to speed things up for drivers meant they occasionally scattered panicked pedestrians while right-turning through populated crosswalks. State traffic engineer R. E. Hefron could barely suppress his disdain for Port Huron's foot travelers: "If you take care of the automobile traffic you will find that pedestrian traffic will take care of itself."

Even walkers trying to thumb a ride found themselves pilloried, and from both sides of the hitchhiker question. As police and the Auto Club saw it, the "thousands of both men and women wandering over the country" as hitchhikers during the depression either preyed like wolves on automobile drivers who picked them up, or met horrible ends as the victims of the fiends who offered them rides. The warnings weren't entirely unjustified, as Savage Smith of Port Huron learned when three hitchhikers he picked up on the south side savagely thumped and robbed him of his money and his car. Truly heroic walkers refused to ask for or accept a ride in a car. Two young French Canadians, Elzear Duquette and Pierre Caron, marched through Port Huron, pulling their homemade travel trailer on bike wheels, walking from Montreal to Vancouver, 3,800 miles.

One of the most startling and illuminating facts about the depression is that the United States' overall health improved when the economic situation got worse, because millions of people stopped driving and ate less. In 1932, when times allegedly were blackest, Michigan recorded its lowest death rate ever up to then. As business and driving perked up in the middle of the decade, so did the bathroom scales, with all the attendant problems. The same cycle started all over again beginning with the 1937 slump. Incredibly, while millions of people had trouble setting the table during this decade, America as a whole got fatter during the 1930's.

A compendium of Michigan medical experts warned that obesity led to impaired organ function, mental slowdown, bronchitis, constipation, diabetes, gout, kidney disease, gallstones, apoplexy, skin disease, and "nervousness growing out of the belief that he or she is conspicuous..." Especially kids: "...a fat boy or girl meets with certain disagreeable incidents among playmates." Obesity killed more people over 40 years of age than cancer, and in New York City doctors noticed that obesity-related diabetes had risen 50% in 20 years.[63] Dr. Lewis Newburgh of the University of Michigan, the top expert on obesity, proved it wasn't a disease, and had nothing to do with metabolism or glandular problems. An imbalance in calorie intake caused it. Newburgh only slipped up by completely overlooking the exercise side of the imbalance. He warned against overeating, instead of underexercising.

Middle class Americans bought a million electric refrigerators per year during this decade and now kept too much food too readily at hand for a lifestyle stripped of exercise by the automobile. Processors packed much of that food with sugar and fat, and emptied it of vitamins, said the American Medical Association. The overeating

232

overemphasis led fatsoes to try more quack diets and to scarf down reducing supplements, like Kojena Bonhora from Peck's Drug Store in Port Huron: "Lose Ugly Fat. 14 lbs. in 11 Days. If Fat, You Can't Attract." Heart disease, the natural outgrowth of the automobile, became America's most frequently fatal malady. It claimed a prominent overweight victim in Port Huron druggist, state representative and WW1 vet Marvin Tomlin, who dropped dead at age 44. If only he'd carried Kojena Bonhora at Tomlin's. The same thing happened to Road Commission engineer William Cox, 53, while out on the golf course.

As usual, Ed Snover put his finger, or quill we should say, on the problem, with his immortal *We'd Rather Ride!*

The chap who's feeling under par
Should lay aside his motor car
And travel on his feet.
So our physician tells us when
We totter to his smelly den
And give him a complete
Description of the pains which wrack
Our mortal clay – 'Put up the hack
And walk once in a while',
He says, 'and Nature will restore
The robust health you had – and more
You'll face life with a smile!'

Then for a day or maybe two
Our automobile we eschew
And plod with labored tread
To destinations far and near
And utilize the running gear
Which we inherited
From some old member of our clan
Who never owned a big sedan.
But we don't persevere –
We'd rather suffer aches and pains,
And ride in well upholstered wains
Than have them disappear.(64)

That false hope of of good health, the hospital, continued to sap the strength of the Port Huron community. After a three year halt due to no money, Port Huron scraped together $175,000 from private donors and public works sources to finish an expansion of its hospital into a 7-story, 96-bed behemoth twice as tall as any other building in town, with twice as many beds as necessary. Within a week the new facility welcomed its first traffic casualty, William Rankin, who came in with one of those smashed up faces so fascinating to Dr. Straith. As often happened in these civic projects, Louis Weil did much of the fundraising. Nothing could budge his conviction that the bigger the hospital the better the public health, or get him to see the better sense in an ounce of prevention. Like installing a sewage plant, or getting rid of the car.

The World of Tomorrow might have been out of reach during this decade but

233

the War of Tomorrow arrived in September of 1939 when Germany invaded Poland. Just as they had during slow times in 1914, the European nations came to America's economic rescue and began beating each others' brains out. It triggered an immediate increase in trade with Yankee businesses and farms. In two months time national income hit the highest level since 1929. Auto building picked up nationwide, a development heartily welcomed in St. Clair County where four of the ten biggest industrial firms, with 3,100 employees, supplied the carmakers. The Auto Lite factory in Port Huron expanded by 70,000 square feet, and other facilities like Chrysler put on more room and more workers. Elsewhere in Michigan the car companies landed a big bonus of defense work as part of President Roosevelt's $3.3 billion defense preparedness program. General Motors had $400 million of defense contracts in hand by the end of 1940. GM president William Knudsen resigned to become head of the National Defense Advisory Committee, over the protests of Alfred Sloan, who warned Knudsen that Roosevelt would make a monkey out of him.

Henry Ford reluctantly agreed to build airplane engines for the U.S. military but refused English orders. Ford and Charles Lindbergh and the rest of the 800,000 people in the America First organization intended to keep the country out of the trenches in Europe this time.(65) There seemed to be no immediate threat from the disturbance on the Continent, and the U.S. Navy assured the public that if a war with Japan broke out in the Pacific we'd win it in three weeks. Mrs. Bradford Robbins visited Port Huron from her home in Honolulu, Hawaii and confidently told her friends that the American naval anchorage at Pearl Harbor rested "2,000 miles from any place from which a bomber could take off."(66) Further on the topic of bombs, William Robeson, the Port Huron inventor of "Preservo", a waterproofing treatment, and a former classmate of Thomas Edison's, said the recent discovery of fissioning uranium had powerful wartime implications.

During these years many notable figures of the auto age came to the end of all the tomorrows they were going to get. Horatio "Good Roads" Earle expired at 80, not long after the lobbyists known as the Road Gang erected a commemorative rockpile in his honor at a Thumb crossroads. Frank Beard got a posthumous rock, too, at a bend in a highway outside Port Huron. James Couzens lost his Republican U.S. Senate seat in 1936 after endorsing Roosevelt's reelection, and promptly died, not of regret but of bladder trouble. Henry Ford did duty as one of Stormy Jim's pallbearers. Walter Chrysler wasted away for two years after a stroke incapacitated him, before dying at age 65 in 1940. Harold Wills took a bad fall at his Detroit home and died two days before New Year's Day 1941 in Henry Ford Hospital. Wills' colleague, former Marysville mayor John Barron, died himself of shock when he heard the news about Harold. As the people of Marysville looked at it, if Wills had failed to build a car to last he'd at least left them a city, and in doing so he'd built better than he knew.

Chapter 7. 1941-1950: There's a Bright Day Dawning

I've seen plenty of fellas start out with fifty bucks and wind up with a bank account. And let me tell you, Long John, when you become a guy with a bank account, they got you...The helots...a lot of heels...They begin creeping up on you, trying to sell you something... First thing you know, you own things, a car for instance. Now your whole life is messed up with a lot more stuff. You've got license fees and number plates and gas and oil and taxes and insurance and identification cards and letters and bills and flat tires and dents and traffic tickets and motorcycle cops and courtrooms and lawyers and fines and a million and one other things. And what happens? You're not the free and happy guy you used to be. You've got to have money to pay for all those things. So you go after what the other fella's got. And there you are; you're a helot yourself.(1)

The pitfalls of automobile ownership, according to the Colonel, hobo wise man of Frank Capra's 1941 film M*eet John Doe*. Thoreau himself couldn't have put it any better. The 46 helots selling automobiles to St. Clair County's chumps drummed away full time as this latest decade began, because they suspected that the Second World War intended to visit the showroom someday soon. Once that war came to call on America, it wasn't likely that the auto industry would be allowed to continue swinging along as it had during WWI. All the road signs pointed toward a major detour. The U.S. defense buildup forged ahead. The nation reinstated the draft. President Franklin Roosevelt declared an unlimited national emergency. He vowed to give $10 billion in Lend-Lease assistance to Great Britain, half of it in oil, adding to the $5.7 billion England still owed America from the last war. In plain view of Port Huronites, some exiled Norwegian pilots staged a mock dogfight in the skies over Sarnia to give the locals a taste of European combat action.(2) *Hitler, Beast of Berlin* played in one of the Port Huron movie houses. Fred Riggin of Mueller Brass, boss of the biggest factory in town, penned to the community a public letter almost famished with war hunger: "How Will We Meet Our Date With Destiny?" No, things didn't seem too promising to the auto guys.

Though he had taken on a $480 million contract to build 1,200 bombers for the government, ordered strictly for defense of course, Henry Ford did his best to apply the brakes to the war momentum, just as he had a quarter century earlier. Still a committed war hater, Henry sincerely hoped, he said, neither England nor Germany won their fight; the U.S. should supply both sides until they collapsed; nothing but greed motivated both the Allies and the Axis; and the invasion threat to America was a hoax. However Hank's credibility suffered a bit in this hour because he'd accepted in 1938 the Grand Cross of the German Eagle, Germany's highest civilian honor.(3) At General Motors Alfred Sloan played it cool, and speculated on how marvelous the postwar car market would be. Faced with what looked like a pending deadline, the car industry pushed more than 5.2 million new cars and trucks out the door during the 1940-41 model year, the biggest total since 1929.

235

To help accomplish this feat car sellers used the usual promotional song and dance. That included the Easy Financing two-step, of course. An anxious buyer in one ad protested: *We can't afford anything but one of the three lowest priced cars.* The helpful car company responded: *But Listen, Lady! On a monthly time-payment basis, you'll hardly notice the difference at all.* Detroit also flogged a bewildering variety of superficial surface choices and price-boosting accessories. Along with 40 body styles and 261 interior trim combinations, Packard offered a new gas-waster: *real, mechanically cooled air-conditioning.* Plymouth addressed a previously unmentioned automotive hazard by headlining its *New Safety Rims to prevent 'throwing' a tire in case of a blowout.* How handy were these rims? Well, according to a press report from Salem, Illinois, when their vehicle threw a tire,"Twenty members of a professional roller-skating troupe died a horrible death in the blazing wreckage of a huge motorbus that sped crazily into a bridge abutment."

Ever the crowd pleasing showman, Henry Ford in person unveiled a 1941 car body entirely made of soybean plastic, and pounded it with an ax to demonstrate its collisionability. Henry correctly preferred vegetable plastics to the petroleum-based kind, and now baked two bushels of beans into every Ford.(4) Automatic transmission gained more ground with buyers, and provided the biggest sales hook in '41. The different carmakers variously called this advance Hydramatic, Simplimatic, Vacamatic, and Electromatic, all at higher cost than gear-grinding regular models. According to Oldsmobile, Hydramatic justified the extra money because it *Minimizes The Human Element...relieves driver of responsibility of pressing clutch pedal and shifting gears by hand.* Cadillac said further of automatics: *Safety is greater, the engine can't stall!* which looking back explained a great many past stalled-engine traffic accidents, especially some of those car-train encounters.

Lest buyers fear that automatic transmission cut down on speed, dealer John Cawood had this reassurance ready about his Buicks:

Come on! Drive a Car with 'Second Wind'! You say a racehorse has 'heart' when he can turn on the drive turning into the stretch and bring the crowd to its feet with an all-out finish. Okeh – come try a car that can turn on extra wallop like water from a tap – and see what you would say about Compound Carburetion.

Compound Fracture is what Cawood's doctors said when he and his wife Merle rear-ended another car on an icy street in Port Huron while driving a Buick with just 41 miles on it. Bound for Florida on a vacation by car (ignoring the ready train service available) the Cawoods didn't even make the southern city limits. Their Buick ejected them when the doors flew open on impact. The bouncing Cawoods suffered a broken arm for John and some of those inscrutable internal injuries for Merle. As to any police charges against John for driving too fast for conditions, let's just say they didn't make the newspaper.

The Human Element had struck again! Where would it stop? It wouldn't. At least the police could recognize the Cawoods when they picked them up off the pavement. When Chester Smrch of Marysville slammed his car into a tree in early 1941, his own brother didn't know him when flagged down by police to render assistance at the accident scene. Cops knew well enough the two corpses in a car clobbered by a Chrysler semi full of auto parts a week later: they were St. Clair County Assistant Prosecutor Richard Holt and Undersheriff David Hanton. They'd been out on the road at

2:30 a.m. looking for blind pigs. To prosecute, presumably, not patronize. Another victim of 1941, prominent Port Huron contractor Leo Noffs, died in a 65 mph head-on smash-up on the Gratiot Pike, not far from where his only son Bernard had been killed the same way in 1934. Auhorities blamed the Noffs wreck on another of those confounded dogs in the road.

In the worst auto event of the year, two oncoming drivers thought they could simultaneously cross a narrow culvert on a dusty county road near Port Huron at 45 mph each. But they couldn't, and five more names joined the 50 other locals on the 1941 auto fatality roll. A record 40,000 people died that way across America, plus, at a wild guess, one million injured, at a cost of $1.8 billion in damages, medical bills, undertaker's fees and such. If you're willing to combine dead and wounded, the country suffered as many casualties on the road in that single year as it did in military action during the entire Second World War.

And for what? The sacrifices of war could be accounted for, sometimes honestly sometimes dishonestly, as the price of the nation's independence, but what did the automobile stretcher cases accomplish? Was this the American Way of Life Fred Riggin believed to be under threat? This mad conceit? This turning away from the controlled sensibility of the rails for the near anarchy of the highway? The St. Clair County Road Commission tried calling them not highways but "happyways." This didn't mollify David Smith's family, after the 81 year-old pedestrian danced out of the way of one car on the 10th street happyway in Port Huron, only to be killed by another one coming the other way. Five traffic accidents of one kind or another per day occurred in Port Huron alone.

So many motorists got away with murder, figuratively speaking, in 1941 that in keeping with these war-shadowed times, Police Chief Thomas Davidson finally followed through on the traffic espionage idea. He enlisted "Twenty trustworthy citizens" to go undercover and denounce bad drivers to the cops, including, on the lighter side, violators of the "state anti-horn-blowing law," those nuts with loud musical car horns who blew them day and night, saluting their friends on the sidewalk with *La Cucaracha* for the umpteenth time. Together the police and their spies tossed 300 people into jail for traffic offenses during 1941. Like 62 year-old John Scef of Port Huron, convicted for the 9th time since 1929 of drunk driving. A judge sentenced him to 90 days or a $100 fine, but he couldn't pay the fine, so he did the time. The cost of liberty.

Some more unsettling facts about automobile liberty turned up for Port Huronites during these days of 1941, by way of the the war news from Britain. It seemed that London had recorded a lower death rate during the German bombing blitz than in peacetime, and observers cited the ban on most civilian driving as the number one reason. "By taking automobiles off the highways, by exercising caution in the home and in industry, by improving diet, by safeguarding self and community from the threats of epidemics through sanitation, vaccination and immunization, the English are saving more lives than their enemies are able to take," reported James Forgan of the American Red Cross.(5) Even with driving restrictions in place, two Britons died in auto accidents for every one killed by enemy action against the home island. "War is hell. But it is not quite so hellish in some respects as automobile traffic," admitted the *Times Herald*.(6) During the bombing campaign, the British gave first repair priorities to their railroad lines and canals, and found both very resistant to aerial destruction.

There were lessons to be learned from the British, but Americans by now were impervious to the suggestion that they'd live longer and better without cars. The physical unfitness of the United States, formerly just a vague suspicion, proved to be a dismal reality on the brink of war. Up to 50% of the new draftees washed out of the service with bad bodies. Doctors first suspected bad nutrition for this shortfall. Dr. Earl Wilder of the Mayo Clinic said America had the poorest national diet in its history, despite the alleged wonders of agricultural Fordism: the tractorized farming, the food processing for "convenience," the chain grocery stores supplied by long-haul trucking. The small-time fresh food grower-vendors, like Elizabeth Voet, who with her mare Molly had traveled their door-to-door vegetable route in Port Huron for 30 years, were fading from the scene. Roger Babson stepped away from his usual business beat to say he was no fan of industrial farm products *vis-a-vis* the real thing of yesteryear:

Not only were the vegetables and other products of the soil much better in those days but also the cattle and poultry, including the milk, eggs and butter. If you have any doubt as to this compare the taste of the blueberries which you yourself pick, and the trout which you yourself catch, with the frozen food and fish which you buy at the market.(7)

Bad chow obviously didn't account for the whole picture, though, and President Roosevelt inaugurated a "Make America Fit" campaign. Director John Kelly, an ex-Olympian rower, announced "It's unpatriotic to be unhealthy," as in lack of exercise, as in automobile sickness. Kelly had his work cut out for him, seeing as how fitness headquarters, Washington DC, qualified as one of the most unpatriotic / unhealthy spots in the country, with 2,500 automobiles per square mile. Navy Lieutenant Commander Gene Tunney, former world heavyweight boxing champion, observed with some disgust that the latest naval recruits were in worse shape than those in 1917. He might have been thinking about Henry Ford II, tubby grandson of the original. Young Henry had been kicked out of Yale University for academic cheating, but he at least declined to pull the same draft-dodging tricks his father Edsel had stooped to in the first war, and ended up at the Navy's Great Lakes training center.

One look at a generation of young Fords told Tunney that "First and foremost, we are not getting as much unconscious muscular exertion." Why not? "There is the automobile – a first evil, though a blessing in many ways." Today's inactive youngster spent way too much time with passive entertainments like movies and radio, said Tunney, and riding around in that other bad idea, the school bus "to carry him to the school doorsteps."(8) Colonel William Ganoe of the University of Michigan military department said every teenager in America needed a 10 mile hike every day. How could they get it if they drove every place? Another athlete, tennis star Alice Marble, recommended that Americans, "Park the car a mile or so from the movie, your place of business, and other spots. Start walking half-mile to mile distances, then increase it to miles, and weekend hikes of 15-20 miles."(9) Marble lived to regret not parking her first evil permanently. She attempted to commit suicide during the war when she suffered a miscarriage following an auto accident.

Just as insidiously, the automobile helped to undermine the nation's political health at this critical juncture. Though a blessing in many ways, Port Huron decided to dismantle its municipal democracy in 1941 by installing an unelected city manager to run things. The automobile's transformative effects on the community was the prime mover. Though a strong argument could be made for the city fathers getting expert advice in governing the community, Port Huron's Labor and Trades Council correctly denounced the city manager idea as "one-man rule." Nevertheless, Charles Rettie, Louis Weil, Edgar Kiefer, and a raft of other business leaders pushed through a charter revision by a razor thin public vote. That left the City Council with two primary duties: 1) Rubber stamp the manager's decisions or 2) Fire him and hire somebody else.

The council named as Port Huron's first dictator 47 year-old Leonard Howell from Ironton, Ohio. He'd been the city manager there, and previously the superintendent of the Federal Asphalt Paving Company. He'd never set foot in Port Huron in his life until this job opened up. A total stranger with a love for paving had been handed almost complete power, and this arrangement proved to be a powerful accelerator for the further evisceration of the community by the automobile. Within weeks of his takeover, Howell purchased, leveled and covered in asphalt an entire city block in downtown Port Huron for a municipal parking lot. He also put 315 parking meters back on the streets (they took in $2,000 per month along with numerous slugs and washers), and laid plans for ever more paving and wider streets.

Paradoxically, at the same time in the private sector, the days of one-man rule were fading fast for Henry Ford. The bell tolled for the old-style Ford Motor Company in early 1941. President Roosevelt had won another big election victory the previous autumn, his third. The United Auto Workers union had helped put another of its friends into the Michigan governor's office, Murray Van Wagoner. The FMC remained the last big holdout against unionization, and Henry knew full well what was coming. He said he'd close the company down before he'd accept a closed shop, or maybe lease the whole outfit to the government for $1. Even Ford workers expressed mixed feelings about the idea of a union, but not farmer's son Lawrence Rumenapp of St. Clair County, who commuted 120 miles back and forth to Dearborn to work at Ford. He called the Rouge factory "the Madhouse," and welcomed more labor say so for the inmates.

On April Fools Day the UAW's fifth column inside the Rouge plant called an illegal sitdown strike, and subsequently beat up any strikebreakers who took exception to this act, especially Negroes, when the unionists could catch any alone. Governor Van Wagoner called in the state police to restore some semblance of order, but by and large he just twiddled his thumbs. At first Henry Ford vowed to fight on, but later claimed his wife Clara had threatened to leave him if he did, which would have been about as likely as the Moon leaving its Earth orbit.

Throwing himself into reverse, Henry okayed a union election, and afterward handed the victorious and somewhat dumbfounded UAW the most generous contract it had ever seen: a 10 cent per hour raise (about 12%), a union shop, dues checkoffs, seniority rights on layoffs and callbacks, grievance procedures, time-and-a-half for overtime, doubletime for Sundays and holidays, plus a week of paid vacation. Congress of Industrial Organizations president Phillip Murray called it "one of the finest labor contracts in the nation today," and ordered an end to all wildcat strikes at the FMC. The UAW blithely ignored this directive. Reputedly now the world's largest labor union, it assumed more power in running the auto industry than, say, Port Huron taxpayers had in running their own town.

Ford's outraged security boss Harry Bennett called the labor agreement "...a great victory for the Communist Party, Governor Murray Van Wagoner, and the National Labor Relations Board." But Edsel Ford genially vowed to "go all the way" with the new state of affairs. After all, it wasn't the Ford family but Ford customers who would end up footing the bill. It marked the end of unfettered Fordism at Ford Motor. The FMC simply had grown too big and enmeshed too many people to go on functioning purely at the whim of its namesake, like a family machine shop. The auto industry now became semi-public property, the hope and despair of not just the hundreds of thousands of people on its own payrolls, but the untold millions of minions laboring in its wake. In St. Clair County alone, 7,100 people toiled at 12 different companies making or handling parts for Ford and the other automakers. That head count had doubled in two years.

One last, leisurely prewar summer of aimless, mindless, meandering motoring occupied much of Michigan in 1941. "Drive and Eat" summarized the general theme of the Times Herald's summer travel supplement for the Thumb region; not, admittedly, in full compliance with "Make America Fit." A correspondent painted a picture of Port Huron's downtown on the weekend, still the center of gravity for much of the county:

Streets and stores were filled with shoppers and visitors. Clerks hated to see Saturday night roll around each week because the amount of business tired them. Corners on the 'main stem' of the city were scenes of little crowds of persons chatting or renewing old acquaintances. Going downtown...was the chief thing to do after a week of work or staying at home. Scores of 10, 11 or 12 year old children could be seen near the shows and in the restaurants.(10)

Overseas, things went from bad to worse as the former allies Germany and Russia turned on each other and began the battle which would really settle the Second World War, irrespective of what the United States did. At summer's end the bummers began to fall in earnest on Auto America. The federal government ordered a 50% cut in automobile manufacturing, and President Roosevelt set limits on installment car buying: he required at least a one-third down payment and set a maximum of an 18-month loan to buy a new car. At the other end of the auto life cycle authorities put out a call for junk cars, to supply the steel industry for defense production.

The junker edict opened the *Times Herald's* eyes a little to the revolting mess the automobile made of much of the landscape.

As we drive about cities and country we notice thousands upon thousands of these old cars rusting and rotting away in yards and open fields, which quite evidently will never be used again in any way except for just this purpose.(11)

An estimated 4 million junk cars lay scattered like a disease over the whole United States, almost a full year's production for the auto industry. 350,000 of them rested in Michigan, about 5,000 in St. Clair County. Port Huron set up a jalopy hunting committee, and its chairman Leslie Holden, normally a tire dealer, soon received a letter per day from locals wanting some auto carcass or other hauled away to boost defense and incidentally clean up the neighborhood.

Even more momentously on the automobile front, top Roosevelt aide Harold Ickes began the gradual implementation of gasoline restriction in the United States, to the heartfelt lament of Louis Weil's newspaper: "...likely to disrupt business and industry, social life and recreation, without corresponding benefit to our defense preparation." Translation: tough on *Times Herald* deliveries. Most of the 194 filling stations in St. Clair County started closing early, which for them meant at 7pm. Ickes didn't dare tell the public that he sent the gasoline they saved to England, where just a five week supply remained for the defense forces at one point.

America turned off the oil spigot to Japan, part of the punishment of that country for its war of conquest in China. Japan had imported 17 million barrels of petroleum from the U.S. during 1940, barely a drop in the barrel compared to the way Americans drank up the stuff. But the loss of this resource helped tip the increasingly rash leadership of Japan into the desperate strategic gamble of war against the United States and Britain, in order to secure oil supplies in the Dutch East Indies. In the December 7th, 1941 edition of the *Times Herald,* Louis Weil quoted International News Service correspondent Jimmy Young in Tokyo to the effect that "as a first-class power Japan is a myth."(12) 2,000 American servicemen, including Port Huron native Fred Jones, learned differently and died the same day in Hawaii.

In the shocked aftermath of the surprise attack at Pearl Harbor, America forgot its own part in bringing about war in the Pacific. Virtually a straight line led from the American seizure of the Spanish Philippines in 1898, and the armed suppression of the Filipinos – an action correctly interpreted by both Japan and China as the establishment of a forward military base threatening *them* – to the defeat in Hawaii. During the intervening 40 years America regularly had insulted Japan and threatened that nation with war. Now the tables had been turned. Just for good measure, a numerically inferior Japanese force, thousands of them mounted on bicycles, overwhelmed a huge American and native army in the Philippines and took control there with relative ease in early 1942. To fill out the fight card, Germany obliged its Japanese ally by declaring war against the United States, so America had a two-theater battle on its hands.

How did Port Huron react to this calamitous news? Why, with a song! Satisfied apparently that the Date with Destiny had arrived, Fred Riggin sat down at his piano and composed *There's a Bright Day Dawning*, which became the theme music on the Mutual Broadcasting System radio show "Rainbow House":

Let's store away our pleasure and work for Uncle Sam
And try our best to treasure freedom for ev'ry man.
Stop worrying, start smiling, have nothing to regret
For better days are coming, remember, never forget.

There's a bright day dawning, some sunshiney morning
When soldiers come marching home from war.
There'll be love and gladness and maybe some sadness
But peace will reign again once more.

And the skies will be brighter, and hearts will be lighter
And clouds will lift from ev'ry shore
So it's now or never, to tie the world together
To hold our peace for evermore.(13)

Immediate sadness, and no maybe about it, descended on the tire stores in Port Huron when the government ordered national tire rationing less than two weeks after Pearl Harbor. An outright ban on new tires sales came days later. For all the defense preparation that had been underway in America for more than two years, the widening war triggered an instant rubber panic for the auto-nuts Allies because supplies from the Far East had been cut off. One Roosevelt adviser called the rubber famine the single biggest threat to victory, and it naturally could have been avoided had America followed the rail pathway in land transportation. Instead, a shocking calculation now told President Roosevelt that the country needed at least 20 million rubber-footed motor vehicles just to operate the economy, in addition to those needed for war. Rubber topped the agenda at a crash meeting of FDR, British Prime Minister Winston Churchill, and Canadian Prime Minister Mackenzie King in December. They promptly approved building a $40 million plant to make oil-based synthetic rubber in Sarnia next to the Imperial Oil works. 5,500 workers tackled the construction job around the clock, hoping to get out the product in a year's time.(14)

Meanwhile, gas station attendants around Port Huron lectured drivers to the effect that patriotic, tire loving Americans did not underinflate their rubber friends, run them over curbs, dive into chuck holes, speed or overload, and did rotate tires frequently and get wheels aligned often. Port Huron and St. Clair County set up tire rationing committees. Dr. Alexander Campbell of the Michigan Health Department advised women in particular to embrace this blessing in disguise: "Tire rationing will mean more walking this year and that will be good for women who are going to have babies...make a virtue out of necessity by walking..."(15)

Less devoted folks decided to make a profit out of necessity, and a vigorous black market in new tires sprang up, which County Sheriff Ferris Lucas vainly tried to stamp out. In light of all this, it came as a major surprise when the first local rubber scrap drive in Port Huron uncovered 100,000 lbs. of mainly old tires and tubes lying around alleys, garages, vacant lots, and junk yards in town, the kind of auto litter most people had stopped noticing long ago. Enough waste rubber turned up in the state of Michigan alone to fill 1,000 freight cars.

In January 1942 Uncle Sam stopped most civilian new car and truck production for the war's duration. For millions, this action transmuted any existing running motor vehicle into gold. It proved to be fool's gold for most Port Huron auto owners, as they emptied their pockets to keep their cars out of the junker committee's grasp. A single dirty spark plug wasted 10% of the gas in a car, warned Standard Oil, trying to entice car owners onto the hoist for a tune-up. Gulf Oil started an Anti-Breakdown Club, outlining for worried owners "39 Danger Points" by which their four-wheeled children might come to grief. Wreckers dragged up to ten accident-damaged autos each weekend into Lauth's Body Shop in Port Huron, the former Lauth Hotel livery stable, which operated around the clock to keep these beaters alive: "The steady pounding of hammers on fenders and car bodies, the rasping of files smoothing out small dents, the odor of the special paint for matching body color all go to give the shop a factory-like atmosphere."(16)

First aid for sick and dying cars couldn't always be procured immediately because half the auto mechanics in America went into the armed forces or war factories during 1942. In addition, Port Huron's used car lots starved, as private transactions handled most auto sales in the city during the war. With mechanical help scarce and little new or used stock on hand, Albert Parfet thought the immediate prospects so poor that he turned over his Port Huron Ford dealership to pinch-hitting Mercury man George Hoyt for the duration, while Parfet entered the military. To one factor or another, General Motors lost 20% of its own dealers during the war.

Now that new cars were out of the way and used ones hard to come by, a minority of Americans briefly recovered some small semblance of mental health about transportation. The national amnesia lifted a little and even Washington DC's Highway Department remembered that streetcars were "the most economical means, both in cost and in use of space, of moving large numbers of people on surface streets in urban areas. We are convinced that with rapid, direct, and comfortable service, mass transportation can and should supplant much of the individual vehicular service into the central business area." And whaddya know? a pedestrian used only 1/200th as much room on the street as an automobile, and no rubber or gas, and worked out 500 muscles in the process.(17)

These revelations came too late to save the Port Huron streetcars, but a collection of local lawyers and court workers formed the Rubber and Gas Conservation, or Kill 'Em or Cure 'Em Walking Club, to actually walk back and forth to work. This seemed to them a pretty unusual and patriotic sacrifice to make, as though walking involved some sort of exotic, strenuous effort like yoga or acrobatics. The club's pledge: "Let's get out of the habit of driving to work. We're going to have to do it eventually so let's have some fun out of it." The "give walking a try" campaign frequently aimed at even unpregnant women during the war: "So you complain that you'd like to look less hippy in your new spring suit and in the same breath reaffirm your dislike of exercise? Well, try walking with an objective in view. Walking is not dull if it gets you places."(18)

The healthful and pleasant habits of hiking didn't register with everybody, even during a war. Standard Oil used the examples of Great American Walkers Dan O'Leary, Eleanora Sears, and Edward Weston as a warning rather than encouragement: "Mr. Weston enjoyed being a pedestrian. Many car owners are becoming pedestrians and they're not enjoying it." And Johnny Appleseed: "How could Johnny Appleseed do it? We don't know. Better ask one of the thousands and thousands of motorists whose cars have worn out. They're learning more than they want to know about walking." By Standard's logic a child's learning to walk involved an unnatural intermediary step on the path to the organic act of driving.

The depression era's revival of the bicycle came in especially handy during the war. Planners approved a special allotment of steel and rubber for the nation's 12 bicycle makers to build Victory bicycles, on the sound theory that one 34 lb., $30 bike could replace a 3,000 lb. Chevy for most uses and mass transit could handle the rest.(19) A commercial delivery bike advertised to Port Huron's "grocers, druggists, butchers" set them back $50, and reasserted the gas-saving logic that it made more sense for a retailer to deliver by bicycle to his customers than have all those people drive to him. Two Port Huron teens, Wayne Bovee and Orrin Ramsey, set the pace for bike vacationers, pedaling 50 miles per day around the Thumb with their homemade luggage carrier, and shaming a lot of adults in the process. A number of prominent Port Huron matrons who hadn't been seen on bicycles since girlhood now cut familiar figures pedaling back and forth around town, even in winter weather. Of course, fewer than 20% of the women in America knew how to drive anyway.

Even with fewer motor vehicles on the streets in 1942, a lot of moms worried

243

over letting their younger kids cycle. They debated the pros and cons, according to the *Times Herald*. On the plus side: "Parents are finding the bicycle a blessing..for youngsters derive so much health-giving fun from pedaling their bikes, that they are more willing to start for school on time, and to run errands for mother and dad."[20] On the negative: there'd been 21 car-bicycle accidents involving children in Port Huron during the previous year.

The war reminded one prominent American, Ernest Hemingway, who returned to France as a war correspondent, of the pleasures and local feel that a bicycle gave: "I knew the country and the roads around Epernon, Rambouillet, Trappes and Versailles well, as I had bicycled, walked and driven a car through this part of France for many years. It is by riding a bicycle that you learn the contours of a country best, since you have to sweat up the hills and can coast down them. Thus you remember them as they actually are, while in a motorcar only a high hill impresses you, and you have no such accurate remembrance of a country you have driven through as you gain by riding a bicycle."[21] This came as quite an admission from a diehard Ford man like Hemingway, who once bragged that he could hand assemble a Model T in a day if somebody gave him the parts. The same year he wrote this, 1944, Hemingway suffered a bad concussion in a serious car wreck, his second.

Many millions of Americans couldn't even be persuaded by the greatest war in history to give up their cars. Like Franklin Roosevelt, who drove a model with all hand controls for a paraplegic, and nearly backed himself and British Prime Minister Winston Churchill over a cliff on one occasion. The public resisted driving restrictions so ferociously that, gripped by the same political nervousness that had hobbled it during WW1, the federal government didn't invoke full nationwide gas rationing until almost a year after Pearl Harbor. In the interim, German U-boats slaughtered one-quarter of all U.S. coastal oil tankers and their crewmen, who died trying to keep the auto culture above water.[22] Finally, following a regretful national directive, in November 1942 people lined up at Port Huron's elementary schools to grab 7,600 of the first gas ration cards intended for the nation's 27 million passenger cars and 5 million trucks.

Five different grades of coupons assigned gasoline on the basis of alleged driving necessity, most of it bogus. These ranged from grade A, 4 gallons per week for the average schmuck, up to grade X, unlimited for doctors, clergymen, and, naturally, government officials. This system presented another window of opportunity for sneaks, according to economist John Kenneth Galbraith, who served on the federal price administration staff: "...there was no form of rascality, chicanery, thievery, larceny that people wouldn't engage in to get extra gasoline."[23] The gas rascals were not above siphoning the rations out of other cars in Port Huron, and the local Montgomery Ward's store offered for sale a previously little-used innovation, a locking gas cap.

The *Times Herald's* Victor Spaniolo reported that, at first, "Automobile traffic in St. Clair county has dwindled to such a point in two months since gas rationing started that today pleasure driving has been all but eliminated and deserted roads and highways are the rule instead of the exception."[24] Not for long. Soon gas coupon counterfeiters were filching 2.5 million gallons of gasoline across America per day, and ration-busters thought up many other deceptions. Even at the summit of the war effort, American civilians burned through 52 million gallons of gasoline daily, five times as much as the rest of the non-Axis world *combined*. This strained supplies from both ends, because petroleum in all its forms was the single most vital and most extravagantly wasted military resource of the Second World War.

America furnished 6 billion of the 7 billion barrels of oil consumed by the Allied forces after Pearl Harbor. "I drink to the American auto industry and the American oil industry," said Russian dictator Joseph Stalin. Once they got to Europe, American military units used 100 times as much gasoline as they had during WWI.(25) One military bomber on a single flight used enough fuel to drive the average car around the world. Supply services built 20 different oil pipelines between Britain and France, and pumped a million gallons of fuel per day to Allied armies on the Continent. American and British forces squabbled incessantly about who got how much, though both would have been cut to pieces by Axis armies if the Russians hadn't borne down on Germany in the east. In the Pacific, American oil also carried the day. Just one U.S. air base on Guam received six times as much aviation fuel as the entire Japanese air force. (26) And in this theater of war as well, the fear of a Russian attack on the Asian continent forced the Japanese to maintain millions of extra soldiers there, opening the way for Allied forces to move against Japan across the islands in the south.

Despite assurances from the *Times Herald* editorial page to Port Huron readers that "...there are no indications that our supply of petroleum is not going to last forever...one less thing for folks to worry about," within nine months of the first civilian rationing, "A" cards had to be cut back to 3 gallons per week. After a few more weeks, Harold Ickes penned a dire article for the press, "We're Running Out of Oil!" and he reduced A rations to two weekly gallons in some areas, including Port Huron. It didn't set well with the home folks at all when reports surfaced of American G.I.'s in Europe hijacking "hundreds of thousands" of gallons of military gasoline per week to sell on Europe's black market.

President Roosevelt tried imposing a national 35 mph speed limit during the war – not as a sanity measure, but as a conservation measure – and a maximum annual car mileage limit of 5,000. Neither could be enforced in any practical way. After a promising start, the Auto Club estimated the average speed on American highways by mid-1944 at well above 50 mph. For $1 at the B.F. Goodrich store in Port Huron you could buy an optional "Speed Warden" attachment for your automobile accelerator that increased pedal resistance as the car neared 35mph. Speed governors on automobiles had been talked about for more than 30 years and had been stonewalled by the auto companies for just as long. Why didn't the government make these devices mandatory during this crisis? That's what people like Undersecretary of War Robert Patterson wanted to know. He urged the administration to cut the comedy, and get tough about conservation. He also wanted to seize 7 million private autos (leaving 20 million still roaming around) plus all spare tires, ban Sunday and holiday driving, halt long haul trucking and busing, and stop commercial trucks from carrying non-essentials like beverages and luxuries.

It never happened. Roosevelt's kowtowing to Drivin' America with half measures probably stemmed from both political concerns and the country's continuing lack of any overall transportation plan, in war or peace. Under a happier scenario, if America had collected and melted down all the motor vehicles in the country, it would have liberated enough steel not just to meet war needs but to build 100,000 miles of new railroad and streetcar lines, and re-route the country's entire future for the better.

Instead, wartime scrap hounds sniffed out and tore up the old streetcar tracks in Port Huron.

It is not too much to say that the astounding performance of American railroads constituted the single biggest logistical factor in the Allied victory of the Second World War. Just as in the first war, the train companies again bailed out a nation which during the intervening 25 years had leaped at any opportunity to badger, reduce, and impoverish them. Although they had in 1942 about the same operating capacity as in 1917, the railroads carried half again as much freight annually during the second war as they had during the first, reaching an incredible peak of 737 billion ton-miles in 1944, at a cost of less than a penny per ton-mile.(27) Both locomotives and boxcars grew in size, and a good thing, too. The war effort piled a mountain of extra goods on top of regular railroad business. Somehow the rail system squeezed a mile-long, 1,000 person circus train for a Cole Brothers show into the crush of traffic and delivered it to Port Huron during the frenetic summer of '42. Not for nothing did the Times Herald marvel that the railroads accomplished "miracles."

Passenger volume doubled, and reached 95 billion passenger miles in 1944. (28) It amazed Louis Weil when he took the Santa Fe Super Chief to Los Angeles in '44 that the train arrived in 48 hours, *twice as fast* as on previous trips. 97% of American armed services personnel (making 47 million individual trips) and 90% of their supplies and equipment moved by rail. The Grand Trunk in Port Huron justifiably bragged of handling 2,500 troop trains without a single mishap, including many loaded with German POW's. This was a unique performance; the huge increase in traffic inevitably killed and injured more people nationwide in train accidents: 2,300 dead and 29,000 injured in fiscal 1943. But this still amounted to a minute fraction of the auto toll. As to the auto competition, the trains even helped delay gasoline rationing, by moving as much as a million barrels of oil on 550 trains per day during the U-boat crisis of 1942.

The federal government made no serious attempt in this war to take over operating control of the railroads, as it had during WWI. President Roosevelt, who had served in the Wilson administration, remembered the McAdoo train debacle all too well. But despite the rails' remarkable achievements, they still met with plenty of interference. War bureaucrats allowed only a small increase in production of railcars and locomotives to meet the greater demands placed on train companies. Employment on the railroads grew to 1.4 million people, and wages increased 30% during the war, but regulators granted only modest rate increases. The government paid for little or no upkeep or improvement of the railbeds, again refusing to acknowledge any public responsibility for the care of a track system that during these years literally meant life or death to the nation. To cite another example of this criticality: one of the biggest and most secret projects of the war, the production of the atomic bomb, would have been utterly impossible without American railroads delivering supplies to nuclear sites in Oak Ridge, Tennessee and Hanford, Washington.

A local example of gross governmental neglect of rail lines in the face of war cropped up less than two months after Pearl Harbor, when the Interstate Commerce Commission approved the abandonment and dismantling of 40 miles of Pere Marquette Railroad track leading out of Port Huron to the village of Almont. Neither federal nor state leaders thought it prudent to maintain the 60 year-old line as a public necessity, like a highway. This act of destruction meant pulling down a 100-foot tall iron bridge which apparently had whetted the appetite of some scrap metal wonk. Conversely, with a War Department guarantee of business, new track appeared with emergency speed. Workmen finished in just three weeks a needed spur to a defense plant producing magnesium in Marysville.

On top of everything else, the federal government, which said yea or nay to railroad rates, took the time to sue 47 railroads for alleged rate fixing during the war, which the *Times Herald* called "the screwiest thing we've heard of in years. They [the railroads] should not be compelled to have their attention distracted from the colossal job they have by silly law suits..."(29) Somehow, while paying out $3 million per day in federal income taxes, American railroads managed to make money anyway during the war, a 5% return on investment. That amounted to a feeble enough reward under any circumstances, and a return which would have gagged Alfred Sloan over at General Motors.(30)

Sloan didn't have to cry in his beer, because GM continued to make healthier profits than the railroads all through the war, $673 million dollars worth, and dished out annual dividends of $2-$3 per share to Sloan, to new company president Engine Charlie Wilson, and to the other thousands of stockholders.(31) Big executive salaries kept coming. Wilson took home $459,000 in pay in 1943. Though money poured in, Sloan didn't find life easy, due to the huge turnover in those annoying instruments of the assembly line, workers. 750,000 came and went at GM during the war. "The sheer numbers involved were distressing enough," Sloan groaned, "but in addition, the workers we got were generally at a very low level of industrial skill. Many of them were not physically fit; many, especially the women, had no prior industrial experience at all."(32)

While Sloan feathered his nest, the Roosevelt administration and the UAW mocked Henry Ford as a senile old man for losing money during the war, for refusing on moral grounds to enrich himself from the worldwide suffering that Sloan was completely indifferent to. Ford shouldered personal suffering of his own in 1943, when his son Edsel died of stomach cancer. Henry felt plenty of fatherly regret over the way he'd browbeaten his amiable only child. "Dynamic" was the antonym for Edsel, who once at the Detroit Auto Show listened patiently for 30 minutes to a sales pitch from an unsuspecting Mercury dealer before introducing himself.(33)

Henry Ford took over the FMC presidency again, despite having suffered a couple of small strokes in recent years, which we've speculated might have been the after-effects of his 1927 car wreck. Ford still felt up to it physically at age 79, telling the press he still jogged regularly. "If there's anything ever wrong with me I just get out and run. There's nothing better for you, you know." In assuming overall command again, Henry also may have had qualms about the qualifications of his grandson Henry II to run the FMC, which were, generally speaking, none. The Second cut something of a slack figure, and manifestly didn't get in much jogging. The Navy released Young Henry from the service following his father's death, and he hung around the company waiting while his mother Eleanor plotted to put him on the throne.

Altogether, under the industry-wide coordination of a young executive named George Romney, U.S. carmakers turned out 20% of the war material produced by the country during WW2. About $29 billion of it.(34) This was a significant contribution, but far from being the salvation of the nation that auto worshipers like General Brehon

Somervell claimed with unwonted irony: "...when Hitler put his war on wheels, he ran it straight down our alley. When he hitched his chariot to an internal combustion engine, he opened up a new battlefront, a front that we know well."(35) We sure did. America's own war on wheels, with itself, had lasted forty years by this time. The global automobile industry, America's not excepted, facilitated and amplified the death, destruction, and waste in the Second World War just as it had in civilian life, whatever Somervell's or even Joe Stalin's opinions.

American auto firms mass produced military equipment of mediocre quality at best. 660,000 jeeps for example, and 2.7 million military trucks, plus 7,000 tow trucks. All built simply to overwhelm the opposition with numbers, just like indifferently built automobiles overwhelmed America. The jeeps, originally designed by the Willys company, required parts from 850 subcontractors to assemble. These overpowered, unstable, roofless, comfortless general purpose automobiles encouraged military over-reliance on mechanization and killed or injured thousands of unwary Allied personnel by rolling over more often than a recalcitrant mule. Willys chairman Ward Canaday promised that after the war was over, "the beloved jeep" would *dig wells, saw wood, fill silos, run electric light plants, act as a tractor, then a truck, hauling people, hauling milk and produce, herding cattle, fighting fires, running a snowplow, spraying orchards, spray-painting barns, road building, railroad grading.* The pitch for this miracle machine sounded suspiciously like something out of an old Model T brochure.

In view of claims like these, one of the surprising post-WW2 scandals involved the junking of thousands of American military motor vehicles overseas, many of them brand new, tossed away like so many Spam cans after the fighting stopped. On the Pacific islands of New Caledonia, military personnel simply dumped several hundred GM trucks into the ocean, along with thousands of tires, just at one disposal site alone. Another car graveyard in the South Pacific filled up 10 acres of ground with American war chariots. At home, 40,000 new Army vehicles rusted away in a Georgia depot without seeing any action at all.

Apart from ground vehicles, the Ford Motor Company also built 8,700 flimsy, uncomfortable, and dangerous-to-fly B-24 bombers, designed not by Ford personnel but by somebody else, an arrangement extremely distasteful to the Founder. The 24's made a poor contrast to the reliable Tri-Motors, now out of production. Snooty aircraft experts maintained that an automaker building something as complicated as a B-24 amounted to a blacksmith building a watch, but at least the planes came off the line quickly. The entire manufacturing setup, on a formerly sylvan 1,000 acres of open country west of Detroit called Willow Run, furnished a textbook example of America's automobile-induced dimwittedness about transportation. Officials gave little or no intelligent thought as to how the plant's complement of 40,000 workers would get there. Instead of installing comprehensive rail passenger service between Detroit and Willow Run, authorities built a no-stops 33-mile long divided highway, called interchangeably a freeway or expressway, the first like it in Michigan. This road exacerbated the gas and rubber and speed limit and old car problems already straining the region. Police sometimes stopped drivers on the new expressway and reprimanded them for driving too *slow*, unaware that traffic accidents cost Michigan factories 5 million lost man-days of labor in 1942 alone. The Willow Run commuters included in their number the original factory mom Rosie the Riveter, alias Rose Monroe, a Kentucky transplant

248

supporting two children after her husband had died in a 1940 car accident.(36)

If Rosie and her colleagues made it in one piece to factories like Will It Run, as skeptics called it, they found themselves in almost as much danger as if they'd been sent into combat. Wartime work weeks lasted up to 70 hours, and a tired workforce inevitably suffered a higher injury rate. An average day in Michigan's war factories in 1944 resulted in one death, 100 injuries, and five amputations. Labor no longer took this sort of thing lying down, and plagued the auto industry with wildcat strikes during the war, 700 at Ford alone.(37) War production in Detroit auto plants also suffered from racial reverses. Instead of treasuring freedom for ev'ry man, white members of the UAW struck more than a dozen times in protest over the hiring of more black workers to ease the manpower shortage. One of his members collegially informed UAW president R. J. Thomas, "I'd rather see Hitler and Hirohito win than work beside a nigger on the assembly line!" After a preliminary racial street bout in Detroit during February 1943 resulted in nine deaths, an even bigger riot broke out in June, and only ended after 5,000 soldiers came in to control things. This event toted up 25 black and 9 white deaths, 700 injuries, and $2 million in property damage.(38) Pretty bad, but it only equaled about as many people killed and injured in U.S. traffic accidents every 6 hours or so.

Because they fell so ridiculously short of Britain's civilian driving ban, America's modest wartime driving restrictions did not lessen appreciably the human toll on the happyways, to the disgust of National Safety Council executive director Ned Dearborn. In the first 20 months of America's war 22,000 service personnel died in combat, 65,000 suffered wounds or went missing. During the same time traffic wrecks killed 46,000 and injured 1.6 million civilians, permanently disabling 110,000. "This comparison should shame every loyal American," said Dearborn, but it did not, far from it. For millions of people loyalty to the country now meant loyalty to the car. Give me my four wheels or give me death. Liberty and driving, now and forever, one and inseparable.

After all, what else did Mrs. Thomas Gleason's two Port Huron sons, John and Robert Smith, die for in WW2 combat? And 200 other St. Clair County men. Here at home, didn't 3 year-old Lawrence Stoll really perish for auto freedom when a truck backed over him in Port Huron's Pine Grove Park as he waited for the Memorial Day parade? That driver had a right to back up his truck, didn't he? These sacrifices had to be made. America's automobile struggle knew no surrender, no truce, no quarter. Funeral director Arthur Smith's ambulances flew the flag by carting the automobile casualties to Port Huron Hospital at speeds of up to 90 mph, smashing the national speed limit, giving the injured a second chance at the glory of dying on the road, and everyone else en route the patriotic duty of diving for cover.

During the war years the automobile received full citizenship in Port Huron, everything except the right to vote. Edgar Kiefer, chairman of the city's new Planning Commission, helped author a wide-ranging zoning law designed partly to ensure civil rights for cars. From now on each and every home and apartment house and store and factory and church and theater and restaurant and public office and indeed any building of any description except maybe a doghouse constructed in Port Huron had to have off-street parking. The law set the number of parking spaces according to a complex formula as to how many people were likely to be in the building at maximum capacity, so that no automobile need be discriminated against and turned away. For some stores

249

that meant as much parking space as floor space, or more. A self-serve supermarket opened under the new code with three times as much parking as store footage.

Every time an owner altered a pre-code property to a new purpose the parking rules kicked in, unless the Zoning Appeals Board granted a dispensation, which the new Kresge store downtown humbly requested in lieu of destroying any neighboring buildings. In other cases, as a result of the ordinance, large cavities started to open in earnest in the cityscape, barrens covered in asphalt or gravel, lots partly filled with a motley herd of autos for a few hours per day, but which sat empty most of the time. These erasures sometimes sparked regret:

Once one of the handsomest dwellings in Port Huron, the residence of A.D. Bennett, retired banking executive, was torn down to provide parking space north of the H.A. Smith Warehouse Market on Main Street.

Sometimes celebration, courtesy of Howard Furniture:

WE ARE ASHAMED in having neglected to keep you informed about our FREE PARKING LOT directly in the rear of our store reserved especially for our customers.

Churches did some of the most aggressive demolition, flattening homes left and right so parishioners could put up their cars for an hour off the street during Sunday services. Slumlords converting some of the older homes into apartments on busy streets shoehorned extra tenant parking spaces into the backyards, front yards, side yards, accomplishing this with the cheerful acquiescence of City Hall. The downtown A&P grocery tested the limits of auto indulgence by digging a 125-vehicle underground parking cavern beneath the store: "The advantage of this undercover parking 'lot' is protection from weather and theft of precious automobile tires."

It all hastened the auto rot process which the *Times Herald* had warned about even before the war.

One of the most noticeable conditions [in] *American cities is the large number of people who are moving out into suburban areas. And city governments are worried. For this emigration is cutting down city income and speeding up the degeneration of city residential areas into slums. Going about a city like Port Huron even, we find streets and areas which once were almost fashionable sections so physically degenerated that almost everybody who can afford to moves out.*(39)

That sounded like Port Huron's south end Negro and Hispanic section, denounced in 1943 by the Michigan Tuberculosis Association as especially nasty. Inhabited by 1,200 people, only a quarter of whom had so much municipal service as running water, under Port Huron's at-large City Council and City Manager system this neighborhood had less in the way of practical representation in their government than an automobile did.

Another wartime issue in Port Huron which needed fixing before the bright day could dawn was the surprising outburst of juvenile delinquency that took place, much of it car-connected. Baffled authorities generally blamed this uprising on lack of supervision by parents. Not only were most fathers busy in the armed services or at work, but adult women held down 3,000 of the 11,000 war jobs in Port Huron, often to the neglect of children. From someplace or other teenagers still found the gasoline to go joyriding, 30 miles for a steak sandwich in one much-played-up incident. More seriously, amid an epidemic of juvenile car thefts, three boys aged 15 and 12 used a car to stage 30 break-ins around the area, with gasoline they drained from farm tractors, which stood high on the gas priority list. Another 16 year-old stole a car, gas coupons, and a federal car tax stamp, then drove at 100 mph out Griswold Street before police warning shots finally reined him in. A judge ordered a mental exam for a 14 year-old who'd stolen 12 cars in succession, the last while on probation for car theft.

17 year-old Robert Buckingham of Marysville beat neighborhood gas station owner and former blacksmith Frederic Ritter to death with horseshoe tongs and a hammer (he went at it hammer and tongs) to get $24 and gas stamps to drive to a party. The impatient young Buckingham still wore his bloodstained trousers when arrested at his host's address. In light of all this, Port Huron ordered an 11pm to 6am curfew for kids under 17. This measure, claimed the press, "will cut deeply across a whole body of social customs, most of which came with the automobiles. The curfew, coupled with gas rationing, may result in a return to the home movement.."(40) But don't bet on it. Buckingham didn't join the return to the home movement; he moved in for life with the other 800 teenagers in Michigan's state prison system.

If you couldn't beg, borrow, or steal them, or murder somebody to get a car, gasoline, or tires, then you could board one of the buses carrying billions of people around Port Huron, the Thumb, Michigan, and America during the war. Nationwide, in 1942, 7 billion passengers rode the buses, and another 7 billion caught the streetcars. The Carpenter company implored local patrons to be patient about jammed-to-capacity Port Huron city buses. Squeezed-in riders had to pass fares hand to hand from one person to another up to the driver at rush hour. 12.5 million people took the Port Huron buses during the war, a combined distance of 2.8 million miles, without a single serious injury accident, and you couldn't do much better than that with these conveyances.

Greyhound buses offered seven daily round trips between Port Huron and Detroit. A bus couldn't compare to a streetcar or interurban in most respects, but the Greyhound office reminded folks that next to an automobile it looked pretty good. Bus tires carried people much more efficiently than car versions and lasted up to 40,000 miles. Streetcar wheels lasted more or less forever, didn't go flat, or need recapping, the streetcars were cleaner than buses, etc., etc., but that story belonged to a fast-receding past in Port Huron, some of whose children by this time had grown up never having ridden on a trolley.

Carpooling enjoyed a vogue during the war, spurred on by the slogan "When You Ride Alone, You Ride With Hitler!" Carmakers had bragged for years that their products could carry up to six adults in comfort. Now came the test. The verdict: around the block, maybe. Most Americans connected the idea of the automobile with privacy so intensely that they resisted regularly carrying passengers, even if it meant Hitler had to come along. Nor did they like being driven by someone of whose skill they weren't as certain as they were, rightly or wrongly, of their own. This rasped the male ego especially. And, of course, a car carried a full load of people with no more safety than a single occupant; less, probably.

Five carpoolers, including Lawrence Kaufman and his daughter Luella, drowned when their car skidded into the St. Clair River during a snowstorm just a few hundred yards from their jobs at the Chrysler plant in Marysville. Those conditions probably would have defeated a bus, too, but had the Rapid Railway interurban still been running, no problem. Another carpooling accident claimed the life of "Wide Streets" Whitemore, Earle, Port Huron's City Engineer. While driving one car of a two-vehicle X-coupon caravan taking City Manager Howell and the entire City Council on a shopping tour of Michigan sewage plants, an instant's distraction caused Whitemore to pile into some cars parked right in front of the State Police headquarters in East Lansing. He died, aged 62.

No local passenger ship service operated during the war in St. Clair County despite the presence of one of the world's best waterways at its doorstep. Although the big burgs on the Great Lakes like Detroit, Cleveland, and Buffalo enjoyed regular intercity boat connections (8 hours Detroit to Cleveland), neither the state nor federal governments thought it expedient to substitute for cars the cheap and efficient and safe daily vessel operations between smaller shoreline cities and towns, which had been a staple on the St. Clair River for almost a century, before stopping in 1936. Instead the Navy converted two Lakes passenger liners to aircraft carriers to train pilots like Lieutenant George H.W. Bush.

The Chris Craft powerboat factory in St. Clair County built 8,000 military landing craft during the war, as well as patrol boats, but why, one might ask, no civilian landing craft? Why not whip up a quicker, modern river ferry? There seemed to be plenty of enthusiasm still for boat travel. A single church excursion by steamer from Port Huron to Detroit's Belle Isle park attracted 2,000 people. The Canadian liner *Harmonic* found plenty of passengers for its pleasure cruising of the upper Lakes out of Sarnia during the war. Sadly, the *Harmonic* burned at the dock in mid-1945, killing 11 people, which seemed like a heavy toll, but amounted to five hours worth on American highways at the time. If you wanted to go it alone in your own motorboat, you could get a gasoline ration for it, about the same as a car's, but that wouldn't take you and Adolf very far.

Cargo traffic for war boomed on the Great Lakes. To the 300 freighters working at the outbreak, shipping companies added still more. Its owners even re-launched the old sailing schooner *J.T. Wing* to help out. As a wartime measure the Coast Guard expanded winter navigation on the Lakes through the use of icebreakers. To facilitate the extremely critical iron ore and coal shipments through it, the federal government built an additional lock at the Sault Ste. Marie canal for $8 million, and ringed it with the heaviest defenses of any civilian installation in the country. Perhaps even more importantly for the war effort, 422 million bushels of wheat were shipped on the Lakes in 1943, though due to the heavy traffic not all arrived at its destination. 90,000 bushels went to the bottom of the St. Clair River when the brand new carrier *William Brewster*, bound for England, collided with another vessel.

The Axis massacre of American shipping in the Atlantic and U.S. coastal waters early in the war (500 ships and 5,000 crewmen in six months of 1942) reminded the *Times Herald* of the general underappreciation and underdevelopment of the Great Lakes, as well as the nation's other 27,000 miles of secure inland waterways. A Mississippi River barge tow, for instance, could haul 16,000 tons per trip, equal to 300 railroad cars. Barges moved 1.7 billion barrels of oil around America during the war. Far from the comparative safety of the Mississippi and the Lakes, torpedo attacks sank five Ford Motor Company ships requisitioned by the government and sent to sea. The remains of one unfortunate captain, George Hodges, were later found inside a shark.(41)

No other form of transportation in America profited so handsomely from World War Two as commercial aviation. One way or another, the federal government spent $4 billion on airports alone, according to industry historian T. A. Heppenheimer. $3.25 billion went to build military air stations, half of which Washington handed over to state and local governments after the war. The feds put up $500,000 to upgrade the St. Clair County airport, one of the 500 civilian fields improved at a total cost of $400 million.(42) Aircraft design also leaped forward, thanks to a virtual blank check for experimentation on designs for bombers and air transports, and on both prop and jet propulsion systems. The resulting Lockheed Constellation transport demonstrated how a large prop aircraft could now fly with relative ease from coast to coast. This research effort carried over into the postwar years, when the Boeing B-47 jet bomber, built at government expense, established the prototype for future passenger jetliners.(43)

Back on the ground, amid the tire-anxious millions of resolute motorists, the most colossal wartime construction project in the Blue Water area, the factory to make plastic rubber out of oil over in Sarnia, finally reached full production by 1944, though whether it justified the $48 million cost remained to be seen. The 185 acre facility, now known as Polymer Corporation, needed the biggest steam powerhouse in Canada, cranking out enough energy to have lit half the table lamps in the country. Its water pumping station could have supplied all of Toronto, the biggest city in Canada. This polymer city unto itself, with its own own hospital, fire hall, general store, bowling alley, post office, police department and ball park, made 60 million pounds of ersatz rubber in 1944, primarily to meet a shortage caused by automobile tire demands. To do this it used 20 million gallons of petroleum, a resource already in short supply due to automobile fuel demands. This typified the crazy tail-chasing induced in wartime by the automobile culture.

Due to the war, the number of motor vehicles in America declined for the last time during the 20th Century, though not dramatically when compared to other nations. Wear and tear and the relentless search for steel and iron culled as many as 6 million from the U.S. herd (2,500 from St. Clair County), leaving 28 million. In comparison, Britain's pre-war car and truck population of 2 million shrank to 250,000. America scrapped about 4,000 cars per day in 1945. Some took the shortcut to the junkyard via traffic accidents. Crackups destroyed 250,000 American cars in 1944. Saboteurs hardly could have done a better job. A lengthy series of patriotic ads published in Port Huron played up the subject of irresponsible wartime driving:

3 Americans Killed by the 7th Column! No, they weren't lined up against a wall and shot! They were killed by a man who thought he was above the law. They were killed by a man who believed the 35 mile speed limit was meant for others. They were killed in a needless automobile accident. Does this make you mad?(44)

A "needless" automobile accident, but how many needed ones had there been? No, it didn't seem to make anybody mad, or even wary. "Autos wanted" outnumbered "Autos for sale" in the Port Huron classifieds for most of the war.

As the dust finally settled over the battlefields in Europe and Asia, the restraints on the pent-up American automobile dementia tore loose. Victory swept away most of the good travel habits laboriously if imperfectly relearned during the previous four years. Gas rations doubled after the German defeat in May 1945 and rationing disappeared completely the very day after Japan surrendered in August. On the first derationed weekend in Port Huron the headline "Postwar Traffic Jams Highways" told the story. A few weeks later the panicky cry of "City Faces Gasless Weekend" announced that oil workers had struck for a 30% pay hike. September traffic fatalities in Michigan soared 54%, injuries 48% compared to 1944.

The automobile meat grinder resumed its normal routine in Port Huron. Furnace dealer Edward Klump died when he drove in front of a train crawling along at 8 mph across Main Street. Deputy Sheriff Mathias Stine and two prisoners were killed the same way on the south side of town. Pilot Russell Moran's car collided with a horse-drawn hay wagon north of town and Moran expired, underscoring the recently discovered fact that flying now beat driving for safety in America. A car fatally sandwiched city employee Gustave Pethke against his dump truck while he spread sand on the icy streets on Christmas Day.

National newspaper columnist James Marlow told Port Huron readers, "Cars are killing people at a startling rate. It's so startling that President Truman has called a national conference to halt it." Why President Truman and Marlow and the rest of the country should be startled over the resumption of the natural pattern of full blast auto traffic presents a mystery. The stress and strain of war must have erased the memory of the previous national conferences on auto safety stretching back 20 years to the Coolidge era, none of which had changed a thing. Invitations again went out to all 48 state governors and their highway directors. Port Huron held a local version of this conference. All the top cops in St. Clair County met with City Manager Hansen under the auspices of Louis Weil's up-and-coming son Granger at the newspaper office. They mapped out a "safety campaign," primarily for getting those nimrods, drivers, to stop smashing up themselves and other people. Talk about a lost cause.

Under Granger Weil's direction, an editorial "Letter to a Motorist" appeared in the *Times Herald*, pleading with Mr. Motorist not to run over the writer's children Joe and Frankie: "I understand, Mr. Motorist, that it's an awful temptation to speed it up when you are in a hurry. Please don't. Especially in my neighborhood." A few weeks later Mr. Motorist hit and killed David Tholen, the 5 year-old son of the *Times Herald's* city editor, while David walked home from the market. Granger Weil served as one of the pallbearers. Another driver, 21 year-old John Zeros, under an awful temptation, almost mowed down several kids in front of a Port Huron Township school, forcing them to jump for their lives into a ditch. This, Zeros' 6th traffic offense, put him in jail for 60 days. Marion Smith of Port Huron received two years probation for negligent homicide: she'd been speeding, with defective brakes, when she struck and dragged 10 year-old Eileen Mann for 40 feet along Main Street before finally running her over. Automobiles hit 40 children in Port Huron in 1946, the year of the safety campaign.

Port Huron drivers condemned reckless Mr. Motorist, until they found themselves on the same hot seat for their own indiscretions. Then the special pleading started. Just as Louis Weil had admitted a decade earlier, "extenuating circumstances" and behind-the-scenes influence continued to undermine auto law and order in St. Clair County. Exhibit A: Sheriff Ferris Lucas. He'd cut quite a figure for himself as a lawman. A six year veteran of the auto assembly lines before he'd won election as the youngest sheriff in Michigan, Lucas not only had talked the county out of abolishing his department during the depression, he'd enlarged the staff to 12 men and half a dozen cars, and even added a 300 foot tall radio tower in Port Huron to keep tabs on

254

everybody. He served a term as president of the Michigan Sheriffs Association.

But Lucas also helped whitewash the reckless driving killing of a teenage girl by one of his own deputies. Officer Ezra Tomlinson ran down 13 year-old Dora Hollis as she crossed the Gratiot Pike in the rain one day south of Port Huron. Tomlinson passed another car at excessive speed with poor visibility, and struck Hollis. "The Sheriff Department's slogan on the backs of their cars 'Lose A Minute – Save a Life' should be written in blood – the blood they've spilled of (our) daughter and others," wrote Dora's parents, both Chrysler employees it turned out.(45) After engineering a coverup for Tomlinson, months later Sheriff Lucas pulled a U-turn on this issue when a car struck his own 6 year-old daughter Linda, leaving her with a broken thigh, broken arm, a concussion and permanent disfigurement. In that case, Lucas sued the driver, 74 year-old Alfred Caulkett of Port Huron, for $50,000 in damages, blaming Caulkett's bad brakes, bad eyesight and bad speeding.

"Automobile accidents are seldom accidental," lamented Michigan Mutual Insurance, as the all-time number of auto dead in America surpassed the number killed in all the country's wars, 852,000. And the insurance men were so right, but carsickness had fixed its grip again on the faculties of the nation. The inherent and ineradicable flaws of the automobile now faded even further from public consciousness. After a particularly bloody 4th of July weekend, the Safety Council's Ned Dearborn unleashed another indignant blast, "Instead of using our holidays as periods of national honor we are turning them into periods of disgrace by committing mass suicide." Nice try, Ned. Car insurance rates went up 25% in 1946, then another 30% in 1947.

In the immediate postwar years car speeds rose as fast as insurance prices. Hardly before David Tholen had grown cold in his grave, his father's employers at the *Times Herald* gave their approval to Detroit's latest fantasy, that of building 400 mph cars by the 1970's: "...kids will be able to get into the family car and spin to New York and back for the evening." Some kids couldn't wait for 1970, and two teenagers paid $50 fines for staging an 85 mph spin on Main Street. Others went out to the Sunset Speedway, 6 miles west of Port Huron, for a legal speed fix watching the "Hot Rod Races" out there. Half price for children. The idea of speed governors on cars, a patriotic notion during the war, now seemed in poor taste to Port Huron dealer Andy Falk, who defended the privilege of excessive horsepower for the Cadillac owner:

He understands that his last two inches of throttle were not put there for the ungracious purpose of dominating the highway. They are there for an emergency – and for that lovely, floating, cruising ride which only a great reserve of power can provide.

After spending four years building products of military destruction, the American auto industry lusted to begin again building products of civilian destruction. From Washington came the okay to manufacture 200,000 new passenger cars during the last four months of 1945 if carmakers could lay hands on the materials, which for the most part they couldn't. The war production board gave the FMC an early start due to worry over Henry Ford's latest stroke. No one quite knew who ran the company anymore. After Ford designers quickly hammered together a 1946 model, Henry II took this vehicle all the way to the White House and ceremoniously presented it to that dangerous driver President Harry Truman. In view of Truman's 1938 car crackup and his now daily habit of taking a long walk around the capital, this friendly gesture by Ford didn't seem entirely appropriate. However, as a sales call it apparently worked, since later the White House ordered some custom-built Lincoln limousines from the FMC.

The '46 Ford subsequently attracted 1,500 people at its Port Huron debut on the George Hoyt lot. Not a bad turnout, but slim compared to past unveilings, perhaps because Ford made no guarantee as to when buyers could take delivery, due to manufacturing delays. Hoyt handed the Ford franchise back to Albert Parfet and Parfet's son-in-law Sanford Ladd. The two men had been mustered out of the service, both rarin' to get back into the auto game. Parfet even rented back his old Ford headquarters on Main Street which he'd sold during the depression.

Marriage paved the way for a changing of the guard at John Cawood's Buick and Pontiac dealership in Port Huron. John's own son-in-law Charles Barrett joined the team as his heir apparent. The son of a local bean dealer, Barrett had trained as an accountant at the University of Michigan before doing a hitch in the armed forces. He didn't know beans about selling cars, but this quick learner had a nose for a buck, and when had a car dealer needed any other qualifications? Now, where were the products?

In September 1945 Henry Ford II assumed control of the Ford Motor Company, overcoming his declining grandfather's resistance with the backing of Mom's shares in the company. Like Charles Barrett, Henry II didn't really know or care much about how to build cars. However he had enough sense to realize that he needed the help of people who did. Young Ford possessed none of his grandpa's mechanical aptitude, self-discipline or wide-ranging curiosity about the world, but he inherited the invaluable knack for persuading people of ability to work for him, and the willingness to boot them out the door if they threatened his authority. After somewhat petulantly firing about a thousand non-union FMC white collar workers, Henry II assembled his own crew, most importantly hiring a team of eight former Air Force efficiency experts known as the "Whiz Kids." The FMC also took on an engineer trainee named Lido "Lee" Iacocca, who actually owned a Ford vehicle, and reasoned "Anybody who builds a car this bad can use some help."(46)

At the very top of the new hire list at the FMC sat a one-time General Motors luminary named Ernest Breech, who became Henry II's guide and mentor. Ford profoundly envied the competition at GM, and the way they made money come hell or high water. For his part, with the infernal nuisance of war out of the way, Alfred Sloan announced plans to use some of GM's profits to build a gigantic technical center in Detroit's suburbs, "a city of science and art," if either of those terms could be applied to automobiles. Sloan stumbled a bit when he made this announcement, since if he could afford to blow that kind of money on the office boys, the United Auto Workers figured GM must be flush enough to put up more cash at the hourly payroll window. Under the orchestration of the union's GM division leader Walter Reuther, the rank-and-file staged the first big strike of the postwar era, shutting down the company for four months, beginning in 1945, until they extracted a 15% wage hike. That success won Reuther election as president of the entire union. He severed his past Communist connections and kicked the Reds out of the UAW altogether, which earned him and his brother Victor a couple of assassination attempts.

Now that the UAW held virtually a labor monopoly over the unionized portion of the auto industry, what workers at one firm got, the rest expected, too. The 2,700 UAW members making auto parts at Mueller Brass in Port Huron launched an 80-

256

day strike in 1946 to get their share of the melon. Auto prices went up to pay for more pay, and this game of wage-and-price leapfrog continued for the balance of the 20th Century. A big frogleap came after the UAW won automatic cost-of-living adjustments in 1948 from GM, and pensions from the Big 3 in 1950. Learning quickly, Henry II called this process an "insane spiral of mounting costs and rising prices." A standard Ford sedan cost $1,470 by 1949, about twice the prewar charge, and that didn't include sales tax, license and accessories. Driven in no small way by the auto industry, the federal minimum wage nearly doubled, from 40 cents to 75 cents per hour.

What did auto workers do to earn their dough? Lee Iacocca got the chance to find out, during his assigned tour of duty on the assembly line at Ford, so he could learn the engineering ropes from the ground up. "My job was to attach a cap to a wiring harness inside a truck frame. It wasn't hard work, but it was tedious as hell." National newspaper columnist Hal Boyle spent a day at a Chrysler assembly plant. The facility put together a typical vehicle in one hour and twenty minutes, completing 700 operations, one for each line worker. A car moved at an average speed of 25 feet per minute along the 2,000 foot-long assembly line. Not a lot of opportunity there for fine craftsmanship. It also gave Boyle some insight into why so many wildcat strikes occurred over speedups on the line, like the 24-day walkout at Ford in 1949, which cost the FMC $500,000 per day. The factory routine, and in fact the whole unappetizing production side of carmaking, bored Iacocca so much that he abandoned the engineering course halfway through: "I was eager to be where the real action was - marketing or sales."(47) The helot department.

The ocean of money created to bankroll America's $300 billion war effort left the nation feeling unnaturally wealthy following the end of hostilities, even given the inflation of wages and prices (about a 63% increase in prices between 1941 and 1950), and the fact that the national debt amounted to about $2,700 per person. State and local governments paid off a gigantic amount of their own debt during the war, in effect shifting it to the federal level, which furthered the illusion of well-being. The median household income of $2,400 in 1945 rose to $3,600 by 1950. Taxes took about a quarter of it. The public went on a buying binge after the minor deprivations of first the depression then the war. Cars, homes, appliances, clothing, schools, stadiums, highways, hospitals, shopping centers, airports, utilities; almost everything made the shopping list except land-based mass transit. But especially cars. The auto industry estimated at the end of the war that Americans needed and wanted 13 million new motor vehicles. Battling a variety of headwinds like supply shortages, construction bottlenecks, price controls, and a wave of postwar strikes across the entire economy, it took the auto companies most of the rest of the decade to ramp up production sufficiently to satisfy this demand.

During the shortage of new cars, Port Huron dealers worked the used car game like never before:

Wanted Dead or Alive, Age '34 to '42 Cars & Trucks. We're just crazy enough to pay you about twice as much as your car is worth.

1937 Terraplane. 2-Door Sedan. Motor runs darn good. Tires are pretty fair. Body is holding together good. Interior is fair. I'll sell it for $60 – want it?

Nude – Practically Bare of Any Profit.

I Deal for Anything.

The poetic muse visited the classified ad writers often in these days: "Don't Get a Horse, Call Harry Morris!" "Why keep waitin' – See Jack Paton." Parfet and Ladd's Ford lot sold 100 semi-nude used cars per month, no matter how beat up.

The never-failing service angle remained a reliable source of dealer income. *Driving is Hard on Your Car!* warned Harvard Chevrolet – though what else was the thing good for? Better get it checked out. George Hoyt asked: *Is Your Car a Hospital Case?* You and the car both if it failed at the wrong time. The makers of a new specialized rustproofing procedure, "Underseal," said go ahead, crawl under there and see for yourself, *Your car is being WRECKED from below.* Preparation for winter driving, according to Standard Oil, required a new battery, oil change, radiator flush, transmission fluid, lube job, new tires, spark plugs, new belts and hoses, and gas additive. Cawood's summarized the state of the postwar auto nation: *Nearly every car on the road is at least four years old. Radiators Boil! Brakes Fail! Motors Miss! Bearings Burn! Clutches Fail! Tires Blow Out! Any one of a thousand things may happen to cause you trouble – damage your car – endanger your life.* For once an ad that contained no exaggeration. In New Jersey, half the vehicles examined under America's one and only mandatory safety inspection program failed the grade.

With the country panting for brand new cars, retailers who obtained any demanded and got under-the-counter premiums of up to $500 on some high-priced models. They squeezed buyers in other ways, too, according to a Congressional committee estimate. Dealers buncoed customers for $450 million in undervalued trade-ins and unwanted extra gadgets in just six months of 1948. But once he got his hands on a new vehicle worth about $1,500-1,800, the owner could frequently drive it down the street and sell it for $1,900-2,200 to a used car dealer. The used car man then turned around and sold it a third time for an even bigger markup. Americans went crazy to get new wheels. Buick acknowledged these clucks with heartfelt gratitude: *They smile in deep and blissful content over its comfort – fondle this wheel like a long lost friend returned – vow it's better than Old Home Week to get the good solid foursquare feel of Buick underneath you again.*

A black parish of 150 Baptists on Port Huron's downtrodden ("blighted" in the City Council's words) south side pulled together $2,600 to put the feel of a top line Buick Roadmaster underneath their pastor George Taylor. He'd have been better off with a bicycle and a few shares of General Motors stock, which paid $8 in dividends on a $10 par in 1949. At the other end of the the GM price list, a Negro icon of the day, ready-mix pancake batter queen Aunt Jemima, helped out Harvard Chevrolet with a personal appearance at one of the Port Huron Kroger stores. *I'se Comin' to Town, Folks,* said AJ, *The sales force of Aunt Jemima drive several hundred Chevrolets.*

Chevrolet advertising also favorably compared its product to that American landmark Old Faithful geyser at Yellowstone National Park; or rather vice versa, the geyser's dependability resembled a faithful Chevy's in GM's way of thinking. Dodge likened the successful purchase of one of its postwar cars to the birth of a new baby*: When a new Dodge comes to its permanent home, the whole neighborhood is often its reception committee. People troop out from doors, peep out of windows – pop up from nowhere, full of excited admiration and noisy congratulations. Each new Dodge delivery becomes a little local triumph shared and enjoyed by all.*

258

A farm implement dealer in Port Huron, Norman Cosgrove, an old Wills Sainte Claire hand, agreed to sell the Jeep. At first he tried a sales ad featuring a Jeep pulling a plow. When that didn't work the Jeep quickly turned into the Jeepster, not for plowing, well-digging, or silo-filling, but for cruising: *We don't recommend one-hand driving but you'll wonder why you need two! 'Easy to handle' doesn't say it.* Easy to handle didn't describe it, either. Mordern's Studebaker in Port Huron alluded to physics in assessing its new models: *The new Studebaker is low to the ground for safety as well as for looks. Most of the weight is down where gravity works in your favor.* Somebody in the FMC advertising department inadvertently hit the nail on the head about American driving habits: *I Love the 'feel' of the Ford...You don't drive it, you aim it.*

The postwar introduction of widespread television broadcasting gave automobile advertising far and away its biggest push of the 1940's, or maybe the century. Not the most reliable of devices at first, Port Huron's Ritter Appliance had to reassure customers that "When you buy an RCA television – YOU KNOW IT IS GOING TO WORK!" For its $325 table-top model General Electric promised a picture "So clear, so vivid, you can enjoy it in broad daylight." The first Detroit TV station (to which Port Huron tuned) went on the air in 1947 and the national networks linked up the next year. Right from the get-go, cars and the idiot box made a loving couple, as RCA executive Thomas Joyce had predicted as early as 1944: "Television properly used has the power to make people want merchandise more than they do money, thus creating the necessary turnover of goods and services with which to create jobs."(48)

TV furnished the perfect medium for stage-managed, information-free, Empty Roads automobile hawking in motion, without having to go to a theater to see it. TV didn't sell with the facts, but by creating a 60-second mood, and nothing suited the carmongers better. The fewer and foggier the details, the less chance of being held to account for them. On one of the first big network hits, Ed Sullivan's variety show, beautiful girls fawned over a Mercury sedan while the announcer mooed hypnotically: *Soft foam rubber seat cushions are your invitation to the many happy motoring days ahead, and they will be happy days because nothing has been overlooked to make the road-proven new 1949 Mercury your perfect highway companion.*

Thus stimulated, Americans bought cars and every other kind of consumer items so quickly after the war that the government slapped installment buying curbs back on in 1948 to try to hold back the tide. Automakers nevertheless built 6.2 million motor vehicles the next year, eclipsing the 1929 record, and this came as especially welcome news in Detroit because the industry as a whole now had to sell 2 million units per year just to break even. Ford unloaded 1.4 million 1949 cars, trucks and tractors, and planned to build its own new $20 million headquarters on 175 acres in Dearborn.

Port Huron area parts suppliers raced to keep up. An entire trainful of parts and five dozen more truckfuls left the Chrysler depot in Marysville daily for the assembly plants in Detroit and beyond. Pressed Metals could barely ship it's "Knee-Action" patented suspension parts fast enough to supply Ford and the rest of the industry, and ordered a $1 million expansion. Auto Lite grew into a 250,000 square foot operation. A newcomer, Standard Products, took over an old foundry building and hired 400 workers to make more parts, and more.

American cars and trucks numbered 48 million by the end of the decade according to one robust estimate.(49) The census takers of 1950 reckoned America spent

$28 billion on cars that year. Half of all families owned at least one. More than 30,000 motor vehicles roamed St. Clair County, one for every three people, sold to them by 70 different helots offering new or used models. The number of cars in Detroit climbed a mind-boggling 31% in just six months in 1950. The beginning of the Korean War in June of 1950 pushed car sales even higher. Buyers in Port Huron snapped up 1,200 vehicles in a month, trying to get the jump on what they feared would be another dreaded automobile production freeze.

The automobile continued its landscape-bending ways post WW2, pushing and pulling residents and businesses out of both big cities and small farm towns and transplanting them in suburbia. In Detroit, the Hudson department store company, the largest in town, announced construction of a 100-acre shopping mall named Eastland just outside the city limits, with 6,000 parking spaces, the equivalent of 25 city blocks. At the same time, in the village of Applegate out in the Thumb, five stores, a hotel, a poolroom, post office, doctor's office, and undertaker vanished as the farm population shrank, and Applegators drove miles away to shop. They'd driven at first out of curiosity, now of necessity.

"Building Spreads Outside City Limits," announced the *Times Herald* in a report on Port Huron area housing. Developers tossed up batches of 10 and 20 houses at a time, pretty much anywhere they wanted, made out of 2x4's and that new "plywood" stuff, averaging 900 square feet plus basement, costing $10,000, with an attached garage and no front porch, on a lot 100 feet wide or wider. Along the desirable Lake Huron shoreline north of town, builders erected $1.6 million worth of homes and cottages in a single year. A great many suburban dwellings also appeared on the upper Black River. The total for the five postwar years of the decade came to 2,000 homes built within easy driving distance of Port Huron.

In addition to the old Federal Housing Administration, which by now had backed $10 billion in mortgages, another federal home loan program from the Veterans Administration aimed at millions of discharged servicemen helped to fuel the suburban movement with 4% loans for new homes. To give suburbia another official blessing, the state of Michigan okayed creation of the "chartered" township, basically city government with no city, a scheme primarily intended to ward off annexation of these low-tax bedroom communities by the cities they'd sprung from.

The 1950 census showed Port Huron's population had increased 8% since 1940, while numbers in two adjacent townships jumped by 70% and 100%. The Census Bureau called suburbanites "rural non-farm" folks, who now made up one-quarter of St. Clair County. Naturally, all this extra suburban automobile traffic took its toll, to the misfortune of William Stanley, a 96 year-old farmer, and Bethel Paul, a 12 year-old Girl Scout, both run over and killed by cars while walking near their homes on the same stretch of road in the formerly peaceful Gardendale. The once auto-indulgent architect Frank Lloyd Wright changed his mind about cars somewhat when he built a handful of suburban homes in Michigan during these postwar years. A Wright admirer described these homes later as being "shielded from the road," "carefully screened from the road," "protected from the road," "away from the road."(50)

The auto industry carefully monitored sales of its pickup trucks and six-passenger station wagons, the signature vehicles of rural non-farmers, to stay abreast of the suburban osmosis. In its own response to this trend, Port Huron created with the help of the automobile industry shills at the Michigan Highway Department a car-friendly city "master plan" that included parking, parking and more parking. Plus, of course, wider streets. Fifteen avenues needed widening, although if they got any wider in some spots the traffic would crush pedestrians up against the building facades. 22,000 motor vehicles penetrated the Port Huron downtown district per day, carrying 33,000 people. Pondering these figures, Planning Commission head Edgar Kiefer worried that for lack of parking, "People cannot shop in the business district because they cannot get out of their cars." Look at Trese's Meat Market on Main, for example. Closing after 69 years because customers wanted parking right outside the door to cut down on the distance they lugged their meat.

Port Huron's central district already featured three municipal parking lots, 30 private lots and more than 1,000 street parking spots, but department store boss Clare Sperry waved away these facts in demanding more: "The need for off street parking space in the downtown area is so obvious it needs no discussion." Discussion adjourned, the city government spent $500,000 to install 600 more lot spots. A man who put an amusing twist on this situation, and literally couldn't get out of his car, paid a visit to Port Huron at about this time. Oregonian Don Haynes had made a $25,000 bet that he couldn't live imprisoned in his sedan for 14 months. He'd had himself welded inside it. Equipped with a makeshift lavatory and a bed, Haynes drove something far worse than a rolling jail cell around the country for publicity purposes, and filled an honored spot in Port Huron's 1949 centennial parade in front of 75,000 spectators. He took parking pretty darn seriously.

"People cannot get out of their cars." Was that phrase music to Detroit's ears, or what? In a self-congratulatory mood, the auto industry took the opportunity in 1946 to celebrate its unofficial 50th birthday in Detroit with a parade, street dancing (if enough cars could be cleared off the streets), and "solemn moments of dramatic tribute"...to itself. The Automobile Manufacturers Association opened its own Hall of Fame, inducting Ford, Durant, Olds, Sloan, Charles Nash, the Duryeas, and Charles King. The Hall also conferred its knighthood on that perfect symbol of the American driving public, Barney Oldfield, who'd killed three people as a race driver, who'd been arrested for driving 87 mph while drunk, who'd said driving a car at less than 50 mph made him drowsy, and who'd recently gotten into a road rage fistfight at age 66. "He tried to crowd me off the road," said Barney after the bout. "We exchanged a few words, then got out of our cars and started to swing at each other."(51)

The Auto HOF coincidentally opened during National Noise Abatement Week, intended to reduce "civilian shell shock" from incessant city noise. Far and away the biggest racketmakers, cars and trucks could induce fatigue, emotional disturbance, impaired hearing, and neuroses, according to Dr. A.L. Callery of St. Clair County's Health Department. Just look at what they'd done to Barney Oldfield, for instance. More evidence surfaced after the war that not just the noise, impact, and sedentary effect of cars wore people down. The phenomenon of smog made its unwelcome debut in Los Angeles during the 1940's. Science writer Alton Blakeslee reported that both auto exhaust and tar dust from roads might be carcinogenic because investigators found a high correlation between automobile ownership and cancer rates. Car engineers worried that carbon monoxide sucked from one motor vehicle into another in city traffic cut down on driver alertness, just as illness, fatigue, age, alcohol, eye strain, roadside distractions, and drugs did. Michigan's Department of Health fielded 144 air pollution complaints in 1950, and spokesman John Soet said, "The air is free, it's all around us and invisible, so people don't think much about it – until it begins to go bad." Anecdotally, the Associated Press called Michigan the sinus trouble capital of America.

The automobile also made Michigan's state government sick, according to Port Huron lawyer Eugene Black. After his election as Michigan Attorney General in 1946, Black discovered that auto dealers pretty much controlled the governor and the state legislature, and automobile advertising dollars corrupted the press as well. Dealers cheated on millions of dollars in sales taxes, and paid bribes to political candidates. Prosecutors convicted 18 Michigan dealers in 1948 of breaking the Corrupt Practices Act. Black also found that the Highway Department blundered along without any coherent overall plan, responding to whoever had the most pull in the state capitol. It cost $8 million annually just to staff the highway office, and none of the state's main trunk lines had yet been finished end to end due to the piecemeal construction methods. Black's accusations amounted to one Republican pitted against other Republicans, but when the governorship changed parties in 1948, the new man, Democrat G. Mennen "Soapy" Williams, mustered no more independence from the auto industry's pressure than his predecessor had. Like Democrats Frank Murphy and Murray Van Wagoner before him, Williams governed practically as a shop steward for the United Auto Workers.

While World War Two halted most street and highway construction in America due to material shortages it didn't stop the road lobby from writing to Santa about the future. Just two months after Pearl Harbor the American Road Building Association met in Detroit to propose a solution for the coming, someday, postwar recession: build more roads. Prompted by an auto-friendly advisory committee whose members must have seen the 1939 World's Fair, President Roosevelt tentatively had outlined a 34,000 mile national highway system, price to be determined once the shooting stopped. This idea later expanded to 40,000 miles, with a $3 billion price tag. But even those figures weren't set in concrete, and the projected cost increased with time to $11 billion.

Michigan's highway director Charles Ziegler, the man Eugene Black virtually called a saphead, kept 100 draftsmen and 24 surveying crews busy during WW2 creating $36 million worth of new road proposals, even though he had drawersful already. There must be new roads, new bridges, and a 90% rebuild of the entire state highway system, said Ziegler, disregarding the $2.5 billion from all sources which already had been spent on Michigan's roads and streets since 1913. City leaders in Detroit put two big World of Tomorrow freeways priced at $8 million on the drawing board. St. Clair County's top road engineer Kenyon Goeltz included $3 million worth of goodies on his wish list.

After the war ended, contractors managed to get their hands on a little steel and concrete, so road construction slowly resumed. Ziegler, still smarting over the hiding he'd taken from Eugene Black, turned his attention to Port Huron, and finished the by now legendary "bypass" road to try to decongest streets by routing traffic around downtown. No dramatic congestion relief followed. Part of this project, an $850,000, 700 foot-long fixed bridge across the Black River, hindered and even blocked many commercial and sailing vessels from the upper river. Despite the pleas of people more enlightened than himself, Ziegler magisterially rejected proposals for a drawbridge. A five minute delay in auto traffic to allow ships to pass could not be contemplated. The very idea shocked him. Ziegler also connected the bypass to the Blue Water Bridge, in the process cutting nine local streets in half, and eradicating several dozen homes and businesses standing in the way.

Auto-owning Port Huroners clamored for more paved streets after the war, submitting petitions for 11 miles worth in 1948 alone, although the city could only afford 4 miles that year, about $200,000 worth. Not everyone signed the petitions. One elderly homeowner cried in front of the City Council about the paving assessments placed on her home. Clam up, Granny, responded Port Huron's latest city manager Jay Gibbs – or words to that effect. He served as president of the Michigan Good Roads Federation and wanted another $3.7 million in new streets and bridges built in his city, though like all good roadsmen, he projected no maintenance figures for them. To tend the auto infrastructure already in place Gibbs had to employ a three-man crew just to look after the 5,000 traffic signs and signals.

Maintenance – the bane of the happyways! Especially in winter. Once upon a time, you just waited until snow melted. Nowadays, coping with a single bad snowstorm required the efforts of 25 Port Huron city employees, some on duty driving plows 24-30 hours straight, not the safest arrangement, while police wrote a blizzard of 200 snow parking tickets in two days for cars left on the streets. That same snowfall cost St. Clair County's Road Commission $13,000 in emergency costs and 8,400 man hours working 40 different vehicles to try to clear the decks. "It is a shame to spend all that money, and it seems like pouring it down the drain," observed maintenance man Donald Belyea thoughtfully. Winter kept public works departments all over Michigan on pins and needles because even a "2-Inch Snowfall Endangers Traffic," according to the press. Efforts to remove the white stuff cost $10 million per year in the Great Lakes State. Curious engineers put a test electrical grid on a section of highway to see about melting snow with heat. They learned it would cost $112 million to wire the state's 9,000 miles of highways and $98 million per year to slow cook them.

Once winter departed, the spring thaw came along and chewed up the roads in its own way. Take the Ford Motor Company's word for it: *Turn off the highway onto a country lane. It's there you discover how easily Mercury absorbs the jolts and jars of rutted roads.* The breakup of a single spring did $600,000 damage in St. Clair County, 100 years after the first such impassable roads crisis. Almost at wits' end with anxiety, engineer Goeltz declared a "near emergency." He also had on his things-to-do list: dust control (1,300 gallons of calcium chloride per mile), litter ($25 per mile to pick up the junk alongside St. Clair County roads), weeds (mow them once the trash had been cleared away), dividing lines ($350,000 to repaint Michigan's highways every year), and taxes (Goeltz said the county's roads "will be sunk" without a 5 cents per gallon state gasoline tax, currently 3 cents). Just collecting Michigan's gas tax cost $2 million per annum. Thinking the whole thing over, Goeltz decided to retire, worn out at age 57.

The Road Commission dispensed $1.6 million in 1950. Out of one pocket or another, the people of Michigan as a whole unloaded $100 million that year on their roads and streets. Still, no matter how much taxpayers invested, the Road Gang kept up its continual propaganda barrage for more spending. And not without cause. For example, the state highway laboratory rated half the thoroughfares in Michigan deficient because traffic had increased 900% since 1920. Michigan Secretary of State

Fred Alger predicted for the Port Huron Kiwanis Club that toll roads were the next step, a return to the old plank roads setup.

Having been on a gasoline diet, however half-hearted, during the war, American drivers gorged on it in peacetime. By the end of 1946 the country consumed more oil than the civilian and military sectors combined had used during the height of WW2. In 1947 all these uninhibited cars and drivers combusted 100 million gallons of gas per day and outstripped the supply. Oil and gasoline shortages came back again in the USA for several months, along with talk of new rationing. Like the late Franklin Roosevelt, President Truman feared alienating the great motoring public, and he called for voluntary cuts in pleasure driving to deal with this shortfall. His predecessor's widow, loyal Eleanor Roosevelt, found it easy to comply with Mr. Truman's request, because she'd fallen asleep at the wheel of her car recently, triggering a three-car, five-injury pileup, after which authorities had revoked her driver's license.

The postwar trend of replacing coal with oil on railroads, in ships, and in home heating added to the petroleum problem. Diesel fuel powered 90% of all new locomotives, and took over on new Great Lakes freighters. Heating oil warmed 10 million dwellings by 1950, a 50% increase in seven years (natural gas use also climbed).(52) The coal industry and United Mine Workers had made themselves so obnoxious with their endless series of strikes and delivery stoppages during the past 40 years that business and residential users could hardly get rid of their coal bins fast enough. Standard Oil hatched a scheme to pick up the slack in coal sales by brewing gasoline from it. The company said that potentially 3,000 years worth of coal gasoline lay there just waiting in the ground. It was still waiting there at the end of the 20th Century.

As if cars and trucks and tractors and buses and homes and ships and airplanes and even railroads didn't burn enough, another way to use petroleum, crazier than all the rest, the gasoline-powered lawn mower appeared at Sturmer Hardware in Port Huron right after the war. The Reo Royale mower came from one of the companies founded by Ransom Olds, Mr. Oldsmobile. For all the stink and noise emitted from the poorly mufflered mower, a machine perfectly capable of mowing off an operator's fingers or toes, or hurling an object like a missile off its cutting blades, or starting a fire from gasoline clumsily poured over its hot, inefficient engine, it didn't appreciably speed up or improve grass cutting. At $120 a Reo cost five times as much as a reel mower. President Truman missed a bet in not banning these entirely to save gasoline. Better yet, get rid of gasoline powered golf carts, the first of which rumbled down a fairway in the Thumb in 1950, carrying hackers too auto sick even to walk a golf course.

America's oil habit, still primarily for automobiles, led to the first successful well drilling in the Gulf of Mexico following the war, and U.S. oil reserves increased 20% by 1950.(53) But rather than live within its means, the nation allowed petromania to further warp its foreign policy. In 1946, the State Department calculated the country would need to import half its oil by 1965. The number one source of supply looked to be the Middle East, where American companies like Standard Oil and Texaco controlled 40% of the reserves. This region already furnished the States with 120 million barrels per year. It also suffered from a host of political, cultural and religious divisions inscrutable to Americans. The *Times Herald* commented on one of the many crises wracking this region almost with an air of entitlement, "...we need the oil. If we need it badly enough the situation in Iran may be loaded with dynamite. " Right your are, added Roger Babson, "That's what all the shootin' is about."

Even America's good intentions went wrong in these lands. Regret over the Nazi slaughter of European Jews during the wartime Holocaust, combined with Zionist political clout, prompted the USA to help the newly formed United Nations erect on the stilts of religious fairy tales the nation of Israel, a massive provocation in this solidly Moslem part of the world. Oil and Israel, a thoroughly unhealthy combination, became the "American interests" in the Middle East. The defense of these interests generated almost nothing but trouble for the United States for the rest of the century.

Across the river from Port Huron the Imperial Oil refinery grew and grew, until it covered 500 acres, and turned out gasoline and 600 other products from 53,000 barrels of oil per day. Another company, Canadian Refiners, set up shop nearby to churn out an additional 105 million gasoline gallons annually. A third, Sun Oil, broke ground on its own plant. A big oil discovery in the Canadian province of Alberta stimulated these exertions. Why couldn't Port Huron have its own oil refinery like Sarnia's? That's what the envious *Times Herald* wanted to know: "Let's Go After Them." Of course, that meant also going after those pesky explosions that dogged Imperial. This time a 50,000 gallon tank blew up with a blast which shattered windows in Port Huron and echoed across 25 miles of St. Clair County.

It also meant going after the filthy remains of the petrochemical process. Investigators pinpointed Imperial and its plastic-making neighbors Polymer (renamed Polysar) and Dow Chemical as three of the major pollution sources fouling up the Great Lakes. Some of Chemical Valley's noxious discharge showed up in the water 65 miles away in Detroit. The postwar demand for petroplastics in cars, toys, kitchen utensils, containers, construction, furniture, packaging, and clothing increased American plastic sales by 3,500% in a decade. 500 women rushed the Penney's store in Port Huron after nylon stockings re-appeared in 1946 and cleaned them out in an hour.

Gasoline delivery to retailers continued to carry its share of perils. The trucking companies moving it didn't always hire the most reliable people. Three 21 year-old Port Huron WW2 vets, now junior college students Alan Davis, David Crimmins, and Darwin Currens, died when a gas tanker truck hit their car on the Gratiot Pike. The truck driver, Robert Campbell, an ex-con with 11 arrests on his record, had been paroled specifically to drive gasoline trucks. Prior to the wreck he'd dropped off 8,000 gallons of gas in Port Huron before stopping at the Harrington Hotel bar to get snockered. Campbell ran from the death crash scene, afraid no doubt that one of the new "intoximeters" to measure blood alcohol content might be used on him by the police. Register over 0.15% and he was done for. After 14 weeks on the lam following this misdemeanor, for that's all the deaths of these three innocent men amounted to under automobile law, Campbell received a sentence of two more years in stir, mainly because he'd been on parole when it happened.

Virtually everyone in Port Huron admitted by now that too many gas stations did business there. Everyone except Detroit stockbroker Edward Roney, a summertime resident, who looked to make a killing on a prime location for yet another one:

Once again the old gives way to the new. The old Danger home, which for nearly 80 years occupied the northeast corner of Tenth Street and Lapeer Avenue, has been razed and workmen are replacing it with a streamlined super service station. The nine room brick dwelling, which housed three generations of the Danger family, was built by John Danger and his wife, Elizabeth, who settled in Port Huron after coming to this country from England. For many years the old homestead stood as a landmark. It was never occupied by anyone, except descendants of the builder and their families. To make room for the service station, which is being erected by the Socony-Vacuum Oil company, many huge shade trees were felled.(54)

That act of progress placed the fourth gas station at the intersection, one on each corner. Of course, some people liked the country's 250,000 filling stations. The Coca Cola company, which installed Coke machines in a lot of them, sentimentally pronounced the gas house "one of America's meeting places." The St. Clair County gasoline retailers cartel, a perfectly legal one at the time, set prices at about 26 cents per gallon at the end of the decade.

Seemingly back on their feet financially again, the railroads entered the postwar period with some exuberance. Adding to their good feeling, the federal government finally relieved train companies of furnishing a 50% discount on shipping rates to Uncle Sam to pay off the 19th Century land grants. By one RR industry estimate, those land grants had been paid for 12 times over. The Chesapeake and Ohio system formally absorbed one of Port Huron's rail lines, the Pere Marquette, and came to be called the C&O or Chessie. Down the C&O tracks the roving national exhibit known as the Freedom Train rolled into Pine Grove Park to celebrate the end of the war. 9,000 people climbed aboard to look at replicas of the Declaration of Independence, the Gettysburg Address and more than 100 other historical documents worth fighting a war for. For many youngsters it marked the first time they'd ever boarded a train. And the last.

Businesswise, the Chessie gave a great big affectionate bear hug to the automobile industry in 1945, ecstatically hailing the coming boom in production of freedom wheels:

Postwar Jobs - Delivered by Automobile! Here's one of the greatest opportunities for mass employment, mass buying power, mass prosperity, that any nation has ever had! Jobs by the carload! On railroads! In factories! In banks! Shops! Stores!(55)

The Grand Trunk railcar shops in Port Huron had orders in hand to build another 5,900 freight cars after the war, many of them for automobiles.

The diesel locomotives furnished by General Motors and General Electric also pleasured the railroad industry though not necessarily the public. While not as powerful, fast, cheap, picturesque, or musical as the chugging steamer, the droning diesel did have major advantages. It started up immediately, multiple units could be combined easily, it was cleaner, and a diesel didn't have to stop every 100 miles or so for coal or water. In many ways Alfred Sloan seemed prouder of GM's locomotives than any of the autos he built. The Port Huron and Detroit shortline railroad became one of the first in the country to switch entirely to diesel. The last steam locomotive built for U.S. RR lines left the factory in 1949.

Elsewhere in America electric trains gained some ground, though the U.S., which 40 years earlier had envisioned 120 mph interurbans, now lagged woefully far behind Europe and the Far East in the development of these engines superior to either steam or diesel. Electric rapid transit systems got some bad press in February 1950, when two commuter trains crashed into each other in New York, killing 29 and injuring 100, the worst train crash ever in that city. On the scale of American auto traffic this equaled eight hours of dead, and an hour of injuries. Trains still demanded careful attention, even from experts. They didn't get it from Capac station master Harold Jones, when he absentmindedly stepped in front of an oncoming Grand Trunk freight train one day. The public needed no further details.

After the war the Port Huron GTRR freight sheds for a time did more business than any other stop in the company's entire system, moving 110,000 tons of freight for business and industry per year, and picking up 22,000 full carloads. Every 30 minutes another train crossed through the St. Clair River tunnel. The Trunk planned a $5 million upgrade in Port Huron, and in fact lowered the tracks in the tunnel to allow bigger freight cars through. But readjusting to peacetime brought its share of troubles. Like the automobile industry, the railroads encountered plenty of strikes. But unlike the automakers they remained virtually powerless to prevent or settle strikes alone, since government regulators effectively controlled wages, prices and working practices. One particularly crazy but successful union demand forced diesel engines to carry firemen, though these locomotives used no coal to shovel.

Roger Babson still had his qualms about railroad securities, and rated only 12 of 200 public railroad companies as investment grade. Rising costs still outpaced revenues, said Babson: "Railroads for years have been the football of legislation, regulation, unionization and lack of appreciation." After more than 100 years of train service, America still had no single coast-to- coast railroad. C&O president Rodger Young pointed out that a hog could cross the country without changing cars, but a passenger couldn't. The natural evolution of trains had been hogtied.

If they couldn't get better transcontinental connections than swine, perhaps some proud passengers felt justified in giving up trains for automobiles again after the war. Despite upgrades on featured trains, like greater speed, luxury compartments, and amenities such as movie cars, passenger numbers declined. Railways lost money on standard fares of 2.5 cents per mile, 3.5 cents for a Pullman berth. In vain did they point out the overwhelming advantages of long haul travel by train instead of by automobile:

Let storms sweep the skyways. Let sleet snarl holiday traffic on the highways. Aboard your New York Central daylight streamliner or overnight Dreamliner you can settle back and enjoy every minute. Because you're traveling the world's safest way and you know you'll get there as planned, weather or no.

The Interstate Commerce Commission raised the possibility in 1949 that Congress might have to subsidize railroad passenger service someday. In another bad development, an important money making load, the mail, migrated away from trains to trucks. The Post Office canceled a C&O mail contract between Port Huron and Bad Axe in the upper Thumb after 65 years, just one day after a blizzard completely shut down truck travel along the route, but not the train.

Railroads abandoned more trackage in Michigan for these reasons, reducing the total mileage to 6,800. According to historian Willis Dunbar, railroads encouraged the end of service on some unprofitable routes by deliberately offering lousy service. "Abandonment planning" they called it.(56) Far from being unsympathetic toward rail companies, Port Huron turned out 200 people strong in 1946 for yet another banquet to honor the Grand Trunk for its role in the community, a starring role since it employed 1,300 people. Louis Weil played toastmaster again, this time to GTRR manager C. A. Skog, the featured guest.

Skog didn't feel entirely festive when he reported that the railroad industry's return on investment had skidded back down to just 2.2%, despite its making progress on many other fronts. For example, over the previous 25 years the average length of American freight trains had increased 39% and speed 39%, while the employee injury rate had declined 60%. Cost factors didn't look promising; wages were up 84%, taxes up 76%, rates up just 23%. A locomotive engineer now averaged $5,000 a year in pay, a fireman $4,000, twice as much as an auto worker. The company needed a 20% rate hike, and what chance did it have of getting it? asked Skog. (Later, the ICC okayed 10%). When Grand Trunk closed the books on 1947, it had lost money on a record $45 million in revenues.

Skog no doubt wondered from time to time if he shouldn't have entered the trucking business instead of railroading. After all, national newspaper columnist David Lawrence said the latest "heavy duty trucks...have reached such size that they look like railroad freight cars on rubber tired wheels." More of those street monsters rolled through Port Huron every day, and, unlike freight cars, they each individually belched noise and exhaust in every direction. Eight trucking companies operated from the city and they built two more big truck terminals during the last half of the decade. On the drawing board a truck terminal looked as green and lush as a park, in person as dead as a lava field.

More trucks lined up to use the Blue Water Bridge and invade Canada, which had opened its highways to American trucking during the war. A single Port Huron trucking concern, Ogden & Moffett, logged 1.75 million miles per year to Canada and destinations around Michigan. Caesar Scarvada, a former State Police captain, now a flack for the Michigan Trucking Association, bragged to the Port Huron Lions Club: "Life today is built around our highways; communities are spreading out and main streets are disappearing due to transportation. Today in Michigan, 1,500 communities receive all their supplies by truck only."(57)

Captain Scarvada left out the part about the trucking strikes shutting off those supplies. About the higher prices and erratic service, about the highway and street destruction, and about the public menace of the Robert Campbells on the road. Strangely, for an ex-cop, Scarvada neglected to mention the rampant corruption and criminality in the trucking industry and the Teamsters Union. The Teamsters especially now stank to high heaven. The union had used the world war as a shield behind which to enlist and in some cases to strong arm more drivers and other workers like store clerks into its ranks. Dozens of Port Huroners underwent this Teamster treatment, which brought the organization into increasing disrepute.

Even the normally union-tolerant Franklin Roosevelt had ordered a brief federal takeover of 100 strikebound Midwest trucking companies during WW2. Worse, the Teamsters had joined ranks with organized crime to accomplish some goals. In 1946 prosecutors charged 50 Detroit Teamsters leaders, including James Hoffa, with

268

extortion. But, to its credit, the union undeniably did come through in securing better deals for most of its one million members, though the rank and file often worked long hours. The Port Huron city bus drivers on the Teamsters rolls received $65 per 54-hour week in 1948, and some over-the-road truck jockeys made $80 weekly plus benefits.(58)

On one important trucking subject Captain Scarvada could gloat to his heart's content. Railroads paid 20% of their revenues, $1.77 billion per year, to maintain their railbeds. Trucking companies paid only 4% of their gross on highway taxes, and stuck those numbskulls, the general public, with the lion's share of the bill.(59) Scarvada could enjoy another laugh at the railroads' expense when President Truman seized control of the major train lines, this time during the Korean War in August 1950, and held on for 21 months, but made no similar move against truckers. Or for that matter against automakers, or airlines, or bus companies, or even streetcars.

A thoroughly converted fan of heavy rail, Alfred Sloan took grateful note of the 17,000 freight cars that had hauled away the excess inventory and redundant machinery from General Motors plants after the war. And he promoted a passenger "Train of Tomorrow" tour around the country pulled by one of his GM diesels.(60) But Sloan never relaxed his enmity for light rail. His campaign of destruction against America's street railways ended in 1949, after he'd bought 45 streetcar systems around the country and replaced them with buses. The streetcars in New York, Los Angeles, Baltimore, St. Louis, and Philadelphia had been routed. GM then disposed of its National City Lines operation. Sloan caught a little flak over the NCL, certainly nothing to worry about. Prosecutors indicted General Motors and corporate partners Phillips Petroleum, Firestone Tires, and Mack Truck for monopolistic practices connected to NCL activities. GM paid a $5,000 fine, which for Sloan amounted to walking around money.(61) In 20 years the streetcar mileage in America had shrunk from 40,000 miles to 15,000, the number of streetcars from 62,000 to 24,000.

The large bus passenger crowds of the Second World War dissipated with the dawn of the bright day in Port Huron. Ridership numbers started their decline within a year of the war's end. Just like with the automobiles on the streets, aging vehicles posed one of the biggest problems in busing. The Carpenter company promised Port Huroners nine new buses to get back on the right foot, but only two showed up. That left most of the old fleet in place, with each ancient machine covering another 120 miles per day. Rickety rigs especially aggravated bus riders after the fare doubled from a nickel to ten cents, with little to show for it. The fare increase zipped through the City Council with amazing speed, in just three weeks, compared to the multi-year fare war that had put the streetcars out of business in 1930.

Eventually, though, even the council lost patience with Carpenter's procrastination about getting new buses, and in 1950 they canceled the franchise. This threw the bus rights into the lap of Port Huron Plymouth dealer Jack Paton, of "Why Keep Waitin?" fame. Jack did no waitin' on this occasion, he sprang for 16 new buses. Why keep buses at all? The city's master plan looked to buses for a single reason: "everything must be done to retain and improve bus service for the downtown area since bus passengers need no parking facilities." The Greyhound Company, or The Big Dog as people knew it, still provided Port Huron with intercity bus service throughout St. Clair County and the Thumb, at about the same 2.5 cents per mile allowed trains.

Passenger ferry service reappeared between Port Huron and Sarnia following

269

the war, one of the happier transportation developments. Fed up with the expense and bother of crossing the Blue Water Bridge, pedestrians patronized a privately financed new ferry built around two 50-foot converted wartime landing craft. These vessels outran cars or buses, and crossed the St. Clair River with up to 80 passengers in as little as 10 minutes, operating 18 hours per day, at 15 cents per head. Patrons went back and forth between America and Canada looking for cheaper goods or legal bingo. Even with two boats running, the ferry needed fewer employees than the bridge's fulltime crew of fare-takers, mechanics, janitors, and painters.

As one might expect, the Port Huron bridge builders – Marshall Campbell, Dale Moffett, and Louis Weil – who had put the original ferry out of business, did everything in their power, pulled every political lever, told every lie they could think of, first to prevent the new ferry service from starting, and then to ruin it. The principle untruth promised that the Blue Water Bridge would someday be free to the public, if only they'd pay the higher fares now to cover the construction bonds. Nobody believed it. Equally encouraging for the local maritime forces, passenger ship service between Port Huron and Detroit got a new lease on life in 1950, when three excursion trips a week commenced for the summer aboard the Put-in-Bay steamer, and attracted 1,800 customers on the first run.

The World War Two development of radar, courtesy of government research, proved to be the single greatest aid to navigation since the compass, greatly assisting watercraft on the Great Lakes. The War Department spent no research money on trains, of course. Both marine speed and safety improved as a result of radar, though occasional mishaps still occurred, like the 1950 collision off the Thumb between the *City of Cleveland III* passenger ship and a Norwegian freighter. Four people died. Another big wreck on the Lakes took down the freighter *Emperor* with 12 victims. Nevertheless, these incidents now had become noteworthy primarily for their rarity.

Looking at its ledger, the Ford Motor Company calculated it spent only 67 cents to ship a ton of iron ore from Duluth to Dearborn on the water. After that ore had been converted into automobiles, the steamer *Mastaafa*, an independent auto carrier once salvaged by Port Huron's Reid family, hauled 500 vehicles at a time from Detroit to cities across the Lakes. Modest commercial bulk shipping traffic continued in and out of Port Huron following the war, but another effort to revive package freight service using war surplus ships sadly came to naught. The master plan for Port Huron called for greatly improved docking facilities, with direct dockside railroad connections, but no special sense of urgency pushed it ahead, as it did parking lots.

Just as it did during the war, the federal government continued to subsidize air travel in peacetime, in sharp contrast, as ever, to the railroads. The Federal Airways Act of 1946 earmarked $20 million per year to underwrite airports. About 13 million passengers flew commercially on U.S. airlines in 1949. Transcontinental fares could be had for $160. It took about 7.5 hours flying time coast to coast, though air patrons had to put up with customer service almost comically bad next to the best passenger trains and ships.(62) As commercial aviation advanced, the automakers began comparing their products to aircraft. Nash: *World's Only Cars Designed and Built On Aviation Principles.* Buick: *Looks like a Jet Plane, Travels the Same Way.* Buick did not, however, similarly embrace the flying saucers of the late 40's, first spotted over Port Huron on the 4th of July, 1947. Somehow "Looks like a Flying Saucer, Travels the

Same Way" didn't send an automobile customer the right message.

The end of the war cooled off the enthusiasm for adult bicycling in Port Huron, and boys and girls again did most two-wheeling. Sears occasionally offered an adult bike for $44: "Ride for pleasure, ride for convenience...the roomy luggage carrier is handy for small loads." Ralph's Bike Shop sold used bikes for all ages for $15. The automobile lobby now began actively persecuting and bullying bike-riding children. A handbill distributed in the Port Huron schools told kids: "Bike Boners Kill." 1947's 550 dead and 25,000 injured young bicyclists across America had only themselves to blame if you believed the car propagandists: "The Greatest Cause – Careless Riding." The *Times Herald's* hardline view on dumb kids on bikes softened somewhat when a driver ran over and killed one of its carriers, 12 year-old Ronald Winter, while he delivered newspapers by bicycle on the bypass road. That didn't seem to fit the bike boner profile. Could it actually be that car boners were the greater threat?

"Pedestrian's Rights Are Nonexistent Here – Watch Your Step!" Walking convert Ed Snover sprang this revelation on his Port Huron readers following the war. The pandemic car sickness that raged in the community after the end of the fighting stigmatized the poor foot traveler worse than ever. The author of *We'd Rather Ride* bucked the times, and found out in a hurry about the perils walkers had to put up with:

If the pedestrian, caught in the middle of the street by changing lights, does not get out of the way, too many motorists honk their horns impatiently instead of waiting for the pedestrian to complete his journey across the thoroughfare. He has to scramble through moving traffic to prevent being run down by drivers who seem to think that the automobile – not the man on foot – has the right of way. One can hardly go down the street without being forced to jump out of the way of some motorist who refuses to recognize that the pedestrian has any rights at all on the street.(63)

In light of these dangers the "walking is bad for you" theme continued to crop up in auto advertising: *Why Walk When It's So Easy To Ride*, counseled the Nash dealership. But not just motorists ignored pedestrian rights. Though the city of Port Huron put in five miles of new sidewalks in 1946, it abandoned the practice of horse-plowing the snow off them. It left that job almost entirely to property owners, and many didn't bother, according to annoyed pedestrian Floyd Surline: "Everyone cannot jump in a car to go a block. We have to walk."

Surline could take some satisfaction in the fact that people who didn't walk paid a price for their indolence. The Kill 'Em or Cure 'Em Walking Club of Port Huron didn't have to walk anymore, they'd disbanded after the war, and it killed one of 'em. Lawyer Laurie Telfer dropped dead of a heart attack at age 56. He followed fellow attorney Miles Benedict, aged 41, to the grave. U.S. Supreme Court Judge Frank Murphy succumbed to heart trouble at 59, one of many notable national victims. Heart disease claimed 600,000 people annually, more than the next five causes of death in sedentary America combined.

Nothing of a medical nature spawned more uneasiness than the growing national fat, directly traceable to national sit. Even in the middle of a world war, in spite of the rationing of some food and of course automobiles, fat crept up on people who didn't get in enough walking. "Not nearly all of America's 65 million women are overweight as most people seem to think," one anonymous author told Port Huron gals

271

in 1944. Nevertheless, for the rest of the decade, false cures for flab by the score filled the stores. "Ayds," "Vee-Mor," "Trymm," "Rennel," "Mynex," "Wonder Bread – Burns Off Fat Without Drugs or Violent Exercise," "The Stauffer System – Wise Women are Slender. No Exertion, No Disrobing, No Drugs, No Electricity." Hollywood starlet Marilyn Monroe endorsed "Kyron" condensed food tablets: "It's Fun to be Slender Like a Movie Star." Marilyn did not yet need or endorse the "Futuro Abdominal Brace – For Waistline Bulge, Indigestion, Constipation, Heart Strain due to Obesity," but who knew what the future might hold? Nothing helped. Nothing, that is, but the walking cure, said Ed Snover: "Want to lose weight? Follow the Postman's program. Ever see a fat one?"

An 82 year-old Detroit grandmother, Sylvia Carlen, introduced her own fitness plan to Port Huron in October 1950, by walking the 57 miles from her home to the city in 11.5 hours. At the end of her journey Mrs. Carlen was greeted by her embarrassingly overweight friends, Dr. and Mrs. R. M. Patterson. Physician, heal thyself. This wasn't Sylvia's first long-distance march, either. She'd done 90 miles to Lansing on another trip and a short 46 mile hop down to Monroe. "Mrs Carlen began her strange hobby of 'walking' a number of years ago when she joined a hiking club," marveled *Times Herald* reporter Annette Matthews.

"Strange hobby" indeed! If only Alex Jacobs could have heard such talk. A dangerous hobby, maybe. Days after Mrs. Carlen's feat, 75 year-old Port Huron pedestrian Mary Lau set out to walk not to Detroit or Lansing, but just to the mailbox to drop off her Christmas cards. A car intercepted her, knocked her 114 feet, and broke her skull, both arms, leg, jaw, neck and chest. Miss Lau didn't survive this, one of the last of the 1,915 traffic accidents in the city in 1950. But the driver, 19 year-old Elmer Richter, had a Happy New Year, absolved of any blame although he'd been speeding and passing another vehicle on Main Street at the time he killed his victim. 270,000 people luckier than Miss Lau required only hospitalization following car accidents in America in 1950. To keep pace with auto casualties, heart cases, and other medical malfunctions, Louis Weil announced a $2 million campaign to enlarge the Port Huron Hospital by almost half again, and build a second hospital, Mercy, this one to cater to Catholic superstitions.

Health concerns did not readily dissuade Port Huroners from their automobile ways, for the simple reason that while folks grew physically more feeble due to their wheels, they lived longer, 68 years on average, thanks largely to improvements in public health measures. Mass vaccinations increased. The breakthrough antibiotic penicillin saved a lot of lives in Port Huron after the war, as it did everywhere. And after 30 years of abysmal ignorance and folly, and delays caused by public spending on the car culture, Port Huron finally bowed to state pressure and agreed to build a sewage treatment plant to clean up the rivers. Water customers paid 80% higher water bills for this.

The automobile warping of the education system also picked up pace during this decade. Port Huron's school board named a committed Fordist, Howard Crull, as superintendent. The WW1 veteran and longtime educator from the Detroit suburbs became a dedicated enemy of the small neighborhood elementary schools that dotted Port Huron. He launched a program of deliberate neglect of these sturdy masonry buildings, coupled with a campaign of falsehoods that they were falling apart. Crull dreamed of replacing them with a few of the new factory-type monolith schools. Plus plenty of busing, just as Gene Tunney had feared. "In general," said Crull, "a building which contains fewer than 12 rooms does not permit efficient use of supervisory and operating personnel. School buildings are expendable."(64)

Crull pulled down three of the old elementaries and also bought a 40-acre site on the west side of the city near the new War Memorial stadium, so he could move the high school out of the downtown eventually and build something more to his liking, awash with parking. Outraged, 2,000 people signed an unsuccessful petition demanding Crull's removal. Similarly, out in the country, the number of one-room rural schools in St. Clair County declined by one-third, down to 115 by 1950, despite the population growth in the suburbs. Consolidated warehouse schools replaced the one-roomers. Buses increasingly carried country kids back and forth, as in cattle trucks, a legitimate comparison since no responsible farmer would have allowed his cattle to roam rural roads anymore in the face of the growing automobile traffic.

National newspaper columnist Paul Mallon blasted the use of mass production methods in schools, which he traced back to the late 1920's. "Education got to be big business and the classroom an assembly line. Grown up educators, with apparently adult minds, today openly advocate that every child be passed regardless of his mental capacity, so he will not be personally ashamed of his deficiency." Ed Snover, who now handled editorial writing for the *Times Herald*, agreed. "There is something radically wrong with our school system. We sometimes think the boy and girl who went to school half a century ago accumulated much more by the time he was through eighth grade than the pupil of today by the time he is through his high school course."(65) Snover said graduates of the high school, the Port Huron Junior College, and even the University of Michigan who came to work for the paper couldn't spell or add, and knew little geography or civics. Michigan taxpayers spent $125 per year per student in the public schools.

Fordism made further inroads in agriculture as well. Partly as a result of an all-out farm effort during the world war, the number of tractors in use doubled during this decade, to 3.4 million. 3,300 of them tilled the soil of St. Clair County.(66) Farms combined into bigger spreads on the lines of Fordist principles. 40% of the farms in America now measured 1,000 acres or larger. While the general population grew, the farm population gradually declined. Just 18% of Americans lived on farms, a dramatic fall off from the 50% of 1900. By 1950, farming employed only 7% of adult males in Michigan. Despite the revved up methods now in use, 50% of U.S. farmers made less than $3,000 per year. Time magazine painted a picture of the country's baffling agricultural practices:

One arm of the massive Department of Agriculture was feverishly shuffling schemes for limiting farm production; another arm was busily showing farmers how to grow more. Already the U.S. had stored up enough wheat and corn to fill a freight train stretching almost halfway around the world...(67)

To manage their bigger places farmers turned further and further away from organic methods. Artificial fertilizer use increased, and so did the spraying of 15 new classes of pesticides. Arsenic and lead had been the original poisons of choice, but the world war introduced DDT into the bug killing arsenal. "Goodbye to mosquitoes, moths, other insects, with chemicals," cheered the Chesapeake and Ohio Railroad, which delivered DDT to commercial firms. This compound worried plenty of more sober people right off the bat, since it killed off beneficial as well as harmful insects, and didn't seem to do the wildlife any good either. The Food and Drug Administration thought it extremely likely that "the potential hazard of DDT has been underestimated."(68) This insecticide had barely gone into commercial use before DDT-resistant strains of insects appeared, just as Charles Darwin might have forecast.

Another technique of modern American farm life created a stir in the late 40's, the "confinement rearing" of livestock. A veterinarian in Goodells, Howard Conrad, erected a four-story concrete assembly and disassembly plant for chickens. Dr. Conrad crammed 32,000 birds at a time permanently inside the building, with one square foot of space each. He fed and watered them for 16 weeks, then slaughtered them. The fowl had to be electrically de-beaked in order to prevent cannibalism under these conditions. The set-up shocked the few chicken fanciers with backyard coops left in Port Huron, who weren't in touch with modern ways. The Conrads of the day defended confinement life for chickens and other species with the twin claims that the animals were better off and didn't know the difference anyway. Automobile companies said about the same thing of their customers.

The first generation of American auto pioneers began passing away in earnest at the end of this decade. Hardly had the doors to the Automotive Hall of Fame swung open in Detroit before the members of its honor roll departed for the cemetery. Ransom Olds of the Merry Oldsmobile, William Knudsen the "Vun for Vun" Ford man turned Chevrolet boss, Barney Oldfield the terrible, Charles Nash who ran Durant carriage then Buick then General Motors then his own Nash auto company, John Raskob the architect of GM's installment financing arm, all died. In early 1947 three of the largest figures of this history died within weeks of each other. Billy Durant expired in New York City where he lived in an apartment he couldn't afford, subsidized by old friends like Charles Mott, who never forgot what he owed Durant. With his last throw, Gambling Billy had opened a bowling alley in Flint, and he'd occasionally served hamburgers in person there when he visited town.

In Port Huron, George Yokom by 1947 had all but retired from the automobile business, having closed his dealership. He sold an occasional used heap for old times sake, and lived in an apartment building he owned. Yokom sometimes reminisced to the press about his early days in the industry, and like the original auto huckster he was, he inaccurately inflated his accomplishments, backdating this and misremembering that. But he remained indisputibly the man who'd done more than any other to introduce the automobile to Port Huron, St. Clair County, and the Tnumb. When he died he left a $100,000 estate to his common law wife Mary. A variety of Yokom relations anxious to get their hands on this money subsequently sued her, and took their case all the way to the Michigan Supreme Court before Mrs.Yokom prevailed. Perhaps in her distress over this unbecoming lawsuit the matter slipped her mind, or maybe she just felt unsentimental about him, but Mrs.Y allowed her husband to disappear into an unmarked grave.

And finally, in a scene reminiscent of the movie *Citizen Kane*, Henry Ford died during a spring storm at his Fair Lane mansion in April. He was 83. During the last 18 months of his life after he left the FMC, while his grandson shut down projects like Fordlandia and the soybean lab, abolished the no-smoking rules, and turned the company into a General Motors clone, Henry sometimes went for long drives in a chauffeured car. Typically, he gave the driver orders to avoid those joy killing devices, stop lights. Ford told his coachman that he longed most for the days when he tended his woodlot and tinkered with steam engines, in the house he'd hand-built for himself and Clara, before he ever turned a hand to automobiles. After 100,000 people took a last look at him at Greenfield Village, and a 1942 Packard hearse carried him hence, his family buried Ford next to his parents "...at the busy intersection of Joy and Greenfield Roads. Its crumbling white headstones are dusted by ashes from the stacks of the huge River Rouge plant, symbol of the motor empire that Henry Ford created."(69) Ford had accumulated a $700 million estate, and a global reputation, but for all the wrong reasons. And when a man of Henry Ford's ability, a genius indeed, takes a wrong turn, the world trembles.

As the half century closed, something else symbolic happened which disturbed the city of Port Huron. Thanks to the automobile, the community dispersed further and further each day. The more driving people did, the less they walked their town, the less they actually saw of their neighbors and neighborhoods, the less they knew of the community as a whole. Suburbanites knew next to nothing. In abandoning walking people increasingly concerned themselves only with their starting points and destinations. The intervening spaces became simply an annoyance, what one later historian called "the curse of distance." Reduced to just a blur from a passing car, to all intents and purposes Port Huron became for many an invisible city. Store owners slapped aluminum facades over the masonry of their buildings, with just a single large-lettered name in front, to try to catch the attention of auto travelers going by at 30 miles per hour. Or in 17 year-old Alva Gross' case, 80 mph, which is how fast he drove up Main Street one day "to see how many lights we could make." Modernism now ruled the design of new buildings in town, what critic Jane Holtz Kay later called "fast-read architecture." One night in 1949, the city's premier slow-read architectural centerpiece, the City Hall, caught fire.

The top floor of the majestic three-story Victorian building collapsed, along with the tower in which a massive weight-driven clock had chimed away for 70 years. It marked one of the last times Port Huroners stood in the streets and wept over something they all shared. The pastor of the Catholic church, E. J. McCormick, put it this way:

I've lost a fine friend who never has faltered
Who year after year has been faithful to me.
Through winter and summer it never has altered
But called my attention to things I should see,
The passing of time our most pressing treasure,
The throngs of the town, the strange passer by,
The heartbreaks and sorrows that no one can measure.
It ticked out the minutes sometimes with a sigh,
The old faithful clock so high in the belfry,
The faithful old clock of our old City Hall.(70)

Chapter 8. 1951-1960: You Don't Drive It, You Aim It.

...we waited, hoped, prayed for a new hard top road to take the place of a bumpy, dusty gravel one. We thought it would be heavenly to have such a hard top. A year ago we got it! Now we find it's not heavenly, not by a long shot! We wish we had the old road back. Families with children live with fear for their youngsters. Old folks are afraid to cross the road to the mailbox. Women drivers stay at home, afraid to venture out. We're kept awake nights and aroused early in the mornings. Our road has become a speedway! Cars and motorcycles are tested out on this level stretch. Cars traveling 60, 70, 80 miles per hour create enough noise to rouse the dead. The vibration and vacuum created by high speeds rattle our doors and shake TV antennae so programs are interrupted. One of these days there'll be a butcher shop accident. (1)

So saith Mrs. Ida May of suburban Port Huron Township in the summer of 1951, having been introduced to the progressive modern combination of unlimited speed Good Roads, and what Ford Motor Company called *flashing, jet-away performance.* Or it might have been Chrysler's *"FirePower Engine...most powerful engine ever put in an American passenger car."* Or General Motors' descendant of the Merry Oldsmobile, the Rocket: *What a thrill to take the wheel / Of a Rocket Oldsmobile / In performance it's a star / It's a rocket engine car.* Chrysler asked "*How much more of TOMORROW do you want TODAY?*" But of course Mrs. May didn't want either, she wanted YESTERDAY back again.

For much of the 1950's America's automobile industry, known collectively now as just "Detroit," concentrated on building bigger, more powerful, and above all faster automobiles. Horsepower levels leaped up from the mid 100's through the 200's and into the 300's on some models by 1956. As conflicted as ever, designers excused this both ways as a "joy of driving" thing, and a "fear of driving" thing, in Cadillac's words: *It works for your safety...because a great reserve of power is a wonderful safeguard in most of the driving emergencies that present themselves....it works for your* peace of mind, *for it is unbelievably comforting to know that you have tremendous acceleration, should the necessity for it arise.*

John Cawood's ads said the same about his new $2,300 Buicks:

Here's Where the Pounds Pay Off. This isn't 'deadweight'. Though a Buick like the one pictured here tips the scales at more than two tons, it's as nimble as an antelope at play. It has a generous hoodful of valve-in-head Fireball power – packing a powerful punch of velvet velocity. That gleaming new push-bar forefront, which greets your eye with flashing beauty, contains 25 grille bars made of stamped steel, individually mounted to 'give' and come back unharmed. Combined with a massive, wrap-around bumper, fortressed by two stalwart 'bumper bombs' and two added uprights, it gives unsurpassed protection.

On the receiving end, of course, it gave unsurpassed demolishment. At about

276

this time a powerful punch by a hit-and-runner rocketed Islay Freeman of Port Huron 200 feet from the spot where he'd been walking on an unsidewalked portion of Main Street one night, reducing the father of three to deadweight. Police estimated the impact at a velvety 35,000 foot pounds, from a vehicle moving at about 75-80 mph. Another gentleman, Elvester Moss, given the same treatment at about the same spot, died from a broken neck, fractured skull, and two broken legs. Police found his shoes 100 feet away. Detroit's parrot talk about the necessity of souped up engines flew in the face of the conclusion by the National Safety Council that excessive speed caused one-half of all car accidents, which totaled 170 in Port Huron during the month of June 1951 alone. Not even the addition of one-fingered power steering and head-wrenching power brakes to ride herd on overpowered automobile engines managed to steer drivers clear or stop them from piling into more and more wrecks during the Fifties.

What kind of driver was Detroit in love with and Mrs. May afraid of? How about 19 year-old Edward Zeros, who drove out Mrs. May's way one night with his headlights off at 80 mph trying to shake off a police pursuit. Luckily a blown tire stopped him before he could butcher anybody. Not so another 19 year-old from Mrs. May's neighborhood, Darren Maes. While on probation for speeding, racing, and running a stop sign, he ran over and killed 55 year-old Margaret Wallen as she walked at night along the road with a flashlight. Maes' velocity measured 50 mph when he met Mrs. Wallen. "I know I have a bad driving record, but for the last 10 months I haven't done anything wrong," pleaded Darren. Another fellow for Mrs. May to keep an eye on, 42 year-old Clarence La Turno, a convicted drunk driver with a 12-year history of violations, and no license, backed his car out of his driveway on one occasion that summer, and in the process killed 18 month-old Diana Gardner as she played outside her foster home. Diana's final adoption by her new parents had been scheduled for the next day, but instead she found a home in Lakeside Cemetery in Port Huron, one of 27 people killed in the 2,450 traffic accidents across St. Clair County that year. That figured to about one accident per 14 motor vehicles. Cleared of any negligence by the forgive-and-forget traffic justice system, La Turno lived a reformed life, for 12 days. Then following a high speed chase police arrested him for drunk driving again and he spent a year in jail, a little late for Diana Gardner's sake.

Traffic cops now clocked 85, 95, 105 miles per-hour speeds with a fair amount of regularity on Port Huron's city streets. 27 year-old Frank Penno actually outran a 120 mph patrol car, and some gunfire, until he stopped like a good sport and accepted a $25 fine and 2 days in jail. The less accommodating 21 year-old Jack Griffin resisted capture until police finally hauled him into court for "auto terrorism," racing around and around neighborhoods and thumbing his nose at protesting homeowners. Griffin paid a $50 fine, and the finance company took back his car. 26 year-old Keith Thornton took a couple of 90 mph laps around town at 3 a.m. before he finally spun out on a patch of ice into the clutches of his police pursuers. 25 year-old Donald Christner's drunken 105 mph flight from police ended when he careened off a milk truck, and he'd face arraignment for it just as soon as he got out of the hospital. After incautiously motoring up a Port Huron avenue at 75 mph, 23 year-old ex-convict Kenneth Davison landed in a cell for four months, for his fifth reckless driving rap. Another couple of speed fiends also in their twenties (you may notice an age pattern here), Gerald Van Wormer and Frank Bond ended their lives at Lakeside Cemetery, next to Diana Gardner, but in their case by crashing into a tree on the cemetery grounds.

277

A few columns of newsprint away from the Van Wormer / Bond death story in the *Times Herald* the FMC excitedly proclaimed that its new 205 horsepower Lincoln car engine had taken away from Chrysler the title of: *The most powerful engine in any standard automobile...* It seemed that the Lincoln had swept the first four places in its class in a Mexican road race, covering 1,938 miles on public roads in 21 hours, about 90 miles per hour on average. Better get out of the way there, *amigos*. Lincoln went back to Mexico the following year and, *que lastima*, the field killed eight spectators watching this same race.

In Detroit cops arrested the near legendary figure of 22 year-old Richard Heathfield 16 times for hot rodding. They once fired some wild gunshots at his car to try to stop him, and killed a 14 year-old bystander instead. Finally Heathfield went to a psychiatric hospital where doctors found him to be psychopathic, though not insane. The same diagnosis could be said to apply to most automobile designers in Detroit. Luminaries like stylist Pinin Farina made good ad copy by boasting about the speeds they achieved in their designs: *I have driven the Nash Golden Airflyte and I tell you it is magnificent. So responsive, so fast, so eager to go.*

"It's about time somebody slapped down these young punks!" That's what Port Huron City Councilman Kenneth Ramsey said, meaning the hot rodders not the car companies, though both needed it. Mayor Thomas Woods, a junior college teacher turned car salesman, agreed, and said these "race track terrorists" posed the same danger as a man firing a rifle down the street. At a meeting of the Citizens Traffic and Safety Committee at Port Huron's Lauth Hotel, Michigan Auto Club official Ernest Davis blamed public apathy for the situation: "We impose fines which in many cases are mere gestures, while in the case of a thief, who most of the time has inflicted far less damage on society than the traffic violator, we mete out two to five year prison terms. A single accident caused by someone not observing a traffic law may result in thousands of dollars worth of damage and in many cases serious injury or death."[2]

And as far as effectively disciplining juvenile traffic offenders, don't make me laugh, said Davis. One 16 year-old St. Clair City boy who'd cracked up his car and killed his 15 year-old friend in the process, had pleaded guilty to negligent homicide, then received two years probation and a court order to attend church. Another 16 year-old, Gerald Lindsay, paid $150, accepted two years probation, and wrote a court-ordered 500-word essay "My Carelessness Cost a Life":

If only I had kept the speed under 50 miles per hour...my friend, Bernard Martin, would be alive today and my other friends and myself would not have been maimed, scarred and crippled.[3]

At the time of this wreck Murphy had been hauling a carful of friends, including Martin, to a hayride. He'd just come from a meeting of the Twin Carbs car club, dedicated to "SAFETY at all times and places," when he plowed into a bridge support.

Shaking off their apathy, 100 petitioners demanded action from the Port Huron council about maniacal speeds on Main Street between 3p.m. and 2a.m., a pretty wide window of lawlessness. Cars and trucks frequently went by at 70-80 mph. These voters wanted more cops out there, but this idea cooled off the council's ardor on traffic safety in a hurry. Hold on, said the mayor, let's not go overboard, additional cops will be expensive. Splitting the difference, Woods and his colleagues ordered the city manager

278

to institute a crackdown by the present-sized police force. Don't jail any "respectable citizens," just the punks. This seemed a safe temporary alternative. The council also passed a new comprehensive traffic ordinance, duly published in several columns of the newspaper, in case anybody was interested. Port Huron police had to enforce so many state and local traffic laws on the books, laws of such complexity, that by one estimate 262 of these statutes contradicted each other.

Obliging their employers, the police ticketed 195 drivers for speeding in October 1951, compared to 29 in June, which gives some idea of the easygoing liberality which had been observed previously. Police could have written several hundred more citations because their new electronic speed meter found half the drivers in Port Huron broke the limits. So officers upped the ante, and ticketed 81 drivers in a single day at a single intersection. The speed problems went right on. Traffic cops caught 27 year-old Robert Zuehlke twice in one hour on the same street, going south at 60 mph, then north at 75. Another apprehendee, August Lasky, took one look at the Port Huron police car that had stopped him and said, "You got me this time but the next time I come through town you won't catch me – not with that thing." Lasky's record already included three reckless driving busts and one for negligent homicide, so this was no idle threat.

Detroit Times reporter Harry Taylor dug a bit into the phenomenon of unstoppable road outlaws like Lasky. His startling conclusion: "The State of Michigan is issuing licenses to kill!" One reason for the kill permits: the state still had no uniform procedures for issuing driving licenses. It left the matter up to local authorities in most cases, the only state in America to do so. Many locals required no test of any kind for a license renewal – no vision, hearing or written exams. Some public servants okayed licenses over the phone. The cops in one town filled in the examination for the applicants. One county sheriff approved licenses for two blind people. Port Huron's Yager Optical seized on this issue: "Safe Driving Demands Good Vision. Wise motorists know that if driving is hampered by poor vision you are heading for trouble..."

Thousands of phony names and addresses on file prevented the service of 40% of Michigan traffic summons. One driver turned up by Taylor carried four different Michigan driving licenses, all with different first names, because he thought it would be handy to have some spares. A complete lack of record-keeping coordination led to hit-or-miss license suspensions and revocations for drivers like August Lasky. As had other investigators before him, Taylor also found much too much leniency for traffic offenses. When Charles Bankson attended a hearing in Port Huron about his third traffic ticket in three months, he faced license revocation or probation. Let off with six months probation, Bankson celebrated by rolling his car over on top of himself in a fatal crash the same evening. Michigan's chief law enforcement officer Attorney General Thomas Kavanaugh racked up five traffic tickets in 18 months, three of them for speeding. To nobody's surprise, Kavanaugh also drove off with just probation, and eventually he became Chief Justice of the Michigan Supreme Court! Harry Taylor's investigation eventually helped get more of the licensing process assigned to the Michigan Secretary of State, along with responsibility for keeping a centralized record bureau, but neither he nor anyone else knew of a way to stop the unworthy from driving without a license.

"...[T]he killing and maiming of human beings by automobiles has reached the point where it is a national emergency," said the President's Conference on Highway

Safety. A fine sentiment, but nobody treated it much like an emergency. America in 1951 struggled with another mess in the Far East, the Korean War, but the fighting didn't compare to the Horsepower War when it came to piling up the casualties. In a replay of the embarrassing WW2 parallel, during the first nine months of hostilities in Korea, 9,600 American soldiers died, while back home during the same period 28,400 people expired in traffic accidents, which injured 25 times as many as the war wounded. This moved President Harry Truman to call the automobile "the most deadly weapon man has yet invented," and this came from the man who had ordered the dropping of the atomic bomb.(4) At the present rate of attrition, statisticians calculated that one-half of all Americans could look forward to death or injury from the Highway Hiroshima of auto accidents in their lifetimes. Maybe more if they kept driving like the contestants in that new entertainment attraction out at St. Clair County's Sunset Speedway, the Demolition Derby.

52 year-old Elma Wishmeir of Cleveland fell like a flipped coin into the Too Bad half of the American population. The National Safety Council nominated her, posthumously, for the title of the 1 millionth person killed by automobiles in America. A truck clobbered Elma in her home town during December of 1951, she lingered along for 11 days, then died a Levassor death. Herman Dengel, who hailed from no place else but Dearborn, Michigan, Henry Ford's hometown, drove the death truck. The Safety Council didn't bother to sort out for special recognition the 50 millionth American injured by automobiles so far.

In another of its regular spasmodic attempts at virtue on this issue, the *Times Herald* agreed that, "The greatest killer of them all, as far as the United States is concerned, is the automobile, not war." Mixed in with its idolatrous praise of the car culture, the voluminous new and used car ads, and the auto companies' public relations handouts masquerading as news, the paper now published photographs of mangled accident vehicles, and occasionally a corpse, like the above mentioned Elvester Moss. The paper made a further effort to shake people up by running "10 Seconds to Live," a syndicated moment-to-moment "you are there"- type story about an imaginary car crash. The fictional protagonist, a man driving in the rain with bad wipers, rear-ended a truck: "Horror numbed everything into slow motion. He was floating right into the near corner of the truck bed. He opened his mouth to scream. NO SECONDS TO LIVE." The author of "10 Seconds", Raymond Eastman, ran out of seconds himself when he drove his Jaguar into a bridge abutment in Iowa.(5)

A nagging litany of driving instructions also flowed across the *Times Herald's* pages: slow down, be cautious, obey the laws, don't tailgate, drive courteously, drive defensively. Readers even were subjected to a series on "Unwritten Rules of the Road," and a fat lot of help they were, just make up your own as you go along. More constructively, editors continued Louis Weil's policy against unwritten drunks of the road, and published with intent to humiliate the names and facts about intoxicated local drivers like Clarence La Turno on the front page. These became nearly as regular a feature as the weather report and the comic strips.

The paper profiled a few local survivors of bad accidents, an interesting look at some aftermaths. Case File #1: An anonymous 18 year-old whose spine had been crushed in a 1947 wreck. His family had spent $7000 on medical bills, sold their home and business, exhausted their savings. State aid amounted to $60. The victim, who'd had no insurance, lived in a wheelchair and revolving bed to allow him to turn over. File #2: The similarly afflicted 21 year-old Ervin Sager, paralyzed from the waist down after his brother rammed their car into a snowbank. Sager now spent 21 hours per day face down in a hospital bed, the other 3 face up. File #3: The story of a young widow and mother whose husband missed a curve on the Gratiot Pike and met a tree. "With three children to take care of, the mother can't very well take a job," sympathized the reporter. "Even if she could, she has no car to get to work."(6) In other words, no car to lose her own life in.

The uncomprehending attitude about the inherently dangerous nature of automobiles, even when they had obliterated immediate family members, the epic conceit of auto sickness at work, the Ford euphoria, all left the American driving public as a whole convinced: it can't happen to me. But happen it did, to Port Huron native Evelyn Korzynski, whose believe-it-or-not story also made the *Times Herald:* "A Detroit woman, on her way to see her husband, was killed near Emmett Sunday when the automobile in which she was riding collided with a car driven by her husband. He was on his way to meet her."(7)

With Granger Weil at the wheel, who'd taken command from his ailing father, the *Times Herald* veered back and forth on the subject of automobile life as wildly as any drunk driver. And no wonder. The leading newspaper advertisers in America were, you guessed it, General Motors, Ford and Chrysler, who spent more than $100 million combined annually. In a single edition lovesick columnist Louis Dunn wrote that the American automobile "has grace and style about it that makes it a thing of beauty and a joy forever." This bound Port Huroners emotionally to their cars, said Dunn. On another page readers learned that the joy forever had ended forever for two people in fatal city crashes the previous month while 125 others had had their feelings hurts in lesser wrecks.

Granger Weil served as chairman of the Michigan Press Association's traffic safety committee, but one day his sheet roared like a lion on the safety subject, the next day it bleated like a lamb. When readers demanded lower speed limits in Port Huron, the meek editorial reply said no, just "set a good example" and maybe other drivers would follow. Were deafening engine noises, screeching brakes, loud horns, and defective mufflers a problem? "We have to depend on the respect every American is supposed to have for the laws...it's just too bad that our dependence so often is misplaced." After all, friends, 59 million drivers in America were using 53 million cars and trucks daily in 1952, driving a billion miles per day; you couldn't babysit them all. Reversing course a few days later, the editors damned "Jekyll and Hyde" drivers: "honorable men, men of politeness and good manners, men who would not think of trying to rush through a door, who will break their necks to beat you to the next stoplight."(8) Men like Detroit Traffic Judge Joseph Gillis, arrested for a road rage brawl, trying to beat some sense into another motorist.

Another national auto safety congress held in Chicago at this time took on some of the tones of a revival meeting, especially when Paul Jones took to the pulpit on behalf of the National Safety Council to lash American driving habits as: "...the greatest mass demonstration of gutter manners ever seen in this country. The marvel is not that so many people are killed and maimed but that so many manage to survive. This boorish traffic behavior goes deeper than mere lack of manners. It reflects the same attributes of greed, selfishness and disregard for the rights of others that bring about black marketing, bribery, corruption and the current slump in old fashioned morality that is bothering us so much right now." The psycho argument also got another workout at this meeting, courtesy of psychiatrist Dr. Alan Canty of the Detroit Auto Clinic: "The chronic traffic violator is a social problem child. His behavior is but a symptom of his personality maladjustment. The fellow who blasts his horn to bully his way through traffic, the fellow who wants to race you in a traffic light getaway, and the smart alec who defies traffic regulations are mentally off."(9)

"I figure all the other drivers on the road are crazy." A roomful of listeners at Port Huron's Harrington Hotel heard this happy motoring tip in person from renowned race driver Ab Jenkins of Salt Lake City, the Mormon Meteor. Ab calculated that he'd driven 2,000,000 miles among the crazies over the years, without an accident, and he'd never so much as paid a heavy fine, just spent a few nights and weekends in jail, but hey, hadn't everybody? The loonies behind the wheel killed or injured 1,300,000 Americans less adept than Ab in 1953. Naturally, the bigger the perpetrator's name, the more press it got. In one incident which tickled the public's fancy, entertainer Bing Crosby's Mercedes Benz collided with another car in Los Angeles, breaking a back, a jaw and a nose belonging to the riders in the other vehicle. Later the victims sued Crosby for $1 million, claiming the Groaner had been drunk when this happened. They extracted a $100,000 settlement from him.

The celebrity car miseries also tripped up TV and radio star Dave Garroway, who'd barely finished a promotional film for the new Chevrolet sports car before he had an auto wreck in Miami. This news made an interesting counterpoint to the Garroway ad campaign: "*They call her Corvette, and she belongs to the highway, just for the sheer and simple joy of driving. For the open road and the country by-way, for Mr. and Mrs. America in a carefree mood.*" Ed Sullivan suffered a head-on crash going home from his Lincoln-Mercury sponsored TV show. His broken ribs and bruises knocked him off the air for a while and he missed the debut of Elvis Presley. Broadcaster Arthur Godfrey, the soul of amiability on the air, a man who counted General Motors president Charles Wilson as one of his personal friends, and who hosted a TV broadcast of the GM fantasy pageant "Motorama" at the Waldorf Astoria Hotel in New York, limped into the hospital for further treatment of traffic injuries 22 years old. The details: "The 49 year-old Godfrey suffered 27 fractures when his car collided with a truck in Washington, D.C., in 1931 and he has been in almost constant pain since then."(10)

The most significant car accident of the decade probably occurred to U.S. Congressman Kenneth Roberts of Alabama. It happened on the way back from his 1953 honeymoon. Roberts and his wife found that their wedding presents survived the crash better than the couple themselves did because the gifts had been wrapped in protective packaging. A light bulb went on. The lawmaker persuaded the House of Representatives to create a subcommittee on automobile safety with himself as chairman. He subsequently earned the nickname "Seat Belt Roberts" after recommending that car seat belts be made mandatory. "Brother, were we laughed at!" Roberts recalled later.(11) But the American College of Surgeons didn't laugh, and issued a blast against carmakers for only offering seat belts as optional equipment. The surgeons rang down damnation on excessive horsepower, too. So did Maryland governor Theodore McKeldi ("horsepower derby of death and destruction") and Illinois governor William Stratton ("absurdity of the automaker horsepower claims in light of the present speed laws").

These people just didn't get it, according to Buick. Extra horses meant a "safety-surge of power...Words just can't describe it." But they tried.

You can hardly hear its whispered might – but man, you sure can feel it. It's power almost without limit – power that humbles the hills, melts the miles, makes you monarch of all you survey. First time you tickle the gas pedal you'll know what we mean. When you need a still greater flow of get-up-and-go for safety's sake, you merely switch the pitch and you zoom out of tight spots.

However, switch the pitch as much as the industry tried, Seat Belt Roberts wouldn't be put off so easily.

The political power of the U.S. automobile industry probably reached its zenith during the early 1950's, when for a short time it reigned almost supreme. Coming as it did in the middle of the Cold War, Russia's *Soviet Encyclopedia* published an embarrassingly accurate description of the situation: "Michigan's automobile magnates not only keep the economy, the administrative apparatus, and the press of the state in their hands, but they also play a big part in the economic and political life of the whole country."(12) Although President Truman placed only trivial production curbs on the automakers during the Korean War, even these modest reductions aroused resentment in Henry Ford II and GM's Charles Wilson. How dare foreign policy interfere with auto policy? Fed up anyway with union friendly Democrats, the Big 3 got busy for Republican candidate General Dwight Eisenhower during the 1952 Presidential campaign, squeezing their dealers for contributions.(13) Of, course, the United Auto Workers union did nothing less in its own fashion for Eisenhower's opponent, Adlai Stevenson.

Once in the White House, Eisenhower rewarded victorious Autodom with three Cabinet seats, one for Engine Charlie Wilson as the new Secretary of Defense, another for Flint Chevrolet dealer Arthur Summerfield as Postmaster General, and the last for former Chevy and Cadillac dealer Donald McKay as Secretary of the Interior. What Summerfield knew about the job could have been written on a postage stamp, and Wilson famously told his confirmation hearing "I always thought what was good for the country was good for General Motors, and vice versa."(14) But far more importantly, Eisenhower put a member of the GM board of directors, his former military aide General Lucius Clay, in charge of drawing up a gigantic World of Tomorrow national highway program, which promised to be plenty good for General Motors, and the rest of the automakers too, though not necessarily for the country. Not wanting to give the impression that he was in GM's pocket, President Eisenhower also made time for a chummy get-together with the Ford Motor honchos not long after assuming office. It seemed that the prez once had owned a souped up Model T he'd used for road fun back in the 1920's, until some parts thieves stole its carburetor and ignition system, and probably struck a blow for public safety in the process.

Ford appreciated a Presidential pat on the back in 1953, its 50th year in business, a year the company spent rolling in self-love. *How beautiful is a Ford? A great English poet, John Keats, once wrote 'Beauty is Truth, Truth is Beauty.' Well, he could have been writing about our car...* The depth of this infatuation filled the pages of the FMC's industrial autobiography *Ford at 50*, published the same year, a book in its own way as remarkable as the Founder's *My Life and Work*. This volume *Ford at 50* revealed one of the most unsettling auto facts of the day, that looks now almost entirely

283

governed car design:

Few Ford people work with less restriction than Gil Spear, Jr., and the designers on his staff in the Advanced Styling studio. Nobody tells them what to do. Their job is simply to draw sketches of any kind of idea for a new car that happens to come into their heads. A magazine picture of a tropical fish may inspire a sketch for a fender, or the nose of a jet fighter may lead to a contour for a hood. Recent trends have been toward cars built as low, long and wide as possible. Considering the limits of parking spaces, garages and visibility, the present type of automobile, with its engine in front of the driver, can hardly be made much lower, longer or wider.(15)

Of course, the buyer still had the last say, but Ford reckoned:...*he always buys the biggest car he can afford. Today's Ford is larger, heavier and more elaborate than the Ford of 1930 because the public wants it that way.* The FMC offered a 1953 product line with 378 possible passenger car combinations from fish fenders to fighter nose hoods. It could crank out 9,000 vehicles per day through its network of 50 plants and parts depots in America. The company cleared $200 million on $4 billion in sales in 1954.(16) The following year Ford offered the public some non-voting shares in the company, making them silent, powerless partners, just the kind Grandpa Henry would have wanted. The company's net worth reached $2.4 billion.

To keep the good times rolling at the manufacturing end, Ford started a sales practice known as the Blitz among its dealers. According to industry critic John Keats (not the poet), blitzing typically began with a big PR campaign involving musical bands, free eats, giveaways, and deceptive advertising, the latter a Ford tradition as old as the company. Customers foolish enough to be lured into a Ford dealer's premises were bounced back and forth between salesmen, who quoted a constantly shifting price on a new car, cheated on trade-ins, and slapped buyers with a list of surprise option, delivery, preparation, tax, license, and miscellaneous charges as long as your arm. American carmakers padded their profits by $200 million per year just in phony shipping charges.(17) In some extreme cases Ford salesmen "unhorsed" their bewildered victims; took a potential trade-in into the dealership garage allegedly to examine, then refused to return it.(18) Automobiles carried no listed prices, leaving dealers free to make them up on the spot, a valuable tool in working the Blitz picked up by the other auto companies. After enough of this chicanery the feds finally ordered prices displayed on vehicles beginning in 1958.(19)

The biggest share of the average auto dealer's profit, when he made any, came from financing and insuring the 150 new and 225 used cars he sold in a year. Draper Chevrolet in Port Huron reaped an extra $240 on a $1,764 Chevy by financing it for a customer who wanted something new.

Chevy puts punch in the old word 'new' because it's totally new, temptingly new, youthfully new, and truthfully new. See, drive, and get the feel of the all new '58 Chevrolet. It's all new and almost too new, too great, too good to be true.

By mid-decade installment contracts lasted up to 36 months on an average $2,000 new car. A Ford customer typically bought a new one every three years, jumping back into the financial hole he'd just climbed out of. And the hole deepened. Wholesale car prices rose 50% during the Fifties, twice the overall inflation rate.(20)

According to one cost breakdown, a family with $6,000 in annual income spent 25% of its money on taxes, 25% on food, 20% on housing, and of the rest $650 on a car. Farmers on average spent $1,700 per year on mechanized equipment, three-quarters of that on cars and trucks. Not surprisingly, a University of Michigan study in the mid-50's found that the average American family held just $350 in liquid assets. By 1960 80% of U.S. households owned a motor vehicle, while experts as diverse as the U.S. Treasury and Institute of Life Insurance warned against consumer overspending. "Get Out of Debt!!" urged a loan consolidator in Port Huron. Get Out of Your Car would have been more practical advice.

Nothing guaranteed profits at the auto retail level, and nothing much guaranteed the cars either. Warranties on new ones lasted 4 months or 3,000 miles in the early 50's, later extended to 1 year and 12,000 miles on "major parts." Even that timid a promise cramped some dealers' style. They lost money selling new cars while the manufacturers rolled in dough. The Ford and Chevy dealers in Detroit sometimes redressed this imbalance by conspiring to fix prices. Fix or no fix, in Port Huron, after 34 years as a Ford tradesman, Alfred Parfet chose the Golden Anniversary year of 1953 to call it quits. His son-in-law Sanford Ladd already having left the business for a slightly less disreputable career in lawyering, Parfet conferred the Ford franchise on his sales manager, Charles Rossie.

Rossie enthusiastically announced his inheritance to Port Huron: *Headache or Joy...which will it be this winter? Make it Joy by buying one of our A-1 Used Cars!* Rossie quickly found out why Parfet had left, more headaches than joy. Used car prices dropped 42% in 1953, and 25% of all the used car dealers in America went out of business. A saturated market for used cars spelled serious trouble indeed because secondhand car sales outnumbered new by 2 to 1, and underwrote the whole ball game. Trade-in's furnished the down payment on most new car purchases and then had to be redisposed of themselves. In 1954 39% of all U.S. car dealers lost money, and 1,700 new car dealers went under completely. Rossie threw in the towel after one year, the first of three men who came and went as the Ford agent in Port Huron during the balance of the 1950's, before a man named Ken Gardner managed to get a foothold.

This parade of losers did business from the new FMC-subsidized showroom on 10th Street, which replaced some homes knocked out of the way for this Albert Kahn-style modernist glass and concrete emporium. Port Huron architect Walter Wyeth bafflingly said that he'd designed the new Ford shop "to increase neighborliness in what was formerly a residential neighborhood." None of the remaining homeowners nearby showed much reciprocal neighborliness at having a new car lot next door. Or even worse, a used car lot. The used iron inventory grew so enormous that dealers needed to move further and further away from the city center to get more room, biting into new territory across the city and in some cases out into the suburbs. Aghast at this invasion, Gardendale passed its first regulation of used car lots and auto junkyards. Ground-hungry Harold Draper abandoned downtown Port Huron completely, the first big-time car dealer to do so. He took the whole Chevrolet bandwagon, new and used, out to a farm-sized undeveloped 27-acre site on Port Huron's south side, and put up a 28,000 square foot store surrounded by asphalt.

In addition to its other troubles in Port Huron, Ford's spectacular automobile bust of the decade, the Edsel, proved to be especially disheartening locally. Ford introduced the Edsel – again copying General Motors' methods – to fill a "price gap" in the FMC car lineup. A dealer recruit from Detroit with the agreeable name of Tony Carr put up the Edsel banner at a separate Main Street salesroom in Port Huron in September 1957. After 30 years in the auto business, Carr's big chance to run his own show had arrived. The big chance lasted five months before Carr closed his doors. Ford launched the clumsy, boxy, 345-horsepower Edsel with the familiar brag that it contained the biggest passenger car engine in America, but this couldn't overcome the vehicle's homeliness. One outsider said the Edsel's puckered grille looked like an Oldsmobile sucking on a lemon. *Dramatic Edsel styling is here to stay,* insisted the FMC, a couple of months before dropping the brand. The $250 million national failure of the Edsel in just two years left its mark on Henry Ford II. He'd told his staff that they could name the project anything *but* Edsel, rather than risk equating his poor father's name with a flop. Then he let himself be talked into it by by his right-hand man Ernie Breech.(21) Breech's star waned at the FMC from that point.

Like his longtime rival Al Parfet, John Cawood also hung up his guns during the 1950's, and handed the Port Huron Buick and Pontiac dealership to his son-in-law Charles Barrett. In Cawood's case, though, it made a generous legacy. The average GM new car dealer cleared $2,700 profit per month in 1955, and Cawood did a lot better than average.(22) John's decision to retire came after he suffered yet another traffic accident, hit by a car as he walked across a Main Street intersection, which landed him in Port Huron Hospital with a broken leg. Journalists did not exempt car dealers from the traditional blame-it-on-the-pedestrian assumption, and in reading the press report of this incident Cawood learned that he had "walked into the side of a car." Considering how much physical punishment the 70 year-old dealer had taken from automobiles over the years, he could count himself lucky still to be on his feet at all. And he'd dodged another bullet just months earlier when a furnace explosion and fire destroyed his downtown dealership, burning up 36 cars and doing $500,000 in damage. The initial blast occurred as Cawood and his salesmen met in the front office, congratulating themselves on their best month ever.

Hobbling about on his crutches with the broken leg, the old snake charmer bowed out with a farewell used car sale, offering to bring one of his bargains to the shopper's door for inspection, like the prize '48 Buick going for $53, about a 97% loss of its original value in eight years. Sonny boy Charles Barrett took over not just the new car dealership, but also Cawood's two used car lots, a repair shop and a car wash. Since the war, Barrett had picked up the knack for auto trading and repair hijinks from his boss right handy. He bragged of personally making $100,000 per year during the Fifties, and as a sideline used his car swag to build a $200,000 autocentric Howard Johnson's chain motel and restaurant next to the Blue Water Bridge.

Their dealers might be having a mixed time of it, but by mid-decade the FMC and General Motors fell under government suspicion of being a little too successful, too muscular. Despite the Eisenhower administration's close ties to Detroit, the Justice Department started a probe of the near monopoly of the auto industry by GM and Ford, who together took a combined 84% of a market of 9 million new car and light truck sales in 1955.(23) Alarmed by the suggestion of collusion and monopoly, the two companies ordered their executives to stop socializing together. It hardly needs emphasizing that had any two railroads cornered 84% of the American train market the heavens would have shaken with the government's wrath. In '55 GM alone earned $1 billion, a 28% return on investment.(24) That meant that a big shareholder like the redoubtable Charles Mott reaped $5 million per year in dividends. Harlow Curtice, a flamboyant Flint resident who succeeded Charles Wilson as GM president, made the cover of *Time* magazine for realizing the firm's bonanza.

Alfred Sloan had stepped down as the grand old man at GM, which left Curtice to open the huge and handsome new technical center, all 900 acres and 27 buildings of it, on television in 1956, in front of a band and a cheering grandstand in the Detroit suburb of Warren.(25) Eliel and Eero Saarinen, two of the few architects who actually could make modernism work, designed the place. 1,200 of the 4,000 tech center employees labored at that most critical element of auto construction, styling, but unlike the Saarinens they couldn't make it work.(26) Curtice also presided over the parades, pageants and dinners at GM's 50th birthday party in Flint. He dedicated a new $7.4 million Flint cultural center, built mainly on the theme that automobiles equal happiness. "Sometimes I go to the park and place my car in the lot, give it a nice pose and admire it, the way the sunshine catches it and how pretty it looks. I'm almost in love with it." A Flint teenager said this in 1958, and the cultural center immortalized his declaration on the walls of the Alfred Sloan Museum. It is the east, and General Motors is the sun.

Sharply different from Sloan in operational methods, Harlow Curtice had been cast more in the mold of Billy Durant, as a committee-hater who made snap decisions on his own. Curtice later accidentally shot the head off a former GM vice president in a duck blind not far from Port Huron, when he made a snap decision about the angle of fire. GM's 50th didn't pass unnoticed in Port Huron, where Blue Water Auto Restorers Club leader J. Kenneth Weller, a pickle company president, proudly displayed his 50 year-old 1908 Buick, a zombie which he proudly had raised from the dead.

General Motors also continued to expand its test track space during the '50's, as did Ford, Chrysler, and the remaining carmakers. Ever since the 1920's they'd spent millions building these tracks, on tens of thousands of hidden acres in Michigan and Arizona, allegedly to perfect cars and trucks. However, since the manufacturers didn't run these tracks with thousands of vehicles crowded together in stop and go city traffic jams or in high speed bumper to bumper highway traffic; didn't litter them with trash, potholes, distracting billboards, or confusing and unintelligible road directions signs and signals; didn't populate the tracks with pedestrians, bicyclists, children or animals at all hours of the day and night; didn't use test drivers in various stages of sobriety, sanity, or senility, or any suffering from epilepsy, palsy or angina, or any under the influence of sedatives, narcotics or antihistamines (all of which doctors cited as dangerous for driving), the tracks fell short of duplicating actual driving conditions in America. One notable point of similarity achieved on the 4.7 mile-long banked six-lane Chrysler track, boredom, required installation of special signals to keep the drivers awake during long test runs.(27)

Occasionally the Ford test drivers, who collectively put in 5 million miles per year, took camouflaged new models out onto the streets to mingle with millions of real drivers. So did Chrysler, with hood masks like the Lone Ranger's tied over the front grilles. They disguised these vehicles not to protect them from damage but from copycats. To hear Detroit tell it, letting another carmaker get even a glance at the trivial and superficial styling differences in a new model meant ruin, millions of dollars up the

287

chimney in retooling costs. This obsession reached the point where General Motors had a couple of policemen and a turncoat security guard arrested for selling photos of its unreleased designs for $1,000, about what Harlow Curtice earned by lunchtime every day.

It was a bum rap in any case, because the automakers themselves often fed these photos to car magazines and newspapers in order to whet the appetite of a public easily bamboozled by a lot of noise over nothing. GM in fact supplied major car parts to both Ford and Chrysler, so how secret could these things be? (28) Not for secrecy but mainly for their own safety, test drivers for all the auto companies preferred motoring on their own private preserves because tracks were 25 times safer than the mean streets of America. The test track also served as the best place to stage favorite advertising stunts like the old blindfold gag. Flacks took handpicked consumers wearing blindfolds around the track a few times in a car and extracted a few helpful quotes: *The Dodge Blindfold Test Really Amazed Me - bumpy roads felt smooth as highways*!

Dodge's parent, Chrysler, had difficulty in negotiating its bumpy financial roads during the 50's. The company tripped up badly after a long UAW strike early in the decade, and even more than its competitors fixated on 1) big engines and 2) tail fins, *the style touch of the future.* In a decade full of promotional excess Chrysler's advertising at times amounted to little more than incoherent babbling:

Suddenly It's 1960...In one flaming moment, Plymouth leaps 3 full years ahead...Step into the wonderful world of AUTODYNAMICS...It tames a tornado of torque...It breaks through the vibration barrier...It is swept-wing mastery of motion...It unleashes a hurricane of power from a thundering new aircraft-type Super Red Ram V-8 engine that's a spitfire in action....more wheel-turning power than any other passenger car engine in the world...a good companion as well as an obedient servant...Adventure begins the moment you rev the lion-hearted '59 Chrysler...Want to pass a car or a truck on the highway? You don't have to kick the throttle to the floor. Just touch lightly...and ZOOM!

The rest of the American automaking competition faded fast during this decade. *Sooner or later, every quality-conscious family falls in love with a Packard,* or so Port Huron dealer Bob Lane thought in the early Fifties. But nothing is fickler than car love, and Packard went the way of the 4,000 by the end of the decade. Studebaker sales collapsed 60% in just one year, 1954, putting many of its assembly line workers up against it. Former Indiana farm boy Robert Milner, married with 2 kids, had been making $350 per month at Studebaker in brighter days. He'd bought a 5 room house, a new car every year, a TV, fridge, and furniture on time, and saved little. Now he scraped by on $120 monthly working part time, his savings had disappeared, he'd sold his latest new car and replaced it with a secondhander, the family had purchased no new clothes in a year, and shunned restaurants or travel. Milner now lived life as a Studebaker customer wannabe, unable to afford his own product.

Nash and Hudson merged under duress in 1954 to form the American Motors Corporation, and struck a deal with Walt Disney for an important TV endorsement:

A dream is a wish your heart makes
When you see a star.
A Nash is the star of car makes

It outshines all others by far.
If you keep on believing
The wish that you dream will come true.
You'll love Nash for '55 or my name isn't Jiminy Cricket.

But neither Jiminy nor Davy Crockett nor the offers of free trips to Disneyland moved enough product, and if you kept on believing in Nash you were out of luck. AMC chief executive George Romney, the auto industry coordinator from WW2, replaced both the Nash and Hudson brands with a distinguished bicycle name revived from the past, Rambler. Romney lobbied the government hard to get the big boys, Ford and GM, broken up into several smaller companies, and he sometimes spoke with alarming forthrightness about the crummy quality control in American cars:

Recently I overheard two men talking about cars. One said, "I'm just sick. I paid $5,000 for my car and in less than six months it rattles and squeaks like a milk wagon. And they can't seem to do anything about it!" Unhappily this is a remark that is heard far too often.(29)

Romney made a concerted effort to promote smaller, more economical cars, figuring not everyone wanted a 19 foot Cadillac, or a 9-passenger "bowling alley big" Ford station wagon, about the maximum length passenger cars reached. However, Romney didn't want anybody mistaking Rambler for a sissy car: *Look at this honey! Look at its sleek, low lines. It's pure 'custom' and a powerhouse! Whips along the highway, romps over the hills, handles and parks easier than any sedan you've known before.* The smaller-is-beautiful angle met with some success during the late '50's. "Compact" European imports like the French Renault and German Volkswagen and the first trickle of Japanese models all combined to take 10% of the U.S. market in 1959. Port Huron dealer Andy Falk sold the mini, 40 miles per gallon Renaults next to his behemoth Cadillacs, which were more than four feet longer, what critic Edward Durrell Stone unkindly called "four feet of vulgarity."

In response to the compact fad the Big 3 turned out their own brand of small cars, like the rear-engined, air-cooled Chevrolet Corvair, which resembled the Volkswagen, only less compact, less solid, less stable, and more expensive. The Corvair promptly ran up an uneviable accident record. The son of Cadillac's general manager died in a Corvair crash, the son of a General Motors executive vice-president suffered brain damage in another Corvair wreck, and the niece of Semon "Bunkie" Knudsen, Chevrolet's general manager, took a bad mangling in a third Corvair incident. Knudsen threatened to quit the company if he didn't get an okay for a Corvair redesign.(30) American compacts barely had hit the market before they started growing larger in size and price, into "luxury compacts." As Henry Ford II put it, "Small cars mean small profits."

While foreign carmakers sent compacts to America, the export of standard sized U.S. autos to other countries virtually halted. "There is no heavy demand for American style cars in other countries," reported Associated Press, "because they are too big, too powerful and too costly, both to buy and to operate."(31) They cost more than 10 cents per mile to run in America (even with cheap gas), sometimes much more, not including repairs.(32) When the inevitable malfunction occurred, the newest features on these vehicles meant higher repair bills. Author John Keats counted 50 electrical devices on a single model alone. Goofy gadgetry meant 120,000 Ford mechanics had to

289

be retrained after a single model changeover, while GM ran 30 different training centers for its grease monkeys. This training also fully qualified these men, once they got a vehicle up on the hoist, to look for ways to add unneeded work to repair bills.(33)

What with breakdowns, maintenance, unnecessary tinkering, and of course crackups, all on a rapidly expanding automobile population, the amount of service work done on cars at one typical Ford dealership increased 500% in seven years.(34) GM expected its average franchisee to keep 1,600 cars on the road. The Plymouth dealer in Port Huron ran his service bays from 7:30 a.m. to midnight seven days a week to cope with the workload. Independents like Herber's Collision also toiled away to meet the demands of the rolling nation, because, said Herber, "In these great United States of ours, the citizens practically live on wheels..." Just as in Henry Ford's day, the quality of repair service frequently came into some question, as when a mechanic for Bezenah's Brake Service in Port Huron died in a crash while test-driving a machine whose brakes he'd allegedly just fixed. The public wondered as to whether these $10,000 a year wrench jockeys really knew how to handle everything from an $11.95 tune-up (parts extra), to blown tires, to the 10% of the automobiles involved in Port Huron accidents which had to be towed from the collision scene to a garage.

Owing to the growing complexity of auto design, do-it-yourselfers now undertook less than 10% of auto repairs and maintenance. In one respect this improved things, since home mechanics in Port Huron sometimes choked the new sewage treatment plant by pouring used motor oil down their garage drains. Plenty of people just decided to skip expensive maintenance altogether, with the result that a 1954 survey rated 1/4 of all motor vehicles in the U.S defective, usually with bad brakes, lights, steering, exhaust, tires, etc.

Another refrain in the cyclical song of the auto industry broke out in the middle of the decade. Hardly had the record new car sales year of 1955 closed than the Big 3 automakers, having glutted the market once again, started their own round of worker layoffs. Legions of factory hands went through the back end of the same binge and purge routine Robert Milner had lived through at Studebaker. The 16% of American businesses now tied in some way to the automobile industry backtracked rapidly. *U.S. News and World Report* magazine took a look-see:

Already Detroit and her sister industrial cities are being hurt by the layoffs. Savings are being depleted. Evictions are increasing. Some workers buying homes are losing them. Cars, home appliances and TV sets purchased on credit are being repossessed. Neighborhood merchants generally appear to be hard hit. So do dealers in new and used cars..."(35)

As though this sort of thing had never happened before, the UAW on its 20th anniversary in 1956 threw a conniption fit about the layoffs, blasting the "unbelievable greed and inhumanity of the automobile industry." The fact that in some years auto executives numbered 9 of the top 10 best paid business people in America deepened the UAW's resentment. But if automakers were so greedy and inhumane, why work for them? The union wouldn't own up to its own avarice. Michigan paid the highest unemployment compensation in America, but the UAW demanded and got from the car companies extra layoff bucks for its overextended membership, half a million of whom lived in Michigan. As a result, the Big 3 looked more closely at the idea of moving assembly operations to "right-to-work" states that banned closed shops.

290

During the subsequent recession, when new vehicle sales fell as "low" as 5.5 million in 1958, federal labor bureaucrats dubbed Detroit and Port Huron "chronic surplus labor" cities for their high unemployment in both good times and bad. Port Huron's jobless rate hit 17% during this period. The Michigan state government went back to the same financial cliff edge it had teetered on during the 1930's. The 29 new and used auto dealers in the Port Huron area and their 400 employees joined hands in the touching "You Auto Buy Now" national public relations campaign of '58, imploring consumers once again to empty their savings and bail the industry out of its jam:

Live Better By Far With A Brand New Car – because owning and driving a sleek, sweet sounding, smooth riding '59 model will give you a brand new outlook on life. Sure, buying a new car is a major investment. It's one of the big accomplishments in your life. It sets you apart as a person who is going places and doing things...

The unpredictability of the car trade kept Port Huron's manufacturing sector jumping during this decade. A new technical idea, ball joints, surprised the bejeezus out of auto parts maker Pressed Metals. The company's "Knee-Action" suspension parts had been trumped. The new ball joints went into Ford cars first (...*it lets your Ford take the corners almost as if on rails!*). Pressed Metals had been one of 6,000 suppliers to the FMC, warmly described in *Ford at 50* as "6,000 partners." Now, Ford bid Pressed a regretful, "*Adios*, partner." Employment levels at PM went from 1,000 to zero in three years, and after almost 40 years in business the company closed up. More durable local parts punchers like Autolite, Mueller Brass and Yale Rubber prospered and expanded during the up-and-down 50's, but only after threatening to pull out of the state if the UAW didn't behave. Chrysler Corporation decided that it had overstaffed its mammoth parts depot in Marysville. The firm shifted 2,000 of its 2,500 workers closer to Detroit, leaving many with the choice of either quitting, moving to a new community, or making a 100 mile round trip commute daily.

A surprising number, like 30 year-old John Angerbrandt, illogically chose the commute, by automobile, despite the heavy costs in driving time, car expenses, and the risks involved. Angerbrandt's commuting days came to an end when he drove into a train while heading for work one morning. Some Port Huron laborers drove further than Angerbrandt, commuting daily back and forth to the General Motors factories in Flint, 70 miles each way. A car carrying home five of these men at 75 mph on Highway 21 blew a tire and bounced across the countryside for 400 feet before hitting a tree and flipping over. Two Navy vets died, Shirley Mitchell and Anson Dennison.

2,500 of St. Clair County's 29,000 workers now commuted to work outside its boundaries, mostly by car. The Ford brothers – (Edsel's boys) Henry II, Benson, and William – took out a joint advertisement celebrating the commuter life: *We live in one place, work in another, send our children to school in a third, and enjoy recreation in a fourth. We think nothing of going fifty miles to dinner.* Commuter Arnold Lenz thought nothing of it either, until he, too, drove into the side of a train after a night out in the Thumb, killing himself and his wife. Lenz was the general manager of GM's Pontiac division, and his vehicle skidded 100 feet before the impact, suggesting he'd been using a little too much whispered might as he approached the crossing.

Which leads us to revisit the safety beat. President Eisenhower had been in office just a year when he learned that the 1953 traffic accident toll had cost the country an estimated $4 billion. A lot of that money came out of insurance company profits.

291

Industry spokesman Thomas Boate didn't mince words in beefing about it: "The manner in which the automobile is used, or perhaps better stated, misused, in America today, is, by my book, one of the cruelest and most blatant expressions of arrogant mass selfishness of which mankind has ever been guilty."(36) Traffic cases now outnumbered all other civil and criminal cases in U.S. courts. Traffic lawbreaking caused more loss of life and damage than any other crime. The American Medical Association said more people had their health impaired by car accidents than all illnesses combined. This prompted Eisenhower to call another White House Conference on Traffic Safety, chaired by Harlow Curtice. Like asking Brer Fox to chair a rabbit safety conference. Ike announced a new D-Day, National Safe Driving Day, for December 14, 1954, though a National No Driving Day would have been a lot safer.

As it did in many places across America, a Safety Crusade began in the Thumb. Motorists promised in writing to be good, as God was their witness, at the First Methodist Church in Port Huron. Governor Soapy Williams visited Port Huron to bless the Crusaders, and the city hosted a conference on safety just for teenagers, sort of a children's crusade. State police handed out booklets containing 18 pages of stomach-turning car crash death photos as shock therapy for the young drivers. "No one likes to look at bones sticking through flesh from compound fractures," said state policeman Tom Masterson, "or faces smashed beyond recognition by windshields, or heads and arms severed from the body – but that's what happened 105 times a day last year."(37) The doctors of St. Clair County's Medical Society made their own pitch for traffic safety, by condemning speeding ambulances, after one snapped off a utility pole and collided with three parked cars in Port Huron while racing to pick up a heart patient. "Two or three minutes which may be gained by exceeding legal speed limits," said the docs," can be of no value to the injured person but may, in fact, result in harm either to the patient or to the innocent motorists or pedestrians."(38)

Some new weapons in the crusade for safe driving came to hand at about this same time. Dr. Robert Borkenstein at Indiana University finished work on the "breathalyzer" in 1954, a device to deduce a drunk driver's blood alcohol content from a few gasps of air. This seemed like a breakthrough, since drunks caused an estimated 20%-40% of all fatal accidents, and who-knew how many less serious crackups. However, the breathalyzer only corralled drivers already drunk, and its results were inadmissible in Michigan courts. The breathalyzer couldn't stop motorists from imbibing at bars, liquor stores, restaurants, or at home. When Michigan Secretary of State James Hare went undercover to make a personal bar investigation, he found the average customer downed between 3 and 8 drinks before driving away. Prevention remained a practical impossibility.

Traffic radar also made its debut in St. Clair County, and it promised to be more convenient in reading speed. But like the electric speedimeter, which used cables laid across the road, radar just confirmed what the cops already knew, there were too many speeders to count, much less catch. General Motors and Columbia University dredged up again the by-now 20 year-old promise of driverless cars, safely steered by buried mistake-proof electrical cables in the road. Look for these cars in 1976, said GM, with a marked lack of urgency. Statistics suggested one more possible path to safer driving – ban male drivers, because women suffered only 1/10 as many accidents.

Ready or not, National Safe Driving Day arrived, December 14th, and lo and behold, nobody died in Michigan traffic that day, and "only" 48 across America. Half the average. Two days later the hallelujahs stopped when 11 people died in a single day's traffic in Michigan, twice the average. The awful national carnage over the Xmas holiday ten days later moved Ned Dearborn, the Cotton Mather of the Safety Council, to unleash another blast at the sinful nation: "Hurricane Hazel, which swept up the East Coast last fall, was a piker compared to the tidal wave of carelessness, selfishness and cold indifference that is piling up a holiday death toll on our highways which should shame any civilized nation."(39)

Which raised an interesting point. Were automobiles compatible with civilization? Was America civilized now, or overrun with mechanized barbarians as Dearborn suggested? In Rome, automobile traffic as bad as earthquakes shook to pieces that remnant of an earlier civilization, the Colosseum, requiring $250,000 in repairs. Automobiles also started shaking Port Huron to pieces, not just with vibrations but with their spatial demands. At a cost to the community of $1.3 million, plus an equal amount of federal cash, city officials wiped out the entire 1st Ward in the 1950's as part of an "urban renewal" project. 200 homes and businesses across 48 acres of the city's traditional waterfront district disappeared. This had been the spot where generations of ferries, sailing ships, steamers and passenger vessels had docked and unloaded and refitted, where sailors found refreshment, repose and comfort. Its rich assortment of shipping offices, warehouses, docks and drydocks, hotels, taverns, homes, shops, and brothels had made it Port Huron's signature neighborhood. First and foremost, Port Huron destroyed its 1st Ward for more parking.

Nobody mentioned in public the secondary reason, the ejection of inappropriate minorities, or as author James Baldwin put it about these programs, "Urban renewal means Negro removal." You could say that again, complained removee Cecil Mickens. Real estate prices came in two colors in Port Huron, said Cecil, full price white and sharply discounted black, and the city naturally had offered him the latter. Families of Irish, Greek, Indian, Russian, Scots, and Italian descent also got the heave-ho. Many never forgave it, like Sal Barzone, who defended the honor of the 1st Ward ever after: "You could leave your door unlocked, go away for a month and when you came back nothing would be stolen." Future Police Chief Herman Dusellier, a 1st native, said the same: "People respected each other's rights and property." An overweight ex-Navy officer from Port Huron named John Hume, who'd been known as "Fats" as far back as his U.S. Naval Academy days in 1920, took charge of the urban renewal project on the city's behalf. As one might expect, Hume didn't live in the renewal zone himself, and he didn't respect its rights and property, either. He happily kick out anybody. Dozens of 1st Ward families and business people fought Fats in court to the last appeal, but lost.

Once the ground had been cleared, the Port Huron and St. Clair County governments joined forces to erect the centerpiece of the "reclamation," as they insultingly called it, a $3.2 million replacement for the old City Hall – County Building. This defied the overwhelming sentiment of the community, which wanted the old hall repaired. Instead, a blank, mud-colored box with no clock tower went up, its ugly bulk half-heartedly excused by the dispirited architect Walter Wyeth:

..it was decided to use permanent materials which would reduce decoration and the cost of maintenance to a minimum. The cost of maintenance alone of a classical or

293

Georgian building would undoubtedly be in excess of a less ornamental type, to say nothing of the initial cost. The simplicity of the exterior design indicates an endeavor to obtain the desired architectural effect thru proportions rather than thru the use of ornament.(40)

In the face of Wyeth's opprobrium not another decorative ornament appeared on a new Port Huron public or commercial building for the rest of the century.

That universal ornament of the automobile age, a 100-space parking lot, decorated the rear of the new City/County building. It also served a new, bigger county jail put up beside it. That jail now frequently bulged with more than 100 prisoners at a time, another consequence of the auto age. The old City Hall so beloved of Fr. McCormick got some new proportions thanks to the wrecking ball – flat. Henry McMorran's descendants very generously donated $1.2 million to build a public auditorium and arena with a non-chiming clock on the old site, but even this offer translated into a death sentence for 8 nearby homes and the junior college gymnasium, in order to make way for the auditorium's automatic-gate parking facility.

At the urging of city officials, the YMCA relocated to the urban renewal zone, sometimes called Reclamation Park, while the city erased the old Y for a parking lot. Sears did the same, and built a parking area at its new store considerably bigger than the store itself, as zoning laws now mandated. Sadly, a new Wrigley grocery store with a voluminous parking lot flopped completely in the reclamation area; because no grocery-buying families lived there anymore. The A&P steered clear of Reclamation Park, and with the help of Fats Hume demolished six homes for the parking lot at its new downtown supermarket, and presented Hume with a bouquet of flowers in remembrance of this achievement.

Elsewhere, Port Huron Hospital knocked down several adjacent homes for a 45-car parking lot. Another Main Street mansion disappeared to make way for a new factory-style post office, with plenty of parking for the fleet of new 3-wheeled urban postal vans called "mailsters", and for the trucks that had replaced railroad intercity mail service. Grace Episcopal Church got into an unchristian zoning brawl with neighboring homeowners over building its new parking lot. The city tore down the Majestic theater and the Chamber of Commerce building to complete the latest of 11 municipal parking lots, built at a cost of $1,000 per car space. All over town bricks and dust flew. The combination of heavy traffic and a cityscape chopped to pieces to try to park it all began to drive patrons away from downtown Port Huron hotels. The once grand Harrington fell into foreclosure and its kitchen closed.

At the direction of school boss Howard Crull, Walter Wyeth put up an undecorated warehouse-style high school at the very edge of town, with parking for hundreds of cars, many belonging to students. The traditional 1908 downtown high school, one of the handsomest buildings in town, managed to escape destruction by the skin of its teeth, but four more of the traditional neighborhood elementary schools did not. Their replacement – the large, parking-enriched Woodrow Wilson school – looked exactly like the new jail. All these public "improvements" helped to get Port Huron chosen as an "All-American City" by *Look* magazine in 1955. Another architect of the day, Edward Durrell Stone, had a different opinion from *Look's* about the automobile's aesthetic impact: "We do everything rapidly in this country and I think in 30 or 40 years we have converted it from the most beautiful country to one of the ugliest."(41)

Apart from the ruin it inflicted on its surroundings, the ugliness of Port Huron's automobile population blighted the community all by itself. This population consisted not of thousands of gleaming new factory-fresh cars out of some advertising agency fantasy. Instead several dirty, shoddy generations of older machines dominated the scene. Some dated back as far as the depression, "transportation specials" in various stages of decay, clung to by some of the 2 million American car owners who earned less than $750 in annual income but who wouldn't give up their jalopies.(42) These people stashed their four-wheeled litterbuggies here and there, every which way throughout the city. When dying cars landed one last time in used car lots, they disgusted even dealers, as Andy Falk advertised: *It's a SCANDAL....but we want a divorce...from these cars. We've Looked At Them Long Enough.*

Not only did automobiles displease the eye, but they actually hindered travel. After a half century of civic rearrangement for their benefit these devices made it more difficult, not easier, to get around Port Huron, as even the newspaper admitted "...it's often quicker and easier to walk someplace than it is to drive and find a parking place." When a tornado swept through the city in 1953, killing 2 people, flattening 40 homes and damaging hundreds of others, Louis Dunn reported, "The traffic jams (of sightseers) in the storm area created about as much hardship on police and ambulance drivers and emergency cleanup crews as the storm did."(43) In any case the twister did small potatoes worth of destruction compared to the damage wrought in Port Huron by the car culture in the guise of urban renewal.

Renewal of a different sort reared its head when, after several hints and rumors about somebody building a car-based shopping center in Port Huron, developers put up "Northgate," straddling the northern edge of the city limits. Just one of 1,800 similar centers in America by 1955, Northgate offered parking for 700 cars. That was plenty for its purposes, but nothing on the scale of the new $30 million Northland Center, the biggest in the world, which opened just outside Detroit in 1954. The 150-acre, 100-store Northland floated in a sea of asphalt, enough parking for 10,000 cars. Big and small, the Northlands and Northgates rode the automobile-powered wave of sprawl and displacement that by 1956 ate up 1 million acres of American farmland per year, and which drained Detroit of 9% of its population during the decade. Port Huron's population barely changed during the 50's as continued home building inside the city – a lot of it on the old Driving Park property – offset the scorched earth policy in the 1st Ward. But Port Huron's two adjoining suburban townships grew 16% and 56%.

As people scrambled for more space for more automobiles and other forms of household clutter, middle class homes and lots grew larger every year. An average 1957 home of 1,150 square feet occupied a lot with 75-100 feet of frontage, usually in the suburbs. And let's not forget the garage, measuring 230 square feet. Most builders no sooner would put up a house without a garage than a house without a roof. This suburban villa set you back about $11,000-$12,000, for which you fairly easily could obtain a federally insured loan, and pay about $100 per month. By comparison, prices for downtown Port Huron homes lagged, ranging from $5,000-$7,500, with tougher loan terms. In the townships quick, haphazard home building required hundreds of septic tanks which when poorly installed often drained into open ditches. Of these suburban building practices the National Planning Association warned: "...irresponsible developers and inexperienced local officials [are] laying the basis for bad communities for tomorrow and for suburban slums."(44)

295

A new suburb-oriented business association clustering around Northgate gradually attracted 25 members. Charlie Barrett used his Cawood money to put up another shopping strip at the north end of Port Huron. A trailer court full of tin can homes appeared up there. So did a lumber yard, some new markets, gas stations, and a Burger Chef. The Institute of Life Insurance promised more to come, and took credit for financing the spread across America "of many of the shops, stores and small factories you see sprouting up in the suburbs." Taken all together, this trend definitely didn't look too promising to the downtown Port Huron commercial crowd.

They hired a consultant to suggest ways to jazz up Port Huron's central district. The grand design handed down by this seer of tomorrow really shook people up. Basically he wanted to convert downtown into Northland. This meant building 180 acres of parking lots in a crescent of concrete around the present 90 acre business section iteself. The proposed path of obliteration spared nothing; it even meant tearing the baseball field out of Pine Grove Park. Maybe a couple of $1 million multi-story parking garages should be built, too. As the U.S. Chamber of Commerce put it, cities like Port Huron needed to be "broken apart and reconstructed." All but the most seriously auto-deranged citizens gagged at this ludicrous conception, but business people still fretted non-stop about parking.

"They can't get close enough to the store," moaned the Main Street Fruit Market's manager about his carsick customers, heartsore at the thought of them staggering all of 100 feet to the doorway, for lack of an upfront parking space. Churchgoers too late to grab a parking spot in the lot at their house of worship couldn't get close enough to the pulpit, and Port Huron cops ticketed 200 of them a month for illegally parking on sidewalks, boulevards, no parking zones, driveways and in front of fire hydrants every Sunday. Port Huron's parking spaces themselves grew in length, stretching out from 20 feet to 22, even as car sizes lengthened, an average of 5 inches in 1957 alone. Like some malign form of dark energy, automobiles physically pushed everything in America, including themselves, further and further apart.

To deal with customers who couldn't get close enough to the store, an increasing number of Port Huron businesses added drive-in service. A reporter for the *Times Herald*, John F. Brown, claimed credit for one such innovation, when the accelerator on his car stuck and sent it crashing through the front door of People's Bank: "My head went through the windshield, and I was looking out at the teller windows inside the bank while the alarm was going off. I invented drive-in banking in Port Huron."[45] Two more banks put in their own drive-thrus, a little less violently, as did Troy Laundry and Barnet's Pharmacy. More drive-in restaurants appeared, and so did two of the 4,000 drive-in movie theaters in America ("Great for shut-ins"). Young Port Huron dad Bernie Lyons said these theaters if nothing else at least saved the cost of a babysitter:

...a night out for a movie meant putting young children into their pajamas, depositing them in the back seat with pillows and blankets, and going to the drive-in. The younger the children the sooner they fell asleep, leaving mom and dad to enjoy the movie and the inevitable popcorn.[46]

Even the new bandstand in Pine Grove Park became a drive-in affair.

So let the Colosseum crumble to dust, the *Times Herald* measured civilization by living standards, "Living standards are measured most accurately by material possessions," and the U.S. now owned more of the supreme material possesions, automobiles, than ever. Its cars put America "infinitely nearer being a Utopia than any other country." As to that safety thing, only 20% of the motorists on the road to Utopia ever broke the law at all, according to the editors. Except for them, things would be perfect: Put your minds at ease, New Utopians, all you have to do is watch out for every fifth vehicle on the road.

Not so fast, said traffic savant Harry Smith of Detroit: "Why do careful drivers who travel at moderate speeds under good driving conditions have most of the Nation's traffic accidents?" The *Times Herald's* John Brown saw just such a two-car wreck in front of his own eyes while driving hear Port Huron one afternoon. It happened to sober, responsible adult drivers in broad daylight on a clear day at a rural obstruction-free intersection marked with stop signs and a blinker light. Thankful that he'd avoided the incident himself, Brown swung into action as a reporter. "The injured moaned and screamed as blood ran from their wounds. All but one begged for help. The silent one was dead." Brown discovered that 6 people had been killed and 50 hurt in crashes at the very same intersection in the last half dozen years. "It's too safe-looking," a wrecker driver told him.

Civilized countries usually have some laws on the books to discourage anarchy, and the state of Michigan in 1956 reinstated a rural speed limit in peacetime, after a 28 year hiatus. The legislature approved it over the opposition of the governor, the highway department, and the Auto Club. 65 mph in daytime, 55 at night became the law, not exactly a strict crackdown, especially on the gravel roads that made up most of the 110,000 miles worth of byways now in place across the state. Three weeks after the return of the speed limits Michigan drivers set a new single-day fatality record of 23 corpses. The state also now mandated driver's training to obtain a first license. This required 30 hours in the classroom, and 6 behind the wheel, though as Harry Smith had observed, it probably wouldn't do all that much good.

Even before speed limits came back, 1 out 10 Michigan drivers received a traffic ticket annually, amounting to 391,000 in 1955. To get ready for the expected flood of new citations under the speed law, the state police hired 200 more troopers, making a total of 1,100. The FMC took this opportunity to point out that 70% of state police drove Fords cars, in case you wanted to race one: *For police cars must have the 'scat' to get going quick – to pass other cars lightning quick. And a mighty Ford V8 engine can pay off in your Ford, just as it does in a police car.* The number of annual traffic tickets in Michigan nearly doubled again during the next two years, to 722,000 in 1957. One Detroit man stopped by Port Huron police, 37 year-old William Krause, got his 65th ticket in 20 years, and a year in jail, his seventh stretch in the slammer for illegal driving.

As the auto culture threw more and more business the cops' way, St. Clair County Sheriff Ferris Lucas wangled six more deputies from the county's governing supervisors, making a total of 32 employees for his department. He ordered 24-hour 'scat' road patrols, which now covered 36,000 miles per month. Shortly afterward Lucas came to the end of his 20-year tenure as sheriff when voters kicked him out of office for trying to blackmail his election opponent. Just to show there were no hard feelings, 300 admirers threw Lucas a going-away banquet, and gave him the ultimate tribute, the full measure of a community's esteem – a new car.

Port Huron Police Chief Dan O'Leary and his department, also guardians of the new civilization, now employed 14 different vehicles in their work. Patrolmen spent much of their time driving around town, with up to six patrol cars in service at night. National newspaper columnist and broadcaster Paul Harvey didn't like this rolling cop trend: "When we had most policemen walking beats we had lots less crime. Today the sense of comfortable aloofness that comes with riding in a car gives (police) only a tourist's eye view of the community."(47) But since people in cars committed most crimes nowadays, cops had little choice but to follow the bad guys.

In a reflective mood one day Chief O'Leary informed the Rotary Club that driver attitude played a big part in the life-and-death derby on the streets. He recounted the true life story of the Port Huron woman who, in a fit of anger with her husband, took out the family car, drove it off into a field and around in circles until it overturned. Just one of the 1,400 local accidents in 1957, including 5 fatals and 175 injury affairs. O'Leary also mentioned that traffic controls actually *generated* collisions at some of Port Huron's 279 intersections. The amber slow-down light on three-color stoplights actually encouraged many drivers to speed up to beat the red. A new traffic light at a formerly safe 10th street corner triggered 7 accidents in 12 months, because of drivers' misplaced faith that everyone would obey the signal. The correct motto of the auto age: trust nothing and nobody.

They relied primarily on big engines to protect their customers, but every now and then during the 1950's American carmakers made a token effort about increasing passenger safety inside their products, which seemed the civilized thing to do. The most significant attempt came from Ford during the 1956 model year. After some experimentation with a couple of crash dummies named Ferd 1 and 2, the FMC offered extra padding, a collapsible steering wheel, and seat belts in an optional safety package. It marked a turning point in the career of Ford engineer turned sales exec Lee Iacocca. His hadn't been a steady rise at Ford. During one of the periodic shakeups that still occasionally roiled the company, the FMC had fired a third of its corporate sales staff and demoted a number of others, including Iacocca, who briefly considered quitting and opening a chain of hamburger stands.

The Ford safety campaign got off to a bad start for Iacocca when he tried to demonstrate the extra-cushiony dashboard padding to a sales conference, by dropping eggs onto a swatch of this material from a step-ladder, and scrambled them instead.(48) A major live national TV commercial by Ford for its new "lifeguard design" safety stuff, endorsed in person by North Carolina state police major Charles Speed, drew only an ominous silence from the studio audience. It shocked viewers to hear an auto manufacturer actually discuss the deadly potential of its product, something Americans preferred to forget. When the safety campaign flopped completely at the showrooms, it reduced Port Huron Ford dealer Russ Dawson to the desperate expediency of offering a 2-year, 25,000 mile guarantee on his cars: *No major repair bills. The Old Horse Trader Means Business!* Old Russ also made a freedom appeal for the *14,000 Captive Wives In The Port Huron Area Because There's Only One Family Car!*

In this hour of trial, Iacocca recouped his fortunes at the FMC by thinking up a catchy $56 for '56 installment sales plan to save the day. It set him on the road to becoming the Ford Division's general manager in 1960. The misfire of the safety campaign gave birth to the conviction at Ford that "safety doesn't sell," which governed the company's attitude for years to come. Ironically, Iacocca himself believed wholeheartedly in seat belts after seeing some color slides of fatal car wrecks: "It was pretty horrible stuff, and I had to leave the room once with nausea." (49) The American Medical Association also had seen enough and demanded that the decision of whether or not to put safety devices in cars "should be removed from the jurisdiction of the auto companies."

At about this time Congressman Kenneth "Seat Belts" Roberts brought his federal automotive safety investigation to Detroit to meet with the Big 3. The auto men treated him to a front row seat at a field test: an empty car rolled down a slope at 35 mph, hit a 15 ton wall and shove it back two feet. Pretty suggestive about a car's impact potential. But the most fascinating, and alarming, information provided to Roberts came from Ford driving analyst Fletcher Pratt.

As an average driver moves along an average road he observes various different things happening...other vehicles moving, potholes in the road, pedestrians or animals crossing in his path, traffic signals and the like. We call these 'events' and on the average they may occur at a frequency of 200 per mile. Some will require decisions...There may be as many as 20 such decision in the course of a mile's driving...since the average driver's judgment is not perfect he will make a wrong decision once in a while. (50)

Once in a while meant that a driver made a mistake once out of every 40 decisions, or every two miles. Once every 12 miles a near collision resulted. Pratt's figures showed an accident occurred every collective 61,000 automobile miles that Americans drove, an injury every 430,000 miles, a fatality every 16 million miles. The driver in fact made his worst decision by getting into the car at all. In addition to Pratt's work, Ford helped sponsor the automobile research lab at Cornell University. There the lab director John Moore reported after looking at some cadavers that people killed in cars suffered a "generalized crushing. People in these accidents seem to get hurt all over." Another Cornell boffin, Irwin Bross, urged that speed governors be installed on cars, and where had that argument been heard before? (51)

A few weeks after Pratt revealed his calculations, a 1-in-430,000 miler happened to Michigan Secretary of State James Hare, boss of autos. Somebody making a wrong decision at a stoplight T-boned Hare's car, leaving the secretary with five broken ribs, beat-up innards, and $3,000 in medical bills. Like 750,000 other drivers in Michigan, the guilty party in Hare's crash carried no insurance. In his own interest, Hare proposed that the state reimburse victims of uninsured motorists, who did $10 million dollars in damages annually. Only one state in America required compulsory auto insurance, Massachusetts, and coverage there cost 4 to 5 times as much as in Michigan. The actuaries had more troubling news for Hare. In just ten years Michigan's auto accident rate had climbed 79%, injuries 77%, and repair bills 400%. In three years, 1954-7, the yearly national auto accident price tag rose from $4 billion to $7 billion, culminating with 11.7 million accidents in 1957. St. Clair County's annual share of the damage came to $3-$4 million.

Even in the face of generalized crushings, internal injuries and uninsured drivers, the American automobile civilization turned to its popular arts to hail the spirit of the era. Car music moved into a new phase during the 50's, especially for teenagers.

299

Only squares dug that safety stuff, in many Port Huron kids' minds; the sort of "do what I say not what I do" doubletalk adults were so great at. Why, look at Mr. Draper's Main Street Chevy ad: *We'll wager that the first thing you'll say when you drive the new Chevrolet is: 'Who changed Old Reliable into a flash of fire?* Did that sound like a safety crusade? The uptempo dance number *Rocket 88* by Jackie Brenston had the younger set jivin' pretty good in 1951: *You women have heard of jalopies / You've heard the noise they make / But now let me introduce my new Rocket 88.*(52)

Brenston didn't write this as a commercial for Oldsmobile, though he might as well have. Another free spirit attuned to brand names, St. Louis guitarist Chuck Berry, who'd done prison time for auto theft, then more prison time as an auto assembly worker, concocted the rock and roll classic *Maybelline* in 1955. It told of a man who spotted his girlfriend right out there driving around in her Cadillac Coupe de Ville without him. The nerve of this woman! He gave chase in his V8 Ford, and the story ended happily with the lovers racing side by side at 110 mph along a rain-slicked highway. Less optimistically, the Jeff Barry – Ben Raliegh weeper *Tell Laura I Love Her* released in 1960 eulogized a hometown Romeo who entered a local stock car race in order to win $1,000 for his girl's engagement ring. He lost, and was burned up in a crash to boot, singing his last goodbye as rescuers dragged him from the wreckage.

Nothing could have suited Detroit better. Perfectly prepared to tug on the old heart strings to sell autos, if power and size didn't get it done in the 1950's, the auto industry didn't hesitate to pitch romance to all ages.

Stepping Out With His Two Loves... his two favorite companions – the lady in his life...and the car in his life! Cadillac.

In spring a young man's fancy likely turns to thoughts of...a new Plymouth convertible! And small wonder, for just look at this long, low, lean, excitingly styled automobile.

My Darling: Years ago I promised that if you married me I'd give you the moon and the stars. Look out the window, darling. It's yours...a new DeSoto.

The 1955 motion picture *Rebel Without a Cause* further exploited the special teenage brand of carsickness. A couple of young drag racers in this story challenged each other to launch their cars off a cliff, and one of them neglected to jump clear. How rebellious could you get? The film's star, James Dean, didn't make the Hollywood premiere of this epic, because after finishing his role he didn't jump clear of the real-life crash that killed him. This particular accident had a cause; Dean had been driving a Porsche to a car race, and speeding. The Big 3 carmakers vowed to get out of car racing forever after a rash of headline accidents like Dean's, but they didn't mean it. Authors Jeffrey O'Connell and Arthur Myers described this no-racing pledge as "a pack of wolves agreeing to turn vegetarian."

In a Port Huron salute to Dean's *Rebel* "chicken run", two local leadfoots, both drunk, staged a side-by-side drag race down the two-lane Scenic Highway one night to settle a $5 bet. One of them had the presence of mind to stop before he entered the city limits, but Robert Fraser roared on until he collided with a party of roller skaters driving home from the rink that evening. He bounced them into another car, then crashed himself into a store in the Northgate center. Fraser admitted fuzzily to police that his license had been revoked "6 or 8 years ago." He'd borrowed the car he killed 12 year old Tommy King and injured eight other people with. In a memorably rare instance of judicial severity, Fraser received a 4-5 year sentence in state prison. The lawsuits between the victims, the drivers, the car owners, and the bars who'd served Fraser ricocheted around the courts for years. There's no such thing as bad publicity in some trades, and the movie business cashed in a second time when the Family Theater added to its schedule *Dragstrip Riot – "Murder at 120 Miles Per Hour."*

The car culture alternately bored and excited Americans like Dean and Fraser. They used crazy driving to try breaking the monotony of everyday driving, instead of just giving it up altogether. The Gratiot Pike became the most popular spot for the Maybellines of St. Clair County, but it also claimed a lot of other people. Gratiot was three lanes wide, one going north, the other going south, and a middle lane for passing in either direction, called the "suicide lane." State police named Gratiot as one of the three most dangerous stretches of road in Michigan. In one particularly bad span of five months, car accidents along that stretch of road took five lives and injured 22 people.

Among those who met their ends, Harrington Hotel manager Tom McConchie just drifted across the centerline one day, killing another oncoming driver as well as himself. The Reverend John Hollis, 68, of Port Huron, expired in a broadside crash with an 18 year-old driver. William Wismer, a man already on probation for reckless driving, killed 12 year-old trick-or-treater Patricia Hardy on Halloween. The police didn't trouble Wismer with another criminal charge over Patricia; why make it hard on the guy? The asking price on a dead daughter in an automobile civil suit now averaged about $25,000, open to negotiation, as were all the hundreds of traffic accident actions filed in the Port Huron courts during the 1950's. The estate of a top-rung GM executive Fred Wiles of Oldsmobile, who wiped out in a Highway 21 crash, put a price of $175,000 on his hide before the matter was settled.

By 1960 St. Clair County's 50,800 private motor vehicles choked Gratiot, Highway 21, the Scenic, Main Street and the rest of the hundreds of thoroughfares with about 25 units per mile, just fewer than 1 for every 2 residents. 74 million crisscrossed America. 11 million trucks, three times as many as at the end of WW2, carried triple the amount of cargo, 240 million ton-miles per year. An increasing number of industries abandoned railroads entirely, and set up their factories next to state highways for shipping purposes. If the neighbors objected to the heavy trucks running in and out all the time, too bad. Those trucking luminaries of Port Huron, Myron Ogden and Dale Moffett, found business so good during this decade – 400,000 tons in 1951, and a $1.5 million gross – that they built their fleet up to more than 200 different rigs. Competitor Oscar Richards counted 700 trucks in his collection when he sold the business in 1953 and retired to his horse farm.

The Michigan Trucking Association took a modest bow for its achievements during Truck Transportation Week of 1953:

...folks should say a prayer of gratitude every time they see a truck. They should thank Providence whenever grace is said at table because without trucks we wouldn't eat, we would have no clothing, shelter, comfort or newspapers.(53)

The following month Anthony Jawor of Port Huron forgot to say his prayers when he saw a truck coming on Gratiot, and an inattentive semi driver accordioned Jawor's car into a tree, killing the 35 year-old father of six. The trucking company settled up with

Anthony's widow for $50,000.

Apart from their sustaining an otherwise helpless nation, truckers also took credit for helping push sprawl and the general disorganization of American society along. "They've enabled us to go out into the rural and suburban areas and build homes and business projects," bragged the industry. Truckers also hawked "just in time" delivery service for manufacturers, showing up at the last minute with parts, which lowered inventory costs at the expense of jamming the public roads with more trucks. Michigan State Police called them warehouses on wheels. Trucking shipments cost more than four times as much as rail, 18 times more than barges, but with the speed game rigged in its favor many businesses saw little or no alternative to using the most grossly inefficient, corrupt, and under-regulated freight-hauling industry in America.

Many trucking companies still didn't bother to check their drivers for criminal records, so inside job hijackers made off with $65 million of goods in 1951 alone. Even if honest, their employers subjected poorly educated, poorly trained drivers to as much as 16 hours of driving out of 24 in a day. "Those trucks just beat hell out of you," confessed one road warrior at a Port Huron physical therapist's office. Ford Trucks tried appealing to the profession's sore butts with new *Driverized Cab Comfort to cut fatigue – make driving easier. Prove it yourself, take the 15-second Sit Down Test*!

Nobody thought much about the safety of materials on board trucks, like the 900 quarts of nitroglycerin on a Pringle Powder Company truck that rolled nonchalantly through Port Huron and across the Blue Water Bridge before authorities even learned about it. Nobody objected to a 90-foot truck loaded with steel girders tying up the highway for 40 miles on the way to Port Huron under a police escort, then shutting down Main Street for delivery to the job site. By comparison, the railroad delivered a 500,000 pound electrical generator to town with no police escort, no closed streets, no fanfare. It looked for a time as though 90-foot trucks might become the wave of the future, when 98-foot, 65 ton supertrucks called "turnpike trains" actually got a tryout in New York State.(54)

Truckers still regularly ignored the weight limits on Michigan roads. State Auditor John Martin called this "the rape or our highway system from overweight and overloaded trucks..." Martin wanted these trucks impounded, which would have required a lot of parking, because weighmasters ticketed 33,000 of them for violations in a typical year, and warned 70,000 more. The inspector working out of Port Huron, Leo Msiolek, drove 175 miles per day on his beat with his portable scales, looking to catch overloaded trucks in the act. He admitted, "It's difficult to prove that a truck owner deliberately disregards regulations...but intentional or not it's tempting economically to use one overloaded truck where it would take two with legal weight."(55) Especially tempting since Michigan only fined overweight trucks 2 to 10 cents per extra pound. The all-time record fine for a single truck, overloaded by 15 tons, came to only $3,200. Rather than drive all the way through their own country, 40 different Canadian trucking companies regularly drove through Port Huron on a shortcut across Michigan to take advantage of the free ride.

On the labor side of the trucking industry, Teamsters President James Hoffa, master of America's biggest union, spent much of his time in court, fighting a never-ending string of indictments of his unsavory administration. Apart from bribing, perjuring, and racketeering where he would, Hoffa allegedly converted the Teamsters

302

pension fund into an $800,000 per month piggybank for its pals in organized crime.(56) Hoffa's criminality eventually got his union kicked out of the AFL-CIO labor federation. Most of the 1.1 million Teamsters members remained loyal to the top boy, partly because he negotiated skillfully for them, and partly because he didn't brook turncoats too well. In Port Huron, police arrested Teamsters agent Walter Sacharczyk for repeatedly ramming his car into that of a strikebreaker, a typical example of the union's methods of persuasion. Hoffa threatened to cut off the food, clothing, and newspapers in Michigan for a weekend, after somebody in the state capital suggested that trucks be banned from the highways every Saturday and Sunday. Seldom was a government proposal withdrawn so quickly.

Those mongrel descendants of the streetcars, the bus systems of the United States, had a far less successful decade than truckers. Bus ridership had fallen 50% in most cities since the end of WW2. For Port Huron's 16-bus Paton company the continually declining ridership, escalating costs, and regular annual losses of thousands of dollars meant service schedules shrank while fares tripled during the 50's. Bus ads truthfully but unsuccessfully recommend that residents "Ride City Busses...It's Cheaper By Far Than Parking Your Car." It cost less for a Port Huroner to ride back and forth to his job for a year on the bus (at a 20 cent fare) than keep up an automobile for a month. The Chamber of Commerce and Mayor Thomas Woods appealed to the reason of the 1,000 or so downtown workers to please use the buses instead of driving to work and clogging up parking spaces. They didn't get much response.

Bus company owner Jack Paton found himself in an awkward spot complaining about his $1,000/month losses, since he also sold Plymouths and DeSotos, one business sapping the other. Privately owned city bus systems failed all over Michigan, notably in the state capital of Lansing, and even across the St. Clair River in Canadian Sarnia. Paton cut out holiday service in Port Huron, then Sunday service, and for this latter act Mrs. Charles Stanley accused him of fomenting a Communist conspiracy to undermine church attendance. Weeknight service stopped, and due to the financial astringency the bus fleet broke down more often.

Finally Paton threatened to stop the buses entirely, prompting an amusing though inaccurate used car offer from Charlie Barrett: *Chief Cawood says Ugh! No Buses After October 8th. These Ponies Cheaper Than Riding Buses Anyway!* Cawood's patron General Motors won either way in these to-bus-or-not-to-bus situations. GM built 85% of the buses in America. So many that the U.S. Justice Department sued the company for hogging the market. The city of Detroit loaded up on 150 more GM diesel buses in 1956 and shut down the last of its 93 year-old municipal streetcar system, surrendering the streets completely to automotive chaos. Chicago's remaining streetcars vanished the same way.

"It would work untold hardship on individuals who do not own automobiles," the *Times Herald* said about bus abandonment, "and there are thousands of them in Port Huron."(57) The Port Huron buses still carried 1 million passengers per year at this stage. 3,000 people signed a petition urging the city to step in with subsidies, but Councilman Kenneth Ramsey said if these people would ride the buses instead of signing petitions there'd be no problem. Ramsey also called the fleet "...those ambulatory pieces of junk on our streets that you facetiously refer to as buses..." Paton obtained another fare increase, but a year later another shutdown loomed, and "Honest

303

John" handed the franchise over to city taxi operator Leo Shovan. Eventually an arrangement to give the bus system quasi-municipal status helped it limp into the next decade.

Intercity bus service between Port Huron and the larger world also declined during this decade. Greyhound's local office offered service to Detroit, New York, Chicago, Boston, Los Angeles, New Orleans and to the upper Thumb. 18 Big Dog buses departed the combined downtown station and lunch counter daily, charging about 2.5 cents per mile, and traveling roughly 50% slower than trains, but on the whole providing service vastly superior to automobiles. "This Winter Travel in Comfort and Safety by Greyhound. 10 Times Safer Than Driving." But safety didn't sell, as Ford could have told the Hound, and nationally intercity bus passenger mileage fell 20% during the 1950's.(58)

About the only growth market for busing during the Fifties came in education. With the same fine illogic and disregard for expense shown by automobile owners, the Port Huron school district mostly shunned the city bus system. Instead it assembled its own parallel fleet of 7 buses, costing $17,000 apiece, to fetch rural children for the high school, and to shuttle city kids back and forth across town according to the redistribution schemes of superintendent Crull. Some 76 school buses employed by the various school districts now rolled across St. Clair County, lugging 6,000 students a total of 830,000 miles per year. That took an hour per day per average youngster, and often a good deal longer in snow or spring mud, for which school buses were notoriously unsuited. More than once rural children stranded in buses had to be rescued by parents in sleighs, like that of the intrepid Mrs. John Flinchbaugh of Port Huron Township. Nationwide, one quarter of American schoolchildren rode buses, 9 million kids in 137,000 vehicles, at an annual tab of $312 million. Fordist school consolidation pushed forward with a rush. Half of the rural districts in St. Clair County merged during this period, obliterating Hazel Ketelhut's school. The Michigan Rural Teachers Association disbanded.

American buses, trucks, and cars running up 718 billion miles in the single year of 1960 needed about 60 billion gallons of gasoline and diesel fuel. The Imperial Oil refinery across the river from Port Huron visibly enshrined these mammoth figures. Imperial, its refining competitors, and chemical and plastic-making neighbors in Chemical Valley continued to expand along the eastern Canadian skyline during this decade, and their home city of Sarnia grew by as many as 4,000 people in a single year. Imperial now handled 70,000 barrels of oil per day, with a production potential of several hundred million gallons of gasoline per year.(59) When a 1,700 mile-long 20 inch-wide pipeline from the Canadian oil fields commenced to flow into the Imperial works the company expanded again, to 94,000 barrels per day.

Another explosion at Imperial, this time on board the tanker *Imperial LeDuc*, shook things up again in Port Huron, lest the city become too complacent about the nature of the elixir that ruled the world. Audible five miles away, the blast did $200,000 damage, and charred four Canadians, one mortally. At the time of the mishap, the *LeDuc's* captain had been in the ship's hold testing for explosive fumes, and found some. Petroleum also took the lives of two Port Huron mariners, Captain Louis Guyette and helmsman Ray Richardson, who died at their posts when their freighter *Penobscot* collided with a barge carrying 800,000 gallons of gasoline in Buffalo's harbor. The resulting firestorm killed nine other people as well. On a much smaller scale, a wrecked truck casually abandoned in back of Port Huron's shuttered Jackson elementary school in the 1st Ward blew up when a child dropped a lighted test match into its gas tank, burning his 7 year-old playmate Ronald Edward to death.

The gasoline retailers of America did their best to push the speed mania along during the Fifties. Standard Oil: "Premium Volatility at Regular Price! Higher than ever in octane! Makes the old family bus feel as lively as... *Animobile*. Red Crown the greatest GO on earth!" Battling for market share, dealers in Port Huron dished out nine different brands of trading stamps along with their gas, introduced oil company credit cards, and hyped imaginary advantages in their products, like Speedway 79's "Platofuel," gasoline supposedly juiced up by refining with "precious platinum."

Margins shrank at the gas pump, and the chain retailers like Standard started shoving the independents out. The number of filling stations in Port Huron actually declined in number, to a mere 70, but stations expanded in size. On-site storage tanks swelled from 5,000 to 12,000 gallons. One of these station enlargements leveled another historic home, that of Port Huron's great 19th Century physician Cyrus Stockwell, along with a pink chestnut tree, the only one of its species in the city. An interesting comparison suggested by a calculation of the Associated Press showed that 14 times as many gas stations did business in Port Huron as in the entire Soviet capital of Moscow. The reason? 80,000 Muscovites who attended a game at a soccer stadium left a grand total of 12 cars parked outside. American reporters accounted this a sign of Russian primitiveness.

Enormous expansion of the U.S. petroleum industry, now worth a cumulative $58 billion, boosted U.S. oil reserves to an all time high, 35 billion barrels. But America also drew like a helpless oil drunk on foreign sources, and became a net importer of petroleum by 1954.(60) A number of these foreign producers got together to form the Organization of Petroleum Exporting Countries (OPEC) in 1960, largely so they wouldn't be chiseled on prices by domineering, auto-crazy countries like the United States.

The petroleum industry in general, Sarnia's Chemical Valley not excepted, didn't always contain its raw materials, or products, or wastes too well. Some of it ended up in the St. Clair River. More and more downstream consumers like the Detroit water board and the Michigan Waterways Commission objected to this discharge. So did Port Huron, where the new municipal sewage plant, constructed after 40 years of agonizing, actually began to clean up the water and lure back some fish. St. Clair County's Health Department, which took into account petroleum effluent, septic tank leakage, storm drain overflows, and farm and lawn chemical residues, warned the public against drinking any natural source water from lakes, streams, or springs. First add bleach, or iodine, or chlorine, or boil it – one of the auto age's signal accomplishments. The oil and plastics companies – Imperial, Sun Oil, Dow and DuPont – finally bowed to pressure on this issue and formed a St. Clair River Research Group, but with only a measly $6,000 kitty to look into the pollution situation.(61)

In the air as well, when an east wind got up over Port Huron, residents still held their noses against Chemical Valley's odors, which were "making breathing outdoors almost impossible," crabbed one complainer. The fumes of semi-combusted gasoline and diesel fuel bursting from cars and trucks into the air came under more serious study and criticism during this period. U.S. lung cancer deaths had increased 200% in 20 years, and the American Cancer Society suggested that both auto exhaust and the dust from asphalt roads played a part in this. The Pollution Control District in America's smog capital, Los Angeles, by this time employed 170 people on a $1 million annual budget. They faced a monumental job. The 2.7 million cars and trucks in Los Angeles County cranked out 90% of a smog blanket that sometimes cut visibility to one-eighth of a mile. Visitor Paul Harvey called it "aerial sewage" that subjected air-breathers to the equivalent of smoking 100 cigarettes per day. L.A. County supervisor Kenneth Hahn needled Ford with a letter about cleaning up its auto exhaust. In response he got back a baldfaced lie about the FMC's harmless tailpipe gases, even as scientists at California's Institute of Technology proved a link between cars and smog.(62)

When Los Angeles proposed banning any new cars not fitted with pollution control devices, Detroit Mayor Louis Mariani stood by his home boys and loyally scoffed at the Angelenos, "How silly can they get!" The chief air pollution inspector for Detroit, Milton Sterling, chimed in, "The easiest way to stop pollution is to stop living, or go back to the stone age."(63) The U.S. Public Health Service said plenty of people already had stopped living due to the air pollution of the auto age, which in money talk cost the country $7.5 billion per year. Eisenhower cabinet member Arthur Flemming warned automakers to cut down the skunk air from their products or he'd demand regulation. Chevrolet advised customers worried about all this bother just to stay in their cars, because with Chevy's new ventilation system, *Even the Air You Breathe is Better*! Port Huron convened an air pollution fact-finding panel, and invited two Michigan Health Department officers to a meeting over the issue, though unfortunately the gentlemen suffered a car wreck on the way to this get-together. Eventually the department installed half a dozen air monitors around town, but aimed these detectors at industrial plants, not motor vehicles.

A single subject dominated the topic of auto-friendly roads during the 1950's. As mentioned, President Eisenhower had set his administration the task of coming up with a grand interstate highway plan. The proposal placed before the Congress in 1956 envisioned something considerably more grandiose than the network of mainly two-lane U.S. highways which had grown up out of the postal roads during the past 40 years, highways encumbered with innumerable cross streets, railroad grades, and traffic signals. General Motors largely directed the design of the proposed new Interstate Highway System (IHS), with help from that slayer of neighborhoods Robert Moses of New York, and assisted by lobbyists from the rest of the automobile manufacturing and support industry, plus truckers, road builders, land developers and a host of others. The job: build 41,000 miles of high speed, limited-access, non-stop, toll-free, multi-lane divided highway to connect most of the major cities of the United States, at a cost of...well, nobody quite knew what it would cost.

Almost every IHS story coming out of the nation's capital cited new figures. The optimistic guess said $31 billion in construction costs over 13 years, about $750,000 per mile. To be paid for on a 90%-10% basis, with the feds eating the 90% share, states and locals the rest. That meant higher federal taxes on fuel, vehicles and tires, with the money to be sequestered in a Highway Trust Fund, the same setup the auto industry had pushed through in Michigan. The trust fund idea prompted some skeptics to ask why not put railroad taxes into a Railroad Trust Fund, or alcohol taxes into a Liquor Fund, and so on. The federal government itself didn't plan to build or maintain the IHS; that chore it left to the lower-downs. In the usual American Way, nobody seriously explored the subjects of future maintenance or policing costs.

The Road Gang got busy promoting the plan. J.R. Buckley, the chief engineer of Alfred Sloan's Automobile Safety Foundation, broke new records for optimism by promising America that no more traffic congestion would exist by the year 2000 thanks to World of Tomorrow IHS expressways. Drivers on the sacred way of this Via Automobilia would encounter no obnoxious pedestrians, bicyclists, railroads or streetcars to impede them. Happy motorists only would travel in perfect safety across the triple-decked, heated thoroughfares, lit bright as day on the darkest night. To give the IHS further sales sock with the Congress and public its backers called it the National Defense Highway System. These highways, so it was said, would facilitate the defense of the nation through rapid military movement in case of a Red invasion. Why they wouldn't facilitate the Red invaders at the same time remained an open question.

The automobile and highway lobbies also suggested in all seriousness that in the event of a nuclear attack city dwellers could hop in their cars and drive on Defense Highways out from under the falling A-bombs into the countryside, wait there until the fallout settled, then drive back to the ruins of their homes to rebuild their lives. It says plenty about the jangled nerves of Americans during the Cold War with the Soviet Union that this argument actually carried some weight. If all this didn't satisfy the doubters, the IHS backers relied on spiritual appeals. If the nation drove more often and faster and farther, the level of American happiness just naturally would rise.

The titanic scale of the planned construction had the press rolling as happily in the statistics as a dog in manure. The largest public works project in history would require the condemnation of 750,000 pieces of property, totaling 1.5 million acres. At a cost 25 times the price of the A-bomb project, a million workers would cover 400 square miles with pavement, enough concrete to build six sidewalks to the moon or 80 Hoover Dams, etc, etc.(64) This appeal to national pride of size didn't convince everybody, especially those concerned about the sheer size of federal government spending, up 1,600% in 20 years even without the IHS.

Troubling information from Detroit indicated right from the start that the costs and timetable of the IHS had been grossly underestimated, like the cost of owning a car. Two six-lane freeways, the Edsel Ford and John Lodge, already being gouged through Detroit, displacing thousands of families and businesses in the process, had rung up $200 million in charges. A single interchange with 12 different "overpass" bridges, so motorists could be spared the torture of stopping for cross traffic, cost $15 million. Work on these expressways had dragged on for seven years and they still weren't finished. Traffic on the Ford and Lodge, far from being liberated, moved no faster during rush hour than on regular surface streets, according to the Auto Club. Elsewhere in the USA, various states admitted they didn't have even the 10% match money ready to begin work on the IHS, nor the rights of way secured, nor enough civil engineers on hand to do the work.

Pressing on regardless, Dwight Eisenhower, in remembrance of his 1919 Army truck trip across America, put his John Hancock on the IHS legislation in August, 1956. In the words of two critics, Ike

paid little attention to the warnings that easier (motor vehicle) access to cities would

307

simply aggravate congestion, that the more efficient railroads would suffer and the less efficient trucks would gain; and that instead of improving the nation's transportation system it would simply make it far more destructive and expensive.(65)

Passage of the 1956 Interstate Highway Act ensured the complete triumph of the automobile over mass-transit alternatives in the United States and killed off, except in a few large cities, the vestiges of balanced public transportation systems that remained in 1950's America.(66)

Reality set in early. Within four years estimates on the IHS costs rose 50% and time-to-completion lengthened to 25 years. Engineers quickly saw that driving the x-ways could be dangerously monotonous, lacking in even the limited visual variety afforded on regular highways. They'd need special rest areas, and constant police patrols. "Take a long trip by car today on our modern super highways and what happens?" asked the Associated Press. "You see an endless ribbon of concrete before you and very little else. You eat food almost as standardized as the gasoline your car consumes. The restaurants and filling stations look alike and too often they serve the same menus."(67) As far as the IHS being a defense system, the Congress learned in 1960 that the Defense Department hadn't even been consulted on the design, which meant that 2,200 of the bridges had been built too low to allow weapons vehicles to pass underneath them.(68) Eventually the Pentagon proposed getting some use out of the IHS by loading 50,000 nuclear missiles onto low-clearance trucks and driving them continuously around the country to baffle the Russians.

At first, the highwaymen in Washington left Port Huron and St. Clair County entirely off the IHS map. Frantically, local officials lobbied to overturn this unrecognized blessing, certain that a spot along the national Mississippi of pavement meant nothing but prosperity. They succeeded in adding an entirely redundant extension of Interstate-94 from Detroit to Port Huron, paralleling the Gratiot Pike and the Grand Trunk railroad, crossing St. Clair County for what they called the bargain basement price of $13 million. The catch: the county had to pay an extra $3 million and acquire 280 parcels of property on which to build 43 miles of access roads and bridges to get on and off I-94. State Highway Director John Mackie tried dressing up this boondoggle as the "'Seaway Freeway' (which) holds the promise of economic growth we feel will be unsurpassed anywhere in the nation."

All of this IHS construction came *on top* of the regular road and street wheeling and dealing in America, and it might be said that the pitch of begging and threats by road interests in the state capitals and city halls of the nation ratcheted up several notches to try to get some attention back from the big interstate push. Everybody everywhere wanted more, more, more. "The organized lobby of the State Highway Department has made itself felt everywhere in Michigan," said state Senator Donald Gilbert. "I understand that there's an entire division there that does nothing by write (press) releases, contact people and make friends for the Department."(69) The folks at Highway needed all the friends they could get when "gross irregularities" in the buying of rights of way led to a rash of department firings. Such things didn't come as a complete surprise in a bureaucracy dishing out $300 million per year. Loyally, the Portland Cement Association tried reassuring the public about what they got for their tax dollars: "Michigan's new concrete highways are being built to last 50 years – and more." Don't expect a warranty on them, though.

In St. Clair County, Road Commission boss Charles Ash lamented that he had only $1.7 million to spend in a year, and as many as half the county's roads, 800 miles worth, still broke up something terrible in the spring. Farmers and truckers and school buses should keep off them when possible. The suburban migration mentioned above required more road improvement and maintenance, which in itself spurred more development in the townships, increasing Ash's work load further. Port Huron had 70 miles of unpaved streets left, and citizen petitions to pave them rolled in so fast the Department of Public Works bought its own asphalt plant. And did you want some salt with those streets? You got it in Port Huron. Salt trucks spread 200 tons during one December alone, more than a ton per mile. Road salt came into its own on Northern American roads as a snow cure during the 1950's, melting snow all right, but fouling groundwater, poisoning plant life, attacking the steel reinforcement in the pavement and structural steel in bridges (a single county road bridge cost $100,000), and rotting away automobile bodies faster than ever.

The clamor grew louder from public officials like Fats Hume for wider streets in Port Huron. Fats wanted 10th Street widened from two lanes to four. Homeowners on 10th objected: "I could sit on my front porch and shake hands with people driving by." "Is this city for the homeowners or for the out of towners that race through the city without a stop?" When voters turned down the 10th Street widening by a 2-1 margin, Planning Commissioner Edgar Kiefer felt his old Fascist distaste for democracy stirring again: "...be careful not to disturb the Rip Van Winkle existence of the people of Port Huron...Of course it is pleasanter to live in a small, tree shaded village. The only trouble is there isn't much work to be had among ideal residential surroundings."(70) How dare anyone ask for ideal residential surroundings?

Straddling the fence again, the *Times Herald* editors came down first on Kiefer's side in the wider streets debate, "Wider Streets Needed. Port Huron needs more streets that will accommodate four lanes of traffic – a lot more." Then, two days later they took up the Van Winkle cause, "Getting Back to Nature – Man belongs to Nature...to the trees and the grass and the stars...a rich reservoir of spiritual happiness." So which to choose? Why not have both? Even without 10th Street, road builders found their spiritual happiness in widening the deserted 1st Ward urban renewal streets for $125,000 per mile. All except two prominent local paving contractors, Archie Baker and his son Robert, who needed a wider street the day they drove into a tree, dropping them permanently out of the widening sweepstakes, and life.

Despite having every conceivable obstacle flung in their paths, American railroads still operated 40% of the world's rail capacity at the beginning of the 1950's. But U.S. system shrinkage continued steadily. An enormous tax burden, amounting to $1.3 billion in 1951, consumed all the railroad passenger and express revenues in the country. Union featherbedding cost another $500 million. While the government lavished billions on the highways, it created no Interstate Railroad System, and spent nothing for Defense Railroads, except some loan guarantees. "The railroads are the only form of transportation that pays its own way; no free roads, no free waterways, no free airports, no subsidies of any kind!" reiterated the Michigan Railroad Association. The Interstate Commerce Commission steered its same perverse course with respect to the railroads, in the words of one Detroit area company, "...as it is now, the ICC often denies proposed *lower* rail rates because (they) might win too much traffic away from trucks or barges."(71)

Bit by bit operators began giving railroad freight routes in the Thumb, some of them dating back to Henry McMorran's time, as more farm products shifted to trucks. Due to fading agricultural business, cattle and refrigeration railcar numbers in America fell by more than 50% during the four decades ending in 1960.(72) But gloom and doom didn't reign completely. Not all rail companies lost money. The C&O, for example, inheritor of the McMorran Line, earned $42 million across its entire network in 1960. The industrial freight picture looked somewhat more promising in Port Huron. Customs house agent Elmer May, who handled 50,000 shipments coming across the border from Canada annually, insisted that rail held the real key to Port Huron's future development. The city dedicated a new 130 acre industrial park on the west side of town, and planned to install railroad service to every factory site. Technically, the railroads gave the trucking industry a kick in the pants during the 50's, by starting piggyback service, loading truck trailers onto flatbed rail cars and moving them more cheaply, quickly, and safely than truckers could do themselves.

The passenger train service between Port Huron and Detroit came to an end in 1954 after 95 years in operation. "Ease the strain, go by train," a 50's railroad slogan said. But whereas at one time five daily round trips had connected the two cities, by '54 an average of just 10 Port Huroners eased the strain and climbed aboard the day's single train. The Grand Trunk had to go to court to win permission to drop this lone, poorly scheduled service, leaving buses as the only mass transit link to Detroit. Port Huron's passenger rail service to another important Thumb city, Saginaw, also ended. 1,200 other passenger trains halted in America during a five year span in the 50's, when rising expenses outran fare increases by more than 250%, and railroads lost $700 million per year on passenger service.(73) They abandoned 4,700 miles of track during the same period. American passenger railroads fell further behind other countries technically. An electric French locomotive set a new speed record of 195 mph in 1955, far beyond anything the Yanks could manage.

Though with decreasing frequency, and in trivial numbers compared to automobiles, trains still suffered wrecks. 81 people died and 500 were hurt in a 1951 New Jersey commuter train crash, one of the worst ever. On the local scene, 34 freight cars derailed west of Port Huron, tearing up $100,000 worth of track and rolling stock in a bad accident. These smashed freight cars usually ended up in Port Huron's Grand Trunk repair yards, still rebuilding 1,500 units per year at a cost of $2 million. And the iron horse still suffered pesky bites from those autos. The law mandated that trains blow their horns at every road crossing, which translated to as many as 800 blasts per trip, but still couldn't convince some motorists to get out of the way. To the list of previously mentioned St. Clair County drivers who met their ends tangling unwisely with trains during this decade, let's add with unfeigned regret the name of 74 year-old Walter Sparling, father of that early automobile suburb of Port Huron he modestly named Sparlingville. And John McKay, former three-sport standout at Port Huron High, done in on his way home from a bowling league at 2:30 in the morning.

Passenger ships continued to fade away from the Great Lakes. The last major American passenger line on the Lakes, the Detroit and Cleveland, went out of business in 1951, citing rising costs and government regulation as the reasons. The five big D&C ships were scrapped. The fact that the world's largest freshwater system had no significant American passenger traffic across it save the occasional cruise ship or ferry raised no alarm bells in government halls, and certainly no suggestion of operating public passenger vessels, or creating an Interstate Waterway System. Port Huron's Chamber of Commerce occasionally charted the 40 year old steamer *Put-in Bay* for pleasure cruises in 1951. Two years later this ship, too, docked for good in the scrapyard.

The passenger ferry from Port Huron to Sarnia, which carried no autos, stopped in 1956, undone by the decline in pedestrian traffic, as fewer and fewer people walked. One million people per year crossed the Blue Water Bridge, almost exclusively in motor vehicles. Michigan erected another bridge, similar but five times as long and 30 times more expensive, between the state's two major peninsulas. The $100 million Mackinac Bridge opened in 1957, strictly limited to automobile travel, and there too ferry service shut down. Ferries thrived in only a few special spots on the Lakes where bridges were impractical. For instance to St. Clair County's Russell Island. No automobile had ever set tire on Russell, and its residents with justice called it the most "quiet, exclusive and beautiful piece of real estate" in the county.

Bulk shippers continued to thrive on the waterways for the best of reasons, they made money. The FMC's new freighter *William Clay Ford*, 647 feet long, built for $5.3 million dollars, carried as much tonnage as 700 trucks or almost 300 freight cars. 164 million tons of iron, coal and grain crossed the Great Lakes in 1953. One million annual tons of marine cargo (33,000 trucks worth) flowed in and out of Port Huron in the form of cement, coal, wood pulp, sand, limestone, and, the biggest consignment, petroleum products. 4,000 towing vessels and 14,000 barges worked the other inland waterways of America, and there bulk traffic increased 700% between 1930 and 1960 to 300 million tons per year. U.S. Coastal shippers handled about 200 million tons.

After 40 years of dilly-dallying the United States finally agreed to join with Canada in expanding access between the Great Lakes and the Atlantic Ocean via the St. Lawrence Seaway project. The American share of the cost of deepening channels, improving canals and locks, and building new hydroelectric plants came to $450 million, a fraction of the sum spent per year on the IHS. Work completed on the Seaway in 1959 and grain exports in some cities boomed, up 900% in Chicago. One drawback: the sudden intermingling of the regular Lakes traffic with foreign vessels unfamiliar with these waters led to 38 collisions and 2 sinkings in 1960.

Port Huron felt only a negligible effect from the Seaway at first. It meant just the deepening of the St. Clair River channel; and a visit by Queen Elizabeth to Sarnia in her royal yacht to celebrate the Seaway's opening. A city commission led by the ubiquitous Fats Hume looked into getting some of this overseas business, and residents approved by a 4-1 margin a $300,000 bond issue for port development. St. Clair County farm agent Ned Netherton backed it to the hilt: "Water transportation is cheap. A quantity of anything can be shipped anywhere in the world for about one cent a pound."

A group of local businessmen joined forces to run the Port Huron Seaway Terminal, and at first leaned on beans for business. 29,000 tons of freight, including locally grown beans and some Chrysler auto parts, shipped through the terminal the first year. But Port Huron found itself handicapped by a major development in cargo transportation: containerization. American shipping pioneer Malcolm McLaren hatched the practice of packing manufactured goods and food products into standard-sized containers, to facilitate their movement by anything – ships, railroads, trucks, even air cargo planes. It was a brilliant, world-altering concept, but handling these containers

311

required a scale of operation and crane equipment that Port Huron simply couldn't manage.

Although Port Huron's commercial shipping legacy hung fire, pleasure boating flourished, and construction started on a new $36,000 city marina on the Black River. Thousands of small craft patronized public and private boat wells all over St. Clair County, and the state government build harbors of refuge for boaters around the Thumb. The Port Huron to Mackinac Island sailboat race, an escape to another one of Michigan's automobile-free island paradises (where trucking magnate Myron Ogden kept a cottage), became the major event of the city's summer. But the use of small boats for freight or mass transit purposes, uses still common in many places all over the world, just didn't click any more in this part of it.

Commercial airliners thrived as never before during the 50's, with the helping hands of the federal and state governments, who assisted this growing child at every step. In 1954 Boeing unveiled its four-engined 500 mph jet, the 707, which by 1958 had inaugurated the age of American domestic jet travel. The jetliner design was the direct descendant of armed forces bomber and transport research. U.S. airlines carried more passengers than did railroads as early as 1956. That year two planes collided over the Grand Canyon, killing 128 people, and as a consequence the Congress created the Federal Aviation Administration, and accelerated development of the air traffic control system, at no cost to carriers. Lawmakers offered nothing similar to the railroads, naturally.(74) Small cities like Port Huron couldn't support commercial air service. Barely two passengers per day boarded a trial run by an air carrier at the county airport.

In the 1950's America backslid on bicyclism once again. 21 million people rode them, but few adults took bikes seriously as a vital method of transportation. 80 year-old Charles Duncan rode a bike half a mile to the Marysville city hall one day and found this epic journey headlined on the *Times Herald's* front page: "Marysville Old-Timer Pedals Half-Mile To Keep Tax Date." Not a single dedicated bicycle path of any kind existed in St. Clair County, and road builders paid no more attention to bicyclists than to roadkill. Teenage bicyclist David Wolfe had no bike path or even a decent road shoulder to escape to when impatient 67 year-old geezer George Rich recklessly drove his car past another vehicle on Highway 21 one evening, and slammed into Wolfe, severing his leg and his life. Wolfe's grandfather Stanley Church reacted:

This afternoon I stood at my gate and watched a funeral procession pass by. So you ask what is so important about that? Well sir, I'll tell you. You see, in the hearse was our grandson, a 14 year-old boy, who was loved by everyone who knew him. And I ask myself 'why?' And then, although an old man, I cried and cried, and I am still crying, and so is my wife and my daughter and my son in law, and many, many others who loved this young boy.(75)

Bicycles still topped many childhood Xmas lists, and intrepid young bicyclists still sometimes defied the killer drivers who menaced the Thumb roads. 14 and 13 year-olds Ken and George Stommel with two friends covered 200 miles in five days on their summer bicycle vacation of 1955. "I'd like to put everybody on bicycles," said Dr. Paul Dudley White, President Eisenhower's physician, "not once in a while but regularly as a routine. That's a very good way of preventing heart disease."(76) But President Eisenhower, who suffered a heart attack and stroke while in office, never appeared on a bicycle, nor did U.S. Senate Majority Leader Lyndon Johnson, who also

312

had a bad heart attack. Future journalist David Lamb found only losers used bikes on the college campus he attended: "...if I had shown up at college with a bicycle in 1958, I would have immediately been dismissed as a twit and had no more luck finding a Saturday night date than I would have a bike shop."(77)

As bad as matters had become for American pedestrians since the opening of the 20th Century, they became significantly worse during this decade. National newspaper columnist Hal Boyle of New York sensed downright hostility against him. "People always seem startled when they meet a grownup man who admits he can't or won't drive a car. They tend to put you down as either an idiot or perhaps a secret conspirator against the American way of life." Police in Los Angeles stopped and questioned author Ray Bradbury for the suspicious activity of walking at night on Wilshire Boulevard, an incident reminiscent of Bradbury's anti-Utopian science fiction. Louis Dunn described a typical Port Huron pedestrian's winter day: "Between ducking a slushy splashing from those motorists who put folks who walk in the same class as clay pigeons at a trap shoot, and treacherous footing beneath the slush, the pedestrian earned every mile they had to walk Friday."(78)

Traffic "experts" routinely blamed pedestrians for 50% of the traffic accidents that killed walkers. Sometimes 70%. But since the victims couldn't give their versions of the events these statistics seemed a little suspect. A federal appeals court ruled that "drivers of motor vehicles have no monopoly on streets and highways," but by the 50's this seemed more an arcane theory than a practical fact. Cars hit as many as 3,000 children per year in Michigan, and occasionally these children fought back, as in this rebellion by a gang of Port Huron boys at Washington Junior High:

The hoodlums have been...throwing stones and snowballs at passing cars, nearly causing two bad accidents when drivers lost control of their vehicles; walking down the center of the street five and six abreast and refusing to yield the right of way; holding cars on ice while their wheels spin; swearing at drivers, especially women; snowballing the drivers when they stop out to complain; and pushing parked cars out into the street. (79)

More often, though, children compliantly swallowed the auto propaganda fed them. Some Port Huron fifth graders put into rhyme this watch-out-for-cars advice:

Never play in the street
If you don't want some broken feet.

If you want to save your soul
Always mind the Fillmore [School] *Patrol*

Don't walk between parked cars
Or they'll knock you up to Mars.

Watson Major regretted that his 6 year-old granddaughter Marianne Tipa had been too young to absorb these warnings: "Yes, the name of Marianne Tipa may have long been forgotten in your memory, but not for her parents and her small circle of friends she called 'her gang' and maybe the driver of the car who was responsible for her death." (80) The driver, unaware that he had no street monopoly, killed Marianne as she tried to cross an avenue in her neighborhood.

Nor did the names of 4 year-olds Gary Anglebrandt and his pal Maurice Meyers linger long on Port Huron's conscience, after 18 year-old driver Phillip Morris blasted into them at 50 mph on the residential street outside their homes, knocking them 100 feet to their deaths. City officials refused afterward to put up a traffic light at the spot, saying it was too risky. This incident occurred about the time that Dr. Jonas Salk announced his polio vaccine, and church bells rang, factory whistles blew, cannons fired, schools and offices closed in celebration. But American Medical Association President Elmer Hess said, "Sometimes I can't see why we get so hysterical over polio. More children are killed by automobiles in a month than are killed by polio in a year. Perhaps it's time to get hysterical over traffic deaths."[81]

The car-crazy adolescent youth of America fell more and more out of shape during the 50's, mainly from leg disuse. A survey found 56% of U.S. schoolchildren failed simple muscle tests, compared to 8% in Europe. Infantry from automobile-free China physically far outmatched young American soldiers in the Korean War, and 80% of the Yanks who died there had early stage heart disease. National medical columnist Dr. William Brady unloaded on the public school systems for overlooking physical education: "Our public schools are training a nation of flabby muscled and dull witted youngsters who grow up to find 'relaxation' through alcohol, and 'recreation' in paying to watch sporting events instead of playing the games themselves." True enough, though Brady overlooked the fact that the schools did what the public demanded, indoctrinate children into the physically debilitating car culture. After all, today's young flabbies and dimwits grew up to buy tomorrow's automobiles.

Not just cars but television drained the well of fitness. American often devoted as much as four hours per day to watching auto-loaded and auto-sponsored shows like *Highway Patrol,* and *Traffic Court.* 20% of American adults weighed too much, and became so averse to walking that some couldn't be bothered even to push a lawn mower, so the first riding mower appeared in Port Huron advertising. "Good muscle tone, elasticity, resiliency is acquired by regular daily exercise...and no other exercise is better for the purpose than a brisk daily walk," said the 71 year-old Brady, one of the most prominent physicians in the pedestrian's corner.[82] Dr. White scoffed at anti-exercise members of his profession: "The general warning to stop all vigorous exercise at 40 seems to me to be ridiculous and, more likely than not, actually to lead to an increase in coronary arteriosclerosis." America, said Dr. White with disgust, had become "one of the unhealthiest countries in the world today."[83]

A sedentary life, warned Dr. Hess' AMA, caused heart attacks, diabetes, backaches, tension, obesity, stiff neck, ulcers, cancer, appendicitis, cirrhosis, varicose veins, blood clots and hemorrhoids. 20 million Americans suffered from high blood pressure, and bad hearts felled a lot of middle-aged Port Huron men: bank exec and school board president Gerald Collins, 57; former Chevy dealer Howard Henderson, 58; *Times Herald* controller Ralph Dupes, 37; Port Huron Paper president Norman Seagrove, 58; former ferry boat owner and state senator Gilbert Ibister, 57; Ralph "Ham" Irvin, ex-traffic division chief at the Port Huron Police Department, 57. Just to pin down one year, 382 people died of heart disease in St. Clair County in 1953, the county's favorite cause of death. Preferring to avoid membership in the American League of Dead Fat Men, columnist Hal Boyle embarked on a walking program, and peeled off 40 pounds in 90 days by walking 7-8 miles per day. "Solitary walking can be a great joy," said Hal. "You learn the trees, the store windows, and the people in your town as you can in no other way." But Boyle lost his resolve, and after an idle winter his wife cuttingly told him, "The fat man's back again."

Many older Americans pedestrians presented the nation with better examples than did President Eisenhower or the other slackers. Mrs. Sylvia Carlen, who had dumbfounded Port Huron by walking there from Detroit in a single day at age 82, made a similar excursion to Algonac two years later, covering 40 miles in 9 hours. Retired customs man Joseph Roesch made a 5-10 mile walk around Port Huron part of his daily routine. A Pennsylvania hoofman named Mote Bergman walked 65 miles, Detroit to Pontiac round trip, on his 65th birthday. U.S. Supreme Court Justice William Douglas at age 55 walked 189 miles along the old Chesapeake and Ohio Canal route as a publicity stunt to prevent the canal's being paved over for an automobile highway. 71 year-old farm wife and mother of eleven Emma Gatewood walked from her Ohio home to Portland, Oregon – 2,000 miles in three months – and 5,000 admirers greeted her when she arrived. Gatewood also had walked the entire Appalachian Trail at age 67, the first woman ever to do this solo and in one season.

Attendees at a University of Michigan Conference on Aging heard that regular physical exercise "begun early in life and continued into the advanced years can add 10 years to your life." The corollary that regular automobile use usually subtracted rather than added years went unspoken. Medical advances ran a neck-and-neck race with the degenerative and often violent automobile-based lifestyle in America. The Rx of "get rid of your car" vanished from the lexicon of Port Huron's doctors, because every durned one of them owned an automobile. Health care became the fastest rising U.S. cost-of-living component (transportation was second). One-eighth of the public visited hospitals annually. Port Huron's second hospital opened during the 1950's, the $1.4 million Catholic Mercy Hospital, built on 25 acres of Henry McMorran's former property on the city's south side. Did the city really need it? That converted Catholic Louis Weil apparently didn't think so. He sat tight in one of the beds at the secular Port Huron Hospital for six long, sad years, reviewing his sins, after suffering a stroke in 1953. When he died there at age 82, Mueller Brass boss and songwriter Fred Riggin exaggerated not at all in calling Weil Port Huron's Number One Citizen, though Riggin did not set this sentiment to music, more's the pity.

315

Chapter 9. 1961-1970: Infinitely Nearer Utopia

What if we fail to stop the erosion of cities by automobiles? There's a silver lining to everything. In that case we Americans will hardly need to ponder a mystery which has troubled men for millennia: What is the purpose of life? For us, the answer will be clear, established, and for all practical purposes indisputable: The purpose of life is to produce and consume automobiles.

- Jane Jacobs, 1961(1)

Only a man with a heart of stone could resist temptation like this! Sensible talk about the budget, the good years left in your present car, any kind of rational thought, forget it!...you might as well stop by the bank on the way to the Chevrolet dealer's. It's fate, man!

– General Motors, 1963

The mantle of First Citizen of Port Huron now descended not onto the shoulders of Louis Weil's son Granger, but onto one of his employees, John Francis Brown. Nobody immediately recognized him as the heir apparent, but over the course of the next 35 years reporter Brown gradually assumed the role of your typical Mr. Port Huron. Born in 1935, raised by his grandmother in a home about halfway between the bells of the old city hall and those of St. Stephen's Catholic Church, Brown and a platoon of friends spent their childhood scampering through a neighborhood they knew well enough to have walked blindfolded. He pulled the usual boyhood pranks, and Sheriff Lucas once booted him in the butt for throwing rocks at the jailhouse windows. Brown also served as an altar boy, and sold the *Times Herald* on the downtown streets. Though heavily near-sighted, he played football and basketball at St. Stephen's High, then did a stretch in the Army, worked as a repo man, and finally joined the hometown paper. Before long he was covering the police beat expertly, sometimes with tips from his aunt, who worked as secretary to the police chief. He married, started a family, bought a middle class home on the expanding north side of town, and occasionally relieved the tensions and stresses of a working member of the press by throwing open a window and unleashing his version of the Tarzan yell across the neighborhood. Known as Jerry, or sometimes Brownie, he captained no industry, didn't move or shake politically, but Brown's stories, interviews and personal travails practically defined the city of his time. Brownie came from a generation that not only had never known an automobile-free Port Huron, they couldn't even imagine such a place. To Americans of his age, half-human half-sedan, if you traveled anywhere outside of your yard, you drove. Even so much as a block or two away, no joke. Car travel was expected, a badge of responsible independent adulthood, the normal – indeed the only – way to get around.

Brownie proved especially adept at writing that staple of American journalism which took a permanent and valued place in the editorial bag of tricks during the 1960's, Heroic Sick People. These profiles featured as a standard subject somebody in a bad way physically or mentally, who faced the future, sometimes an abbreviated future, with resolution, a poignant smile, maybe with a sigh and a few tears mixed in. "Doomed By Rare Disease, Youth Isn't Surrendering – Plans Active Life," typified the genre. Jerry could really work up a sob story over some of these cases, abundantly supplied by the auto culture. 15 year-old Meredith MacRury came tailor-made for the treatment, though she wasn't smiling, sighing, or crying. She lay inert in a eight month-long coma in a nursing home following a three-car traffic accident north of Port Huron on the Scenic Highway. At the time of this wreck she'd been riding home with her 20 year-old employer from a babysitting job.

Understandably, Meredith's mother had to fill in the gaps a little for her daughter in Brown's story:

Unforeseen Traffic Accident Shatters Life of Teenage Girl – Her Smile is Gone.

What once was a world of imagination, joy and an eagerness to learn isn't even a memory. A bed, four walls and meaningless footsteps of unknown persons, as well as persons she once knew, are part of her new world. Her mother: "Hope for her now is only a word. The doctors have given us little hope that she will recover and if she does it will be with probable severe brain damage. Unless you have had a loved one confined to a hospital bed or have seen him in helpless pain, you can't measure the hurt.(2)

Neither Mrs. MacRury nor Brownie expressed the slightest hint of resentment or disillusionment with the device that nearly had destroyed this girl. Neither swore off using automobiles forever or for so much as a weekend. Meredith eventually ended up in another hospital, her fourth, as doctors strained to discover whether she could still see or hear. Her high school classmates earned a few dollars from fundraisers to help out the family with medical expenses. The MacRurys had insurance but "it's just not enough."

The headline writer, not Jerry Brown, hatched the fumbling expression "unforeseen traffic accident." After all, how many foreseen traffic accidents had there been? A sad enough story, yes, only a man with a heart of stone would deny that. But at least Meredith had done her bit in the consumption of automobiles, the real meaning of life in America. It's fate, man. It got to be a progressively more crowded fate, what with 4.5 million motor vehicles on the roads of Michigan, and 105 million in the United States by 1969, one for every two people in the country. The 13-16 million traffic accidents that year involved one out of every ten people in America, and killed or injured 178,000 victims like Meredith in Michigan, and 4-5 million nationwide.(3) And for the benefit of the humane society, let's mention the one million animals pancaked *per day* on U.S. roads.

The accident tally sheet furnished yet another awkward war casualty comparison. More Americans died and suffered injury in traffic in a single year than in combat action during the entire 14-year course of the Vietnam War, the Far Eastern adventure in world management that the U.S. stepped into in 1961, though it couldn't even keep its own house in order. We may well wonder who served the higher purpose: Meredith MacRury, or Dewayne Williams, the St. Clair County Marine who covered a grenade in Vietnam on his 19th birthday and won a posthumous Medal of Honor.

Traffic accidents cost the nation about $15 billion per year, or $285 for every single household in the country. Michigan Secretary of State James Hare calculated the

317

accident rate at three times higher than estimated, because most people didn't report the minor ones which might bump up their insurance rates. During the decade that ended in 1969, the numbers of Michigan motor vehicle numbers rose 40%, drivers 26%, mileage 65%, accidents 67%, deaths 69%, injuries 170%. Achieving yet another apogee of gall, auto company stooges in the Swinging Sixties used the declining ratio of outright-killed-per-mile-driven as some sort of crazy source of hope to distract the motoring public from the soaring millions of broken but still-breathing victims. Since no one kept track of Levassor deaths, for all anyone knew their numbers climbed proportionately as medical science invented new ways to keep the gravedigger temporarily at bay. Detroit rooted for Meredith MacRury because, statistically, if she didn't conk out within a year of her accident, authorities didn't record her in the automobile fatality ledger.

A single victim's story like Meredith's made an easy assignment for Jerry Brown in 1969, compared to the six-corpse crash he'd worked on as a young reporter back in 1961. Seven youths packed into a single car on their way home from a high school graduation party had piled into a bridge railing in rural St. Clair County. Each of them got a personal profile send-off in the *Times Herald*, loaded with wistful details. The dead driver, for instance, 22 year-old Alvin Meddaugh, had been part owner of a Port Huron gas station. Meddaugh's mom admitted that Alvin had been a little car-crazy, and the 290 feet of skid marks at the accident scene seemed to verify it. This graduation crackup supplanted in the public mind a crash of just few weeks earlier, when four Canadian soldiers expired after their car collided head-on with a pickle truck on the Gratiot Pike coming back from Detroit. Sheriff William Pettengill pronounced it one of the worst auto accidents in St. Clair County history, until Meddaugh went it two bodies better. By the 1960's it took either something pretty spectacular in the way of highway mayhem to get the public's attention, like a lot of bodies laid out in one fell swoop, or else the close up and personal tearjerker treatment in the press to put a face on an individual victim. Outside of his circle of family and friends, the public barely noticed a run-of-the-mill fatal during these same few weeks, Lloyd Solomon's dive into some roadside trees, after the father of eight fell asleep at the wheel of his car.

The perfection of the automobile driver still seemed uncomfortably far off for a nation on the verge of Utopia. How many people in Port Huron actually followed neighbor R.R. Smith's advice and recited the *Driver's Prayer* by S. Barlow Bird before taking the babysitter home, or departing a graduation party, or making a run to Detroit, or even heading to the Ross Drive-In Bible Church, for that matter?

Each time I feel the urge to roll
At speeds my hands cannot control
Let me recall the eerie blare
Of sirens on the empty air
And see the grim faced men in white
Bear a sheet draped form from sight.
Let me not numb, by drinking booze,
The brain that I attempt to use,
Nor range myself with those whose sin
Is killing when too full of gin.(4)

Bard Bird hit the mark squarely about gin sinners, like Port Huron teenager Cornelius Gross, who drunkenly pulled his carload of friends into the path of a family of churchgoers one night, triggering another six-fatality wreck. Drunks piloted one out of every 50 vehicles on American roads, according to United Press correspondent Robert Buckhorn. Booze slowed their reaction times by at least 15%, and reduced their eyesight acuity to the equivalent of wearing sunglasses at night. Booze left drivers 25 times more likely to have one of the 800,000 drunk driving collisions rung up in 1968, which accounted for almost half the fatals. When the state of Michigan finally okayed breathalyzer evidence in courts, and passed "implied consent" rules to force drivers to give it, the number of drunk driving arrests quintupled in one year. This meant embarrassing exposure in the *Times Herald* for more local sots. Friends and relatives of drunk drivers regularly accosted and yelled at Jerry Brown for printing these names. Buckhorn wondered whether America's 6 million alcoholics should have driving licenses at all. They got them because states didn't require breathalyzer tests for license applicants.(5) Thinking back to the days of Happy Jack Welch in the Port Huron of 1900, one could warmly appreciate the fact that he'd only traveled afoot.

Many more defective drivers besides drunks menaced the roads as well. For example, recreational drug use picked up substantially during the 1960's. A big 1969 pot bust in Port Huron collared 22 people at one party, and the breathalyzer couldn't detect grass. Aside from Pennsylvania, not a single state required a medical certification for driving. Nobody methodically weeded out the 24 million people in America with physical shortcomings that might not bear up too well behind the wheel – the crippled, the deaf, the semi-blind, the 5% of the populace with convulsive disorders. (6) And the senile: "I am 86 years young. When driving my car I find there are two white center lanes in place of the true one. It is deceiving and inconvenient. This has bothered me for two years. Are there any vitamins that would remedy this?" So wrote one oldtimer to medical columnist Joseph Molner in the *Times Herald*.(7)

Mentally disoriented drivers proved especially elusive. Social scientists of this decade speculated that suicidal drivers caused an estimated 5% of all fatal crashes, and who knew how many sub-fatals. One California motorist deliberately drove into a head-on collision which killed everybody but him. "I wanted to teach the #@$% to dim his lights when he sees a car coming," remarked the survivor. Another unhinged Californian cried out before triggering a fatal wreck, "What's the matter, are you afraid to die?" He too recovered from his injuries.(8) Traffic expert A. E. Florio of the University of Illinois didn't call it a new idea, but he suggested that an occasional mental exam for drivers might be helpful. He identified four main types of road crazies: "the egotist," "the overemotional," "the rationalizer," "the showoff." Failure with the head shrinker on these terms would have looked a little silly on some license applications: "Rejected for rationalizing." Still, the process might have diverted from the road people like 39 year-old James Shaw of Port Huron, who pointed a .357 Magnum at a fellow motorist during a traffic argument. Clearly overemotional. Port Huron insurance man Robert Odle proposed a broader category for mental study, "under 25 single men," half of whom had traffic accidents annually.

Agents like Odle also reported big trouble from the driver type known as "the swindler," who staged crashes, and reported phantom crashes, designed to milk insurance companies. Fraud of all kinds drove six insurance firms out of business in Michigan within two years, while others canceled thousands of policies. Car insurance premiums in America averaged $170 per year by 1970. Companies paid out $8-$10 billion in padded repair bills each year, and called an estimated 10% of all auto accident

319

claims pure phonies, like the following: "A young boy was wheel-chaired into court in California after being 'crippled' in an automobile accident. A fire engine went past the courthouse...the youngster jumped from his wheelchair and ran to the window."(9) To honest traffic accident victims a personal finance column in the *Times Herald* offered this insurance advice: "Keep your big mouth shut." Easy enough to do if you were dead, but if you blabbed to a crooked driver or witnesses after your crash it could cost you thousands.

Professor Florio should have made room in his catalog of dangerous motorists for "the impatient," what most drivers became after spending too much time behind the wheel. None other than the *Times Herald's* head man and traffic safety fanatic Granger Weil talked a little screwy sometimes about waiting for a 30 second traffic light: "Somehow I hate to think that over the next five years I'm going to spend a full work week waiting for a red light to turn green." Longer than that, Granger, more like six months over the course of a lifetime. Alongside Weil, 40 year-old Mabel Dixon of Port Huron could be slotted into this same fretful category. While driving herself and her husband home from a vacation (and 90% of all vacationers went by car), Mabel got a little ahead of herself on the last lap (most auto vacationers traveled about 300 miles per day). She tried passing two cars and a travel trailer simultaneously at night, on Highway 21. The resulting crash into an oncoming car killed the Dixons and three other people and backed up traffic a mile in both directions. Fascinated gawkers broke into tears over the awful scene and could barely stand to keep on looking. The Dixon disaster also underscored the extraordinary dangers of night driving, dangers most drivers preferred to ignore. Headlights carried brand names like "intense-beam turnpike Super-Lite," but remained completely inadequate for illuminating the road ahead. Drivers at night steered mostly from instinct, making their moves based on an educated guess about what should be in front of them, and trusting to luck. Rationalizers.

The *Times Herald's* editors, numb in the brain not so much from booze as from decades of failure in promoting auto safety, attempted to use their heads more philosophically about the matter, and achieve a stoical inner peace on the subject:

Every day we blithely duck into a couple of tons of steel, hunch over the steering wheel, and send it hurtling along the ground at anywhere from 30 to 70 miles an hour. And every day hundreds of us discover that when those tons of steel are forced to come to an abrupt halt, they – and us – get smashed up. Of course, the nice thing about it is that although we know it happens every day, we don't really believe it will happen to us.(10)

When another four teenagers died in a crash on the north side of town, the paper added with a sigh: "...soon dull routine spreads its analgesia over the warning and we become once again a part of the hurried, harried, it-can't-happen-to-me motoring public." Almost everyone in America tangled up the the automobile culture by the 1960's qualified as a Heroic Sick Person.

The guardians of the law didn't really accomplish very much in the circumstances. Police handed out 6,000 tickets and attended to 3,000 traffic accidents in St. Clair County per year. Sheriff William Pettengill's deputies tried another speed survey around the sticks, and found one-third of the 900 cars they clocked broke the law. During a check at a single intersection, Port Huron police issued 57 tickets in 5 hours, as fast as they could write them. "Sometimes it appears that we almost need one officer for every driver to see that the regulations are obeyed," wrote the *Times Herald's*

Louis Dunn helplessly. Port Huron Police Chief Carl Falk defended his cops for chasing speeders at 120 mph: "Unless the violator is apprehended there will be no regard for the law." But few regarded it in any case.

Civil disobedience on that scale all over the state led the Michigan legislature to increase expressway speed limits to 70/60 mph in day/night. They condemned 25 mph, once regarded as a dangerously high speed, as now being dangerously slow on highways, and ordered motor vehicles traveling that slowly to carry big reflectorized warning signs. Lawmakers created a new category of driving offense, careless driving, a lesser version of reckless. They hoped careless would be easier to prove in court than reckless, though the dividing line looked a little subjective. Somewhat careless and reckless themselves, 10% of Michigan's legislators drove on expired licenses. 83% had tickets or accidents on their records. State Senator Basil Brown of Highland Park, birthplace of Henry Ford's moving assembly line, racked up 21 driving convictions in 20 years, and sponsored a bill banning public disclosure of this information. Two weeks later police jailed him for drunk driving again. The phenomenon of dumb driving by public officials didn't occur just in Michigan. U.S. Senator Ted Kennedy zoomed a car off a ferry landing one night in Massachusetts, drowning his presidential ambitions and a friend at one stroke. The President of the United States himself, leadfoot Lyndon B. Johnson, reportedly cranked it up to 90 when he drove himself around Texas. Maybe from a bad conscience, LBJ beat his breast over the "carnage on the highways," calling it the nation's biggest problem, next to Vietnam.

Michigan's new governor, former Rambler president George Romney, appeared in a traffic safety film broadcast across the state, *The Michigan Massacre,* but warned children not to watch due to some of the nauseating crash footage included. Romney convened a 219 member Committee on Traffic Safety, called for more state police and more driver training, and also ordered enforcement crackdowns. All pretty tired gambits by then. As researcher David Klein put it, "There's not a nickel's worth of proof that these things ever prevented an accident. And the same goes for motor vehicle inspection."(11) The state police could hardly crack down any harder since they patrolled a million miles a month and wrote 14,000 citations every 30 days. At a loss to say anything new or original on the subject of automobile law, police just took refuge in cliches. "I believe safe driving depends on the individual," said Port Huron traffic officer Ed Cole tiredly. Cole had just settled his own individual $15,000 accident lawsuit over a collision with a dairy truck. Depending on the undependable individual for safe driving gave him too much credit, as St. Clair City Police Chief John MacDonald found out when a car killed him while he directed traffic at a high school football game.

If only raw signage had helped, America's 50 million traffic signs should have made highways as tranquil as canals. 9,000 of them decorated Port Huron's streets, an average of 64 per mile, in 300 varieties, including 758 stop signs. Even with that many around, some intersections still had no signs at all, and usually an intersection crash happened somewhere in town every day. Resident Elmer Malone wanted another stop sign placed in his neighborhood:

Take this evening for instance: the usual blood chilling sound of brakes, and this time, the sudden sound of metal crunching against metal. Or consider the other day when my wife Faye saw a young girl hurled through the air after [one] *car smashed into another.*

Faye tells me that the thud of a body as it hits and then slides along the pavement is quite unlike any other...(12)

Stop signs were better than nothing, but far from foolproof, as Jerry Brown detailed in another gutpunching article:

"We were just going for a little drive – I thought that other car would stop for the intersection." The man who spoke those words had just walked away from the smoldering wreckage of his car. Two blankets covered the lifeless bodies of his wife and young daughter. Just a little drive.(13)

By comparison, the widespread disregard for the 700 parking meters and 1,500 No Parking signs in Port Huron, and the resultant 1,000 parking tickets per month, seemed pretty trivial.

The American Bar Association, whose membership revered the automobile as a gift from the litigation gods, nevertheless took alarm over the amount of traffic work drowning the nation's courts, especially in big cities. U.S. courts at all levels spent 57% of their time on automobile matters.(14) Chicago faced a backlog of 4 million tickets, and even in a small city like Marysville traffic cases lingered as long as four years. Some courts spent as little as 2 minutes apiece in adjudicating these matters. Brand new Port Huron City Attorney Anthony Bonadio had a reckless driving case tossed in his lap the day the jury trial began. As a result of this courtroom crush, traffic justice varied wildly. The ABA cited the file of a man who ran a stop sign at 100 mph, killed two people and injured seven, and after his day in court got off with a $22 fine.(15) And a lot of this traffic court work involved repeat business. Edward Zeros of Port Huron, mentioned in our last chapter, now 30 years old, convicted five times for reckless driving, once for drunk driving, and twice for driving without a license, on his latest trip to court finally pulled a nine month stretch in the county jail to allow him time to think things over. Secretary of State Hare uncovered the incredible record of a Detroit driver who somehow ran up 125 violation points in two years, the equivalent of 20 negligent homicides, but still hadn't been jailed.

A scholar at Michigan State University, James Carnahan, found that only 1 out of 25 drivers responsible for fatal accidents in Michigan actually went to jail. 20 year-old Robert Carson, of Port Huron's Gold Coast up on Lake Huron, now the richest neighborhood in town, avoided the hoosegow for killing 62 year-old Janet Gaiefsky in a head-on crash. He peeled off $200 in court costs and drove away with three years probation for negligent homicide. When 78 year-old Steve Saladucha ran over and killed his best friend George Kotyk in the village of Emmett, he argued that a dog barking in the car had distracted him and really deserved the blame. Not even the dog went to jail.

It didn't do any good, but for conscience's sake, the media urged American motorists throughout the decade to drive more carefully. On television the device called the Public Service Announcement slipped in discreetly between the avalanche of automobile-promoting commercials and the car-filled episodes of dozens of entertainment programs on the air, everything from *Route 66* to *My Mother the Car.* A typical 30 or 60 second PSA told motorists to slow down and live, bring 'em back alive, drive defensively, watch out for the other guy, and designate a driver – somebody at the party to abstain from alcohol so he could enjoy the privilege of chauffeuring all his

322

plastered friends home afterward. A modestly catchy jingle on the virtues of seat belts drilled its way into the consciousness of Americans through sheer repetition:

Buckle up for safety, buckle up.
Buckle up for safety, always buckle up.
Show the world you care by the belt you wear,
Buckle up for safety, when you're driving buckle up.

The more pertinent and direct advice of "Don't drive a car for safety, take the train" never made it onto the air, nor did the simple declarative truths that "Automobiles are inherently unsafe." An interesting parallel occured when U.S. Surgeon General Luther Terry announced in 1964 that cigarettes caused cancer and numerous other maladies. The government mustered the courage to order that every package sold in the country, and every cigarette ad, carry a health warning. They slapped no such health warning on the cars and trucks which constituted a vastly greater danger than all the smokes ever consumed, nor on even the most irresponsible automobile advertising:

Wildcat! Buick's Torrid New Luxury Sports Car! First with the Sure-Footed Sock of Advanced Thrust! Now – all the fun of red-hot, sports car action while you sit in the lap of luxury. Advanced Thrust that places the rip-snorting Wildcat V-8 over the front wheels. This Wildcat has more horses than you'll ever need. Wild.

By now the automobile sales year moved to a rhythm as familiar and comfortable to Port Huron dealers like James Moore Chevrolet as the seasons on a farm. The matching of suckers to bait at Moore's Main Street dealership began in October, when the newborn Chevy models appeared. Chevy sold as many as six different sub-brands, big, little, and in-between. Each of these sizes enjoyed in turn a year or two of public favor during the 60's, as drivers' tastes in cars swung back and forth between economy and voluptuary. To alert potential buyers about the new arrivals, Moore had to cook up just the right kind of swill for the local newspaper ads. The hoopla high season still lavishly used the word "new":

New Caprice – Shimmering new interiors. New Chevrolet – no Chevrolet has ever had a ride like this. New Chevelles – as all new inside as they are outside. All New Chevy II – It's so different, we should really call it Chevy III. Corvair – Lots new.

The *Times Herald* could be relied on to work the publicity bellows every year with a feature story or two during new car month, and the paper assigned reporter Mike Patton to huff and puff over one such introduction, throwing in some horsey imagery:

The '68s are in the showroom in all their gleaming multihued glory, sleek as thoroughbreds, powerful as Percherons, enticing as sin and virulent as flu. The symptoms are those of puppy love – loss of appetite, weakened knees, a peculiar distortion of view. The victim sees what he wants to see.(16)

To make sure the victim saw what Chevrolet wanted him to see General Motors aided Moore with generous national support during the annual launch. All the automakers papered mass market publications with ads. The Big 3 bought up an October edition of the national Sunday magazine supplement *Family Weekly* which the *Times Herald* stuffed into its newspapers. Typical headlines: "Those 1968 Cars – Safer, Roomier, More Powerful!," "The 1969 Cars – A Step on the Road to Perfection." But just in case, tucked in between these picture-packed feature stories, *Family Weekly* introduced a little cautionary advice about the road to perfection. "How to Be a Safer Driver: Don't assume anything, except to assume that all other drivers are blind or homicidal." And: "Would You Survive These Driving Emergencies?"

Suddenly you feel very sick because you might die. There's a car coming at you head-on. You have one chance – a split second one. Do the wrong thing and you'll end up one of the six Americans who die on our highways every hour. Do the right thing and it's possible to come through the incident with nothing worse than a cold sweat. The difference, according to new research by the National Safety Council, is knowing what to do without thinking about it – know what to do automatically.(17)

The possible driving emergencies placed before the *Family Weekly* reader together cast some doubt on the mechanical perfectitude of automobiles: an engine fire in the Mojave Desert, brake failure in the Mexican mountains, headlight outage on a Texas highway, accelerator jam on the Kansas Turnpike, and a dive into Lake Geneva in Wisconsin after taking a curve too fast. Two weeks after this story appeared, Port Huron auto mechanic Clark Christy took a curve too fast just north of town, but had no lake to plunge into, so his car rolled and tumbled for 560 feet across a field before tossing him out and killing him. Too much thinking there, Clark, not enough automatic.

Fresh broadcast ballyhoo filled the television and radio channels for a month or more at new car season. Sometimes the soft sell fitted the occasion, as when singer Dinah Shore, famed for the song *See The USA in Your Chevrolet*, probably the most appealing spokesperson the industry every hired, emceed a mellow Chevy special:

Oh, when the fall comes along
And the leaves come tumbling down
The eyes of the nation turn to Detroit town.
That's where the cars are.
Brand new cars.
And that's where we're going to go
On this Chevy show.

Sometimes the situation called for the hard sell, as in this apotheosis of Empty Roads TV advertising: arguably the worst car built in America struggled up an incline at the Inyo National Forest in California, urged on by a panting announcer:

Land of the oldest living things on earth: the more than 4,000 year-old bristlecone pine. Arid highlands two miles in the sky, windswept and tortured by sand. Mountain rocks left gaping and jagged by endless erosion. Now, to this land, a visitor! By special permission of the United States Forest Service, the incredible Corvair...Chevrolet's rear-engine success steps out with spirited sports car flair! If there's a skeptic left, let him watch now...a deep-throated engine...the fight is fought...the last leg of a brutal climb!

Once the fervor of the fall dissipated, Moore Chevrolet got down to cases in January with a plain vanilla *New Chevrolet Sale,* soberly expressing the dealer's willingness to hand over a 1966 Chevy II for $60 per month for 36 months, plus $99 down and any old car trade-in. Carefully, so as not to antagonize the losers who'd already forked out full price, in April Moore set about suggesting a certain degree of sticker leeway: *Chevrolet Double Dividend Days! Buys on those big beautiful*

Chevrolets have never been better! In August it came time to sweep out the chaff: *"Are there really any sound reasons for buying a Chevrolet in August? In a word: Six.* And with October's return came renewed newness: *'67 Chevrolet. Everything new that could happen...happened!...massive new grille...new-type body...new rear window...new safety.*

Thanks to these time-tested methods, St. Clair County families, head count 120,000, now owned 56,000 motor vehicles. They spent $1,400 per vehicle per year, a total of $78 million. By decade's end the average new car price topped $3,500. To pay for it, as author John Jerome said of this period: "...the universal practice of computing car loan interest rates on a nondeclining balance commonly result(ed) in true interest rates of over 18% per annum."(18) Americans typically wasted 20% of their income on cars; in two-car families 30%. Private spending on U.S automobiles, all in, totaled $94 billion in 1970.(19) Americans also bought and maintained cars they never drove or thought about, like the municipal vehicles in Port Huron. At a single meeting, the City Council helped themselves to a $21,000 tree truck, 2 vans for $2,800 each, a $2,600 pickup, $4,000 dump truck, $10,000 dump truck with crane, and 2 empty chassis for $20,000. After a meal like that the council thought it wise to table a $25,000 bid for 8 police cars and a $3,000 stake truck.

As usual, Autoland's business fortunes went through ups and down during the decade, but enjoyed mainly ups. Auto profits, and wages, mounted like hotcakes during much of the period. GM executive John Delorean later expressed his gratitude: "We were living off the gullibility of the consumer combined with the fantastic growth of the American economy in the 1960s."(20) Fantastic except at Studebaker, which gave up the ghost entirely in 1966. That left four American automakers, plus the foreign importers who now sold 1 million vehicles per year, much to the discomfort of the Yanks. By 1970 auto industry bosses regarded the sale of more than 8.5 million new cars and trucks in the United States during a single solar orbit, an all-time record back in 1950, as a recession. They reckoned the 9.5 million sales year of 1969 their just due.

Not even the strains of war were allowed to decelerate U.S. assembly lines any more. Instead of operating under constraints similar to those imposed during WW2 and the Korean War, the industry's rate of automobile production, and the amount of buyer financing, went completely unchecked by the government during the enormously expensive, unpopular, seemingly endless, and ultimately unsuccessful Vietnam campaign. The fact that former Ford Whiz Kid and FMC president Robert McNamara served as Secretary of Defense may have played a part in this inflationary scenario.

Ford Motor constructed a new 300,000 square foot headquarters in Dearborn, where in these salad days top executives ate $100 meals at lunch, for which they paid $2.(21) What little self-control Henry Ford II possessed went by the board as he divorced his wife, married an Italian jetsetter, roamed the world's hot spots, and drank more than he could hold. Henry the Deuce, as he came to be called, reenacted a scenario from his grandpa's days that had many wondering whether he'd lost his marbles. He first hired Semon "Bunkie" Knudsen, son of the late Ford and Chevrolet stalwart William Knudsen, as the FMC's new president, its fourth of the decade. Henry then fired Bunkie 19 months later, just as grandfather Ford had canned William, and for the same reason, uppitiness. Henry subsequently tagged Lee Iacocca as Ford president #5 of the Sixties.

325

Iacocca's self-confidence belonged to him, but his leadership style came right out of the Ford manual. Later he was loath to admit this after his own trip to Henry II's scaffold. Iacocca paved his way to the presidency when in 1964 he overrode company skeptics and masterminded the introduction of the Mustang, a souped up version of Ford's compact Falcon. He also broke the horse barrier at Ford in naming this car. Iacocca launched a gigantic marketing campaign for Mustang that almost carbon copied the 1928 Model A2 rollout, with TV added. His Mustang pitch also reworked some refrains of the Universal Car, "We wanted to develop a car that you could drive to the country club on Friday night, to the drag strip on Saturday, and to church on Sunday," said Lee.(22) The ad agencies translated this to:

You know these people. They're the go ones, the exciting ones, the young ones, millions of them, they're all around us. Bright, charming, attractive, vibrant. With a whole new concept of tomorrow. They have taste, judgment, unmistakable flair. Ford knows they search for the unexpected. Ford has it. The Ford Mustang.

The Mustang sold like mad and earned over $1 billion in profits in two years, largely from overpriced options attached to it. Hollywood gave the Mustang its seal of approval in the motion picture *Bullitt*, when hero Steve McQueen drove his high-power version around San Francisco in a lunatic pursuit of a Dodge Charger (*Comes on like Genghis Khan!*). The episode ended in a simulated fiery crash of the Dodge, nearly worthy of real life, and the immolation of two bad guys. See you in church. Henry Ford's great-grandson William Clay Ford, Jr. flipped over this picture: "This was one of the coolest scenes I'd ever seen in a movie. From that point on I was hooked..."(23) Just like Barney Oldfield and the *999* of 1902. Great grandpa would have been proud; the next generation of Ford boys were coming along fine.

Bright, charming, attractive, vibrant auto assembly line workers commonly put in 10 hours per day, six or even seven days per week during the go-go Sixties, and absenteeism among the go ones on Mondays and Fridays registered as much as 20%.(24) In exchange UAW members took home almost $9,000 per year by 1970, wages 25% higher than average manufacturing employees received, wages often extracted by a strike at one or the other of the Big 3 when the latest labor contract expired. Despite this high rate of pay, the FMC still had trouble hanging onto its 250,000 workers, the same problem it faced in 1913, and the company sent a mobile recruiting office to Port Huron to try to enlist bodies for a plant 80 miles away. GM offered similar jobs 120 miles away at Lansing.

Ford nearly adopted Port Huron permanently and in one gulp during this period, when it considered the city as the spot for a humongous new 327-acre, 2.5 million square-foot stamping plant. It was a close call, but the FMC instead built the 4,000 employee operation in Woodhaven, Michigan, south of Detroit. Alumnus Steve Deak later remembered that the work at Woodhaven wore out some new hires so quickly that they didn't last past lunch time on their first day. "Things like ergonomics weren't considered back then. But the people who stuck with the job and worked hard took pride in coming home exhausted."(25) This precisely inverted the relaxed style the first Henry Ford had promised his workers, before the company double-crossed them with speedups and mandatory overtime.

Established St. Clair County firms continued to manufacture auto parts aplenty even without a Ford presence. The Prestolite (formerly Auto-Lite) auto wire plant kept 900 people at work and paid out $7 million in wages annually. Chrysler built 427 cubic-inch engines in Marysville for both boats and cars, threatening the lives of Americans on land and sea. Port Huron redoubled its efforts to lure new faces in the auto business to its Industrial Park. It succeeded with some nickel-and-dimers. Assembly Specialties built luggage racks for station wagons, in case you had so much treasure to haul that it overflowed the wagon's interior and had to be strapped to the roof. County unemployment rose and fell between the tolerable limits of 4% and 11% during the decade.

Quality control remained as bad as ever in auto manufacturing, not least because of the retooling needed for the annual model changes. The average new car arrived at a dealer's showroom with 24 defects in it – bad leaks, bum brakes, shorty electrical systems, and wheel misalignment ranked among the usuals. Auto recalls, which dated as far back as Buick's bad gas tank latches of 1915, became a regular fact of ownership in the 60's. Recalls came in all sizes. Chevrolet summoned owners to bring back 1.5 million vehicles to fix sticky accelerators. GM recalled 24 Port Huron area school buses for faulty brakes. Just be careful driving them in.

Considering their cost, automobiles were unconscionably flimsy. A simple 5 mph bump meant an average $200 repair bill thanks to the largely decorative nature of bumpers on U.S. vehicles.(26) Most cars came with a kind of warranty, but it usually required exacting maintenance and often exasperating negotiation with retailers to get repairs. One wrathful car owner wrote "All the warranty means is that 'We have your money, now whistle *Dixie*.'" The Federal Trade Commission summed it up:

...many new cars are delivered to the buyer in poor condition; car owners experience difficulty in having repairs made simply and expeditiously, often causing them great inconvenience; workmanship in warranty repair work is frequently shoddy; and exclusions, limitations and conditions in the warranties are not made clear to the purchasers.(27)

At General Motors, suspicion grew that the dominance of the company by accountants undermined product quality. When he reached the rank of vice-president, Thomas Murphy, a numbers-cruncher himself, admitted it: "I suddenly realized I didn't know the first thing about an automobile, let alone the mechanics of meeting a production schedule."(28) Even an engineer, like Pontiac boss DeLorean, couldn't help but notice that his Tempest model "rattled so loudly it sounded as though it was carrying a half ton of rocks." Delorean creatively attacked this problem by jamming a bigger engine into the vehicle, marketing it as a "muscle" car, and commissioning a pop song about it, *Little GTO: Gonna save all my money and buy a GTO / Get a helmet and a roll bar and I'll be ready to go.*(29)

In a rare dissent, the Auto Club condemned the GTO idea, or any other muscle car, which it called "motorized missles": "These cars are powered far too strongly for the needs of any motorist in any foreseeable circumstance, and far above the capacity of present streets and roads."(30) And built no better than the regular brand in the bargain. When one lemon owner complained about his problem vehicle to an auto worker he knew, the fellow replied, "Come on down to the plant anytime and I'll show you cars that come off the line every day that are a lot worse than yours." Ford battled these bad vibes about quality by driving one its cars off a ski jump at Lake Placid, NY and another one up and down the steps at the Los Angeles Colosseum to try to show

how slamworthy they were.

Aside from quality, the tide of public opinion also turned against Detroit on two other counts: safety and smoke. Attorneys filed as many as 5,000 lawsuits per year over accident injuries which they claimed had been caused by unsafe, badly designed vehicles.(31) This prejudice gained traction, to the dismay of automakers, who reckoned that this was not their just due. General Motors president John Gordon blasted "self-styled experts" and "amateur engineers" for hassling him. The *Times Herald* couldn't have agreed more: "There's a conspiracy afoot to rob you of your horses – or, rather, your horsepower. The conspirators won't admit thoughts of larceny, but you will be walking if they have their way."(32) The paper sent Jerry Brown over to a Port Huron Rotary Club meeting to hear one of the conspirators, accident researcher Paul Gikas of the University of Michigan. Brownie came away from the luncheon in shock after Gikas gave him and the stunned Rotarians a look at some crash slides, one of which "showed a young girl with a gearshift lever through her throat."

Another of the self-styled experts, lawyer Ralph Nader, published a book called *Unsafe at Any Speed,* for which GM sicced some private detectives on him because of his nasty remarks about the Corvair. Nader's book not only doomed "the incredible Corvair," it helped persuade the federal government to found the National Highway Traffic Safety Administration (NHTSA), which 70 years late imposed the first government regulation on car design. Michigan State University's Traffic Safety Center pointed out that, heretofore, government in America had inspected building construction, electrical equipment, plumbing conditions, and meatpacking, but not car manufacturing, which when gummed up did more damage to the public weal than the others combined. Certainly no government man graded car carcasses as "grade A choice" when they came off the assembly lines, as he might a cow or hog.

Not everyone in the auto industry opposed safety regs. American Motors styling chief Richard Teague had lost an eye at age 6 in a car wreck, then his father in another crash the following year. Teague admitted that car interiors could use some softening up. Chrysler safety chief Roy Hauesler allowed a car should be more "forgiving of driver error, driver inattentiveness, and driver inebriation." A noted ambulance-chasing lawyer from Detroit, Harry Philo, who could be said to have made his living from automobiles, ventured that maybe traffic accidents were foreseeable after all. Everybody had one eventually, and car companies should build accordingly: "They should see that the product they put out is safe for foreseeable use - and it's foreseeable that cars are going to be in collision."(33) Forewarned is forearmed.

More interior padding, breakaway mirrors, and collapsible steering columns introduced by the industry didn't mollify the new critics. NHTSA director William Haddon set 23 safety standards for new cars beginning in 1968. This touched off a chorus of whining among the Big 3, who immediately added $100 each to the price of their cars. "You're looking at a worried bunch of guys," said an FMC spokesman. The U.S. Public Health Service, the National Safety Council, and the American Medical Association all got behind the seat belt idea originally hatched by Congressman Kenneth Roberts in the 50's. The *Times Herald* ordered belts on company cars, and quoted a Port Huron doctor: "I wouldn't drive the few blocks from my office to the hospital without using my safety belt." He might just as well have walked the few blocks in the first place but his opinion seemed to carry some moral authority.

The seat belt campaign resulted in the federal government's requiring them on its 300,000 cars. Belt mandates followed for vehicles in individual states like Wisconsin, California, and even Michigan, and finally the industry made them standard equipment in the '66 models. Nothing yet compelled people to use seat belts, not even doctors. When he ran a red light while driving to an emergency surgery call in Port Huron, a collision tossed unbelted 75 year-old Dr. Edgar Sites, the leading medical figure in St. Clair County, from his car to his death, just a couple of days before his planned retirement party. Many people thought it would be safer to be thrown from the vehicle in a crash, than belted into it. What a choice either way! 29 year-old Linda Sopha of Port Huron flipped her car over three times and died in it, but her unbelted children, 7 year-old Jeffrey and 8 year-old Cindy, and a neighbor's child as well, flew through the windshield and lived. " They sure were lucky their injuries weren't more severe," commented Sheriff's Deputy Andy Hahn.

By the end of the decade, a general consensus had been reached on young kids in automobiles, called "car orbiters" by the National Safety Council. They should be strapped down like cargo. Otherwise "the infant becomes a missile, threatening himself and others in the car with injury and death." Himself a parent, Jerry Brown wrote sagely, "Standing on the seats, lying on the back seats, sitting on the driver's lap, leaning out the window, standing on the front floor, and playing with car door handles and lock buttons are dangerous practices than can lead to needless suffering."(34) Example: Detroit Mayor Jerome Cavanaugh's playful 2 year-old son closed a car power window on his head and turned blue in the face before rescuers freed him and applied mouth-to-mouth resuscitation. Kids naturally didn't like riding around tied up in a car. Contrasted with the freedom of movement afforded on a train or ship or even a bus, the interior of a car cramped a passenger tighter than any prison cell, and seat belts made this worse. To prevent kids from losing their minds on long trips, expert child soothers recommended checkers, magic slates, crayons, spinner games, cards, counting games, and reading out loud. "Motion sickness medicine is a must," advised Port Huron mother of four Pat Polovich.

Instead of following up seat belts with something practical, like GTO crash helmets and roll bars, or speed governors (which locomotives carried), or limiting horsepower, the federal government moved on to a wholly eccentric frontier of collision-proofing, the "passive restraint." The explosive airbag favored by regulators amounted to a super balloon hair-triggered to burst instantaneously out of the dashboard, with the equivalent noise of a shotgun blast, into the faces of the front seat occupants, and to restrain them in the event of a crash.(35) The bags wouldn't be of much use in side-impact or rear-end or rollover or multiple impact crashes but Washington began dickering with the industry in 1970 over a deadline for their required installation.

Then, in addition to the automobile's safety failings, there was that smoke problem. By the 1960's 90% of Americans, in 7,300 cities, breathed bad air from vehicle exhaust, "the nation's single greatest source of air pollution," according to the federal government. Cars annually discharged 85 million tons of contaminants, including, just to pick one out of the air, an incredible 260,000 tons of lead.(36) Detroit breathed the 3rd dirtiest air in America, behind New York and Chicago. Michigan's last governor of the decade, William Milliken, cited Port Huron as one of the seven worst cases in the state, though at first he couldn't bring himself to finger the automobile for this. Port

329

Huron Kiwanians heard pollution expert Dr. William van Hoogenhuize estimate that air pollution cost the U.S. $11-$13 billion per year. Emphysema cases doubled every five years, and asthmatics in the country numbered 5 million. Congress passed a Clean Air Act in 1963, and strengthened it in 1970. In 1965 federal rules came down from the Department of Health, Education and Welfare to cut hydrocarbon and carbon monoxide emissions from motor vehicles by 60%.

None of these regulations placed any limit on the number of motor vehicles to be built or operated in the United States, nor laid any plans for the eventual removal of the #1 environment wrecker, and for those reasons alone they had failure built into them. As we noted in Henry Ford's case, no one who owned or operated an automobile, or condoned them, could simultaneously be an environmentalist. U.S. Senator Robert Kennedy mustered the courage to express the unthinkable: "We need to substitute mass transportation for individual cars if we are to obtain a significant reduction in the amount of carbon monoxide and hydrocarbons in the atmosphere."(37) That sounded good to Eileen Pavlov of St. Clair County: "Cars are one of the main polluters, so stop the cars. By this I mean get streetcars back in the running." After the Justice Department concluded that the automakers were conspiring to delay vehicle pollution controls, U.S. Senator Gaylord Nelson of Wisconsin called for the abolishment of the internal combustion engine by 1975, which just floored sputtering American Motors president William Luneberg: "astonished...shocking." Ford put the cleaner but now extinct electric car back on the drawing board. A Detroit Edison representative came to Port Huron to tantalize the Kiwanis Club with an electric car promotional film, *Watts Under the Hood.* But like the driverless car, the electric ultimately figured as just another empty promise, an auto industry shield from criticism, always just out of reach, awaiting a battery breakthrough to equal the petroleum engine.

Nor were the auto industry's hands clean on other forms of pollution. The federal government named Ford Motor as the single biggest despoiler of Lake Erie, accountable for 20% of the filth pouring into that Great Lake, which had aged biologically according to some some accounts by 15,000 years in just 50. The main culprits were Ford's Rouge and Monroe, Michigan plants. Ford spokesman Frank Kallin took a "Who, us?" stance on this question. "I don't think the Rouge River has ever looked as good as it does now." This convinced nobody. In 1969 Congress created an Environmental Protection Agency to watchdog automakers and other polluters.

The last generation of unregulated American motor vehicles now hastened to their end. Approximately 12 million used cars changed hands each year by the end of the Sixties. On big days, classified used auto ads took up as much as 19 columns in the *Times Herald.* Ken Gardner Ford simultaneously warned the public about used cars (*Every day you drive your present car, it's costing you money. Every day is just one day closer to what might be an expensive repair job*) while at the same time Ken offered a 10 year-old Buick 4-door for sale for $4.95 (no misprint). A typical new car lost one-half its value in just two years. Consumer advocates cautioned shoppers when buying a used car to watch out for, among other things, bad steering, leaky valves, smelly (that is, shot) transmissions, spongy brake pedals, misaligned wheels, rust. Mainly through used cars, auto ownership continued to penetrate to the bottom rungs of society. A welfare food handout in Louisville, Kentucky sparked a traffic jam of clients' cars outside the distribution center, including one foodie driving a lavender Cadillac.

Mandatory vehicle inspections had spread into 32 states in an effort to keep tabs on road hulks. Michigan was not included, but in a random safety check of cars by Michigan State Police near Port Huron, 60% failed. Governor Milliken wanted to start mandatory inspections in the Great Lakes state as well, to retire the $4.95 models ASAP. Like virtually everybody else in Michigan, Milliken saw driving as an inescapable fact of life:

Their brakes are sluggish, their lights dim and even out, their steering erratic. I don't think anyone drives them for the sheer pleasure of inhaling their engine fumes and listening to their squeaks and rattles. They drive them because they have to, because they can't afford better cars. This is the wider social problem, that while the garages of suburbia hold two or more late- model cars, the streets of the inner cities are filled with rust heaps that long ago should have been consigned to the junk-heap.(38)

With this many basket case cars around, the good times rolled on for Port Huron's auto support businesses. The five different tire specialty shops in town – Goodyear, Goodrich, Firestone, Royal Tire, Tireville USA – battled it out with big department store chains like Sears and Yankee for the honor of rubbering your wheels. The Federal Trade Commission didn't think too much of some of the tire practices employed on new or used cars these days, becuz: 1. Many new cars came with inadequate tires for the size, weight and speed of the vehicle. 2. Owners had no ironclad method of selecting the right tire. 3. Manufacturers often stamped inaccurate sizes on tires. The newly formed U.S. Department of Transportation maintained that as many as two-thirds of new tires contained potentially hazardous defects, "time bombs" in the words of Senator Gaylord Nelson.(39) Every year America threw away 100 million used tires, which became environmental time bombs, a well-nigh indestructible addition to the republic's landscape and landfills.

The auto trade also encouraged Port Huron car owners to empty their meager bank balances on tune-ups, wheel balancing, rustproofing, car washes, mufflers, paint jobs, windshields, body repair, and general overhaul. What with one thing or another the average car owner spent $220 per year on maintenance and $100 per year on parts, for a grand total of $36 billion across the entire auto nation. 670,000 mechanics kept busy, 18 at Gardner Ford alone. Some said the country needed half a million more. Thus the field of opportunity grew for the chiselers Henry Ford had cautioned everybody about. Michigan's own U.S. Senator Philip Hart admitted that mechanics botched one-third of all car repairs. Jerry Brown tucked into a profile of 24 year-old mechanic Irving "Skip" Tuschling of Port Huron. Skip nourished a love of cars, a perverse love in view of the fact that his father had run over him with the family sedan at age 2, leaving Irving on braces for life. Skip managed a gas station, and was happy, until a head smash in a second car accident left him clinging to life, another Heroic Sick Person. Even at that, Skip made out better than 61 year-old repair shop owner Chris Herber, whose love affair with cars ended fatally when one of his patients fell on him as he worked on it.

Once their jalopies had aged past helping some families simply parked the deceased in the backyard, and awaited Automobile Resurrection Day. Port Huron city inspector Roy Munro counted 60 junkers on residential lots in a single eight block area, which resulted in the first municipal ordinance on the subject. Soon the city found itself hauling away almost 100 per month. Junk cars not only littered the city of Port Huron but had spread into the suburbs, where Gardendale wrote up its own heap ban. "It is a

331

plague on the land," thundered the *Times Herald's* Floyd Bernard, about the 6 million cars deactivated annually.(40) Though WW2 had stripped the nation of them, by 1970 the national junk car population had grown back to somewhere between 10-40 million, a pretty wide estimate range. 15,000 U.S. auto scrappers employed 100,000 people. Five auto junk yards operated in St.Clair County.

If you couldn't keep up a car, and didn't mind hanging your hide outside, you always had the motorcycle alternative available, and a lot of people took it. Port Huron's police force got rid of theirs during the 60's, but Michigan's civilian motorcycle registrations increased 60% in 1965 alone. Cycle accidents went up 90% that same year, and riders coped with a fatality rate 5 times that of cars. Port Huron insurance salesman Burt Frane acquired some expertise on motorcycle risk when, after ramming a phone pole during a two-block test ride of his brother's machine, he spent 40 days in the hospital and underwent five major operations for his broken pelvis and two broken legs.

The motorcycle's snow cousin, the snowmobile, a miniature single-tread tank, also entered the lists in a big way during the Sixties. "New Toy Skims the Snowlands: The heretofore silent woodlands, once deserted from December to March, resound with the whiz of 18 to 35 horsepower engines, encased in colorful, streamlined chassis. They whiz over the terrain with red-cheeked passengers, bringing them into the great outdoors in a swift and thrilling way." That was the good news, courtesy of the *Times Herald's* women's page editor Grace Crimmins.(41)

Four days later, Jerry Brown brought in the bad news: "The snowmobile is not a toy." It could hit 100 mph, couldn't turn well, tore up wildlife habitat and private property, especially golf courses, and sent a lot of red-cheeked passengers to the doctor, like drivers who'd been clotheslined on wire fences they couldn't spot in time to avoid. Port Huron banned snowmobiles from public streets, but the frozen Black River became a favorite snowmobile course, treating residents within a mile and more of the river to the roar of the virtually unmuffled engines. Thin ice and open water presented two more hazards not always immediately recognized by river sledders. Snowmobiler Duane Barnes went through the ice and drowned in the Black River the same day the Crimmins story appeared. Apart from the snowmobile, another automotive innovation of destruction appeared in sports showrooms in St. Clair County, the All Terrain Vehicle (ATV), like the "Lil' Buckaroo," built in the Thumb. This buckaroo didn't need a street or road, it could pursue its victims across hill and dale, with or without snow.

One of the most expensive four-wheeled vehicles in St. Clair County by the end of the decade worked on the farm, the tractor. A top of the line, air-conditioned, soundproofed, 115 horsepower tractor cost $13,000, compared to a $5,800 Cadillac. The tractor also killed more people than any other farm implement, according to Jerry Brown. It dispatched 35 folks in Michigan per year, as when 2 year-old Christopher London's father backed one over him near Capac. Though valiantly opposed by the Blue Water Organic Farm and Garden Club, one of the biggest in the state, Fordism drove the dwindling numbers of St. Clair County farmers (down 50% in 30 years) to ever greater excesses in total farm mechanization and agricultural mass production, in "confinement rearing" of chickens, cows and pigs, and the use of questionable chemistry. "Without agricultural chemicals insects would eventually rule the world," warned Michigan State University. Why hadn't they ruled it before the invention of chemicals? Just biding their time.

The horse, which we last visited in the 1930's, had done its bit like any other loyal American during WW2, helping to save gas and tires. Nevertheless, by the 60's it had been driven largely out of the municipality of Port Huron, like some sort of foreign invader. The proposed opening of a new stable in the city back in 1947 had drawn an eruption from neighbor Annie Carpenter: "Said stable and horses will draw RATS and FLIES...this neighborhood should not be subject to, nor have to put up with the ODORS and STENCH..."(42) Refugee horses found homes on fewer farms these days, like Harry Roehl's place near Marysville, where the state champion draft horses Bob and Dean earned an organic living. Sometimes Sheriff William Pettengill deputized the remaining horses for a posse to help with searches or rounding up escaped cattle: "Horses still can get many places where an automobile is stopped by the terrain and where a person loses valuable time in walking." The new St. Clair County Farm Museum in Goodells, the first in Michigan, memorialized the workhorse of yesteryear – flies, odors and all.

If horses or anybody else thought they'd found safety in the countryside from the "chrome smeared monsters," as a *New York Post* story described the automobiles of the 1960's, they could think again. The expanding threat to rural America came primarily from the growing number of suburban moms behind their steering wheels, a generation of American women undivorcably married to their cars. To get to this stage in her life, a single girl first had to endure the humiliation and danger of a car-based courtship quite different from that of 1905, as depicted by Chrysler:

The Eternal Triangle. You'd think Ralph's new love would have been curtains for me. I mean, it was all he talked about. Well, I learned to live with it. As it turned out, I think his new Charger R/T really brought us closer together. He's taught me how to shift the 4-speed synchromesh. He lets me pick out the stereo tapes. And clean the vinyl buckets. It's not all bad. He's even mentioned marriage once.

American women started asserting a good deal more independence of mind during this decade, except about automobiles, and so sometimes bought their own, making it woman's fate now just as much as man's. National reporter Aileen Snoddy offered women readers a list of 20 tips for buying a car. The highlights: Shop around among car dealers. Walk out on a dealer if he tries to bait and switch you with a different model from the one advertised. Check your chosen car's background. Test drive it. Take it to a mechanic and pay for his opinion. Take it back to the dealer. Figure operating costs; shop for insurance; shop for an auto loan; put at least one-third down; keep the finance contract to just two years; review the contract for language, itemized costs, and refund procedure. Repeat as needed. Or let Ralph handle it.

Once they tied the knot and set up housekeeping, 30% of St. Clair County couples acquired two motor vehicles. More than a million families nationwide owned three. Local housewives had no trouble recognizing themselves in Ruth Millet's syndicated column in the *Times Herald*:

Most wives spend more time driving than they do preparing food...If they ever faced the fact that they are as much slaves to their cars as their great grandmothers were slaves to the stove it would really give them a jolt....chauffeuring, running errands, driving long distances to meetings, shopping...(43)

These women and their families fled on wheels further and further away from Port Huron into St. Clair County's countryside, to randomly placed subdivisions like

Charmwood ("A Quiet Suburban Neighborhood...It's like a long vacation") and Old Farm. Neither of these outposts stood really close to anything, not stores, workplaces, schools, theaters, libraries, churches, etc. But they had room, plenty of room, for the family's most important members, its automobiles. Homes and garages grew large out there in the townships, as carsick Americans, revolted by the ugly mess their cars made of everything around them, withdrew into the great indoors. The median house price topped $20,000, with a 30 year mortgage attached, guaranteed by one federal agency or another.

Old Farm indeed once had been an old farm in the former Gardendale district, until the bulldozers carved up its 83 acres. Its residents permitted no farming in Old Farm now, none of the backyard chicken coops or cow barns of just a generation past, and any fruit trees left served strictly for decoration. Without the regular chores of the farm to keep suburbanites occupied, and with no city amusements close at hand, it could be pretty boring. The typical "restricted community" of St. Clair County's suburbia, white as the driven snow, didn't always furnish the quiet oasis promised. The sheriff's department did 85% of its business in Port Huron's three adjacent bedroom townships, attending to crime. Deputies also cleaned up the growing number of traffic wrecks out there, like the head-on that killed former County Prosecutor Richard Schonk.

By 1970 more Americans lived in the suburbs than in cities or on farms. Realtors redeveloped 3,000 acres of farmland per day. Promoters tried building an imitation suburban subdivision inside Port Huron itself, Colonial Village, with the same kind of "estate" look, two-car garages, and crooked colonial streets (Monticello, Brandywine, Mt. Vernon) designed to frustrate speeding cars. And no sidewalks. Who wanted those skunks, pedestrians, around anyway? Lee Iacocca thought the suburbs were just the ticket for America's future: "The only real solution to the traffic problem is to spread people out enough so they can move around without bumping into each other."[44] Somewhat illogically, Port Huron's City Council members agreed, and decided to furnish more water and sewage service to their runaway former neighbors outside the city limits, without requiring annexation of these developments, a sure fire recipe for more sprawl and urban decay.

While the council cozied up to the suburbs, the ethnic-heavy southwest side of Port Huron, studiously ignored by City Hall, wondered when it would get an occasional hug. Dissatisfied resident Pablo Santiago itemized the south side's deficiencies, "...houses falling down, outside wells, outside sanitary facilities, and people living like sardines in a can." Even dirt floors in some homes. No Charmwood, in other words. And parked beside many a dilapidated home, an equally crummy car. Or two. A permanent welfare class had taken root in America following the depression, and now numbered 6% of the populace. St. Clair County disbursed $3.5 million in federal and state cash per year on welfare payments, and 3,000 people qualified for food stamps.

Browbeaten into it by the state of Michigan to accommodate auto-powered suburbanization, ten rural school districts, some of them 100 years old, encompassing parts of eight different townships, voted to merge with the Port Huron schools in 1961, creating under the maestroship of superintendent Howard Crull a huge, 14,000-student Fordist school system guaranteed to be more efficient in operation and effective in teaching. Luckily for Crull it wasn't a money back guarantee, because the merger achieved neither goal, and Crull wisely retired before the roof fell in. He received a farewell banquet from his supporters, while his successor Gerald DeGrow, after grappling with Crull's clumsy handiwork for a time, received a 1,600 signature petition demanding his resignation. Assembly line schooling fell flat on its face, and the U.S. education commissioner Francis Keppel admitted that American schools sometimes graduated "functional illiterates."

Port Huron schools got larger, student performance lagged, costs and taxes soared, and 66 buses motored 7,000 children a total of 900,000 miles per year, back and forth. The district's bus feet required a 13-acre compound just for storage and maintenance. Many of these vehicles serviced a second huge high school, Port Huron Northern, built for suburbanite kids. It resembled a shopping center surrounded by acres of parking for buses and teachers' cars, students' cars, visitors' cars. Because of increasing suburban traffic, laughed-at speed limits, and no sidewalks or shoulders on paved roads out there in the green acres, many rural children couldn't walk to elementary schools in safety. Busing did them no favor either, because (1) a large percentage of American school buses used diesel power, which exposed their passengers to unwise levels of exhaust fumes, and (2) 1,000 school bus accidents occurred per year in Michigan.(45) Sixth grader Bryan Fuller didn't climb onto his Port Huron school bus nimbly enough one day and got caught in the closed door, unnoticed by a prize bus driver, who dragged Bryan to his death.

The school district appointed a Director of Traffic Safety, Albert "Tiny" Renaker, a hulking ex-Marine drill instructor turned elementary school teacher and principal. Tiny, as one might imagine, expected instant obedience, and sometimes became a little frustrated that children didn't snap to when he gave them instruction. "Don't do your homework or eat your breakfast on the bus. Think what might happen if the bus went over a bump or stopped suddenly. You might choke on a mouthful of food or jab yourself with a pencil." Car drivers also failed to perform up to Marine standards: "WE, the drivers of any type of vehicle must at all times be on our guard when on the highway. We cannot for a moment take time to stare off into space, look in the back seat at a passenger or start to daydream."(46) 5,000 children living in Port Huron still walked or biked to school, and Sergeant Renaker observed that contrary to orders, city kids often walked with childlike insouciance in the face of car danger, and sometime rode bikes in the streets like circus performers, one pedaling with another aboard the handlebars, which drove Tiny nuts.

Port Huron's schools by now also had been saddled by the state formally with the task of educating new drivers to perform the single most dangerous act of their lives. Driving instructors didn't give a great deal of actual street practice to their eager pupils because these teachers quite reasonably feared for their own lives. A lot of rehearsal took place in the school parking lot until technology came to the rescue, and provided a driving "simulator." The Drivotrainer cost $28,000, partly paid for in their own best interests by the Port Huron Association of Insurance Agents. "Students view movies accurately simulating driving conditions on the highways with all of the hazards portrayed on color film. Students' reaction to each situation are recorded on tapes. The only thing lacking is the feeling of motion..."(47) Given this kind of instruction, no one could be too surprised when Michigan State University traffic expert Robert Gustafson told a Port Huron lecture audience that "drivers' ed" didn't lead to safer drivers.

335

Driving license examiners showed a similar reluctance to put applicants through real life paces on the streets. The local cop who usually handled it didn't really want to discover the hard way that a neophyte driver didn't know what he was doing. The CBS TV network did a little examining of its own when it ran a *National Drivers Test* special after the network's president Fred Friendly received a ticket for speeding. The promo: "The program uses spectacular photography to test your driving judgment. You'll see high speed head on collisions. Potentially serious driving hazards. And you'll be asked questions as though you were driving." Like a Drivotrainer at home. Port Huron's gasoline distributor Star Oil picked up some of the local sponsorship cost for the program. Nationwide, 30 million viewers watched and 40% of the audience participants failed the test.

About 18% of American high school students owned their own cars, and 30% of those who did flunked their classwork. At Port Huron High School 55 kids formed a car club, the Magwinders. The 'Winders busied themselves with plans for building a $60,000 drag strip, much to the dismay of police. The cops had formed a low opinion of dragsters after two competitors roared through the downtown business district on a Saturday afternoon, one slamming into a tree in front of the new McMorran Auditorium, scattering shoppers in all directions. This incident hurried up passage of an anti-dragging ordinance by the City Council. Port Huron had the worst reputation in Michigan for street racing, according to Algonquin Hotel owner Maynard Smith. Street heats regularly awakened his customers at 2-3 a.m., which didn't encourage repeat business. Dragsters used some of the rural highways in St. Clair County so often that they painted the pavements into quarter-mile courses.

The Marysville Drive-In theater celebrated this lifestyle by showing the movie *Hot Rods to Hell* – "Call Them Punks. Call Them Animals. But you'd better get out of their way!" Hotshots like Gary Sinda drove around with treadless racing tires on their rear wheels. "Slicks" didn't work too well on slick surfaces, as Sinda found out when his out-of-control car first ejected, then ran over and killed him. American automakers continued to pander to speed addicts like the Magwinders, only now manufacturers used the euphemism "high performance" instead of high speed or high power in company advertising: *The biggest Plymouths ever built. Big,beautiful hardtops, with big high performance engines. These are the Roaring 65's!* In that context, one might say that 22 year-old Wallace Smith did some high performing when his car hit an embankment off the road near Marine City, flew 100 feet in the air, and somersaulted another 100 yards. This high performance was Smith's farewell performance. He joined 55 others killed in traffic in the county that year.

Port Huron's parking mania escalated during the 1960's as car numbers grew. When the movie *West Side Story* appeared at the Family Theater, its opening helicopter shots showed New York City crawling with mechanical lice – cars – and Port Huronites sometimes felt the same itch. The city launched another urban renewal scheme to wipe out 200 more homes and businesses across 60 acres in the central city, at a cost of $10 million, primarily to furnish 1,000 parking spaces for the community college (a sort of remedial high school) and the McMorran civic center. Author Jane Jacobs knew well how this decimation worked from her observation of similar programs in New York: "people who get marked with the planners' hex signs are pushed about, expropriated, and uprooted much as if they were the subjects of a conquering power."(48)

The renewers destroyed without a qualm the ornate, picturesque mansion of Port Huron lumber and paper pioneer Jacob Haynes. They did the same thing to Jerry Brown's childhood home, a loss that took some time to sink in for this teller of tales. One of the very anchors of the community, the 115 year-old St. Stephen's Catholic Church and school, sold out and departed into the townships. The purge of this neighborhood triggered some token resistance by hard cases. The Port Huron Saw Service refused to go quietly, and won a $52,000 judgment before it, too, moved on. Even outside the renewal area the destruction continued. Much to the disgust of historian Helen Endlich, the First United Methodist Church tore itself down, including its 180-foot steeple, which had been a landmark to passing mariners for generations. The First replaced itself with an uninspiring modernist structure that also required the removal of half a block of homes for parking.

The Chamber of Commerce declared the start of Operation Facelift, to eliminate or cover up the 19th century character of as many downtown buildings as possible, and provide more parking. The owner of eight side-by-side storefronts making up the old Union Hotel on Main Street donated the place for $1 to the city, which vaporized it for a 90-space parking lot. This left such an ugly gap in the streetscape that it disturbed even some of the most obsessed parking devotees, which took some doing. Port Huron beat up its parks further to make room for drivers, by selling 120 feet of Sanborn Park to a supermarket for parking, gouging more parking spaces out of Pine Grove Park, and cutting down 75 trees and spending $112,000 to allow 500 more cars into Lakeside Park. People now called it Lakeside Parking Lot, with an asphalt area so enormous that racers used it illicitly as an after-hours drag strip.

At about this point Port Huron's seventh City Manager in 24 years departed the community for greener pastures: a bigger city and salary. City Councilman Robert Cook announced that he'd had enough of the revolving door city manager system: "...the typical city manager is only here on his way to a larger city. After two to four years of building everything he can by borrowing every dollar our legal limit will permit, plus what he can beg from the Federal Government, he will take pictures of all he has built [and] paste them in his resume as evidence of his ability to manage a city."(49) However, with no alternative legally left to a city hamstrung by its own charter, the search began for a new man.

The council found a successful candidate in 33 year-old Gerald Bouchard. Like every one of his predecessors in the manager's job, Bouchard knew next to nothing about the city of Port Huron, its people, its history, anything. Barring that, Port Huron's civic fathers hardly could have found a better prospect had they searched for a decade. Bouchard came from a Maine family of French-Canadian ancestry not unlike that of Port Huron's founders, the Petits and others. He spoke French fluently and played ice hockey – which gave him an agreeable Canadian pedigree in a border town like Port Huron. An Army veteran, a family man, a masters degree holder from the highly regarded Wharton school at the University of Pennsylvania, he'd served as an assistant city manager in Saginaw, Michigan, about 100 miles distant, so he wasn't entirely unacquainted with the Thumb region.

Bouchard's shortcomings were hardly of his own making. He was somewhat standoffish, but this need not necessarily have been a demerit in a job in which the city *caudillo* supposedly made impartial decisions on behalf of the entire community. He

337

had little or no aesthetic sense. This didn't make him unusual in America in the mid-1960's. The automobile had destroyed the aesthetic values of most of the country. In fact one could say that no one who owned an automobile had any appreciation for beauty or harmony, manmade or natural, at all. Bouchard's training in the automotive school of city management constituted his greatest deficiency. When Jane Jacobs wrote the following in her perceptive volume *The Death and Life of Great American Cities*, she might have been writing about Gerald Bouchard:

It is disturbing to think that men who are young today, men who are being trained now for their careers, should accept on the grounds that they must be "modern" in their thinking, conceptions about cities and traffic which are not only unworkable, but also to which nothing new of any significance has been added since their fathers were children. (50)

In taking on Port Huron's top job, Bouchard allowed as he might stay all of five years in it. In fact, he spent the next 30 years running the government, a legacy. Gerry and Jerry, Bouchard and Brown, effectively became the two faces of the community.

As one of his first major assignments, Bouchard completed the leveling of another city block for even more parking. It meant goodbye to one of the oldest areas in Port Huron, packed with some of its most traditional and pleasing structures, masonry buildings with walls up to eight bricks thick. Prize-winning Michigan newspaper columnist Jim Fitzgerald, an ex-Port Huroner from one of the city's oldest families, marked the passing of the National Guard Armory: "I read they are going to tear down the Port Huron Armory. They need space to park cars. Egad. The day is coming when the law will require people to walk sideways to cut down on the room needed between cars."(51) Fitz remembered the Armory from his school days as the "dance center of the Universe." Other nearby buildings just as memorable vanished. A saying hatched in opposition to the Vietnam War – "It became necessary to destroy the village in order to save it" – now came true in Port Huron. It became necessary to destoy the city in order to park its cars.

Despite the best efforts of preservationists, an investor bought and polished off another handsome and potentially recyclable building, an 1873 vintage fire hall, to build a car wash. Historically minded residents *did* manage to save the classically beautiful Carnegie Library by the skin of its teeth, and transform it into a museum. A headache-inducing $1 million replacement library, based on another Walter Wyeth modernist design, went up in the 1st Ward reclamation area, not far from a new black glass-faced office tower six stories high, the largest and most threatening-looking business edifice in town. Both structures had a wealth of parking.

Bouchard also okayed the demolition of the landmark Washington School, renamed the McVety Youth Center. An energetic teenager named Robert McVety had helped convert it into a kids' hangout before he enlisted in WW2 and died in combat in France on Christmas Day 1944, aged 18. Regrettably, coming as it did so early in his administration, the destruction of the McVety, still "straight and strong after 107 years" in one admirer's view, sealed for good with many residents Bouchard's image as an insensitive and duplicitous philistine.

It should be said in his defense that Manager Bouchard worked at first from a city master plan that he'd had nothing to do with designing, and he dealt with a business community panicked at the thought of a major shopping center appearing either in the north end of town or in the suburbs. The Chamber of Commerce looked with alarm at the GM-dominated city of Pontiac, Michigan, just outside Detroit, where two big new suburban malls had emptied out 40% of the downtown retail stores in a matter of months. 3,000 shopping malls populated America by 1970.

Port Huron office products dealer Harry Blomquist suggested something akin to ritual municipal suicide to meet this threat: level 20 acres of the business district to build the city's own mall. Other hand wringers floated plans to roof over Port Huron's downtown Main Street business section for a few blocks, push traffic to the perimeter, and convert these blocks into a mall. Reporter Floyd Bernard tried imagining the result: "...plantings and fountains and benches and congenial bustle without much hustle... (people) browse about in unhurried comfort, unworried about passing trucks and free to enjoy pleasant, uncrowded surroundings."(52) In other words, the Port Huron of 1900.

Another new element introduced into the retail mix during this decade raised a sweat in Port Huron, when the Kresge company opened one of its new all-in-one Fordist superstores, a K-Mart, just across the city limits in Port Huron Township. This behemoth sold cheap goods of all descriptions, everything from underwear to corn flakes, in an 80,000 square-foot building with 1,000 parking spaces. It dwarfed the competition. Even Santa Claus deserted Sperry's downtown department store to make his seasonal debut by helicopter at K-Mart, an event which jammed with thousands of cars the surrounding streets, which hadn't been designed for a store that size.

Some prominent old businesses pulled out of the downtown, most notably the Beard-Campbell company. Once the buggy, wagon, bicycle dealer, and hardware store deluxe, and the city's first automobile agent, B-C now largely did a wholesale trade in electrical and automotive supplies. The firm decamped for a new site in the suburbs, which had a 60-car parking lot. Other retailers closed up, including the 102 year-old Ballentine's furnishings store. Some business firms remained in town, but joined the 1960's trend of consolidation in America that spread sameness from coast to coast. Sperry's department store sold out to a retail chain, though it kept the old name. The Weil family got out of journalism, handing the *Times Herald* off to the established but relatively faceless Gannett multiple newspaper organization.

Half the neighborhood grocery stores in Port Huron shut down, and no new ones could be started due to zoning and parking restrictions in residential areas. Grocer John Wolfel ended 63 years behind the counter. Customers preferred driving to the distant supermarket so beloved of Henry Ford – which had a 3% markup on 10,000 items – rather than pay 10% on 600 or so selections at the corner store. Fordism in food meant 85% of supermarket fare required processing, dousing with preservatives, and trucking hundreds or thousands of miles. The very essence of a Fordist assembly line restaurant, a McDonald's, opened across the street from Port Huron High School, offering the Universal Meal: "100% pure Beef hamburger, crisp golden brown French Fries, rich Triple-Thick Shake...come and get acquainted with one of the good things in life." Franchise operations like McDonald's did 25% of all retail trade in America.

The 1960's version of Port Huron remained the home to more than half the retail and service businesses in St. Clair County. And it still ruled as the region's social center. 200 different clubs and sports leagues and civic groups of various kinds still met

339

and played and worked and partied there. Though the days when thousands of people had gathered on foot in Pine Grove Park for evening concerts were long gone, and the city band had disbanded, as many as 100,000 people jammed the streets on big days, like for the Blue Water Festival summer parade. But who knew how long this would last? Although overpopulation became one of the environmental concerns of the day, the revelation of the 1970 census that Port Huron's population had begun to shrink didn't spark any parade.

Many of the central city homes spared from destruction for Port Huron's parking lot push declined in health anyway, attacked by automobile rot that stemmed from having too many cars crammed awkwardly onto properties never built to hold them. Auto-crazy upper and middle class owners abandoned to the slumlords or to public housing contractors Major Nathan Boynton's spacious home and many other 19th Century structures that once had distinguished the community:

In some of the homes, vestiges of once gracious living are evident, despite the fact that many were long since cut up and divided into apartments. These once ornate dwellings, and others built along more prosaic lines, were scarcely vacated before becoming the target of looters, who hauled out marble washstands, paneling, furnaces, fireplaces, and practically anything else that was movable.(53)

In many of the original one-car-garage neighborhoods, automobiles sat permanently in the driveways, because owners had filled their garages with other living standards: "There are few things worse for a householder than a garage so full of junk even ye owner can't get in, let alone the car," admitted reporter Louis Dunn, whose own garage held a lawn mower, rakes, hoes, grass chemicals, an end table, croquet set, old tires, and 24 cans of paint. His neighbors jammed extra concrete parking pads onto front, side, and back yards to make way for that ego-expanding second vehicle, rather than fit two in the driveway and go crazy backing them in and and out to free one or the other.

As Port Huron defaced itself with more and more commercial and residential parking blight, the Sixties inaugurated as well more destruction for street "improvement," – widening, of course. The Michigan Highway Department converted two of Port Huron's principle east-west streets, Griswold and Oak, into what it aptly named "penetrator" streets. The department widened the penetrators and made them one-way affairs with higher speed limits, to give traffic quicker access to Highway 21 outside of town. Too bad for homeowners along a penetrator, which stabbed them to the heart as it cut their front yards and property values in half. Too bad for drivers as well because the penetrators became two of the most unsafe, crash-prone streets in town.

Next, the state road dictators proclaimed that two-lane North Main Street must be improved into a five lane, no parking thoroughfare. About 400 vehicles per hour used North Main at peak periods, and the street could handle 1,700 in a pinch, but in the Department's crystal ball, usage would rise to 3,000 by 1980. That was all the legality the street surgeons needed to start work, a "projection" of increased traffic. Business people at older locations on North Main implored the state to allow continued street parking, but they got the big raspberry in reply. When traffic speeds picked up on wider North Main, homeowners, too, protested fruitlessly. "I would like to know why North Main was allowed to become a race track, " asked Mrs. Percy Boult. A similar chorus of complaints arose across town, when another edict from Capital City jacked

340

apart the once-stately Lapeer Avenue by another two lanes, with the same disastrous results for people living there.

Disputing the Highway Department in Lansing on these issues became virtually impossible. They were the road-builders from hell: call them punks, call them animals, but you'd better get out of their way. The richest, most powerful branch of the Michigan government, now ruled by an appointed board, occupied a four-story headquarters two blocks long, the biggest building in the capital. In their mad rush to clear the way for motorists, road bureaucrats ran roughshod over the rights of in-place residents and property owners in Port Huron and a thousand other communities. The department had one mission and one only: the continuous and limitless increase of car and truck traffic into every corner of the state, regardless of the consequences. The corruption at highway HQ prompted Republican George Romney and Democrat Frank Kelley, Governor and Attorney General, to join forces to get a one-man grand jury impaneled to investigate kickbacks, bribes, graft and organized crime influence within the department. But after 50 years of dodging similar charges, the Road Gang proved to be too fast on its feet, and a friendly judge buried the issue.

In the matter of another important Port Huron street over which they lacked direct control, state wideners pressured the City Council into simply ordering the building of two more lanes for 10th Street, without one of those messy municipal elections like the one that had voted down the same project less than a decade earlier. They helped draft a phony cost estimate of $700,000, but maverick Councilman Robert Cook, the only dissenter, judged the real cost from the general obligation bonds required for this project to be $2 million. Like all the city managers of his generation, Gerald Bouchard suffered from the same widening and no-parking compulsion when it came to streets as did the state honchos. On his own say-so he added to the expansion list a couple more avenues he felt needed more elbow room.

"Our city," said native Helen Endlich, "often has been called a City of Trees." Now it became a city of stumps. The *Times Herald* proclaimed grim satisfaction as the chain saws went to work on hundreds of trees lining 10th, North Main, Oak, Griswold, Lapeer, Erie, Glenwood, 24th, etc., etc.: "It is sad that so many trees, many of them old and revered specimens, must be cut down to make way for the wider street. Erie isn't really Erie anymore, even though it will be continued to called that...the aura of Old Erie, of the falling leaves and speckled sunlight will be no more. Yet Port Huron has no time for stagnation. A thoroughfare geared to the future is essential..."(54) "Thoroughfare" was a polite name for what these streets turned into. A future critic more aptly called multi-lane, no parking streets "traffic sewers."(55)

The national tab just for maintenance of streets and highways hit $3 billion per year by 1965. At the end of the decade, 85% of Port Huron's streets had been paved and the upkeep bill grew proportionately. After a solemn report predicted that, "...the City now and in the future will experience a great expenditure for highway needs," voters reluctantly okayed a municipal income tax of 1% on residents, 1/2% on non-resident wage earners. Suburban sprawl increased road costs everywhere outside the city limits as well. One rural matron in St. Clair County, Mrs. Harry Parsons, measured the collapsing road in front of her home against her tax bill with increasing displeasure: "During last week's warm weather, we who use our country roads were again sweating it out, wondering if we could get to our homes, and if we accomplished this, could we

341

get our again...we get less from our road tax dollar than from any other tax-supported project."(56) Twenty years earlier the Parsons had been one of four families along that mile of road, now there were 19.

Parsons' complaint and others like it saddened Road Commission manager Charles Ash. He was spending $2.3 million per year by 1970, dispatching 450 pieces of rolling equipment across the countryside, directing the superhuman labors of his road nurturing crews. They battled rain and snow, frost and thaw, summer heat, and just plain increasing traffic. The chafing of snowplows and graders echoed across the land. They took down 10,000 trees in a single year, making Port Huron's tree cutting look pretty tame. Yet by Ash's reckoning all this effort left 55% of the main county roads and 80% of the secondaries inadequate to their purpose. "No matter in what direction you drive this summer in St. Clair County you are bound to find road construction activity," ran one typical annual warning.

1969, the original 13-year deadline for the completion of the $31 billion National Defense Interstate Highway System, came and went without its completion. The price tag for the IHS had inflated like an airbag by 150% to $80 billion. An expensive complication had arisen when the interstates started falling apart even before the system had been half finished. The completed portion needed $200 million in repairs. Federal planners set a new target end date of 1978. Rex Whitton, administrator of the 5,000-employee Bureau of Public Roads in Washington, appeared in person to Port Huron in 1964 to open the brand-new IHS section known as Interstate 94 in St. Clair County. It seemed the least he could do after the taxpayers had put up $16.5 million for this 26 miles. Whitton wielded his scissors at the ribbon-cutting following a blessing by Reverend William Knack. According to author Helen Leavitt, a typical highway builder's prayer of the era went something like this:

O Almighty God, who has given us this earth and has appointed men to have domination over it; who has commanded us to make straight the highways, to lift up the valleys and to make the mountains low, we ask thy blessing upon those men who do just that.(57)

At a luncheon for 250 people, Whitton promised his Port Huron audience that after the whole interstate system had been made straight it would save 8,000 lives per year. Hearts were light that day, so Rex didn't have much to say about the chaos and suffering being wrought in the name of building the IHS system. Though not present for lunch, social critic Lewis Mumford had noted that: "Currently the most popular and effective means of destroying a city is the introduction of multiple-lane expressways..." (58) Down in Detroit, freeway building was in the process of destroying so many homes and neighborhoods, and kicking so many dislocated black families around that it helped lead to the race riots of 1967, in the opinion of Governor Romney.

In Lansing, the IHS obliterated the home, hotel and office block built by the late Oldsmobile founder Ransom Olds, plus scores of other buildings. In General Motors' birthplace, Flint, it displaced 3,000 households and destroyed several of the best neighborhoods. Nor did Rex touch on news headlines like "Federal Highway Program Marked by Charges of Collusion, Waste, Bribery." Nor on the complaint of Conrad Wirth, head of the National Park Service, that the interstates: "...destroyed a lot of wonderful scenery by slapping our high speed roads down the fastest routes, regardless of anything else." Luncheon guests did not munch over the statistic that St. Clair County

342

paid $1.4 million in taxes per year for the IHS system. That kind of table talk just didn't suit this special occasion in Port Huron.

On the first day the freedom of the expressway bloomed in Port Huron motorists got a surprising tip from the *Times Herald* on how to navigate the new I-94: Don't pay too much attention to your driving while using it:

The secret of safe driving on superhighways lies in violating one of the oldest rules of the road. Look at the scenery one in a while, the American Automobile Association recommends. The motorist who stares fixedly at the pavement ahead may become a victim of 'highway hypnosis' and doze off, crashing into an abutment or hurtling off the highway...(59)

In addition to rubbernecking it might be a good idea when expressway driving to also get plenty of fresh air, stop and rest frequently, in fact avoid long drives entirely, especially at night (hard to make out the scenery then anyway), skip heavy meals, wear loose clothing, listen to a "snappy radio program", don't smoke too much, talk with your passengers, or sing. How about a couple of choruses of *Dead Man's Curve* by Jan and Dean? Or you could try staying alert by reading the billboards. Congress passed a highway beautification bill to tear down billboards within 660 feet of the 400-foot wide interstate right-of-ways, then found it didn't have the money to do this. Bad as they were, billboards looked no uglier than the interstates themselves. Michigan authorities proposed painting the blank concrete overpass bridges maroon, beige, green, cinnamon, and ivory to spruce them up and give highway hypnotized drivers a wakeup jolt of color.

More hints came to hand about handling expressway driving. Develop telepathic powers, for one: "Try to anticipate what other drivers around you intend to do." There had been a 100-car pileup on the Edsel Ford freeway in Detroit when motorists failed to anticipate each other one icy morning. Don't forget to study the map of your target destination in advance so you'll know which exit to take. At expressway speeds you had little time to sort these things out on the fly, and if you missed an exit it could be miles before you had the opportunity to turn around and go back.(60) Watch out for "The Invisible Car," the driver lurking in back of you in the rear view mirror's blind spot. All this seemed a little discouraging, but General Motors offered an answer to anybody anxious about expressway driving: *How to put in 600 Miles in a Day and Love it? Simply start out in a Cadillac.*

Unimpressed by his test drive on the new I-94 superhighway, Port Huron motorist James O'Brien called it a "maniac strip." Casualties promptly mounted up. 23 year-old Eric Swanson of suburban Port Huron did not qualify for the 8,000 lives saved annually. Not long after the opening he hit an I-94 bridge abutment when a tire blew. Swanson had survived a 1954 car crash that killed five members of his family; but not this one. The day after Swanson's fatality two hypnotized drivers from Detroit died within a mile of each other on I-94 in St. Clair County. Maybe they forgot to loosen their clothing, or look at the scenery enough; instead they fell asleep at the wheel. One of these vehicles "...meandered 441 feet along the shoulder of the road before it hit the second and third tier of a drainage ditch abutment, bounced into the air, soared 110 feet in space, and then plunged into a stone bank." Close calls aplenty also rattled some nerves. When the first snows fell on I-94 a family of five took a bad beating in Port Huron after "their station wagon was ripped apart by a skidding trailer truck" on a snow

343

covered bridge.

A few weeks later three more people died on the dream highway when a 78 year-old Detroit driver got on the wrong side of the road and wiped out himself and another couple. Newspaperman Charles Wrzesinski discovered the hard way that crossing the I-94 median took less than half a second at 70 mph. Another car did so in front of his sedan, and the writer barely survived the ensuing crash. Once recovered, Wrzesinski dug into the matter a little and learned that effective median barriers to prevent this sort of thing would cost $60,000 per mile, so don't expect any. Negotiating the IHS safely looked like a job not for mere man but instead for the driverless car, coming in 1970 according to the University of Michigan: "Instead of fighting traffic, crunching fenders, and swearing, the commuter within five years will be able to relax while reading his newspaper as his car rolls down the highway."(61)

Hardly had I-94 been connected to Port Huron's Blue Water Bridge before a new 100-room motel with two swimming pools, a bowling alley, health club, steam bath and conference rooms opened next to the junction, for travelers who wanted plenty of noise and car pollution off the road as well as on. Despite the unattractive and unhealthy location, this facility ended up sucking hotel business out of the downtown area a mile south of the bridge. The new motel overlooked the I-94 exit and entrance that intersected with North Main and several cross streets. Motel guests got a good view of what instantly became the three most accident-prone intersections in the city, "positively lethal," in the newspaper's opinion. It turned out that just getting on or getting off a defense highway could be a dangerous proposition.

The principal beneficiaries of the interstate highways were truckers. Much of the IHS system amounted to nothing more than a costly road version of major railroad routes, and the trucking industry used these publicly financed motorways to the hilt to compete with the trains. The federal government's General Accounting Office named trucks as the villains pounding the interstates to pieces practically before the concrete cured. U.S. President John Kennedy demanded and got higher truck license fees and diesel fuel taxes, and said they still didn't cover truck damage to roads. A single normal semi-trailer truck inflicted as much of a beating as 5,000 cars. 15 million trucks up to 60 feet long now traveled the nation's roads, racking up more than 400 billion ton-miles per year.(62) The trucking lobby tried again to get approval for super-long tripletrailer rigs on the federal interstates, but this failed after analysts predicted that it would cut useful highway life by 40%.(63) The state of Michigan already allowed the highest truck weights in America, 80 tons, and endured some of the worst roads in the country as a result.

1,300 trucking companies across the U.S. grossed more than $1 million per year apiece during the 60's, and the return on equity for these companies averaged almost 9%, compared to 2.6% for railroads.(64) Port Huron's Ogden and Moffett company branched out to 82 cities in Michigan and Ontario, and doubled employment. O&M owned one of 10 trucking company terminals operating locally, as trucking to all distances grew by leaps and bounds. Cross country drivers earned as much as $12,000-15,000 per year, thanks in large part to efforts by the 1.7 million member Teamsters union. Their leaders often lined their own pockets in the process, and prosecutors convicted 40 Teamsters officials of corruption charges during the first half of the decade. After a career of jail-dodging, Teamsters President James Hoffa finally ended up in a federal prison in 1967.

The inefficiency of trucking meant it required a massive army of drivers, a demand that couldn't be met safely. Companies still often ignored operator qualifications, and had little choice but to do so. According to the Michigan Trucking Association, only four adequate semi-trailer truck driving schools operated in the entire country. As a result undertrained drivers by the thousands sat at the steering wheels of enormous rigs which often weighed ten tons *empty*. They spent illegally or illogically long periods behind the wheel. Jerry Brown looked over one typical long-haul rig, 53 feet in length, eight feet wide, with tires costing $110 apiece. Its driver admitted to averaging 10 hours per day driving this $30,000 isolation chamber. Truckers consumed $200-$400 million worth of pep pills per year to stay awake, and 30% of heavy truck accidents involved drivers who were high, drunk, or physically unfit to drive.(65) The Teamsters lobbied through the legislature a bill to give Michigan truck drivers twice the number of traffic violation points that regular drivers could receive before they had their licenses yanked, a bill which Governor Milliken vetoed in disgust.

Let the driver of an average car run into a semi, or vice versa, and the civilian died 40 times more often than the truck driver. Robert Perz doubled those odds when he had the ill luck to be sandwiched between two big trucks while making the 55-mile commute from his northern St. Clair County home to a job at a suburban Detroit Ford plant. The resulting explosion burned him up so thoroughly, like the *Bullitt* villains, that it took some time to identify the body of the 34 year-old ex-Marine, Korean war vet, married father of two, Little League president, and Parent-Teachers Association leader. In regularly covering long distances, many trucks operated in no better shape than their drivers, liable to shut down at any time. When a semi's brakes failed near Port Huron, *Times Herald* photographer Ralph Polovich's car slammed into it. Polovich, reported his employer, "...climbed out of his demolished car, took this picture, and then got into an ambulance and was taken to Port Huron Hospital for first aid."(66)

Averaging 14 miles per gallon per car and a lot less for trucks and buses, Americans autoed more than 1 trillion miles in a single year for the first time in 1968, the equivalent to about 44 times around the solar system.(67) Getting enough oil out of the ground to sustain this travel habit entailed an increasing number of risks, which began to trouble the nation's conscience in a modest way during the decade. Particularly when the oil ended up in a body of water before it got to the gas tank in your car. A serious oil well blowout near Santa Barbara, California in 1969 covered 300 square miles of Pacific with petroleum, and inspired a lot of teeth-gnashing and platitudes, and a $1.4 billion lawsuit. But very few people gave up their cars as a result. St. Clair County's oil wells produced 500,000 barrels per year, fortunately without any catastrophes, about half of the 350 gallons per person used locally.

Imperial Oil, Dow Chemical, DuPont and the rest of the denizens of Sarnia's Chemical Valley went through good times and bad during the 60's. Imperial cranked out 110,000 barrels of refined oil products daily, and installed another pipeline from the oil fields. The government even added a portrait of the C-Valley to the Canadian $10 bill, in honor of its robust business and massive infrastructure, the very symbol of the country's industrial prowess. Named Canada's fastest growing city, Sarnia erected a new city hall, library, and a $5 million railyard on the back of this prosperity.

Less pleasingly, another explosion rocked the Imperial works, destroyed 140

345

feet of river dockage and injured five people. Also on the bad side, leakage of Valley output into the St. Clair River produced some humiliating headlines, as when Michigan Governor Milliken banned fishing in the river due to mercury poisoning. Dow admitted it had been dumping 30 pounds of mercury into the river every day for the past 20 years, and an employee alleged collusion with Ontario officials to cover it up. Mrs. Otto Mohni of Port Huron complained about Chemical Valley's airborne assault of its American neighbors: "It is a rather pleasant September evening but we have all rushed indoors, tightly closing our doors and windows about us. It helps a little but the gagging odors manage to creep in. A soot filled cloud envelopes the house and the houses around us, for blocks and even miles. Our cars hardly stay clean overnight."(68) Check the gas tank in your dirty car, Mrs. Mohni, for the real problem.

The number of operating gas stations in Port Huron continued to decline during this decade, a welcome development. But getting rid of the vacant stations proved no easy matter, and they often lingered as useless hulks in the city landscape for years. And even with some empties still standing, station construction continued. When a gas station chain in 1970 leveled another of Port Huron's grand old Main Street mansions, the 1885 James Goulden place, to build a new "Gas for Less" outlet, hawking fuel at 19.9 cents per gallon, resident Mike Soule exploded like a barrel of high octane:

Will this gas station with nice cement and asphalt be more aesthetically pleasing than the old house it is replacing? Otherwise tell me what cultural value does a gas station offer? What alternative use might you have for the use of this building if our nation ever wakes up to the fact that our internal combustion transportation system and its supporting industrial complex are the greatest single plague on the air we breathe.(69)

Very likely a great many Port Huroners agreed with Soule, but gas for less sounded so good that they put aside their consciences and filled up to save half a buck per tankful.

Some oil companies hawked the product not with low prices, but by leaning on the mean streak in drivers: "My dad's pump can lick your dad's pump...Sunoco 260...highest octane gasoline at any station in the world. We call it 260 Action. Action to be used...not abused." Other firms emphasized the homey side to their stations. Gulf Oil hired a registered nurse from Port Huron, a graduate of Henry Ford Hospital, Linda Lalley, to drive 1,000 miles per week from station to station inspecting the bathrooms. She received a salary, expense account, and the use of a sports car for what was described as "glamorous, stimulating...any girl's dream job."

Not everybody who stopped into a filling station wanted to fuel up or use the john. Since they took in $16 million per year, St. Clair County's gas stations still provided a source of ready cash for criminals. Port Huron police discovered after they shot and killed 19 year-old James Gostinger, Jr in the middle of a gas station burglary that he was on probation for robbing the same station five months earlier. A few weeks later a customer unknowingly interrupted the armed robbery of another station down the block, and the thieves helpfully sold him gas and oil, since they'd locked the real attendant in a back room. Once they had the money in hand, filling station holdup men often found I-94 a welcome route for an expressway getaway from Port Huron.

Mass transit in the Thumb tailed off further during the 60's. Port Huron's city bus service withered and died, as it did in Lansing, Flint, and communities across the country. Bus company owner Leo Shovan had his business permit yanked in 1964 after a car rammed one of his 17 year-old buses when it stalled on the Scenic Highway. Four children in a party of 50 roller skaters burned to death in the resulting fire. Shovan's 500,000 mile clunker had carried no fire extinguisher and no flares on board. The worse thing he'd ever seen, said Deputy Sheriff David Doktor, a familiar refrain by this time. A trucking company picked up the Port Huron bus franchise for four more years, before service ended completely in 1968.

The City Council refused at this point to spend $25,000 to subsidize the bus line for one year, a fraction of what it spent on paving a mile of street. This marked the end of 102 years of municipal mass transit of one kind or another in Port Huron, inspiring Charlie Barrett to address the crisis: *City Bus Service Ends. Your Transportation Begins at Cawood's $60 to $600 Lot.* Gerald Bouchard barely suppressed a yawn over the 1,100 petition signatures that asked to keep the buses rolling. Port Huron made no attempt to secure any of the federal mass transit money beginning to trickle out of Washington.

Port Huron might be in the dark, but it had dawned finally on some national political figures by this time that the country could not build and maintain roads fast enough to keep up with the rate of automobile expansion. "The highway system is not adequate now for rush hours and it never will be," said the country's first Transportation Secretary, Alan Boyd, to the Detroit Economic Club. A bus on the other hand could carry as many people as typically rode in 35 automobiles; two train tracks could handle as many commuters as 80 lanes of freeway. Uncle Sam put up $175 million for mass transit in 1970, but that still compared miserably to $5 billion for roads.(70)

Intercity bus service still rolled in and out of Port Huron, but it was nothing to write home about. When one bus traveler, a Mrs. Curtis, did write home, she complained that her 200 mile trip across Michigan to Port Huron had taken 9.5 hours, longer than her flight from Amsterdam to Chicago: "(I) think about fast trains, buses and trams in Europe and the fantastic Metro system under Paris. Realize that fewer people there float around in big cars like we do here in the US, but must our public transit be like this?"(71) The average American bus celebrated its 12th birthday during this decade, to the discomfort of most passengers. Three daily round trip buses left Port Huron for Detroit, a couple went to Flint, and just one per week traveled to the north. When two ladies wrote to the *Times Herald* requesting more frequent regular bus service from Port Huron into the upper Thumb, they received in reply this helpful hint: hitchhike.

Not that the auto addicts at the *Times Herald* had turned entirely heartless or lamebrained on the subject of mass transit. "When it comes to moving large numbers of people quickly and safely between urban centers," they admitted, "the rails have some formidable advantages to offer." A single rail line could move up to 10 times as many people in an hour as I-94, and a railroad passenger traveled 25 times more safely than in an automobile. Yet only 500 intercity trains operated in America in 1970, compared to 20,000 in 1929.(72) Two daily trains heading east to Toronto and west to Chicago were all that remained of Port Huron's service. The prospect of 500 mph magnetic-powered passenger trains of the future, recently outlined for Port Huron readers in *Family Weekly,* seemed a little out of reach. As all this occurred in the USA, electric passenger trains in Europe and Asia commonly hit speeds of 125-150 mph, more than twice as fast as the Port Huron run.

347

While passenger service stumbled, U.S. railroad freight efficiency continued to run rings around trucks. A Grand Trunk engine pulling a train at 65 mph between Port Huron and Chicago could move as much cargo with a fraction of the fuel needed by 160 trucks. A single freight car, the world's largest, delivered an 850,000 lb. load to a St. Clair County power plant with ease, the equivalent carrying capacity of 25 trailer trucks. It cost 66%-75% less to move a ton per mile by train than truck. Nevertheless, while 30-35 Grand Trunk freight trains passed through Port Huron daily, locally generated cargo shifted more and more to trucks. Whereas Kimball Appliance once had staged carload refrigerator sales during the 40's, the retailer had switched to truckload sales by the 60's. The *Times Herald* glimpsed the light again about the mistreatment of America's freight railroads: "The Nation's railroads are in trouble...as mounting costs and the competition of government subsidized waterway and highway transport combine to lock them in a economic vise."(73)

Author James Burby got more specific: "It is Interstate Commerce Commission policy to deny railroads any rate that might take business away from trucks and barges, a so-called 'umbrella' approach to setting prices that costs Americans somewhere between $500 million and $5 billion a year in higher...freight charges."(74) The train businesses managed to score at least one win for sanity in the 60's when after 16 years of lobbying and legal shenanigans they won the right to remove from their locomotives thousands of wholly unnecessary firemen left over from the steam era. These hands had been riding the diesel trains as the all-time champions of union featherbedding. U.S. railroad employment shrank to 700,000, down 50% since WW2. In Port Huron, 900 of those workers remained at Grand Trunk, 100 at C&O, 40 at the Port Huron & Detroit. The 400 surviving railroads in America, one-third the number that had existed in 1915, were so strapped financially that they could only afford one-quarter of the capital expenditure needed on equipment.

Aside from one or two bright spots, America continued to make a shambles of light rail also. The city of Seattle built a monorail from its downtown to the 1962 World Fair site, and passengers rode from one to the other in 90 seconds, compared to the 20 minutes it took driving. But in Los Angeles the last line of the Pacific Electric street railway, the one-time transit wonder of America, closed, marking one of the ugliest episodes in the country's transportation history. Reporter Ward Cannel described L.A. County as "6.5 million people caught in an endless and paralyzing traffic jam," with more registered cars in it than in all of Africa.(75) Streetcars also disappeared from Washington, DC, a significant statement about the nation's overall backwardness in land transportation.

As Mrs. Curtis noticed, the rest of the developed world regularly lapped America in mass transit. Particularly galling was the superiority of streetcar service in Communist countries, like the 1,400 streamlined streetcars operating in Czechoslovakia. (76) U.S. autoheads tried using patriotism, the last refuge of a scoundrel, to disparage Red transit achievements, calling them a symptom of weakness compared to the supposed liberty of the auto. "You can stand in front of the Kremlin for an hour and never see a private car," sniffed correspondent Esther Tufty, forgetting that similar conditions on Mackinac Island made it the vacation Mecca of her home state of Michigan.

Trying to right past wrongs, some government officials made stumbling efforts in the late 60's to begin rebuilding regional mass transit in Southeastern Michigan, with plans for buses and light rail and rapid transit. Short memories at the *Times Herald* responded: " A regional system of rapid transit, reasonably priced and suited to the travel and time needs of a great many people would be a fine service to have. Whether it can ever be realized is problematical at best."(77) Of course, such a system already had been realized once before, in the interurban era, 60 years earlier, and dismantled at its Port Huron end in 1930.

Although another effort to start air service in Port Huron failed during this decade, 169 million passengers climbed aboard airline flights in America in 1970, which represented 10% of all intercity travel.(78) Government ran virtually all the major airports in the country, and taxed passengers and carriers appropriately to pay for them. This admirable system should have been applied to the rails decades earlier. Many of the sub-500 mile flights around the country would have been entirely unnecessary had the railroads been permitted to evolve during the 20th century. The private flight of 250 miles in Michigan that crashed and killed UAW boss Walter Reuther in 1970 presented a fair example.

It wouldn't be right to let the Sixties go by without mentioning another transportational method born in this era, space flight. Within a period of nine years an astounding burst of American ingenuity, plus $24 billion dollars, put astronauts first into orbit around the Earth, then two of them on the surface of the moon in 1969. They had no particular reason to go to the Moon, since remote and robotic examination had determined it was just a heap of rocks and dust. A disparaging comparison came into fashion following this event: "If we can put a man on the moon why can't we...." do this, that, or the other thing. For our purposes we'll say that with a similar effort, America could have rebuilt its railroad and streetcar networks, with an infinitely greater reward to the nation.

Time can turn a natural idea into a pretty Utopian concept. The design for a grand canal system stretching across Michigan's Lower Peninsula, which came to such a bad end in the 1840's, then revived briefly but unsuccessfully in 1910, reappeared again in 1966. With a change of heart worthy of Paul the apostle, the former State Highway Director, John Mackie, who'd spent much of his public career as an unabashed member of the Road Gang, now outlined a $600 million project to link up existing rivers and lakes with a series of canals, creating 900 miles of waterway 300 feet wide and 15 feet deep. The price would be a third of what the IHS cost per mile; the work to take five years. Port Huron businessman John F. Adams served as president of the Trans-Michigan Canal organization. He said the main route from Port Huron across to Lake Michigan would tie together most of the major cities in the state, and could be 85% privately financed as a water utility, furnishing hydroelectric power, irrigation, potable water, improved recreation opportunities, and home and factory development. Now did auto-sickened Michigan have enough good sense left to build it?

Abundant evidence demonstrated that any expansion of the 27,000 miles of inland waterways in the U.S. with projects like the Trans-Michigan could be amply repaid. The same sized engine on a towboat could move eight times as much weight as it could on rails, carrying a ton a mile for 3/10 of a cent, compared to 1.5 cents by rail, cents by truck, 20 cents by air. This comparison was distorted to some degree by the fact that the federal government spent $500 million per year maintaining waterways and charged no user fees, compared to nothing spent on railroads which operated under the baleful eye of the Interstate Commerce Commission. The ICC regulated fewer than 10% of the 1,700 shipping companies on inland waters.(79)

The worthy dream of increasing water transport couldn't offset the real-world decline of passenger travel on the Great Lakes. In Port Huron the arrival of the occasional chartered ship at the dock in Pine Grove Park marked a special occasion. One pulled in carrying 2,000 members of the Michigan Railway Club. The vessel *Aquarama* pulled out carrying 1,200 Port Huroners. But these events were as rare by the 60's as they'd been commonplace in 1900. The last cruise line on the Lakes, the Georgian Bay, first organized by Detroit and Chicago investors in 1913, closed up in 1968. This company had enjoyed a banner season during its final year of1967, carrying passengers to the Expo '67 World's Fair in Montreal. But the Coast Guard declared the last Georgian Bay vessel, the wooden-hulled *South American*, to be unseaworthy, and company directors refused to build a steel replacement. At one time 60 cruise ships had plied the Lakes. Now, none. Sailing the Lakes never had been safer than in the 60's. The sinking of the freighter Daniel Morrell off the Thumb in 1966, which killed 28 (a holiday weekend's worth of fatalities on Michigan roads) made out-of-the-ordinary headlines for days.

Commercial shipping lessened in Port Huron, though it still serviced the cement plant, the paper plants, and an aggregate company. The Seaway Terminal busied itself with about 50 ships per year, handling shipments of beans, wood pulp, auto parts, and even whole cars sometimes. Freighters also hauled coal to the Detroit Edison power plants in Marysville and St. Clair City, but this fuel had gone entirely out of most other uses. Port Huron looked enviously across the river at Sarnia, where 17 of the big ships laid up during one winter, a valuable source of revenue when these vessels refitted for the coming season. The Great Lakes fleet counted 700 vessels these days, none of them based in Port Huron, though 150 captains, mates and engineers lived in St. Clair County. Lake veterans founded the Lake Pilots Association, headquartered in Port Huron, to assist foreign vessels in navigating through tight spots on this section of the St. Lawrence Seaway.

The Coast Guard station and cutter, and the light house remained in Port Huron (at government expense, with no corresponding service like a Railroad Guard), and the old port spirit hadn't died by any means. But for most St. Clair County people, their only contact with the water came through taking the ferries out of Marine City or Algonac, or through recreational boating. 350 men labored at the Chris Craft plant in Algonac on sportboats; but nobody built commercial. Waterfront homes with docks sold at a premium, and a developer put in a new neighborhood in Port Huron along a series of short canals dug along the Black River for residential use only. Canals but no sidewalks. The city started work a new $1.8 million pleasure boat marina to service more of the county's 5,000 private craft, a marina that had twice as many car parking spots as boat slips. And no bike rack.

The bicycle held its own as a plaything, that's the best that could be said for it in 1960's America. The number of recreational riders grew to 30, 40, 50 million by various estimates. Fads came and went in Port Huron's three bike shops, like a tandem bicycle flurry in the mid-60's, but adults very rarely indeed mounted up to get to work, to travel, to go to the store. You'd have looked in vain to find a bicycle rack at Mueller

Brass' factory door, at Sperry's department store, at the McMorran Center or the Grace Episcopal church. Mrs. Curtis, the world traveler from Port Huron, had some thoughts on this as well: "...how healthy people looked in the countries where there is much bike riding, and I wish we would make bike paths along our roads and highways."

Right you are, Mrs. C. It might be only a niche vehicle in the USA, but around the rest of the globe the bike still worked its magic in the workaday world when called upon. The Congress learned that Vietnamese Communists used 5,000 bicycles to surreptitiously and efficiently transport up to 500 lbs. of equipment apiece during the war there. "I wonder what kind of tires they use?" pondered U.S. Senator Strom Thurmond, himself a biker. American troops resorted to no such tactics, but filled yet another foreign landscape with that warped expression of U.S.freedom, automobile junk.

For most of the decade, only children made everyday use of the bicycle in Port Huron. The hostility of motorists towards cyclists, which always lay just below the surface, found regular expression in the continued scolding or threatening of kids on bikes. During one American Bike Month his paper assigned Jerry Brown to throw the Fear of God into youngsters, and incidentally their parents, on behalf of the car dictatorship which ruled the city.

The twisted wreckage of his bicycle lay near the center of the intersection. As the 9 year-old child was lifted into the ambulance, the motorist who had struck the child on the bicycle tried to wipe tears from his eyes. Fortunately, the child suffered only a broken leg, and someday he would ride another bicycle.(80)

And his assailant continue driving his car.

Two undeterred Port Huron teenagers, Rob Grambau and Russ Salton, bicycled all the way to Boston, making their way through Ontario. They discovered after several close calls with annihilation that "Canadian truck drivers, like their counterparts in America, don't take kindly to those dudes out there on the road, riding their cycles..." Pack riding kept cyclists a little safer, and a large group of teenage high school students from Washington State came through Port Huron on a 2,800 mile trip to New York. They averaged 85 miles per day, in a large enough convoy to hold their own against predatory truckers. A *Times Herald* summer intern, Tom Winters, gave his colleagues a brave example one year by biking to his story assignments. Another area resident, Jerry Hickey, biked solo 2,300 miles from Port Huron to Los Angeles in 42 days.

The bicycle returned to the spotlight as serious transportation on Earth Day, April 22, 1970, the starting point of America's facetious environmental movement, when citizens all too briefly questioned the direction their country traveled by car. Elementary school teachers Lynne Nelson, Rita Stark, and Marilyn Winters decided to bicycle from Port Huron to their jobs in suburban Sparlingville, about five miles away. They had to rent bicycles in order to make this dramatic statement, and they first rendezvoused at Nelson's house by car. A couple of more serious Port Huron bicyclists celebrated Earth Day, James and Carol Worthey, who'd ridden bikes to and from their wedding ceremony the previous autumn. They didn't own a car. James worked as a college math and physics instructor at the community college. He wrote a letter to *Time* magazine calling for birth control for automobiles, and heard in reply from a White

House lawyer in his late 50's who biked 25 miles per day - not, unfortunately, President Richard Nixon.

Elsewhere on Earth Day, students at Henry Ford Community College reverted to the FMC Founder's once-preferred mechanical transport method, bikes, and announced that "Pedal Power Doesn't Pollute." Yet, an informal survey by the *Times Herald* found 77% of Port Huroners drove rather than biked or walked to destinations within a mile of their homes. Not too Earth-friendly. William Kramer of the St. Clair County Health Department had to point out to the community that burning a gallon of gasoline generated 3.4 pounds of bad air. The bicycle got some nonpolluting competition during the 1960's with the introduction of the skateboard, which several million American boys took up with push power. But tinkerers subverted even this innocent and healthy pastime by motorizing some of these boards, making them easily the least controllable vehicles on the street.

By the 60's, all the elements that significantly expanded American life expectancy during the 20th Century had been put into place in Port Huron: water and sewage treatment, garbage pickup and sanitary disposal, mass vaccination against communicable diseases, antibiotics, pasteurization, and aspirin. Beyond these six, the additional and increasingly expensive labors of the medical world accomplished very little. "It had long been known that medical care, especially when compared with the environment or social behavior, has relatively modest effect on mortality rates," in the words of historian Paul Starr.(81) The debilitating lifestyle in overtransportation by the automobile worked against longevity. Cars could either a) knock you down, or b) wear you down. About alternative a) Port Huron's Dr. John Coury, a future president of the American Medical Association, said "I would like to see a large color print of a horrible traffic accident printed on the front page of the *Times Herald* every Friday as a reminder to weekend motorists." The doctor could not, however, bring himself to say get rid of your cars.

Under alternative b) the obesity epidemic in America grew with the number of automobiles during the 1960's, although people consumed less calories than they had 20 years earlier.(82) An estimated 30% of the populace, 40 million people, weighed at least 15 pounds too much, and 20% of children were overweight. The U.S. Public Health Service crowned the American male the fattest in the world. The same Public Health Service crowd ignored the primary fat-builder, the automobile, at all costs rather than make an unpopular diagnosis. Instead the USPHS reinvented the fantasy that obesity had a genetic component, because so many fat parents had fat children. This idea had been disproven 30 years earlier, and it ignored the bad habits that a fatso Ma and Pa transmitted by example to their kids, like car ownership.

While his employer promoted summer outings around Port Huron of "driving and eating fun," Jerry Brown, who at 6 feet tall weighed 240 pounds, heard some alarming news from his doctor, "You'll be dead in 15 years if you keep on eating." Splitting the difference with starvation, Jerry embarked on a crash "once and for all" diet and dropped 57 pounds in four months. He had plenty of fad diets to choose from certainly, dozens in fact – the Hay diet, Air force diet, magic pairs diet, liquid diet. Plus amphetamines, laxatives, and diuretics. And a growing array of "low-calorie" foods in the stores. After dropping the 57, Brown could look down and see his belt for the first time in five years. But the "once and for all" cure wasn't for all after all. This slimdown

352

didn't include dumping his car, and building enough walking into his life. Brownie grew large once again and repeated the whole process several times in the years to come.

Most middle class adults of Brown's type had a bad attitude toward exercise. A few fatties tackled the gym now and then at the YMCA, but most looked for less strenuous programs. Diet clubs and fat parlors geared mainly to women sprouted across the city, like Weight Watchers, and the Elaine Powers Figure Salon in Northgate, where 7 instructors armed with 42 pieces of "light movement" equipment promised to carve four dress sizes off the customer in a month. "Every woman is weight conscious, unless she's unconscious." wrote *Times Herald* reporter Marianna Goodman. The first whispers reached Port Huron medical circles in 1968 about stomach bypass surgery as a treatment for obesity, a procedure which required a brain bypass first. The declining intelligence of Americans ready to grasp at straws like stomach stapling itself resulted from a lack of exercise; they didn't get enough oxygen to their heads. The IQ Index of Automobile Advertising proved this every day:

Young Dodge. New Dodge. Go Dodge. New Dodge Coronet coming on big for 1965. See Dodge. A young beauty, all new hot new Dodge at a new lower price. Go Dodge. New Dodge Coronet. Big on action, too. Power? Wild. Ride? Smooth. Response? The most. Drive Dodge. New Dodge Coronet, with the look of it, feel of it, go of it. Check the price of it, you'll drive home in it. New Dodge Coronet coming on big for '65. Go see Dodge.

Apart from the stomach and head, the trend in American inactivity struck most forcibly at the nation's heart, giving it the highest coronary disease rate in the world. Port Huron and Mercy Hospitals vowed to be ready when Jerry Brown's generation seized up and needed cardiac services. 60% of St. Clair County deaths were now heart related. Cardiologist Richard Bates told a Port Huron convention "Americans like the swiftness of dying from a heart attack because they always want to get things over quickly and get on to something else." If after surviving their first attacks people couldn't be bothered to give up the car and live a healthier lifestyle, medical specialists, somewhat like car mechanics, could get under the hood with anticoagulants, antibiotics, heart lung machines, artificial heart valves, grafts, pacemakers, and artificial kidneys to prolong matters. The two hospitals added another 200 beds between them. A "medical village" replaced one of the McMorran family's twin Main Street mansions. All this required a corresponding expansion of parking, which apart from demolishing several more homes encouraged more driving, which encouraged more fat and bad tickers.

The increase in heart disease among youngsters also accelerated. Dead young American soldiers autopsied in Vietnam had even more heart decay than those examined during the Korean War, which had been alarming enough. The nation's heart expert, Dr. Paul Dudley White, shamed the country's parents for inflicting automobile sickness on their children. On a typical school day "Most children will arrive by bus. Others will emerge from private automobiles. As mother sees it, 'Junior's physical stamina should not be overtaxed.' What mother fails to realize is that Junior is being set up for a life of slothfulness."(83) White insisted that children should walk or cycle to school, "instead of being enclosed in a school bus." Both young and old, per Dr. White, needed one hour of walking per day as a "must," 2 hours would be better, which jibed with Thomas Jefferson's figures from 200 years earlier.

Columnist Paul Harvey laughed at government efforts to encourage exercise:

353

"Washington did not have to tell my generation of schoolchildren to stretch their muscles. But that's before roller skates and jumping ropes and hopscotch and walking were replaced by TV and two cars and self indulgent lethargy." Out of shape brats made terrible drivers once they grew old enough to get licensed, according to researcher James Crumbaugh, who speculated that wimpy teenage boys thought of a car as a substitute "machine body", and drove wildly to prove their masculinity.(84)

Body disuse inflicted a catalog of other miseries on America's auto-fixated population. By the 1960's the image of the senior citizen had been firmly established as that of a fat, jowly, stiff, slow-thinking wheezer who could barely stumble back and forth to the garage and climb in and out of the car. 13 million people in the country suffered from arthritis, 5 million from migraine headaches. An indeterminate number had "urobphrenia," said Dr. Igho Kornbleugh, from too much indoor living, "the wearisome monotony of an immured existence within the confines of the residence and the place of employment." 30 million people had chronic backaches, the #2 reason for visits to the doctor. Back pain sometimes nearly crippled the country's most famous patient, President John Kennedy. Back man Dr. Ira Rumney had no doubt as to where the national sacroiliac problem originated:

Automobile riding is bad for backs, not only because it promotes lack of exercise but also because the plain old mechanism of just sitting there promotes a distorted postural position, like debutante slouch.(85)

Health spending in Auto America tripled during the decade to an annual $70 billion by 1970. Both private health insurance and new government programs like Medicare and Medicaid fanned the inflation flames. Costs at Port Huron Hospital had risen 250% since 1949, five times the national inflation rate. The *Times Herald* called this "...unbelievable, almost impossible. For large numbers of families serious illness can mean instant poverty." A day in a hospital bed with meals, exclusive of any doctoring or medicines, set you back $86. The same stay in a hospital usually revealed to the patient that automobile-bound doctors and nurses waddling around the halls were in no better physical shape than anybody else. The automobile worked against health progress in another way, because very few scientific studies of medical matters in America took fully into account the unnatural physical background of the car culture, which twisted the results and their interpretation.

As always, the only legitimate and certain cure for automobile disease in general came from walking, but by the Sixties many people would rather have died, and did. Not everyone, however. The oldest man ever to live in Port Huron, William Vertican, credited physical fitness, especially walking, for his great age. He continued to walk until his very last years, though admitting he had to be cautious since he sometimes forgot where he was. The former railroad man, Great Lakes sailor, Pinkerton agent and coal miner had never seen a doctor or taken any medicine until the age of 108, and he finally said his last goodbye in 1968 at 111.

People saw Mrs. Gordon Bliss walking the four mile round trip from her Port Huron home to her Women's Benefit Association job every day, and she continued on into her 32 year retirement, which ended at age 97. Christian charities and the March of Dimes made a sterling example to the community by sponsoring fundraising walks of impressive distances, like the hike from Yale to Port Huron, 25 miles, and from Algonac, 28 miles. Enough joggers began running the streets so that people like James

Baird were "No longer considered oddities on the roadways..." for putting in 20 miles per week around town. Michigan produced a genuine walking hero in the tradition of Edward Weston and Emma Gatewood during this decade. 49 year-old Andy Horujku walked from Anchorage, Alaska to Tierra Del Fuego in South America, to protest pollution, mainly car pollution. The former engineer refused car rides during his odyssey, and averaged 30 miles per day, covering the immense distance in 21 months. But Horujku and pedestrians like him who enjoyed public esteem were still the exceptions.

While Port Huron dished out fortunes for streets, some of its oldest sidewalks buckled and crumbled. Since no municipal sidewalk maintenance program existed, sidewalkers perforce became streetwalkers. And in places like Colonial Village, significant gaps yawned in the sidewalk network. Sidewalks were obstructed for extra parking areas at downtown businesses. In winter, public and private snow plows negligently blocked sidewalks all over town, or owners refused to shovel them, to the annoyance of walkers like Harold Blake: "...Mr. and Mrs. Citizen who ride Shank's mare must negotiate [them] unaided at the risk of a serious, perhaps cripping fall." Blake could sue private homeowners for this, but if he fell on a municipal sidewalk he had to grin and bear it because a new state law forbade suing cities for sidewalk tumbles; inviting more neglect .

Many Americans have long lamented the fact that people have foregone walking for the automobile - even to the extent of driving half a block to the grocery store, admitted the Times Herald. *Maybe a contributing reason is that we have become too oriented toward auto travel, spending too much time and effort on street and parking problems while forgetting entirely the plight of the pedestrian - or the plight of the motorist who might become a pedestrian if walkways were made safe, comfortable and inviting.* And, *Until recently anyone who walked dogless through a neighborhood was looked upon with suspicion as a possible sinister character bent on no good.*(86)

The desertion of the sidewalks by responsible adults didn't only foster sinister grownup characters, but juvenile delinquents, a trend that began during WW2. Adolescents who formerly interacted daily with grownups on the streets of Port Huron now rarely saw them there, or anywhere, except in structured settings like schools. Without the example constantly before them of how to behave in society, and without the supervision they'd formerly received on the streets, a minority of children ran increasingly wild, smashing up public and private property. Like the bathrooms at the McMorran Center, garage windows at Ogden & Moffett, school buildings (66 windows at Washington Jr. High in two months), even churches. They committed larcenies and burglaries, set fires, stole cars, and more. On one occasion six boys aged 10-16 walked away from the juvenile detention home in Port Huron, stole two cars, and roamed the county before their spree ended in two traffic crashes. Police arrested 800 kids in St. Clair County annually. Granted, the sum total of youthful vandalism didn't amount to much compared to the mauling of society committed by automobile drivers, but it injected another element of disorder into the community and took a toll on the quality of life.

The quality of Alfred Sloan's life came under review when he died at 90 in 1966, in the New York City hospital he and General Motors pal Charles Kettering had helped endow, Sloan-Kettering. Supporting this institution seemed the least they could do to thank the millions of people who'd been put into hospitals by GM's products. The last of the early American auto giants still kicking, Charles Mott, eulogized Sloan in a carefully phrased fashion: "Stockholders of General Motors owe a great deal to this man..." The GM stockholders, yes, but how about everybody else? Looking at the alarming decline of the city into which he'd invested so much of his life, Flint's ex-mayor Mott wondered about the ultimate effect of Sloan's, and his own, automotive handiwork.

In Detroit, a city which ahead of any other should have been infinitely nearer Utopia by this time, the week-long racial riots of 1967 killed 43 people, did $50 million in damage, and sent the one-time "Paris of the Midwest" into complete freefall. "Looters Use Luxury Cars to Steal Anything Moveable," reported the press. The riot dead amounted to as many people killed every seven hours on the nation's highways, and the destruction equaled a day-and-a-half worth of traffic property damage in America. 40% of Detroit's white citizens moved out of town during the 60's, fleeing mainly along the defense highways, never to return. Maybe the production and consumption of automobiles weren't the purpose of life after all. At about this time prominent attorney Chase Osborn III, grandson of the walking Michigan governor of 1912, committed suicide by jumping off the Blue Water Bridge. Port Huron police arriving at the scene found only his abandoned Mustang.

Chapter 10. 1971-1980: It's a Necessity

The automobile is one of the absolute necessities of our later-day civilization.
— Henry Ford, 1906 (1)

...an every-day necessity... — Scribners Magazine, 1913

...an economic necessity... — Buick, 1918

...a year-round necessity... — Henry Ford, 1922

...the fad of yesterday is the necessity of today... — Prof. William Frayer, 1933

...a 'necessity' in the depression. — Robert & Helen Lynd, 1937

...the necessities of our American standard of living. — Port Huron Times Herald, 1942

...no longer a luxury - it's a necessity... — PHTH, 1951

...a family necessity...a personal necessity... — George Romney, 1957 (2)

...a common necessity... — John Keats, 1958

...a pleasure, a chore, a necessity... — PHTH, 1961

...the second car's becoming a modern day necessity... — Ruth Millett, 1964

...a necessity for sustaining life... — John Jerome, 1972

It was a necessity for sustaining life in an American automobile to fill it with gasoline once in a while, and this practice came to have nation-rattling consequences during the 1970's. The country's memories of World War II gas rationing, "a war time necessity" according to the U.S. Fuel Administration, and of the periodic gas shortages which followed in the late 40's, had faded almost completely away. For 20 years afterward, gasoline prices had remained amazingly low, lower at times than the price of distilled water. Taxes on gasoline had increased during the 50's and 60's, but still only averaged a trivial 12 cents per gallon. The underlying product price barely budged, and even retreated when adjusted for inflation. No other factor played a larger role than this in America's automotive narcissism. The country mistook cheap gas for an unvarying fact of life, an inalienable right of drivers. But now, to the disbelieving eyes of the highway hypnotized, the mirage of everlasting 19.9 cents a gallon regular at Port Huron's Gas for Less station vanished forever. It had been adjusted for reality.

The chickens of unrestrained spending and borrowing by consumers and government alike, at home and abroad, finally came home to roost in 1971. A step-up in the cost of just about everything, plus the onset of the first U.S. trade deficit of the 20th Century (caused mainly by the purchase of foreign cars and imported oil), prompted President Richard Nixon to implement wage and price controls. Though they didn't last very long on most items, price controls stayed put for the rest of the decade on much of the country's domestically produced oil. The president also abolished the $35 per ounce gold exchange rate for the dollar, violating Henry Ford the First's commandment that "A dollar that stays 100 cents is as necessary as a pound that stays 16 ounces and a yard that stays 36 inches."(3)

America's oil industry felt that price controls made a pretty strong production disincentive in the face of inflation that averaged 8% per year during this decade. So, to keep its 150 million motor vehicles running, the USA was obliged to buy 3 million, then 4 million, then 6 million barrels per day, eventually one-half of all its oil, from exporting countries who gradually hiked their $2 a barrel price to $40. Not only had U.S. money declined in value, but the idea finally had dawned on foreign producers that they had the car junkies in America over a barrel when it came to the petroleum necessity.

Some of these nations in the Middle East had had enough as well of America's client state Israel dropping bombs on Arabs during the recurring wars in that region. Following the latest desert brawl in 1973, outraged members of OPEC slapped a 2 million barrel per day embargo on the U.S. for four months. In a twinkling a minor gasoline shortage across the country turned into a major drought. Pump prices vaulted to as much as 60 cents a gallon at Port Huron stations. This triggered what came to be known hyperbolically as the "energy crisis," the "Pearl Harbor of energy," and the "moral equivalent of war," or MEOW for short.(4)

"Drought" and "crisis" are relative terms in this instance because petroleum supplies would have been perfectly adequate if it hadn't been for America's harebrained automobile culture. The U.S. accounted for 6% of the global population but used one-third of the world's energy. 98% of the rest of humanity sustained life without automobiles, while Americans single-handedly burned through 96 billion gallons of gasoline per year. The U.S. spent 20% of its gross national product on the transportation of people and goods, about $170 billion per year. No other nation came close to this kind of egregious waste.(5)

Would that at this point in our history we could relate that Port Huroners took these developments to heart. That their eyes opened to the foolishness of their ways and they redirected their steps onto the path of mobility righteousness. They did not. Like the rest of the country they refused absolutely to acknowledge that the energy deficit in America boiled down to one cause and one only: the buzz wagon. When gasoline dried up, frustrated St. Clair County motorists lined up, at filling stations like the new-fangled "Fill 'Em Fast" self-serve on Main Street in Port Huron. If people at the pump didn't fill 'em fast enough, those further back in line fumed and whined and threatened and pleaded. Their lifestyles depended on it. Commuter Ken Conley spent $100 per month on gas *before* the 1973 embargo, nonchalantly driving 120 roundtrip miles a day from his home north of Port Huron to his General Motors job in Detroit. John Wescott covered 150 miles to a Chevy factory in Flint. Mr. and Mrs. John Gallourakis drove a combined 150 commuting miles daily to their separate jobs in opposite directions from their hobby farm in the township boondocks. Thousands more did likewise.

Together St. Clair County drivers consumed 50 million gallons of gas annually, more than 300 gallons per capita, in 1.8 vehicles per household, if you can envision 80% of a car. In a way, the county should have been almost self-sustaining,

358

oily speaking, since 400 local wells produced a million barrels of petroleum each year. Somehow, it didn't work out that way at the gas pump. Eight life-sustaining oil and natural gas pipelines crisscrossed the St. Clair County landscape, most on their way to Chemical Valley in Sarnia, where refinery and petrochemical giants commissioned another $1 billion dollars in expansion during the 70's to deal with the MEOW panic.(6) On the U.S. national scene, Congress greenlighted a gigantic Alaska pipeline to get arctic crude down to the lower 48 with dispatch.

Screwball conspiracy theories abounded to explain the gasoline shortfall, like the one about the secret Nazi formula for cheap synthetic gas brewed from coal. In the feverish imagination of drivers suffering from gasoline withdrawal, a cabal involving the oil companies, the government, and the Arabs withheld this magical car fuel elixir from the public in order to push up petroleum prices. Gas-famished millions scanned the horizon for gasoline replacements supposedly coming to the rescue – fuels concocted from natural gas, compost, garbage, alcohol. Promoter Gordon Blake promised to put up a 100 million gallon home-grown ethanol plant in Marysville if only he could lay his hands on $24 million.

The situation from coast to coast drove some mentally unbalanced people over the edge. In Hollywood, California, where gas station lines sometimes stretched seven blocks, a motorist held off a crowd of 50 people with a gun while he filled his car from a station's pumps out of turn. In Washington, DC, White House assistant Stuart Eizenstat found himself seized by "almost uncontrollable rage" after sitting 45 minutes in a gas line.(7) Luckily he had no gun handy. Many speed fiends raged against the national 55 mph speed limit imposed to save the country 250,000 barrels of oil daily. Since drivers crashing at 70 mph died 15 times more often than those traveling 55, lower speeds also helped cut traffic accident deaths in St. Clair County from 63 in 1973 to 43 in 1974. But did basket case car owners care about that? They instead outfitted their vehicles with the new police-avoiding, radar-detecting "fuzzbusters" to beat the road cops, and defiantly attended the "Rod-o-Rama" at the McMorran center in Port Huron to gape with desire at the fuel-hogging custom cruisers.

Speculation about the possible return of gas rationing and of a 50-cent per gallon tax to cut consumption rattled people still more. Resentment about everything oil ran so hot that President Gerald Ford, the first president ever from Michigan (and no relation to Henry), refused to rule out the idea of taking over by force the oil fields in countries ornery enough to boycott the USA. Understandably this put these nations somewhat on edge over what the Yankee maniacs might do next. The eventual overthrow of the pro-American government in oil-rich Iran by Moslem nationalists in 1979, and their kidnapping of dozens of American hostages, could hardly be said to have occurred in a vacuum. The subsequent cut-off of Iranian oil to the U.S. following this action doubled gas prices again, to $1.30 per gallon.

Not everybody saw these things upside down, it should be mentioned. Up until these tumultuous days, the *Times Herald's* editorialist Floyd Bernard had functioned as a more or less reliable car dope: "The American people will give up their cars about as quickly as they will stop breathing. One way or another the symbol of American freedom is here to stay." Now the press of events inspired in Floyd some intermittent days of rationality about transportation, days almost of fondness for walking, biking, and mass transit:

359

People are likely to become more physically fit, and more fit to live with. That is to say they will be more social because they will have to mingle more with other people. People have been riding when they should have been walking, going when they should have been staying and moving farther and farther away from their daily activities, while leaving nearby areas to decay. Sometimes interesting people live next door whom we only see coming and going or at an occasional stop light. Many people are relearning the art – and the joys – of bicycling...a bicycle is a great way to become reacquainted with the community where a person lives. You can see the same scene from a car, but from there the exposure is brief and the tensions of traffic distracting. From a bike you get a renewed impression of what nice towns we live in hereabouts.(8)

Looked at that way, OPEC practically was doing the U.S. a favor. In the same general vein, a study by the Federal Energy Administration showed America could live well on half its energy consumption if it switched to mass transit and ditched freight trucks for trains. But would it?

For the Big 3 car companies, this sort of unsettling talk, plus the increasing demands of auto regulators, occasionally lowered a pea-soup fog of uncertainty and discouragement, one might almost say despair, over the immediate future. "The real mass transit system in the United States is the highway system and the automobile..," insisted Henry Ford II.(9) In addition to the changing fortunes in the petroleum world, the auto men now dealt with safety, emission, durability, and gas mileage requirements from the national and state governments, new anti-trust accusations, and competition from imports. The public's favorite sizes of cars got smaller at the start of the 1970's, then got larger again, then got smaller again, as buyers adjusted and readjusted to the ups and downs in gasoline supplies and prices.

General Motors and Ford spent more than 200 million advertising dollars per year, and Chrysler another 100 mil, reaching out to the masses, catering to their varying moods. In doing so, Ford leaned even more heavily on the image of the animal so repugnant to Henry I.

If the gasoline shortage has got you scared, partner, get a horse. Your Ford dealer has three little thoroughbreds named Maverick, Pinto and Mustang II. They're easy riders, dependable and economic. So see your Ford dealer and saddle up.

Chevrolet tried custom tailoring its TV ads for both big and small vehicle sizes:

You know, I thought about buying a smaller car, but the more I thought about it...Impala's the only car that makes any sense for us.

You know, I wanted a bigger car, but I'm glad we got the Chevelle...it fits all of us and it's a handy size to drive.

Big and small, Washington put Detroit on notice to start tightening up the gas mileage until their "fleets," as they were called, met an overall average of 27.5 miles per gallon by 1985, twice what they achieved in 1974.(10) Those manufacturers who didn't comply faced a big penalty per car. No other single edict wrung more tears out of Motor City executives and engineers, who kept pinups of gas guzzlers – such as the 5,500 lb., 8.5 miles per gallon Impala – beside their desks, like long-lost girlfriends. Many of the guys, the Dodge boys for instance, had a hard time letting go of this romance gone wrong:

Wanted: Men who can handle a real road machine. Dodge Challenger Rallye. There are special men who develop an almost spiritual attachment to their cars. They want a no-nonsense road machine that grabs a rough, winding stretch of road and holds on. One that stays low and close to the road like a snake.

Automotive advertising came to include gas mileage figures supplied by the Environmental Protection Agency on each new model, for both highway and city driving. A fortunate owner in town might get two-thirds of the highway rate, but neither was guaranteed. The EPA admitted, in fact, that it overestimated gas mileage by between 7% -16%. Careful readers of these ads noted a number of "your mileage may vary" disclaimers, according to the car's condition, the driver's habits, the climate, the terrain, the load. Ford said its new cars needed 4,000 miles of break-in to get to top gas mileage. Of course, once broken in, a car began to break down, and engine efficiency declined. They were not long the days of wine and roses and top gas economy with any car. The sole ray of sunshine for the industry on this gas mileage topic came from the partial exemption granted light trucks – pickups – those overpriced gas gulpers providing almost half the profits at the FMC.(11)

Gloom hung even heavier in Detroit when Transportation Secretary Brock Adams suggested a target of 40-50 miles per gallon by the turn of the century. Enjoying a joke at motordom's expense, writer Dick Dougherty said the favorite method of American carmakers to get better gas mileage by lightening up their vehicles was rust. Somebody in Washington thought about that subject, too, and intimated that the auto industry should guarantee their cars for 74,000 miles against rust holes and 24,000 against surface corrosion. The gas mileage quotas invigorated alternative car ideas both new and old. But by and large, that's all they remained, ideas. Electric cars got yet another new lease on life in the nation's admiration, but only 3,000 made it onto the road. Marysville dealer George Lang lost patience with a new electric model sitting unappreciated on his lot, so he cut the price from $3,400 down to $2,000 just to get rid of it. A few plastic and pedal cars went into limited production, and a couple of these engineless quadricycles were spotted in Port Huron. According to Robert Sobel of the newspaper *Newsday,* by the year 2000 customers could expect the average auto to be made of wood (1900 A.D. all over again), weigh 1,700 pounds, and get 60 mpg from a gasoline fill up costing $6. Believe it or not.

Two small economy cars put out by Ford and GM to get on the right side of the gas mileage question, and to retake some of the 15% - 25% in market share now owned by imported cars, made headlines for the wrong reasons: fire, crazy handling, jammed accelerators, bad brakes, etc. Chevrolet built its Vega model on the world's fastest assembly line, in Lordstown, Ohio, slapping them together at a rate of 100 per hour, with the quality one expected at that pace. Ford's "new little carefree car," the aforementioned Pinto, acquired a reputation as a rolling crematorium when subjected to a rear-end crash.(12) Port Huron Pinto owner John MacDonald practiced unbuckling his seat belt quickly to escape in case of a fire, but a policeman cautioned him, "You can't unbuckle any belt fast enough in one of those cars."

After a particularly gruesome triple-fatal Pinto fire wreck took place in Indiana, a criminal charge of reckless homicide compelled the FMC to defend itself in court. The indictment proved to be a slight exaggeration. From court testimony it turned out that *all* cars were fire prone when hit from behind. This revelation didn't save 1.5

million Pintos from a recall, nor Ford nor the rest of the industry from more barbecued-driver lawsuits. General Motors lost a $2.5 million judgment in the matter of a Dearborn man whose Chevy blew up when rear-ended at 60 mph and cooked his goose.

The question of whether cars should be built lighter for better gas mileage or heavier for collision resistance, which dated to the industry's earliest days, came up again for rehashing. The issue boiled down to: Would you rather spend more for gasoline or end up on a slab? Cawood auto mechanic Walt Heimbach in Port Huron voted for heavy over economical. He said of the newer gas-savers: "There is too much plastic in place of metal, and everything is made so light." Sure enough, the appearance of lighter cars on the roads to meet gas mileage limits sent the death and injury toll higher again after it first took the initial 55 mph dip.

The public indignation about imperfect cars like Pintos seemed a bit forced, since both manufacturers and public alike had known of the profoundly dangerous nature of all automobiles since Henry I wheeled out the first quad. The FMC also experienced issues during the 70's with millions of jumpy transmissions, almost as unpredictable as a real horse, partner. Pedro Walls of Port Huron sued Ford for $5 million after a Pinto allegedly jumped out of park into reverse, pinning him against a phone pole, fracturing his ribs and shoulder and puncturing a lung. Walls later dropped the matter but others insisted these bucking cars killed 100 people and injured 1,700 others the same way. Under the now keener eye of government watchdogs, the scope of automobile recalls increased. A recall record fell when Chevrolet summoned back 6.6 million products to fix bad engine mounts. On another occasion the Falk Cadillac-Olds dealership in Port Huron had to plead with 100 customers to return their vehicles before the brakes failed.

One General Motors recall of Buicks with wobbly front ends set Michael Payionk of Port Huron to thinking. His ma had purchased one of these cars at Cawood's, and she'd taken it in several times for unsuccessful surgery. Michael subsequently wrecked it, and himself, and killed a passenger in the bargain. After doing a 30-day stretch in the county jail for negligent homicide, Payionk lost his job, quit college, and become anxious, distressed, and depressed. The solution: a $1,000,000 lawsuit against GM and $500,000 against Cawood's over the bum Buick. Like Pedro Walls' Pinto case, this legal gambit didn't go very far either.

As the Payionks knew, bad quality meant more trips to repairland – no place for the innocent. Apart from legitimate work (about two fixes per year per car), Americans paid $10 billion annually for phony repairs. As in 1911, typical Ford dealers still stocked thousands of spare parts, and offered the customer this ominous salute: *When we sell you a car we never want to see the last of you.* Nor were they likely to, considering the average car contained 15,000 - 30,000 fallible pieces. These parts weren't bargain-priced, either. The Alliance of American Insurers estimated it would cost $23,000 to replace all the parts on a $5,000 car. The upscale Ford Thunderbird used 39 sets of light bulbs and 16 different fuses and circuit breakers, all waiting to blow. A new T-bird needed a total of 87 regular maintenance procedures performed during its first 50,000 miles. The FMC advised owners to check 30 different potential trouble spots themselves from time to time, and make sure to use the 17 different kinds of fluids and lubricants the car required. If you just gave up and had it crushed into a bale of scrap, a Thunderbird was worth $50.

362

60 different service stations, shops, and auto dealers ministered to automobiles within Port Huron's city limits. "From here they spread out into the County...like fleas on a dog's back," wrote Jerry Brown irritably. His topic: bad repair jobs, and attorney Miles Benedict entertained Brownie with the story of paying $65 in labor charges to re-attach a $10 gear shift knob. The community college in Port Huron offered a course in Powder Puff Mechanics for women, "so when they take their cars in for service, they will know whether they are being taken or not." Down south, prosecutors indicted 125 Detroit area businesses for price fixing on repairs. The Michigan Citizens Lobby called the auto repair industry "an organized crime against citizens...The real question here is who controls Michigan – the auto industry or the people?"(13) This was more of a rhetorical question since everybody already knew the answer.

St. Clair County auto mechanic Tom Wilson objected to this badmouthing. He didn't get paid $23 per hour, he said, as some ill-informed persons speculated. More like $10, and his employer took half of that. He didn't cheat anybody, and he often spent hours investigating imaginary problems reported by nutso customers, who paid nothing for that time. Port Huron mechanics made about $10,000 per year. In the interest of fair play to mechanics, and ad revenue, the *Times Herald* ran a semi-annual 32-page Car Care supplement, basically intended to get car owners into the nearest service shop by spooking them with alarming headline hints: "Dew, Humid Air Can Cause Uneven Brake Action," "V-Belts Must Be Checked," "Air conditioning should be inspected often," "Repair Those Dents," "Wheel shimmy is common trouble," "Forty-one states now ban bald tires," "The Battery is Not Always to Blame," "Emission Controls Can Only Be Maintained By Tune-Ups," "Thermostat culprit behind hot, cold engines," "Do It Yourself? You've Got To Be Kidding!"

Many do-it-yourselfers, like those who used self-service gas stations, actually worked a blessing on repair shops by neglecting their vehicles. One survey at a self-serve station found half the cars were running low on oil, brake fluid, radiator coolant, or tire pressure. Sometime all four. If you insisted on going it alone, one expert in the latest Car Care issue specified what color to look for in leaking fluids from a typical car. He cataloged seven different kinds of drips, all of them deadly poisons, plus gasoline, of course, so no smoking please while leak hunting. Another DIY tip: keep at all times in the trunk of your car a "survival kit" of windshield cleaner fluid, windshield washer solvent, sponge, squeegee, paper towels, tire gauge, Lincoln head penny for measuring tread depth, a jug of distilled water, hydrometer, two or three cans of oil, oil can spout, hydraulic brake fluid, transmission fluid and funnel, pliers, wrench. screwdrivers, battery post cleaner, flashlight, work gloves, bath towel, hand cleaner, and the owner's manual.

Another Car Care expert led *Times Herald* readers down the garden path by recommending an auto oil change every 500 miles using only the most expensive oil available, 10 times as often as most manufacturers suggested. Americans already poured a Niagara of 1/2 billion gallons of used motor oil into sewers and landfills yearly. To keep spark plugs clean "take the car out on a freeway and run it like crazy once in a while." But did this mean normal crazy or crazy crazy? When assessing a used car, "Drive down a quiet, narrow street at 20 mph with both front windows open, the better to hear clanks and grinds that reveal worn or broken parts in the powertrain, steering, axles...mysterious noises."(14)

363

The general manager of the National Car Care Council, lobbyist Arthur Nellen, happened to live right in Port Huron. To celebrate Car Care Week of 1975 he bought a 1966 Mustang off a college student. "It was just what we were looking for – it had everything wrong with it...an accident going someplace to happen." Bad brakes, bald tires, bad shocks, misaligned wheels, bad steering, rusted out body and exhaust system, loose water pump, bad headlights, faulty ignition, even mysterious noises. The delighted Nellen christened it "Calamity Jane" and towed this derelict around town to evangelize jalopy owners: *This could happen to you.*

And it happened more often in Michigan, one of the minority of states *still* without mandatory vehicle inspections. Many people around Port Huron drove cars just as bad as Calamity Jane, with their own fond nicknames like "the Tank," and "Old Turkey," vehicles just waiting for the chance to put their owners in harm's way. On the plus side, though, if you hung onto Old Turkey long enough you might qualify to join the 64 members in the Port Huron chapter of the Antique Automobile Club of America, and get into the Blue Water Festival parade on the strength of your junker's nostalgic or curiosity value.

One 1975 headline went the limit in optimism about car care: "The service free, accident proof car is expected to be in widespread use by the year 2000." But until then, Michigan lawmakers ordered licensing for mechanics and written estimates on car repairs. From now on an auto shop must get the owner's okay on any repair cost overruns above 10%, or eat the extra expense. In just the first eight months this requirement spawned 2,000 written and 12,000 telephone complaints from consumers to regulators about estimate violations. Mechanics complained too. Why weren't doctors and lawyers put under the same guidelines?

Fully aware of the temper of the times, Japanese car builder Honda, represented at the Cawood dealership in Port Huron, made hay out of car customers' well-founded suspicions and fears about American automobile reliability and repairability. Honda pointed out that shoddy Pontiacs and Buicks depreciated more in their first year on the road – $2,000 – than a Honda cost new. Soon a waiting list formed for Hondas at Cawood's, which nevertheless still sold Pontiacs and Buicks. Invasive foreign carmakers like Honda intensified their onslaught against native American species during the 70's. Japan and Germany, those two losers America helped beat up in World War II, took their revenge by flooding the victor's home country with their own versions of the #1 weapon of mass destruction. A trivial 4% U.S. tariff on imported cars proved no barrier, compared to the 45% charged during the auto industry's startup years.

Henry Ford II vowed about imports to "beat them back to their shores," although the FMC imported its own made-in-Germany models. The subject of German cars especially annoyed Henry because he'd been offered the Volkswagen company lock, stock, and barrel, absolutely free of charge in the days after WW2, but hadn't taken it. Now the Seaway Terminal in Port Huron unloaded as many as 900 VW's at a time, while the German company set up its own American factory. In a contemporary war arena, South Vietnam, cars, motorcycles, and American war vehicles did more damage to the capital city of Saigon than the war itself, which came to a conclusion with Communist victory in 1975.(15) Now when would the first Vietnamese auto exports arrive on U.S. shores?

When in America, advertise as the Americans do. The Japanese nameplate

Datsun got into the swing of the U.S. market with TV commercials just as drippy as the home brand.

Feelin' free and rollin' easy,
You've got places to be goin'.
Leavin' troubles miles behind you,
You can keep a smile inside you.
Freedom's just another word for Datsun.
Cause Datsun saves, and sets you free.

American viewers might have been spared this if the federal government had followed up its 1971 ban on TV and radio advertising of tobacco products by also kicking cars off the air. Perhaps to ease the anguish of tightening regulation, Congress left the Autonauts free to spin their usual 30-60 seconds of fallacy and fraud across the airwaves. And in the face of the overseas challenge, some Yankee ads took on a decidedly combative tone:

American cars guzzle gas. American cars are all style and no substance. American cars don't last. To all that American Motors says 'Nuts!'

Frank Sinatra*: "America's not going to be pushed around any more!"* Announcer*: "The Chrysler K-cars are here!"*

Craving more room to deal with the various contingencies of their trade, most of the major car dealers in Port Huron finally uprooted themselves from their downtown locations and flocked together in the vacant acreage available on the far north side of town, on both sides of the city limits. They covered forest and field with massive inventories of both new and used autos. Don Brewer Dodge needed 7 acres for this, plus a 16,000 square-foot building, and, most critically, a 21-bay repair shop with 10 hoists and elbow room for 12 busy mechanics. In spite of the visibility of these layouts, some dealers now shunned widespread personal recognition in the community. They did not wish necessarily to be identified one-on-one with the industry's shortcomings. "By a wide margin, automobile dealers are the businessmen Americans distrust most," reported *Fortune* magazine.(16) And they were fewer in number. Half the new car dealers in America had closed since 1945, leaving 24,000. During that time Port Huron's new car dealerships had changed hands 56 times.

After Don Brewer bowed out of the business his successors in the franchise ownership, who included Granger Weil, retreated behind the corporate name of Eagle Chrysler-Dodge. Barney Wood, the new Ford man, came to be better known as Northgate Ford. Northgate wanted you to know that

We're not just car salesmen. We're Ford salesmen. Because being ordinary car salesmen just wouldn't be good enough...Not just a car dealer. A Ford dealer...he can arrange financing and insurance for you, too.

The grave responsibilities of being not just ordinary car salesmen but Ford salesmen didn't prevent Northgate's boys from having a little fun in the good times.

Warning! First there was the Swine Flu, then Rocky Mountain Spotted Fever, Now It's Ford Fever. Possible Symptoms (with your present car): Bald Tires, Ripped Seats, Shakes and Rattles, Poor gas mileage, Rough Ride, Dull Paint.

In the bad times, said Northgate sales manager Thomas Wood, "We pray a lot." Sometimes these sinners penitentially unloaded cars at up to $2,000 below list price, so hurry in.

A new guy in town, 38 year-old Bob Fox, promised some more of the old time dealer huckstering at his 7-acre, 200 vehicle Chevy lot. GM did car patriotism up big with a schmaltzy *Baseball, Hot Dogs, Apple Pie and Chevrolet* advertising campaign in the 70's, which suited Fox's personality to a T. The son of a Detroit dealer, as a young man Fox suffered some pangs of guilt over Dad's profession: "When I was in school, and we had to tell the class what our parents did, I never told them my dad was a car salesman." Those qualms disappeared forever one day at the Fox lot, when at age 12 Bob awakened to the call of his heritage and sold to some schnook a 15 year-old Model A2 Ford for $800; his first score.

But no more rousing exception to dealer anonymity existed than Charles Barrett, the kingpin of Cawood Auto. A mere adjective like "flamboyant" hardly did Charlie justice. His new Cawood all-in-one lot near the Blue Water Bridge looked relatively modest in acreage compared to some of the auto ranches his competitors built, but the 27,000 square foot showroom and accompanying facilities still set back Port Huron's most successful car dealer $500,000. He could well afford it. Barrett was in no way shy about informing the toiling carbuyers of St. Clair County that he'd made a million dollars at their expense by the time he turned 40, all the way back in 1959, and he still was piling it up. He owned 32 buildings around Port Huron, and on these he collected $250,000 in annual rents. He owned great swatches of empty township land just waiting for Port Huron's sprawl to push up its value. He developed real estate on the side – building homes, shopping centers, motels, restaurants, and a seniors mobile home park in Florida. In honor of his own 50th birthday, Charlie threw a party for 100 guests on board a rented yacht, and for his 60th he flew 60 friends to Nassau at a cost of $100,000.

He also intrigued locals with his messy divorce from Helen Cawood Barrett, whose father John had introduced Charlie to car retailing. Barrett went to court, suing not just his ex-wife but his two sons, Tom and Young Charlie, for allegedly trying to kick him out of the dealership presidency. It seemed in its own Port Hurony way a fascinating counterpart to the personal scandals that dogged Henry Ford II during the 70's. Police caught The Deuce driving drunk one day in California, and tossed him into jail until he posted a $375 bond. Henry'd been in the company of his young mistress when this happened, and he subsequently traded in wife #2 for this low-mileage model. Not all car salespeople ascended the enviable heights of celebrity and riches as did the Barretts and Fords. Former Port Huron Studebaker dealer William Morden, who'd once acted on stage with the Marx Brothers and George Cohan before becoming an automobile comedian, died broke in the county nursing home at age 86.

Despite the uncertain state of American car building and selling, and the high attrition rate among small-time auto parts makers during the 1970's, 110 manufacturers with a total of 8,000 employees made pieces of automobiles in Port Huron and four surrounding counties. City manager Gerald Bouchard continued his single-minded pursuit of more parts companies for the Port Huron Industrial Park, traveling as far away as Europe and Japan, grubbing for them like a truffle-hunting hog. He knocked down 50 more homes and businesses, many owned by blacks and Hispanics, to make more room in the I-park. Great rejoicing broke out at a City Council meeting one night when he revealed that automobile ceiling maker PCI planned to expand its operation in the I-park by 150 jobs. The celebration was more muted among PCI employees, and all the I-park workers. Their wages came to about two-thirds of the median U.S. family income, and they did even worse compared to what UAW members earned on auto assembly lines.

Most unskilled, dead end factory hands all over the country envied UAW people. Labor columnist Victor Riesel called that union's membership "the world's best paid, the best inflation-protected, the best pensioned, and the best cared for employees dentally and medically."(17) The union's arrangements were so plush that the big Port Huron employers with UAW workers, Mueller Brass and Prestolite, began shipping jobs out to cheaper, open shop, right-to-work southern states as fast as they could. True, a lot of UAW members spent a stretch on the unemployment sidelines in 1974 and '75, one of those auto slumps that came and went almost as often as the tide, when the national jobless hit 10% (19% in Port Huron). 200,000 people went without work in greater Detroit at one point during this period, and the city treasury fell $40 million into the red as a result. The usual run of strikes during the decade also halted production for brief periods. But when they were busy, UAW workers made anywhere from $12,000 to $15,000 annually by the mid-70's, and could retire after 30 years service. Alas, even more foolishly than the general public, car assemblers threw their money away on their own products. Thanks largely to automobile impoverishment most lived so deeply in hock from outspending their wages that only a quarter of eligible UAW veterans actually took the "30 and out" option, the rest kept right on working.

60 years after the $5 day went into effect to stop it, turnover remained a big issue in the factories, 25% annually at Ford.(18) So did absenteeism. GM utility man Willie Rawles appeared in a TV ad to explain: "My job is to replace any absentees. I'm here, there, all over the plant. You're not tied down to one job all the time." With a smile for the camera, Rawles compassionately patted some of his tied-down fellow employees on the shoulder. From the Ford executive suite Henry II advised Lee Iacocca to "Keep your people anxious and off-balance," and Iacocca obligingly called for more and more productivity from his people. Anxious and off-balance auto hands sometimes resorted to sabotage to halt the relentless assembly lines for a breather. Some used stronger methods. In one extreme case of imbalance a Chrysler employee murdered three co-workers. The subsequent ruling by the Michigan Workman's Compensation Bureau entitled the culprit to $75 a month plus psychiatric costs until he recovered his mind sufficiently to return to the job. That might take some time, since he'd just tried to kill a fellow inmate at the insane asylum.

It took the Swedish car company Saab to admit the truth about auto factory life in the most startlingly frank car ad of the decade:

The assembly line has made Detroit the automobile capital of the world, because it allows manufacturers to make cars faster and faster. And cheaper and cheaper. But the assembly line does something else, too. It bores the people who work on it. And boredom, in the end, is often responsible for poor quality.

The average new American car cost $3,400 in 1971, about one-third the median family income, and if kept 10 years required $6,600 to run, plus gas.(19) When inflation went into orbit, it jacked up the average Ford price to $5,500 by 1976. The first generation of government required auto equipment accounted for $500-$800 of that higher bill, with much more to come. Gas prices, as we've seen, had tripled by mid-decade. "New cars were always a major expenditure for the average family. Now they are an economic calamity and getting more so," admitted the *Times Herald,* glumly.(20)

Port Huron banks by 1976 wanted borrowers to put 25% down on a new car to qualify for an average loan of $4,100, at 13% interest, for 37 months, amounting to a $132 per month payment. Throw in gas and expenses and that car cost a family $215 per month. Some dealers offered 48-month loans, which piled up more debt and ran the risk of outliving the car. Credit delinquencies in Port Huron nearly tripled. Loan officer John Di Pompeo said the typical Port Huron Joe earned $13,000, his wife worked part time (66% of married women did so), and still "They can't make it. The cost of living is too high." Inflation heated up still further, and by 1980 the cost of buying and operating a mid-sized car reached $4,000 per year. Outstanding consumer loans in the U.S., many of them for automobiles, rose to $300 billion, 36 times the amount in 1948. No more cautious than its citizens, the federal government doubled the national debt to $1 trillion during this decade.

Henry II and Lee Iacocca repeatedly went to Washington to whine, whimper, and growl for special relief from regulations and imports. "We are in a downhill slide, the likes of which we have never seen in our business," said the Deuce in 1971, with more feeling than accuracy. The very next year auto sales soared, thanks to a tax cut on cars from President Nixon. Annual new car and light truck sales in America varied between 10.5 million (not exactly starvation pace) and 15 million during the 70's. Sandwiched in between the lean times both Ford and General Motors set single-year sales and profit records. In 1976 the industry sold 13 million new cars and trucks, and auto people rolled in clover. In 1980 colossal losses, $4 billion worth, heralded the day of doom all over again.

The confident Henry II of the fat seasons alternated with the Hangdog Hank of the thin, who once predicted to Ford shareholders an industry-wide shutdown without a regulation rollback. We're "backed to the cliff edge of desperation," added Iacocca. Ford's sales vice-president N.S. McLaughlin also stepped up the defensive fire when necessary. Auto critics sowed "unwarranted seeds of destruction, dissatisfaction and depression" about cars, said McLaughlin. They dastardly implied "that owning and driving a car is some sort of antisocial or anti-environmental behavior..."(21) Imagine that!

In other words, the big boys meant that the American auto industry, the nation's 3rd largest, should not be pressured unduly, since it employed an estimated 15 million persons in manufacturing, sales, and support. This number took in a vast array: the 938,000 folks in auto assembly plants, 700,000 in service stations, the tricksters toiling at Ford's 6,283 dealerships, and more esoterically people like 240,000 motel and trailer park attendants.(22) So back off, DC. Recycling the automobile's waste, pollution and brutality into economic virtues compared to saying that war and disease shouldn't be tampered with because of the numbers they employed. But as a last ditch defense it wasn't bad.

Corvair-destroyer Ralph Nader admitted as much when he dropped by Port Huron for a speech at the McMorran civic center. Nader predicted that the threat of layoffs would be used to delay auto regulation, which proved to be exactly correct. The head men at GM and Chrysler and even United Auto Workers President Leonard Woodcock joined Ford at the wailing wall in Washington, and the feds eventually issued a series of regulatory postponements on gas mileage, safety equipment, and pollution, including four straight years of delays on the Clean Air Act.

In conducting the industry's fighting retreat, the public relations offices got busy in Detroit and hatched consumer friendly slogans like *Ford has a Better Idea, Chrysler Cares, Chevrolet: You've Changed, We've Changed.* General Motors turned out a children's book about air pollution starring Professor Clean versus villains Harry Hydrocarbon, Ollie (Nitrogen) Oxide, and Pete Particulate Matter. We've eliminated 80% of Harry and 40% of Ollie, said the automakers, who also claimed that meeting these standards had cost just one of them 5 million miles of test driving, and a file of supporting documents 200 feet thick. GM spent $4.7 billion annually on government regs by 1977, which included its primate lab at the Tech Center in Warren, where researchers gassed unfortunate test monkeys with car exhaust.

Ford Listens Better, promisd the FMC, but the company didn't hear too well on some points, and the feds dinged Ford $7 million for phonyng up engine emission reports. Hard to figure it for a mistake by Ford since 6,500 company engineers worked on this subject.(23) Even with these new emission controls in place, cars and trucks of all brands still tossed 125 million tons of pollution into America's atmosphere every year. It took the intervention of the EPA to force the gradual elimination of lead from gasoline starting in 1973, reversing 50 years of mass poisoning by car in the United States. The tires on the nation's 140 million vehicles fouled the atmosphere too. They ejected 340,000 tons of Pete Particulate Matter and tire gas each year.(24) Auto factories still made a mess. Air marshals charged Ford with 140 counts of releasing "Obnoxious, offensive, damaging and harmful" air pollution from the Rouge plant.

Another topic literally blew up in the faces of the auto dons during the 1970's: airbags again. The government at first mandated 1974 as the year that front seat passengers in 30 mph head-on automobile crashes had to be protected from injury by restraints like airbags. "A lot of baloney," is what Henry II said about that better idea, and he didn't miss the mark much. Some researchers in Virginia used live pigs as substitute children in airbag tests, and half a dozen porkers subjected to air bag explosions ended up as baloney makings.

Racing driver Mark Donohue also said "ridiculous" to airbags when he appeared for a talk before the Detroit Sports Broadcasters Association. "If a driver is stupid enough and unaware of the evasive capabilities of his car that he gets himself into trouble then he deserves to die." Asked about innocent victims of stupid, unaware drivers, Donohue philosophized: "There are some dangers we are unable to avoid. It's a free country and we have the choice of driving or not driving on the highways."(25) Or not walking or bicycling on them. It wasn't a necessity. Donohue himself ran into a danger he was unable to avoid, and died in a 1975 race track accident.

America and the World, automotive division, stood as firm as Gibraltar, as they had for decades, on another familiar regulatory topic in the 70's. No speed governors:

93 miles per hour? We obviously don't recommend it, but it is reassuring to know that as you get onto a hectic expressway a new Volkswagen Rabbit Hatchback has the power for incredible acceleration.

The idea of entering a hectic expressway at 93 miles per hour in a Volkswagen didn't sound too reassuring in itself, but even that velocity failed to satisfy the industry. Together they successfully stonewalled the NHTSA's 1971 plan to limit car speed to a dawdling 95 miles per hour. General Motors said governors cost too much and were too complex, though Port Huron writer Jim Fiebig offered his own homemade version – a block of wood bolted to the floor board beneath the accelerator. Ford pointed out that most accidents occurred below 95 anyway, so why worry?

An exception to this rule occurred a month later on Easter Sunday in Detroit, when a 20 year-old driver doing 100 mph killed 7 people, including himself, and injured 26 in a multi-vehicle wreck on I-94. The culpable driver, John Giddens, Jr., had been involved in three previous accidents, he'd been convicted of reckless driving, he'd been busted for speeding at 75, 80,and 90 miles per hour on various occasions, and his license had been suspended twice. Victim Lance Derderian, aged 5, survived the catastrophe, his parents and two grandparents did not. Port Huronites had reason to be glad that Vietnam veteran Wesley Alexander didn't take anyone with him when he died at the end of an ungoverned 105 mph police chase on Main Street in Port Huron.

Bad drivers like Giddens and Alexander still easily eluded the half-hearted efforts of authorities to sideline them before they hit the streets. So did the incompetents. A license renewal in Michigan involved no road test, just a 10-question multiple-choice written exam. Applicants seldom flunked, according to Secretary of State clerk Sulo Nieme in Marysville "because too many wrong answers usually indicate a reading problem rather than a driving problem." No medical exam kept heart patient 59 year-old Michael Cain of Port Huron off the road, before he died at the wheel one day. His car slammed into a house, crossed several more lawns and hit a tree. Consensus of the neighbors: a miracle Cain didn't kill somebody else. Even if perfectly healthy Mr. Cain might have been among the two-thirds of all drivers whom researchers found battled drowsiness at the wheel from time to time.

Drivers took no hearing tests. Vision as poor as 20/70 in daylight passed. Ancient geezers surmounted tepid opposition. 100 year-old former postman Frank Trese told Jerry Brown that license examiners "tried their darndest to get me off the road." Their darndest plainly didn't amount to much. When Trese reached age 104 Brownie expressed sympathy but couldn't suppress entirely a little concern: "Affectionately known as 'Dad', Trese is believed to be the oldest driver in the United States. In Michigan he is. But for how long is another question."(26) The state positively welcomed crippled drivers. A Capac resident with an artificial leg, numbness in his good leg, spinal disease, stroke damage, and severe arthritis kept right on motoring. So many over-aged, disabled and otherwise beaten up drivers (even one-armed motorcyclists) secured motoring rights that by the 1970's Michigan issued privileged "handicapped parking" passes to clear reserved parking lot spaces for them, spots set as close as possible to building entrances, so that once released from their vehicles these decrepits needn't drag themselves any further than necessary.

The 6,800 alcoholics in St. Clair County still breezed right through the licensing process. Robert Borkenstein, inventor of the breathalyzer, estimated drunken Americans made 2.7 million driving trips every day. Not once but twice police arrested rumhead and former Michigan Governor John Swainson. "I am mortified," said

Swainson, and so was his boyhood home town of Port Huron. Swainson had been a standout high school student and athlete who lost both legs as a teenager fighting in WW2. Fitted with artificial limbs, he took up sports again, and driving, then moved away from Port Huron for college and law school. Following a lightning political ascent Swainson served as governor in 1961-62, and later won a spot on the state Supreme Court. But after this promising start hooch and marijuana got the better of him, and after a perjury conviction he left the court. Now this.

Luckily for him, Swainson's drunk driving rap happened in America. *Times Herald* readers learned that drunk drivers in Malaysia went to jail with their spouses, in South Africa they faced $2,800 fines and/or 10 years in jail, and in San Salvador got the firing squad. In Port Huron fines averaged $85-$125 plus a pittance of jail time if any; firing squads were almost unheard of. As a result, as many as 40 cases of drunk or impaired driving showed up monthly in traffic court. "Impaired driving," another of those diet-version criminal charges, like negligent homicide or careless driving, spared the defendant the full consequences of his actions and got him back into the auto economy as fast as possible. Drunk driving, the most frequently committed crime in the United States, cost society an annual $24-$40 billion, and not just in liquor bills.(27)

When Jerry Brown poked into the drinking and driving situation one local lush told him, "Everyone is drunk in Port Huron on Saturday night. I just happened to get picked up." Said another, a 28 year-old woman: "I hit a boy on a bicycle and I didn't know what happened until I came out of the jail the next day. It's the first time I've ever been stopped and I've been drinking and driving since I was a junior in high school. Thank goodness I never lost my driver's license. They let me plead guilty to impaired driving."(28) 22 year-old Richard Manee got off with 90 days in jail and probation after killing Margaret Koryba in a Port Huron crash while he was looped. Koryba's daughter refused to change with the drunk driving times, and carried a grudge about this: "Here is an example of the...so-called justice in this country. (Manee) is driving and continues to work. Is this the correct punishment for one person taking another's life?"(29)

The drunk driver liberation movement scored another victory in the '70's when the Michigan Liquor Control Commission agreed to let gas stations sell beer and wine once again. It seemed that some service stations getting out of the repair business wanted to make up the lost revenue with alcohol sales. Another innovation, the drive-thru Beer Dock, made itself a popular spot in Port Huron for tight motorists. About the only glitch in allowing more drivers to get hammered occurred when the state of Michigan lowered the drinking age to 18, but then had to boost it back to 21 after traffic accidents in this age group jumped 120%.

Michigan reduced the acts of speeding, running a red light, and careless driving to civil infractions. Violators no longer went to jail. That came as a relief to the 5,000 or so drivers in St. Clair County ticketed for speeding each year, but didn't much encourage driving within the limits. The Sheriff threw in the towel to some extent on this issue, and forbade high speed chasing of speeders through cities, for fear of getting sued, or wrecking another police car. Deputies had totaled five in six months. Cops gave Brownie a rundown of some of the speeding excuses they heard from people they caught:

– Late for a funeral.
– Dog sick, didn't want him to mess up the car.

– Trying to keep up with traffic.
– "My tires are too big."
– "I've got new shoes and they seem to be sticking to the gas pedal."
– "You can't ticket me; I was only 9 miles per hour over the limit and it has to be 10."
– Racing to get to K-mart sale. To get home to make lunch for kids. To get hair done.
– "You can't ticket me, I just paid a speeding ticket this morning."

Acquiring enough of these tickets for too much velocity, or committing other highway infractions, supposedly stripped Michigan drivers of their licenses through suspension or revocation, but an estimated 400,000 suspendees just kept right on driving.

Mandatory "no-fault" auto insurance became the law in Michigan. "No-fault was something of a misnomer; actually it was "everybody's-fault" insurance. Theoretically, under no-fault, people involved in the 5,000-6,000 reported traffic accidents every year in St. Clair County wouldn't hassle each other any longer in court over a simple unavoidable fact of life like a car wreck. Instead they would go each to his or her own insurance carrier for compensation. This innovation was intended to cut insurance costs (a typical auto insurance premium ran $200 per year) and litigation, but did neither at first. People just sued their insurance companies instead.

No-fault "created rights that did not exist before," in the words of one Port Huron lawyer. For one thing, it provided for unlimited medical coverage for traffic accident victims. This left the Auto Club insurance office in Port Huron fuming over another teenager who'd been put into a coma in a crash, like Meredith MacRury. "Who knows? He may live for another 50 years," said the Club's John Julien, exasperated over the $3,200 per month tab for the young man in question. Better off dead, from the Auto Club's perspective. Let's mention here that Meredith, hurt before no-fault appeared, eventually awoke from her coma with no further damage than confinement to a wheelchair for life and impaired mental "reflexes" that ended her hopes for a medical career.

If another driver went so far as to kill or disfigure you, your estate or guardian could still sue the perpetrator and his insurer directly under no-fault, but traditional practice meant 80%-90% of plaintiffs settled. The estate of Mrs. Irene Morrison of Port Huron, who'd been run down and killed by a window cleaner's truck, asked for $100,000; got $6,000. Richard Kretchman sued for $7 million dollars to make up for his wife Vicki Sue, killed in a car whose drunken driver Barbara Coleman drag raced through downtown Port Huron one night and crashed into the Sports Shop storefront. Vicki Sue had been a great wife no doubt, but $7 million great? In another memorable case, boozer William Hamm, son of a Port Huron traffic court judge, faced a $500,000 accident lawsuit for mangling plaintiff Russell Clark in a drunken crash. Hamm then fell into more serious difficulty by stabbing his psychiatrist to death, and went to prison for life. Hamm pleaded insanity over the stabbing but not the driving.

How many traffic accidents occurred per year in America at this point? The Insurance Information Institute figures suggested about 15 million reported and unreported.(30) Another source said bad rear view mirror vision alone caused 6 million. How many people injured? One congressional study put it at 4.4 million, costing $40 billion per year.(31) $2.4 billion of that tab belonged to Michigan. "What one thing do most of us automobile drivers have in common? Answer: sooner or later, we'll all be in an accident." Writer Martin Porriss took the Boy Scout view in the *Times Herald*: Be prepared. Stock your car with a first aid kit, blanket, flashlight, candle, matches, tape measure, two towels, a pillow, a whistle, a black grease pencil for writing HELP on the windows, flares, writing pad, pens, chalk, a Polaroid camera, and payphone money. Also keep handy your medical insurance ID number, and your auto insurance agent's phone number. After the accident, presuming you're still on your feet, chalk mark the road and measure distances. "Say nothing, sign nothing." St. Clair County Sheriff Norman Meharg didn't have to write HELP on his windows after he flipped his patrol car and crashed into a house on one of the penetrator streets in Port Huron. Cops were all over that mess in a jiffy, said homeowner Florence Walker. "They got it out of here a lot faster than they get some other accident wrecks." The Auto Club called Port Huron's accident record one of the worst in Michigan, especially along the North Main Street section widened in the public interest by the state highway department.

The whole loosening of driving morals affected the *Times Herald's* news desk, which now often buried reports of bad accidents in a couple of paragraphs back with minor community happenings. After all, why upset the readership with unpleasantness? A typical daily summary: "Train sideswipes car; Woman hurt by car; Motorcycle – car collide; 2 injured in collision." Port Huron fatals like Rufus Middlebrook's encounter with a tree off Highway 21, or the death of Sheriff Meharg's nephew Dennis, or Richard Combs' 150 foot flight through his windshield now received less column space than Pet of the Week. It cut down the scope of Jerry Brown's police beat work, but left him more time for his Working World and Heroic Sick People profiles.

Without close attention to the road toll, who knew for sure but that the 2 millionth traffic death in America didn't happen right in St. Clair County, and went all but unnoticed? This event occurred sometime during the month of July 1973 according to the rough reckoning of statisticians, but they pinpointed no single victim. To fill the void we'll nominate as Dead Citizen 2 Million Father Edward DeMars, 71, the ex-pastor who had pulled St. Stephen's church out of downtown Port Huron for the suburbs. He died in a head-on crash near Marine City. Or how about 10 year-old Vicki Wilson, Keewahdin School 4th grader, catapulted by a motorist's impact into the air to her death as she walked to the family mailbox in Port Huron. 20 year-old Michael Kampanka deserves consideration, dead in a collision at the intersection of two recently "improved" streets in the county seat. Well, whoever it was, Port Huron held no Memorial Day observance for them or for the 57,000 other Americans killed in traffic that year, erected no monument in Pine Grove Park nor built a stadium in their honor as it had for the war dead, staged no parade, placed no flags on their graves. Their ultimate sacrifice in the cause of national mobility didn't get the nation too excited during this Bicentennial Decade.

Not that Americans had turned entirely callous on the subject. St. Clair County experienced subdued regret over its 393 traffic deaths during the 70's. "It doesn't hit you as you leave the cemetery," a traffic widow told Jerry Brown. "You don't feel it that much when people are around you, but when you are alone sometimes it's just unbearable."(32) The occasional traffic conflagration still sometimes struck a distant chord, like the fiery clean-sweep head-on that claimed all five people one 1978 night on Highway 21. Or the celebrity wrecks that killed President Ford's half-brother Leslie King, or John D. Rockefeller III, or Port Huron's leading black citizen James Leonard. Or the bizarre coincidences, which still amused or shocked people according to their tastes.

Muncie, Indiana. Mickey A. Summer, 27, was driving to meet his fiancee, Deborah Darlene Bricker, 21, and she was driving to meet him when their cars collided head on. Both were killed.(33)

How was that for romance on the road? A similar-sounding high school essay from Michigan on the death-by-driving subject made the national Ann Landers column in the *Times Herald*:

In Love with Life – or How It Would Be if I were Killed in an Automobile Accident.

The day I died was an ordinary school day. How I wish I had taken the bus! But I was too cool for the bus...I wheedled the car out of Mom. It doesn't matter how the accident happened. I was goofing off – going too fast. The last thing I remember was passing an old lady who seemed to be going awfully slow. I heard a deafening crash and felt a terrific jolt. Suddenly I awakened. A police officer was standing over me. Then I saw a doctor. My body was mangled. Hey, don't pull that sheet over me head. I can't be dead. I'm only 17. I've got a date tonight.(34) A date with the undertaker.

More in love with driving than life, Port Huron high school students and their parents kicked up a big fuss when officials dropped driver education from the curriculum to save money. Bigshots like utility president Robert Thomson vowed: "Driver education affects every student...all students must learn to drive. If they don't they are handicapped." Thomson himself suffered the handicap of obesity, but he didn't see the connection with driving. No evidence connected driver education with better drivers, but it seemed to ease some consciences. Far more sensibly, local resident Lou Johnson suggested mass transit education might be more appropriate. "With the gas situation the way it is, we should be teaching students alternate methods of transportation to help ease the energy crunch."(35) Not to mention the kid crunch. Automobile accidents killed more children than any other factor. Obituaries of these dead youngsters treated the subject discreetly. "Died unexpectedly" covered it, though "died of necessity" might have been more accurate.

Jerry Brown's police blotter skills still got a workout from time to time on other aspects of auto life. Thieves stole 133 cars in and around Port Huron during 1973. An exciting carjacking took place at K-mart, during which the culprits threatened a school teacher with death unless he handed over his wheels. Automobiles threatened people with death every day, of course, but in this case: "Police fired several shots into the rear of the fleeing car before it stopped, but not before the chase reached speeds in excess of 80 miles an hour...The car, bullet riddled and smoldering, was towed by a local wrecker service to the police garage."(36) And the teacher-victim had to pay the $20 towing charge.

Car thefts and break-ins rated as the most expensive urban crimes in America, amounting to $500 million per year. Oldsmobile faced the disappearing vehicle issue head-on via TV:

These police experts are trying to break into this car without setting off the invisible alarm system. You can order it on this Olds 98 Regency, Toronado, and 88. It's so good even these police experts can't get into the doors, hood or trunk without setting off the alarm. It's a good feeling to have an Olds around you.

For many, the good feeling didn't last long, since malfunctioning or owner-triggered car

374

alarms soon became so commonplace that no one paid them any attention, except as just another nuisance of the auto age.

In addition to car alarms, the automobile's general insult to society's peace and quiet grew progressively worse. The noise along Port Huron's traffic sewers, North Main and I-94 for instance, often averaged 70-90 decibels, and sent nearby homeowners climbing their walls. The Michigan Highway Department, which built these roads, admitted it couldn't afford to put noise barriers along them. Although in theory the law limited truck racket to 90 decibels within 50 feet of a truck traveling at 35 miles per hour, enforcement existed only in theory. The same with souped up passenger cars. A steady audio diet of that kind of noise could lead to hypertension, stomach ulcers, heart disease, immune system disorders, hearing loss, sleeplessness, and mental problems, according to assorted authorities like the EPA. The mental problems of teenagers who added $150, 12 watts-per-channel music systems to their vehicles increased the ear assault. Youthful drivers making what one observer called the "idiot circle" cruising up and down Port Huron's Main Street, took special pleasure in entertaining a city block at a time with the blast from their personal music collections.

Ford Motor Company offered this solution to traffic noise: live in your car. *In the last five years the noise level in American cities has risen 20%. In the last five years sales of the very quiet Ford LTD have risen 160%.* Very helpful, but not good enough for the *Times Herald.* "A few passing cars with faulty mufflers and overstressed tires, can match the noise of a huge bulldozer. The racket they produce moves like a wave through a neighborhood, affecting everyone within earshot."(37) And as for motorcycle noise, the editors added succinctly, "We've had it."

Port Huron motorcyclists denied that their machines made extra noise just to gratify the rider's infantile need for attention. Motorcycle mama Peggy Platzer maintained that these vehicles needed to be obnoxiously loud to alert car and truck drivers to their presence in the building wave of traffic, so easy riders wouldn't be ground like rabbits into the pavement. That's your problem, replied irritated Port Huron resident Edna Carrothers. In her end of town motorcycles were "quickly making the neighborhood uninhabitable." Motorcycles provoked 75% of street noise complaints to Port Huron police.

Loud or quiet, crashes injured 200 motorcyclists around Port Huron during a single summer in 1971. Paralyzed 23 year-old ex-motorcyclist Peter Parker of Marysville, whose machine had dived into a drainage ditch, admitted his resulting paraplegia presented something of "an inconvenience." This Heroic Sick Person quickly learned to drive a van using no feet, to give himself another shot at death on the highway. Roy Thornton attained that goal on 10th Street aboard his motorcycle, when a summer breeze blew hair into the eyes of an oncoming car driver, fatally obscuring Roy.

Vehicle crackups of all types, and how to prevent them, remained a "knotty" problem of traffic control in Port Huron. "Knotty," as in "practically impossible." To put in a traffic light or not, for instance, framed the question at the Jefferson School, where a two-car crash had injured 28 children who'd been standing in front of the building when it happened. 1,000 cars per hour sometimes passed Jefferson along the 10th Street traffic sewer, while 150 pupils at a time crossed the intersection. Port Huron's four dozen existing traffic lights cost about $8,000 each, and the Citizens Traffic Safety Committee did not wish to erect another of these expensive and often counterproductive devices. Finally, after weighing the matter, they okayed installation of a light at Jefferson, but it operated during school hours only. After school dismissed, let the good times roll. Port Huron High School students wanted a light, too, or tunnel, or overpass, or guards, or anything to help them cross the jammed street in front of their school, but for the time being the community left them to fend for themselves.

In the spurious name of safety, as well as the all-purpose excuses of "congestion relief" and "access," Port Huron transformed another traditional two-lane street into a four-lane, no parking traffic sewer. Water Street got the treatment this time, courtesy of manager Gerald Bouchard and the traffic engineers, the men urban planner Victor Gruen once called human animal trainers.(38) Naturally more trees had to be hacked down, more front yards reduced by half, and another neighborhood thoroughfare turned into a slumway. Street widening hadn't improved the community anywhere else, and the city's streets were deteriorating more quickly than they could be repaired under the crush of increasing traffic, but the Bouchardist generation of 2,200 city managers across America were incapable of learning from experience on this subject.

More Port Huron historical structures, including the downtown First Baptist Church, crashed to earth at Bouchard's "serene and regal" command, as one observer described him, to purge the town of the first deadly sin of modern communities, street parking. To no avail preservationist Mrs. Paul Russell pleaded for the First Baptist, "That white spire, spotlighted at night, and the original church, now nearly a hundred years old, are worth more to us than space to park a few more cars." Historian Mary Lou Creamer later remembered the church in further detail:

It was the crown jewel of downtown Port Huron. Designed in English gothic style, the red brick structure offered the congregation plenty of comfort and amenities. Four entrances revealed oak and cherry woodwork, a thirty-six gas jet chandelier, and the choir's gracefully arched alcove. The 365 plush, upholstered chairs sat on 400 yards of carpeting. The zinc-lined baptistry was supplied by pipes with both hot and cold water. Even a dumb waiter was installed to facilitate movement between the kitchen below and the church socials and festivals above. (39)

To tell the truth, replied First Baptist member Janet Jones, the congregation couldn't wait to get out of downtown, and away from Bouchard's spreading asphalt jungle. "The desire to move to a more affluent section of the city was the desire of the majority." Automobile religion grew stronger in America than any other form of worship. No one could be an honest Christian, or Jew, or Muslim, Buddhist, Hindu, Confucian, or any religionist while owning an automobile. The conceit of car ownership, the antithesis of the personal humility that supposedly underlay all the major faiths, required one to ignore the destruction this device did to fellow human beings and the world in general.

The launch of yet another urban renewal scheme, Port Huron's third, combined with the recurring dim-bulb scheme of building a downtown shopping mall, gave manager Bouchard more license than ever, and $3 million, to smash away at any structure still standing that had the effrontery to remind him of the pre-automobile past. That included another church, the Universalist, long since abandoned by that sect, but still in use as an apartment house. Till its day of destruction, the Universalist stood firm, just as the skillful brick masons had built it in 1885. The *Times Herald* liked it better after the wreckers reduced it to another "sight-pleasing and spacious" parking lot.

The business address known as the Drescher Building went the same way. Its cutstone foundations and arched windows enthralled the crews hired to tear it down. "You couldn't reconstruct that building today, regardless of how much money you spent," said owner David Drescher bitterly. The proprietor of the less classically proportioned Wonder Bar, Mike Geikas, put up a stink of his own after being kicked out of his location of 37 years, at age 78. Like many naturalized Americans, Geikas was especially touchy about his rights. Since when had he become a second-class citizen?

Bouchard's were not the only dirty hands in pulling down Port Huron's beautiful structures during this decade. The six-story 1884 Bush building, which stood as a sentinel at Main and Water streets for decades, came to the same sad end. "Really it's too bad you have to tear down an old building like this," said businessman Shaker Touma. He joined the rush of people who bought the still beautiful fixtures and trim before the Bush disappeared. The original home of the *Times Herald*, the Loren Sherman building, along with nine other solid structures, fell victims to an orgy of destruction, clearing the way for a bank headquarters and parking garage.

The culmination of Port Huron's demented self-erasure, and the low-point of Gerald Bouchard's career, came when he bought up and destroyed an entire block of Main Street stores in the very heart of downtown, the original starting point of the city, home to some of its best-remembered firms. Davidson's home furnishings, the Barnet pharmacy, Orttenburger's leather goods, MacTaggart's book shop, the City Opera House, and many others did trade there at one time or another. In their place arose the new $9 million home for the *Times Herald*, a single blankfaced bunker so shockingly ugly it left the city aghast. Employee and truck parking took up half the property. If the automobile age in Port Huron needed a single physical symbol to mark its course of perversity, this was it.

If it needed a second, the new City Hall in the former 1st Ward qualified. The six-story, 60,000 square foot, $7.5 million riverfront structure looked like a huge pile of Playskool blocks. One architecture critic called this style the "New Brutalism."(40) It's most brutal feature, costwise, was a 160 car underground parking garage, built in part to prevent police vehicles from being stolen, an embarrassing criminal accomplishment which had happened more than once. The underground garage cost one-third of the building's price tag, and still couldn't hold everybody, so 90 more parking spaces had to be added outside.

One might reasonably have supposed by now that adequate parking space existed in central Port Huron to contentedly nestle down every vehicle that might want to go there. The municipality operated 1,226 parking spaces in attended lots, 850 spaces in 11 metered lots, and 591 street meters. It took two full-time employees just to empty the meters of $276,000 in 1980, while seven more personnel worked on other parking chores. Thousands of additional spaces waited in public and private lots and along street curbs. The late lamented 1st Ward resembled one colossal parking lot with a scattering of buildings here and there. The community college and high school campuses contained more asphalt than school. Port Huron Hospital treated cars more tenderly than patients, and knocked down another row of houses to put in 160 more parking spaces. It then closed a street to build a $1.4 million 3-story parking deck for 400 more. Even the giant new county welfare office in Port Huron provided 200 parking spaces to welcome in the mobile poor. But all was not sanguine, traffic sergeant Orville Leibler

377

informed Jerry Brown. His department issued almost 20,000 parking tickets per year, took in $51,000 in fines, and held 300 outstanding arrest warrants for criminal parkers. The most common excuses given meter maid Joy Wyatt by expired meter scalawags: no change, meter broken, coins wouldn't fit, plenty of time on the meter when I left it.

Despite the best efforts of its promoters, the downtown Port Huron mall idea sparked no interest at all from developers – not enough parking, they said. City fathers dreamed up their own plan for a 140,000 square foot shopperland with 1,200 more parking spaces. But nobody offered to chip in $12 million to build it. Instead more and more suburban mall proposals floated by. One of them outlined a 58-acre, 30-store spread with 2,500 parking spaces, on a spot just inside the north end city limits, starring a second K-mart. Port Huron insurance man Jerry Marcozzi flew off the handle at this suggestion: "For Pete's sake why do we need or want another K-mart in our town? Let's not kill off the best things that are ours just for the economics of the thing. There are more things to life than economics and we should not destroy that which is good and beautiful for money. Downtown Port Huron is beautiful even when the stores are closed during non-business hours. But it won't be beautiful if the stores have to vacate because of no business!"(41) Fine sentiments, though a little late in the day.

Parts of the central city definitely had gone to seed during the last two decades, because of, not in spite of, urban renewal. The Algonquin and Lauth Hotels for example. Once busy, respectable spots, beautiful structures dating to the 1900 era, in these latter days they played host to welfare bums, parolees, and drug users. The Lauth finally came tumbling down in one of the Bouchard land purges. The Harrington Hotel was in rough shape as well. Owner Jack Paton, the former car dealer and bus company operator, discovered this the hard way when he fell down an elevator shaft to his death one day. Again and again vague proposals stirred hopes of luxurious new hotels replacing the passing generation of downtown structures, hopes which were never realized. The closure of more downtown business fixtures, Woolworths and Detroit Edison among them, troubled the waters as well.

Mayor Timothy Lozen and others finally began to worry that the destruction and neglect of the communty's neighborhoods to make way for the age of auto worship, wider streets, and perfect parking might be having something of a negative overall impact. More beleaguered Port Huron residents, businesses, and churches fled the city for the roomier township suburbs, lower property taxes and no city income tax. The city population shrank another 5% during the 70's, to 34,000. Federal officials found themselves with 50 abandoned Port Huron homes on their hands, the result of busted loans. Insurance man Merlyn Allen created a bumper sticker which read "Happiness is Living in Port Huron," but Allen lived 10 miles outside of town. With no foot police anymore, fewer pedestrians about, and 300 narcotics users driven on by prohibition, street crime increased enormously. 3,000 thefts of various kinds took place per year, at almost twice the rate reported in the rest of the county. "I can remember the days when you could walk to Pine Grove Park at midnight and have no fear of being robbed," said a 72 year-old woman, after having been robbed in broad daylight in a supermarket parking lot.(42)

The theme of decreasing safety played a part in the *Times Herald* saga of "Mom Provides Taxi Service," which told readers about the trials of policeman's wife Mrs. Stewart Appel, mother of eight. "The younger children never walk home from

378

school anymore. And because the high school is too far away, the teenagers are taken and picked up too. It makes for a two-way trip every day for Mrs. Appel, who has accepted taxiing as part of being a mother." That hard-to-define desirable, the good life, seemed to be eluding them, said Mrs. Appel: "It's really too bad. Out children don't have the kind of freedom we had. I remember when we didn't hesitate to pick up a hitchhiker...take a walk at night, or leave the back door unlocked. Now it is simply not smart to be too brave."(43)

Incredibly, when it came time to get away for a while from this tedious routine of shuttling themselves around town, families often embarked on a driving vacation trip. Even in these MEOW times they took 85% of their vacations in a car. Port Huron High School football coach James Bates and his wife loaded up their four children for a drive-til-you-drop 8-week tour through 18 national parks. "With enjoyment," ran the press account, "comes the long, grueling hours of travel as the highway stretches ahead, sometimes endlessly. For the children in the entourage, the boredom takes many forms. They whine, get tired, they cry, they are unceasingly hungry, they argue...they endlessly plead for stops to go to the bathroom."(44)

The number of Bates families on the road tempted America's national parks to lock the gates against their cars. Especially against their 10 million off-road vehicles and 3 million misnamed recreational vehicles (RV). The particularly unwelcome $11,000 bus-sized motorhomes had a Thumb pedigree, if you believed Ray Frank of Brown City. He claimed to have invented the motorhome in his barn in 1958, and now built 1,000 Travcos per year. The enormous Winnebagos motorhomes for sale at Cawood's seemed an equally ridiculous indulgence in MEOW times, comparable to dragging a motel room around with you from stop to stop. High gas prices didn't discourage Port Huron retiree Mary Hauk from driving a 35-footer RV 20,000 miles per year all over North America, or another Port Huroner from parking his "within spitting distance" of the Old Faithful geyser at Yellowstone. The state of Michigan incidentally required no special license for Mary to pilot her vehicle, twice as long as the average car, nor for any of the thousands of others who pulled indifferently attached boat, camper, and utility trailers behind their automobiles.

Motor vehicles of all sizes destroyed parks just as surely as they did every place else they went. The two state parks in St. Clair County functioned as little more than parking lots for visitors and ersatz "campers." Vehicle users systematically trashed the 7,000 acre Port Huron State Game Area which lay northwest of the city, and which had no park rangers to protect it. Apart from ruining the ground and killing the wildlife in this supposed sanctuary, vehicle users lay down a Cenozoic deposit of junk cars and snowmos, bottles and cans, refrigerators, clothing, water heaters, boxes, plastic bags, and some of the 2 billion old tires now laying around America.

No automobile problems troubled one famous Michigan nature spot, Mackinac Island, finish line of the annual Port Huron-to-Mackinac sailboat race, the biggest maritime event in Michigan. The *Times Herald* tried analyzing what the mysterious appeal was about Mackinac:

It doesn't have cars or exhaust fumes. It doesn't have a strip of fast food restaurants. It doesn't have modern high rise buildings. It doesn't have expressways. It doesn't have a shopping mall. In short, Mackinac Island doesn't have progress. The ban on cars, in addition to providing peace and quiet, makes the island seem larger than it is.(45)

379

Or looked at the other way around, the automobile made Port Huron seem smaller than it was, by throwing much of it away.

The idea of turning Port Huron into a Mackinac Island rather than a shopping mall lay somewhat outside the locals' range of vision. So too in Detroit, where Henry Ford II launched his own urban renewal scheme for that community, a $1.2 billion office and retail development on the waterfront, optimistically called the Renaissance Center. Critic Jane Holtz Kay described the finished product as a "detached fortress, wrapped by roads and stuffed with parking..." No renaissance resulted for the 107 year old Grand Trunk railroad station in Detroit, which had to be knocked down for Henry's plans. "Detroit must have revitalization throughout its entire central city area," said Ford, "more businesses, more life, more good architecture, and all the other features that would make it a more attractive place in which to live, work and seek recreation."(46) None of which was compatible with the automobile.

Henry also proclaimed a renaissance at the FMC by firing Lee Iacocca. In sending the 32-year Ford veteran on his way the Deuce explained, "Sometimes you just don't like somebody," a sentiment that Iacocca repaid with interest in his 1984 autobiography. (47) His life's work concluded, Henry the 2nd subsequently retired, but Iacocca found new occupation at the Chrysler Corporation, which in 1979 teetered again on the edge of bankrutpcy during the third auto industry slump of the decade. Chrysler hired Lido as chairman to try to rescue the #3 American automaker from the circling wolfpack of federal regulators, inflation, OPEC, and importers. 240 Chryslerites lost their jobs in Marysville, and things looked grim for the few of them left, but Iacocca, a natural-born actor, put his innate hamminess to work to get $1.5 billion in loan guarantees out of the Congress and keep Chrysler on its feet.

"I hate sending people to Detroit," an executive recruiter told author Vance Packard. Rather than move there herself, she vowed, "I'd divorce my husband first...there is so much ugliness." In addition to auto blight she might have been thinking of the thousands of abandoned homes. Another visitor wrote about the Motor City: "A drive along any of the major streets...is a journey through an urban war zone...where the battle for a viable city has been lost to the suburbs."(48) Packard christened Detroit's victorious neighboring suburb Warren, home of the General Motors Tech Center, as the "Spillover City."(49) Many of the 180,000 white residents of Spillover, through a combination of bigotry and genuine fear for the future, had driven away from the chaos overtaking Detroit, which in 1973 elected its first ever black mayor, Rouge plant veteran Coleman Young. Flint, still a General Motors town, found itself in almost as bad shape as Detroit, chewed up by expressways, deserted by whites, and wracked by the instability of a one-industry economy. Shortly before his death in Flint in 1973, GM luminary Charles Mott asked startled interviewer George May this question about the automobile revolution: "Are you satisfied with what happened?" clearly implying that Mott was not.

Spillover life around Port Huron became progressively more dispersed, disorganized and traffic-fouled. Every single township in St. Clair County grew in population during the 70's while cities for the most part lagged. Port Huron's suburban populace increased by double digit percentages. A growing wave of commerce followed the emigrants. "I mean, you have to have controlled growth. This is more like a cancerous growth," observed Gardendale's Marc Polack. It upset him when the

380

proposed K-Mart #2 hopped like a bunny from its first intended location inside the Port Huron city limits out into his township neighborhood. Polack soon had even more cause for concern: designs for an 80-acre enclosed shopping mall, a little Northland so to speak, planned for a patch of land just a mile further up North Main Street. It took time to come to fruition, but this project eventually proved to be the undoing of Gardendale and downtown Port Huron both. "I think it's just super," said Polack's neighbor Jean Stoutenberg, "I live just a mile from where it will be." Less enthusiastically, another witness accused the developer of "gutting the city of Port Huron so that he can make a dollar."

Crime mobility continued to bother the suburban scene as well as the city. Though it's worth noting again here that all the crime in America combined did far less damage to people and property than the automobile, it wasn't a necessity. Crooks and vandals regularly hit homes, schools, churches, stores, and the old reliables, gas stations. Thieves even broke into the dog pound near Port Huron, took $150 and let 20 dogs loose, many of whom were flattened by traffic while trying to make their getaways. Sheriff Meharg complained that the Port Huron suburbs still didn't pay their fair share for cops and that he'd need another two dozen deputies, twice his present force, to cope. At $20,000 each in salary, and $24,000 per patrol car, Meharg's staff steadily grew to 70 people (the Port Huron Police Department numbered 80). The prosecutor's office kept six attornies busy, and the the jail overflowed.

Semi-rural life became more expensive. Homes grew bigger and bigger. The average new suburban wigwam encompassed 1,700 square feet, plus a 400 sq. ft. garage, and often a basement. An abode in Old Farm now drained you of $60,000, and a lakeshore haven $85,000-$130,000. Driven by demand from two-income families, America's mortgage debt mounted to $550 billion, 30 times what it had been at the end of WW2. Health officials cited St. Clair County townships repeatedly for bad home septic systems installed for sprawl. Where they were available, mandatory sewer connection to Port Huron's system cost $1,200 per buildable lot, and priced some teary-eyed old township residents clean out of their modest homes.

The far-from-minor question of just plain American ugliness troubled people, those not too auto-blinded to see it. Lagoons of parking asphalt surrounded stores in the new commercial strips along North Main and Highway 21, at the rim of the city and out into the townships. Pushed back from the roadside by these requirements, the stores needed bigger and more garish signs to try to flag down potential patrons passing by in their "homes away from home – their cars." Up to 50 billboards and signs per mile graced some stretches. Retailers wheeled portable electric flashing signs to the curb to further emphasize the point: here we are. More drive-thrus of all kinds appeared. Fast food restaurants did 50% of their chow trade now at the drive-thru windows in and around Port Huron.

More auto-sprawl ate up farmland all over the state of Michigan. Governor Milliken discovered in 1973 that Michigan farmers no longer grew enough food to feed the state's population, while other less populous states ran up gigantic surpluses, "awash in an ocean of excess wheat." At the nexus of the fouled-up agriculture picture, the federal government spent $10 billion per year for price supports on one hand and food stamps on the other; one to keep food prices up and the other to allow the poor to afford them. As suburban building and Fordist farming practices crowded them out, the St.

Clair County farm population declined another 34% during the decade, leaving just 1,000 full-time farm workers. The 200,000 cultivated acres amounted to just over half that of the year 1900. These two bad trends collided head-on near the Krause Swine Farm, where 1,200 oinkers stank up their suburban neighbors' air, homes, and clothing something fierce.

In St. Clair Township 90% of the 300 farmers had called it quits since 1949, including township treasurer Fred Meiselbach. Said Fred, he couldn't afford to farm with property taxes so high. Farm villages continued to shrink or disappear. The town of Jeddo once had supported its own farm equipment store, feed store, lumberyard and a railroad depot. Today, just a small market stood there. Periodic energy crisis panics about tractor fuel shortages and lack of petro-fertilizer also shook up the non-organic farms, which used 10 times as much energy per unit of food output as they had in 1946. Horse-based Amish farmers used less than 1/4 the energy of their gentile counterparts but the U.S. Department of Agriculture still opposed organic farming with dedicated fanaticism.(50) At the cash register, farmers only collected 19 cents of the food dollar, compared to the 50 cents they'd once gotten. Some Thumb dairymen staged an old time farmers' market sale in Port Huron, selling eight tons of cheese to protest the truckers, processors, packagers, marketers, more truckers and retailers that stood between the cow and the consumer. The typical food item landed in a supermarket after six trips end to end on the nation's roads.

Build how they would, spend how they would, the American road makers and repair crews simply couldn't keep up with the swelling millions of ground-pounding cars and trucks driving altogether 1.5 trillion miles per year. The 3.8 million miles of navigable roads in the USA swallowed $6.4 billion yearly in maintenance, and they still were pockmarked with more than 110 million potholes. The 1973 spring breakup in St. Clair County rendered 10% of all the roads in the county impassible, and did $500,000 worth of washout damage to a single primary road. The Federal Highway Administration counted 89,000 critically deficient highway bridges in America, and just one, on Wadhams road, the biggest of 169 rural bridges in St. Clair County, needed $400,000 in repairs. 80% of the rest of the county's bridges were more than 60 years old and inadequate for modern loads. These local issues brought in a 3,000 signature citizens petition demanding action by the Road Commission. From his desk in his new $2.3 million headquarters, Road Superintendent James Little replied that all he needed to put everything right throughout the county – roads and bridges and the rest – was $200 million. He had $7 million per year to spend. The national fix-everything everywhere estimate was $329 billion.

Even when enough money collected in the Road Commission kitty to launch some successful "improvement" projects on major roads, they backfired when the wider, smoother pavements filled up with more traffic. Scenic Highway resident Joanne Goodrich called the repaved stretch in front of her home "a comedy of horrors. It has become a do as you please freeway...People are merging, speeding, cutting across traffic, driving two abreast and going the wrong way on a one way lane indiscriminately...The squealing of brakes is no longer occasional, it is constant."(51) She and her neighbors lived with the threat of collision just pulling in and out of their driveways. And someday too soon the work crews would be back in front of the Goodrich home, because the average pavement lasted just 16 years.

Additional pampering and fixits contributed to an endless workload. Budget busting snowfalls led the list. A single blizzard along Michigan highways in 1978 marooned 100,000 cars, some of the drivers too stunned by adversity even to walk to safety. A heavy snowfall in the Thumb, which couldn't be cleared away quickly enough at any expense to suit drivers, unleashed woe and lamentation among housebound suburbanites. School buses couldn't negotiate even the most modest snow drifts in the Thumb flatlands, and one school district had to close eight times in a single winter on account of it. The Road Commission stockpiled so much road salt – 17,000 tons – that it had to be shipped in by lake freighter. Road workers ran hazards (and created plenty) just plowing and salting the roads: "While operating the 5- or 10-speed [23-ton] trucks the driver must watch for obstacles in the road, regulate the flow of salt, note where the plow is dumping the snow, raise or lower the underbody blade as needed and watch for motorists and pedestrians."(52) The 10 million tons of salt spread every year across snowline America inflicted as much as $3 billion damage on roads, water, vegetation and cars. Rustproofing specialist John Lukovich gratefully acknowledged that his Port Huron garage owned its very existence to salty roads.

Skidding automobiles in all seasons knocked down 60,000 roadside utility poles in America annually, with the attendant mess. Organist John Breakie killed himself against one of these poles while driving home along the Scenic Highway one night from his gig at the Fogcutter restaurant in Port Huron. Another issue, bad road shoulders along Highway 21, cost the state of Michigan a $600,000 accident damage award in a Port Huron court case. The narrow, traffic-choked, broken up "21" killed 17 people in a six month stretch. Almost a minor annoyance by comparison, the Dead Man's Curve on Belle River Road deposited a car on the Timothy Koury family's lawn at least once a month, and that glitch needed $10,000 to straighten out. The comparative triviality of roadside weed-cutting now cost $200 per mile. Road signs disappeared by the hundreds every year. Just maintaining the Road Commission's own 550 vehicles cost $300,000 per year. Even at that strength they couldn't keep up with all the trash dumped roadside. And so on, and so on.

Still plodding along after 24 years of construction, the estimated costs-to-completion of the Interstate Highway System, pushed by runaway traffic and inflation, rose up and up to $113 billion, or $2.7 million per mile, with the end still nowhere in sight.(53) Michigan's cost share now stood at $3 billion, triple the 1956 prediction. By comparison, rebuilding a mile of railroad cost $60,000 per mile. Of those interstates already completed, 50% were wearing out faster than they could be repaired. So many craters marred some spots they resembled the Moon's surface, on which the USA abandoned during this decade an $8 million lunar junk car. President Eisenhower originally had intended it to be maintained by the states, but now, five presidents later, Jimmy Carter glumly acknowledged that the IHS needed a permanent federal repair fund.(54) Investigators made another startling finding; the safety installations on the interstates – signposts, light poles, embankments, guard rails – actually caused most of the damage in fatal accidents. Can't live with 'em, can't live without 'em. U.S. Senator Edward Kennedy had had enough, and tried to abolish the federal Highway Trust Fund, which dispensed $6 billion in fuel, tire, truck and bus taxes per year. America had "the best highways and the worst transportation in virtually the entire industrialized world," said Kennedy, who pointedly blamed auto obsession for undercutting mass transit.

A working component of the world's worst transportation system came lumbering into Port Huron one day off Interstate 94 – a semi-trailer truck with a church built into it. The $60,000 mobile chapel of Transport for Christ roamed the nation's truck stops looking to turn truckers aside from their evil ways. Few industries needed it more. Several items required repentance. *Fuel gluttony*: the average long haul truck extracted only 3 miles per gallon out of its two 80 gallon tanks, a poke in the eye to fuel conservationists. Some truck stops pumped 350,000 gallons of fuel per month.(55) *Theft*: $800 million worth of cargo hijackings, many of them staged, occurred per year, 100 per day sometimes in New York City. *Litter*: uncovered dump trucks scattered debris over the roads, like tire-flattening scrap metal, which cost $300,000 per year to clean up just in Detroit. *Road destruction*: trucking lobbyists turned aside efforts to downsize maximum 80-ton monster vehicles in Michigan, which each did as much damage to roads as 16,000 cars, and didn't readily forgive mistakes at the wheel. Driver George Kenner of Port Huron found his 76-ton highway-busting scrap steel hauler a little too much to handle when it rolled over on I-94 and killed him.

Discrimination: federal investigators uncovered "disgraceful, deliberate and patterned" employment practices against blacks, women and Hispanics in the $13.5 billion trucking industry. One woman who managed to break the barrier, 27 year-old, 5'1" Darlene Koenig of St. Clair County, delivered bagged salt to Chicago, and unloaded 600 80-pound bags by hand in 2 1/2 hours. *Illegal licensing*: truck drivers frequently held licenses in different states illegally. One of these multiple license men crashed into a Virginia school bus and killed three people. He'd racked up 25 citations, several accidents, and five license suspensions in North Carolina, plus three more tickets on a Florida license.

Dangerous vehicles: a spot check by the U.S. Department of Transportation found 40% of the big rigs in "imminently hazardous" condition. *Dangerous cargoes*: an imminently hazardous propane tank truck which developed a leak in Port Huron reportedly had the explosive potential of 40,000 sticks of TNT. "It was like having a rolling bomb drive through town," said shaken police Lieutenant Ed Cole. In Colorado a truck from Super Safe Transport carrying atomic bomb grade plutonium slid off a highway and lay there for 18 hours before it could be righted. *Mooching*: truckers continued to pick taxpayers' pockets, as railroad exec William Lashley complained to Michigan's Public Service Commission: "...(it) costs truckers about five cents of each revenue dollar to use the highways, whereas it costs the railroads about 25 cents...to own, maintain and pay taxes on their trackage."(56)

An estimated 11,500 big and small commercial trucks operated in St. Clair County. The industry kept 16 trucking terminals in the Port Huron area busy. Local trucking companies employed 5,000 people, and their professional drivers made $18,000 - $25,000 per year, if they pushed their rigs 60 hours per week and didn't mind some back trouble, hemorrhoids, and prostate issues from being rooted to the saddle that long. The work schedule didn't leave much time for television, but those truckers who did catch it probably got a chuckle out of director Steven Spielberg's 1971 TV picture *Duel*. In this tale, traveling salesman Dennis Weaver inadvertently annoyed a tanker truck driver who subsequently pursued Weaver's car all over a western desert. The film enacted a series of close calls with trucks that the viewer could easily relate to: tailgating, fender benders, broken radiator, treacherous passing, a near collision at a railroad crossing. Weaver adopted numerous stratagems to avoid his road rage antagonist, except the obvious one, stop driving. That idea lay beyond the bounds of the

American imagination by the 1970s.

A Port Huron motorist and *Times Herald* reporter, Michael Duffy, got fed up with some of the local truckers who might have driven right out of *Duel*. "Boors of the road," he called them, who used "tailgating terror tactics" to push law-abiding drivers out of the way. Though trucks made up only 1% of U.S. traffic, they accounted for 9% of the fatal accidents.(57) In an especially nasty and ironic incident, Nazi death camp survivor Chaskiel Slabia burned to death under an overturned gasoline tanker in the largely Jewish Detroit suburb of Oak Park. Author Steven Brill found that independent truckers carrying unregulated goods often drove coast to coast in 72 hours in rigs the size of a studio apartment, "...which should have given other drivers on the road more than enough reason to be afraid of a truck with a pilot asleep at the wheel plowing into them."(58) Still more reason poured from a bottle. State police often saw working truck drivers load up at bars along Highway 21, while their vehicles waited outside, rarin' to go.

Battling back against these bad truck vibes, the popular song Convoy shone an admiring light on the trucking fraternity in 1975. This tale told of an imaginary drivers' rebellion against those cruel 55 mph speed limits, driving time logs, paperwork, road tolls, fuel prices, etc. It also saluted the citizens band radio craze of the 70's. Four million two-way CB radios installed in the nation's vehicles almost overnight allowed truckers to "start jabbering" with each other (in the Federal Communication Commission's words) and coordinate their lawbreaking.

Ah, breaker one-nine, this here's the Rubber Duck. You got a copy on me, Pig Pen, c'mon?
Ah, yeah, 10-4, Pig Pen, fer shure, fer shure. By golly, it's clean clear to flag town.
Chorus: *Yeah, we got a mighty convoy*
Ain't nothing gonna get in our way.
We gonna roll this truckin' convoy
Across the USA. Connnnvoooyyyyy! (59)

This musical scenario sounded a little but not wholly far-fetched to Port Huron truck driver Clarence Ogden. He'd joined a truckers strike in protest against high fuel prices, the "double nickel" speed limit, and the $2,000 fine he'd paid recently for overloading his truck, a business practice Ogden endorsed as almost a necessity. Unlike the Rubber Duck, Ogden parked his vehicle rather than convoy. During a 1976 strike Port Huron Teamsters acted pretty peacefully, content to do some picketing while Brotherhood members elsewhere indulged in the traditional shooting and beating of opponents. A 12-day trucking stoppage in 1979 completely shut down the Prestolite auto wire factory and other local Port Huron businesses dependent on truck shipments.

The Port Huron Industrial Park once had been designed to provide each factory with railroad service. By the end of the 70's only one used it. The rest shipped by truck, despite the strictures of MEOW. Vast parking lots for trucks and employees alike on each factory site wasted scores of acres of land. This transportation inversion obliged Gerald Bouchard to lay waste to more homes and small businesses, cut down trees and widen another street around the industrial park to meet trucking demands, to the fury of Thelma Spigner and other homeowners. Port Huron residents also complained about new truck routes unofficially being pushed through their neighborhoods elsewhere in town by semis barging through. City officials had the authority to ban large trucks from municipal streets but virtually never did so.

Last minute truck deliveries between auto parts makers and assembly plants – Port Huron to Flint for instance – filled the highways with rolling warehouses, sparing General Motors, Ford and Chrysler the need to keep large inventories on hand. "For example, we used to ship transaxles by train from Kokomo, Indiana to Belvidere, Illinois," explained Lee Iacocca. "By switching to trucks we got them there the same day, which streamlined the whole operation."(60) And stuck the public with the bill and the dangers of the streamlining. "Just in time" deliveries (or rather "just in trucks") took over in other industries as well. Cattle trains became a thing of the past in America, now that 99% of all beef on the hoof arrived at slaughterhouses by truck.(61)

If the energy crisis brought no relief from the plague of trucks, it benefited the people of Port Huron by restarting the city buses in 1976. There'd been agitation to bring back the buses from the moment they stopped in 1968. New state and federal subsidies coaxed the revival along and so did, very surprisingly, an enthusiastically passed local property tax for bus support. The tax issue won by almost a 2-1 margin at the polls, backed by most of the civic groups in Port Huron. Even the Auto Club got behind the idea, and convinced guinea pig members Richard and Diana McDonald to actually try to bus and walk for a week to their jobs three miles across town, instead of driving. The McDonalds not only survived this ground-breaking experiment, but thrived, saving two-thirds of their gas consumption, $24 cash. Another convert, former auto commuter Ray Daggett, saved $1,500 in a year bus-riding a few miles to his Marysville job.

Port Huron's City Planning Director, 36 year-old Raymond Straffon, Jr., took the wheel of the area's new 6-route municipal bus system, in place of his boss Mr. Bouchard, who'd made his distaste for mass transit plain years earlier. Michigan Governor Milliken also deserved much credit, because he'd pried a half cent per gallon of gas tax money out of the Michigan legislature to support 45 bus systems and assorted other mass transit ventures across the state. Not so felicitously, Milliken merged responsibilities for highways, buses, trains, planes, and ships into a single Michigan Department of Transportation (MDOT), an office dominated by the Road Gang's nefarious front men. Despite road lobby opposition, the federal government now disbursed up to $500 million annually for mass transit purposes, some of it from the previously inviolate Highway Trust Fund.

Not everyone welcomed Port Huron's new bus service and its customers with open arms. With no central passenger terminal at first, patrons awaited buses on the sidewalks downtown. Business owners chased them away from several locations as *ipso facto* loiterers and bums, before bus officials finally found a real home. Once aboard, a 40 cent ride (20 cents for seniors and kids) took passengers to within a few blocks of pretty much anywhere in Port Huron, and to a few township stops, and Marysville. That price compared to a $7.75 cab fare across the 7-mile length of town.

The Blue Water Area Transit system carried 2 million people during its first four years. Passenger #2 million, homemaker Jenny Boman, no loiterer or bum, had given up her car because the bus cost less. It still cost less after a fare hike to 50 cents. Very importantly, the new bus system enjoyed the freedom to raise rates to keep up with inflation, a privilege the franchised, privately run Port Huron streetcars and buses of yesteryear never knew, and which automakers, dealers, and gas stations obviously employed with abandon. The various subsidies involved amounted to $1.12 per bus passenger on the Blue Water Transit, but county planner Peter Malley defended them, by pointing to the huge hidden costs of individual auto transportation – roads, fuel, police, courts, jails, parking, pollution, hospitals, cemeteries, etc.

As far as energy efficiency, buses ran far behind walking, bicycling, rail, or water, but compared to automobiles worked almost miraculously. Buses achieved up to 150-200 passenger miles per gallon, trains up to 400, the average car carrying 5 people 57, a car carrying the average 1.4 passengers, 16.(62) Unfortunately, these arguments carried no weight with planner Malley's bosses, St. Clair County's board of governing commissioners, who refused to join forces with Port Huron and expand the city and suburban buses into a countywide intercity operation. For all practical purposes regional mass transit throughout the upper Thumb had ceased. Just one bus per week rambled from Port Huron up the Thumb to the end of the line at Port Austin. One more went to Saginaw. Many rural areas of Michigan lived under a similar state of affairs, though relieved here and there by limited minibus dial-a-ride services.

Twice a day a Greyhound bus left from Port Huron to Detroit or arrived coming back. One a day made the round trip to Flint, where passengers connected through to Chicago. During the gas squeezes these vehicles sometimes traveled standing room only. When gasoline was in adequate supply about 10 people boarded in Port Huron. Many private bus companies now required state subsidies to underwrite intercity service. They made most of their profits through exclusive charter services. The number of passengers on America's intercity buses peaked at 300 million in 1970, but then declined, which pretty clearly belied the alleged "crisis" in the energy situation.

Port Huron school buses, which continued right along even while municipal buses were halted for eight years, now traveled a total of 1 million miles per year, at a cost of $1 per mile. This kept students who rode them busbound an average one hour per day. All Port Huron district children living more than 1.5 miles from school, and some closer than that along heavily trafficked roads, were entitled to ride the buses. It near to broke the heart of school transportation director Pauline Morton to think of kids walking to school at all, "We would all like door to door service for our children." Jerry Brown found irony aplenty on this subject when he interviewed 90 year-old John Machesky, a retired auto engineer and Ransom Olds associate of old, who lived in St. Clair County. Machesky reminisced about the 12 miles a day he'd walked as a boy, making his milk delivery route first, then walking back and forth to school. Compare that to the sissy kids of the 1970's, said John. "Brother, haven't times changed! I hear now that some school children don't even walk a few blocks to school. They have to be bused."(63)

Despite his considerable intellect (he spoke five languages) Machesky somehow couldn't connect his lifetime's work in the auto racket with this non-walking routine. Another local, J. R. Ganhs, wrote more perceptively: "Children today are finding it much easier to be driven, even the very short distances, than to get much needed exercise walking, and parents are accommodating them in this respect by driving them everywhere...When are parent going to 'allow' their children the pleasure and benefits of walking?"(64) But look the other side of the coin, J.R. Automobiles killed students Lynn Slowinski and Barbara LaVere within a week of each other as they walked no further than to their school bus stops outside Port Huron. So which child danger should a parent choose, sloth or a skull crushing?

The tried and true streetcar concept, so vastly superior in economy, cleanliness, and safety to buses and cars, seemed now almost a hex from a darkened past, a taboo to the car worshippers in Port Huron. Some shopping center developers jolted the community by offering to link a proposed suburban mall, which they ridiculously called a "lifestyle center," to downtown Port Huron by an automated 3-mile long elevated train. The general reaction: You can't be serious. The train system at least provided a useful idea, though neither the lifestyle center nor the el ever took shape. Only seven American cities kept streetcars in use at this point, some 1,000 in number. Detroit made a stab at rebuilding a 9-block section of trolley to service its Cobo Hall convention center, but didn't ban automobiles from the route. Now that would have been a real renaissance, though not necessarily to Henry II's liking.

One of the most compelling demonstrations of effective light rail mass transit during the 1970's came from none other than the Walt Disney company. A 14-mile long monorail around the immense Disney World park in Florida, which opened in 1971, carried 50 million passengers per year. Disney also built much of its World on an elevated platform, so that subterranean service vehicles ran invisibly beneath the customers walking above on the carfree streets. Although offered plenty of distractions, Disney patrons spent 97% of their time in the park just enjoying a world without automobiles.(65) The opening of the Bay Area Rapid Transit system in San Francisco marked another notable triumph of the decade. Along with the urban train systems in Chicago and New York it posed a standing challenge to the Southeast Michigan Transportation Authority, which encompassed Port Huron, Detroit, and seven counties, to get its own act together.

America's shameful neglect and outright subversion of its heavy railroad intercity passenger system reduced what had once been the world's best to a dire strait by the early 1970's. Service halted entirely in Port Huron on May 1, 1971, as it did that spring for much of the United States. In place of private rail companies, a semi-autonomous federal agency known first as Railpax and later as Amtrak hammered together some passenger routes. A meager 200 daily trains stopped in 400 cities along 21,000 miles of track. Amtrak found its hands full even managing that much. Of the 63,000 passenger rail cars servicing the country in 1926, only 3,000 had survived to 1971, and Amtrak subsequently junked half of them. The price of diesel fuel for locomotives soared like all petroleum products during the 70's, up 800%.(66) Runaway inflation on other train equipment prices and wages didn't help, either.

In the shadow cast by the energy and pollution concerns of the day, a few people elevated their outlook above America's entrenched auto conceit, and remembered the sunnier days of the rails. People like journalist Don Oakley:

Picture an America whose great cities are laced together with gleaming metal rails over which literally thousands of passenger trains run each day...an America whose suburbs and small towns are similarly linked by fast, pollution-free rapid transit systems... an America whose streets and highways are not clogged with poison spewing automobiles, which kill and maim tens of thousands each year and whose manufacture and operation drains the nation's resources...an America where no superhighways are slashed across the countryside, entombing God's living greenness in a killing mantle of concrete...an America where there is no such thing as a Highway Trust Fund, lavishing billions in

gasoline and oil tax dollars on new highways...it is a picture of America at the
beginning of this century.(67)

Restoring that picture would prove to be no easy task. Starting with a 3 billion passenger mile year in 1972, Amtrak improved that to 4.5 billion by 1979, but during the latter year the corporation ran a half billion dollar deficit, much like its private predecessors had done. Passenger railroad service returned to Port Huron in September 1974, courtesy of Amtrak, but only after the city's once handsome Grand Trunk station had fallen into a ruin during the passenger stoppage, finally to be torn down. John DeLora of the Michigan Association of Rail Passengers reacted sadly to the station's demise, "With the best of intentions, the City of Port Huron is trying to make 'improvements' without realizing that some of these improvements are letting the soul of the city die a little each time, never to return." He further vowed "to bring Michigan and America back to a sane transportation policy."(68) Concerned citizens rescued for use as a museum the small waterfront station Al Edison had worked from as a train newsboy. But another former railroad station dating to the Pere Marquette days was knocked down to give auto traffic a better sightline.

A new $400,000 Port Huron passenger station appeared, with all the aesthetic appeal of an outhouse, and in fact the restroom was its only amenity. 1,000 people turned out to hurrah the new train service on its first day, but only 16 boarded. The one train to Chicago and back daily cost $42 round trip, about 12 cents per mile. Initially it took 8 hours to reach Chicago, slower than in 1900, though this speed later improved by an hour. "With a train there isn't the rush-rush mentality," observed reporter Mike Duffy. "You can lay back, read, do nothing or just watch the country roll past. Better still, you can get up and walk around."(69)

Though railroad passengers traveled in comparative safety, they did run some dangers. A Chicago commuter train crash in 1972 killed 32 and injured 200. The sad state of many railbeds, Amtrak's predictable teething troubles with old equipment, and the now open antagonism of the railroads to passenger service using their tracks led to a series of mishaps. Yet all of the railroad passenger casualties in the decade combined didn't amount to a week's worth of dead and wounded on the highways. The rush-rush mentality still cost a lot of car drivers their lives when they tried jousting with trains. A thousand died in America in a typical year at railroad crossings, and in messing around the rights of way. Charles Woodley's snowmobile made so much noise that the 22 year-old rider didn't hear the train overtaking him from the rear as he rode on railroad property in St. Clair County, resulting in his dismemberment. Another 22 year-old, Harry Kerr, tried skirting the stopping gates at a RR crossing near Port Huron. For this rash act a freight train dragged his body and his car more than half a mile.

Grand Trunk train engineer Paul Hicks hit 10 vehicles in his first 11 years operating out of Port Huron. One woman drove around 12 cars and ran the stop gates to get in front of Hicks' train, which totaled her car. She walked away without a scratch. An unluckier casualty hit the side of Hicks' train 40 cars behind the engine and died. It made such a negligible impact that Hicks and his colleagues on board didn't learn about it until police called them later. Freight trains typically weighed up to 5,000 tons by this time. Even in the face of that datum, the Port Huron City Council chose to ban the use of warning horns on trains at night within the city limits, after one harried homeowner counted 106 horn blasts in one night. The city demanded instead silent flagmen at

389

railroad crossings. They placed no similar restriction on automobile or truck horns.

Railroads continued to set new freight records during these times, moving 17 billion ton miles in a single week in 1973, averaging 2 million ton miles per train employee annually by 1980.(70) That still didn't guarantee profits. Another government rescue squad, Conrail, attacked the problem of what to do with the freight service on bankrupt railroads in 17 northeastern states, including 4,000 miles of lines in Michigan. In addressing the situation the federal government clung to the same major misconception that had dogged railroading in America ever since its inception. Instead of acquiring the railbeds for public ownership, and subsequently licensing them for private operation, as highways operated, officials like U.S. Transportation Secretary William Coleman insisted that the RR right of ways be left largely in private hands.

So, another 1,000 miles of unwanted, unloved orphan rail lines in Michigan were abandoned, including some along the McMorran Line right of way built out of Port Huron in the 1880's. This step isolated, among other businesses, Port Huron's Peacock Lumber Company, which had received 95% of its goods by rail, and which not long afterward disappeared in a blaze of arson. Equally shortsighted Port Huron city officials tore up 3.5 miles of abandoned tracks instead of converting them to municipal use. The trackage through Pine Grove Park, which in a saner age had delivered and retrieved thousands of park-goers in a single day, Gerald Bouchard now described as "blight," and removed. Naturally he had no qualms about covering the same right of way with asphalt blight for automobile parking. The huge black Pere Marquette railroad lift bridge across the Black River in Port Huron now stood uselessly in a permanently raised position, pointing 80 degrees up to the sky, the city's monument to the folly of its ways, its own bridge of sighs.

Here and there in the Thumb some short-line railroad entrepreneurs decided to carry on and save some of the track mileage. "It is physically and geographically and economically impossible to ship corn from Michigan to Maine, Vermont, (and other states) by truck," said grain elevator operator Jim Stein. Up to 50 carloads of grain at a time still traveled by rail from a rural elevator near Port Huron. Trucking it would cost 7 cents a bushel more than rail. Moving lumber cost $15 more per 1,000 board feet. "Why not haul more of this freight...by rail instead of by truck?" asked farmer Sam Work. "Wouldn't that be an economical move in light of the current energy shortage?"(71) It sure enough would. Supporters of short-line railroads had a ready example in front of them. One of the best short lines in the country, the family-owned Port Huron & Detroit, first built in 1900 to service the salt plant erected that year, still operated from Port Huron to 25 clients across St. Clair County.

Apart from the PH&D, the two major rail lines in town, Grand Trunk and C&O, stayed financially solvent during the 70's but together employed about half as many as they did a generation earlier; 700 or so. The Grand Trunk continued to handle a large amount of finished automobiles and trucks shipped through from Flint, bound for America's east coast. In fact one-half of the GTRR's revenues came from the auto industry. The firm carrying the infirm, so to speak. A lot of petroleum products from Chemical Valley moved by rail through Port Huron, some of it uncomfortably flammable or toxic. Salt, paper, propane, scrap iron and some auto parts departed from Port Huron these days by rail.

The decade ended on a note of hope about railroad law at last. President

390

Jimmy Carter and Congressman Harley Staggers won wide scale federal deregulation of train business practices. This largely ended 100 years of serfdom at the hands of the Interstate Commerce Commission. During the last tortured years of its reign, the ICC took an average seven months to approve or disapprove a railroad rate change. One railroad merger got the ICC runaround for 12 *years* before the applicants called it off. The government also deregulated 15,000 trucking companies from much ICC governance on routes and rates. That act of reform got a cooler reception from its subjects. A large number of truckers had been cozy with the ICC, because it made life difficult for startup companies. Without the ICC crutch to prop it up, the owners of the Ogden & Moffett firm in Port Huron, now operating 13 terminals, with 300 employees, and nearly 1,000 pieces of trucking equipment, promptly sold it.

The airlines, too, faced a new era of deregulation as the result of legislation passed late in the decade. It took the wraps off rates and routes previously okayed or not by the Civil Aeronautics Board. Although jet fuel prices soared 900%, to $1 per gallon, the number of domestic passengers on U.S. airlines doubled during the 1970's to almost 300 million. Even before deregulation the Boeing company and its airline customers enjoyed the freedom to simply dump the giant new 747 jet carrier onto the market and leave it to the government-run airports to build the larger facilities needed to handle it. The Federal Aviation Administration took over air traffic control of all air space in America between 18,000-60,000 feet, and policed it free of charge, another pointed contrast with the rail network.(72)

The last great 20th Century shipwreck on the Great Lakes occurred in 1975, when the 700-foot ore carrier *Edmund Fitzgerald* went to the bottom of Lake Superior during a November storm, taking 29 crewmen with it. Somehow this particular mishap sparked a fascination that lasted for years for an American public wholly ignorant of transportation history. The media rehashed the *Fitzgerald* story annually, and it inspired a popular song by the Canadian folk singer Gordon Lightfoot, as well as the foundation of a Great Lakes Shipwreck Historical Society in Michigan. Needless to say, nobody founded a society to commemorate great Michigan automobile wrecks or wrote songs about them. The 125 Americans who perished in traffic crackups the day the *Fitzgerald* sank didn't die romantically enough to inspire Mr. Lightfoot's muse.

The *Fitzgerald* might be no more, but the first 1,000-foot freighter on the Great Lakes filled its place. Thousands of people lined the St. Clair Riverfront, blew whistles, and lit fireworks to mark the *Stewart Cort's* first passage past Port Huron, just as crowds had turned out 70 years earlier to celebrate a ship launching. No more launchings took place anywhere in Michigan, the Great Lakes State, after its last shipyard closed in Bay City in 1976. Four local Port Huron men helped crew the *Cort*, among them first mate John Presly, a native of the former 1st Ward, the traditional sailors' home.

For all the maritime enthusiasm that lived on in Port Huron, the commercial waterfront tradition continued to slip away. "There's no need to locate industry on the river," said city planner Straffon, expressing the common wisdom by now. Port Huron spruced up and rebuilt miles of riverfront on both the St. Clair and Black Rivers, and dredged two more miles of the Black during the 70's, but all for recreational purposes. The St. Clair remained one of the world's loveliest rivers, and water fun there and on Lake Huron drove the county's 2nd biggest industry, tourism, attracting tens of thousands of people annually. Sport fishing had replaced commercial fishing entirely. Port Huron's 300 new boat slips, new seawalls, and new waterfront parks proved extremely popular, a considerable achievement of Gerald Bouchard's. The manager demonstrated an undeniable wizardry in extracting grants and loans from higher-ups in government for his favorite projects.

In his greatest coup Bouchard swapped some unused city property for more than 35 acres of prime frontage on the St. Clair River, owned by the Grand Trunk railroad. For more than 100 years ships had docked along this stretch of ground, once the site of the railcar repair shops, the package freight warehouses, the Standard Oil and Star Oil tank farms, and the Peerless Cement Company. All gone now. Only the headquarters of the 50-member Lake Pilots Association remained. What to do with this potentially beautiful piece of land became a burning civic issue for years, but the idea of restoring the commercial docks received little consideration.

That was because the light amount of business at Port Huron's existing Seaway Terminal provided no incentive to develop another facility. Michigan had 23 ports on the Lakes, a surplus under present conditions of national brain lock about transportation. When the Port Huron terminal handled a single freighter load it amounted to $2 million in commerce, but that's all the terminal handled one season, a single ship. Bouchard characterized this not unfairly as a poor return on the city's investment. The Canadians made fuller use of a mixed waterfront on the Sarnia side of the St. Clair River, where side by side with sports marinas as much as 8 million tons in oil, lumber, grain, tobacco and chemicals arrived or departed by ship in a year.

Even in the face of MEOW, America failed to fully appreciate or take advantage of its inland waterways. As part of the energy crisis brouhaha icebreakers kept the Great Lakes open year round during the winters of 1975 and 1976, as a test project for permanent year-round use. The Army Corps of Engineers reported, "Lakes shipping is cheaper than by rail or truck, companies would no longer have to stockpile goods waiting for the normal shipping season to open, and overall freight charges would come down because Great Lakes ships would always be in use."[73] But fears over shoreline damage done by ice-breaking in narrow channels foolishly stopped winter Lakes shipping dead. No such concern for property damage stopped the monumental amount of road plowing and salting each winter.

The Port Huron to Lake Michigan Trans-Michigan canal project remained at a standstill. Its original designer, John Snell, tried again to interest public and private resources. He hoped, futilely, that the new public awareness about energy efficiency would jump start the idea. Misdirected environmental concerns actually halted another major canal project in America, the trans-Florida canal, which just led to more trucking, the most environmentally destructive kind of transport. Better sense prevailed on arteries like the Ohio River system, which moved 174 million tons of cargo in a year, and on the upgraded Arkansas River, where the shipping of 13 million tons annually along its 450 mile length spared the landscape further degradation by the equivalent of 400,000 semi trucks.

Since Americans measured almost all transportation questions in miles per gallon during this decade, it came to light that with the energy in a gallon of gasoline you could pedal a bicycle 1,000 miles. Just don't drink the gas to get that energy. Furthermore, bicycle rides could easily replace the 80% of all automobile trips that

392

covered less than 10 miles.(74) The nation bought almost 12 million bicycles in 1972, the first time since 1908 that bikes outsold automobiles. The next year two-wheeler sales reached 15 million. $90 bought you a new 10-speed at the Port Huron Sears. Better get a lock for it, though, because around town thieves anxious to save $90 stole 400 bicycles one year.

The bike's advantage came as no news to some Port Huroners. 80 year-old Grand Trunk retiree and former County Board member Howard Bell rode his bike every day in Port Huron, summer or winter. 58 year-old Ted Hedberg, night watchman at Grand Trunk, rode to work eight months of the year on the $27 bike he'd bought new in 1929, carrying his nightstick to bash pursuing dogs with. Harriet Edie often biked 15 miles into Port Huron from Gardendale at age 63, and mother of three Mrs. Martin Sopha, 32, who held no drivers license, caught the eye of neighbors by cycling across town to the stores, bank, schools, parks. "It's my way of getting around, especially if I'm in a hurry." John Feeney joined thousands of others on the "Bikecentennial" trail across America for a coast to coast 3,000 mile spin in the spirit of 1976. An inspiring British couple in their 60's, Bert and Queenie Barnes, rode through Port Huron on a similar trans-America trip. "We're used to cycling more than Americans," said Bert. "Bicycles are used much more often in England than here. Sometimes, I think Americans were born in cars."

A Port Huron couple during the 70's might still rent a tandem at Dino's Port Huron bicycle shop and set out cautiously on a quiet side road into that part of the countryside outside town which hadn't yet been converted completely into a death trap by motorists, or into a suburban garrison by real estate profiteers. The American Diabetes Association and American Cancer Society both staged regular fundraising bikeathons in Port Huron, and there'd have been a lot less of both diseases if bikes had been used daily. The adult tricycle, which hardly had been seen since the 19th Century, reappeared for sale at the Port Huron Bicycle Center: "Schwinn's new Town and Country Adult Tricycle will whisk you off to the market and help you enjoy the fresh air and sunshine. An easy riding 3 wheel vehicle for the adult rider who wants a sense of security."

For a real sense of security, cyclists stayed on the sidewalk when riding the busier streets in town, to avoid joining the 41,000 U.S. bikers killed or hurt annually. Car-versus-bike accidents averaged 5 per month in Port Huron. Nine year-old William Hachee died under the wheels of a fire truck he followed too closely one day. When a car "bumped him off his bike," in a reporter's offhand phrase, it left 32 year-old Gary Peck partially paralyzed, with double vision and memory lapses. Another member of the infamous Zeros family, motorcyclist Frederick this time, killed 78 year-old John Zotter as the latter bicycled through town. Zeros' sentence: a year in jail.

Still not a foot of bike path existed anywhere in St. Clair County, though the state of Michigan began offering some money to local communities to build them. 400 people petitioned the Port Huron City Council for bike routes, but Gerald Bouchard didn't like the idea any more than he liked buses, and he had a point. Maintaining in a city setting three sets of thoroughfares – streets for motor vehicles, sidewalks for pedestrians, plus bike paths – seemed pretty extravagant. Additionally, did bicyclists really want to surrender their right to ride on the streets? Why not close the streets to cars? Port Huron had not yet achieved that degree of enlightenment.

In rural and suburban areas building a mile of bike/walk path cost just $15,000 compared to $2 million for a mile of rural freeway. Paths would have made a welcome addition alongside some of the murderous paved township roads. The late 9 year-old Stephen Jerry and 12 year-old Timothy Sawdon might have avoided drunken hit-and-run driver Donald McLean while out riding one evening in Port Huron Township. Ditto Anthony VanLoon and Gary Rosenberg, 15, run down by the truck of killer David Genaw, who couldn't be bothered to stop at the scene of his crime either. The idea of converting abandoned railbeds into walking and biking paths gained ground. The 14 miles of the McMorran Line immediately north of Port Huron looked pretty appetizing. Backers said conversion would keep the rights of way in use for efficient transit and recreation, and preserve them if America ever regained its reason and needed them again for rail. But property owners along these old rail lines, afraid that passing walkers and bikers might fall on them like ravening hyenas, opposed rails-to-trails.

By the 1970's irrefutable evidence had established an inverse relationship between driving and good health. The Jacobs Effect, as we know, linked walking and good health. It didn't make any sense to talk about health without talking about walking. "Our lifestyle has almost negated every major achievement made in medical technology in the last 100 years," said Dr. Lawrence Lamb, physician to the American astronauts. "They didn't have automobiles, so they walked and exercised. As a result the people were fit."(75) He wasn't the only doctor looking backward with admiration from the vantage point of this decade.

The figures backing up Dr. Lamb made dispiriting reading. 20 million U.S. citizens suffered from hypertension. "Scientists Seek Origin of Hypertension," ran one headline, though the origin stared scientists in the face whenever they drove their cars over to the lab. 50 million people moaned and groaned with arthritis of one kind or another, and doctors installed 40,000 artificial hips into their cyborg patients annually. Obesity-induced diabetes reached number 5 on the cause-of-death hit list. 35 million Americans suffered from "allergies," real or imagined, as the natural world relentlessly sought to invade their hermetically sealed automotive existence.

Conspicuous non-walker Henry Ford II was perhaps the most prominent of 12 million U.S. heart patients suffering from auto sickness. General Motors paid the price for the debilitating effect of its products, spending $875 million on employee health benefits in 1975. This amounted to $175 per car; more than GM spent on the steel in it. Blue Cross Blue Shield medical insurance topped the list as the single biggest of Chrysler's 19,000 suppliers.(76) The total annual U.S. health bill came to $250 billion by 1980, $1,000 per person. Health spending increased twice as fast as inflation, and only 4% of that sum went to prevention, like a good pair of hiking shoes.

A limited fitness fad triggered by American Frank Shorter's marathon victory in the 1972 Olympics passed right by most of the overtransported country. Not many in St. Clair County put in 15 miles of running every day like 15 year-old state high school champion Miriam Boyd of Port Huron, or 10 miles alongside 68 year-old James Lux of Yale, or even 1.5 miles with 81 year-old Frank Levy, also of Port Huron. Even many of those who took the trouble to exercise did it bassackwards. Patrons of the new Port Huron Racquet Club and the downtown YMCA climbed into automobiles and drove to these venues, for workouts designed to replace the walking their cars had denuded them

394

of in the first place.

Half of American men and a third of women weighed too much, an average 15-30 pounds. Linda Leffler thought more like half the gals in Port Huron were too chubby, size 14 or higher, and why didn't the city have more rag selection for them? A magazine dedicated to overweight women appeared in stores, named *Big Beautiful Woman*, in lieu of *Fat Lazy Slob*. For sheer make believe, the weight control advertising pages of Family Weekly targeted at the distaff ranks would have done Hans Christian Andersen proud. "Eat Fat Destroyer Foods Till You Groan and Still Lose Weight." "Lifetime Freedom from Fat with Doctor's Amazing 'Coffee-off' Program." "We Were Identical Twins...until Slim-Skins reduced my sister 17 inches in 25 minutes!" "Burn Away More Fat Each 24 Hours Than If You Ran 14 Miles A Day!"

Let's get real, ladies, said University of Michigan physical education professor Charles Kuntzleman: "Unfortunately some women avoid vigorous physical exercise because of a socialized bias against it. American cultural patterns tend to overprotect women and discourage them from physical activity after puberty." And especially after driver education. Kuntzleman advised gals and guys alike to get walking, and "Look at your physician's waistline. If it seems too big don't trust his exercise advice."(77)

Bloated kids worried Harvard nutrition scientist Jean Mayer: "Every farmer worth his salt knows that the best way to fatten an animal is to feed it and keep it penned up. I'm afraid that this is just what our society is doing to far too many of our young people."(78) Mayer's study found that fat kids didn't eat any more than thin ones, they just exercised less. They also got razzed in school, as one Port Huron girl heard: "Fatty, fatty, 2 by 4, can't get through the kitchen door!" 60% of American schoolgirls had been on a diet by the time they left high school.

Medical quackery subjected underexercised St. Clair County schoolboys to special abuse through the galloping fraud of "attention deficit hyperactivity disorder." Too bored and restless with unused energy to sit still in schoolrooms, these kids were drugged into submission through the combined offices of misguided and incompetent doctors, teachers, and parents. One prominent Port Huron pediatrician prescribed the drug Ritalin for 80% of the hundreds of children he examined for this fantasy ailment. School performance sagged along with the physicality of children: "the reading, writing and computational skills of American students from elementary school through college are now in a prolonged and broad scale decline unequaled in U.S. history," reported the *Los Angeles Times*.(79) Some of the 25% of students who dropped out of Port Huron schools barely could read at a third grade level.

Young and old alike nowadays suffered from "exercise deficit disorder" if you asked St. Clair County centenarian John Rahbein. "My father, sister and myself would do our chores, walk seven miles to my older brother's and there we bound all of his wheat by hand. That's healthy. That's 'medicine.'" Pedestrians got a comical, and not very exaggerated, endorsement from humorist Art Buchwald, thanks to the gasoline shortage. "For years people thought of a Pedestrian as someone who couldn't afford a car. The entire economy was based on reducing the Pedestrian population of the country. Those who couldn't be shamed into buying an automobile were run over to teach them a lesson. Our biggest problem [now] is teaching people how to walk again. Most adult Americans have forgotten how, and children have never known. It's actually quite simple, and most of them get the hang of it in a week."(80)

Funny stuff, but American publishers put out 7 new books in 1979 alone on the benefits of walking, just as though it were a new discovery: *The Complete Book of Walking, The Walking Book, Walk!, The Wonderful World of Walking, Walking!* So thoroughly had the automobile distorted the perception of distances and rudimentary human locomotion in America that one local pedestrian he nicknamed Walkin' Bob Tucker left Jerry Brown well-near awestruck. What had Walkin' Bob, a salesman for the Mueller Brass Company, done to win this sobriquet? Had he walked across America in 80 days like Edward Weston? Had he marched from Alaska to Chile like Andy Horujku? Or done the Appalachian Trail like Emma Gatewood? No, Tucker built his legend by Walking! back and forth to work at Mueller's every day. Five miles round trip. Less even than the Jefferson Minimum.

"For nearly 40 years Tucker has been the topic of conversation by people in Port Huron as the man who walks to work," wrote Brown in wonderment. "They say there isn't an inch of Port Huron he hasn't walked...I'd like to accompany Walkin' Bob one of these mornings," added Brownie wistfully, as though writing about Johnny Appleseed. Tucker never had owned the absolute necessity of a car, either. He disliked what he'd seen happening up close and personally in Port Huron, the destruction and rearrangement done at the behest of the car culture, and the ghastly results appreciable only by a pedestrian. "I've really seen the face of the city change, and it's been with mixed emotions," said Bob diplomatically. "I resent dark streets and parking lots where lights are being wasted. I'm not opposed to progress but I don't believe concrete (is) a step in the right direction. Personally, I'd rather see a tree than a stone."(81)

Pedestrian Helen Endlich vented some unmixed emotions about what she saw these days:

Today – 1976 – our sidewalks are in sad disrepair. Some property owners build new ones, the majority just leave them cracked, some so bad that much of the cement is gone, the grass has grown higher than the sidewalk...after every rain the walks are flooded...(once) sidewalks were kept clean of snow by the city with a man behind a horse drawn plow. Now we have "progressed" to none at all. Why should not the sidewalks be kept plowed by the city as well as the streets? (82)

A brief, imaginative throwback to the Port Huron of 1900 demonstrated that it wouldn't take much to revive the commercial power of pedestrianism. When a sidewalk sale closed a portion of Main Street to traffic, the result surpassed every expectation. It produced "an unbelievable mob," according to Mosher's Jewelry store. "It's about time they gave the streets to the people," offered a shopper, and the proprietor of Diana's Sweet Shoppe called it "the best thing possible for business." For a day or two, Port Huron relearned the spatial rule that one less parked car makes room for 20 more pedestrians, one reason why a carless city seemed so much larger. And its citizens so much more attentive. A similar revelation overtook Floyd Bernard when he joined a Bicentennial walking tour around Port Huron: "...going to and coming from these places by automobile gives small chance to notice much else along the way. It is an intensity tour just to window shop in the downtown area. A stroll around the stores almost always reveals changes that one hasn't noticed before."(83)

If only America had exploited that thought. But ignorance still meant bliss to plenty of pedestrian-hating drivers out there in the 1970's. To them the solution to the energy crisis meant getting rid entirely of traffic impediments like walkers. Algonac mother Rose Shagena didn't understand the example of Walkin' Bob, the appeal of the Sidewalk Sale, or the joke from Buchwald: "I have told (my children) that if they ever get hit by a car while on the street it is their fault. The roads were made for cars." The requirement that drivers at all times must be able to avoid other travelers legally on the roads might as well have been ancient myth to the destroyers of 350 Michigan pedestrians in 1978.

No, not everyone on foot in Port Huron received the respect accorded Walkin' Bob Tucker:

An aged man was observed trying to cross the street at Main and Water Monday noon. He was using a cane. Moving slowly, he had just made the middle of the street when the light changed. Immediately the horns started blowing. Flustered and perhaps exhausted, the man put his free hand on the hood of a car. And the horns kept sounding. Finally the man slumped to the street and started crawling the rest of the way on his hands and knees. Several Times Herald *printers, out for lunch, saw the man's plight and ran to his rescue. They were nearly run down before they reached the man and were able to assist him to the other side of the street. And still the horns kept blowing.* (84)

"Why are people like this?" high school student Bonnie Thayer wanted to know, her young conscience as yet uncoarsened by the answer. It was a necessity.

Chapter 11. 1981-1990: Leave The Real World Behind

What does it all mean, this place called AutoWorld?

– Flint Journal, 1984

Some people didn't find America's real auto world amusing enough, so they built an amusement park version in the 1980's just a few dozen dangerous miles west of Port Huron across Highway 21. The massive General Motors fortune that Charles Mott had left behind in his Mott Foundation helped bankroll the world's largest indoor entertainment complex in "Flint, Michigan: The City That Wouldn't Die," as the press sometimes now called that community. On the former site of a riverside sawmill that had belonged to Billy Durant's grandpa stood a derelict 6,000-seat auditorium originally built in downtown Flint in 1929 with GM workers' donations. The Industrial Mutual Association auditorium served as a notable Flint civic venue in good times and bad for five decades before closing in 1979. Now, a team of designers and a battalion of construction workers attacked it, and armed with $70 million reincarnated it as "AutoWorld: A place for people who dream, design & drive cars. Leave the Real World Behind."

What an interesting choice of expression by the promoters: Leave the real world behind! Hadn't that been the original purpose of the automobile in the first place? Wasn't it still? As Chrysler put it: *Somewhere out there is a place you've only dreamed of finding. So don't hold back. Find that place in our Dodge Power Ram 50.* But now here was a friendly invitation to leave the auto-ravaged landscape of America behind and get some relief in a still higher plane of car fantasy. We might ask whether the real world still existed at all underneath the automobile shambles, but that's probably pushing the philosophical significance of AutoWorld past its carrying capacity. All the organizers would say for sure was that they had packed the 300,000 square-foot center with hip attractions expected to generate some honest fun.

A 3-story tall, transparent moving model of an automobile engine greeted patrons at the door of AutoWorld. Moving, not working, so it didn't have a 3-story appetite for gasoline, or pump out 3 stories worth of noise or exhaust, which on that scale would have cleared AutoWorld out in one quick hurry. Next came a multimedia version of a car assembly line, called the "Magical, Musical, Motorcar Machine," on which one saw motor vehicles built somewhat fancifully without the bothersome real world details of speedups, overtime, retooling, recalls, layoffs, strikes, injuries, etc. Get ready for excitement on "The Great Race" ride, a salute to the world's #1 spectator sport, auto racing: "...you'll feel yourself barreling down the straightaway at Indy, exploding down a drag strip, dodging cars in a demolition derby, and white-knuckling the Grand Prix street course at Monte Carlo." This concept probably didn't go far enough; why not feel yourself getting killed in a race crash like Mark Donohue, and winning a $20 million posthumous lawsuit as a result?

Admittedly nothing in The Great Race compared with a civilian white-knuckling his way down an ice-covered expressway at 55 mph, or angrily exploding in a traffic jam at 0 mph, but those thrills really belonged in "The Humorous History of Automobility," another spot to get taken for an AutoWorld ride. Elsewhere, a specially built example of that popular new innovation, the computer video game, allowed patrons the chance to simulate honest-to-goodness drunk driving. Twenty or so cars designated as "classics," though no different fundamentally from any others, posed here and there around AutoWorld, staged in jokey scenes of Auto Americana: the drive-in hot dog stand, the gas station, a day at the auto-cluttered beach, and so on. AutoWorld's mascot, a banjo-playing robot named Fred the Carriageless Horse, and a movie dedicated simply to *Speed*, shown on a six-story high screen, also played their parts in the 'World.

The operators of AutoWorld confidently predicted that 900,000 patrons per year would pay $8.95 each to leave the real world behind for five hours. A cinch. "You don't put a $70 million project together on a wing and a prayer," bragged one.(1) Self-assurance ran so high that they even paid condescending tribute to Flint's pre-automobile past, and put under the AutoWorld dome some re-created 19th Century homes and streets, a Chippewa Indian camp, a version of Governor Crapo's sawmill, and a Durant horse cart like the one that had transformed Flint into "Vehicle City" in the first place. They installed a simulated Flint River, although the real one flowed just past AutoWorld's front door. For nostalgic entertainment, a barbershop quartet, jugglers, and other street performers populated the indoor village.

The *Flint Journal* newspaper made just one serious objection to AutoWorld: it required "a lot of walking" to take in.(2) Others felt AutoWorld's mixture of raucous car celebration with allusions to life before automobiles might not provoke the desired reaction. As historian George May had pointed out, those quieter bygone days almost always seemed more attractive in retrospect than the automotive present: "...when one compares the descriptions of a town like Flint in the 1880's, with its tree-lined streets and leisurely small-town atmosphere, with the reality of Flint the factory town of today, one cannot help but wonder what history's final judgment will be."(3)

While not all the auspices read fair, Michigan Governor James Blanchard stoutheartedly proclaimed his faith in AutoWorld at its opening in 1984, "I believe today is the rebirth of the great city of Flint." "No longer will Flint bring to mind a gray industrial image of smokestacks," added Mayor James Sharp, a sharp turnaround indeed in America's former love affair with smokestacks.(4) At last the gates swung open. Nobody wondered for long about history's final judgment on AutoWorld. To use an expression suitable for The Great Race, the park crashed and burned in the first turn. Attendance never came close to projections, and within six months the whole works shut down.

Awkwardly, the closing came one day before a big story appeared in *Family Weekly,* describing AutoWorld to Port Huron readers as "The Symbol of Flint's Revival." The title at least proved to be all too accurate. The revival of this auto-cursed city went nowhere fast, and another big renewal project, a "festival marketplace," for which a good part of downtown Flint had been demolished, also collapsed in short order. A couple of attempts to resuscitate AutoWorld in the following months did no better. As an automobile lemon it towered almost as high as the Edsel, and carried what passed for the world's biggest new car loan. Flint's city treasury found itself on the hook for $360,000 in annual payments for 20 years to cover AutoWorld's construction debts and maintenance costs. The Mott Foundation paid a bruising $1.3 million per year for the same purposes. Within five years of its brief, backfiring life, AutoWorld's losses totaled $40 million.

Whatever had possessed AutoFlint to try such a crack-brained scheme in the first place? Well, town fathers thought something extravagant had to be done to try to get the city back on its feet. Inflation, oil prices, and the recurring habit of automobile overproduction all had put the American car industry back on the ropes by the beginning of the 1980's. U.S. car output and sales fell to their lowest point in 20 years, when 5.5 million domestically-built vehicles sold during the 1982 model year. That once had been a lot of wheels, but now weren't enough to turn a profit. As part of the USA's huge trade deficit, 2.1 million import car sales took a big chunk of the 1982 market. Japan, with a cost advantage of $2,000 each, shipped 1.8 million vehicles to America, pushing aside in the process U.S. workers by the hundreds of thousands.

That meant 17% unemployment in Michigan, the worst in America. Flint's jobless rate stood at 23%, the worst of the worst. National newspaperwoman Ellen Goodman looked into the situation at the Flint welfare office, and found a lot of broke autoworker families, weighed down with clutter and debt that had piled up way beyond any real material needs. "These are people who have bought homes and cars, maybe two of them...washing machines...dishwashers... snowmobiles...lawn tractors...cabins up north. What they have not got is work."(5) With luck, Flinters on the dole received $450 per month for a family of four, about one quarter of an autoworker's normal pay. AutoDetroit looked kinda sad too these days with 20% unemployment, property tax revenues falling, and the Renaissance Center stores two-thirds empty. Detroit couldn't even afford to collect 2 million unpaid parking tickets, worth $15 million. The Ford Motor Company folks at the RenCen owed $20,000 of those tickets.

In the Thumb, St. Clair County endured 18% unemployment, which meant 10,000 people without work. Several Port Huron area businesses rolled over and croaked. St. Clair Rubber Company, an auto parts firm which went all the way back to the Wills Sainte Claire era, died at age 65. The gasping Prestolite wire factory laid off 300. So did many more parts plants all over the region. The aptly-named Lowell Driver, manager of one of these concerns, said, "It's disastrous. It's never been this bad before." The considerable ripple effect of all this through the Port Huron economy permanently knocked out some downtown retailers and pushed two shopping centers into receivership.

At the end of the previous decade, the Federal Reserve System's Chairman Paul Volker had embarked on a kill-or-cure program of tight interest rates to get the country's runaway inflation under control. Now, this pushed new car loan rates as high as 21% at Bob Fox Chevrolet in Port Huron, one of the five new car dealers left in town. Bob had to downsize right quick, lay off 40 people, auction off 50 cars, and eventually give the Chevy franchise to somebody else. The fact that millions of American households during this period actually paid these loan shark-type rates to purchase depreciating assets like new automobiles, at an average price of $9,200, on an average annual per person pay of $16,000, mustered pretty strong evidence of just how far wrong the country had gone on the subject of transportation. Only the large number of two-income families made these transactions possible at all. Volker's choke hold finally had its intended effect after a grueling recession, and inflation retreated to less than 4% in 1983, or about the same level which had triggered the Nixonian panic in the first place a dozen years earlier. Car financing rates then fell back as low as 2.9% by 1986.

The decision by President Ronald Reagan a week after his 1981 inauguration to fully decontrol the price of oil helped dispel petroleum shortages in AutoAmerica, as did the 2 million barrels per day saved through higher gas mileage requirements on cars. (6) In their eagerness to cash in, domestic and foreign producers poured so much petroleum into the American market that prices declined at one point during the decade to $7 per barrel, and gasoline prices in Port Huron, from a peak of $1.50 a gallon in 1981, slid to less than 90 cents by 1986. Together these factors, cheaper money and plenty o' gas, triggered another parabolic boom in the automobile industry.

The good times began again in 1983, and while they lasted set new sales records. Sixteen million new cars and light trucks left the showrooms in 1986. Big cars came back into vogue. The average new car price reached $14,000. Big 3 profits in 1988 cleared $11 billion. America now owned more cars than it had drivers.(7) Ecstasy! But the party, as always, ran its course. In 1990 another war in the Middle East, the return of $40 per barrel oil, and higher gas prices than ever, sent carmakers into the dumps again. They pronounced the 14 million sales year in '90 a "slowdown." For seat of the pants thrills, this real world business saga left AutoWorld behind.

What seemed at first to be a personal catastrophe – getting the boot from the Ford Motor Company presidency by Henry Ford II in person in our last chapter – turned out to be the best thing that ever happened to Lee Iacocca. His charged-up personality gained full sway at Chrysler Corporation during this decade, and he used near-dictatorial powers to reshape the company his way. Iacocca suffered some pretty bleak first months at Chrysler, marked by immense losses. He cut the company in half, bid adieu to half its work force, and closed or consolidated 20 factories. Clutching at straws, he even offered a 30 day money back guarantee on Chrysler cars, and approached the FMC about a merger, unsuccessfully.(8) Fate had determined to free Lido forever from the clutches of the Ford family.

Iacocca took to appearing on television as Chrysler's #1 pitchman in its commercials, the first top auto executive ever to do so. His enthusiastic razzmatazz rapidly made him the most recognizable and popular businessman in the country. It seemed as if an especially dynamic and personable car salesman had crowded through the TV right into the viewer's home. When the tide turned for Chrysler, Iacocca received full credit for it, and huge salary packages to boot – $20 million in 1986 alone. "We see him as walking across water," Chrysler dealer Dick Huvaere told the *Times Herald* about his savior. Iacocca's autobiography became a best seller, and he toyed with the idea of running for U.S President, *a la* Henry Ford the First.

None of this happened because Iacocca made commercial appeals any more factual than those of other car companies:

The Chrysler LeBaron series. Nobody has anything like them. Not Ford, not GM, not the imports. I challenge you to compare their quality and technology with anything that comes out of Germany or Japan. No cars are perfect, but these come pretty close. Drive 'em... If you don't agree they're the best Chryslers ever made, the best America has to offer at a sensible price, then I'm in the wrong business.

401

Belying the Chrysler chairman's promises, 60% of American car engineers now admitted the inferiority of their own products to foreign brands. One-third of these disloyalists planned to buy imports. "U.S. cars have a poverty stricken appearance," groused one, "flimsy construction, inadequate transmissions, and engines, and idiot lights."(9) One of Iacocca's sales successes, the minivan, required 10 miles of assembly lines with 1,837 stations, each point an opportunity for something else to go wrong.(10) In any case, all cars came from rehashed designs, admitted Chrysler's big guy. "These days," said Iacocca," 'new' cars are an illusion."(11)

Back at the FMC, the company operated for the first time ever without Ford family guidance in the executive offices. Henry the Second and Iacocca had been replaced in the top jobs by much lower profile men, Philip Caldwell and Donald Peterson. At first the pair did some heavy recessionary cost cutting of their own: ditching 7 plants and 64,000 employees.(12) But they next achieved a sales breakthrough in the 80's with a very minor reintroduction of streamlined design. Their simple decision to round off a few corners on the industry's standard boxy car shape struck people with little background in auto history as a triumph of imagination and daring. By such trivialities did fortunes and careers rise and fall in Auto World.

The usual dosage of Ford promotional claptrap attended the debut of the round car: *Its sophisticated shape not only permits it to move easily through the air but also helps it to hold the road.* Spurred on by the heavy sales of "jelly bean" shaped cars (GM's opinion) or "potato" shaped (Chrysler's), the FMC started making more money annually than 'Generous' Motors, $5.3 billion in 1988.(13) That warmed the cockles of every heart in the expanding Ford family. Caldwell wisely retired in 1985 in their good graces. Drunk with power, to exaggerate some, the expansion-happy Peterson bought up the English sports car makers Jaguar and Aston Martin, and then the Hertz Rent-a-Car company. He built Ford's financing business into the second biggest money firm in the country. Mistakenly, he then tried crossing lances with two young Fords, Edsel II and William Ford, Jr., on the FMC board of directors. This last act put him into the bad graces of the family, which as always meant a ticket to the ejection seat at Ford. Peterson departed under a cloud in 1990.

For General Motors, the 1980's by and large belonged to Chairman Roger Smith, a diminutive, unprepossessing accountant who somehow acquired the knack for attracting attention he just as soon would have done without. It was Smith who introduced an entirely unnecessary 6th GM car brand, Saturn, which required construction of a $2.5 billion factory on 2,700 rural acres near America's Mule Capital – Spring Hill, Tennessee. It was Smith whom the public and press blamed for bulldozing 1,600 homes and businesses to build a new Cadillac factory in Detroit – leveling a Catholic church for a parking lot in the process – a plant subsidized by the government to the tune of $325 million. It was Smith who caught the flak for ordering the closure of 11 other General Motors factories during a major retrenchment late in the decade. And it was Smith who unwillingly headlined a popular, sarcastic documentary motion picture, *Roger and Me,* which portrayed him as the wrecker of the city of Flint.

This last beef came from filmmaker Michael Moore, a man with Flint family ties to GM and the United Auto Workers union that went right back to the 1937 sitdown strike. *Roger and Me* stigmatized Smith for the permanent dismissal of 30,000 Flint auto workers, and the resulting near collapse of the city's economic and social structure.

402

Item: the film's premiere took place in the suburb of Burton because no more theaters operated in Flint proper. Item: *Money* magazine had tagged Flint at the worst place to live in America, and not just because of no movie theaters. As far as Smith's responsibility went, the producers might just as well have indicted Billy Durant. For decades General Motors had said "Jump" and Flint had asked "How high?" leading to the present set of circumstances. The fact hadn't dawned on Michael Moore or much of anybody else yet that the sooner Flint shed itself of the automobile industry altogether the sooner the city could achieve some kind of stability. *Goodbye and Good Riddance* might have been a more appropriate theme for Moore's epic, but he remained as blind as Smith to the automobile's ultimate destructiveness.

As the FMC had demonstrated, style not substance still ruled the roost in the Motor City's design studios in the 80's, despite the magical, musical assurances of the Ford people:

From the folks in engineering
To the people in design
From the factories to the showrooms
To the people on the line
We say you're going to love the quality.
Ford!
Quality is Job One.

In fact, so many quality issues dogged the Big 3 that on one occasion they announced five recalls in one day, which summoned a total of 4 million vehicles back to the barn for bad axles, brakes, distributors, fuel leaks, and wheel misalignment. Forget quality; General Motors' chief of chic Chuck Jordan said Job One was, "When it hits the road it has got to have emotional appeal. You've got to look at that thing and say: 'Wow! I want it, I want it.'"(14) Cadillac General Manager John Gerstenburger seconded that emotion, when he announced plans for a $50,000 model: "The Allante is an image, a dream. It will mosty be bought on emotion, rather than how much it costs."(15) "I have gasoline in my bloodstream," emoted Pontiac's chief stylist Terry Henline, who lived in Port Huron, and commuted 100 miles daily to his drawing board at the GM Tech Center.

For individual car buyers (GM's or anybody's), if your "I want it, I want it" feelings cooled later and you decided that because of the car's numerous defects and mechanical problems you didn't want it, well, marry in haste, repent at leisure. No returns. Just go ahead and wrestle with the manufacturer about who paid what under the vehicle's limited warranty, such as the $100 deductibles per repair visit. To redress this imbalance, California's legislature passed a law giving the buyer of any brand of lemon his money back, or a new car from the manufacturer. They defined a lemon as a car with a major defect that either hadn't been fixed in 4 tries, or required 30 days in the shop during the first year after purchase. Governor Jerry Brown (no relation to the Port Huron writer) sipped a glass of lemonade, ha-ha, as he signed this bill. Michigan followed suit with its own lemon law, though this version provided for an arbitrated settlement to give the industry every chance to weasel.

Lemons notwithstanding, when the motor industry's sales fortunes improved, as so often in the past, it triggered increased aggression in advertising, powered in General Motors' case by a $1 billion per year ad budget.(16) Other automakers also spent plenty to get a word in edgewise:

403

Margaret: *My palms use to sweat when I had to get on the highway. Now with my Camry V-6 I just PUNCH it.*
Passengers: *Yeah! PUNCH it, Margaret!*
Chorus: *My Toyota, I love it!*
Margaret: *We just fell in love with life in the fast lane.*

Mercury Cougar. Just because it's reshaped doesn't mean it's reformed...the heart of something ferocious still beats under the hood.

"Lighter, leaner, and meaner is the general rule for '85," ran another promotional headline. Lighter and leaner, true: the average weight of a passenger car decreased from 3,800 pounds in 1975 to 2,700 in 1985.(17) Flimsy lightweights made up 40% of the cars on the road. When it came to meaner, heavy still ruled the roost. In collisions with heavier gas guzzlers, riders in skimpies like the 2,200 pound Ford Escort, the FMC's latest Universal Car, died 8 times more often than their opponents. "It's my privilege as an American," said Thumb resident Alan Loding about his heavyweight Lincoln. "I drive one because I can afford it."(18) This suggested a possible epitaph for less privileged accident victims: "Couldn't afford enough car."

Alarmed, more people began to see it Loding's way, and dug deeper into their pockets to buy the heavier, bulkier, semi-armored jeep descendants miscast as Sports Utility Vehicles or SUV's. "Dealers are selling weight," explained Lee Iacocca, "they're selling 'put a lot of iron around you' for safety reasons. So what if you only get eight miles per gallon and your SUV pollutes like hell? Your children are safe."(19) The same held for pickup trucks. The industry got away with this because of the lower gas mileage requirements for SUV's and pickups under the "light trucks" definition. Heavier/meaner also meant more profitable. It cost only $500 more to build a standard sized car than a subcompact, but the former sold for thousands more, and dealers made a 25% margin on them, compared to 17% on midgets.(20) This disparity gave more room to build phony discounts and rebates into prices of larger models, too.

Averaging the leaner with the meaner, operating an automobile required about 50 cents per mile, $4,000-$5,000 per year for a new one, even when the thing functioned perfectly. Three quarters of new car buyers sold or traded in their vehicles before paying off the loans, which lasted as long as five years, netting them more losses. 22% of personal income went to car support, while the national savings rate fell below 2%.(21) It was all part and parcel of an orgy of post-recession acquisitiveness that brick by brick raised still higher the U.S. edifice of heedless debt. That tower reached as high as $4 trillion in household IOU's and a $3 trillion national government debt by the end of the decade.(22) Proportionately, the country consumed twice as much stuff as in the 50's. "America has spent too much, borrowed too much, saved too little," warned ex-President Gerald Ford when he spoke at Port Huron's Town Hall series, though as a true Michigander he didn't make "get rid of your car" part of his message.

The relentless increase of the trade deficit seemed unstoppable as well, and St. Clair County's car customers forcefully debated the relative merits of foreign versus American wheels. Janet Barnum called her Pontiac a pile of junk because she'd taken it into Cawood's six times for leak repairs. Plus, she said, the valve lifters had failed on the typically lousy GM engine. Hold on there, replied Fred Bauer, he found American cars more comfortable, reliable, solid, serviceable. He'd owned an import lemon which wouldn't work and couldn't be repaired. Why not just skip both foreign and domestic alternatives, suggested columnist Art Buchwald: "...the sooner it gets out the better I'll feel about it. I don't drive a car."(23) Buchwald ran some risk in admitting this. More auto crackpots than ever looked at the consumption of cars, especially American cars, as the main qualification for good citizenship, or rather good consumership, now the same thing.

The UAW got into the argument, and swore not to support any political candidate who drove a foreign car, especially Japanese versions. Port Huron's Congressman David Bonior threatened to can any of his 35 staffers he caught driving an import. His pal Congressman John Dingell of Detroit ranted about America's yearly $150 billion trade imbalance: "The foreigners are skinning us alive with all sorts of unfair trade practices." Yet, Japanese car sales continued to grow, reaching 2.3 million skins in the USA by mid-decade, despite an insurance industry report that Japan built 12 of the 15 unsafest car models on the road.(24) Finally, to take the onus off themselves, the Japanese firms – Toyota, Honda, Nissan, Mazda – set up their own auto assembly plants in America. To be fair, U.S. carmakers had complicated this issue by using foreign parts in their own products. Parts like Ford's Mexican engines, and the duty-free Canadian-made auto innards imported through Port Huron over the Blue Water Bridge. But putting the matter of auto sickness on a nationality basis dodged the bigger issue. An idiot light should have gone on whenever you climbed into an automobile from any country.

Once a car descended to used vehicle status, patriotic passions cooled a bit. Just be careful of anything on wheels, wrote Jennifer Harsha in the *Times Herald*. Harsha once had worked for Michigan's Attorney General Frank Kelley, and presented her own version of that consumer advice staple, a 20-point checklist for buying a used car, whatever nation it haled from: "Look for breaks in the frame...Make sure the keys fit properly...Look for burnt wires...As you drive let the steering wheel go. Does it veer and pull to one side?"(25) Don't try that steering wheel test on the freeway, incidentally. Other potential pitfalls: jimmied odometer, hard hoses, chipped glass, mismatched paint, bent bumpers, jammed windows, worn carpets, sputtering, shakes, rattles. You could have spent the rest of your life looking for a used car that passed all 20 criteria.

One of the biggest hazards of a used car came from the person trying to sell it to you. Even a spokesman for the industry admitted, "The consumer is such an amateur at buying or negotiating that he can't really distinguish between the ethical and the unethical car salesman." Port Huron's Eagle Chrysler Dodge dealership on a typical day trolled for amateurs with these hooks, lines, and sinkers: "Rock Bottom Prices Now on Every Used Car on Our Lot!" "Extra clean, 1 owner." "Special purchase from Chrysler Corporation." "Loaded, 49,000 miles." "MUST SEE, 36,000 miles." "Like New." The depth finder on Eagle's rock bottom prices ranged from $3,000-$11,000 on listed cars. Nationwide, the typical used car changed hands for $5,400 in 1985.

By the year 2010, "Cars will diagnose their own problems and service themselves automatically," predicted John Diebold, an "authority on technology and management."(26) In the meantime, despite the attempts to bring law-and-order to the automobile repair business of America, plenty of holdups still took place. 60,000 bad mechanic complaints flooded the In-trays of Michigan's regulators per year, and similar reports to a White House consumer hotline outnumbered all others 4 to 1. A survey of Michigan repair shops found only 56% of the test equipment used gave accurate readings. Ball-joint testers did worst, and car owners who came in for unrelated service at deceitful garages always heard an additional earful about the "loss of steering control" awaiting them when their ball joints failed.

The average car owner spent almost $1,100 per year for maintenance of his increasingly complex vehicle. Goodbye to do-it-yourself, said Cawood mechanic Fred Riehl: "You can't use your ears and eyes anymore. It's all computers now and you need special diagnostic equipment. It can be a real nightmare if you don't know what you are doing."(27) The more expensive the car, the greater the maneuvering room for repair crooks. They smiled ear to ear when the most expensive car for sale in Port Huron, a Mercedes Benz, pulled into the shop. A single accoutrement on this vehicle, a Mercedes muffler, cost nearly $1,000. One Port Huron supplier stocked an awe-inspiring 500,000 individual automobile parts for all makes, ready for installation by your dealer's $28/hr mechanics, known collectively as Mr. Goodwrench at General Motors. Officials at City Hall bypassed Mr. Goodwrench, and kept seven full-time mechanics laboring over Port Huron's municipal fleet, everything from road graders to dump trucks to pool cars to the 15 automobiles assigned personally to top city employees. Gerald Bouchard's luxury sedan expenses came to $7,000 per year.

The *Times Herald* did not provide its reporters with Bouchard-style perks, and like many millions of Americans, they found themselves driving limping old cars, as prices outstripped their means. Stories about their travails on the road frequently made distressing reading in the paper. Dave McVety: "traveling...at midnight in a blizzard on icy roads, almost out of gas with a car backfiring and barely moving is not the way to spend a winter vacation." James Irwin on running his used 1973 Oldsmobile, purchased for under $1,000: "I may spend a four-figure sum within a year's time for the gasoline needed to power the 455 cubic inch engine." Bill McMillan:

The worst sound in the world is the thwap, thwap, thwaping of a very flat tire at 6:30 a.m...I tried to ignore the fateful sound by turning up the radio and continuing on. But the sound of ripping rubber turned to grinding steel. I gave up and pulled over. Main Street is not the place to be when your car is kaput. Maniac drivers heading for Detroit pretend the road is a race track... I assessed the damage to my car – a 1976 pile of Bondo [body filler] and rust. There was no safe place to put a jack except under the axle – waaaay under the car. My hat flew down the street and my new gloves tore as I tried to jack up the car. Lugnuts get rusty. I felt like a fool jumping up and down on the long wrench trying to get the buggers off. But the thing got even with me – it bent.(28)

Nothing reduced a modern American woman to the role of damsel in distress faster than a flat tire, or almost any auto mishap for that matter. Reporter Roberta Stevenson elaborated on a woman's breakdown etiquette: Keep the windows closed and the doors locked, attract attention (from inside the locked car somehow), get the car off the road if possible (from inside a locked car?), don't panic. Colleague Michael Benscik suggested that if immobilized in a car in winter, women (and men) should roll up in a ball like a possum and stuff newspapers into their clothes to stay warm while awaiting rescue. Not bad advice, since most wintertime drivers underdressed woefully for the weather in the hostile RealWorld outside their car doors.

What to do when the end came for your Bondo buddy? It might seem like a natural progression, first new then used then rust in peace, but Port Huron car retailers refused absolutely to deal in dead vehicles. If a trade-in couldn't be sold, it went to an auctioneer, and then to parts and scrap operators like Bob Anger, who ran a 14-acre auto dissection and squeeze yard near Port Huron. Bob paid $25-$35 for the husk of a car, picked up 40-50 per week, crushed them, and sold the remains to metal dealers for a healthy profit. He also could acquire auto hulks from the hundreds of vehicles totaled in local accidents per year, or the thousands of informal car junkyards that low IQ types kept on their properties in city and country, in yards, alleys, and fields, scattered promiscuously here and there, across the length and breadth of St.Clair County, often in defiance of blight laws.

Farms were a rich mine of automotive junk. American farmers owned 1.5 trucks on average, and often the half-a-truck rusted away in the barnyard or under a rickety shed. The same with tractors; there were more than two per farm.(29) Port Huron Township grew especially overripe with dilapidated vehicles of all kinds. The township supervisor Robert Lewandowski ran an auto junkyard of his own in competition with Anger, and he felt inclined to be tolerant of sentimental car owners reluctant to part with their metal memories. The 5'1", 280 lb. Anger – practically a poster child for automobile sickness – told Jerry Brown that from the wrecker's viewpoint the older the vehicle the better, the more metal in 'em. Who needed plastic?

Anger wanted nothing to do with old tires, either. Very few people did. The few and far between practical uses for them led to unchecked tire pollution. Tire manufacturers themselves shunned worn out product like the plague. Some entrepreneurs tried shredding tires for re-use as mats, fuel, or building material. Burning sounded like a good bet, to get at the 2.5 gallons of oil in each tire. When 2.5 million old tires ended up in a heap on a lot in Port Huron Township during the 1980's, and as old tires were wont to do, caught fire, they burned for 8 months. A pile of half a million more sat on the ground in Capac after a local tire capping business burned down without, unfortunately, taking its stock with it.

Laborers on car assembly lines in the 1980's didn't concern themselves with how the product met its end, in car crushers and tire dumps. They didn't think about much of anything. Unlike the AutoWorld version, no magic or music characterized the real world line, according to UAW man Larry Weber, who polished 78 finished Chryslers per hour as they exited the works. "It's the most monotonous, boring job you'll ever get [but] you show me an unskilled, uneducated worker in America who does as well as I do, I'd be surprised."(30) Larry made $11.54 per hour plus $11 in benefits. With overtime, his take home amounted to $22,000 annually.

Mr. Car Polisher and his colleagues cost entirely too much, in the Big 3's opinion, and efforts quickened to replace more workers with robots. The Japanese followed suit. During one hectic season, Japanese carmaker Mazda decided assembly line mechanism Rachel Lesko didn't function robotically enough and fired her for missing too much work at the company's suburban Detroit plant:

...functioning more like a machine than a human, she screwed bolts onto the frames of passing cars. Every two minutes for 10 hours she fired her vibrating air gun. Within months, Lesko's hands swelled up like bear paws.(31)

Membership in the UAW dwindled by a third during this decade. The same sad stories cropped up again and again about those gone missing from the ranks. Larry and Vivian Davis of Detroit spent two years on layoff from Ford, sold their three cars, and eventually ended up on welfare. Overall, 1.3 million manufacturing jobs disappeared from the auto-devoted states bordering the Great Lakes.

Despite the plain evidence of history before them – an unemployment rate in Port Huron consistently higher than it had been before the Industrial Park ever opened – city officials continued to urge more auto parts makers to move in. 16 of the 22 tenants in the I-park worked in the car field. Governor Blanchard, so badly misled about AutoWorld, now came to Port Huron to hail the opening of four more plants in AutoPartsWorld. These four Port Huron factories, if everything went well, might furnish 400 jobs, but they started life with about a quarter of that number. Not too much later, a top U.S. trade negotiator, Mark Santucci, warned a Port Huron audience that car parts companies in fact wanted to leave the state: "Michigan is not going to grow as a parts maker."

In the slough of the recession during the early 80's unskilled, uneducated people, whom Port Huron schools turned out in abundance, lined up to seek work in these parts factories for $6.26/hour. That might be far less money than Larry Weber made, but look on the bright side, it dwarfed the 90 cents an hour handed to Mexican auto workers. Applicants braved some risks, too, because 3% of Michigan's auto parts workers suffered serious injuries on the job every year. 1,200 prospects crowded the Port Huron unemployment office when a single parts company said it might start hiring. "We'll take anything that's available." "I've got a family to support." "It's a full-time job looking for work," said the jobless, but many prospects had such poor reading and math skills, or drank or used drugs so much, that even parts makers, almost the bottom of the barrel, found them unemployable. Those hired discovered the work to be so stupid and dull that some said flatly they'd rather flip burgers, and left to take up a spatula in Fast Food World.

Monsieur Gerald Bouchard flew to Paris four times in two months to land one of these parts companies, Labauto, instead of spending his time encouraging established firms like Mueller Brass (which since WW2 had shrunk from 4,500 employees to 700) or tending to more mundane matters. Labauto promised 250 jobs, but the French concern opened its doors in Port Huron with only 7 employees. It closed down completely after just 18 months. This left Bouchard looking pretty ridiculous, and so did the closure of the 55 year-old Prestolite automobile wire plant behind his back, throwing out of work its last 180 people (there once had been 1,000) when their jobs moved to Arkansas.

Battling back again, Bouchard rolled out the red carpet for auto carpet maker J.P. Stevens and its 120 jobs. Stevens got a city-paid-for $1 million makeover of a vacant plant, plus a 12-year, 50% tax break. Stevens shipped its carpets by truck to assembly plants in Flint and Detroit, a mere 2-6 hours before workers glued them into new vehicles there. This meant more truck traffic in and out of the I-park to bedevil the sorely-tried southend residents living nearby. Thanks to antics like these, dissatisfaction with the industrial park grew among voters, and in 1989 they crushed a proposal to further expand the park by rubbing out more homes and a nearby athletic field.

Meanwhile, in another part of town, its owner demolished the first-ever auto plant built in Port Huron, the almost forgotten Northern Automobile factory of 1907, used in recent years as everything from an iron foundry to a boat warehouse. To this end all earthly car ventures eventually came. Did anybody remember the Wills Sainte Claire

408

automobile at this point? About 80 units survived of the 14,000 built, prized by a few "Gray Goose" collectors for nothing more than their scarcity. A less nostalgic legacy waited to be cleaned up at the old Wills plant, later the Chrysler depot: some 50,000 cubic yards of paint, solvents, metal, lead, chromium, and construction debris dumped onto 12 acres of ground. Other unpleasant memories of car building lay scattered around the Blue Water Area. America generated a ton of hazardous waste per person per year, and 90% of Michigan's came from car production, including the 1,000 leaking barrels of unused automobile paint found at a private disposal site in Port Huron Township, and 130 barrels of toxic material left behind at the bankrupt St. Clair Rubber Company in Marysville.

It endangered your health while under construction, and the Consumer Federation of America now anointed the completed automobile as the most dangerous everyday item around, beating out cigarettes, alcohol, children's toys, and bicycles, the latter of which would have been considerably safer with no cars around. Nationally, the countable dead in traffic accidents averaged about 900 a week, not including, let's emphasize again, those whom medical science nursed along until they fell outside statistical notice, Levassor deaths. An ungraspable number of millions suffered injuries annually, including 180,000 with brain damage and 5,000 with paralyzing spinal cord crushing or breakage. Traffic accidents in the Thumb cost every man, woman and child the statistical equivalent of about $700 per year, but this figure, like all the rest, couldn't be nailed down precisely, because of under-reportage, and because every estimate included a different set of variables.(32)

This raft of figures impressed Port Huron's Frank Warren enough that he decided that when it came to maintaining a safe and civil society, give him a handgun over a car anytime:

Automobile accidents claimed approximately 45,000 lives last year. Why not ban cars? It would save thousands more lives. Also, cars are used criminally each and every day to commit thousands of crimes. Read your paper. Compare the numbers of cars used illegally by people to the number of handguns used illegally. Cars have it, hands down.
(33)

The press in Detroit did a dance of mourning for 155 people who died in a 1987 air crash at Metro Airport, the second deadliest U.S. air accident ever to that time. That number equaled about five weeks of auto victims in Michigan. 93% of all transportation deaths in America happened in cars.

The typical citizen took part in an auto accident about once every 10 years, which disabled 1 out of 3 at least temporarily. One out of 60 left the real world behind, for good. The leading cause of death for Americans under 35 erased the teenaged Empson sisters, Amy and Heather, and made the *Times Herald* front page one day. Not because of anything especially unusual about the wreck, just the irony that their father Theodore had passed the head-on crash scene on his way home from work without recognizing his girls' vehicle. Famous last crash words also made good front page fodder, as in 27 year-old Kerry "Huck" Steinhaus' case, when he ran into a bridge abutment near Port Huron: "A doomed man pleaded for a passing Samaritan to help free him from the wreckage of his car in the seconds before it burst into flames today. 'To watch a man burn – I felt so totally helpless,'"witness Tom Thornton told Brownie.(34)

The accident toll among young people dismayed government onlookers particularly, because the entire automobile operating system in America – driver's controls, signage, roads, licensing – had been designed for the level of physical and mental ability found in healthy 25 year olds. If *they* couldn't make it in Auto World where did that leave the elderly? In 76 year-old Rosaria Petrice's case it left her sitting in the sporting goods section of the Port Huron Sears store, after she hit the accelerator instead of brakes and roared through a plate glass display window. Apart from the slow decline that wits and flesh were naturally heir to, America's seniors operated their cars under the influence of the 15 prescriptions they each took annually. Furthering the cause of dangerous motorists, the National Association of Driver Educators for the Disabled worked diligently to put more deaf, retarded, paraplegic and quadriplegic jacks and jills to driving, a task even perfectly healthy people couldn't handle with any degree of certainty. "I helped one guy get a driver's license even though he was considered to be legally blind," said association president Bill Ramsey with satisfaction. "In our society...you've just got to be mobile to be able to live anything that resembles a normal life."(35)

The normal life. Ladies and gentlemen, boys and girls of all ages and abilities paraded through the accident reports of the *Times Herald* on a single day's normal life:

A Capac motorist told police he was looking for UFOs when he drove his pickup truck into the side of a house Saturday.

When relatives of hundreds of Michigan residents killed in alcohol related accidents hold statewide vigils tonight, Charles Morris will light one of the candles. His mother died with a friend last February after they were struck by a drunken driver outside an Alcoholics Anonymous dance in Birmingham.

Two women died early today after their car went into the St. Clair River at Champion's Auto Ferry dock on M-29. "They maybe missed the ferry by two minutes, three at the most," Officer Kevin Labuhn said.(36)

After years of debate over whether to curtail a driver's personal freedom to be tossed around or out of a crashing car, Michigan ordered mandatory seat belts for almost everybody in 1985. In effect the government admitted the fact of accident inevitability. Car accidents injured somebody or other in the immediate Port Huron vicinity every day, and most victims didn't wear their seat belts. Port Huron cops dished out 475 tickets for unbuckled belts during the first year of the new law, but only to people they stopped for other offenses. Drivers could not be halted simply for unbuckled belts, and many thumbed their noses at the idea.

Jerry Brown had to be talked into belting up by his 7 year-old granddaughter, "...so you don't fly out the window in an accident." Larry Kearns of Port Huron couldn't be talked into one, and died on his 37th birthday when he drove into a utility pole on the way home from jogging at the Court Rooms North health club. Mr. and Mrs. Wilbur Davidson luckily had their belts buckled when they ran off a freeway; as a result they only suffered broken backs. Looking down memory lane, we find that Wilbur's own father had died in a 1920's auto accident, and it was his grandfather, Wilbur the Elder, who brought the first car to Port Huron, way back in Chapter One.

Seat belts, of course, weren't always feasible on a motor vehicle:

410

Did you see that Globe of Death over there? With a 13 foot diameter it's the smallest globe that anyone rides a motorcycle in anywhere. Would you believe one of the guys' wives stands inside it while they ride around?(37)

Thus did a member of the Shrine Circus describe one of their acts in Port Huron not long before Brownie went to the scene of a Highway 21 motorcycle crash that put the Globe of Death to shame. General Motors designer Daniel Lange and his wife had slammed head-on into the car of a 16 year-old motorist. Upon impact Lange rose from his chopper seat and soared into the path of another car, which dragged him 260 feet. "One of the worst *I've* seen," a sheriff's deputy rated the wreck, though it typified the variety that killed 1,800 motorcyclists per year in the USA. "Investigators are still trying to determine why (the Langes) had to die," wrote Brown philosophically, invoking the theme of malevolent fate stalking the innocent.

Bob Garbutt protested that motorcycles seemed to get nothing but bad press these days, not just because of their risks but because of their widely despised users. We are not a gang, the 40 year-old president of the Port Huron Motorcycle Club emphatically stated, we are middle-aged, middle-class and respectable. Member Bob Hammar, a welding company owner, said please, don't jump to conclusions: "My wife and I have friends who think motorcycles don't even belong on the road. I've even been run off the road a few times. People get the impression that we're a bunch of crazies."(38) A few weeks later 38 suspected crazies on Harley Davidsons, members from an entirely different club with an entirely different outlook, followed the hearse of 23 year-old William "the Demon" Langolf to the cemetery, after he punched out in a cycle crash. "He was a little devil," said one of Langolf's mourners appreciatively. The Demon became the third member of these independents killed in six months.

A new tone entered the public sagas of people mangled but not killed in Port Huron traffic accidents. These victims, to achieve full Heroic Sick People status, must consider themselves *lucky* to have survived the crash at all. Granted, you wouldn't want to take that sort of luck to a casino, but looking on a wreck as a piece of good fortune spared people from facing up to the inherent unworkability of the auto culture. St. Clair County Deputy Sheriff Tim Donnellon nearly lost a leg when his motorcycle collided with a car in downtown Port Huron one night, as the officer rode home from work. After he'd spent nine months in recovery Donnellon told Jerry Brown, "I count myself lucky."(39) In her own bad crackup, Beverly Palmer suffered a left leg broken in two places, several broken ribs, a broken right shoulder, a torn kidney, ruptured intestines, both lungs punctured, a blow to the head that caused some nerve damage, and a bruised heart. "It could have been a lot worse," said Bev.

"Erick Harrison – a profile in courage" was the title of another Brownie pick-me-up. The 17 year-old Harrison had been horribly burned and disfigured in a car wreck which also killed his two parents. After 40 operations, and with the prospect of seven more years of surgery ahead, Harrison had not a bad word to say to Brown about automobiles. "All I can do is make the best of the situation." However, Lady Luck didn't always smile on the driving residents of the Thumb, as she had on Erick. Thirteen people from the modest-sized town of Brown City, about 1% of the population, died in traffic accidents over 15 months. These mishaps ran the gamut: missed stop signs, unmissed trees, drunk drivers, sleeping drivers, head-ons, T-bones; one woman spent more than 2 years in a coma before expiring, etc, etc. "It's just bad luck," sighed State

411

Police Lieutenant Gary Parks.

When luck ran out for three mobile teenagers living a normal life who died in a suburban crash into a tree in St. Clair County, one of their parents had a hard time accepting the spin of the auto roulette wheel: "There must be a lesson in this somewhere." One observer blamed TV and the movies for fostering a lighthearted approach to reckless driving among the young, the idea that "you can run through fences and have a good time." Of course alcohol played its part. After one of their boozed up classmates landed in traction with busted ribs following a crackup, some students at Port Huron High School formed a chapter of Students Against Drunk Driving, SADD.

National SADD president Robert Anastas came to Port Huron to urge parents and offspring to sign a mutual "contract for life."

Kid: *I agree to call you for advice and-or transportation at any hour, from any place, if I am ever in a situation where I have been drinking or a friend or date who is driving me has been drinking.*

Parent: *I agree to come and get you at any hour, any place, no questions asked and no argument...or I will pay for a taxi... I expect we would discuss this situation at a later time.*(40)

Discuss it all you liked, but examplewise no one who owned or operated an automobile could be a good parent. You just infected the next generation. SADD meant well, but only a Students Against Driving contract made any real sense. A month after Anastas' speech Port Huron police broke up a beer-soaked high school graduation house party of 200 students, who fittingly had parked their cars all over a nearby cemetery, and who conked three cops with bottles in the melee.

Not so young but just as impulsive, 35 year-old Port Huron divorcee Wanda Rawlings stopped at five different bars for a snort before heading into a 90 mph crackup that took down four people. Prosecutors stacked four negligent homicide charges on her but the judge tagged Wanda with only 1 year in the county jail, $300 costs, and probation for five years with no driving and no bar-hopping. That compared to the 90 day sentence John Zeros, member of the notorious Zeros clan, served for drunkenly stomping a cat to death in Port Huron. 1 dead cat = 1 dead traffic accident victim. That's how the scale of justice balanced in St. Clair County during the 1980's. A long-time drunk driver himself, Zeros forgot that if you wanted to kill a cat with impunity you just used a car.

"Liberty as I understand it gives me the constitutional right to drink and drive," maintained Port Huronite James Mullins, the day before the following story unfolded in town:

An 82 year-old Port Huron man was injured when he drove his car through his garage into his family room, then backed his car across the street into a neighbor's house. Frederick D. McElroy...was ticketed for drunken driving.(41)

"We've all driven home from the bar or a party a little drunk, haven't we? I have. And how many times have we even joked about it?"(42) A chastened Bill McMillan wrote that after a drunk driver nearly paralyzed his niece with a broken neck. Two-thirds of all

412

fatal traffic accidents in St. Clair County involved alcohol. More than 100 arraignments took place monthly for drunk driving, including the guy Prosecutor Robert Cleland personally placed under citizen's arrest for motoring backwards up the Scenic Highway. And the drunken Clay Township volunteer fireman who rolled over a $120,000 fire truck. Many arrestees were old hands at the game but fresh waves of newcomers kept coming. In theory, first offense fines went as high as $500, plus jail time of as much as 90 days, plus $100 costs. In practice, the courts punished deer poaching more heavily.

"There are definitely too many people drinking and driving in this county. Something has to be done to stop it." Judge Walter Turton's solemn declaration in Port Huron echoed many, many of his predecessors on the bench, with as little result. 60% of drunk drivers pleaded down to impaired driving. 40% were never reported to the Michigan Secretary of State. 86% of those who'd had their licenses revoked restored them again through court appeals. Less than 50% of drunk driving fines were collected. Only 40% of those sentenced to jail actually did time. The jail threat was an empty one because St. Clair County's jail wasn't empty. Even after officials expanded the jail by 40% in size, 140 criminals and suspects stuffed it beyond capacity. When no more bodies could fit in the jail, the extras had to be sent to lockups in adjacent counties at $40 per head per day, exhausting the budget. So judges like Turton often kicked defendants loose without incarceration.

Like many, many of *his* predecessors, Governor Blanchard formed a task force to try to reduce the 800 or so drunk driving deaths in Michigan every year. Simultaneously, Blanchard had to declare state prison overcrowding emergencies as often as twice a year and reduce sentences, which put a lot of drunk drivers back in action again. Under a sentence of 2-5 years for hitting a girl on a bicycle during his third drunk driving offense, St. Clair County's Lewis Byrnes served 46 days. The drunk driving accident toll in America numbered 3 dead and 80 injured every hour.(43) Half the population could count on finding themselves in booze-related traffic crashes during their lifetimes. Police never even tested most of the drivers in fatal driving accidents for alcohol, so as bad as the statistics about this practice looked, they certainly were grossly underestimated.(44) So President Reagan formed a national drunk driving task force.

Task forces didn't prevent 27 bus passengers in Kentucky from suffering the last wreck of their lifetimes in a collision with drunk Larry Mahoney, as he drove his pickup truck the wrong way on I-71, the most spectacular American car crash of the decade. Nor did they dissuade 33 year-old Bettyjane Vanpeolvoorde of St. Clair County, who landed in a mental hospital after drunkenly driving 20 miles through oncoming traffic on I-94, and finally killing 19 year-old Richard Lee as he came home from an amusement park (not AutoWorld). If only task forces had been effective then Thumb resident Joseph Zink would have been as sober as Judge Turton. Instead police arrested the 65 year-old Zink for his 9th drunk driving outing. Again, theoretically, he could have been sentenced to life in prison as a habitual offender. In fact, he got a year in jail, and a lifetime revocation of his license, which only relieved him of the bother of carrying it the next time he drove.

How many drunk drivers took to the road at any one time? Michigan State Police found that 0.5% of the people they checked through sobriety checklanes on the highway had been indulging. Applied to America's 167 million drivers this figure suggested a potential of 800,000. One of them, Port Huron City Attorney Dean Luce, had enough presence of mind and experience with such cases to flee the scene of his drunken fender-bender that injured two people, and go home to sober up. Police tracked him down. "I blacked out," Luce told them at first, then he pleaded guilty.

Jerry Brown mounted up for a tour of duty with sheriff's deputies on special patrol for drunk drivers. Officers Joel Davies and Warren Head pulled in more than 200 per year, including one they found sleeping in his underwear in the middle of Highway 21. This man thought he had arrived home, undressed, and gotten into bed when he lay down on the asphalt. Most boozer cruisers were 30-50 years old, and men outnumbered women by an astounding 18 to 1! Davies and Head had learned never to go easy: "The pair once arrested an 83-year-old man and took some heat from fellow officers when they would not give him a break. Three months later the same man, now 84 but just as drunk, drove across a center line and was killed when he hit another car head-on..."(45)

Alcohol being a depressant, in fact auto life in general being a depressant, the number of drivers dejected unto death still presented an unaddressable problem. Cops at one point figured on about two suicide crashes per six months in St. Clair County. Port Huron psychiatrist Dr. Frederick Greiling told the *Times Herald* that he'd treated a number of patients "who said that because of depression they had contemplated driving into the river, a tree, or an abutment of some kind." Trains also made handy end-it-all implements, according to the Michigan Railroad Association's J. Allen Gross. "Engineers all tell the same story. The motorist will stop at the crossing. As [the engineer] nears the crossing the motorist will look him right in the eye and accelerate in front of his train and kill himself." One engineer from Detroit polished off seven drivers that way. "It's caused him a lot of emotional problems."(46)

The car wash industry thought it might be able to help out pschologically troubled drivers. The owners of Port Huron's new "detailing" shop looked at it this way: "The automobile more than any other physical possession is an extension of a person's personality. Detailing meets the beauty shop needs of your car." After all, who'd want to run a sparkling clean car into a train? The detailers offered to superwash your personality top to bottom for $130. Another alternative path to good driving mental health came from video game maker Nolan Bushnell. Echoes of AutoWorld: Bushnell had under development a super realistic racing car video that worked out a player's demons "emotionally," with steering wheel in hand, even to the point of smelling the exhaust. Look for it soon in one of the four video game arcades doing business in Port Huron, or a home version on the increasing numbers of home TV and computer consoles.

No lawsuit video games had been invented yet, so plaintiffs filed thousands of real world traffic accident torts in Michigan yearly. Settlement in these suits averaged $11,000, but as always, wide disparities existed in how much loot changed hands. A full set of broken legs, wrists and hands won Robert Friederichs $635,000 in a Port Huron case against the elderly gal he'd collided with. Martin Esquibel only received $49,000 for the death of his wife Ann and 19 year-old son Tony in a wreck on the south side of town, for which the other driver got a year in jail for manslaughter. Suing an institution with deep pockets raised the stakes. Nicole McDonald's mother wanted a steep $5 million after a Marine City school bus crushed the 5 year-old girl on her birthday. Nicole had been trying to fetch some papers from under the vehicle, as indicated by the tire tracks found on her lunch box. The three children of Esther Fisher of Yale won $2.8

million from the public treasury over the lack of stop signs at the intersection where she'd been killed.

Some accident cases showed amazing stamina in the courts. After 17 years a St. Clair County action finally concluded in 1981 with an award of $33,000, which forced the loser into bankruptcy. Other legal battles were byzantine beyond belief. Plaintiff Douglas Hamm sued himself over the traffic death of his wife Carol and injuries to their son Gregory. Mr. Hamm had had nothing to do with the crash, which occurred when Mrs. Hamm plowed into a semi on Highway 21. But this sue-yourself gambit offered the best way to squeeze as much cash as possible out of the insurance company. In court or out, imagination played an important part in making an auto insurance claim of any kind, if you believed the statements filed with one insurance company.

– A pedestrian hit me and went under my car.
– In my attempt to kill a fly, I drove into a telephone pole.
– The pedestrian had no idea what direction to turn, so I ran over him.
– The telephone pole was approaching. I was attempting to swerve out of its way when it struck my front end.
– I saw a slow-moving sad-faced old gentleman as he bounced off the hood of my car.
– I pulled away from the side of the road, glanced at my mother-in-law, and headed over the embankment.(47)

Auto insurance rates across America doubled during the 80's. Policy holders paid an average national premium of $486 per year. Apart from injury and property damage coverage (recommended for $300,000 per accident), wise owners kept up insurance for theft, just as in Louis Weil's day, since nowadays nogoodniks stole one million vehicles per year in the U.S. Fraud accounted for a third of car thefts. Police arrested 78,000 Michiganders for boosting autos in 1984. Three-quarters of the suspects had been arrested for this crime before, but, here again, Michigan didn't have enough prison space to hold them. Auto thieves wouldn't even let Michigan Attorney General Frank Kelley alone; they grabbed his car twice.

A single small group of ambitious St. Clair County thieves took 10 cars per month in Detroit and netted $5,000 apiece for them. Police found another wild bunch in the county with parts of 30 different stolen vehicles spread around their chop shop. Port Huron car thieves held nothing sacred, not even the souped-up American Motors subcompact treasured by Tyler and Diane Crockett's son: "Someone has seen this car and knows where it is hidden...a bright orange Gremlin with the name GRUMPY painted on the doors in gold letters. We hope someone will help bring GRUMPY home."(48)

Since this decade proved to be a turning point in Port Huron's history, it's fair to ask just what prospect did downtown Port Huron present to Grumpy's abductor as he drove his hot car around during the mid-1980's? Depended on your point of view. The new owner of Sperry's department store also took an automotive tour, and liked what he saw, at least from a moving car: "I drove around and didn't see any empty stores, saw people moving around downtown, the boats, the grass, and said this city is too good to be true." Though still gripped by parking paranoia, and mall fear, business owners made every effort to pull together, as when they sponsored a charitable event, the ultimate sacrifice, "Park Free Today In Downtown Port Huron." And they commissioned a new

415

radio jingle: *Downtown Port Huron, Downtown Port Huron / More shops, more shows, more people you know / There's just no topping downtown shopping.* "We now have an alive downtown," said Chamber of Commerce President Miles Benedict. Enough people agreed with Benedict that the same 100,000 or so still jammed the city for its annual summer parade.

Spectators also turned out in droves for a carnival of that civic nuisance, automobile cruising, when the first organized Cruise Night took place in 1984. 100 special pet cars driven by their proud owners did the traditional, aimless Main Street meander up and down for 90 minutes. The next year 500 cars showed up, the next year 800, eventually 1,000. Grumpy may have been there somewhere. On the fifth such outing, a "mini-riot" broke out despite the presence of police from four agencies. The car-loving rioters exuberantly flipped over an automobile to crown the night's event. Police arrested 30 people, ticketed 40 more for careless driving, and suffered two injuries themselves. The next year, when a Port Huron-built 1911 Havers starred as the guest of honor on Cruise Night, 103 people ended up in jail.

Cruise Night also coincided with Noise Night in Port Huron. Police acquired a noise meter with which to measure hopped-up engines and car stereos for excessive decibels during the 80's, but under the press of more life-threatening auto business rarely used it. 300 watt car stereos with "automatic loudness," costing up to $2,000, could push a noise meter off the scale anyway. The City Council finally passed a law banning car sound systems audible more than 50 feet from the vehicle. "Nobody's going to tell me not to play my stereo," said owner Doug Jones defiantly, and nobody did. The cops ignored the problem and the law totally, despite one news report that sprung this major surprise: "...some statistics relate traffic accidents to loud in-car music." Some freaks spent so much money on car stereos that a Port Huron audio dealer offered a free used car with one of his pricier sound systems, and 12 people took him up on it. Another gizmo for distracting a driver, the cellular phone, made its appearance in 1984, and it became another menace to life and limb on the roads within a few short years.

From the other side of the "How's Port Huron making out?" opinion fence came this assessment: "I think the city has pretty well torn apart the downtown area." Peter Whipple said so not long before his Howard's Furniture store, the oldest retailer in town, closed. The K-Mart company, formerly Kresge, shut its 84 year-old central city store in favor of its two suburban locations. The owner of Sperry's who'd been so impressed by the city gave up on it after four years, and sold the store again. The buyer of the relatively new People's Bank Building, built in 1968, called the 14 year-old Albert Kahn-type steel and glass structure, "a bit bland." The last central district movie theater closed (there once had been eight), and a six-screen replacement with parking enough for a dozen screens appeared on the burgeoning, auto-friendly north side. And the last of the downtown new car dealers, the Oldsmobile/Cadillac shop, moved to the suburbs, to fresh territory it bought from competitor Charlie Barrett.

City Manager Bouchard didn't exactly bolster public confidence in Port Huron's future when he invested in some Gardendale land, which turned into a restaurant and a strip mall. Another shopping strip, a mobile home park, apartments, a pornographic theater, and an office center all arose in the same general area in short order. The burgeoning suburban sprawl in this northerly direction transformed the Scenic Highway into one blinding headache. "Now you can hardly see the lake for all the houses," said one resident. Heavy traffic often kept those haggard homeowners along the Scenic bottled up their own driveways, waiting for a break in the flood so they could wheel out themselves. A pedestrian bridge had to be built over the Scenic at the Lakeport State Park to get visitors across the teeming road in one piece.

Finally, somebody lowered the boom for real on Port Huron's downtown retailing future. The big money which had been talked about wistfully by developers for years finally showed up in 1988 to construct an enormous enclosed shoppers' world in Gardendale along North Main. The backers of the $80 million Birchwood Mall – an Iowa company calling themselves General Growth Development – expected it eventually to hold 120 chain store outlets of various sizes and descriptions. Surrounded by 3,000 parking spaces, on 80 acres of soon-to-be-bulldozed woods and filled-in wetlands a mile north of the Port Huron city limits, this giant nevertheless would tie right into city utilities. The projected interior space amounted to 728,000 square feet, twice as big as AutoWorld, adding to the 4 billion square feet of existing shopping centers in America.(49) It would be "opulent but not pretentious," said its planners, totally different, a paradise of consumption, with real trees and plants growing in a glassed-in "food court." Here came the perfect fulfillment of shopping and eating, which along with driving constituted the three pillars of happiness.

In General Growth's general view, although Americans spent more time and money shopping than any people in the world, and owed $200 billion in credit card debt to prove it, not enough took place in Port Huron's little corner. The company's middle name, "growth," said it all. The Birchwood reconnaissance team made no secret of the fact that they expected to have an especially easy time selling shopping growth to the dumbells living in Port Huron, because only 56% of the locals had so much as graduated from high school, and a lot of these clucks worked in places like auto parts plants. Port Huron people sometimes drove 40 miles away to Detroit area malls as it was. Now these "under-retailed, under-malled" thousands, could stay home to enjoy a higher plane of purchasing existence, inside.

From a transportation standpoint the Birchwood Mall's owners couldn't have picked a worse location, one with only a single major access road and no room to build another. County official Mary Mechtenberg sputtered, "The major concern that comes to my mind is the traffic...It's already a nightmare [25,000 vehicles per day], and with that mall it will become more congested."(50) General Growth expected North Main, already the most accident prone road in the county, to shoulder the added load of their purely auto-and-truck-supplied bazaar. Once upon a time the McMorran Line had run through this area, and Gardendale's farmers had shipped produce away by boat on Lake Huron, but today no rail- or water-borne goods could possibly reach the doors of Birchwood.

The Birchwood project, which might better have been named the NoWoods Mall, benefited from the jumble of various levels of governmental authority in St. Clair County. In essence, the "home rule" provisions in Michigan law denied any higher-ups the right to veto a destructive proposal like this one. Nor did anyone pay attention to St. Clair County's master plan for development when considering the matter. Gardendale's tiny handful of township officials instead rushed to prostrate themselves in welcome before their new rulers, the mall kings. "This change will pave the way for growth. We need this shopping mall real bad. We've got to.have it. We can't get ahead sitting still. This is vital." So Gardendale's leaders said, although 38 retail stores and 18 restaurants

417

already did business in the 9,000-person township.

Within four days of the original NoWoods announcement, 10 other developers had contacted Gardendale about piling into the same marshy area and obliterating the landscape, setting the stage for full-blown commercial anarchy. The Walmart company, the new giant of American retail, rushed breathlessly to the scene, and started logrolling to get more wetlands dried out and repurposed for parking. So did local landowners like the Mueller family, of the Mueller Brass fortune. Just a few weeks later, with public and private parties lobbying like mad, the truculent Michigan Department of Transportation, which hadn't been consulted previously in any way about NoWoods (neither had the county's Road Commission), ordered an emergency widening of North Main at the critical location. They split the $1 million cost 45/55 between the taxpayer and the developers. After that, mail the maintenance bill, as always, to that sucker John Q. Public. Absolutely no one made any provision for bicycle or pedestrian access to the mall.

As work progressed at NoWoods, and the full ugliness of the buildings and surrounding area took shape, Charles Marengo spoke up for a lot of Gardendalers:

How can these elected officials be blind to the hideousness of North Main?...I remember well a stretch where a kiddie park used to be, where vegetables were sold in summer, where birds used to sing, and fields where I as a child used to play. Now this road has become a sterile and hideous cement jungle.(51)

At first, the roughly 150 merchants in downtown Port Huron tried to take heart over the fact that NoWoods charged store rents of $30 per square foot, five times as much as theirs. So high, in fact, that NoWoods shut out local retailers entirely. Profits at the mall, it seemed, would be harder to come by. And surely, loyalty to hometown businesses counted for something with shoppers, thought the Chamber of Commerce. The City Council, as usual at its wits end, could think of nothing more helpful than to order three more downtown lots paved for parking. Then, the big chain store names began to bail. J.C. Penney announced that it would move to NoWoods, trading in its 70 year-old downtown location for one three times as big in the mall. Sears followed suit, abandoning the 87,000 square foot store and enormous parking lot it built in the former 1st Ward less than 30 years earlier. Fox Jewelers made the move, after 50 years downtown. Some smaller local stores closed up completely even before NoWoods opened, crushed by the mere anticipation of the competition .

40,000 people turned out for the mall debut in October 1990, more than a quarter of St. Clair County's entire population, and six times as many as had appeared on AutoWorld's opening day. Although it at least maintained a carfree interior, indoor NoWoods seemed like a strange, claustrophobic, closed world reinterpretation of Port Huron's shopping district. The great cavern admitted of no sky, no horizon, no perspective, no sun by day or moon by night, no weather, no grass or unpotted trees, no waterfront, no public places, no community, just acres of linoleum and tons of imported stuff for sale. It left the real world behind. To the displeasure of adult customers and the mall owners alike, idle adolescents of the auto age, 65% of whom had never heard the word "thrift" mentioned at home, regularly flooded the place. The 1,000 or so jobs behind the counters at NoWoods fell heavily into the minimum wage range. It didn't take long before another township resident, Thelma Reid, joined the clamor of the dissenters:

I have news for you. Not everyone loves the mall. It is one of the worst things to happen to our area, thanks to the greed of the township and the developers. It was not needed. Who needs the horrible traffic, the crowds...and the mess? We have a lovely downtown area for a city the size of Port Huron and I hope it will not be ruined.(52)

Even before the appearance of NoWoods, Gerald Bouchard had said he didn't like the look of AutoPortHuron's population trends: down and poorer. 60% of St. Clair County's poor lived in Port Huron, home to only 24% of the population. Mistakenly fancying himself a housing as well as an industrial developer, the manager now proposed to help things along by midwiving construction of 1,000 new housing units, preferably affluent, on what suitable vacant property could be had, as well as in some of the rattier residential areas where people could be bought, run, or bluffed out. A minority of City Council members led by Mayor James Relken instead wanted to fix up the existing older neighborhoods, the most prominent of which called itself Olde Town. Once a premier district, home to Mayor Fred Moore in 1900, Olde Town now held 3,800 people, 70% of them renters.

The principle street through Olde Town, 10th, had fallen on sorry days since its widening into a traffic sewer. The noise, dirt, danger, and disruption of streets like 10th, and the slumlords who feasted alongside these avenues, caused much of the destruction to residential areas of Port Huron. The police department called the 10th Street area the "red zone" for all its crime and other problems. "Gone are the days of picket fences and the lush green grass cared for along front lawns," wrote resident Martin Switzer. "What remains are barely running automobiles in dirt driveways and dilapidated front porches suffering from rotten wood."(53) Citizens organized a Port Huron Beautification Commission to combat this trend in several parts of town, and offered a free junk car towaway day. But the city really needed an Automobile Elimination Commission to beautify Port Huron by towing away all its cars.

The idea of salvaging neighborhoods came a little too late for former residents of the 1st Ward, whose expulsion had started Port Huron's population decline in the 1950's. They invited Jerry Brown to their latest reunion. No fewer than 275 people gathered to denounce Fats Hume's urban renewal that wasn't, and lamented what they'd lost. Neighbors, for instance: "In your neighborhood today you hardly know anyone around you," said Peter Mainguy. "Even the people next door are strangers sometimes." Brown agreed. He counted hundreds more local crime reports monthly on his beat than he'd seen as a young journalist. Whereas Port Huroners once commonly strolled their streets at night in safety, in the 80's police had to stage an official Night Out to persuade some residents to emerge from their warrens into the real world as a crime fighting tactic. It shocked Brownie to learn that 90% of the churches in town now had burglar alarms. "Neighbors are going to have to become neighbors again. It's time to look out for each other." Hard to do from the driver's seat.

Others besides Brown and the 1st Warders began to smell a rat in Port Huron's "progress" as well. When, oblivious to this dissatisfaction, 20 year City Council veteran Clayton Berdan called street widening the greatest civic achievement of his two decades in office, voters promptly threw him out. Yet, neither the Bouchardists (known as the "Say Yes" council members) nor the Relkenite faction admitted, or even realized, that automobile blight above all else dragged the community down. They didn't do a single thing to retard the carsickness. Gerald Bouchard ignored completely the concepts of the

419

"New Urbanism" school of municipal planning, which de-emphasized automobiles. True, the New Urbanism amounted to a half measure, a compromise with an implacable social evil with which there could be no compromise, but at least it offered something better than Port Huron's total surrender.

Bouchard remained just as dedicated a servant to traffic flow as ever, and even as he plotted building the city's population back again he trashed yet another neighborhood, this one adjacent to Pine Grove Park, by building another three-lane, no parking traffic sewer through it. Homeowners complained in vain: "What the city is proposing...would decrease the quality of a family neighborhood, increase traffic congestion, increase the safety hazards to our families...."(54) Meanwhile, on 80 empty acres purchased by the city for $500,000, the Northern Woods subdivision project began, full of two-car garages with attached homes, loopy, dead-end streets, and no sidewalks. Port Huron's population decline continued.

So did Detroit's. Between 1960 and 1990, one-third of its residents left the Motor City behind. A third of those one million who remained lived on welfare. A racial profile told the story: Detroit 75% black, its suburbs 92% white. Thousands of redundant, abandoned homes, stores, offices and vacant lots littered the Detroit landscape. Many of its most handsome buildings, like the great Michigan Central Railroad depot, fell into ruins. The failing schools faced a state takeover. The city budget needed $80 million it didn't have. Undertakers profited from one of the highest murder rates in America. "Detroit's population decline, in one of American society's bitter ironies, ultimately was caused in no small part by the automobile and freeway, which enabled white flight, daily commuting, and the so-called crescent of suburbs to grow up around the decaying city." So editorialized the *Holland (Mich.) Sentinel*.(55) On the positive side, though, 43% of Detroit's auto dealers closed during the 1980's, and since a third of its residents couldn't afford wheels, people relied on buses. 90% of U.S. households owned cars, but the carless 10% held 25% of the human population. In transportation anyway, poverty now spelled progress.

Detroit looked doomed to become the biggest of America's automobile ghost towns, like the cities born of mining, farming, lumbering, railroading and other hot industries of the past that had faded from the landscape. The sites of long-gone towns peppered the Thumb. The vanished community of Lambs, once a stop on the McMorran Line about 15 miles west of Port Huron, had counted two grain elevators, three general stores, a grist mill, creamery, school, bank, church, and post office to its credit, plus twice-a-day round-trip train service; more train than Port Huron had in 1985. But Lambs also had acquired a Ford dealership, visited once by Lyin' Hank himself, and a John Deere tractor outlet, both of which sold the products that eventually undid the town.

By the 1980's, the farmers remaining in St. Clair County didn't have enough economic clout to keep small burgs like Lambs operating. Town-building power had shifted from railroads and farms to suburban expressway entrances and exits. The former riverside sawmill village at Wadhams, now a prominent x-way ramp and Port Huron suburb, acquired two gas stations, a bank, diner, two hair shops, two restaurants, a hardware store, dentist, laundromat, supermarket, pharmacy, and a huge combined tourist camp, sports, and games center called Sawmill City. Also horrible road surfaces and bumper-to-bumper traffic.

Some members of the media, like Associated Press auto writer Tim Bovee, celebrated the diffusion of American society by cars every which way, the fruits of mobility freedom. "The automobile makes it difficult for a government to control its citizens. Public transportation is easier to police because it concentrates travelers. Cars disperse them beyond the easy reach of authority."(56) They sure did, but St. Clair County suburbanite Zelma Bugaiski didn't sound so enthusiastic about this liberation movement, "It's terrible to live in the country like this and be afraid of big city crime." Something about the burglarized homes, flattened mail boxes, a burned out road bridge, thousands of tires dumped along roadsides, and trashed cemeteries took the pleasure out of rural life for Zelma. Same for Goodells market owner James Nader, who counted 21 break-ins or attempts at his place in 7 years. The 600 folks in Charmwood started a Neighborhood Watch to fight crime, keeping their eyes peeled for "strange cars...driving slowly..." Each month, Port Huron's two neighboring townships called the sheriff 350 times and filed 200 criminal complaints. Thanks to car dispersion, malefactors stayed beyond the easy reach of Sheriff David Doktor, whose 60 deputies, driving 23 patrol cars, had their hands full just trying to control citizens driving at illegal speeds.

Doktor's ranks wrote 3,200 speeding tickets in a typical year, out of the 1.2 million moving violation citations issued in Michigan. Again, for a first hand look, Jerry Brown tagged along with deputy Gary Miller on an 8-hour, 200-mile road shift. Miller began the day by snaring a driver doing 105 mph in a 50 zone. "I was just trying out my new car," said the offender. "I wanted to see how fast she would go." Sixteen speeding tickets, seven verbal warnings, four other violations, and a drunk driving arrest occupied the rest of Miller's day. Brown heard more of the regular speeding excuses police got: hurrying to gas station to fill gas tank, looking for a bathroom, important golf date, doctor's appointment, drying just-washed vehicle in the wind, tailwind pushed car over speed limit. Brownie took another ride on the interstates with a pair of state troopers who clocked almost 100 drivers *per hour* breaking the speed limit.

More and more drivers got antsy about the 55 mph national speed limit set during the 1970's. The defiant anthem *I Can't Drive 55* by rock musician Sammy Hagar got a fair amount of airplay: *Write me up a 125 / Post my face wanted dead or alive / Take my license, all that jive / I can't drive 55!* (57) Not can't really, just won't. Only 10% or so of expressway drivers obeyed the 55 as things stood, and state police working the x-ways didn't ticket anybody below 70. The very Secretary of State himself, Richard Austin, driver's license czar of Michigan, clocked a 70 one day on police radar. Father Dennis McMahon couldn't drive 55, and lost control of his car while doing 75 on a Detroit freeway, flew up an embankment and killed a 6 year-old girl. Turned out the priest's license had been suspended after 10 speeding tickets in five years. Although many automobiles now came equipped with automatic cruise control speed adjusters, no one talked anymore of speed governors to prevent the breaking of speed limits.

To give Sammy Hagar and Fr. McMahon more cushion, the U.S. Congress finally hiked the speed limit in some areas back to 65, and in the first year traffic fatalities on Michigan's affected highways jumped 19%, injuries 40%, property damage wrecks by 2,200 in number, for a total cost of $62 million. "We're trading off people being killed, people being maimed for the convenience of driving faster. It's not a free lunch," said one analyst. The cost of lunch didn't deter GM from introducing its new prototype car, the Express, at this same time: *It's a streamlined, whisper- quiet, turbine*

421

powered, ground hugging, four passenger, 150 mph alternative to the hassle of short distance air travel. In joining the renewed speed push, auto parts maker Bendix even revived one of GM's old 1939 World of Tomorrow fantasies, the driverless car: *By the year 2010, cars may travel routinely at 130 miles per hour over long hauls without the need for a driver,* steered by, what else?, buried electronic cables in the pavement.

Higher speeds also sped the decimation of animals on highways, all the while America hypocritically claimed to do more for wildlife protection than any other country in the world. 400 cars crashed into deer in 1986 on St. Clair County roads; 100 times that many across the state of Michigan. How dare these or any other animals obstruct traffic, wrote one impatient *Times Herald* reader: "Roads were made for cars to travel on, not for animals to play on." Giving a playful deer a break actually cost the county $2 million, after driver Craig Smith ran off the road at 55 mph in order to avoid it. Crippled for life in the crash, Craig's successful lawsuit claimed that bad road conditions had hampered his deer-avoidance maneuvering. "Most people's only contact with wildlife is with dead animals on the roadside," Thumb naturalist Dan Farmer pointed out. This fact prompted publication of a book in the 80's on how to identify roadkill by species, *Flattened Fauna.* In fact, no real animal lover could own a car.

Port Huron police tried to deal with their city's own speedbusters by keeping up to 9 patrol cars on the streets at a time, each getting about 6 miles per gallon, or considerably less than a Cadillac Allante or a motorhome. Despite their efforts the cops couldn't stop what exasperated resident Betty Greene called the South Main Street Grand Prix: "Anytime, day or night, is a good time to see the cars speeding down the stretch. If you're lucky, you might see one of the accidents.." The state wideners at MDOT opened up South Main another 7 feet across to speed things up still further. Why didn't MDOT try some "traffic calming" as an alternative? A fair question. New Urbanist planner Andres Duany and his associates had outlined the concept: "Speed bumps, rumble strips, hammerheads, flare-outs, doglegs and other combinations of geometry, landscape, and street furniture can be effective in lowering drivers' speed on local streets."(58) These measures might not lower drivers' tempers, however. Add it all up and the only calm car was a scrapped one.

Police often decided to chase or not to chase speedsters on the spur of the moment. They pursued three-time drunk driving loser Gary LaFave one night, and the suspect crashed into and killed popular local hockey coach Roger Jones, an incident which floored the community. A witness claimed that the police had driven just as recklessly as LaFave, but it was the latter's sentence which set a local precedent: 15-30 years in prison for 2nd degree murder. Eighty years after St. Clair County drivers began murdering people with cars, someone finally had been convicted of it in court. The speeding practices of Port Huron's fire trucks, and the running of stop lights to answer fire calls, also received some scrutiny during this decade, after one of these trucks collided with two cars on a false alarm run. This killed both 78 year-old Marion Schotzline – the former head of the national organization Blue Star Mothers of armed services personnel – and 79 year-old retired Mueller Brass engineer Louis Currens, whose son Darwin had died at age 21 in that triple-fatal collision with a gasoline truck way back in 1948. Like son, like father.

Speed limits weren't tied as closely to oil limits in the 80's as they had been in the previous decade, now that supplies seemed more bountiful. When the U.S. Interior

Department predicted the exhaustion of domestic oil reserves by 2015 it got zero response. So many similar predictions had been made over the years that people brushed this one off. The American oil industry pumped 7.6 million barrels per day, and imported another 7 million. Significant shrinkage continued in the number of Port Huron gasoline stations, down to only 40, but each location sold a lot more gas, almost all self-served. Most filling stations offered no repair service, but instead ran a small grocery shop where the old hoist had been located.

A "recession" in the gasoline business during the decade's opening years meant Americans still lapped up 400 gallons each per year, a total of 90 billion gallons. Motoring miles and oil consumption, as usual, set new records once the economy picked up. Michiganders drove 61 billion miles in 1982, 78 billion in 1988, and America as a whole 2 trillion in 1990. Notwithstanding the lessons of the last 15 years about volatility in gasoline supplies and prices, the USA still wasted it prodigiously in long hauls and short. 93 million people still commuted to work by car, while fewer commuters used mass transit than in 1960, just 2% in Michigan. Mike Garavaglia typified the 98 percenters in covering 200 miles per day between the Thumb and Detroit. St. Clair County commuter Paul Szelestey laboriously took another route to a distant General Motors job for 26 years until that afternoon he inattentively drove in front of an Amtrak train. "Wall to wall traffic," is how one harried commuter described I-94 from Port Huron to Detroit. Equally guilty short-trippers, those drivers going less than five miles by car, burned one-third of all the gasoline used in the country. The average household made six such trips per day.

Petroleum-burning cars and trucks coughed out 35% of the air pollution in the United States. Half these vehicles violated government-ordered emission standards. Nine million people in the country suffering from asthma could just as well have done without the 11 million tons of hydrocarbons set floating about by cars every year. Port Huron found itself under "ozone alerts" on a regular basis from air conditions unfit to breathe, and Port Huron Hospital organized a Breathers Club if you needed a little help catching your wind. No doubt some wheezing Breathers members also belonged to the Auto Club.

Rather than ban cars in Los Angeles for the two-weeks of the 1984 Olympic Games, something too fantastic apparently even for discussion, organizers tried to schedule events around peak smog hours. Running half an hour in automobile air equaled smoking a full pack of cigarettes, but UCLA doctor Henry Gong reassured athletes that they would get used to it after some initial discomfort. Like GM test monkeys. The ancient Greeks had declared a holiday from war during the Olympics in their day, but the automobile hostilities of 1984 admitted of no holiday. It made a sad spectacle of the city that once had led the world in clean mass transit.

Oil companies still struggled to differentiate their gasoline brands one from another by how much good they did your car's health, if not yours. They used the familiar ploy of higher priced octane grades: regular, super regular, and premium. That's what the station signs said anyway. Half the stations checked in Detroit scammed the public on that one, dispensing the same gas for all three grades. The clean-out-your-engine promise also persisted:

This is the world as you know it. But let's move 10,000 times closer...into a car's carburetor and you may find...dirt. Fortunately, you can wash dirt away before it accumulates, with Mobil detergent gasoline.

America needed some serious detergent to clean up the gasoline that had leaked into the dirt out of 500,000 service station storage tanks across America during the past 70 years or so. One dealer went out of the gasoline business at his station on Highway 21, rather than pay $150,000 for government mandated replacement of his tanks and pumps, plus a $24,000 per year insurance premium against further leaks.

And speaking of leaks, a considerable one in the tanker Exxon Valdez messed up several hundred miles of Alaskan coastline with 11 million gallons of crude oil in 1989. That spill amounted to about half an hour's worth of American consumption. The Valdez load had been pumped out of the Arctic on the Alaskan pipeline built during the 70's MEOW crisis, then transferred to a tanker for the last leg to the States. In cleaning up the spill at a cost of $1.1 billion, scientists discovered petroleum to be about 1,000 times more toxic than previously thought.(59) The half million birds, 5,000 otters, and 22 whales who'd choked to death on it convinced them. The nation with some justice blamed the ship's skipper for crashing into a reef, but the real responsibility lay inside America's garages.(60)

Not that everybody disliked spilled oil. Not long after the *Valdez* crash the Automotive Hall of Fame in Detroit inducted Soichiro Honda, founder of the eponymous car company, and he fondly reminisced about the oily deposits left behind by the early Model T's in Japan:

Every time that Ford car stopped, it left a little bit of an oil slick underneath and I smelled that oil slick. I enjoyed it thoroughly and I still remember very vividly the kind of enjoyment I had by smelling that oil slick.(61)

Now if only Alaska would take that attitude. Or the Great Lakes states, where 5,000 oil and chemical spills into those waters occurred during the 80's.

Leaky motor vehicles in need of oil and gas or plastic parts drew down harder than ever on Sarnia's now immense Chemical Valley, which represented a total investment of $6 billion Canadian dollars. Its busier than ever workers processed or transshipped 600,000 barrels of oil per day. (62) One study described the Valley as the fountainhead of pollution on the lower Great Lakes, discharging 442 million gallons of waste, cooling, and storm waters into the St. Clair River daily. As its reputation suffered for this, the Valley disappeared from Canadian currency. Angry Greenpeace environmentalists climbed up the Blue Water Bridge superstructure in protest of PetroWorld affairs, although they never bothered to climb up on top of Plum's gasoline station, or Northgate Ford, or Fetterly's Tires for Cash in Port Huron, businesses further down the oil food chain.

Well beyond the Blue Water horizon, America's entanglement in the Middle East to guarantee enough oil to support the automobile culture grew much uglier during this decade. Just for starters, 240 American servicemen supposedly on peacekeeping duty died in a truck bomb blast in the middle of a civil war in Lebanon. Later, U.S. Navy vessels patrolling the Persian Gulf during a huge war between Iran and Iraq offered protection from the fighting to Kuwaiti oil tankers. That conflict ended in Iraq's favor shortly after the *USS Vincennes* shot down an Iranian domestic airliner by mistake. This disaster stoked even higher Iran's already profound loathing of the States, and also left America in the awkward position of seeming to favor Iraq's dictator Saddam Hussein.(63)

The USA's foreign policy mess came to a head in August 1990 when Iraq annexed Kuwait in an unprecedented oil grab. World petroleum prices shot up from $18 to $28 per barrel in a week. The latter development really caught the attention of Port Huron motorists, when gas prices consequently rose 10 cents per gallon overnight and kept on going. Fearing that Iraq's Hussein, now with 20% of the world's reserves under his control, would wield too much power over Oil World and American gasoline pumps, the United States prepared to use force to dislodge him, under the guise of liberating the Kuwaitis.

"We are now hostages to the whims of the oil producing countries, and there is no guarantee that Middle East friends today will be friends tomorrow," observed the *Times Herald's* Tom Verdin.(64) American war opponents accurately called the coming conflict Detroit's War. The threat of war steepened the latest downturn in the auto sales cycle into a nosedive. Port Huron dealers began wheedling again: *Northgate Ford is Selling Lots of Cars Despite What You Read in the News!* And rolling out sales guff: *The $1,000,000 Clearance Sale! The No Money Down Sale. The Guaranteed Rebate, Down to the Wire Sale. Emergency Bargain Blast.* Half the new car dealers in America lost money in 1990, and together the Big 3 dropped $2 billion.

Gasoline taxes continued to advance lazily during this decade, but they still amounted to just a paltry 24 cents in Michigan. Vehicle license fees also rose 15-30%. *Times Herald* editor and sturdy auto shill Bernard Lyons threw a taxpayer fit over even modest increases: "...the gasoline price explosion touched off by OPEC has already shaken our economy quite enough. To look at the hapless motorist as a source of additional [tax] dollars adds sadism to cruelty."(65) Lyons' tantrum notwithstanding, the fuel taxes, tolls, license charges and assorted other fees paid by American motorists of all stripes didn't come close to raising all of the $30 billion needed annually to maintain almost 4 million miles of roads.

With virtually all its streets paved by now, Port Huron laid out $1 million per year to maintain them – $50,000 just for potholes, but the crumbling continued. The deficiencies ran end to end. On the south side, Mrs. Harold Marlette complained that some of the streets hadn't been repaved in 45 years. On the north side, a *Times Herald* contest selected the avenue along "millionaires row" on Lake Huron as the worst in the city. The millionaires said their street had more patches in it than asphalt, it rattled their tailgates like castanets, it rode like a rollercoaster, it slammed heads against car roofs, it induced childbirth in pregnant women driven across it a few times. Appropriately for millionaires row, the street needed a $2.1 million repair job for just a two mile stretch. Rich and poor, the entire city of Port Huron lacked $10-15 million for needed street fix-ups, or about $100,000 per mile. Nobody gave serious thought to closing streets to traffic, or cutting traffic, or imposing weight limits on trucks.

However, the street repair tab paled in comparison to another gigantic bill of the auto age which came due and stunned public officials in Port Huron. Rainwater runoff from 140 miles of paved streets, 300 acres of parking lots, and thousands of paved driveways, regularly flooded the sanitary sewer system and carried tons of untreated waste into the St. Clair and Black Rivers. Fix it, said the Michigan Department of Natural Resources, by separating the storm and sanitary sewers, at a cost

425

of $50 million, which eventually escalated to $186 million. This bill overshadowed the entire city budget process for years.

The St. Clair County Road Commission suffered from its own coin shortage in these days, having a mere $10 million to spend per year. The responsibilities for keeping up suburban thoroughfares, both old and new, easily outran resources. The late Keith Lindke's family sued, blaming stingy road-grading for the "washboard-type conditions" on which he bounced to his death in an accident along one of the 1,700 miles of county road. "It just jars your teeth. You can't even go 5 mph," said another resident of Washboard Lane. Judging exactly when a washboardy gravel road needed re-grading remained an inexact science.

The Road Commission put off repairs on one of the county's rickety bridges a little too long and two cars crashed through the 46 year-old structure on Sterling Road into the creek below, killing 54 year-old Florence Elliott. It seemed that a 41-ton truck had preceded the victims across this particular bridge, rated for 12 tons. "Truckers don't pay attention to the posted limits. I"m amazed it doesn't happen more often," said a bridge engineer. Overweight trucks tried to avoid the weight scales on the expressways by ducking onto side roads, like Sterling. "You can hear them on the CB," said the bridge expert. "They ask each other 'Is the chicken coop open?', meaning the scales." The $100 fine for exceeding the weight limit on a bridge amounted to 1/2000 of what it cost to repair this one. Collectors of "Bridge Out" warning signs carried away 8 barricades and 16 lights from the Sterling Road disaster scene as souvenirs during the following weeks, inflating the repair tab. The Road Commission rebuilt 10 bridges per year, at a cost of $3,000 per foot, and at that rate would need 27 more years to get to all of them.

MDOT spent almost $600 million per year on highways but at a one point in the 80's still faced $220 million in lawsuits over defective roads and bridges. Three St. Clair County families split $1.4 million in legal recompense after each lost a member in a fiery pile-up on the I-94 bridge in Port Huron, which didn't have shoulders wide enough to accommodate stalled vehicles. An attending policeman called it the worst wreck *he'd* ever seen. MDOT set aside $10 million just to rebuild the Main Street drawbridge in downtown Port Huron, the state's busiest moveable bridge, the city's principle traffic pinch point. The same sum would have bought 100 bridges a couple generations ago. When repairs finally began they disrupted the middle of town for two years.

St. Clair County's second expressway, Interstate 69, slowly crawled west-to-east across the landscape toward Port Huron and the Blue Water Bridge, like a "lazy brown snake" by one description, during the first half of the '80's. This 40-mile piece of divided highway, with 45 bridges and 9 interchanges, supplemented but did not replace the infamous Highway 21, and paralleled the Grand Trunk railroad route, at a price of $101 million. Plus right-of-way costs, plus design costs, plus a $1.4 million rest area. The federal and state governments split the charges 3:1. This extravagant outlay compared dismally to the privately paid cost of repairing 66 miles of Thumb railroad line for $1.5 million at the same time. Since no new Michigan train lines were being built, no basis existed for comparing new railroad vs. new freeway construction costs.

When six years of leisurely labor finally completed it in late 1984, Port Huron civic leaders decorated I-69 with the same false hopes of fresh prosperity they'd

426

crowned I-94 with twenty years earlier. Those hopes faded almost immediately. As an alternate expressway route between Chicago and Toronto, I-69 wrought only one change of any consequence. The number of heavy trucks crossing the Blue Water Bridge jumped by 22% in the first year alone, and with them the noise, vibration, fumes, and dirt flowing from this aerial traffic sewer. "It was incredible," said homeowner Janice Willey about the shaking from 60,000 passing overhead trucks per month, which knocked pictures off the wall, rattled the windows, and shook her awake at night. Five million vehicles of all kinds used the Blue Water Bridge annually, turning it into a certifiable public nuisance. The bridge authorities called out Port Huron police, firefighters, public works and ambulance personnel more often than any business in town.

MDOT named a section of the new interstate the Dewayne Williams Highway, in honor of the county's young Medal of Honor winner of the Vietnam War, who deserved a better memorial. How long would the Williams last? The figures suggested 20 years before a major re-build was needed. A single 18-mile stretch of Williams Highway required its own groomer and his tools, in this case 48 year-old Larry Dresser. He cut grass in the summer, plowed snow and dropped 5 tons of salt per mile in the winter, and dealt with the various other hazards of the seasons ("Danger, Leaves Ahead. Covered road can be dangerously slippery.").

Dresser rapidly discovered that the public still mistook the freeways for a long garbage dump. He found bottles, cans, hubcaps, mufflers, mattresses, car parts, refrigerators, and tires strewn along the shoulders. "Believe me, people are real litter bugs. They toss everything out there they don't want." Their driving habits didn't impress him, either. "It's as if a third of the people can't read, a third can't hear, and the other third don't care. I've seen people driving reading a paper over their steering wheel, or turned around talking to kids in the back seat. The drivers are crazy out there."(66) When they got too crazy, tow truck operators like Larry Cote had to be called in. If he found the client still alive when he arrived, Cote often caught some motorist frustration over the disruption and delay. "There are customers who call and expect you to be there before the dispatcher hangs the telephone receiver up."

As Cote knew well, freeway driving these days still mesmerized people. When their driver fell asleep, five persons died in a somersaulting car wreck on I-75 in Ohio while motoring home from a drum and bugle show in Port Huron. "A real shame," said the pageant's organizer. Not everybody took the subject very seriously. A *Times Herald* profile of Port Huron auto parts executive Isaac Lang approvingly quoted him to the effect that he'd worked so hard building his business that, "There were a few times I fell asleep and drove off the road," as though this testified to his diligence. Some drivers tried to break the spell of the open road through the new distraction of listening to recorded books, though, wait a minute, driving distraction caused 90% of all accidents. You might try reading overpass graffiti instead. So much of it rapidly covered the bridges on the new I-69 that highway workers spent $1,000 per month cleaning them.

To otherwise liven things up for bored drivers, vandals occasionally dropped objects from overpasses onto expressways in St. Clair County. A water filled milk carton smashed through a car windshield on one occasion, some firebombs missed a couple of other drivers, and an auto transmission came down on another. Elsewhere in Michigan assorted rocks, a bowling ball, and a pumpkin fell on passersby. State trooper

427

William Nowicki predicted, "Somebody is going to be killed if these things continue," and indeed, somebody was. When pranksters hung a scarecrow from an I-69 overpass near Port Huron on Halloween, driver Tracey Pearson mistook it for pedestrian, flipped her car in a panic, and died.

Expressways triggered snoozing at one end of the reaction scale, and road rage incidents at the other; ten shootings in two months in Detroit. "It certainly makes people anxious," admitted a Detroit psychiatrist. "The car has been known as a sort of sanctuary, but now that's not the case." A toymaker invented the dashboard-mounted "Revenger" weapon, which allowed a driver to spray other motorists with simulated machine gun fire, death rays, and hand grenades. "It's a fun way of dealing with your frustrations," said a spokesman. Eschewing gunfire, some drivers tossed bottles onto the pavement from their speeding vehicles just to see them explode. This happened on I-69 in front of Marysville motorist Bill Gignor: "When I got home, I discovered that a piece of the bottle glass had flown into and punctured my truck's radiator. My immediate reaction was that I wished I had put a slug through the other car's radiator." Better get a Revenger instead, Bill.(67)

Deregulation of trucking further decreased safety on the interstates. Big tractor-trailer rigs in greater numbers posed a greater menace than ever. Michigan counted 155 fatal wrecks involving big trucks in 1985. 4,500 took place nationwide. Trucking fatalities grew 4 times faster than overall traffic numbers. The number of truck accidents in Michigan doubled in four years time, to 23,000 in 1986. "You have to be extra careful with these rigs because if you catch a wheel the wrong way on the shoulder, you'll buy the farm," admitted one trucker as he drove through Port Huron. "You have to start turning that corner half a block away," is how another described its maneuverability. Trucks regularly somersaulted or jackknifed on the interstates in St. Clair County, as when within a week of each other driver Leo Paige turned his rig over avoiding another of that troublesome species, a deer, and Darrell Kaufeld fell asleep at the wheel of his auto parts load. A chemical tanker crackup took place about once a month in the Thumb.

Federal trucking deregulation in the 1980's didn't noticeably decrease the prices consumers paid for the growing numbers of goods mindlessly trucked around the country. The tangle of *intrastate* trucking rules still cost Americans $12 billion per year in higher prices.(68) Nevertheless, with less federal interference the number of trucking companies in America increased 90% in five years, to 33,000. Some old-time firms with Teamster contracts couldn't compete with non-union start-ups, and fell by the roadside. The Ogden and Moffett firm of Port Huron liquidated after 60 years in business. The new companies operated just as dishonestly as the oldtimers. Michigan State Police inspected 54,000 trucks in fiscal 1987 and ordered 28% of them off the road as unsafe. A special crackdown inspection of 93 rigs at the Blue Water Bridge resulted in police citations against 47 drivers for safety violations and 22 for carrying phony logbooks.

An unwitting public still massively subsidized the trucking industry, the most parasitic in America. Taxpayers footed the bill, for instance, to build a new $40 million truck inspection plaza on the Blue Water Bridge, for which dozens more civilian buildings had to be knocked down. Joe Dokes covered the damage done to roads everywhere by undertaxed and overweight monsters like 40-wheeled gravel train trucks, and that 41-tonner that wrecked the Sterling Road Bridge. And they put up with the airborne filth from the dirtiest vehicles in transportation. For the same amount of hauling, a truck used a minimum of 4 times as much fuel as trains, usually much more, and 12 times as much as barges.(69)

It cost about $60 per hour to operate a semi-trailer truck. A Port Huron couple, Gene and Julie Renaker, tried driving an interstate moving van together for 10 months. They first received from the moving company a grand total of 3 weeks training in this enterprise. Their slim degree of experience behind the wheel remained a little secret from the customers. Sleeping in their 55-foot truck, coping with flat tires, bad weather, tight schedules, and underestimated loads, the Renakers covered 46 states on their odyssey, lived to tell the tale, and claimed to have made money. Julie said truckers lived with a bad public image: "They are not the greasy, scarfaced, long haired, toothless people you think they are." "They're not all drug addicts and whoremongers," added another sympathizer. Maybe not, but they weren't knights of the highway, either. During a 1983 national job action against rising truck taxes and fees, protestors shot up 300 trucks and trashed another 800.

Although it now carried 60,000 people per month, the reach of the Port Huron area bus system contracted during the 80's. Ignoring the pleas from riders in outlying districts, adjacent communities voted down tax subsidies for this service. This fractured method of obtaining money from a wide assortment of taxing authorities greatly impeded regional mass transit in Michigan and elsewhere these days. The car driving majority looked at Michigan's public bus systems with misgivings. "Loser cruisers" is how detractors described buses in some parts of America, though in fact bus patrons saved money while car owners lost their shirts.(70) The *Times Herald* sought to reassure the public about the civility of bus life with occasional glimpses into it from reporters who actually boarded and rode buses, brave hearts. Fine, orderly, clean, warm, prompt, wrote correspondent Diane Delekta about her bus ride, as though writing from a foreign country. Bus driver Mary Meadows had to do some hand holding with new Port Huron patrons leery of, even frightened of the novel experience of climbing aboard.

Port Huron lost its privately-run intercity bus service both to Detroit and Sarnia, as ridership declined and subsidies dried up. This left PH without any regular mass transit to Detroit, or to most other parts of St. Clair County, or to any cities in the upper Thumb, for the first time in 150 years, since the stagecoach and ferry days. The number of passengers on regular intercity runs in America fell by 50% between 1970 and 1984, to a low of 150 million, and profits faded by the same margin. 4,500 cities lost this service during the 1980's. Paradoxically, the number of bus companies nearly doubled, but charter services accounted for most of this increase.

For the dwindling number of Port Huron residents old enough to remember them, memories of the streetcar days stirred faintly when local business people sponsored an imitation street trolley bus to take visitors sightseeing around town. No one could now imagine a revived streetcar system replacing the auto mess. Legitimate trolleys and rapid transit systems did start operations in some cities around the country; in Miami, Portland, and Los Angeles for instance. The elevated, 3 mile-long People Mover began looping around downtown Detroit, after a decade of construction and a $200 million public investment. It carried 10,000 passengers per day at a speed of 12 mph. However well intentioned, the Mover didn't get Detroit back on track with the ground level streetcar and rapid transit system needed to remove automobiles and buses.

Just one eastbound and one westbound Amtrak train per day comprised all the regular intercity mass transit left to Port Huron, and for a while even that much looked iffy. Because the federal government subsidized Amtrak in relatively plain view, while backing motor vehicles, aircraft, and shipping much more clandestinely, cost-cutters in the Reagan administration early on targeted passenger train support for elimination. The *Times Herald* editors, though never steadfast supporters of rail, took the trains' side: "Writing off our nation's rail passenger service will admit defeat in a transportation area every other advanced nation on earth has put to work effectively and efficiently." Barry Williams of the National Association of Railroad Passengers emphatically pointed out the shortcomings of doing 90% of all American travel by car: "It is ironic that an administration so committed to reducing inflation and to strengthening national defense would advocate still greater reliance upon the private automobile. Indeed, our overdependence on foreign oil, half of which is consumed by autos, is a primary cause of inflation in our economy and a significant threat to our national security."(71)

Had America spent on its trains the $21 billion in tax dollars it wasted during Mr. Reagan's presidency on the drug war, America once again could have had some of the best passenger rail service in the world. Instead it took a series of compromises and a lot of financial brinkmanship to keep Amtrak rolling through this latest crisis. Donald Maushund and his wife decided to take a chance on Amtrak, while it lasted, and after riding the rails round trip Port Huron to Los Angeles he called it, "the nicest thing we have ever done. The service, courtesy and friendliness is just fantastic...we saw and enjoyed more on the one round trip that you could possibly do on a dozen flights."(72)

Amtrak still operated with the expensive responsibilities of simultaneously delivering passengers while rebuilding a system its predecessors had neglected for years. By 1988 revenues covered 69% of costs. More than 100,000 passengers caught the Port Huron to Chicago train per year. The Blue Water service achieved a maximum speed of 70 mph, comparable to an auto, but unimpressive when measured against train speeds of 150-180 mph in other nations. Similar speeds in the U.S. undoubtedly would have boosted ridership, especially along the one-third of commercial airline routes that covered less than 500 miles. As things stood, total U.S. rail travel amounted to only about 2% that of airborne. 340 million people flew in 1984, an average of 880 miles. About 20 million rode Amtrak. Americans traveled only 45 miles apiece per year on trains, compared to 570 in Canada and 1,760 in Japan. West Germany operated 20,000 trains daily, Holland 4,300; dwarfing the USA's level of service.

To double passenger train speeds in America (and incidentally speed up freight trains) meant that all road crossings needed gates, and the rights of way had to have better fencing. Don't expect us to pay for it all, said the railroad owners. The mixed heritage of the track system still caused trouble. The railbeds remained private property and public necessity both. Of the 138 grade crossings in St. Clair County, 51 lacked gates or even flashers, and made do with stop signs. Port Huron's James and Margaret Richards and her mother missed the stop sign at one of these crossings, placing them inopportunely in front of a train doing 55 mph. "The (Richards) car was just coming too cotton-picking fast and didn't stop at all," in the opinion of one witness to the triple fatal.

Two more examples of ignored train stop signs around Port Huron:

#1. *John R. Mintz and Karen Lynn Fowler were planning to get married in April. Early*

Sunday morning they were returning home from a wedding reception. They never made it. Their car smashed into a moving freight train at a crossing on fog-shrouded Allen Road. They apparently were killed instantly....The accident was not discovered until about 7:30 am Sunday when a motorist saw the crushed car on its top in a water filled ditch.

#2. I witnessed the death of the most beautiful, intelligent and loving animal in the world. He was my horse, Legendary Ruffay. The train that hit him wasn't very long and it had plenty of time to either slow down or stop. A complete stranger who witnessed it said that every time my horse got a little ahead of the train it seemed to speed up until he couldn't run any faster. Can you imagine the terror he felt?(73)

Another witness to Incident #2 absolved the train engineer, and asked why the most intelligent animal in the world didn't just get off the tracks. People riding inside trains enjoyed America's safest transportation. Outside, discounting horses, car-train collisions killed 49 people and injured 379 in Michigan during the two-year 1981-82 period, virtually all of this attributable to dangerous or careless car driving. On a single 70-mile train trip, a group of state safety officials making a test ride counted 39 cars trying to beat the train to crossings.

Freed from the oversight of the ICC henpeckers, U.S. railroads broke more records for freight loads during the 80's. The total reached 1 trillion ton-miles in 1988, or one-third of all intercity freight, despite the fact that tens of thousands of miles of track had been abandoned since the 20's, and the number of railroad employees had shrunk by 80%. Ancient ongoing battles between railroads and unions (Grand Trunk dealt with 18 labor groups) still continued over work rules, like the 1919 edict that 100 miles made a full day's work for a locomotive engineer. Nevertheless, ton-mileage per employee doubled between 1980 and 1988. It cost 1/10 as much to send a ton of freight a mile by train as by truck, and the train costs actually declined by an inflation-adjusted 21% during the 1980's.(74) Return on equity for train companies rose almost 400%. The Conrail outfit put together by the government from busted RR's in the 70's now looked good enough that investors lined up to buy shares in it.

Every year more than 400,000 railcars of all descriptions passed through Port Huron, one of the busiest border crossings in the nation. Some carried bulk freight, some containers, some truck trailers remounted on flatcars, some finished automobiles and trucks (Ford spent 65% of its transportation budget on rail). A four-man crew could handle a 150-car train. The versatility could be amazing. On one occasion, five flatcars brought to a Marysville power plant the longest piece of equipment ever delivered by the Grand Trunk, 193 feet long, weighing 190 tons. Sadly, though, the Port Huron freight office of the Grand Trunk closed, bringing an end to an era 130 years old, as the railroads largely abandoned to trucks less-than-carload freight hauling.

Select railroad companies grew bigger, others smaller in the deregulated atmosphere of the 1980's. Some did both. In Port Huron, the C&O (whose local operations, just to review, began life as the McMorran Line, then joined with the Pere Marquette, then with C&O) became part of the CSX, one of the biggest operations in the country.(75) Along the way this company snapped up the short line Port Huron & Detroit, while at the same time it abandoned or sold the last of the McMorran property. Some McMorran trackage in the upper Thumb ended up as part of a brand new short line, the Huron & Eastern. Under more nimble owners, starting with just 9 employees and 2 locomotives, the H&E quickly upgraded its equipment, doubled its train speeds, boosted freight traffic 1,000%, expanded operations to 140 miles and 14 cities, and most importantly turned a profit.

After a merger with two other lines, including Henry Ford's former Detroit, Toledo and Ironton, the Grand Trunk promised Port Huron freight customers 48 hour service to as far away as Atlanta, Georgia. Eighteen of its trains passed each way through town on a typical day. At the same time the GTRR abandoned its upper Thumb operation, idling it until new owners, if any, could be found to turn it around. Line abandonment continued during the 80's despite improved railroad prospects. 1,400 miles shut down in Michigan. The failure of the automobile-dominated MDOT to step into the breach and preserve rail lines came in for just criticism: "The state Department of Transportation should live up to its name and do a better job of keeping railroads running in Michigan," editorialized the *Ann Arbor News*.(76) Needless to say, MDOT abandoned no state highways during the decade.

The Grand Trunk railcar repair yards in Port Huron suffered their worst blow in 70 years, a fire that wiped out a major part of the yard, which meant a $2.5 million rebuild. GTRR employees like Yvonne Williams sharply chided local governments for their seeming indifference in the wake of this calamity, in contrast to their pandering to auto parts makers. While the I-park cranked out cheap pieces for Detroit's throwaways, the GT refurbished 10 year-old freight cars which already had covered 1 million miles, and put them back on the rails for another million miles, at a cost of $14,000 each, less than 1/3 what a new Cadillac Allante cost.

The recession of the early 80's visited the worst business conditions on Great Lakes commercial shipping since the 1930's depression. Half the Lakes fleet sat idle in 1982. The principle shortfall came in the steel industry, which depended on automobiles. The car industry's chokehold on America's economy erased 1,500 marine jobs during this period. When auto sales increased, so did Lakes tonnage, and sailors went back to work. Compared to '82, seven times as many St. Clair County shiphands were sailing again in 1987.

About 180 big ships traveled the Lakes. Of his 1,000 footer *Burns Harbor* St. Clair County captain William Jones said, "I drive it just like a car," which didn't strike a very reassuring note about safety. Nineteen of these Lakes vessels carried petroleum products, which caused some concern lest an *Exxon Valdez*-type accident occur. Port Huron's slim shipping trade had little to do with oil or autos any more, it moved mainly feedstuff for cattle. The Seaway Terminal loaded 54,000 tons of ground-up sugar beet feed onto vessels in a good year. "It's been a 30 year struggle to survive," admitted Terminal president William Neal. It needn't have been, had America the eyes to see what was what. A barge delivered a 130-ton paper dryer with ease to the Port Huron Paper Company, in yet another demonstration of what could be accomplished by water.

In the 1950's America had built most of the world's ships. In the 1980's Japan and Korea constructed 80% of these vessels, twice as fast and twice as cheap as the U.S. A quarter of American shipyards closed, throwing 30,000 out of work. A well-built ship still made the best investment in transportation; trucks and cars the worst. The *Kinsman Independent,* a 600-foot Laker built in 1906, tied up at the Seaway Terminal for a decade, used only for storage purposes. In 1988, though still in excellent shape, the *Kinsman* went to the scrapyard, another victim of America's throwaway culture. It once

432

had belonged to the Ford Motor Company, named for Henry II's sidekick Ernest Breech. The FMC sold off the last of its ships during the 1980's.(77)

The Trans-Michigan Canal project idea went nowhere, and faded from memory, but inland ship routes progressed elsewhere. The completed Tennessee Tombigbee Waterway opened up 234 miles of improved mid-American water course, 21 months ahead of schedule, the most significant such undertaking in the U.S. since the St. Lawrence Seaway. For long-term usefulness, a sterling example on the East Coast, the Chesapeake and Delaware Canal, couldn't be beat. It marked 159 years in operation, still going strong, handling 11,000 vessels per year, the largest more than 900 feet long. Finally, the federal government took a sensible step in inland waterway management by levying a long overdue federal marine fuel tax to help pay for maintenance.

The dichotomy of increased individual pleasure boating and moribund passenger shipping (somewhat like cars vs. trains) continued during the 1980's in Port Huron. Not one of the 150 cruise and ferry boat passenger operations left on the Great Lakes did business here, just two ships carrying railroad cars back and forth to and from Canada. A stern-wheeled steamboat tried giving weekend cruises up the Black River for a season. Once in a blue moon, one of a new breed of cruise ships passed by or even stopped in Port Huron, such as the *Caribbean Princess*. They brought back happy memories for local historian Helen Endlich:

We feel that the young people of today are missing much, not having group transportation on boats or trains. The boats were specially nice because one could run all around, upstairs and down, meeting new people as well as coming across old friends. Sitting in an auto is a poor way to have fun compared to the boats and trains.
(78)

The 160-foot *Princess* comfortably carried passengers in 40 cabins around the Great Lakes on a 12-day cruise. The ingenuity of this adaptable ship demonstrated that marine design ideas by no means had been exhausted. It had a shallow draft, could beach itself when necessary, and even had a lowerable pilot house to get under obstructions. At the same time, power plant technology pushed small private boats around St. Clair County at up to 70 mph. Why hadn't power and design married to produce a versatile new generation of speedy commercial watercraft for passengers and freight on the Lakes? One might as well ask where the shipyards of yesterday in Port Huron, Marine City, and Detroit had gone. Michigan's automobile-fixated transportation imagination wasn't up to it. Instead $8 million in private capital built a 500-slip pleasure craft marina in Port Huron, called the Yacht Haven, to house some of the state's 700,000 recreational craft. The Corps of Engineers spent $660,000 dredging the Black River for sports boats.

100 years after local wheelmen organized the first Port Huron Bicycle Club, the Eppley brothers, Kurt and Bob, who opened their Alpine Cycle Shop in 1981, launched a 20th Century version of the club. They inaugurated a road rally under the name of Beat the Boats to Mackinac, which ran along the Scenic Highway roughly paralleling the course of the annual sailboat race up Lake Huron. Though only 23, competitor Michael Hart had been a dedicated cyclist for years. He'd spent $500 on a bicycle while in high school: "...my parents were going to kill me...They thought I should have used the money to buy myself a car."(79) Hart made the smart choice, but his purchase disqualified him from using the number one late-for-class excuse by Port

433

Huron high school students: "My car wouldn't start." When he eventually married, Hart and his bride covered 3,200 miles on their honeymoon by bicycle.

Hardly a week passed during a Port Huron summer in this decade without somebody pedaling through town on a major bicycle trip, or departing on one, heading across the country, around the world, on a charity ride, a vacation trip, or a church excursion. 800 cyclists made the 250-mile Pedal Across Lower Michigan ride-and-campout trip across the state, which ended up in Port Huron. Michigan Bike to Work Day, 1983, a state effort to get more commuters using their legs and heads, turned up some interesting stories, though not the hundreds of cyclists who could and should have commuted by bike in Port Huron. Policemen Richard Klaus, 47, regularly biked and walked to work: "It's economical and helps keep me young and pretty." *Times Herald* worker Jack Barton had done the same for 10 years. Carfree 74 year-old Laura Colgan made any day bike day while traveling about on her tricycle attending to the charitable work that won her the nickname of the Good Samaritan of the north side. She subsequently lived to age 101. Retiree Manuel Gonzales repaired old bikes in his home shop and found a ready market for them during the recession: "A lot of people are out of work and it's easier to ride a bicycle than open the pocketbook to buy gasoline for the car." The 68 year-old Gonzales rode one himself to stay fit, and he lasted another 28 years. Between 1970 and 1990 bicycling among 50-65 year-old Americans increased 400%.

If left alone a bicyclist traveled 20 times more safely than somebody in a car. Unfortunately, no other vehicle on the road aroused more deranged malevolence from drivers than a bicycle. "I resent the cyclists using their fragility to intimidate me," said one crazy St. Clair County motorist. 35 bicyclists failed to intimidate Port Huron's automobiles sufficiently in 1985, and were hit, one killed. Bicycles killed no motorists that year. In 1987 St. Clair County prosecutors tried hanging a 2nd degree murder charge on 17 year-old David Mauer for drunkenly driving off the road to kill bicyclist Richard Goike and injure the victim's son. It didn't stick, and Mauer got off with a year in jail for involuntary manslaughter, plus the $5,700 bill for Goike's funeral.

As to efficiency, all but the oldest and youngest bicyclists did better than the automobile traffic on Manhattan Island in fabled New York City these days, which averaged less than 10 mph north-south, 6 mph east-west. A million motor vehicles every day strangled that 15,000 acre community, and the city as a whole towed away 140,000 abandoned cars per year. Americans spent 8 billion hours in traffic jams, which seemed altogether too many to New York musician and artist David Byrne:

...it soon became apparent to me that biking was an easy way to run errands in the daytime or efficiently hit a few clubs, art openings, or nightspots in the evening without searching for a cab or the nearest subway....I discovered that zipping from one place to another by bike was amazingly fast and efficient. So I stuck with it, despite the aura of uncoolness and the danger...Car drivers at that time weren't expecting to share the road with cyclists, so they would cut you off or squeeze you into parked cars...As I got a little older I also may have felt that cycling was a convenient way of getting some exercise...
(80)

"Exercise. Just say the odious 'E' word, and lots of people will tell you the only thing they care to exercise is their right to sit in an easy chair and fast-forward the remote control." So reported Betsey Marsh in the *Times Herald.* She recommended

434

calling exercise "my fun time," rather than a spade a spade. Her colleague Tom (I'm a) Walker also hid the truth:

The best thing about walking is that you can exercise and no one needs to know. To the unsuspecting public, you are just one more person on their way to some destination. But you know that you are secretly exercising. I guess I came by walking naturally. My father was a postman. I also got a lot of practice as a child because my parents would sometimes drop me off at a museum or a movie theater and forget to pick me up.(81)

32 million American families owned both exercise equipment in the home, and exercise defeating equipment parked in the garage. Predictably, obesity continued to worsen. Two new fitness estimates came down about adult Americans: 60% overweight, 50% no exercise. These habits inflicted on them a comprehensive range of difficulties including respiratory and cardiovascular trouble, varicose veins, embolisms, bad livers, gallstones, osteoarthritis, gout, menstrual and endocrine complaints, 75 million bad backs, and often roaring hypochondria. One or another of these took down the first head of GM's new Saturn division, Joseph Sanchez, a 54 year-old fat man who dropped dead before building a single Saturn. Heart patient Henry Ford II hung in there until age 70, dying in 1987. His motto to the end: "Never complain, never explain." This also could have served as his parting advice for FMC customers and dealers.

Some adult fatties in despair joined Overeaters Anonymous, though they'd have been better off joining Automobiles Anonymous, had their been such a thing. Local Overeaters hotline operator "Eleanor" had clawed her way back from 232 pounds to 180 by walking four miles per day. Dr. David Levitsky of Cornell University, who'd studied the question exhaustively, tried appealing to reason: "The data are abundantly clear now – dieting doesn't work. And I'm totally convinced that exercise alone can cause a clear change in body composition."(82) Other researchers cited exercise as effective treatment not just for obesity, but for its opposite, anorexia. These maladies weren't eating disorders, but exercise disorders.

Reason fell flat with some Port Huronites, who spent hundreds or thousands of dollars on diet plans, fat classes, and clinics (Be Trim, Take Control, Slim Living, Doctors Weight Loss Center, Leaner Weigh). The nation declared zero tolerance for narcotics but greedily gobbled drugs and "nutritional supplements" to try to lose weight ("Cal-Ban...it bonds with the food you eat and ties up calories, preventing their absorption.") In one development that might have arisen straight out some ghastly horror story, gastroplasty, or stomach stapling, became an approved operation. Pathbreaking Port Huron Doctor S. Akram Ali's obese patients submitted to this procedure rather than get the exercise they needed. For $2,000 in doctor's fees, surgeons stapled 97% of the stomach shut. Judy Doan, who at 5'3" crushed the scales at 254 lbs., took this stomach stopper option and became eligible for the support group Staples for Life. Wise up, scoffed Port Huron psychologist Bill Militko: "Surprisingly, many studies show that thin people eat more than most heavier people. The difference is exercise."

Happily, John F. Brown didn't roll over for stomach stapling, or have his jaws wired shut, or join the National Association to Advance Fat Acceptance, as some other carsick loonies did. Following his forevermore diet 20 years earlier, Brownie had fallen from grace and put all the weight on again, and more, reaching 276 lbs. Now he tried another diet kick, with some walking this time, although it took a month before he could

435

cover a mile. Eventually he walked 6-8 miles per day, and dropped 94 pounds in the process. But, auto slave that he was, Brown couldn't stick to the walking regimen, and returned to his slipshod ways. One day a snack of three cheeseburgers, a side of onion rings, a side of fries, a big orange drink and a bag of candy circus peanuts put Brown into the hospital with a suspected heart attack. He might well have been headed for one of the 350 heart bypasses performed in Port Huron annually, until doctor's diagnosed it as just a bellyache.

Brownie felt doubly grateful to the hospital now, for it once had repaired his daugher Jody after a near-fatal car crash. Traffic accident treatment still brought in a lot of business to local hospitals, though it didn't always end so successfully as Jody's. Dr. Elmore Shoudy, the man who settled Brown's stomach, was back on duty two weeks later when the dead body of his own 6 year-old grandson, Dan Shoudy, arrived by ambulance from a car accident. The heartbroken physician could do nothing but stitch up the child's cuts for appearance's sake. "He was such a beautiful boy. So full of life. I couldn't leave him like that." From a helicopter pad at Port Huron Hospital, installed with a complete disregard for the life and limb of surrounding homeowners below the flight path, a flying circus lugged especially busted up car patients to Detroit for more elaborate treatment. They coptered out motorcyclist Leo Burleigh after his run-in with a truck, and no wonder. "Nearly every bone in his body was broken," reported the paper.

Port Huron and Mercy Hospitals continued to expand during the 80's to the tune of $50 million. Like a failed member of Overeaters Anonymous, PH Hospital wolfed down 9 more blocks of homes on which to construct a "medical campus," so that redundant tests and ineffective treatment for auto lifestyle-induced ailments could be administered more readily. Even if this did the patient no good it gave a shot in the arm to the economy, said administrator Charles McKinley, though not quite in those words. An average patient bill of $2,900 helped out the hospital's bottom line considerably.

Every block of the medical campus needed a huge parking lot, which, let's remember, the zoning law required. "When you go to the hospital, the last thing you should have to worry about is parking," patients were assured. Save your worry instead for Michigan's heart disease and cancer rates, the highest in America, thanks to that device you left in the parking lot. "Take good care of yourself! Exercise, and follow good health habits," pleaded Michigan's Blue Cross Blue Shield insurers, but never, "Get rid of your car."

By 1982 America spent $1,350 per person annually for health care, 40 times what it had spent in 1940. "I want you to stop apologizing for the cost of medical care and medicine in this country." Port Huron's Dr. John Coury, Jr., their president, told this to members of the American Medical Association. "You don't have anything to apologize for. You have something to be proud of."(83) Something like medical costs rising 3x as fast as inflation, and doctors salaries twice as fast as average wages. Automobile buyers could be proud of paying not only their own medical bills, but also those of the Big 3's employees, by forking over an extra $700 per vehicle. That amounted to $3 billion per year at GM. At Chrysler it bailed Lee Iacocca out of his wife's $20,000 hospital tab, for which the Chrysler boss only paid $12 under the company's insurance plan.(84)

80 years after Alex Jacobs established his Effect, and 200 after Jefferson discovered the Minimum, to walk or not to walk remained a question in the minds of

436

many Americans old and young. Charlie Barrett enticed patrons to his Colonial Shopping Center by reminding them "You can park directly in front of the store. When you park downtown, you have a block to two-block walk to the store at best." Barrett himself showed the physical bloat of a life spent in the driver's seat, virtually unrecognizable from the man he'd been just 30 years earlier. Such nonsense, said Catherine Edie, who at the age of 86 still walked miles and miles all over Port Huron. "The good Lord gave us legs and we're supposed to use them. There's so much to see if you get out and around. I can't see the sense in just sitting around and waiting to die."(85)

The sitting-and-waiting patients at the Evangelical Nursing Home had to be cajoled to get on their feet at all for a "Walkathon," in a pathetic contrast to Ms. Edie. Many such institutions played up walking as some sort of special effort, a "program." Albert Stephens, winner of the Determination Award, managed 300 feet, total, for an entire week. Nettie Halsey, 494 feet. Champion William Robertson put in 6,200 feet, or about what Catherine Edie covered in 25 minutes every day. Health officials considered one-quarter of Americans over age 65, who lacked Edie's sass, to be disabled. One-half had arthritis, 40% high blood pressure.

The two hospitals in Port Huron, at least nodding to the equation of health = walking, began a "mall-walking" group at NoWoods, marching recruits around and around its halls, a workout for people who didn't want to get too much fresh air or deal in person with real world Port Huron. And of course many drove to the mall to walk in it. The state's biggest mass march, the Mackinac Bridge walk on Labor Day, underlined Michigan's warped view of Walking World. For one day of the year MDOT opened the 5-mile long bridge between the peninsulas to pedestrians (never to bicyclists), and treated this as some sort of special privilege. Few of the tens of thousands of participants walked as much any other day of the year. The Blue Water Bridge remained open for pedestrians and cyclists every day, but so few used it that reporter Tom Murphy investigated the matter for the *Times Herald*. One walk across the 1.3 miles wore him out.

And what of the young? The 30 year-old President's Council on Sports and Fitness, the world's most ineffective council, admitted American children were worse off physically in the 1980's than they'd been in the 1960's, and that had been pretty bad. The Council gave 84,000 elementary school kids in Tulsa, Oklahoma a fitness test and 590 passed. 5,000 Port Huron city pupils still walked to class, in an imaginary sort of way, because many in fact rode to school in their parents' cars, but technically counted as walkers. Fifteen adult crossing guards worked to get the dwindling number of no-kidding walking kids into the schools in one piece. Retired grocer Fred Krohn took the guard job seriously after seeing a woman on foot killed during his second day at his corner, by a car which ran a red light. "You don't forget something like that." Crossing guard Harold Sage, a Golden Gloves champion, winner of the Silver Star, two Bronze Stars, and a Purple Heart in WW2, had seen a lot of unnerving things in life, but he cringed at some of the driving around his corner. "Many drivers today don't use any common sense. Sometimes I have to yell at them to slow down." To make a sad comparison, Michigan set up "drug free" zones around schools, in which it doubled penalties for narcotics offenses, but why no "car free" zones? Call it SchoolWorld – leave the automobile behind.

Chapter 12. 1991-2000: Remorse

What is progress anyway, I mean when it comes to our neighborhoods? Some people call it a forward course, a development, if you will, toward perfection. We can't stop progress. Those in charge are going to find some way to do it anyway. Even if we don't like it. I know our house in Port Huron needed a good coat of paint when I was a kid. But a deteriorating situation? No, I never thought our house or any of the houses in our neighborhood needed a progress jump... [T]he wrecking ball? No way. A parking lot with light posts replaced my house and homes of many of our neighbors. I really never liked the kind of progress that befell our neighborhood.

– John F. Brown, 1997 (1)

By the beginning of the last decade of the 20th Century it was entirely possible, and in wintertime a likelihood, that a pedestrian walking the whole 7-mile north-to-south length of Port Huron wouldn't meet another single soul on foot. The U.S. Census Bureau and other assorted busybodies contrived a picture of the average American you wouldn't meet on this walk: a 32 year old married woman, overweight and on a diet (she'd put on about 8 lbs. during the 80's), with 2 kids, living in Old Farm or something like it, in a 25 year-old house worth $84,000. She'd probably change homes 11 times during her lifetime, and if she shopped for a new house in 1991 the *Times Herald* had a design in mind for a "country cottage" of 2,338 square feet, "which feels and lives much larger." That was triple the size of a new home in 1950. She stocked her nest with two TV's, a video cassette recorder, and six radios. The family had one or more of these devices turned on 11 hours per day.

Mrs. Average worked a job for less than $20,000, and commuted 20 minutes to work driving the family's second car, an eight year-old sedan. Together she and St. Clair County's 145,000 other residents owned about 80,000 non-commercial motor vehicles. Compared to her mother's generation she lived longer (target: 75 years), and had more education, or at least more classroom hours, but suffered from forced mobility (that is, drove a lot more, 5 trips per day).(2) She was more harried than her mom had been, dealing with home and job responsibilities that included 3.5 hours of housework and child care daily in addition to her employment. She and her husband conversed together four minutes per day, and with their children for 30 seconds.(3) Mrs. Average ran a 50% chance of going through a "no-fault" divorce, which usually meant a financial catastrophe for her and the children. While they remained married Mr. and Mrs. A earned a combined household income of about $35,000.

Frau Average found adult life more costly than her parents had, and partly as a result carried 10 credit cards with a cumulative running balance of $2,000. In St. Clair County's case, there'd been a decline of inflation-adjusted income during the 1980's. People looking into these things warned the Averages that this part of Michigan "is likely heading into a future of crowded suburbs, traffic congestion and an economic climate where personal income will barely keep up with inflation."(4) The race between expanding income and the debasement of the currency told the economic story behind

438

the American Century, as some chest-thumping jingos called it. Had she cast her eye back over the past 100 years, Mrs. Average would have been disagreeably surprised to learn that the $1 spent by her great grandmother in 1900 bought about 16 times as much in goods and services as $1 did by the year 2000. In comparison, during the automobile-free 19th Century, while living standards greatly improved, and even taking into account the ravages of a civil war, the value of the dollar *increased*, by 40 percent.(5)

From coast to coast, the national Averages together spent a yearly $158 billion on cars, plus $89b for gas, $34b tires and parts, $20b car insurance, $6b auto registration fees, and $68b for vehicle storage and parking.(6) Plus another $230 billion or so (a very modest estimate, others ran far higher) for roads, accidents, lung disease, congestion, land loss, noise, oil imports, etc., etc.(7) Having made that kind of sacrifice on behalf of the auto industry, the biggest industry in St. Clair County, it came as something of a disappointment just a few days into 1991 for Mrs. Average to pick up her copy of the *Times Herald* and read: "Auto sales skid puts brakes on area jobs." How much more could consumers do to prop this business up? And how many times had that headline been recycled since the dawn of Port Huron's involvement in the car industry? At least once or twice a decade since 1907.

Let's hope that this latest news didn't affect these Averages directly, though the ink hardly had dried on the story before companies at the Port Huron Industrial Park axed 250 more people. Then 150 more, then 130 more. Some of these folks departed from employers that Gerald Bouchard had stood on his head for, like J.P. Stevens. But it was just part of the normal ebb and flow of the car business. Port Huron's unemployment consistently remained among the worst in Michigan's larger cities during this recession, often 12% and more. The laid-off wouldn't find things easy, as redundant ex-Prestolite worker George Hislop could tell them. He wasn't coping too well with the rainy day he hadn't saved for during his 23 years as a relatively well-paid UAW man. "It is sad. I'm 44 years old. They [creditors] are coming to get my truck; they are coming to get my boat. My guts are eating at me...I am dying inside."(8) An ex-convict, Hislop glumly maintained, with maybe a little exaggeration, that he'd been better off in prison.

The state of Michigan, where one-third of America's cars and light trucks still were built, floundered again in this recession, and looked to drop $1 billion from its budget. The knives also came out at the Big 3 car companies. Lee Iacocca warned that he had to carve $3 billion out of Chrysler, though his halo slipped a little when at the same time he opened a new $1 billion company HQ 20 miles outside Detroit, with more space in it than the Empire State Building.(9) General Motors parted ways with 15,000 white collar workers and 80,000 hourly, and started chopping away some of its 8,000 dealers. All part of a push to cut the company size in half by 1995. GM dumped its chairman Robert Stempel, an engineer, for not trimming fast enough, and handed control to former Procter & Gamble soap salesman John Smale in order to really clean house.

While a third of his 4,500 remaining dealers lost money, FMC chief Harold Poling furloughed factories, announced plans to slash the number of parts contractors by a third, and squeezed the rest on prices. Twenty auto parts suppliers went out of business in Michigan in a single year, unhitching some of the 200,000 state residents who'd been working in this industry – in St. Clair County for wages as low as $5 per hour. After selling 8.8 million vehicles and losing a record total of $7 billion in 1991, the Big 3 hoisted the Star Spangled Banner again, warning that the Japanese, now with 26%, meant to take 40% of the U.S. car market.

The Persian Gulf War bore a lot of the blame for the gloomy automobile sales outlook. Nobody in the federal government went so far as to propose the curbing of automobile production in wartime anymore, a nearly-forgotten tactic of the past, but the conflict created among prospective car buyers a sense of unease that didn't jibe with the financial abandon encouraged by industry leaders like Honda: *Don't Put Your Dreams on Hold. If you've been wishing for an Accord, now's the time to start driving one.* The war kicked off in January 1991, following a gigantic buildup of U.S. armed forces in the Gulf. President George Bush, who'd spent most of his working life in the oil and gas business, enlisted an impressive array of auto-loving allies in this war, but he made no secret about which country ran the show. The main event wasn't exactly a fair fight. The enemy, Iraq, had a Gross National Product amounting to $38 billion per year, about what the Pentagon spent per month. In short order the military coalition broomed Iraq out of Kuwait. To use this comparison yet again, 30 times more Americans died in traffic during the 40-day war – 4,500 – than on the battlefield – 146.(10)

But the larger, cultural war didn't end after 40 days. The Persian Gulf incursion stuck America with a running annual military tab of $50 billion to "protect" Middle East oil, which along with other extravagances helped balloon the national debt to $5.5 trillion dollars by the end of the century. Not everyone appreciated the sacrifice. Once, Middle Easterners had viewed the United States as a good petrocustomer, petroholic in fact, who less agreeably used Israel as a military catspaw in the region. Now, some Islamic religious circles interpreted the U.S.-led invasion to secure oil for America's automobile society as the opening phase in an imperial war of conquest, a *de facto* takeover of the entire region. The United States became a major target for terrorists at home and abroad. These malcontents bombed an American destroyer in Yemen, embassies in Kenya and Tanzania, and the World Trade Center in New York, accomplishing that last assault with the helpful weapon of the mobile disaffected, a car bomb. Of course, even when they weren't stuffed with explosives, cars and trucks did infinitely more harm to America through its self-inflicted campaign of standard domestic automotive terrorism than all the bomb-throwers on the planet put together. The 100 Years Auto War killed at least 3 million Americans, and hurt and maimed 200-300 million more, or possibly two to three times those numbers of casualties if you used the multipliers calculated by knowledgeable people whom we've mentioned.

Although it caused a brief spike in gasoline prices, the Gulf War didn't make a significant impact for long at American pumps. Certainly no wartime gas rationing materialized, nor nerve-frazzling gas station lines. Two months after the war ended Port Huron stations sold regular for about $1.10 per gallon, the level folks had become accustomed to over the previous few years. For most of the 90's gas prices hovered in this range, sometimes falling below $1, as America's 200 oil refineries distilled 17 million barrels of petroleum per day, more than half of it imported. Looking back a few chapters in our saga, gasoline cost about 30% less than motorists had paid for it in 1915, adjusted for inflation.

As a result, the mind-boggling waste of this resource by the United States continued and even accelerated. Automakers could hardly give away their high gas mileage models. Sales of the top 10 mileage makers accounted for less than 1% of the market in 1997. RV dealers sold more units than that. Nine million RV elephants roamed the nation, drinking service stations dry, and Port Huronites owned a higher percentage of them per household than any city in Michigan. Big or small, motor vehicles remained astoundingly inefficient in using the elixir that warped the ways of the world. Author Terry Tamminen pointed out that after 60 years of fine-tuning, car engines still lost 80% of their fuel energy in heat, friction, and bad burning, compared to the 92% reported by "This Curious World" in the 1930's. The same tiny 1% of the gasoline poured into an automobile actually transported the driver.(11)

Researchers Stanley Hart and Alvin Spivak dug into the issue of gasoline prices during the 90's and discovered that the American government subsidized this fuel in various ways to the tune of $3-$9 per gallon! (12) This open secret kept better than many classified ones. When during occasional interludes in this decade the up-front cash price for gasoline jumped a few cents, it never failed to provoke a hysterical outburst among crybaby drivers. They called $1.23 a gallon an "astronomically high" price in Port Huron. The traditional bombastic threats by politicians to intervene in the oil industry always followed. "We can't allow Michigan families to be held hostage by runaway fuel prices," said one, though runaway car prices didn't faze him. Hyperbole ran wild during these times, like the *Times Herald's* prediction that the Scenic Highway would be turned into a bike trail if gas prices kept rising – which come to think of it made pretty good sense. In this atmosphere, Mrs. Average lived her life entirely unaware of, or indifferent to, the fact that the world consumed 23 billion barrels of oil annually by the year 2000. If the same percentage of Chinese citizens had owned automobiles as did St. Clair County, Chinese drivers alone would have consumed every drop of petroleum produced in the world, and then some.(13)

Suddenly, in 1999-2000, oil prices tripled to the $34 per barrel range, primarily from an OPEC production cutback. In Port Huron this meant $2 changed hands for a gallon of gas. This *still* came to less than the adjusted 1915 price, but at $2 Port Huron motorist Sharon Pool believed herself driven to the last extremity: "I live close by work and I'm going to start walking to work to save gas." So there. Very, very few Americans adopted Ms. Pool's course. Cheap gasoline, it bears repeating, furnished the primary growth medium of America's automobile illness. By the end of the 90's this sickness drove 210 million vehicles a cumulative 2.6 trillion miles per year, consuming 330 million gallons of gas *daily*.(14) In the Average household, Mr. did 84 minutes of driving per day, Mrs. 64.

"What oil prices? The United States has reserves coming out of its ears." Carl Thompson issued this declaration with the customary chutzpah of the auto industry, at his Chevrolet dealership in Gardendale.(15) And what better use to make of oil reserves than burn them up in a new Chevy Suburban SUV? *On the freeway all men are created equal. Fortunately, all vehicles are not. Chevy Suburban. Like a rock.* – yours truly, Carl Thompson and General Motors. The monster-sized Suburban's equally threatening alternative slogan, *Kickin' Dirt and Takin' Names,* boomeranged on the buyer, who got dirt-kicked and name-taken for $30,000. 200 people worked at Port Huron's new car dealerships, including the senior salesman of them all, 80 year-old ex-Hi Speed gas station owner Sam Napolitan at Northgate Ford. Though backed by Ford's annual $100 million ad budget for the Taurus and Sable jelly bean cars, and by the $40 billion in advertising spent by everybody else connected to automobiles, Sam and his colleagues found themselves in continuous sales, rebate and discount mode during the slow years early in the decade.(16) With the aid of Ford Motor Credit they crafted cunning, impenetrable deals with more fine print to them than a pocket dictionary. The Federal Reserve Bank finally ordered all auto dealers to use a little more plain speaking and less of the "gibberish... that can mask dealer fraud."(17) Consumer advocates also advised Mr. & Mrs. Average to look a little more skeptically at car advertisements, like this one: *Ford Windstar starting at $19,960. Ford Windstar LX shown, $27,685.*

By the end of 1992 prospects for Sam and the rest of gang brightened again with the war over and inflation below 3%. The interest rate on a new 55-month car loan averaged less than 7%. Carl Thompson embarked on a $1.75 million expansion of his layout, while not far away work finished on the new Oldsmobile/Cadillac emporium for a local-record tab of $3 million. Feeling his oats, Carl had a little set-to with the *Times Herald* over a critical story the newspaper ran about the pitfalls of new car shopping. This report recommended that buyers never tell dealers like Thompson what they could afford, only buy from stock, avoid brand new bug-loaded car designs, and skip failure-prone power options like seats, windows, antennas, roofs. "This opinionated and unfactual article...is unacceptable to your largest advertising accounts," Carl told the hometown rag in no uncertain terms, alluding to the seven full pages of car ads carried in the same edition.(18)

Carl had a point. Though the press might throw some spitballs at the Big 3 now and then, the *Times Herald* regularly and unquestioningly published any tripe the auto industry would pay for. Like a Cadillac test drive fantasy, featuring

Stabilitrak yaw control...a more lively platform geared for an enthusiast driver who appreciates hard cornering maneuvers and faster throttle action. At this speed, one wrong motion from hands on steering wheel or feet on stop and go pedals would send several tons of Detroit's finest steel careening headlong off the road on a tangent into the trees. Rooted in a flat stance which hunkered in turns, the sedan felt totally balanced, as if supported by a center ship sky hook as it tiptoed through the apex of the dangerous curve.

Starting price for this Cad, about $41,000, near the apex of American passenger cars.

The yaw-resistant Cadillac, the slippery priced Windstar, and the rocky Chevy Suburban all fell a little outside the price range of heavy-hearted Port Huron shopper Bill McMillan.

My best friend died this week - my car. For six years we drove 130 miles together back and forth to Detroit - more than 187,000 miles. I was hoping the Ford Escort would make it to the big 200,000. But... (19)

McMillan's Universal Car conked out on I-94 in a snowstorm so bad his wife refused to come pick him up in the family's second vehicle. The Escort was done for, and rather than car pool (85% of St. Clair County's 21,000 commuters rode alone), or take the train or bus (there weren't any), or move closer to his job, McMillan bought a new automobile, which cost on average $16,000 early in the 90's but zoomed later to about $20k. Ford broke down the charges this way:

Stuff. We all want stuff. And when we buy a new car we want all the stuff. Dual airbags, power steering, power mirrors, air conditioning, a stereo, automatic transmission, a place to put a cup of coffee. Convenient stuff.

His two-auto arrangement straitened the family's circumstances, but McMillan didn't really want to know where all the dollars and cents went, he just accepted it as a fact of life: "Heck, you don't even worry about the total cost. You're more concerned about keeping the monthly payments down." A week later the remaining used car in the McMillan garage suffered a seizure, and needed an unplanned $122 repair job. Had he been forced to purchase another used vehicle from a dealer, McMillan would have faced an average cost of $10,800 and a loan of 50 months for it.

We'll have over $4 million worth of credit available for this event, the Cawood dealership crowed about one of its used car diasporas, *so we are confident we can arrange financing for anyone with a job, even if they've had problems in the past!* And wanted more problems in the future. Or McMillan might have fallen into the hands of Bob Fox, looking for one last score to wrap up his career. Fox waylaid somebody else and sold him a used Chevy pickup for $31,000. Or McMillan could have picked a used car out on the Internet, from the 1.5 million vehicles listed there by the end of the decade, with all the pitfalls this entailed. For instance the phony odometer readings on 6% of used iron fleeced customers out of an estimated $4,000 per vehicle, perfect for online retail. Whatever channel they used, American buyers and sellers exchanged 29 million used cars and trucks a year by 1996.

Multiply the McMillans by millions and you had the essence of the automobile finance picture for most American households. Not one in a thousand knew, or wanted to know, just exactly what it cost them to own and operate a car. Or two. Estimates figured about $7,000-$8,000 apiece. In another 2-car Port Huron family, the Taylors worked almost 100 hours per week between them, because, said Kristel Taylor, "If we didn't both work, I wouldn't be able to drive a decent vehicle." That kind of devotion pleasured the Big 3 to the nth. But was it just devotion? Psychologists claimed to have put their fingers on another "disorder" during this era, "obsessive/compulsive" behavior. Sufferers needlessly and irrationally performed the same tasks over and over. Who better suited the profile than car owners?

New car sales picked up again in 1993 and Chrysler did a 180-degree spin from its cost-cutting. The company now spent $1.8 billion to boost production by 50%, which included adding 200,000 square feet to its Marysville parts depot. At General Motors assembly lines sped up, work schedules increased to as much as 66 hours per week, and company-paralyzing strikes broke out in Flint among exhausted workers. Members of the United Auto Workers now made $42 per hour in wages and benefits from the Big 3. This rate of pay incentivized the carmakers to shop around for cheaper, less ungrateful, non-American employees. The industry whittled down UAW membership to 680,000, half the 1979 numbers. Passage by the Congress of the North American Free Trade Act (NAFTA) allowed Mexican and Canadian auto products to fly right through U.S. customs duty-free. The jobs of another 300 workers in Port Huron's I-park promptly flew away to Mexico, along with many thousands of others from across America.

Three years after their record losses the Big 3 rang up record profits in 1994 – $14 billion worth on 12.2 million cars and trucks. Then $16 billion in 1997. Sales across the entire American market ascended steadily for the rest of the 90's, to 17 million units in 2000. As usual in good times, the top boys went a little flaky in the head from success. William Clay Ford, Jr., took over as FMC chairman. He gave his

443

predecessor Alex Trotman a $78 million farewell, and promptly laid out $6 billion to buy the Swedish carmaker Volvo, and $2.7 billion for England's Land Rover. Across town, Chrysler's new boss, Robert Eaton, okayed a $92 billion merger with Daimler Benz of Germany.

Michigan's state government, still yoked to the automakers, saw tax revenues swell its new Rainy Day emergency fund to $1 billion. And a good thing, too, because the same old pattern of overexpansion and market saturation in automobile making began to reassert itself late in the decade, and an overcast gathered again. The storm front included 1.4 million personal bankruptcies in America during the '97-'98 federal fiscal year, $1 trillion worth of outstanding consumer debt, a personal savings rate that went negative in 1999, and car loans which grew even longer – 72 months for new, 60 months for used.

A certain amount of strain re-entered the advertising: *It might be hard to believe but these Chevrolet offers are perfectly legal.* And: *How many years of self denial will it take before you crack? Toyota – Be good to yourself every day.* Car floggers in Port Huron mounted a red tag sale, factory authorized clearance sale, customer appreciation sale, minivan markdown sale, spring spectacular, demo sale, construction sale, tax savings time, a swing into spring, and an April shower of savings during a single week of 2000. They put 0% financing on the table. Chrysler's marriage to Daimler went sour almost immediately and the company lost $1.2 billion in the last quarter of 2000. Ford slashed production 9%. GM reduced output 15% and also killed off the Oldsmobile, the vehicle with which Ransom Olds really started the American automobile industry in 1901. *Sic transit gloria carrus.*

In these days, the folks at Dodge claimed to be *Building machines more in harmony with humanity,* but Chrysler executive Robrt Lutz revealed one of the auto industry's more down-to-Earth private sayings, "Good, fast, or cheap, pick any two." The disharmony in the products kept 200,000 auto repair shops and associated feeder businesses busy in America. The tow truck industry alone did $7 billion in hauling per year. A towing museum opened in Chattanooga in 1995 to celebrate this slice of Americana. At one time or another wreckers hitched up to every make on the road. Owners of the Ford Bronco SUV furnished a lot of towing business. These people filed 300 lawsuits against Ford for Bronco-busting rollovers, the eventual settlement of which cost the FMC $2.4 billion. It made just another item in the automotive boner and recall roll call that rolled on relentlessly through the 90's: exploding sidesaddle gas tanks, defective minivan latches, bad seat belt bolts, fire-prone ignition switches, faulty airbags, poor lugnuts, stalling, anti-lock brakes failure, etc., etc. Recalls totaled 20 million vehicles in 1999 alone.

Ford ran into another ravine when millions of the Firestone tires on its vehicles began peeling unexpectedly at high speeds during the 1990's. 271 people, more or less, bit the dust as a result of this phenomenon, and Ford recalled 13 million tires. Once the dust had settled, the FMC was out another $3 billion in make-good costs, and it kissed off Firestone for good, despite the fact that Bill Ford, Jr. was Harvey Firestone's great grandson, too.(20) A new safety law blazed through Congress in record time in the wake of the the collapsing tire case, threatening auto execs with 15 years in jail and $15 million fines if they covered up any more serious defects.

In addition to malformed Firestones, 3 billion other scrap tires decorated the

USA by 1998. That pile grew by 200 million annually, 100 thousand of which landed in St. Clair County.(21) Tires spent just a fraction of their lives on a car, where road contact ground a pound of rubber off each one every year. They lasted a lot longer just laying around in retirement. "If your great, great, great grandfather took a tire off a Model T and left it in his garage, and you opened the garage today, it would still be there." This parable came from the manager of a tire recycling center in Flint, who chopped up 16,000 per day. Tire retailers easily baffled the average customer with a bewildering array of sizes, makes, designs, guarantees, prices, taxes and extra charges. A Port Huron shop quoted prices ranging from $25 to $100 for a single tire size. Tire mileage warranties carried various disclaimers requiring proper inflation, balance, rotation, alignment, and no running over deep potholes or unreasonable road debris. People or animals, ok.

Auto mechanics still created enough problems that the federal government hit three major repair chains – Sears, K-mart, and Goodyear – with fraud complaints. Allegedly, their garagemen on commission were ordering up unnecessary repairs. What a shocker! Insurance companies also nudged mechanics to use inferior replacement parts to save billions in claims money. The gulf of trust between car owner and repair shaman grew ever wider. By one estimate, it took five years for a repairman to become proficient at his job, and customers were not always privy as to how long Mr. Goodwrench had actually been in practice when they turned their cars over to him. One third of mechanics failed their national certification tests.

In their own defense, the repair trade with considerable justice blamed high bills on self-defeatingly complex automobiles laden with gizmos and government-mandated hardware. The parts grew increasingly expensive. A typical set: water pump $155, alternator $321, front brake pads $108, starter $278, fuel pump $240, struts $240, universal joint $207. More and more damaged cars cost more to fix than replace; disposable, in a manner of speaking, a return to Sloanism. A car hospital also needed a lot of expensive overhead. It took as much as $100,000 to outfit a repair shop; not surprising since an engine analyzer alone cost $32,000, plus thousands of dollars more in computer software.

The experts also claimed that motorists neglected maintenance more than ever. "Live by the owner's manual," one Port Huron mechanic preached to his customers, though Leviticus wasn't so exacting as some of these car bibles. Another local greaser blasted motorist ignorance, "I've had people drive in who couldn't turn the engine switch off." These men expected owners bringing a vehicle into the intensive car unit to furnish comprehensive info about knocking, pinging, squealing, hissing, roaring, sputtering ("your car may be trying to tell you something important"), odors, drips, leaks, smoke, warning lights, gauge readings, changes in gas mileage or acceleration, when the problems occurred, at what speed, and were they constant or intermittent? The owner should have told the car something important: get lost.

New cars cost so much that some Port Huroners, at least at first, feared to drive them in heavy traffic, park them next to other cars, eat in them, or report minor accidents that might boost the average $640 annual insurance premium. A scratch, a ding, a stain, a fenderbender inflicted a heartbreaking disfigurement on this metal box into which so many hopes and dreams and bucks had been sunk. The Insurance Institute for Highway Safety ran up an $11,000 repair bill on one SUV with a 5 mph bumper test.

Just washing the thing at home could be an ordeal. If you listened to some people, an auto required a bath twice a month, without fail, no matter how cold the weather, but never when too hot. Why not when hot? Sensitive skin was the problem. Not yours, the car's. Automakers used only 1/1000th of an inch of paint these days, covered with several layers of clear coat lacquer. So, in cleaning, "Never use a rough sponge or cloth...A protective coating is a must...[and don't forget] frequent vacuuming ...thoroughly wash the underside...Under the hood things can get really messy... But there are engine degreasers." When bathing your beauty use protective eyewear, collect engine runoff, patch up the undercoating.(22) Patch it up, but remember "there is no such thing as a rustproof vehicle," said the University of Michigan.

Sentimentalism still clouded the judgment of millions of people when it came to motor vehicles. Trading on this, the *Times Herald* ran a community feature called "My Favorite Car." An early installment spotlighted 14 year-old Ted Koppelberger, who'd blown an inheritance from his grandmother on a 1965 Mustang, and had it photographed at Grandma's grave. Toni Alexander reminisced about her 1968 junker "El Kabong" which she'd bought for $400. She remembered how on the day the tow truck dragged Kabong away to the scrapyard "minus hood and windshield...more than a few heads bowed." In gratitude, probably. Jack Oyler called his 1965 Rambler "Thumper" because the loose tailpipe banged against the floorboards, while a vacuum leak made the engine whistle at high speeds like a tea kettle. David Fitzgibbon rigged a spark plug in the tailpipe of his 1956 Ford to shoot flames 10 feet out the exhaust, which made it his favorite car but nobody else's.

He didn't qualify as a local, but U.S. President Bill Clinton named his restored 1967 Mustang as his most prized possession. Charles McConnell of Port Huron rhapsodized about his 1969 Mercury Cyclone before admitting, "She's now in a self-inflicted state of disrepair due to a license suspension." Motorcycle love just plain carried away Robert "Rocco" Fletcher of the Thumb, after police impounded his favorite seven Harley Davidson motorcycles for insurance fraud. For reporting the scam, Fletcher murdered his wife and two stepchildren, then shot himself. American pickup truck fetishists dropped $5 billion per year draping their vehicles in accessories. 21 year-old pickup owner Nate Noetzel of Gardendale had lavished affection on 23 vehicles he'd owned successively since the age of 15, at a cost he couldn't estimate. Dan Curtis kept on hand 13 cars to pick a favorite from, lovingly housed in his two enormous air-conditioned garages.

With all their other failings, the growing numbers of cars and trucks in the country, especially obese, gas-wasting types like pickup trucks and SUV's, and the growing number of miles they traveled, defeated efforts to control the automobile flatulence problem. Per year their gasoline burning belched 1.1 billion metric tons of carbon dioxide plus various other combustion constituents into the American air. Motor vehicles emitted annually 150 million pounds of pollution over southeastern Michigan alone, including St. Clair County. Each person's share came to 35 pounds. Especially noxious clouds settled over traffic-choked North Main Street and the truck-heavy Blue Water Bridge in Port Huron. Yet some people remained oblivious. "Why is Lung Disease Epidemic in St. Clair County?" wondered pulmonologist Michael Basha in a lecture.

On especially poisonous occasions a coalition of governments, ecology

446

groups, and businesses declared "Ozone Action Days" and mildly urged people to cut back on their driving. Auto exhaust triggered 6 million asthma attacks per year in America (Port Huron now had an Asthma Center), gave a pain in the nose to 33 million people suffering from chronic sinus trouble, and just flat killed off 30,000 folks. That didn't sound like enough to worry Cadillac, which installed emission cheating equipment on 470,000 cars before the Environmental Protection Agency caught on. Honda paid $267 million in fines for covering up its own auto pollution deceit.(23)

The fumes over 104 areas of the U.S. exceeded legal smog levels, and the federal government threatened St. Clair County with a road cash reduction if it didn't cut smog 15% in four years, mainly by tightening up leaky gas pump nozzles. Some people, however, apparently liked the smell of gasoline. Port Huron's City Council for instance voted symbolically against tighter federal smog standards. Gasoline sniffing briefly became a fad among St. Clair County teenagers, until 14 year-old Coy Van Hee's octane fix blew up as he inhaled it, roasting him to death. Like it or not, Port Huron still did a good deal of sniffing of the refinery odors from Sarnia's Chemical Valley, whose 14 different installations stretched for five miles opposite the Michigan shore. And apart from stink, what would the last decade of the 20th Century have amounted to without another explosion in the Valley? This time lightning touched off a 72,000 gallon tank of gasoline additives, one of 70 such tanks on the grounds of a single company.

In his book *Earth in the Balance* U.S. Vice-President Al Gore sent a none-too-subtle signal to the auto industry when he called the internal combustion engine "a mortal threat to the security of every nation." As the EPA leaned harder on carmakers the FMC talked up fuel cell cars and promised again to build electrics to fully tame gasoline gas and waste by the end of the decade. Neither of these vehicles showed up at Northgate Ford or anywhere else. Lee Iacocca also teased the public about building a Chrysler electrocar, but he showed far more excitement about the 450 horsepower gas-gulping Viper model he okayed for production, a car with its own TV show, and "downright frightening speed." Honda found nobody wanted its electric cars, so it tried hybrid gasoline/electrics, as did Toyota, both of which models sold feebly.

Alternative fuels gained very little ground. The Port Huron bus system converted to cleaner burning natural gas vehicles, and some natgas private cars appeared in Port Huron briefly. But an explosion at the local fueling station which wrecked two such autos didn't encourage conversions. It is only fair to admit here that no meaningful effort had been made to control pollution by the big diesels used in railroad and ship engines. Only their greater carrying efficiency mitigated their discharges somewhat. For the amount of work done, a train emitted one-third the pollution of a truck, a Lakes ship one-tenth. The EPA demanded pollution controls on heavy diesel trucks and buses, hoping to cut down their smoke signals by 95% sometime in the early 2000's. A diesel truck ran three times dirtier than a coal-fired power plant per fuel unit. "These dirty trucks and buses will be history," promised EPA director Carol Browner, or at least reduced history. Add it all up, however, and America made no significant reduction of its smog bank in the 90's.

The automobile production process remained a filthy one, a worse mess than that made by the finished product. A German study in the mid-90's found that manufacturing a single car created an astounding 29 tons of waste. GM ran the second pollutingest industrial facility in Michigan, and dirty conditions inside the Ford Rouge plant – coal dust – contributed to a power plant explosion that killed six men. Bill Ford, Jr. wanted to be an environmentalist, but his automobile ties made a fool of him on this issue. As it did of nearly everybody. As long as the automobile hung around, Earth Day in America, now an annual event, doubled as Hypocrisy Day. Bill okayed spending $2 billion to put a greener face on the Rouge plant, at the same time 700 diesel delivery trucks came and went from the factory daily.(24)

The auto lobby fought like lions during the 90's against efforts to increase overall gasoline mileage to 40 mpg in motor vehicles. That target threatened to cut deep into pickup truck, minivan, and SUV profits ($4,000 per Ford Explorer). By 2000 these vehicles made up 58% of sales, and weighed an average 900 pounds more than passenger cars. The arguments went this way: Anti – The 40 mpg standard would mean lighter, more dangerous vehicles, and since gas cost so little nobody needed it. Pro – 40 mpg would conserve resources, improve the environment, and strengthen national security by cutting oil dependence. Leading the way for the Anti's, Ford defiantly announced that it would build the biggest SUV in America, 19 feet long, weighing 3.5 tons, the 10 mpg Excursion. Its sinister slogan: *No boundaries*. The next Universal Car. The Pro's at the Sierra Club described the Excursion as "a garbage truck that dumps into the sky."(25) For their part, high mileage backers didn't just stop at 40 mpg, but talked somewhat ethereally about a future full of featherweight 100 mpg mosquito cars, made of carbon fiber. Not only would these things just sip gas, they'd bounce off each other in crashes, while airbags and seat belts kept occupants from shaking to pieces.

Michigan's 6.7 million motorists paid less and less attention to their driving (of which they did 10% more in the 90's), relying on the vehicle's size and weight and far-from-foolproof safety features to save their necks when worse came to worse. Front-seat airbags became mandatory in 1997, and in celebration of this development bag enthusiasts scheduled a public inflation demo on the steps of the Detroit Institute of Arts. Seeing as how airbags had killed 50 people so far, including a 1 year-old Idaho girl decapitated by a bag in a rush hour accident, and had blinded a Texas woman in a 12 mph rear-ender, and had sidelined Algonac police chief Robert Dumond from duty for 9 months with hand injuries, and had hurt 130 other people by detonating for no reason at all, none of the auto engineers in Detroit saw fit to volunteer as test subjects for this occasion, nor did anyone else. Inside a motionless, empty car the bags exploded with "an ear-popping boom," blasting into the passenger compartment at 200 mph while "white smoke curled out from the steering wheel. The smoke comes from sodium azide pellets that ignite, burning a gas that inflates the airbag..."(26) Bag backers insisted with more emotion than evidence that 1,500 lives had been saved by these devices already, but unpersuaded vehicle owners deluged dealers with demands for bag deactivation. Another way to get rid of airbags popped up at the renamed Blue Water Chrysler dealership in Port Huron when thieves stripped 35 cars of their bags in one night. They were a cinch to steal and could be re-sold for $400 apiece.

Seat belt use topped 60%, or so authorities claimed, but police still ticketed 96,000 drivers per year in Michigan for non-buckling. Anti-lock brakes became commonplace, but didn't prevent accidents or improve driving manners, according to federal investigators and the Michigan State Police. It came in handy in case of a breakdown or a wreck but when used while driving the cell phone made things far more dangerous. "Some nerd nearly ran me off I-94 one afternoon while placing an urgent call," complained Port Huron reporter Roberta Stephenson. 85% of the nation's 80

448

million cell phone users made or took calls while driving, causing about 4,000 accidents per day. "He probably thought my car horn was a busy signal," wrote Roberta. "Telephones should definitely be limited to the home, the office, and the side of the road."(27) But they were not, despite studies that showed phones made drivers as dangerous as drunks, 4 times more likely to get into accidents. As for a drunk using a phone, better steer clear. About 30% of Port Huron car families owned cell phones by the time the decade ended. A distracted phone user hit the road-worker son of St. Clair County's Bonnie Lester at 60 mph. A year later the victim had incurred $1 million in medical expenses and now spent his time re-learning how to walk and talk.

American cops devoted 70% of their time to traffic matters.(28) Port Huron's 52 police officers issued 7,500 citations for auto transgressions in 1995, and handled 2,100 traffic accidents in a typical year. Speeding alone caused many of them, and triggered 740,000 U.S. traffic injuries per year. Nevertheless Congress abolished federal highway speed limits completely during the 1990's, and left the matter entirely up to the states, which meant only one thing to Ford and Pontiac.

Salivating? The new Lincoln LS. 0-60 mph in 7.7 seconds. Be enlightened.

Pontiac Trans Am exists for one reason. To launch you into another dimension.

Chevrolet also celebrated the need for speed when a 70 mile-long, 3,500 vehicle caravan pulled up at the opening of a Chevy Corvette museum in Kentucky, in homage to the fastest and deadliest production car in America.

The forces of the enlightenment in Michigan's legislature pushed expressway speed limits up to 70 mph, which police said translated in practice to an average of 88 mph on I-69. With the help of radar and the new laser velocity detectors, Smokey Bears (CB nickname for police) wrote 600,000 speeding tickets annually in the state of Michigan. This had one strange but signal benefit, for public libraries, which received part of the fine money – $500,000 worth in St. Clair County – though it hardly seemed likely people clocked 88 mph racing over to the library. Wherever they were going, local resident Christopher Balas said enough already:

The increase of speed does not save gas. The increase does not save lives. The increase will not save most motorists more than a few minutes of travel time. For the life of me and my family I cannot think of a good reason or have yet to read one in support of the raising of speed limits.(29)

David Catinella thought he had a good reason for higher speed – fleeing the cops while drunk – when he collided with another vehicle at 110 mph in St. Clair County. This launched Catinella and the other driver, William Smith, into another dimension from whose bourne no traveler returns. The insurance industry revived an old debate, and denounced the Big 3 for making cars that exceeded 100 mph at all. The ghost of Alfred Sloan must have smiled when his successors trotted out his classic defense: the drivers, not the cars, were responsible.

For bad motoring, authorities suspended the driving licenses of 350,000 people in Michigan every year. In trying to avoid this fate, 2,000 traffic offenders contested tickets annually in St. Clair County court. In addition to the threat of losing one's license, just two speeding tickets boosted a driver's insurance rate as much as 50%. Insurers sometimes cut a customer loose completely after he'd picked up three traffic violations against his license. A lot of suspects decided to skip the court scene and licensing altogether and just fade. In 1999 police held 400 unserveable drunk driving warrants and 300 more for unlicensed driving by St. Clair County motorists who'd made themselves scarce. The state champion of this practice, Darrell Johnson of Niles, Michigan, piled up 44 misdemeanors and 15 drunk driving convictions, then drove 20 more years without a license before cops nabbed him. 20% of the drivers in fatal American car wrecks held no driving licenses, whether suspended, revoked or not even applied for.

Driving education, now a requirement for new motorists, accomplished as little as ever. Even after passing the course, 15% of Michigan license applicants failed their road tests. 40% of young drivers suffered accidents bad enough to require a police report during their first year behind the wheel.(30) Driving instructors didn't always make the most trustworthy models, since only reckless people taught driving to begin with. One such teacher, William Bolz, ran a Port Huron stoplight while on his way to pick up a pupil, and died in the resulting crash. But Bolz's bad example didn't noticeably cut down enrollment. Certainly instructors never discouraged their pupils from learning to drive, nor did Port Huron children learn much fact in history class about the most dangerous, destructive, and wasteful form of transportation ever devised. However bad youthful drivers might be, 500 members of this age group drove cars daily to Port Huron Northern High School, which readily granted them free parking at taxpayer expense, and taxpayer risk.

At the other end of the age scale, older Americans often looked forward to retirement from their jobs, but never to retirement from their cars. The number of citzens over 64 years old increased 1,000% during the 20th Century, and these aged car jockeys couldn't be pried loose from the steering wheel for love or money, though they were 3 times more likely to have fatal accidents. Police found 72 year-old Earl McMahon of Momence, Illinois motoring aimlessly around Port Huron one day, having meandered, lost, for 350 miles up I-94 from his home town. 72 year-old Lorraine Erickson ran over and killed fellow senior citizen Milan Barjaktarovich, 76, as he harmlessly pedaled his tricycle across Main Street one day, a familiar and admired figure about town. Jerry Brown profiled ex-driver Lillia McMorran Webb, cousin of Henry McMorran, at age 103: "I've made a few mistakes in my life, but when I quit driving my [40 year-old] 1953 Plymouth last year it was the biggest mistake of my life. I've been driving since 1917 and I never had a ticket, not one. But traffic seemed to be getting heavier, and at 102 years old, I thought it was time to let someone else drive me. But I was wrong. I can't go when I want to anymore."(31) Webb died a few months later, not at the wheel of a car, luckily for the public.

About 41,000 dead, and the usual number of untallied Levassor deaths, plus 2 or 3 million disabling injuries were par for a year's course on American roads during the 90's. Michigan's 1998 share amounted to 400,000 accidents; 125,000 killed or injured. "Virtually everybody has a friend or family member who's been killed or injured," reported *Prevention* magazine, about the American driving public's state of mind. And the effects often lingered long after the road crews swept away the debris. Post traumatic stress syndrome sometimes cropped up in these cases, according to the medical profession. Martin Esquibel saw his Port Huron family whittled down over the years through the loss of his wife, two sons and a grandson in three separate crashes. "It's not easy," he said simply, about coping. 25 to 30 folks died annually on St. Clair

450

County roads. "There's just no rhyme or reason to it," claimed Sheriff Dan Lane during an especially deadly stretch one spring. In light of these unpredictable outcomes, and seeing as how they wouldn't be needing them any more, Michigan Secretary of State Candice Miller asked drivers to okay posthumous organ donation in advance on the back of their licenses, just in case.

Some fatal accidents got a once-over-lightly investigation from police. Code it and load it, as the ambulance people put it. Cops put other cases under the microscope. The head-on wreck that killed teenagers Hart Kinsel and Jeffrey Himmel on the Gratiot Pike so intrigued authorities that they summoned "accident reconstructionists" to the scene, to measure and re-measure every angle with laser exactitude. They created a computer animated cartoon of the incident. Police looked intently for "the exact cause of the accident," and they found it. Dust-Off. Driver Matt English had "huffed" two cans of intoxicating computer keyboard cleaner Dust-Off before crashing into Kinsel and Himmel and had been in no condition to steer.

We may cluck with disapproval but bad crashes, as always, provided grisly entertainment value in Port Huron. On this occasion: "Children on bicycles weaved in and out of slow moving traffic early Friday evening to get a better view of a motorcycle accident that left one man dead." The end of Earl Dicks and his machine after he rammed a car at high speed along a Gardendale road aroused more curiosity than empathy among scores of passersby. "Another foot or so and he would have missed the Jeep completely," mused a cop. (32) At other times bad accidents tapped people's generosity. "Last Wednesday I received the kind of telephone call everyone dreads," wrote Gary Armstrong. Mercy Hospital had admitted his wife with a broken pelvis, broken ribs, and a punctured lung following a crash. Friends rallied round: took in the kids, delivered meals, arranged rides, one with a medical background checked at the hospital on the wife's condition. Greatly cheered up, Armstrong went back to his auto lifestyle without a qualm. Until the next call.

The forces of law and order maintained that drunk driving declined during the 90's, due to tougher laws. Thanks to this increased severity America in 1997 arrested only 1.5 million drunk drivers, while a mere 544 people died in drunk driving accidents in Michigan. Celebration time! But a Michigan Department of Corrections spokesman belied the "get tough" talk somewhat when he called drunk driving that didn't hurt anybody a "lower tier crime." Meaning popular. In Port Huron, Joan Van Gorder didn't feel the full lash of the law, a 15 year sentence, for killing father of two Mark Hazel while drunk. Just the gentle slap of a year in the St. Clair County jail, plus a lecture from Hazel's widow:

...I lost my husband – the man I loved. I lost the father of my children. I wasn't given the chance to thank Mark for loving me. I wasn't able to say thank you for the two beautiful children he gave me...I feel the worst punishment you could get is to come to my home and see what you have put my children through. To watch as they cry themselves to sleep because they miss their daddy...say they want to die and go to heaven just so they can be with their dad...This is the life sentence that you have given us.(33)

This marked the second drunk driving incident for Van Gorder, herself a mother of four. Auto poker had dealt her, too, a bad hand for the Hazel wreck. More than 60% of drunk drivers arrested walked scot free out of court.

451

1,200 drunk driving cases, mixed in with an additional 1,400 felonies and 5,000 misdemeanors, kept a staff of 12 lawyers hopping all year long in the St. Clair County prosecutor's office. In a decade's time, the driving and drug wars in America doubled the number of jail inmates, and left the land of the free with 1.8 million people sitting behind bars. This put a higher percentage of the population in prison than in any other country in the world. The national cost of running these jails came to $16 billion per year. A brand new Michigan state prison opened in 1993 next door to St. Clair County. Its 1,200 beds were almost fully booked before the paint dried.

More no-goods than ever crowded the county jail in Port Huron, 200 head some days (10 times the jailbird numbers in 1900), at a cost of $4 million per year. Storing the overflow in the rent-a-jails of other counties required $750,000 extra. Finally, St. Clair County fathers threw in the towel and rather haphazardly picked out a spot for a new $30 million, 455-bed 21st Century super jail to be built out in suburbia, Port Huron Township, about five miles away from the courthouse. Port Huron's Ron Paul denounced this new slammer as the very symbol of America's malfunctioning society, the nation's "lust to punish...We are on a collision course with social catastrophe." That collision already had occured, Ron.

While the new incarcetorium awaited construction, 27 year-old David Reid stopped in for a stay at the old jail before heading to state prison for 3-5 years. He'd knocked down two motorcyclists while driving flushed to the gills and carrying no operator's license. Reid's driving permit had been yanked 10 times in 7 years for boozing. Jailers also squeezed in 17 year-old Justin Michelsen after he drunkenly crashed into a bridge abutment, killing his teenage passenger. At the time of his latest misadventure Justin had been awaiting trial on negligent homicide charges from an accident nine months earlier that killed another passenger. What would it take to persuade people not to ride with Justin?

Were drunk driving laws tough enough? President-elect George W. Bush ventured no opinion, though he'd suffered a 21-month license suspension and $150 fine for drunk driving as a young man. Port Huron homemaker Sherry Garety spoke more forthrightly: "No. I've been hit by a drunken driver and I have also driven drunk. The laws should be tougher." Port Huron cops wrote about one drunk driving ticket per day. Even this delicate touch prompted responses like "Hey pig, I'm not the real criminal. Go arrest a drug dealer or a murderer." Once in a while, the pigs did. 17 year-old Earl Boughner got 23-60 years in prison for second degree murder after he stole a truck while drunk and killed two people in a crash.

General Motors Vice President Harry Pearce piously endorsed the get tough approach: "As a society we've come to realize that accidents by people who choose to drink are not accidents. They are violent crimes." On another occasion, though, violent crime or no, mercy fell like the gentle rain from heaven on 18 year-old David Muzzy of Port Huron, who rolled his jeep over on I-69, killing his girlfriend and injuring two others, while driving home from a concert. The parents in the case were dumbfounded. "Although empty beer cans littered the accident scene," reported Brownie, "some are having a hard time believing alcohol was involved." Muzzy went on 3 years probation, all charges against him to be erased from the memory of man after he finished up. This ruling came under the obscurely titled Youthful Trainee Act. Training for what? people legitimately asked. Plenty of Muzzies are left on the road, said traffic officer George

Romzek. "I can remember sitting down and chastising some young person for his type of driving, telling him if he didn't stop it he was going to get into a serious accident. Three weeks later he slammed into a power pole. That boy was a really nice young kid."(34)

Nowadays virtually everybody killed in an auto accident, whether victim or perpetrator, was characterized as a nice person. The teenaged Allagreen brothers of Casco Township, Vaughn and Brent, sons of an auto repair shop owner, died within a year of each other, one at the hands of a drunk driver, the other by running into a culvert while sleep driving. They were nice people. So were 41 year-old Amish mother Barbara Shelter and her 10 year-old daughter Fannie, residents of the Thumb, mortally injured when a 16 year-old pickup driver plowed into their horse-drawn buggy. A sheriff's deputy at the scene found a few flickering signs of life in Fannie. "She grabbed my hand and held on." And died. When a jury acquitted the driver, Launce Herron, of manslaughter, he didn't seem quite so nice to outraged Gary Wilkins of Port Huron. "Who is responsible for the operation of a vehicle? It's the driver. In daylight or darkness, you're supposed to adjust your speed to the limits of your vision."(35) But America ignored that principle, 100 years old as the century closed, as fixedly as ever.

Fifty readers deluged the *Times Herald* with complaints about nice person Betty LaRosa's story. She'd died in a traffic wreck at a Gratiot Pike intersection just days after a stop light had been installed there. A million crack-ups took place at U.S. stop lights each year. "Drivers dying to beat the light," ran the headline in this case. A businessman on the corner counted eight cars running the signal in one day. Her neighbors refused to accept the implication that Mrs. LaRosa, a Sunday school teacher, could be one of them. Elsewhere on the nice list, 41 year-old Terry Worden mashed his motorcycle into his stepbrother's car, and 100 riders accompanied him to the cemetery, a good gauge of his niceness. 17 year-old Marysville honor roll student David Currier killed a state policeman by ramming a patrol car with a Corvette. Five months later an erratic driver returned the favor and killed Currier in a head-on. The end of another nice person.

Some of these decedents had been so nice that "grief counselors" were called in to buck up former work colleagues or fellow students after the bad news arrived. These professional mourners descended on Stephanie Lamparski's school when her mother slammed into another car while avoiding a cat and killed Stephanie in the process. Mom Debbie said 7 year-old Stephanie "always said her prayers before she went to bed." She should have saved some for when she climbed into her mother's car. Naturally the grieving process didn't include any apostasy from the auto religion, a promise never to ride in one again. The *Times Herald's* church editor Jim Ketchum remarked on the lack of grief he felt for auto accident casualties, until news about a certain car hitting a garbage truck reached the pressroom:

We ...marveled at how anyone could have survived...how rescuers had to peel the top of the car back to get the driver out. But it was one of those times when the protective defensive walls go up, and the victim ceases to be a person. Too bad, but that's life. Laugh a little and don't think too much about it because it might hurt. It was only an hour later I learned that the driver was my neighbor, Richard Graham. This is a friend, a genuinely good, decent, hard-working man with a smile and a laugh and a willingness to help as big as all outdoors. The news sent the emotional wall crashing down...(36)

Graham died the same day.

Traffic accidents did $12 billion in damage in Michigan in 1993, compared to $5 billion for violent crime. Nice people with lingering auto injuries drained the insurance companies of millions of dollars of potential profits. Gary Belyea made a good example. While he helped out one evening at an I-94 accident scene, a passing truck struck and quadriplegized the 44 year-old Navy vet, Grand Trunk blacksmith, and volunteer fireman. "Why, I'm lucky in a lot of ways," he told Brownie. That kind of luck still annoyed insurers upset with Michigan's unlimited cap on medical expenses from car crashes. They proposed stopping payouts at $1 million. Betty Tomion of Port Huron objected to that idea, pointing out that 10,000 people suffered traumatic brain injuries in car wrecks in Michigan per year. Half the victims were aged 16-24, and ran up bills of $4 million apiece during their lifetimes. What were their families supposed to do when the insurance ran out, put these people out with the trash? Voters rejected the $1 million cap.

The growing popularity of carjacking also bedeviled insurance men and women during the 90's. Thirty-five 'jacks per week took place in Detroit. This method of ejecting the owner from the vehicle at gunpoint and driving it away afforded the thief greater discrimination in selecting his target and sped the whole transfer process up considerably, compared to the older, time-consuming practice of laboriously breaking into and removing an empty car from a shopping center parking lot, the method preferred in St. Clair County. Carjacking so impressed federal authorities that they awarded it a minimum 15 year jail sentence. The average murderer in America only served 6 years. Car theft became the theme of one of he big interactive video game hits of the decade, *Grand Theft Auto*, in which players could enjoy the vicarious thrills of make-believe carjacking from the comfort of home.

The comforts of home spread out further and further across St. Clair County, pushed inexorably by the pressure not of human population but of car population. "Area must be ready for inevitable growth," proclaimed the *Times Herald*, somewhat like the preacher warning that man must be ready for inevitable death. In this case, though, not all preachers endorsed inevitable growth. "The residents of sprawldom insist on much that is urban, but they define themselves against the city," said Episcopal rector Charles Hoffacker of Port Huron. "There is no downtown, no public square, no place where citizens encounter each other casually on common ground. A shopping mall cannot fulfill this vital function because it is not public space, but rather private property whose every feature is designed to stimulate the spending of money rather than the living of life."(37) "Quite frankly," added county planner Gordon Ruttan from his perspective, "Saint Clair County doesn't have the soil composition and public utility infrastructure to handle current growth trends safely, economically, and in a manner that would preserve the quality of life we know today."(38) And the automobile-driven quality of life they knew didn't really deserve preservation in the first place.

Nevertheless, carpenters tossed up more disconnected subdivisions all over the county: Amberwood, Brentwood, Shorewood, Old Country Estates, Pine Ridge Estates, Periwinkle Estates, Cranberry Estates. They fashioned ever-larger homes and attached to each a 2, 3, 4-car garage. Buyers stuffed their buildings not just with cars but with the fruits of universal Fordism; mass produced everything. The junk of nations. Out back there might be a shed to catch the overflow of general stuff. These were the

454

Mound Builders of the 20th Century. Eventually suburban home developments bumped into each other, like tailgaters. When informed of a plan to build 344 new homes near him, Norbert Schneider said oh no, "I moved here because it is rural, to get away from the city. Now the city is coming here." Some suburbanites didn't want to live in a multi-home subdivision, they just dropped a single Colonial into the middle of nowhere. "They are looking for that magic 10 acres so they can have an animal or put up a pole barn," said a realtor. Sandy Pouget moved out to the open spaces for just that reason, to entertain daughter Emily's horse. Then Emily developed an allergy to horses and Sandy to grass. "It breaks our hearts," sneezed Sandy.

The median new home price hit $135,000. At the low end, stocked with dwellings priced well below that median, 27 mobile home parks, full of Fordist factory "manufactured" homes (as dealers preferred to call them) set themselves down across St. Clair County, with a total of 4,000 sites. Occupants crammed their cars and trucks into what little space existed between these cheapjack shacks. Perversely, all new home buyers in all price brackets named "low traffic" as the number one feature desired in their neighborhoods, but none offered to reduce traffic by giving up their cars. They also liked the lower property taxes out in the townships, about half the rate in Port Huron.

St. Clair County's township residential growth outstripped cities 4 to 1 during the 90's, facilitated by eager beaver mortgage brokers like Port Huron's Roxanne Sears. "As long as you have a pulse and can sign your name, we'll try to get you a mortgage." "The safe assumption for local home appreciation is a consistent 6% per year," added a colleague, meaning safe in the suburbs, where twice as many residents lived as in the cities. Suburbanization measures like water line extensions put more pressure – water pressure – on St. Clair County's 1,000 remaining farmers to get out. The runout of Port Huron's municipal water into the countryside hit one farm with a $35,000 service connection bill. A developer bought up a bean farm facing that kind of duress and converted it into an 8-home subdivision cleverly named Harvest Row. 21 square miles of the county's farmland went out of production in 10 years.

Only about half of St. Clair County's remaining farms qualified as "working" outfits in statistical terms at all, with at least $10,000 per year income. Machinery costs alone averaged $54,000 on local farmsteads and this ate up as much as 80% of their revenue. These expensive implements – primarily tractors – killed more than 20 people and injured 8,000 per year on Michigan's 54,000 remaining farms, making agriculture the single most dangerous profession in the state. Late in the decade state farmers dealt once again with "Depression-like" prices according to Michigan's Agriculture Department, which launched an "eat local" campaign about 50 years too late. Port Huron supermarket shoppers commonly found apples from Chile for sale while apples fell off abandoned fruit trees in the Thumb and rotted. The grain and bean elevators, the flour mills, the wholesale and retail farmers markets, the dairies and creamery, the chicory plant, the meat packers, the equipment dealers, virtually any business connected to working agriculture had disappeared from Port Huron during the last 100 years. Scarcely a processing plant of any kind existed anywhere in the Thumb.

America continued to throw away its farm heritage and culture during this decade, convinced by practioners of Fordist industrial farming techniques that with endless mechanization, artificial fertilizers, blanket pesticiding, genetically engineered crops, livestock confinement rearing, and transportation of a thousand miles per product, more yield could be squeezed out of less ground by fewer people. Looking back over the century, 25 million people who'd once made independent, comfortable, healthy livings using largely sustainable organic agricultural practices, had been driven off the land, and into places like Port Huron's Industrial Park. 3,700 unfortunates labored in the I-park by the end of the 90's for $9 per hour, about what Mrs. Average made. Happily, some brave farm families held on here and there, waiting and working for a return to sanity. Thumb farmers Les and Rhonda Roggenbuck used the organic techniques his grandfather had employed 60 years earlier.

Meanwhile, at the forefront of the rural invasion, the NoWoods Mall unofficially became the long-awaited replacement for the McVety Youth Center of Port Huron, which Gerald Bouchard had pulled down to begin his administration in 1966. For all intents and purposes 17 year-old Jason Sontag had moved into NoWoods: "I'm here every day of the week. If I could sleep here, I could be happy. We're like one big happy family outside of home." The big family of 7 million customers passing through the mall per year didn't seem quite so happy to the security guards, who had to break up some ugly fights, and they banned teenagers from flocking together more than four at a time. These feuds sometimes forced the mall cops to call in the real cops. Suburbia kept the 911 line humming in a lot of ways. The sheriff's men spent a third of their time in Port Huron's suburbs, attending to 5,400 calls in a year, while taxpayers in the 22 other townships wondered what had become of their police protection.

The location of NoWoods remained a transit disaster. Traffic jams as long as three miles tied up the streets leading to and from the mall along what became one of Michigan's most congested roads. One of the few homeowners left along North Main Street dealt with "loud music at all hours, many accidents [68 in one year at a nearby corner], cars racing, cars running red lights, and many requests to use my private telephone to help people in trouble."(39) Some 40,000 vehicles per day slowly crawled along North Main Street's 5 mile length, through 20 stop lights, at about 18 miles per hour, slower than the streetcars of 1900, sometimes so slowly that drivers passed the time watching tennis matches on streetside courts as they waited. The *Times Herald* in despair surrendered the matter to the gods of science: "Technology holds key to easing traffic congestion. Computer-synchronized traffic signals, 'smart' roads are long-term answer." This revelation came in a special "Transportation" supplement crammed with 17 pages of automobile ads.

North of NoWoods speeds picked up, and the Scenic Highway for as much as 20 miles turned dangerous enough to give drivers and pedestrians alike the shivers. Resident M. A. Dickinson had seen a son hurt, a friend hurt, and neighbors killed in wrecks on this road. People on foot often found the Scenic too jampacked even to walk across. Richard Courtney's wife watched a car on the Scenic strike and kill her husband of 57 years, as the couple walked from an athlete's reunion for Jerry Brown's high school alma mater. The Michigan Department of Transportation also opened the Scenic to 65 foot-long trucks as a gift to that industry. Anywhere from 10 to 20 semis per hour highballed their way over this thoroughfare, which once upon a time had been promoted as a pleasant little drive through cottage country.

Traffic also filled up the once-placid side roads around NoWoods. One of the 5,000 cars which now passed her home daily caught 19 year-old Lori Castillo off guard while she was retrieving the mail, tossed her 40 feet, and left her with two broken legs, broken ribs, and an injured spleen and kidney. A week in the intensive care unit and several months of rehab followed. Castillo's father worked as an auto body repairman, and Lori didn't blame the car, just the driver, as Alfred Sloan had mandated. The driver in this case didn't stop to ID himself and pick up his blame.

Nothing now could slow down the bulldozers' parade of progress in Gardendale, or Malldale as it might well have been called. Across North Main Street from NoWoods, builders snapped up Bob Fox's old used car lot, which had been padlocked as an illegal junk yard. They redeveloped it into something little better than a junkyard, another shopping center full of chain stores, one of the 2,000 built annually in America, a nation which had more shopping centers than high schools. Another Malldale newcomer – a 200,000 square-foot grocery "superstore" and gas station – set up shop within a can's thrown of NoWoods, submerging more wetlands in pavement and jamming North Main Street with even more traffic.

So did two competing chain giants in the "home improvement" trade who built stores right across the street from each other for a staredown. They rapidly drove most of the locals in the hardware and lumber trade out of the business. A couple of "big box" appliance stores followed suit. In fact, Malldale killed off local businesses not only in Port Huron but in other communities up to 30 miles away. The auto-maddened land rush along North Main swept up everyone. Even Mercy Hospital tore up some wet habitat down the street from NoWoods for a $32 million office and apartment center, though Mercy owned half a dozen acres of empty dry land just in back of its original location in Port Huron.

Did all this commercial development lower the taxes on homeowners in Malldale? Not on your life, said resident Mike Connell; taxes had risen steadily.

If development truly kept taxes down, they should be down to zero after a decade of uninterrupted growth. Come to think of it, maybe they should be paying us to live there. The truth, of course, is just the opposite. There's pressure to add police, to upgrade the fire department, to build parks and trails, to do something about the awful traffic and the lousy roads.(40)

Times Herald writer Michael Eckert voiced similar discord: "It's time we recognized that roads themselves are a pollution problem." Roads brought cars, and in the wake of automobiles came "Strip malls, fast food restaurants, subdivisions and all the trash and litter those things scatter in their wake."(41) In Port Huron Township a trash and litter fountain called a Super K-mart with super parking lots, the descendant of Port Huron's first chain store, opened in the middle of a swamp beside the penetrator highways leading into and out of Port Huron proper. Five years after the Super K started business volunteers pulled 30 shopping carts, 52 pallets, two bicycles, a water tank and several tires out of a small pond in back of it. "The amount of garbage bags and other sundries was beyond description," said one disgusted helper. So ended the first 100 years of the Kresge chain in Port Huron.

Downtown Port Huron experienced no inevitable growth. Loyalists made valiant efforts, and invested millions of dollars in loans, to try to keep the business district healthy. Alas, for the most part, the few significant retailers left dried up and blew away. At the top of the list, Sperry's, the traditional department store that had anchored the district for more than 100 years while it clothed, outfitted, and furnished

457

Port Huroners, shut its doors. Its failure felt like an earthquake. "I used to slide down the banister at the rear of the store," wrote Jerry Brown, "and played hide and seek on every floor with the kids from our neighborhood just around the corner." As an adult he'd also taken a turn at playing Santa at Sperrys, which for decades hosted Christmas parades of epic proportions. "The loss of Sperry's is a blow to us all," admitted the press. "Sperry's is a member of our family. Nothing can make us forget the countless pleasures it gave us. Nothing can shield us from the hurt that Sperry's is no more."(42)

And no more George Innes Men's Wear. "A real class operation" according to one disappointed customer; it closed after 55 years. So did Arden's, a ladies-wear store once the flagship of a 19-city chain. The last downtown pharmacy shut. So did the last supermarket, the former A&P now run privately. So did the last bookstore, the last record shop. The Michigan National Bank building, circa 1927, went up for sale. The good old days seemed long gone. "There was a time that everybody came to Port Huron on Friday and Saturday nights," remembered jeweler George Mosher. "The term was 'go to Port'." They were going to Starboard now. Gary Crankshaw of Arena Sporting Goods admitted, "If I was going to open a business today, I would not do it in downtown Port Huron."(43)

What to do with downtown's remaining landmark structures? The Chippewa Indian tribe, who'd once owned the whole city a few hundred years ago, proposed turning the abandoned Sears building into a casino. But a close city election rejected the idea, despite a favorable comparison of the casino to the auto industry by the *Times Herald*: "It won't relocate to Tennessee five years from now because costs are lower." St. Clair County eventually tore the Sears down to make way for more government offices, which wouldn't move to Tennessee, either. The Ford building that Albert Parfet put up in the 1920's survived, though it went through several owners. One of them hailed it as "...great architecture. You couldn't build another building like this." New owners converted the Harrington Hotel into a senior citizens residence. Some squatters converted the vacant Algonquin Hotel into a pile of rubble by setting it on fire. The 106 year-old, 4-story Algonquin once had been the proud, handsome, luxurious headquarters of the Maccabees, and many a lifelong resident felt deeply depressed by its demise, which seemed in its way, like the end of Sperry's, an indictment of the whole city.

The new chain hotels/motels that came to the area during this decade preferred locations not downtown but at the freeway exits on the outskirts of Port Huron – Knights Inn, Quality Inn, Comfort Inn, Ramada Inn. They weren't really traditional inns, they lacked anything like the dignity and charm of the old-time hotels, but they offered plenty of parking. Critic Jane Holtz Kay called this sort of thing "carchitecture." Rector Hoffacker had a few heartfelt words on this subject, too: "Our landscape has been enslaved to the automobile and its highways for more than 50 years. We have built so much ugly architecture that archaeologists of future generations will wonder what was wrong with us."

Some of the remaining downtown business people asked for the removal of the city's 1,470 parking meters. Why bother with them? The NoWoods mall had solved the downtown parking problem, said shoe store owner Dennis Raetzel sourly. Surprisingly, even with plenty of meter room, $55,000 worth of unpaid parking tickets accrued, as more and more drivers came to expect the largesse of "free" parking, with or without a meter. Only a real cheapskate tried dodging these meters; parking cost a measly 25 cents for 2 hours. Police could impound a car for six unpaid tickets, and actually sold one that racked up 13.

Echoes of its own past parking lot mania sometimes drifted back to Port Huron from the busy suburbs. The Goodells county park put in a parking lot as big as a football field for one of its latest "improvements." How many times had Port Huron heard that "improvement" gag, about itself? All over town patched, aging, crumbling "improvements" of the past left some of the ugliest residues of the auto age. Thinly paved parking lots cracked and broke up with the greatest of ease, sometimes just days after they had been resurfaced for the umpteenth time. The city rarely condemned neglected private parking lots because the buildings to which they belonged legally *had* to have them. Even one of the earliest municipal lots – unused, stripped of its attendant, then of its meters, then of its lights, its stripes faded away, just a desolate acre of concrete with grass pushing up through the fissures – sat year after year behind the Harrington Hotel, its past glories of "improvement" but a distant memory.

Several of Port Huron's older residential areas continued to age gracelessly. Homeowners in these spots enjoyed no safe assumption of 6% price appreciation. Absentee landlords rented out half the homes and apartments. "Severely distressed" is how welfare workers described some of parts of it, meaning too much poverty, unemployment, food stamps, dropouts. "Third World housing, dilapidated, vermin-infested," said an inspector about one auto-ravaged section. In its happier, earlier life, one of the typical homes along 10th Street had been owned for years by a Marine officer, then a school principal. Since Port Huron had widened the street into a traffic sewer the house had declined into a shabby rental, red-tagged as unsafe, a magnet for gangs. "I usually don't go out into the street anymore," said Port Huroner Clotilde Walker. "The neighborhood has just gotten too bad." Some resolute residents got involved in one of the 45 different Neighborhood Watch anti-crime programs, which consisted largely of just walking around, looking out for each other. One of the watch captains, Pam Vaughn, confessed that she'd lived in her area for 23 years but had never gotten to know her neighbors before taking up this walking duty.

But lest we give the wrong impression here, let's be clear about this: the overwhelming majority of Port Huron's thousands of solid citizens hadn't despaired of their neighborhoods, which they strove to maintain in their carsick fashion. The same with their city. They thought their town still fundamentally too nice a spot. They had plenty of spirit left. On Community Paint Works day, 300 volunteers turned out to work on 13 houses. The Garden Club planted 7,000 flowers in Pine Grove Park, and the Beautification Commission sponsored a Yard of the Year award. An annual Black River cleanup regularly pulled tons of debris out of this once-abused stream, including several drowned cars. That inspector's crack about Third World housing got a rental inspection law passed which helped considerably. The Community Foundation and United Way charities supported dozens of causes, and so did lodges, churches, clubs, schools, societies. Taxpayers shouldered a massive municipal budget, far beyond anything remotely imaginable in 1900. Port Huroners wanted a great city. St. Clairians wanted a great county. But they still wanted their cars, and couldn't see through their auto narcissism the fact that they couldn't have both. In view of the devastation the automobile spread, ultimately nobody could own one and function as a good citizen, or even a decent human being.

Jerry Brown remained a firm booster of his hometown, an unshakable loyalist in almost everything. He'd also dedicated himself to the automobile life, dating from the days when he drove his fiance Joan around in a car so rusted out they could see the street passing beneath their feet. As newlyweds they'd upgraded to a 2 year-old 1954 Buick sold to them by Charlie Barrett on E-Z terms. The car-years rolled by from then on. Brown absolutely loathed the McMorran Center parking lot that urban reclamation had put down over his boyhood home. "Our home is gone now, as are all the homes that bordered the Park, Erie, Bard and Ontario streets neighborhood in the 1930's, 1940's and 1950's. The parking lot that replaced our neighborhood is unworthy testimony to the joy of life that once was celebrated there by hundreds of families." But who did they put that parking lot there for, if not for you, Jerry? "As I look back now on the winters of my youth, the beauty of our neighborhood stands out like an artist's painting. The big chestnut trees that stood like sentries on the boulevards appeared to be magically transformed when the snow stuck to their spreading branches."(44) Long gone, Brownie, beneath some of the 38 million acres of parking lots and paved streets in the USA. And as for snow? Ugh! Somebody call for a salt truck!

A private citizen who'd kept score counted that 1,400 housing units had been torn down during Gerald Bouchard's tenure as City Manager, and only half of them replaced. The manager meant to partially redress that imbalance on the prime former railroad property along the St. Clair River he'd so adroitly obtained in a land swap. First he lovingly expanded his pride and joy acreage by knocking down 42 additional homes next to it. Before anything more could be done, Bouchard discovered that the gasoline storage tanks belonging to three different oil companies which used to occupy part of the site had leaked thousands of gallons into the ground over the years, to a depth of 27 feet. The cleanup cost $8 million, plus a whopping lawsuit to get the previous owners to pay for it. Thus did Port Huron learn the sad truth that gasoline was the single biggest cause of groundwater contamination in America.

Once he'd degassed it, Bouchard helped transform the whole parcel into his ideal landscape in three stages. On a ridge overlooking the still brilliantly blue waters of the river, dozens of high end condominiums were built in a gated, sidewalk-free development, at a cost of $19 million. Next door private interests erected a new $12 million, 150-room hotel, the Thomas Edison Inn, with acres of mostly empty parking lots. The *pièce de résistance* ran immediately in front of these homes and hotel, stretching through almost a mile of grassy shore along the riverfront, the three-lane, no stopping, Thomas Edison Parkway, connecting five huge parking lots.

No trees or shrubbery of any kind interrupted the Edison parkway vista, no swing sets, no picnic tables, no barbecues, no pavilions, no fountains, no playing fields, nothing to entertain the human race. Nothing that Al really would have wanted his name put to. The parkway served as a dedicated pleasure cove for automobiles, where they and their tame owners could squat a few minutes and enjoy the view in peace. "The parkway wasn't designed for picnic activity, but rather for a flow of traffic through it," said one of Bouchard's satisfied administrators. Not everybody shared that satisfaction; with the parkway or much else. The decline in Port Huron's population continued during the last decade of the century, leaving 32,300 people in town, a 10% subtraction since 1960. Not good, but modest compared to the 36% missing from Flint, and 43% from Detroit.

460

He had bungled everything. He was the city's savior. Between those two poles of opinion fell the reality of Gerald Bouchard, who retired in 1997 after 32 years. "I never thought he was as bad as some people said," expressed the middle of the road assessment of Adele Stommel, an esteemed judge's widow and long-time resident. 300 other people, including six former mayors, turned out for Bouchard's bye-bye testimonial dinner at $40 per head. In many ways he still resembled the bright young man who'd arrived in Port Huron in 1965. As Jane Jacobs might have predicted, Bouchard had done what he'd been trained to do, what Port Huron's best-heeled, most responsible people had urged him to do. The delusions of the auto age didn't spring from him, nor the ill-conceived city manager system that inflated his self-regard to kingly levels at times. It would be unfair to flay him further for the results. The automobile had victimized him as much as the city he'd tried to do right by. A Heroic Sick Person.

Before he left, Bouchard delivered this benediction to the Port Huron City Council: "It takes a monumental amount of money to keep streets up – especially in this climate. Every city in America has this problem."(45) One of the home video hits of the 90's among the younger set exploited this theme: *Road Construction Ahead.* "Recommended for children ages 1 to 8...[this] 30 minute tape features bulldozers, excavators, rock crushers, buck loaders, and giant trucks...The narrator, a friendly construction worker named George, explains each segment. Drilling, blasting, grading and paving are all shown." Recommended for parents were *Potholes Ahead, Dangerous Bridge Ahead, Gas Tax Increase Ahead,* and a never-ending series of sequels. Michigan now owned 120,000 miles of road, twice the mileage of 1900, and on them the various units of government spent almost $2 billion per annum by the end of the decade.(46) So George was a busy guy. Just how much money did it take to keep passable road surfaces underneath America's one billion spinning tires? The $70 billion spent per year didn't seem enough.(47)

Certainly not enough in the view of the *Times Herald.* Where are "the road repairs Michigan so desperately needs?" cried the editors. Here today, gone tomorrow. A better question: Where was the road restraint Michigan so desperately needed? Why, for instance, did 15,000 of the heaviest trucks in America – 164,000 pounds each – still travel Michigan roads, crunching away at George's handiwork? As is our theme, Michigan desperately needed more rail and water transit, and no cars or trucks. But determined as ever to throw good money after bad, and after suffering the agonies of the damned about it, the legislature raised the gasoline tax another 4 cents to get more road money. The made the state levy 19 cents a gallon, plus a federal gas take of 18, plus state sales tax. Total, about 43 cents per gallon.

At the Port Huron level, Mr. Bouchard's "monumental amount of money" meant it cost $300,000 to resurface and $800,000 to rebuild one mile of city street, which lasted 15-20 years. 80% of streets needed a fix of some kind. Several had been cold-patched so many times they looked like prairie dog towns. The city bowed at last to reality. There would never be enough state and federal tax money flowing in to keep streets in decent shape, nor were the city property and income taxes adequate. Although some Port Huroners said they preferred having potholes in order to slow down traffic, voters passed a special 10-year tax to raise an additional $700,000 per year, just for streets. People quite rightly wondered if this sum, too, would prove to be inadequate, with few limits on the size, weight or numbers of vehicles using the streets. Almost as a rebuke to the city's transportation mess, repair crews working on Main Street found some of the old streetcar rails still intact underneath the fractured pavement.

As Mr. Bouchard had said, the city did not live alone with the bad street and road routine. Next door in Port Huron Township, Supervisor Robert Lewandowski was beside himself over the way his streets busted up: "We have garbage trucks that are so heavy they are overweight when empty...the state legislature should take a look at weight limits because our roads can't take it."(48) And the friendly, graveled Good Roads of Horatio Earle's delight, that once had beckoned so many suburbanites to live in the hinterlands of St. Clair County, were having washboard trouble again. Road engineer Charles Alloway told the Road Commission that he found it next to impossible to maintain unpaved roads under the present funding arrangement. A gravel road could be seriously damaged by the passage of a single heavy truck during a wet period, such as springtime, when conditions closed up to 40 roads at a time. Impassible roads: a problem now 150 years old.

On one memorable township fire call the first volunteers on the scene got stuck in their 4-wheel drive vehicle. Then the fire truck bogged down. And finally after a good deal of struggle everybody had to be pulled out with a road grader. "Ox wallows and obstacle courses," is how the *Times Herald* described some of these thoroughfares. Suburbanite D. Miller Kane itemized his objections about rural driving conditions: potholes half a mile long, water soaked roads with no ditching, 20 minutes to drive a mile or two, outrageous repair bills on cars and trucks, and fearful mail carriers boycotting delivery. Not to mention the summer dust! A car traveling at 35 mph raised a 100 foot cloud in some spots. After he filed these complaints with the road office they told Kane to move someplace else if didn't like it.

But, supposing they were well maintained, the better the roads, the more driving they invited to wear them down, and faster driving too. Most St. Clair County gravel roads came under the 55 mph general rural speed limit of the state, though driving at that speed on gravel compared to driving on ball bearings. A car traveling at a police-estimated 70 mph on a gravel road slammed into 9 year-old bicyclist Adam Schweihofer, knocking him 130 feet to his death. Driver Brenda Leverenz's vehicle skidded for 300 feet in this collision. Brenda felt a little put out over being prosecuted for this. She claimed Adam's dad had hugged her at the hospital. "We were going to try to get through this thing together."

A dogfight broke out during these years over the Road Commission, and the amount of productive work it did on 1,772 miles of county road with its annual income, which mounted from $13 million to $18 million per year during the decade. $10,000 per mile didn't buy enough results, in the opinion of township nesters. Department overhead took half the money. The payroll looked a little top heavy with 45 managers. Accusations flew about extravagant salaries and fringe benefits, "longevity bonuses," and "unused sick time." The road office stoutly denied all this, but it didn't help matters when one of the foremen, Ricky Mitchell, pleaded guilty to driving his county car while drunk. Eventually the Road Commission manager and chairman were shown the door and faint hopes were pinned to their successors.

What with one thing or another, road maintenance costs had quadrupled between 1970-1990. MDOT wondered if maybe the answer to solving this problem lay in volunteerism. Officials tried enlisting some free help to gather up the 5,000 items of

462

trash per mile tossed along state highways in cities every year; 1,000 in the country. The official state litter budget only came to $2.5 million. Solution: the "Adopt a Highway" program. Coax taxpayers into picking up trash along their favorite stretch of orphan asphalt, before it disappeared under the debris. Some Edison Inn employees took a stab at trash-picking along I-69. They weren't on any chain gang, of course. The automobile already had chained Michiganders to their roads, body and soul.

Construction of the Interstate Highway System finished at last during the 90's, 300% over budget, the end of a carnival of corruption, waste, and misconception that had dwarfed the occasional railroad building scandals of the 19th Century. Michigan's last piece of the IHS puzzle fell into place in 1992 after 36 years of work, and a $4 billion outgo. Celebrations were muted, to say the least. This finale concluded just in time to begin $6.5 million dollars in repairs on the stretch of I-94 in St. Clair County finished 30 years earlier, and $1.6 million on teenaged sections of I-69. The federal Highway Trust Fund paid for 80% of interstate repairs, but what did the taxpayer care which pocket it came from? Detroit's freeways presented such a tangled mess of repair work detours, crisscrossing, and traffic jam-ups that officials spent $33 million putting up TV cameras and message boards to help drivers "make smarter decisions on how they get to their destination." Like avoid the freeways.

More monumental money had to be spent during the 90's to keep Port Huron's bridges up. No fewer than five big bridge projects hogtied traffic every which way at one time or another. The Main Street lift bridge cost $9 million. The 10th and 7th Streets lift bridges, $10 million. The Black River Canal bridge, $2.8 million. All four had been punched to pieces by traffic. On top of this a towering 2nd Blue Water Bridge, was cast across the St. Clair River to Canada for $110 million. Port Huron experienced the worst traffic jams in its history, a "traffic zoo" in one observer's words. "For nearly four hours it was as if city streets were a parking lot," wrote Jerry Brown on a bad occasion. "Cars stood still." If only they'd stayed that way.

Traffic crossing the original Blue Water Bridge had increased to 6 million vehicles per year by 1991, double what it had been when I-69 opened in 1984. The bridge's principle beneficiaries, truckers, paid only 11 times the fare that cars did, while doing scores or hundreds or thousands of times as much damage, depending on vehicle size and weight. Michigan allowed a maximum truck size of 8.5 feet wide and 70 feet long; modest compared to the 120-foot long rigs now permitted in some states, vehicles equivalent to rolling 10-story buildings. As many as 2,800 trucks crossed the Blue Water daily, and the bridge needed a $38 million repair job as a result.

Chronic short-staffing left customs inspectors unable to cope with the uncoordinated mob of trucks and cars that had a habit of descending on the Blue Water Bridge all at once, further tying things up. Instead of trying to divert passengers and goods to the superior efficiencies of rail or water, and to facilities such as the railroad tunnel, Michigan Governor John Engler announced that a second bridge would be built in addition to and adjacent to the first one, as another government present for the automobile and trucking industries. It happened that the Grand Trunk railroad built a new tunnel beneath the St. Clair River at the same time, in order to handle larger freight cars. A comparison of bridge vs. tunnel is instructive.

In 18 months Grand Trunk's contractors dug with a gigantic boring machine an entirely new, $160 million tunnel under the St. Clair River, 10 feet wider than the

463

1891 version, large enough to admit bigger freight cars and handle as many as 48 trains per day, traveling at speeds up to 50 mph. It let a train crew of two people move as much as could 200 18-wheel trucks, and electronically file cargo customs documents along the way. It was one reason U.S.- Canadian train traffic subsequently increased by 10% per year after 1994.(49) The tunnel required no new property condemnations or acquisition in Port Huron. Grand Trunk undertook this project despite having lost $250 million in the recent recession. It made a minimum of fuss.

Though Port Huron once had been known as the "Tunnel City," by the 1990's railroads had fallen so far out of the public consciousness that one observer said, " A lot of people don't even know the tunnel exists." 1,500 who did know took a 100th anniversary ride through the 1891 structure, which was still in perfect shape, and had handled 25 million freight cars during its lifetime. Rekindled tunnel love must have spread fast, because when Grand Trunk made an offer to give people a ride through the new one, 25,000 folks turned out, three times the expected numbers, and most unfortunately had to be turned away.

On the other hand, nobody among the boosters of Blue Water Bridge II wanted even to think about building a discreet out-of-sight motor vehicle tunnel. Just like its predecessor in 1938, the Michigan Department of Transportation in the 90's resembled a political milch cow as much as a civil engineering organization, and bureaucrats wanted their handiwork out where people could see it. Transportation officials talked up the second bridge as "a chance for some forced urban renewal that will benefit everyone involved." It benefited 50 property owners standing in the way on the Port Huron side by evicting them. As usual MDOT leveled some fine pre-bridge era homes, tore up yards, and extinguished businesses without a pang of regret:

Tina Cote looks out the picture window of her family's Elmwood Street home and eyes the land that once was a neighborhood. No longer does the 23 year-old mother of two see the houses that filled the four block area between Elmwood and State streets. What remains are mounds of dirt and streets of mud lined with construction equipment.(50)

"I think it's a travesty," said Peanut House bar owner Stephen Armstrong, an unwilling beneficiary of this progress. "I don't want to move." MDOT paid not the slightest attention to him nor to public suggestions that the new bridge duplicate the first one, to at least keep the thing symmetrical. Tacitly admitting that the '38 structure had been a lousy design to begin with, the department mulled over five different plans for Bridge 2, then began work on an tied-arch construction that clashed visually in every way possible with Bridge 1. With a terrific racket contractors pounded 350 pilings into the ground for the span's support, further infuriating the neighbors.

PR types, including the *Times Herald* staff, hyped the dual Blue Water Bridges as an important link on an international truck "superhighway" between Canada, the U.S., and Mexico. It came as something of a shock to these propagandists when the overall number of crossings dropped off dramatically even before Bridge 2 had been completed. Tighter security at the international border, and more truck trailers piggybacking on railroad flatcars, accounted for the decline, which however did not halt construction. Five years after the governor's go-ahead, the second bridge opened in 1997 with a burst of self-congratulation reminiscent of the 1938 celebration, though without a song this time. For a single day Michigan and Canadian authorities allowed pedestrians to march across this structure for an up-close look. 200,000 people took this

464

stroll, the most who had ever congregated within the city limits of Port Huron for anything. This was the most enjoyment many of them ever got from the mismatched, eye-jarring Blue Water Bridges, which both then immediately and permanently closed to walkers and bicyclists, and passed under the unofficial rule of the trucking industry.

As much as 8% of the U.S. labor force worked in trucking, about 3 million as drivers. On some days it seemed as if they were all tearing through Port Huron, penetrating to every corner of the community. These vehicles came in all sizes and shapes. The road-busting sludge haulers out of the sewage plant. The speeding, park-it-anywhere vans of United Parcel Service, whose drivers had to drop off 12 packages every hour. The equipment and product laden panel trucks of every tradesman and vendor in town. But most of all, the ubiquitous 18-wheelers, the most despised vehicles in America, that poured in and out of Port Huron's biggest industries in lieu of train shipment, that crowded into side streets to make store deliveries, that bullied their way through residential neighborhoods looking for shortcuts, that blasted across the sky via the Blue Water Bridges, leaving behind an arc of cacophony and diesel exhaust.

"As you know, truckers have an image problem with the public, who often see them as pill-poppin', road hoggin' missiles-of-doom drivers rather than small business men and women doing an important job."(51) This admission to the *Times Herald* came from G.C. Skipper, editor of the industry's *Overdrive* magazine. A few weeks later a road-hoggin' Saturn auto hauler crashed into traffic backed up by President Clinton's motorcade at Flint, killing 3 people, the latest among the 5,000 dead destroyed by heavy trucks per year. Not long afterward a missile of doom plowed into a Port Huron city lift truck, killing municipal employee Stan Wolfe.

Image problems, indeed. Retired Port Huron businessman Elmer Struyk said he'd made his last car trip to Florida after a hair-raising few hundred miles on the truck-choked interstates. It didn't pay to tangle with them, but exasperated St. Clair City commuter Roy Barnett nonetheless had a set-to with a small businessman doing an important job driving a steel carrier: "I moved over into the left lane," wrote Barnett, "pulled up next to him, pushed the button to lower the passenger window, and swore like a drunken sailor. I am embarrassed to admit that I challenged this inconsiderate moron to a fight."(52) The moron didn't have to fight, he could have squashed Barnett's car like a pop can, but this time he chose forbearance.

An effort to spruce up the trucking industry's image hit American TV's in 2000, a dramatic series called *18 Wheels of Justice*. In this episodic fantasy, undercover Justice Department agent Michael Cates cruised the nation in a semi dealing with criminals. Had such a person really existed he'd have spent all his time on criminal truckers. He could have started with the mobbed-up Teamsters Union, which the federal government took control of in the 90's to try to clean things up. Agent Cates also would have found that due to one legal transgression or another most of the tractor-trailer rigs on the road had no business being there. During one blitz the National Transportation Safety Board stopped 1,500 semis for surprise inspections and parked half of them for brake problems. Even with good brakes it took a big truck 330 feet to stop at 55 mph; with bad, who could tell? A 50% failure rate actually didn't look too bad compared to standards on Mexican trucks. In the southern states, NAFTA threatened to open America's borders to Mexican tractor-trailers, two-thirds of which were mechanically defective, on average 15 years-old, weighed 50 tons, and did almost as much damage to

465

roads as 10,000 cars.

The Federal Trade Commission could have advised Agent Cates that many American truck driving schools were crooked, and stiffed pupils on tuition, training and job placement. Some student gearjammers got only 10 days at the wheel and a handful of want-ads in exchange for their money. A help wanted appeal aimed at Port Huron trucking recruits offered (in addition to "no slip seating") 2,500 miles of driving per week as an *incentive*. To meet mileage quotas some truckers drove up to 16 hours in every 24. Unqualified, overworked truckers hauled almost anything and everything. In one Port Huron reporter's words, "...just about every toxic chemical or explosive substance used in North American manufacturing," rolled through town at the rate of 1,000 dangerous cargo trucks per week.

On top of everything else, a Stanford University study found three-quarters of long haul truck drivers suffered from sleep apnea, which hindered their rest. "When 78% of the people coming toward you on the road in 40-ton trucks have such a disorder, you have a problem," Dr. William Dement understated.(53) Apnea sufferers racked up seven times as many accidents proportionately than better rested motorists. Obesity caused most of this affliction, and commercial truck drivers were even fatter than the general public. Estimates blamed 200,000 U.S. traffic accidents annually on sleep disorders, plenty good enough to persuade Port Huron Hospital to open its own sleep clinic.

Just how tired were the drivers of Port Huron's city buses? Its patrons may have wondered. After all, a bus was just a truck that carried people. Whether for that reason or higher fares, ridership at first decreased to about 50,000 per month during the 90's before springing back to 60,000 by the end of the decade. Port Huron voters renewed the local bus tax regularly at the polls by big margins, but other subsidies waxed and waned, and so did inflation. The fare increased 25% to 75 cents a ride, but even at that figure the price of a single new car would have paid for a round trip bus ride every day for 38 years. Unpersuaded by that calculation, Jerry Brown clambered onto a city bus in Port Huron for the first time in 47 years primarily from nostalgia. He'd ridden often enough as a boy, sometimes to the beach, changing into a bathing suit in the back seats while his pals shielded him with towels. This time he kept his clothes on.

Brownie hadn't been aboard a Greyhound bus in years either. That company closed down its Port Huron charter office during the 90's. Brown reminisced fondly about riding The Big Dog back in the 40's, but added, "I know there are people today who would thumb their noses at the idea or even the suggestion of riding on a bus." The ticket agent in Port Huron, Gertrude Carl, admitted even *she* had never ridden the Hound. One reason may have been the caliber of long-distance coach drivers. They varied considerably these days. When Frank Bedell drove a commercial bus off the road near New Orleans and killed 22 people, police discovered that he had congestive heart failure and diabetes, he was on dialysis, he'd been treated for low blood pressure and dehydration just before the assignment, and he'd been canned from two previous jobs for smoking weed. Bedell tested positive for marijuana after this accident, too. A simple antihistamine used by another driver sent a bus crashing into a semi in Pennsylvania, killing 7 passengers.

The sorry sight of the mass transit picture in the Thumb disgusted well-traveled Port Huron businessman Mike Abdo: "Public transportation in this country is extremely bad. Especially in the winter. This is especially true compared to Europe. There it's easy to get around. Cars are expensive. Everyone can't afford them. There should be more public buses." True enough, 80 million people in America were too young, old or poor to drive a car.(54) Port Huron did its bit for buses, of course, and some Thumb counties ran dial-a-ride programs. Next to many other states Michigan spent generously in underwriting city and regional bus service. But as *Carfree Cities* author Jan Crawford wrote perceptively during this decade, "We must never underestimate the importance of the simple fact that most of the decisions about transport are made by people who drive to work."(55)

Passenger numbers on the Amtrak train between Port Huron and Chicago also declined. Service to Chicago cost a rider as little as 8 cents per mile, but the number of travelers leaving from or arriving at Port Huron dipped below 13,000 in 1999. Officials flirted with the idea of canceling the train altogether. As changeable as ever on this issue for almost 100 years, the *Times Herald* reversed its previous support for Amtrak and now backed cancellation. Fortunately, some remembered how John Bowman, Jr. of the American Association of Railroad Passengers had so ably expressed the wisdom of the trains :

Our excessive dependence on highway and air transport is the main cause of our dangerous dependence on imported oil and also of air pollution, the greenhouse effect and acid rain. The most practical and effective single step toward solving these problems would be to reverse our government's transportation policy and get as much passenger and freight traffic as possible back to the railroads, which are by far the most fuel efficient and land use efficient form of transportation.(56)

In the face of the Amtrak termination threat, Port Huron's pro-railroad stalwarts paused for a little nostalgia. Tom Kerrins remembered back 56 years to the day he'd made his first train trip through Port Huron at age 8. He'd thought the Grand Trunk station the grandest building he'd ever seen. Another rider recalled a system so safe and civilized that "folks never gave a second thought to putting kids on a train with just a note" to get them where they were going. And, oh, for the days of the old McMorran Line. In fact, the first locomotive ever used on the McMorran, the 1878 vintage *D.B. Harrington*, came back to Port Huron in 1991 courtesy of a donation by none other than the Henry Ford Museum. Now just a display piece, the engine arrived by the humiliating conveyance of a truck. The narrow gauge engine still made infinitely more sense than Henry Ford's automotive offspring, and so did the idea of small trains adapted to small communities. The *Harrington* very probably could have pulled a fleet of trucks of the size that carried it back home, had the tracks still been there. Over in Flint, where the last remnants of AutoWorld had been torn down, the Huckleberry Railroad remained an enduring tourism hit. Its 1903 narrow gauge Pere Marquette steam engine, cousin to the *Harrington*, hauled amused visitors around eight miles of track.

Luckily the Port Huron Amtrak line survived its latest threat, pulling through on the strength of a larger state subsidy. But the overall situation looked wobbly. Amtrak continued to chase a break-even performance required of no other national rail system in the world. Revenues amounted to 79% of operating costs in 1992, and reached $1 billion for the first time in 1998. The federal government contributed about $1 billion per year, equivalent to one week's bill for U.S. oil imports. We'll insert here another scolding that if America had spent $100 billion during the 90's not on its crackpot drug war but on rails and waterways instead it could have transformed itself. Amtrak service totaled 5.5 billion passenger miles in 1995, only about 16% of the 1951 load, but considering that only one-third the passenger service tracks available in '51 still existed, and the various other headwinds, not all bad. Amtrak TV commercials tried drawing a favorable comparison with car travel. Dad to daughter: "Do you remember our last trip when you kicked the back of my car seat for about 250 miles? Isn't this better?"

Did America's passenger train velocities catch up again with the rest of the world? Not in this century. Private railroad freight systems, which owned most of the tracks, agreed to work with Amtrak to try to hurry passengers along. "It's about time we prepare for the 21st century," said Edwin Harper, president of the Association of American Railroads, as the 21st bore down on them. Amtrak's Acela train eventually reached a speed of 150 mph on a short stretch of its Boston-Washington run, "one of the world's fastest trains," it claimed. The Detroit-Chicago run might someday do 110 mph. The Port Huron-Chicago topped out at less than 80, and for the entire trip, with stations stops included, averaged 58.

Only 23% of U.S. communities retained railroad service of any kind at the end of the 20th Century. 3,800 miles of track remained in Michigan. Communities had converted 270 abandoned stations to other uses, 55 to museums, like the Edison museum in Port Huron.(57) Rail service had become mighty sparse in the Thumb. Some farmers known collectively as BEANPAC still struggled to keep bean trains running at harvest time. "The highway system could not handle the amount of trucks it would take to haul these products out of the Thumb," said a member, meaning three times as many trucks as railcars.

The railroad business ran much more safely than in 1900; indeed, the 1990's marked the safest years in U.S. railroad history.(58) That didn't mean risk free. Large and small mishaps still occurred. *Large*: a bridge damaged by a barge in Alabama collapsed under a train, killing 47, the worst crash in Amtrak history. A steel hauler with three speeding convictions on his record drove his truck in front of an Amtrak train in Illinois, killing 11 and injuring 100 on board. *Small*: Grand Trunk yardman Henry Kerr slipped under a train in Port Huron and lost both legs. 19 year-old Craig Ruck fatally rammed his car at night into a 7,000 foot-long freight train parked on the tracks near Port Huron, which led to the installation of a $120,000 gate and signal. A train obliterated teenager Michael Weber while he walked the tracks, in an accident reminiscent of the death of Reverend Rowe in 1900. Except in this case Michael wasn't deaf, he'd been wearing a portable CD player. "I was always telling him to turn down those headphones," said his foster mother. St. Clair County train engineer Jeff Roberts had killed six people during 24 years at the throttle. He'd run down a woman who glanced up at him at the last moment. "I can close my eyes and still see her face looking at me right now." 400 people were killed, 1,300 hurt at U.S. train crossings in 1999, mostly in cars, and another 500 or so died while trespassing each year.

Accident risk might be down, but the risk of unemployment grew among Port Huron's railroad workers. The number of local employees shrank steadily. Grand Trunk sold its repair shops to a private contractor, which shortly thereafter closed them, the end of more than 100 years of this service in Tunnel City. The GT laid plans for moving its other operations out of town as well, and also abandoned its name in favor of its

468

parent's, the Canadian National Railway (CN). After several years of deficits the CN expected consolidation of its operations to help put its American division back in the black, as many other of America's 540 railroads managed to do during the 1990's. Which left Port Huron largely out of the picture.

Those 540 companies racked up 1.3 trillion ton-miles of freight shipment per year. A gallon of fuel moved a ton 375 miles, fuel efficiency as much as 15 times better than that of a truck. U.S. rail freight rates of 3 cents per ton-mile were the lowest in the world.(59) The Ford Motor Company shipped as many as 3 million of its vehicles per year by train. The rate of return rose as high as 9% on some freight lines during the 90's. The federal government sold off at a large price to private companies its remaining share of the Conrail freight network, which it had salvaged in the railroad emergency of the 1970's. Though it might have been the most successful federal train venture of the 20th Century, Conrail cut a poor figure against the robust train-building of the 19th. Washington shrank rather than expanded the railroad system, and persisted in the error of failing to establish government control and responsibility over the tracks.

On the community level, light and heavy electric passenger trains continued to battle back in many of America's largest cities. Four dozen systems were either in operation or on the drawing board by the end of the 20th C. They ran the gamut from rapid transit to streetcars, (including the world's oldest trolley line, the St. Charles in New Orleans); all publicly owned. The federal government furnished 50%-80% of the construction costs on new lines. Now if only they could be linked up again in a revived interurban network the country might be getting somewhere.

None of the streetcars systems operated in a community the size of Port Huron, which spoke not a whisper about reviving them. The orderly trolley city of 1900 might as well never have existed. Port Huron blundered ahead on its conceited auto course, adding more and more motor vehicles, vaguely aware that 'we have too many cars but can't possibly do with any fewer.' Let's be positive, though. Someday the civic daze might clear and the patient recover. Just energy-wise, it took 7 times as much to move a traveler in a car on North Main Street as it would have taken on a streetcar.(60) Detroit's modest 3-mile long People Mover monorail remained the only light rail system in the entire state of Michigan. This seems a good spot to drop in the observation that neither the state nor nation even by now had formulated any overall transportation plan.

"They have neglected that waterfront for years." One of St. Clair County's veteran mariners, Captain Morgan Howell, laid it on the line about Port Huron's commercial docks, all but non-existent now. Howell once had captained the *Aquarama*, one of the last big cruise ships on the Great Lakes in the late 50's, and he knew a thing or two. Especially about passenger service. A plan to install a cruise ship dock in Pine Grove Park, and revive some of the halcyon days of water travel went nowhere. A private enterprise to begin a new cross-river ferry between Port Huron and Sarnia died when the Canadian government demanded $500,000 in fees. A novel Canadian passenger service using a 40 mph hydrofoil watercraft up and down the St. Clair River failed to attract enough support. A couple of sightseeing boats worked successfully out of Port Huron and Sarnia during the summer season, but that was all. The Shipmasters Association still survived, and raffled off a popular vacation trip for guests on a freighter every year. But all things considered, hardly a shadow remained of the days of the *Tashmoo* and the busy White Star Line dock and the rest of the passenger facilities on the riverfront. Even pleasure boating retreated somewhat in Port Huron during the 90's, as the waiting list for municipal slips disappeared, and the big sailing race to Mackinac Island grew smaller.

Port Huron retained its connection with cargo shipping primarily through its masters, engineers, and deckhands who worked the Lakes fleets, plus the ship pilots, and the Coast Guardsmen who still operated from town. Much else faded away. The bigger tunnel supplanted the railroad car ferries and they disappeared. Most of the docks owned by industrial concerns sat unused. The Canadian National sold off 31 acres of riverfront it still owned in Port Huron, where once its trains had interacted so smoothly with the shipping trade. Port Huron's Seaway Terminal steered its last erratic, diminished course during these years. The 10,000 tons in cargo the terminal handled in 1999 generated $200,000 in revenue. That amount equaled about 6 hours worth of trucks crossing the Blue Water Bridge. A $2 million fire at the terminal that same year stamped *finis*, at least for the time being, to virtually all commercial shipping in the city once built for it.

Elsewhere on the Lakes 115 million tons of cargo shipped on U.S. vessels in 1999, a decline of about 25% since 1960. Still, more freighter cargo passed by Port Huron on the St. Clair River than through the Suez and Panama canals combined.(61) As usual, bulk materials made up most of the weight – iron ore, for example, much of it wasted in automaking. The owners of the 1,000-foot *George Stinson* charged $5 to move a ton of iron ore 600 miles to the steel mills, less than a penny per mile, and carried as much of it as 7 trains or 3,000 trucks might have managed. Captain Bob Gallagher kept fit by regularly walking a dozen times around the deck of his enormous vessel, a total of five miles. In a way, the *Stinson* was another expression of Fordist immensity, not altogether for the good. The 23,000 barges that traversed the Lakes and America's inland waterways operated with a good deal more flexibility. The standard model carried as much tonnage as could 70 18-wheelers or 16 railcars. As many as 15 of these barges could be towed by a tug at a time.(62) Inland water traffic excluding the Great Lakes had doubled since 1960, to 600 million tons p.a. Shipping between America's ocean ports averaged 200 million tons, about the same as in 1960.

By the 1990's the long distance traveler in America overwhelmingly favored the airlines. Half a billion passengers flew on U.S. commercial aircraft in 1995, and paid $200 billion for the privilege.(63) The airlines calculated that they used 300 million more gallons of fuel annually than they had a decade earlier because American bodies had gained so much weight. Jet planes wasted more fuel in carrying their passengers than any other form of transit, but speed and safety had made them well-nigh indispensable by 2000. With plenty of government help, the country's aviation system had evolved into a near marvel that furnished the model for the rest of the world.

The new Big 3 in American transportation circles meant the three top airlines: American, Delta, and United. Together they offered 60% of domestic flights. None of these three, nor any other, served the St. Clair County airport. Over the last 30 years several smaller lines had tried to start commercial air service there, but none attracted more than a handful of passengers, since the flights all went through Detroit's Metropolitan Airport anyway. Flying Port Huroners (with no train or bus service to get there) first drove 90 miles to Metro, then left their cars in one of the 30,000 parking spaces. Bucking the 34 million passengers who used Metro yearly distressed travelers, one of the many reasons which would have favored high-speed rail service for short intercity hops, had it existed. France furnished an object lesson for America in this regard: fast trains actually had reduced air service on some routes.(64)

We'll begin our final roundup of organic transport with a last visit to the horse barn. Just a scattering of them remained across St. Clair County, so few that the farm census lumped horses together with hogs. Port Huron by now ruthlessly had expelled horses and livestock of all kinds, which once had lived side by side with a less neurotic populace. Now and then horses still pulled a carriage around downtown as part of the Christmas celebrations, or carried an overweight policeman or two in a parade. A young person asked Jerry Brown in all honesty if there'd ever been a blacksmith in town. Resident Sue Butler tried offering regular summer weekend carriage rides as a tourism angle. These departed from Al Edison's train depot on the riverfront, the same spot served by brother Pitt Edison's original horse drawn streetcars in 1866. An 8 year-old animal named Lady, who cost $1,850 including harness, supplied the horsepower for Butler's $3,000 carriage. This arrangement likely didn't highlight Lady's week. For one thing, authorities subjected her to an indignity never inflicted upon her ancestors, though probably a defensible one, horse diapers. For another, those crazy automobiles. If one or two of them on the streets had alarmed the horse's sensibilities in 1901, one can imagine what Lady thought about the situation in 2000.

When University of Michigan architecture professor Gerhard Olving in 1992 assigned his students the design of a mythical city based on bicycles and mass transit, he got badgered about it by *Times Herald* editor Bernard Lyons, who said the idea belonged only in a city like Beijing. The Chinese used half a billion bicycles in their country. Olving replied that he'd rather travel in Beijing than Detroit. Or Port Huron, he might have added. Local bicyclist Bruce Kelchnes described what riding had been like for him over the past 21 years, during which time he had endured

every form of verbal abuse that can emanate from the lips of men (and women, too). I have had rifles pointed out of car windows at me, baseball bats held out at arm's length in an effort to crack me on the back...beer and soda cans and bottles hurled at me, and even been spat upon deliberately by passengers in passing cars. At one time I was knocked unconscious, apparently by a side mirror of a passing vehicle, and left for dead. The driver was never found. I awoke five days later with a smashed head, shoulder and leg, and minus one ear drum. If all of you would only realize that I am not an obstruction on the road but a commuter like you, only using a more gentle means of transportation that doesn't waste our precious resources and doesn't pollute the environment, maybe you would feel more generous toward me and my bicycle.(65)

Fortunately for one's faith in mankind, 68 year-old Frank Bostwick experienced an entirely different bicycle ride from Florida to Port Huron to visit his daughter. "People have been extraordinarily kind," said Frank about his 1,600 mile trip. Bostwick took the precaution of riding the back roads, where bicycles didn't seem to bring out the depravity in motorists quite so readily. His only sad memories of the trip came from riding Jefferson Avenue in Detroit, past the Renaissance Center, which Ford had sold to General Motors for a quarter of its original cost. "That is just a demoralizing part of town." Because no one had yet come up with an orderly way to shrink a city, the Paris of the Midwest looked worse and worse. Visiting musician/artist David Byrne also took a bike ride along some of the Motor City's 2,400 miles of streets. Much as he prized the "cool" attitude in life, Byrne admitted that he'd been thoroughly shocked by the wreckage he saw, the spectacle of the undergrowth reclaiming block after abandoned block. "Riding for hours right next to it was visceral and heartbreaking – in ways that looking at ancient ruins aren't."(66) Further confirmation of what we decided earlier: only a bicyclist, or a pedestrian, can really experience a place.

In an effort to re-experience Port Huron, police did a few bicycle patrols again, reviving a practice they hadn't used in 60 years or so. "The big thing is you're a lot more approachable," said officer Lee Heighton. "In the neighborhood you're more a part of the community than someone who rides by in a big gray tank. I think it brings the officer back to being a person."(67) Cops found bikes especially effective in connecting with children. Ironically, in these days city kids often had more opportunity for purposeful biking (and walking) than suburbanites.

Elementary third grader Kristen Wiley thinks going to school is exciting. So does her sister Jenna and their friend Chelsea Dupree, both first graders. Then again, they all think going home from school is exciting, too. Anywhere they get to go on their bicycles is an exciting adventure for them. "Riding their bikes to school and liking it so much, that surprised me," said Beth Wiley, Kristen and Jenna's mother. "That makes them feel real good about themselves that they're big enough to do that, even if we follow them in the car, which we usually do." (68)

Little did Mrs. Wiley realize that she followed her young bicyclists in their worst enemy, the automobile, the cause of many of the 300,000 bicycle injury cases that landed in hospital emergency rooms per year. Taking this statistic into account, Port Huron insurance businesswoman Bethany Belanger knowledgeably donated several hundred bike helmets to her old elementary school.

St. Clair County residents approved a special $6 million per year recreation tax during the 90's, which promised to get some bicycle/pedestrian paths built. The Parks and Recreation department spent part of this money on converting 10 miles of abandoned McMorran Line to this purpose, though as we've noted obliterating a railroad hardly counted as an unmixed blessing. Michigan had more of these trails than all but one other state in America by 1999. Fine, but the biggest hurdle remained putting the bicycle back to use as a practical everyday transportation tool on the streets and highways. America did only 1% of its travel by bicycle, not nearly enough considering the 120 million bicycles in the USA .(69) Lee Iacocca thought he saw an opportunity here. Now retired from Chrysler, Lido took a stab at bicycle production, though after a lifetime in the auto business he couldn't quite get the bicycle concept straight in his mind. His were electric: "I don't want to get rid of the cars in your garage. It took me 50 years to put them there. I want to complement them."(70) C'mon, get with it, Lee.

Most bicycle-and-walking neglectful, increasingly inert Americans withdrew further and further into the recesses of their cars and the catacombs of their homes. The Surgeon General figured only 22% got enough exercise. "As a result of sedentary lifestyles we are seeing heart attacks and health problems in 30 year-olds that we used to see in people 50 years old," reported Port Huron Hospital dietitian Susan Troop. A lot of the 20 million health club memberships and 10 million home gyms in America went unused. Port Huronite Sean Martin belonged to one such club: "Some days I intentionally drive around it because I feel so guilty." The *Times Herald's* Grace Filion tried countering the auto lifestyle with various abdominal exercisers at home: the Ab

Roller, Ab Sculptor, Abflex, Ab Isolator, Tummytucker. She also took a crack at the Easy Crunch: "an apparatus that looks like a pogo stick and acts like a jackhammer. You push up and down to exert pressure on the solar plexus, thus attacking the protruding area, pounding it down and making it firmer. This is not an exercise you want to do after lunch."(71) Grace sold her Tummytucker at a garage sale for $2.

The annual per-person tab for health care in the USA now passed the $2,500 milepost, almost twice what it had been a decade earlier, and kept on going until it reached $3,500 by the year 2000. The two hospitals in Port Huron vacuumed up $150 million in revenues per year. America's 6,000 hospitals these days averaged record 6%-20% profit margins. Port Huron Hospital became the county's second biggest employer (1,300). Its building encompassed more than 400,000 square feet, and it established outpatient centers all over the county. Hospital president Donald Fletcher might moan and groan at times about busted budgets, layoffs, lawsuits, bad debts, medical bungling, and charity cases, but these niggling difficulties didn't slow down expansion.

Fletcher opened a new $5 million cardiac care unit, which performed $8-$10 million of heart procedures per year. Heart doctors didn't enjoy universal esteem in medical circles. "A monkey can do what they do," is what one Florida family physician had to say about cardiologists.(72) $50 billion in heart treatments could be saved in America if everyone just walked an hour a day, according to Brown University.(73) Instead Port Huron Hospital added 86 more parking spaces, tearing down more sturdy, beautiful homes in the process. Other medical disciplines thrived in the automobile climate. Whether from weight overloading or disuse more of St. Clair County's bones and joints creaked and ached, so doctors offered "Total Joint Replacement" for knees, hips, shoulders. The Orthopedic Associates broke ground on their new $4 million offices in Port Huron, replacing some homes hammered down by Gerald Bouchard in one of the last urban renewal pogroms.

Americans consumed one-half of all the pharmaceutical drugs taken in the world, half of them for cholesterol, high blood pressure, arthritis, nerves...in other words, for carsickness. The nation's 97 million or so overweight or obese adult wide-bodies (60% of all adults) swallowed more than $3 billion of prescribed and non-prescribed non-cures for their poundage per year.

Super Formula Program...absolutely guaranteed to blast up to 49 pounds off you in only 29 days. Your thighs, hips, stomach, and fanny will now be virtually devoid of any visible fat!...without discipline...without one moment of back-breaking exercise.

That claim cost the Super Formula people an $8 million fine by regulators. A little late, the food and drug overseers also found that one of the prescription obesity treatments, fen-phen, to be almost as bad for hearts as the automobile, but unlike the car, they yanked it from the market, at a cost of $4.8 billion to its makers.

Americans heavy laden with grief and fat had become so physically repulsive by the 90's that they underwent 2 million cosmetic surgeries per year, including 170,000 "liposuction" procedures to try to remove fat without back-breaking exercise. Alexander Goen brought his hypnotic weight loss program to Port Huron's Thomas Edison Inn, promising for $39.99 to "destroy your cravings and desires for second helpings, break your compulsive, addictive eating habits or your money back. Plain and simple." But where was the autosuction procedure to pull your car loose, the hypnotists to break your

473

craving for two tons of automobile, the drug to blast the car from your life in 29 days?

Even a definitive report in the *New England Journal of Medicine* restating the obvious failed to stem the tide of fat fraud. Researchers bird-dogging some lardtubs found nothing inherently wrong with them at all, they just ate twice as much as they claimed and got no exercise.(74) Just as Dr. Newburgh had said in the 1930's, obesity wasn't a metabolism problem, a genetic disorder, a disease, or a disability, though some wished it were, simply to excuse their laziness. "Already there are people who ride in electric wheelchairs and motorized scooters for no other reason than with their great bulk they find it easier to do so," observed author Michael Fumento.(75) Basically, they drove an automobile around indoors. "One Test Drive will Convince You!" read a Port Huron scooter ad, a teaser lifted straight from the car folks.

Don Shipley carried his 450 pounds around in a Port Huron city bus; not for convenience sake, but because he worked as a bus driver. "I'm a frustrated dieter," Shipley explained to Jerry Brown, a frustration that put him in his grave by age 50. Shipley had plenty of company – 300,000 folks per year. Blubber trailed only tobacco as the second leading cause of preventable deaths in America. Apart from heart trouble and strokes, the Reaper came in other ways to winnow out unwary fatties; through the 90,000 fat-linked cancer deaths per year, for example.(76) That other close companion to obesity – diabetes – afflicted 14 million Americans; 1 out of 15 people in St. Clair County; triple the percentage of the 1950's. Their condition subjected low blood sugar diabetics to blackouts, but almost half kept motoring with or without this problem, inviting a permanent blackout when their cars suddenly went driverless.

The overweight/obese fraction of 25% among American children, though not as bad as the 30% of the nation's cats and dogs who were too fat, looked like "a situation that seems to be getting worse," to Port Huron pediatrician John Zmiejko. 100 students at a local middle school took a national fitness exam and 7 passed. Michigan and 48 other states required no mandatory physical education programs in their schools to counter car disease. Far from encouraging physical exuberance, the nation's witch doctors by now drugged down 11 million U.S. children as young as 2, including several hundred in St. Clair County, with the heap big medicine Ritalin to ward off the evil spirits of attention deficit and hyperactivity. This allegedly helped kids concentrate, but why not feed it to automobile drivers, too? A new screwball malady, childhood autism in car-abused kids, raised another sweat among parents and quacks alike.

The shrinking number of schoolchildren living in Port Huron, the disappearing neighborhood schools, the final extinction of rural one-roomers, the danger on the roads, all put more youngsters aboard buses. Rather than walk to school, or bike, like the cyclin' Wiley sisters, 22 million American schoolchildren (about half) rode school buses a cumulative total of 18 million miles daily. The National Parent Teacher Association offered children these tips for school bus safety: be on time, never run to or from the bus, stand back from the curb, don't push or shove, stay in your seat, don't yell or shout, always obey the driver, never crawl under a school bus. In other words, don't act like a child. Once they got to school the Port Huron area's 12,000 pupils didn't exactly shine. In 1993 80% of 10th graders failed a state math test, two-thirds of 4th, 7th, and 10th graders flunked the reading test. The annual school bill: $5,800 per pupil. Not as much as owning an automobile but pretty steep. In assessing the lousy performance of the school district the *Times Herald* reached for a General Motors

474

metaphor: "Michigan residents pay Cadillac prices for Chevrolet schools."

Jerry Brown began exercise regimen Number ???, he'd forgotten how many. He took as his model 80 year-old lawyer Milton Bush, who jogged, played handball at the Y, lifted weights, even pushed a lawn mower. Healthy certainly, but did Milton confront the big issue, his car? Another prominent gym patron, Chevy dealer Carl Thompson, hoisted some weights, but who expected him to renounce his life's work, and walk? 44 year-old Joel Thomason walked on a treadmill twice a day, seven days a week for 10 years, though he'd have gotten that same results far more easily by getting rid of his car. Port Huron's firefighters received orders to go on a 1-hour per day exercise course, after somebody discovered that heart disease killed more firemen than fire. "It's the best thing that ever happened to the department," Captain Bob Wagner said. But why not go carless and skip the course? The police department grew ever fatter from riding around in its patrol cars all day.

Jerry interviewed another citizen who had the right idea. 70 year-old Isabelle Haddad had never driven a car in her life. Shades of Walkin' Bob Tucker! "My feet have always been my transportation. Oh, I've taken the bus, and friends have given me a ride, but I love to walk. I walk everywhere and people come up to me and say, 'Hey, aren't you the walking lady?'"(77) The Lebanese-born former French teacher and insurance saleswoman found Port Huron still had plenty of friendliness to go around, provided people got out of their cars to use it. Friendly Mayor James Relken suggested that the City Council actually make some walking tours of the community. He and the school superintendent Larry Moeller tried this tactic, neighborhood walking, in support of the latest school tax issue, trying to persuade people face to face. It was a sign of the times that people thought this a novel approach.

Charitable fundraising walks also tapped into the friendly side of Port Huroners: the March of Dimes, Walk for Warmth, Relay for Life, American Heart Association. Admirable, except that these outings made walking out to be some sort of sacrifice by the volunteers, when for most of them it was their healthiest day of the year. "We walk because they walk," said a lachrymose Marsha Hiller, about the six miles she and the Christian Rural Overseas Programs hunger marchers covered, the Jefferson Minimum, in sympathy with the world's automobile-deprived millions.

Brownie, now in his 60's, gave footwork another try, but it was too late for Charlie Barrett. Had Charlie only listened to the walking lady. Port Huron's auto king spent three miserable housebound years under 24-hour care following a stroke, before dying at 79. Businessman Frank Colby made out better after he took up pavement pounding at 74. Colby staggered along for just 15 minutes on his first outing, but kept at it, worked his way up to 6 miles per day, and lost 127 pounds in a year. 80 year-old former Detroit police chief Johannes Spreen, who'd retired to St. Clair County, reported that he'd found the fountain of youth: walking. He'd also rediscovered the Jacobs Effect: "The more we don't use our bodies, the less time our bodies will last." To get to know their native state a little more personally, Port Huron's Congressman David Bonior and his wife, both in their 50's, marched 325 miles across Michigan. They found it so exciting an experience, for the 1990's, that they wrote a book about it. U.S. Vice President-elect Dick Cheney should have been so active. He suffered a heart attack even before assuming the cares of office, at age 59, the culmination of heart trouble that began in his late 30's.

The last two national American walking heroes of the 20th Century joined the pantheon. Doris Haddock walked from California to Washington, D.C. as a means of urging political reform. She began her pilgrimage at age 88 and finished at 90, covering 10 miles per day, a quite astounding achievement. 79 year-old Earl Shaffer did the 2,150 mile Appalachian Trail in six months of 1998, the same march he'd been the first to accomplish 50 years earlier. This made him the first to walk it in both directions. The world still waited for a local hero to walk the 1,700 mile St. Clair County Trail – its roads – and the Port Huron Path – its streets. Neither would be easy. In some ways the Appalachian Trail offered safer walking than the county or, worse, the city. The same day that the *Times Herald* congratulated Port Huron editorially on recording no pedestrian fatalities in 3 years, drunk driver Michael Miron broke the spell by knocking down and killing 90 year-old Olga Langolf as she walked between the grocery store and her seniors' apartment. Hauled back after running away, instead of something like a second degree murder conviction Miron received only a year's stay in jail for manslaughter, and lost his license for two years. For Doris Haddock, glory. For Olga Langolf, Lakeside Cemetery. Ms. Langolf died as one of the three pedestrians killed by automobiles every week in Michigan, 5,000 in America per year, for which drivers were responsible 90% of the time.(78)

Responsible, too, for mother and daughter Marija Samoilo and Zina Daogaru, who died while walking near Algonac, struck by hit-and-run habitual offender David Sprague. These ladies got even less justice than Olga Langolf. Out of a possible 7 years in prison, the courts dealt Sprague 9 months for this double road killing. Nobody ran Jerry Brown over while walking, but motorists peeved and unnerved him bigtime by roaring past at 50 mph on a 30 mph sidewalkless street up near NoWoods Mall. At about this time government officials in Michigan began a program called "Toward Walkable Communities," but a truly walkable community had to be a car-free one, and the state's autofied bureaucracy didn't want to go there.

St. Clair County had one nearly walkable community left to its name by the year 2000, Russell Island. This small enclave in the lower St. Clair River once early in the century had offered summer vacation camping for 1,500 visitors at a time. Eventually a couple of hundred regular cottages replaced the tents. A small canal separated Russell from an adjoining island infested with cars, but none of those cursed machines crossed this barrier. People walked or bicycled around their autofree domain, and took the ferry into Algonac for shopping. One of Henry Ford's chief inspectors owned a cottage on Russell. In the 1920's he invited the Universal Man himself over for a visit. Ford had a hard time believing that such a place still existed so close to Detroit, as well he might, but he got the proof. Unfortunately Ford's handiwork could not completely be kept at bay forever, even from Russell Island. Powered golf carts had invaded the place in the 1960's to carry around residents too broken down from their auto lives on the mainland even to pedal a bicycle.

Near the end of it, *Fortune* magazine named Henry Ford the Man of the Century. For our purposes this was *Ill Fortune*. Among mighty few people alive in the year 2000, America's oldest man, 110 year-old John McMorran, a longtime Port Huron resident and another cousin of Henry McMorran, could look back across the entire century and come to his own conclusion about Ford. McMorran had bought his first car, a Model T, in 1912, to haul milk cans for a dairy company, just as Henry the Great had prescribed. A lemon, John called the T. "Actually they weren't really built correctly at

476

first." Or ever, John. McMorran's assessment applied equally well to the world of Port Huron and St. Clair County, whose people, culture, livelihoods, sustenance, government, health, history, schools, every building and every square inch of ground, the very air and water, and obviously the transportation, all carried to some extent the stamp of Ford. A lemon, not really built correctly.

How should it have been built instead? Computer-generated alternative reality games became a popular pastime in the late 20th Century. Who could blame the players for wanting to step out of the revolting, overtransported mess the automobile had made of the American landscape, and inhabit someplace else for a while? Why not posit a Carless America evolving from the starting point of 1900? No matter how colossally fouled up, one only had to imagine Port Huron and St. Clair County, and Flint, Detroit, New York, Los Angeles, and anyplace, without the cars and trucks, to see the epic dysfunction and shoddiness fall away. Those places became humane and even beautiful again.

In this parallel 20th Century the rail system expanded according to a comprehensive national layout drawn up by that transportation wizard and Edison confidante Henry Ford, who upon reflection had turned away from his mad course of building individual road engines. Railroads and interurbans further intertwined the nation's communities with passenger and cargo service to every incorporated city and village, feeding the in-town streetcar lines, and furnishing rural service to within a mile of most everybody else, bringing order to the expansion of the population without compromising the blessings of distance. Top train speeds tripled. Airplane service developed as above, but in most cases ignored routes shorter than 500 miles in favor of rail. The inland waterways system grew larger and more sophisticated, with more canals like the Trans-Michigan, and with year round ice-breaking service on the Great Lakes and other routes in the ice belt. Alongside the big craft, middling and small-sized cargo and passenger ships reaped the cost advantages in moving goods and travelers at the lowest possible prices.

Many millions of walkers and bikers ruled the highways and byways. Paved streets and Good Roads subject only to bicycle or pedestrian traffic or occasionally a horse conveyance lasted a century with minimal maintenance. The nation lived easily on its own petroleum resources, and turned its face early against malign theories of farm and school industrialism. It lived more quietly, cleanly, safely, and yes, somewhat more slowly, in a larger world. And as for the healthy, happy, well-adjusted residents of this rewired fantasy, why, we can hardly recognize them! Jerry Brown, is that you?

Game over. Lost opportunities; they weren't to be and there's no point in further lamenting them. Time to go forward. What about the coming 21st Century? Would Port Huron and America succeed in reclaiming their humanity, and redeeming the world they'd made? Was there a cure for these Heroic Sick People? That is a history whose telling I must leave to someone 100 years from now, along with my heartfelt wish for better days.

BIBLIOGRAPHY

Allen, Frederick Lewis *Only Yesterday: An Informal History of the Nineteen-Twenties.* Perennial Library / Harper & Row. New York, NY. 1964

Alvord, Katherine. *Divorce Your Car.* New Society Publishers. Gabriola Island, British Columbia, Canada. 2000

Ambrose, Stephen E. *Nothing Like It In The World.* Touchstone / Simon and Schuster. New York, NY. 2000

American Waterways Operators, Inc. (AWO). *Big Load Afloat: U.S. Inland Water Transportation Resources.* Washington, DC. 1966

Anonymous (HSCC-1883). *History of St. Clair County, Michigan.* A.T. Andreas Co. Chicago, IL. 1883

Barnett, LeRoy. *Getting Southern Michigan Into Line.* Michigan History magazine. Volume 87, Number 1. January / February 2003.

Barnett, LeRoy. *Michigan Gives the Green Light to Traffic Safety.* Michigan History magazine. Volume 86, Number 4. July / August 2002. pp. 22-25

Barnett, LeRoy. *On the Michigan Stage.* (OMS). Michigan History magazine. Volume 89, Number 5. September / October, 2005. pp. 42-50

Berger, Michael. *The Devil Wagon in God's Country.* Archon Book. Hamden, CT. 1979

Berry, Dale.(ed.) *Railroad History of Michigan.* www.michiganrailroads.com

Bessert, Christopher J. *Michigan Highways: Historical Overview.* http://www.michiganhighways.org/historical_overview.html

Breines, Simon, and **Dean,** William J. *The Pedestrian Revolution: Streets Without Cars.* Vintage / Random House. New York. 1974

Brill, Steven. *The Teamsters.* Pocket Books / Simon & Schuster. New York, NY. 1979

Brinkley, Douglas. *Wheels for the World: Henry Ford, His Company, and a Century of Progress 1903-2003.* Viking / Penguin. New York, NY. 2003

Brown, John F. *40 Years Brownie's People.* Reference Publications, Inc. Algonac, MI. 1995

Brown, John F. *John Brown's People.* Reference Publications, Inc. Algonac, MI. 1990

Brown, John F. *Rear View Mirror.* (RVM) Reference Publications, Inc. Algonac, MI. 2004

Brown, Lester R.; **Flavin,** Christopher; **Norman,** Colin. *Running on Empty: The Future of the Automobile in an Oil Short World.* W. W. Norton and Company. New York, NY and London. 1979

478

Bryan, Ford R. *The Fords of Dearborn*. Harlo Press. Detroit, MI. 1989

Burby, John. *The Great American Motion Sickness*. Little, Brown and Company. Boston, MA. 1971.

Burnell, Mary C. and **Marcaccio**, Amy. *Blue Water Reflections: A Pictorial History of Port Huron and the St. Clair River District*. Donning Company. Virginia Beach, VA. 1983

Byrne, David. *Bicycle Diaries*. Viking / Penguin. New York, NY. 2009

Caldwell, Bret, et al. *100 Years of Teamsters History*. DeLancey Publishing. Washington, D.C. 2003

Carson, Rachel. *Silent Spring*. Mariner / Houghton Mifflin. New York, NY. 2002

Clemens, Elizabeth. *Virtual Motor City*. Michigan History magazine. Volume 88, Number 6. November / December 2004. pp. 18-25

Cochrane, Willard W. *The Development of American Agriculture: A Historical Analysis*. 2nd edition. University of Minnesota Press. Minneapolis MN. 1993

Commoner, Barry. *The Closing Circle: Nature, Man & Technology*. Bantam Books. New York, NY. 1981

Crawford, J. H. *Carfree Cities*. International Books. Utrecht, the Netherlands. 2000

Cray, Ed. *Chrome Colossus: General Motors and Its Times*. McGraw-Hill Book Company. New York, NY. 1980

Creamer, Mary Lou, et. al. *Port Huron: Celebrating Our Past*. Sight Creative, Inc. St. Clair, MI. 2006

Damstra, Carolyn. *Bringing Good Roads to Michigan*. Michigan History magazine. Volume 89, Number 3. May / June 2005. pp. 6-13

Davis, Michael W.R. *Images of America: Detroit Area Test Tracks*. (DTT) Arcadia Publishing. Charleston, SC. 2009

Davis, Michael W.R. *Images of America: The St. Clair River*. (SCR) Arcadia Publishing. Charleston, SC. 2011

Detroit Free Press (DFP)

Doner, Mary Frances. *The Salvager: The Life of Captain Tom Reid on the Great Lakes*. Ross & Haines, Inc. Minneapolis, MN. 1958

Duany, Andres; **Plater-Zyberk**, Elizabeth & **Speck**, Jeff. *Suburban Nation: The Rise of Sprawl and the Decline of the American Dream*. North Point Press / Farrar, Straus and Giroux. New York, NY. 2000

Dunbar, Willis F. *All Aboard!: A History of Railroads in Michigan*. William B. Eerdmans Publishing Company. Grand Rapids, MI. 1969

Earle, Horatio S., et. al. *Report of the State Highway Committee*. Robert Smith Printing Co. Lansing, MI. 1903

Eckert, Kathryn Bishop. *Buildings of Michigan*. Oxford University Press. New York, NY. 1993

Endlich, Helen. *A Story of Port Huron*. Self published. Port Huron, MI. 1981

Ertel, Patrick W. *American Steam Tractors*. Motorbooks International. Osceola, WI. 1997

Farber, David. *Sloan Rules: Alfred P. Sloan and the Triumph of General Motors*. University of Chicago Press. Chicago, IL. 2002

Farber, Gene. *Seeing with Headlights*. National Highway Traffic Safety Administration Workshop on Headlight Metrics. Washington, DC. 2004

Feltner, Royal. www.earlyamericanautomobiles.com

Ferry, W. Hawkins. *Legacy of Albert Kahn*. Wayne State University Press. Detroit, MI. 1987

Flink, James J. *The Automobile Age*. MIT Press. Cambridge, MA. 1993.

Ford, Henry, and **Crowther,** Samuel. *My Life and Work*. Doubleday, Page & Company. Garden City, NY. 1926

Ford Motor Company. *Ford at Fifty*. Simon and Schuster. New York, NY. 1953.

Fumento, Michael. *Fat of the Land*. Viking. New York, NY. 1997

Furnas, J. C. *And Sudden Death*. Readers' Digest Magazine. August, 1935. www.rd.com/culture/and-sudden-death-readers-digest/

Gaffney, T.J. *Port Huron 1880-1960*. Arcadia Publishing, Charleston, SC. 2006

Gaffney, T.J. *Images of Rail: Rails Around The Thumb*. (RATT) Arcadia Publishing. Charleston, SC. 2012

Glancey, Jonathan. *The Train*. Carlton Books. London. 2004.

Gustin, Lawrence. *Billy Durant: Creator of General Motors*. William B. Erdmans Publishing Company. Grand Rapids, MI. 1973

Heppenheimer, T. A. *Turbulent Skies: The History of Commercial Aviation*. John Wiley & Sons, Inc. New York, NY. 1995

Herlihy, David V. *Bicycle: The History*. Yale University Press. New Haven, CT. 2004

Iacocca, Lee & **Novak,** William. *Iacocca: An Autobiography*. Bantam Book. New York, NY. 1984

Jacobs, Jane. *The Death and Life of Great American Cities*. Vintage / Random House. New York, NY. 1992.

James, Sheryl. *A Street Called Woodward*. Michigan History magazine. Volume 86, Number 3. May / June 2002. pp. 42-53

Jenks, William Lee. *St. Clair County, Michigan: Its History and Its People*. Lewis Publishing Company. Chicago, IL. 1912

Jerome, John. *The Death of the Automobile: The Fatal Effects of the Golden Era, 1955-1970.* W.W. Norton & Company. New York, NY. 1972

Johnson, D.E. *The Rise and Fall of Detroit's Early Electrics.* Michigan History magazine. Volume 98, Number 1. January / February 2014. pp. 15-20

Kay, Jane Holtz. *Asphalt Nation: How the Automobile Took Over America, and How We Can Take It Back.* Crown Publishers, Inc. New York, NY. 1997

Keats, John. *The Insolent Chariots.* Fawcett Publications, Inc. Greenwich, CT. 1959

Kunstler, James Howard. *The Geography of Nowhere: The Rise and Decline of Ameria's Man- Made Landscape.* Touchstone / Simon and Schuster: New York, NY. 1994

LaBella, Gary M. *A Glance Back: A History of the American Trucking Industry.* American Trucking Associations. Washington, DC. 1977

Lamb, David. *Over the Hills: A Midlife Escape Across America by Bicycle.* Times Books / Random House. New York, NY. 1996

Lazerson, Marvin (ed.). *American Education in the Twentieth Century: A Documentary History.* Teachers College Press. New York, NY. 1987

Leavitt, Helen. *Superhighway - Superhoax.* Doubleday & Co. Garden City, NY. 1970.

Lewis, David L. and **Goldstein**, Laurence (eds.). *The Automobile and American Culture.* University of Michigan Press. Ann Arbor, MI. 1983

Loomis, Bill. *The Great Railroad Conspiracy.* Michigan History magazine. Volume 97, Number 5. September / October 2013. pp. 37-43

Lynd, Robert S. and **Lynd**, Helen Merrell. *Middletown: A Study in Modern American Culture.* Harvest / Harcourt Brace & Company. New York, NY. 1959

Lynd, Robert S. and **Lynd**, Hellen Merrell. *Middletown in Transition: A Study in Cultural Conflicts.* (MIT). Harvest / Harcourt Brace & Company. New York, NY. 1982

Lyons, Bernard P. *Sperry's - The First 100 Years.* F. W. Uhlman & Co. Bowling Green, OH. 1993

May, George S. *A Most Unique Machine: The Michigan Origins of the American Automobile Industry* (MUM). William B. Eerdmans Publishing Company. Grand Rapids, MI. 1975.

May, George S. *Pictorial History of Michigan: The Early Years, The Later Years.* Single volume (PHMEY, PHMLY). William B. Eerdmans Publishing Company. Grand Rapids, MI. 1967, 1969

McCormick, David. *Plank Roads: A Michigan Invention.* Michigan History magazine, Volume 95, Number 6. November / December 2011. pp. 36-39

Myers, Robert. *The Autotram Experiment.* Michigan History magazine. Volume 99, Number 1. January / February 2015.

Middleton, William D. *The Interurban Era.* (TIE) Kalmbach Publishing Co.

Milwaukee, WI. 1971.

Middleton, William D. *The Time of the Trolley*. (TT) Kalmbach Publishing Co. Milwaukee, WI. 1967.

Mitts, Dorothy Marie. *That Noble Country*. Dorrance and Company. Philadelphia, PA. 1968

Mumford, Lewis. *The City in History: It Origins, Its Transformations and Its Prospects*. Harvest / Harcourt, Brace & Company. New York, NY. 1989

Munson, Richard. *From Edison to Enron: The Business of Power and What It Means for the Future of Elecricity*. Praeger Publishers. Westport, CT. 2005

O'Connell, Jeffrey and **Myers**, Arthur. *Safety Last: An Indictment of the Auto Industry*. Random House. New York, NY. 1966

Olsen, Byron and **Cabadas**, Joseph. *The American Auto Factory*. MBI Publishing Company. St. Paul, MN. 2002

Olson, Sidney. *Young Henry Ford*. Wayne State University Press. Detroit, MI. 1963

Otterbourg, Ken. *The Untamable River Trade*. Fortune magazine, 12/26/2011. Vol 164, No. 10.

Owens, Marjorie L. *Index to Port Huron Newspapers 1844-1939*. St. Clair County Library.

Packard, Vance. *A Nation of Strangers*. David McKay Company, Inc. New York, NY. 1972

Paine, Ralph D. D*iscovering America by Motor.* Scribners Magazine. Volume 53. January / June 1913. pp. 137-148.

Pettifer, Julian and **Turner**, Nigel. *Automania: Man and the Motor Car*. Little, Brown and Company. Boston, MA. 1984

Phelps, Edward & **Whipp**, Charles. Sarnia: *Gateway to Bluewaterland*. Windsor Publications Limited. Burlington, Ontario, Canada. 1987

Pitrone, Jean Maddern & **Elwart**, Joan Potter. *The Dodges*. Icarus Press. South Bend, IN. 1981

Pohl, Dorothy G., and **Brown**, Norman E. *The History of Roads in Michigan*. 1997. www.michiganhighways.org/history.html.

Port Huron Daily Times. (PHDT)

Port Huron Weekly Times. (PHWT)

Port Huron Daily Herald. (PHDH)

Port Huron Times Herald. (PHTH)

Rae, John B. *The American Automobile: A Brief History*. University of Chicago Press. Chicago, IL. 1965

Rothschild, Emma. *Paradise Lost: The Decline of the Auto-Industrial Age.* Vintage/Random House. New York, NY. 1974

Schneider, Kenneth R. *Autokind vs. Mankind: An Analysis of Tyranny, A Proposal for Rebellion, A Plan for Reconstruction.* Authors Choice Press. Lincoln, NE. 2001.

Schramm, Jack E. and **Henning**, William H. *When Eastern Michigan Rode the Rails II: The Rapid Railway and Detroit-Port Huron By Rail-Ship-Bus.* Interurban Press. Glendale, CA. 1986

Schor, Juliet B. *The Overworked American: The Unexpected Decline of Leisure.* Basic Books. 1991.

Schumacher, E. F. *Small is Beautiful: Economics as if People Mattered.* Hartley and Marks Publishers. Vancouver, British Columbia. 1999

Schwerin, Catherine A. *Against All Odds.* Michigan History Magazine. Volume 89, Number 5. September / October 2005. pp. 18-23

Shank, William H., et al. *Towpaths to Tugboats: a History of American Canal Engineering.* American Canal and Transportation Center. York, PA. 1998

Sharoff, Robert and **Zbarren**, William. *American City: Detroit Architecture 1845-2005.* Wayne State University Press. Detroit, MI. 2005.

Shaul, Richard D. *Northern Passage at the Soo: The Locks at 150.* Michigan History magazine. Volume 89, Number 4. July / August 2005. pp. 28-38

Shaul, Richard D. *Strait Through Adversity.* Michigan History magazine. Volume 91, Number 4. July / August 2007. pp. 22-31

Sloan, Alfred P., Jr.. *My Years with General Motors.* Currency / Doubleday. New York, NY. 1990

Snider, Clare J. and **Davis**, Michael W. *The Ford Fleet (1923-1989).* Freshwater Press. Cleveland, OH. 1994

Starr, Paul. *The Social Transformation of American Medicine.* Basic Books. New York, NY. 1982

Stover, John F. *American Railroads.* University of Chicago Press. Chicago, IL. 1997

Sussman, Aaron & **Goode**, Ruth. *The Magic of Walking.* Fireside / Simon and Schuster. New York, NY. 1980

Theisen, Harry W. and Katharine D. *Russell Island: Remembrance of Things Past.* Russell Island Press. 1985

Tamminen, Terry. *Lives per Gallon: The True Cost of our Oil Addiction.* Shearwater / Island Press, Washington DC. 2006.

Tarkington, Booth. Edited by John Beecroft. *The Gentleman from Indianapolis.* Doubleday & Co. Garden City, NY. 1957

Thompson, Clive. *Look Both Ways.* Forbes magazine. December 2014. Vol 45, Number 8.

Time Capsule / 1950. Time / Life Books. New York, NY. 1967.

Towle, Herbert Ladd. *The Automobile and its Mission*. Scribner's Magazine. Volume 53. January-June 1913. pp. 149-162

U.S. Department of the Interior. *Chesapeake and Ohio Canal*. (COC) Washington, D.C. 1991

U.S. Department of Transportation. Federal Railroad Administration. Prepared by ICF International. *Comparative Evaluation of Rail and Truck Fuel Efficiency on Competetive Corridors*. November, 2009

Von Keler, Theodore M. R. *Steam-coach Days*. Scribner's Magazine. Volume 53. January / June 1913. pp. 180-185

Vossler, Bill. *The Gold Standard in Steam*. www.farmcollector.com/steam-engines/the-gold-standard-in-steam. July 2008.

Wall Street Journal (WSJ)

Williamson, Samuel H. *Seven Ways to Compute the Relative Value of a U.S. Dollar Amount, 1774 to present*. MeasuringWorth.com. 2010-2017

Withuhn, William T. and **Steeds**, Will (eds.). *Rails Across America: A History of Railroads in North America*. Smithmark Publishers, Inc. New York, NY. 1993.

Yergin, Daniel. *The Prize*. Touchstone / Simon and Schuster. New York, NY. 1991

FOOTNOTES

Chapter 1, pp. 5-39

(1) Ertel, p. 14
(2) Vossler
(3) Bryan, pp. 246-247
(4) Mitts, p. 8
(5) Dilts, James D. *The Early Days*, in Withuhn and Steeds. p. 15
(6) American Waterways Operators (AWO). p. 6
(7) Stover, p. 33
(8) Endlich, p. 17
(9) Shank, pp. 11-12
(10) Shank, pp. 18-20
(11) Cochrane, p. 216
(12) U.S. Deptartment of Interior. COC, p. 14
(13) Shank, p. 40
(14) Cochrane, p. 214
(15) Doner, pp. 29-30
(16) Endlich, p. 95
(17) Anonymous. (HSSC 1883), p. 95
(18) Davis, SCR, pp. 67-70
(19) Scharnhorst, Gary (editor). *Mark Twain: The Complete Interviews*. University of Alabama Press. Tuscaloosa, AL. 2006. p. 167
(20) Von Keler
(21) Glancey, p. 28
(22) North American Steel Interstate Coalition (NASIC). *Steel Wheels or Rubber Tires?* www.steelinterstate.org/topics/steel-wheels-or-rubber-tires
(23) Dilts, p. 10
(24) Stover, p. 24
(25) Dilts, pp. 17-19
(26) Dunbar, pp. 14-24
(27) Cochrane, p. 216
(28) Dunbar, p. 45
(29) Cochrane, p. 220
(30) Schramm and Henning, pp. 165-166
(31) Gray, Walter P. III, *Rails West!*, in Withhuhn and Steeds, p. 43
(32) Dunbar, p. 99
(33) Jenks, p. 391
(34) Phelps and Whipp, p. 38. Dunbar, pp. 220-221
(35) Dunbar, p. 217
(36) Middleton, TT, pp. 13-21
(37) Middleton, TT, pp. 37-49
(38) Middleton, TIE, p. 13
(39) Middleton, TIE, p. 258
(40) Port Huron Daily Times (PHDT), 10/2/1899, p. 6

(41) Munson, p. 23

(42) PHDT, 07/09/1900, p.6

(43) Endlich, p. 26

(44) May, PHMLY, p. 16

(45) Jenks, p. 6

(46) Port Huron Times Herald (PHTH), 02/25/1962, p. 8

(47) Herlihy, p. 39

(48) Barnett, OMS.

(49) McCormick.

(50) PHDT, 09/04/1899, p. 5

(51) Caldwell, p. 11

(52) Herlihy, pp. 75-142

(53) Herlihy, pp. 190-205

(54) Breines, p. 76

(55) Herlihy, pp. 277-280

(56) Lamb, p. 143

(57) Von Keler.

(58) Von Keler.

(59) Flink, p. 2

(60) May, MUM, p. 49. PHTH, 07/08/1951, sec. 3, p. 5

(61) PHDT, 03/03/1900,p. 6

(62) May, MUM, pp. 25-30

(63) May, MUM, p. 35

(64) Olson, p. 55

(65) Olson, pp. 88-89

(66) May MUM, p. 66

(67) PHDT, 6/14/1899, p. 4

(68) Pettifer and Turner, p. 219

Chapter 2, pp. 40-74

(1) Cochrane, p. 210

(2) Damstra.

(3) Port Huron Daily Herald (PHDH), 12/07/1900, p. 8

(4) Rae, p. 5

(5) Cochrane, p. 108

(6) Kunstler, pp. 149-163

(7) Munson, p. 43

(8) Cochrane, p. 188

(9) PHDT, 06/01/1900, p. 6

(10) PHDT, 03/02/1900, p. 3

(11) Olson, p. 38

(12) Starr, p. 34

(13) Jenks, p. 129

(14) Middleton, TT, p. 86

(15) Dunbar, pp. 260-261

(16) Dunbar, p. 263

(17) PHDT, 08/10/1901, p. 2

(18) PHDT, 03/16/1900, p. 3
(19) PHDT, 08/03/1901, p. 11
(20) PHDT, 02/10/1900, p. 1
(21) Phelps, pp. 33, 41
(22) Olson, p. 120
(23) Olson, pp. 118-121
(24) May, MUM, p. 111
(25) Rae, p. 17
(26) May, MUM, pp. 54-56
(27) May, MUM, pp. 118-119
(28) PHDH, 11/13/1900, p. 5
(29) Pettifer and Turner, p. 40
(30) May, MUM, p.85
(31) PHDT, 02/15/1900, p. 4

Chapter 3, pp. 75-112

(1) Ford and Crowther, p. 38
(2) Ford and Crowther, p. 36
(3) Olson, p. 146
(4) PHDT, 11/05/1901, p. 6 ; PHDH , 10/30/1901, p. 3
(5) PHDT, 05/31/1902, p. 4
(6) May, PHMLY, p. 101. May, MUM, pp. 69-70, 127-129, 138. Rae, p. 32
(7) Olson, p. 154
(8) Ford and Crowther, pp. 55-56
(9) Ford and Crowther, pp. 38, 42
(10) PHDT, 09/30/1902, p. 3
(11) Brinkley, p. 70
(12) Wik, Reynold. *Henry Ford and Grass Roots America*. Quoted in Cray, p. 45
(13) May, MUM, p. 265. Brinkley, pp. 69-70
(14) Farber, Gene. p. 2
(15) PHDH, 06/27/1904
(16) PHDT, 07/26/1904, p. 5
(17) May, MUM, pp. 202-213. Gustin, chapters 3-6
(18) Cray, p. 46
(19) Flink, p. 120
(20) PHDH, 11/20/1906, p. 4
(21) Pettifer and Turner, p. 43. Rae, p. 29
(22) PHDT, 09/10/1907, p. 1
(23) Brinkley, p. 99
(24) Rae, p. 84
(25) PHDH. 01/06/1908, p. 1
(26) Sloan, p. 219
(27) PHTH, 08/19/1910, p. 4. Bryan, pp. 217-218
(28) PHDT, 02/25/1909, p. 1
(29) Olson, frontispiece
(30) May, MUM, p. 204
(31) Tamminen, p. 40

(32) Yergin, p. 112
(33) PHDH, 11/04/1903, p. 2
(34) PHTH, 10/26/1903, p. 7
(35) Pohl and Brown, sect. 11
(36) PHDH, 03/01/1902, p. 2
(37) Ford, David. *Heavy Duty*. Michigan History magazine. Volume 89, Number 3. May / June 2005. pp. 28-33
(38) PHDT, 02/24/1910, p. 4
(39) PHDT, 06/08/1907, p. 2
(40) PHDT, 05/25/1905, p. 6
(41) PHDT, 01/15/1907, p. 8
(42) Stover, p. 135
(43) PHDT. 08/19/1907, p. 4
(44) Kay, p. 152
(45) PHTH, 01/31/1967, p. 6
(46) PHDH, 05/29/1903
(47) Doner, pp. 98-99
(48) PHDT,11/27/1905, p. 8
(49) PHDT, 04/01/1909, p. 5
(50) PHTH, 10/15/1972, p. 6

Chapter 4, pp. 113-152

(1) Pettifer and Turner, pp. 16-17
(2) Brinkley, p. 143
(3) Car and Driver magazine. www.caranddriver.com/features/how-to-drive-a-fordmodel-t. July 2009. Retrieved 07/01/2016
(4) PHTH, 11/14/1971, p. 6A; 06/25/1978, p. 1E
(5) Ford and Crowther, p. 68
(6) O'Connell and Myers, p. 168
(7) Ford and Crowther, p. 80
(8) Ford and Crowther, chapter, p. 103
(9) Schneider, pp. 242-243
(10) Flink, pp. 118-122
(11) Ford and Crowther, p. 126
(12) Madison, Charles. *My Seven Years of Automotive Servitude*. In Lewis and Goldstein. p. 19
(13) Herlihy, p. 320
(14) PHTH, 01/01/1913, p. 3
(15) Flink, p. 190
(16) PHTH, 05/18/1915, p.1
(17) PHTH, 04/01/1916, p. 9
(18) PHTH, 01/30/1914, p. 5
(19) PHTH, 08/24/1912, p. 5; 08/23/1913, p. 4; 10/10/12, p. 4
(20) Kay, p. 182
(21) Doner, p. 120
(22) PHTH, 01/03/1920, p. 10
(23) PHTH, 12/20/1956, p. 17

(24) Pitrone and Elwart, pp. 58-59
(25) Rae, p. 70
(26) Yergin, p. 207
(27) LaBella, p. 9
(28) Caldwell, pp. 119-120
(29) Ford and Crowther, pp. 111, 93
(30) Sloan, p. 220
(31) PHTH, 10/11/1920, p. 6; 02/19/20, p. 1
(32) Cochrane, pp. 100, 108
(33) Phelps and Whipp, p. 42. PHTH, 01/08/1913, p. 3
(34) Tamminen, p. 72
(35) Rae, p. 49
(36) Brinkley, p. 209
(37) Yergin, p. 178
(38) PHTH, 06/10/1916, p. 4
(39) PHTH, 02/21/1920, p. 7
(40) PHTH, 02/27/1912, pp. 1 & 7
(41) Stover, pp. 168-169
(42) PHTH, 02/24/1914, p. 4
(43) Dunbar, p. 292
(44) PHTH, 01/19/1943, p. 5
(45) PHTH, 02/05/1923, p.12
(46) Schramm, p. 132
(47) PHTH, 11/20/1911, p. 1
(48) Middleton, IUE, pp. 19, 304
(49) Middleton, TT, p. 386
(50) Snider and Davis, p. 13
(51) PHTH, 06/30/1914, p. 1
(52) Heppenheimer, p. 8
(53) Herlihy, p. 320
(54) PHTH, 06/13/1913, p. 8; 06/30/1913, p. 3
(55) Tarkington, p. 629
(56) Truman, Margaret. *Bess W. Truman*. MacMillan. New York, NY. 1986. p. 81

Chapter 5, pp. 153-193

(1) Wills Sainte Claire Automobile Museum Collection. Marysville, Michigan.
(2) PHTH, 02/24/1921, p. 1
(3) PHTH, 06/11/1921, p. 1
(4) Flink, p. 70
(5) Burnell and Marcaccio, pp. 108-109
(6) Brinkley, p. 275
(7) Flink, p. 251
(8) Bryan, pp. 177-178
(9) Bryan, p. 174
(10) Ford and Crowther, p. 216
(11) Bryan, p. 275
(12) Detroit Free Press (DFP), Special FMC 100th Anniversary section, 06/09/2003

(13) PHTH, 08/13/1929, p. 2

(14) Cochrane, p. 239

(15) Heppenheimer, p. 12

(16) DFP, 06/09/2003

(17) Heppenheimer, p. 22

(18) Brinkley, p. 264

(19) Ford and Crowther, p. 190

(20) Flink, p. 191

(21) PHTH, 03/28/1924, p. 16

(22) Keats, p. 19

(23) Bryan, pp. 227-243

(24) PHTH, 03/01/1924, p. 3

(25) Ford and Crowther, p. 149

(26) Brinkley, p. 339

(27) Sloan, p. 266

(28) Sloan, p. 231

(29) PHTH, 04/22/1930, p. 6

(30) Cray, p. 204

(31) Cray, p. 248

(32) Farber, David, p. 175

(33) Brinkley, pp. 340-341

(34) Rae, p. 118

(35) PHTH, 12/31/1925, p. 4; 11/26/1925, p. 4

(36) PHTH, 7/28/1927, p. 2

(37) Netter, William Bernard. *Eyewitness to the Rumrunners*. Michigan History Magazine. Volume 93, Number 2. March / April 2009. pp.10-11

(38) PHTH, 09/08/1925, p. 6

(39) PHTH, 01/07/1928, pp. 1 & 11

(40) PHTH, 03/01/1924, p. 6

(41) PHTH, 05/20/1926, p. 6

(42) Kihlstedt, Folke. *The Automobile and the Transformation of the American House 1910-1935*, in Lewis and Goldstein, p. 169

(43) PHTH, 01/07/1922, p. 5

(44) Lynd, p. 256. Pettifer and Turner, p. 84. Interrante, Joseph. *The Road to Autopia*, in Lewis and Goldstein, p. 89

(45) Lynd, p. 251

(46) Flink, p. 168

(47) Interrante, p.97

(48) PHTH, 02/17/1930, p. 6

(49) Kay, p. 174

(50) PHTH, 03/21/1930, p. 21

(51) Brinkley, p. 353

(52) Brinkley, p. 359

(53) PHTH, 12/03/1927, p. 2

(54) PHTH, 02/24/1930, p. 6

(55) Flink, p. 188

(56) PHTH, 08/23/29, p. 12

(57) PHTH, 09/01/1926, p. 3

(58) PHTH, 09/28/1921, p. 12
(59) PHTH, 11/02/1921, p. 4
(60) PHTH, 09/27/1927, p. 6
(61) Dunbar, p. 243
(62) Kay, p. 167
(63) Middleton, TIE, p. 402
(64) Crawford, p. 100
(65) Stover, pp. 194-195
(66) Armstrong, John H. *A Golden Age*, in Withuhn and Steeds, pp. 114, 121
(67) PHTH, 12/14/1928, p. 22
(68) PHTH, 11/21/1923, p. 10
(69) PHTH, 08/29/1921, p. 6
(70) PHTH, 12/27/1926, p. 1
(71) PHTH, 02/17/1927, p.2
(72) McGraw, Bill. *Two Detroit Landmarks Reach 80*. Michigan History magazine. Volume 92, Number 3. May / June 2008. pp. 32-39
(73) Flink, p. 212
(74) Rothschild, p. 36
(75) PHTH, 09/18/1930, p. 13

Chapter 6, pp. 194-234

(1) PHTH, 01/29/1934, sec. 2, p. 9
(2) PHTH, 02/22/1934, p. 7
(3) Schneider, p. 123
(4) PHTH, 12/02/1932, p. 1
(5) Olsen and Cabadas, p. 91
(6) PHTH, 03/29/1932, p. 16
(7) Lyons, pp. 54-55
(8) PHTH, 07/02/1931, p. 5
(9) PHTH, 04/06/1933, p. 17
(10) Lynd, MIT, p. 408
(11) PHTH, 12/29/1931, p. 2
(12) Rae, pp. 130-131. Brinkley, pp. 390-393
(13) Farber, David, pp. 165-166
(14) DFP, FMC section, 06/09/2003
(15) PHTH, 09/30/1933, p. 8
(16) Gup, Ted. *The Gift*. Smithsonian magazine. Volume 41, Number 8. December 2010. p. 66
(17) PHTH, 10/31/1931, p. 11
(18) PHTH, 03/09/1932, p. 8
(19) Lynd, MIT, p. 17
(20) Kunstler, pp. 102-103
(21) Cray, p. 265. Kay, p. 217
(22) Herlihy, p. 359
(23) PHTH, 11/09/1932, p. 10
(24) Kunstler, p. 97
(25) Kay, pp. 198-201

(26) PHTH, 05/15/1933, p. 5

(27) PHTH, 07/14/1940, p. 5

(28) PHTH, 12/15/1932, p. 5; 09/30/1940, p. 4; 06/14/1932, p. 7

(29) Furnas, J. C. *And Sudden Death*. Reader's Digest Magazine. August, 1935. www.rd.com/culture/and-sudden-death-readers-digest/   Retrieved 09/18/11

(30) Sloan, p. 278

(31) PHTH, 06/12/1934, p. 2

(32) PHTH, 12/30/1936, p. 4

(33) PHTH, 08/04/1931, p. 1

(34) PHTH, 03/07/1937, p. 4

(35) PHTH, 08/08/1937, p. 4

(36) PHTH, 09/26/1938, p. 8

(37) PHTH, 12/30/1936, p. 4

(38) PHTH, 03/22/1940, p. 3

(39) Farber, David, p. 150

(40) Kunstler, p. 211

(41) Cray, p. 282; Farber, pp. 200-201

(42) Farber, David, p. 179-182

(43) Farber, David, p. 205

(44) Brill, p. 372

(45) Brinkley, p. 441

(46) Burby, p. 379

(47) Cray, p. 327

(48) Rothschild, p. 170

(49) PHTH, 08/04/1938, p. 15

(50) PHTH, 01/04/1935, p. 6

(51) PHTH, 08/24/1937, p. 6

(52) Yates, pp. 258-261

(53) PHTH, 03/22/1940, p. 3

(54) Grant, H. Roger. *Hard Times*, in Withuhn and Steeds, p. 130

(55) Dunbar, p. 28

(56) PHTH, 07/25/1939, p. 2

(57) Heppenheimber, p. 54

(58) PHTH, 02/28/1931, p. 6

(59) Middleton, TIE, p. 70. Crawford, p. 106

(60) PHTH, 06/24/1935, p. 6

(61) Herlihy, pp. 327-328, 355-360

(62) PHTH, 02/28/1936, p. 7

(63) PHTH, 02/24/1932, p. 3

(64) PHTH, 01/05/1933, p. 4

(65) Brinkley, p.451

(66) PHTH, 08/03/1940, p. 5

Chapter 7, pp. 235-275

(1) *Meet John Doe*. Copyright 1941 by Frank Capra Productions. Screenplay by Robert Riskin, based on a story by Richard Connell and Robert Presnell

(2) Phelps, pp. 60-61

(3) Brinkley, p. 448
(4) DFP, 06/09/2003
(5) PHTH, 04/22/1941, p. 4
(6) PHTH, 11/06/1941, p. 6
(7) PHTH, 09/29/1945, p. 4
(8) PHTH, 11/27/1941, p. 16
(9) PHTH, 09/09/1941, p. 4
(10) PHTH, 09/26/43, p. 5
(11) PHTH, 09/15/1941 p. 4
(12) PHTH, 12/07/1941, p. 4
(13) *There's a Bright Day Dawning*, by Fred L. Riggin. Copyright 1942 by Fortune Music, Inc. Sheet music facsimile courtesy of the Lester Glassner African American Experience Collection, Archives & Special Collections Department, E. H. Butler Library, SUNY Buffalo State.
(14) Phelps, pp. 106-107
(15) PHTH, 01/26/1942, p. 3
(16) PHTH, 02/23/1942, p. 10
(17) Leavitt, pp. 242-244
(18) PHTH, 05/14/1945, p. 6
(19) Herlihy, p. 330
(20) PHTH, 08/24/1941, p. 14
(21) Hemingway, Ernest. (ed.) William White. *By-Line: Ernest Hemingway.* Charles Scribners' Sons. New York, NY. 1967. p. 364. Originally published in Collier's magazine 09/30/1944
(22) Yergin, p. 376
(23) *The World At War: Episode 7 - On Our Way.* Copyright 1974 by British Broadcasting Corporation. Interview with J. K. Galbraith.
(24) PHTH, 01/31/1943, p. 1
(25) Yergin, pp. 378, 382
(26) Yergin, p. 362
(27) Stover, pp. 186-190
(28) Grant, p. 145
(29) PHTH, 08/31/1944, p. 6
(30) Stover, pp. 186-190
(31) Cray, p. 217. Sloan, p. 203
(32) Sloan, p. 382
(33) Brinkley, p. 442
(34) Rae, p. 158
(35) Buick Automotive Gallery and Research Center. Flint, Michigan
(36) Brinkley, pp. 459-484
(37) Olsen and Cabadas, p. 117
(38) Olsen and Cabadas, pp. 116-117. Brinkley, p. 484. Hyde, Charles. *Fighting for the Right to Work.* Michigan History magazine. Volume 98, Number 2. March / April 2014. pp. 50-55.
(39) PHTH, 05/04/1941, p. 4
(40) PHTH, 07/20/1943, p. 2
(41) Snider and Davis, pp. 45-62
(42) Heppenheimer, p. 120

(43) Heppenheimer, p. 144
(44) PHTH, 03/15/1945, p. 10
(45) PHTH, 11/28/1948, p. 4
(46) Iacocca and Novak, p. 24
(47) Iacocca and Novak, pp. 30-31
(48) PHTH, 03/14/1944, p. 2
(49) PHTH, 10/05/1950, p. 12
(50) Eckert, pp. 227-229
(51) PHTH, 08/05/1944, p. 5
(52) PHTH, 08/30/1948, p. 5
(53) Yergin, pp. 423-424
(54) PHTH, 01/21/1941, p. 5
(55) PHTH, 12/26/1945, p. 3
(56) Dunbar, pp. 281-283
(57) PHTH, 06/15/1950, p. 5
(58) Brill, pp. 14-15, 283. Caldwell, p. 35
(59) PHTH, 11/20/1949, p. 4
(60) Sloan, p. 385. Glancey, p. 162
(61) Tamminen, pp. 110-111. Cray, p. 345
(62) Heppenheimer, pp. 127-131, 172. Yates, p. 308
(63) PHTH, 02/09/1946, p. 1
(64) PHTH, 09/18/1947, p. 21
(65) PHTH, 04/18/1944, p. 4; 01/24/1947, p. 6
(66) Cochrane, p. 126
(67) Time Capsule / 1950, p. 28
(68) Carson, p. 23
(69) Brinkley, pp. 510-511, 518-519. PHTH, 04/09/1947, p. 2
(70) PHTH, 02/18/1949, p. 1

Chapter 8, pp. 276-315

(1) PHTH, 08/22/1951, p. 6
(2) PHTH, 02/09/1952, p. 5
(3) PHTH, 01/13/1956, p. 1
(4) Schneider, p. 160
(5) PHTH, 01/18/54, p. 10
(6) PHTH, 02/15/1952, p. 2
(7) PHTH, 07/25/1953, p. 1
(8) PHTH, 09/16/1952, p. 6
(9) PHTH, 10/25/1953, p. 4
(10) PHTH, 05/14/1953, p. 1
(11) O'Connell and Myers, pp. 214-216
(12) PHTH, 10/28/1954, p. 19
(13) PHTH, 11/03/1952, p. 19
(14) Cray, pp. 7, 351
(15) Ford Motor Company, *Ford at 50*, pp. 69, 72
(16) Brinkley, p. 569
(17) Keats, pp. 86-96, 122

(18) Flink, p. 282
(19) Pettifer and Turner, pp. 161-162
(20) Iacocca and Novak, pp. 160-161
(21) Brinkley, pp. 575-579
(22) Keats, p. 105
(23) Jerome, p. 26
(24) Cray, pp. 366, 369
(25) Sloan, p. 259
(26) Cray, pp. 355-356
(27) Davis, pp. 107-113
(28) Cray, p. 372
(29) PHTH, 01/13/1959, p. 5
(30) Flink, p. 288
(31) PHTH, 03/17/1960, p. 5
(32) Keats, p. 110
(33) Keats, p. 106
(34) *Ford at 50,* p. 12
(35) PHTH, 06/13/1956, p. 12
(36) PHTH, 05/24/1954, p. 6
(37) PHTH, 07/23/1954, p. 1
(38) PHTH, 12/21/1954, p. 6
(39) PHTH, 01/02/1955, p. 1
(40) PHTH, 01/02/1951, p. 3
(41) PHTH, 06/14/1959, p. 4
(42) Keats, p. 99
(43) PHTH, 05/31/1953, p. 4
(44) PHTH, 04/09/1957, p. 6
(45) PHTH, 12/10/1995, p. 10
(46) PHTH, 06/10/1987, p. 6
(47) PHTH, 12/30/1957, p. 6
(48) Iacocca and Novak, pp. 38-40
(49) Iacocca and Novak, p. 297
(50) PHTH, 08/30/1956, p. 3
(51) O'Connell and Myers, p. 106
(52) Songwriter: Jackie Brenston. Copyright Warner Chappell Music, Inc.
(53) PHTH, 11/16/1953, p. 5
(54) Stover, p.196
(55) PHTH, 03/15/1959, p. 7
(56) Brill, p. 208
(57) PHTH, 01/21/1955, p. 6
(58) Stover, p. 219
(59) Phelps, p. 77
(60) Kay, p. 229
(61) Phelps and Whipp, pp. 80-81
(62) Tamminen, pp. 118-119. Jerome, p. 216. Commoner, pp. 66-67
(63) PHTH, 12/31/1958, p. 3
(64) Schneider, p. 124
(65) Burby, p. 356

(66) Flink, p. 372
(67) PHTH, 12/19/1957, p. 6
(68) Leavitt, pp. 187-188
(69) PHTH, 02/01/1951, p. 14
(70) PHTH, 05/09/1958, p. 6
(71) PHTH, 06/13/1958, p. 18; 04/30/1958, p. 2
(72) Stover, p. 221-222
(73) Stover, pp. 195-196
(74) Heppenheimer, pp. 170-181
(75) PHTH, 05/06/1960, p. 1
(76) PHTH, 03/18/1956, p. 1
(77) Lamb, p. 201
(78) PHTH, 10/12/1954, p. 6; 12/24/1951, p. 6
(79) PHTH, 01/23/1958, p. 1
(80) PHTH, 04/24/1955, p. 1
(81) PHTH, 05/14/1955, p. 1
(82) PHTH, 09/15/1954, p. 4; 01/22/1952, p.12
(83) PHTH, 07/11/1953, p. 3; 03/01/1956, p. 16

Chapter 9, pp. 316-356

(1) Jacobs, p. 370
(2) PHTH, 11/22/1969, p. 1
(3) O'Connell and Myers, p. 41. Schneider, p. 163. Pettifer and Turner, p. 224. Gikas, Paul W., *Crashworthiness as a Cultural Ideal*, in Lewis and Goldstein, p. 332
(4) PHTH, 09/03/1961, p. 4
(5) PHTH, 12/29/1969, p. 1 & 5
(6) O'Connell, p. 80
(7) PHTH, 02/07/1966, p. 13
(8) PHTH, 10/04/1969, p. 3
(9) PHTH, 09/01/1965, p. 8A
(10) PHTH, 05/05/1961, p.8
(11) O'Connell, p. 49
(12) PHTH, 05/20/1965, p. 10
(13) PHTH, 07/07/1966, p. 4
(14) Burby, p. 69
(15) PHTH, 05/04/1962, p. 6
(16) PHTH, 11/11/1967, p. 12
(17) PHTH, 10/13/1968, p. 53
(18) Jerome, p. 159
(19) Jerome, p. 15
(20) PHTH, 05/14/1980, p. 28
(21) Iacocca and Novak, p. 96
(22) Iacocca and Novak, p. 66
(23) Brinkley, p. 617
(24) Olsen and Cabadas, p. 140
(25) Ford Motor Company website.
www.at.ford.com/SiteCollectionImages/2011_U.S._Plant_ Pages/Woodhaven

%20Stamping/Steve%20Deak%20story.pdf Retrieved 03/15/2015
(26) PHTH, 05/25/1970, p. 3
(27) PHTH, 11/18/1968, p. 1
(28) Cray, pp. 496-497
(29) Flink, pp. 288-289, 291
(30) PHTH, 02/02/1970, p. 1
(31) O'Connell and Myers, p. 186
(32) PHTH, 04/21/1966, p. 8
(33) PHTH, 05/24/1969, p. 1
(34) O'Connell and Myers, p. 35
(35) Jerome, p. 203
(36) Tamminen, p. 11; Flink, p. 386; Commoner, p. 167
(37) PHTH, 03/12/1967, p. 10A
(38) PHTH, 04/23/1969, p. 7B
(39) Jerome, p. 197
(40) Kay, p. 250
(41) PHTH, 01/12/1969, p. 13
(42) PHTH, 08/12/1947, p. 6
(43) PHTH, 01/02/1964, p. 15
(44) PHTH, 10/19/1965, p. 4
(45) Tamminen, p. 19
(46) PHTH, 10/01/1964, p. 24; 09/24/1964, p. 26
(47) PHTH, 04/27/1965, p. 2
(48) Jacobs, p. 5
(49) PHTH, 02/09/1965, p. 18
(50) Jacobs, p. 371
(51) PHTH, 04/06/1969, p. 15
(52) PHTH, 09/27/1966, p. 4
(53) PHTH, 04/13/1965, p. 4
(54) PHTH, 06/10/1965, p. 8
(55) Duany, Plater-Zyberk, and Speck, p. 64
(56) PHTH, 02/01/1967, p. 8
(57) Leavitt, pp. 115-116
(58) Mumford, plate 47
(59) PHTH, 01/01/1962, p. 13
(60) PHTH, 01/01/1962, p. 1, sec. 4
(61) PHTH, 12/09/1965, p. 9
(62) Leavitt, p. 12. Burby, p. 344
(63) Leavitt, pp. 144-145
(64) Commoner, pp. 169, 264
(65) Burby, p. 76
(66) PHTH, 06/24/1964, p. 7
(67) Schneider, p. 53
(68) PHTH, 09/21/1967, p. 8
(69) PHTH, 11/05/1970, p. 6
(70) Leavitt, pp. 10, 278
(71) PHTH, 10/03/1969, p. 4A
(72) Stover, p. 234

(73) PHTH, 02/06/1963, p. 10
(74) Burby, p. 269
(75) Rothschild, p. 239
(76) Middleton, TT, p. 325
(77) PHTH, 05/18/1970, p. 4
(78) Heppenheimer, pp. 191, 272
(79) AWO, pp. Fwd, 2-3, 13
(80) PHTH, 04/16/1969, p. 1
(81) Starr, p. 409
(82) Commoner, p. 134
(83) PHTH, 02/19/1968, p. 3; 02/04/1969, p. 4
(84) PHTH, 08/11/1968, p. 2B
(85) PHTH, 07/09/1970, p. 23
(86) PHTH, 09/01/1963, p. 6; 02/17/1963, p. 10

Chapter 10, pp. 357-397

(1) Brinkley, p. 109
(2) Cray, p. 379
(3) Ford and Crowther, chapter 12
(4) Yergin, p. 662
(5) Burby, p. 9
(6) Phelps, p. 86
(7) Yergin, p. 695
(8) PHTH, 07/17/1973, p. 6
(9) PHTH, 09/05/1976, p. 34
(10) Flink, p. 388
(11) Brinkley, p. 693
(12) Rothschild, p. 107. Flink, p. 244
(13) PHTH, 03/15/1973, p. 6
(14) PHTH, 06/01/1976, p. 7
(15) Rothschild, p. 241
(16) Rothschild, p. 78
(17) PHTH, 09/24/1973, p. 22
(18) Flink, p. 347
(19) Rothschild, p. 90
(20) PHTH, 12/08/1974, p. 12
(21) PHTH, 01/20/1972, p. 5
(22) Rothschild, p.184
(23) Brinkley, pp. 660-663
(24) PHTH, 7/30/1971, p. 4
(25) PHTH, 04/01/1971, p. 2
(26) PHTH, 03/22/1975, p. 1
(27) Pettifer and Turner, p. 227
(28) PHTH, 03/09/1980, p. 11
(29) PHTH, 05/16/1980, p. 4
(30) PHTH, 03/27/1977, p. 4E; U.S. Dept of Transportation. Retrieved 02/11/2015.
www.fhwa.dot.gov/policyinformation/pubs/hf/pl11028/chapter4.cfm

(31) PHTH, 03/11/1979, p. 3

(32) PHTH, 01/10/1971, p. 2

(33) PHTH, 03/29/1976, p. 1

(34) PHTH, 09/13/1971, p. 4

(35) Gikas, p. 328. PHTH, 02/05/1980, p. 3; 02/08/1980, p. 6

(36) PHTH, 01/20/1974, p. 1

(37) PHTH, 04/27/71, p. 4

(38) Schneider, p. 216

(39) Creamer, p. 45

(40) Eckert, p. 351

(41) PHTH, 11/18/1973, p. 6

(42) PHTH, 02/01/1976, p. 53

(43) PHTH, 04/08/1971, pp. 1, 7

(44) PHTH, 07/09/1972, p. 13

(45) PHTH, 09/16/1978, p. 17

(46) PHTH, 11/25/1971, p. 2

(47) Iacocca and Novak, p. 127

(48) PHTH, 11/03/1977, p. 4B

(49) Packard, pp. 33, 117-118

(50) PHTH, 12/04/1977, p. 3E

(51) PHTH, 08/24/1977, p. 6

(52) PHTH, 11/27/1977, p. 9

(53) Cray, p. 527

(54) PHTH, 12/08/1978, p. 6

(55) LaBella, p. 49

(56) PHTH, 04/01/1973, p. 15

(57) Brill, p. 274

(58) Brill, p. 273

(59) Songwriter: Carl Davis. Copyright: 1975 Warner Chappell Music, Inc.

(60) Iacocca and Novak, pp. 186-187

(61) LaBella, pp. 38, 24

(62) Brown, p. 66

(63) PHTH, 08/22/1971, pp. 1, 2

(64) PHTH, 10/26/1972, p. 6

(65) Duany, Plater-Zyberk, and Speck, p. 63

(66) Withuhn, William L. *Toward a New Era*, in Withuhn and Steeds p. 175. Stover, pp. 234-237

(67) PHTH, 02/15/1972, p. 6

(68) PHTH, 04/02/1974, p. 6

(69) PHTH, 08/25/1974, p. 1

(70) Stover, p. 244

(71) PHTH, 03/09/1974, p. 2; 02/07/1974, p. 1

(72) Heppenheimer, pp. 258-259, 319, 269

(73) PHTH, 07/22/1978, p. 1

(74) Brown, Flavin, and Norman, pp. 74-75

(75) PHTH, 08/10/1977, p. 6

(76) Iacocca and Novak, p. 306

(77) PHTH, 06/28/1980, p. 13

499

(78) PHTH, 02/20/1974, p. 32
(79) PHTH, 08/29/1976, p. 3
(80) PHTH, 02/17/1974, p. 6
(81) PHTH, 11/19/1980, p. 29
(82) Endlich, pp. 161, 287
(83) PHTH, 05/23/1976, p. 35
(84) PHTH, 06/21/1972, p. 4

Chapter 11, pp. 398-437

(1) PHTH, 04/15/198, p. 3D
(2) Flint Journal, 06/24/1984, pp. A1 & A4; 07/05/1984, *AutoWorld* Section
(3) May, MUM , p 345
(4) Flint Journal, 07/05/1984, pp. 1, 4
(5) PHTH, 02/02/1983, p. 6A
(6) Yergin, p. 718
(7) Kay, p. 291
(8) Iacocca and Novak, pp. 181, 258
(9) PHTH, 09/22/1981, p. 1
(10) Flink, p. 389
(11) Iacocca and Novak, p. 253
(12) Flink, p. 395
(13) Brinkley, p. 703
(14) Pettifer and Turner, p. 143
(15) PHTH, 09/17/1986, p. 26
(16) Kay, p. 17
(17) Flink, p. 398
(18) PHTH, 01/13/1983, p. 15
(19) Brinkley, p. 728
(20) Flink, p. 285
(21) Pettifer and Turner, p. 169
(22) PHTH, 11/12/1991, p. 9
(23) PHTH, 08/03/1983, p. 4
(24) PHTH, 01/06/1982, p. 5D
(25) PHTH, 10/09/1981, p. 12
(26) PHTH, 01/20/1988, p. 21
(27) PHTH, 08/28/1988, p. 25
(28) PHTH, 02/09,1985, p. 1
(29) Cochrane, pp. 197-198
(30) PHTH, 11/30/1984, p. 4
(31) PHTH, 07/05/1989, p. 19
(32) PHTH, 05/26/1990, p. 3A
(33) PHTH, 05/12/1987, p.6
(34) PHTH, 08/23/1990, p. 1
(35) PHTH, 12/27/1982, p. 17
(36) PHTH, 12/12/1988
(37) PHTH, 04/02/1983, p. 1
(38) PHTH, 02/20/1984, p. 4

(39) Brown, John F., RVM, p. 96
(40) PHTH, 11/25/1984, p. 13
(41) PHTH, 06/26/1986, p. 6; 06/27/1986, p. 2
(42) PHTH, 07/12/1986, p. 2
(43) Pettifer and Turner, p. 227
(44) PHTH, 12/01/1986, p. 5
(45) PHTH, 12/09/1984, p. 1
(46) PHTH, 12/12/1982, p. 9; 04/11/1987, p. 3
(47) PHTH, 04/26/1987, p. 4
(48) PHTH, 06/11/1986, p. 6
(49) Schor, p. 107
(50) PHTH, 05/12/1988, p. 1
(51) PHTH, 08/16/1990, p. 4
(52) PHTH, 11/25/1990, p. 17
(53) PHTH, 08/12/1984, p. 9
(54) PHTH, 02/27/1990, p. 6
(55) PHTH, 09/04/1990, p. 6
(56) PHTH, 07/14/1985, p. 24
(57) Songwriter: Sammy Hagar. Copyright Warner Chappell Music, Inc.
(58) Duany, Plater-Zyberk, and Speck, p. 37
(59) Canadian Broadcasting Corporation. *The Nature of Things - Black Wave: The Legacy of the Exxon Valdez.* Writers: Paul Carvalho, Robert Cornellier. Broadcast 01/15/2009
(60) Kay, p. 22
(61) PHTH, 10/10/1989, p. 12
(62) Phelps, pp. 87, 109
(63) Yergin, p. 765
(64) PHTH, 08/15/1990, p. 15
(65) PHTH, 01/21/1982, p. 4
(66) PHTH, 09/28/1986, p. 23
(67) PHTH, 12/07/1987, p. 8
(68) PHTH, 04/27/1990, p. 8A
(69) Thor, Carl and Kirdendall, Eric. *Improving Fuel Efficiency of Trucking Operations.* Kansas Cooperative Extension Service, 1982
(70) Kay, p. 37
(71) PHTH, 04/24/1981, p. 8
(72) PHTH, 08/08/1988, p. 8
(73) PHTH, 02/13/1984, p. 1; 08/02/1982, p. 6
(74) Cochrane, p. 225. PHTH, 06/10/1989, p. 5B
(75) Withuhn, p. 174
(76) PHTH, 08/26/1987, p. 6
(77) Snider and Davis, p. 143
(78) Endlich, pp. 110-111
(79) PHTH, 07/22/1984, p. 32
(80) Kay, p. 121. Byrne, p. 1
(81) PHTH, 03/29/1990, p. 13
(82) PHTH, 09/13/1984, p. 17
(83) PHTH, 04/26/1985, p. 3

(84) Iacocca and Novak, pp. 306-307
(85) PHTH, 03/05/1981, p. 1

Chapter 12, pp. 438-477

(1) PHTH, 05/24/1997, p. 13
(2) Wall Street Journal (WSJ), 01/30/2003, p. 1D
(3) PHTH, 09/01/1988, p. 4
(4) PHTH, 03/03/1991, p. 33
(5) Williamson
(6) Kay, p. 125
(7) PHTH, 07/16/92, p. 4
(8) PHTH, 03/03/1991, pp. 33, 35
(9) Eckert, p. 160
(10) Jane Holtz Kay, quoted in Duany, Plater-Zyberk, and Speck, p. 129
(11) Tamminen, p. 42
(12) Hart, Stanley and Spivak, Alvin. *The Elephant in the Bedroom: Automobile Dependence and Denial*. New Paradigm Books. Pasadena, CA. 1993. Quoted in Duany, Plater-Zyberk, and Speck, p. 94
(13) Crawford, pp. 81, 285
(14) Lamb, p. 234. PHTH, 01/04/2000, p. 3
(15) PHTH, 02/24/1991, p. 102
(16) Kay, p. 17
(17) PHTH, 12/24/1997, p. 12
(18) PHTH, 02/16/1992, p. 15
(19) PHTH, 12/08/1991, p. 21
(20) Brinkley, pp. 739-742
(21) Heartland Institute. 01/01/1998. www.heartland.org/news-opinion/news/what-to-do-with-three-billion-abandoned-tires   Retrieved 02/23/2013
(22) PHTH, 07/15/1992, p.7B
(23) Tamminen, pp. 20, 39, 88, 123-124
(24) Olsen and Cabadas, p. 162
(25) PHTH, 02/25/1999, p. 11
(26) PHTH, 09/01/1996, p. 11
(27) PHTH, 04/25/1991, p. 3
(28) Kay, p. 124
(29) PHTH, 06/28/1996, p. 13
(30) Duany, Plater-Zyberk, and Speck pp. 119-120
(31) PHTH, 03/07/1991, p. 15
(32) PHTH, 05/01/1999, p. 3
(33) PHTH, 01/12/1999, p. 2
(34) PHTH, 07/23/1991, pp. 1, 8; 07/24/1991, p. 3
(35) PHTH, 12/17/1993, p. 12
(36) PHTH, 03/16/1996, p. 16
(37) PHTH, 04/18/1999, p. 19
(38) PHTH, 10/24/1999, p. 16
(39) PHTH, 07/06/1993, p. 7
(40) PHTH, 02/18/1998, p. 3

(41) PHTH, 08/21/1991, p. 14
(42) PHTH, 07/08/2000, p. 9; 10/01/2000, p. 16
(43) PHTH, 07/08/1996, p. 5; 09/12/1999, p. 6
(44) PHTH, 02/05/1990, p. 6; 03/09/1993, p. 7
(45) PHTH, 03/23/1991, p. 1
(46) PHTH, 09/02/1996, pp. 1, 10
(47) Lamb, p. 234
(48) PHTH, 05/08/1994, p. 9
(49) Glancey, p. 76
(50) PHTH, 04/01/1999, p. 1
(51) PHTH, 01/28/1994, p. 3
(52) PHTH, 01/18/1998, p. 13
(53) PHTH, 05/14/1995, p. 3
(54) Kay, p. 33
(55) Crawford, p. 96
(56) PHTH, 12/04/1989, p. 8
(57) Scott, Gene. *Train Stations Restored as Museums: Michigan Towns Lead the Way.*
Chronicle - Magazine of the Historical Society of Michgan. Volume 33, Number 2.
Summer 2010.
(58) PHTH, 11/17/2000, pp. 1, 2
(59) Stover, p. 259. Duany, Plater-Zybeck, and Speck, pp. 95-96
(60) Crawford, p. 105
(61) Creamer, p. 87
(62) Otterbourg
(63) Heppenheimer, pp. 1, 345
(64) PHTH, 01/27/1999, p. 9
(65) PHTH, 12/29/1993, p. 10
(66) Byrne, pp. 24-26
(67) PHTH, 07/08/1994, p. 1
(68) PHTH, 04/30/1997, p. 13
(69) Herlihy, p. 406. Lamb, pp. 202-203
(70) PHTH, 08/20/2000, p. 4
(71) PHTH, 09/27/1996, p. 8
(72) PHTH, 08/21/1993, p. 11
(73) Kay, p. 109
(74) PHTH, 12/31/1992, p. 1
(75) Fumento, p. 255
(76) WSJ, 04/24/2003, p. 3D
(77) PHTH, 08/15/1993, p. 19
(78) Duany, Plater-Zyberk, and Speck, p. 65

INDEX

Accidents and Casualties

airplane - 150, 159, 198, 312, 349, 409

automobile - 14, 37, 72-73, 78, 83, 85, 86, 87, 90, 91, 93, 116, 126-127, 129, 151, 166, 167-169, 179, 194, 200, 207-213, 219, 236-237, 249, 251, 276-281, 282, 291, 296, 299-301, 317-322, 324, 328-329, 334, 343-344, 347, 370, 372-373, 385, 387, 404, 409, 411-413, 422, 426, 440, 449-454, 466

bicycle - 33, 42, 85, 91, 109, 150, 169, 231, 271-272, 312, 351, 393-394, 434, 462, 471, 472, 476

bus - 184, 228, 236, 304, 335, 347, 384, 413, 414, 466

motorcycle, snowmobile, all-terrain vehicle (ATV) - 332, 375, 411, 451, 452, 453

railroad and streetcar - 15, 65-67, 86, 106-107, 125, 139, 187, 228, 389, 414, 430-431, 468

ship - 11-12, 68, 108, 149, 246, 253, 270, 310, 311, 350, 391, 424

truck - 116, 134, 167, 169, 177, 210, 211, 224, 249, 265, 280, 301, 318, 343, 344, 345, 372, 384-385, 393, 426, 428, 465-466

Agriculture 51-52, 140, 160-161, 198, 238, 273-274, 295, 332, 381-382, 407, 420, 455-456

Airbags 329, 369, 442, 444, 448

Air transportation 109, 149, 159-160, 186, 198, 228, 248, 253, 270, 312, 349, 391, 436, 470-471

American Motors Corporation 288, 328, 330, 365, 416, 446

Amtrak 388-389, 429-430, 467-468

Auto Clubs (AAA) 45, 84, 129, 142, 167, 172, 214, 222, 232, 307, 327, 372, 373, 386

Auto Lite (later Presto Lite) 192, 198, 214, 234, 259, 326, 367, 400, 408, 439

Automobile insurance 92, 125, 142, 247, 292, 299, 319-320, 372, 415, 439, 445, 449, 454

Automobile lawsuits 86, 91, 115, 117, 129, 169, 210, 212, 301, 328, 362, 372, 414-415, 422

Automobile parking 98, 127, 173-175, 220, 239, 249-250, 261, 293-294, 296, 336-338, 340, 376-378, 385, 402, 417-418, 439, 458-460

Automobile racing 40, 46-47, 72, 76, 80, 83, 86, 98-99, 327, 300-301, 336, 337, 369, 398

Automobile repairs 81, 83, 87, 98, 113-114, 124-125, 162-163, 215, 242, 258, 289-290, 327, 331, 362-364, 403, 405-406, 444-445

Automobile regulation 84, 116, 127-128, 129, 141, 210-211, 229, 279-280, 282, 319-321, 322-323, 327-329, 331, 335-336, 360-362, 364, 368-370, 404, 413, 416, 428, 439, 442, 447-448, 463

Automobile sales and numbers 41, 47, 77, 79, 87, 88, 90, 95, 97, 113, 114, 118, 119-120, 122-123, 133, 137, 140, 151, 154, 155-6, 161, 176, 178-179, 197, 200, 203, 205, 214, 215, 235, 253, 257, 259-260, 281, 301, 317-318, 323-325, 330, 333, 365, 367-368, 400-401, 404-405, 420, 423, 425, 434, 438-440, 442-443, 446, 463, 469

505

Ford Motor Company (FMC) 80-82, 84, 92, 94, 95, 113, 120-121, 139-140, 146, 162, 164, 177-179, 188, 189, 194, 197, 200-202, 216, 239, 248, 252, 255-256, 259, 270, 276, 278, 281, 283-291, 297, 298-299, 302, 325-326, 327, 330, 360-362, 365-369, 375, 380, 386, 394, 400-404, 424, 431-432, 439, 441-444, 447-449, 469

Gardendale 51, 260, 331, 380-381, 416-418, 442, 451, 457

Gasoline 34, 99-100, 124, 140-142, 165, 171, 179-181, 224-226, 240-241, 244-245, 253-254, 264-266, 304, 345-346, 357-361, 384, 388, 400-401, 422-425, 440-442, 447-448, 460, 461

General Motors (GM) 93-94, 96, 120, 137-139, 164-166, 178, 216, 219, 242, 247, 256, 258, 266, 281, 283, 286-290, 292, 301, 303, 306, 323, 325, 327, 328, 339, 343, 360-362, 368-369, 386, 402-403, 406, 421, 436, 439, 443, 447, 452, 475

Good Roads movement 31, 40, 44-47, 101

Grand Trunk Railroad 17, 19, 64-65, 105, 122, 144, 185-187, 227, 266-268, 308, 310, 348, 380, 390, 431-432, 463-464, 467-468

Gratiot Pike 24, 134, 143, 167, 182, 207, 237, 265, 281, 301, 308, 318, 451, 453

Handy Brothers Railroad 146, 185

Harding, Warren 180, 189

Hare, James 292, 299, 317, 322

Havers Automobile Company 97, 118-119, 416

Health and Hospitals 56-57, 87, 110-111, 151, 156-158, 189, 232-233, 238, 271-272, 292, 294, 314, 315, 323, 329-330, 352-353, 375, 394-395, 435-437, 446-447, 466, 472-475

Hemingway, Ernest 244

Highway "21" 144, 182, 291, 301, 312, 320, 373, 381, 383, 385, 411, 415

Hoover, Herbert 161, 168, 179, 188, 205

Horses 21-22, 29-30, 43, 53-54, 82, 91, 97, 131, 136, 160, 200, 205, 231, 304, 333, 402, 431, 471

Iacocca, Lido (Lee) 256, 257, 298-299, 325-326, 334, 367-368, 380, 386, 401-402, 404, 436, 439, 447, 472

Imperial Oil Company (and Chemical Valley) 34, 99, 140, 180, 224, 242, 253, 265, 304, 345-346, 359, 424, 447

Interstate Highway System (IHS), and I-94, I-69 306, 342-344, 349, 375, 383, 426-428, 442, 449, 463

Jacobs, Alex (Jacobs Effect) 27, 56, 151, 206, 272, 394, 436, 475

Japanese automobiles 289, 364-365, 400, 404-405, 407, 424, 440, 444, 447

Jeep 248, 259, 404

Jefferson, Thomas (Jefferson Minimum) 8, 10, 26, 189, 353, 396, 436, 475

aul war 1859

b 1864   H. Ford
  1876-12   p 14

p 16 HF grandfather 1838
                    -10
            to Am →1828

CPSIA information can be obtained
at www.ICGtesting.com
Printed in the USA
LVHW111655040220
645814LV00004B/638